Communications
in Computer and Information Science 1030

Commenced Publication in 2007
Founding and Former Series Editors:
Phoebe Chen, Alfredo Cuzzocrea, Xiaoyong Du, Orhun Kara, Ting Liu,
Krishna M. Sivalingam, Dominik Ślęzak, Takashi Washio, and Xiaokang Yang

More information about this series at http://www.springer.com/series/7899

Jyotsna Kumar Mandal ·
Somnath Mukhopadhyay ·
Paramartha Dutta · Kousik Dasgupta (Eds.)

Computational Intelligence, Communications, and Business Analytics

Second International Conference, CICBA 2018
Kalyani, India, July 27–28, 2018
Revised Selected Papers, Part I

 Springer

Editors
Jyotsna Kumar Mandal
Department of Computer Science
and Engineering
University of Kalyani
Kalyani, West Bengal, India

Somnath Mukhopadhyay
Department of Computer Science
and Engineering
Assam University
Silchar, Assam, India

Paramartha Dutta
Department of Computer and Systems
Sciences
Visva Bharati University
Santiniketan, West Bengal, India

Kousik Dasgupta
Department of Computer Science
and Engineering
Kalyani Government Engineering College
Kalyani, West Bengal, India

ISSN 1865-0929   ISSN 1865-0937 (electronic)
Communications in Computer and Information Science
ISBN 978-981-13-8577-3   ISBN 978-981-13-8578-0 (eBook)
https://doi.org/10.1007/978-981-13-8578-0

This Springer imprint is published by the registered company Springer Nature Singapore Pte Ltd.
The registered company address is: 152 Beach Road, #21-01/04 Gateway East, Singapore 189721,
Singapore

Foreword

Writing a foreword for the proceeding of an international conference, in the form of an edited volume, cannot but be an intellectual pleasure, which I can ill afford to desist from. But, I would like to avail the opportunity to write a few words for the foreword of the recently concluded Second International Conference on Computational Intelligence, Business Analytics, and Communication (CICBA-2018). The conference was organized by the Kalyani Government Engineering College in association with the Computer Society of India, during July 27–28, 2018, on the Kalyani Government Engineering College campus. The conference was technically co-sponsored by the CSI Kolkata Chapter, IEEE Kolkata chapter, IEEE Young Professionals, Kolkata, as well as the IEEE Computational Intelligence Society, Kolkata chapter. The proceeding of the conference are published by Springer in their CCIS series.

The conference included distinguished general chairs such as Prof. Carlos A. Coello Coello, Investigador Cinvestav, CINVESTAV-IPN, México, and Prof. Xin Yao, Southern University of Science and Technology (SUSTech), China. Prof. Kalyanmoy Deb, Michigan State University, USA, Prof. Hisaob Ishibuchi, Southern University of Science and Technology (SUSTech), China, Prof. Mike Hinchey, University of Limerick, Ireland, Prof. Ashok Deshpande, University of California, Berkeley, USA, were the keynote speakers, and there were luminaries from leading industries and research/academic institutes as invited speakers. The event could attain the true international standard that it intended to achieve.

There were 240 papers submitted from across the globe including countries like Australia, Bangladesh, Indonesia, Lithuania, Nigeria, Portugal, South Korea, USA, and Vietnam – out of which 76 papers were accepted and presented. Three special sessions of the conference were titled Computational Intelligence, Data Communications, and Data Mining and Advanced Data Analytics. The sub-tracks of the conference were Signal Processing, Computational Forensics (Privacy and Security), Microelectronics, Sensors, and Intelligent Networks.

Last but not the least, from my experience, I strongly believe that the conference was undoubtedly commendable, thanks to the organizers, who made it a grand success. CICBA 2019, which will be the third event in the CICBA series, will be organized by, and held at, Jadavpur University Kolkata during December 13–14, 2019, and I am sure that the event will be able to prove its standing as a successful series among the research community in the days ahead.

May 2019   Oscar Castillo

Preface

Kalyani Government Engineering College, in collaboration with the Computer Society of India, organized the Second International Conference on Computational Intelligence, Communication, and Business Analytics (CICBA 2018), during July 27–28, 2018, on the Kalyani Government Engineering College Campus. This was the second activity of the Computer Society of India in an Eastern region with Springer as the publication partner. This conference was organized in technical collaboration with the Computer Society of India Kolkata Chapter, IEEE Kolkata section, IEEE Young Professionals, and IEEE CIS Kolkata. This mega event covered all aspects of computational intelligence, communications, and business analytics where the scope was not limited only to various engineering disciplines such as computer science, electronics, and biomedical engineering researchers but also included researchers from allied communities like data analytics and management science etc.

The volume is a collection of high-quality peer-reviewed research papers received from all over the world. CICBA 2018 attracted a good number of submissions from the different areas spanning over three tracks in various cutting-edge technologies of specialized focus, which were organized and chaired by eminent professors. These three special sessions were: Computational Intelligence, Data Communications, and Data Mining and Advanced Data Analytics. The sub-tracks of the conference were Signal Processing, Computational Forensics (Privacy and Security), Microelectronics, Sensors, and Intelligent Networks. Based on a rigorous peer-review process by the Technical Program Committee members along with external experts as reviewers (national as well as international), the best quality papers were identified for presentation and publication. The review process was extremely stringent with a minimum of three reviews for each submission and occasionally up to six reviews. Checking of similarities and overlaps was also done based on the international norms and standards. Submitted papers came from countries like Australia, Bangladesh, Indonesia, Lithuania, Nigeria, Portugal, South Korea, the USA, and Vietnam. Out of the submission pool of received papers, only 30% were accepted for these proceedings.

The Organizing Committee of CICBA 2018 was made up of strong international academic and industrial luminaries and the Technical Program Committee comprised more than 200 domain experts. The proceedings of the conference are published as one volume in *Communications in Computer and Information Science* (CCIS), Springer, indexed by ISI Proceedings, DBLP, Ulrich's, EI-Compendex, SCOPUS, Zentralblatt Math, MetaPress, Springerlink and will be available at http://www.springer.com/series/7899. We, in our capacity as volume editors, convey our sincere gratitude to Springer for providing the opportunity to publish the proceedings of CICBA 2018 in their CCIS series.

The conference included distinguished general chairs and speakers such as Prof. Carlos A. Coello Coello, Investigador Cinvestav 3F, CINVESTAV-IPN, México, Prof. Xin Yao, Southern University of Science and Technology (SUSTech), China, Prof. Kalyanmoy Deb, Michigan State University, USA, Prof. Hisaob Ishibuchi, Southern University of Science and Technology (SUSTech), China, Prof. Mike Hinchey, University of Limerick, Ireland, Prof. Ashok Deshpande, University of California, Berkeley, USA, Prof. Pabitra Mitra, IIT Kharagpur, India, and Prof. Atal Chaudhuri, Vice-Chancellor, Veer Surendra Sai University of Technology (VSSUT), Burla, Odisha, India.

The editors express their sincere gratitude to Prof. Kalyanmoy Deb, Michigan State University, and Prof. Mike Hinchey, University of Limerick, Ireland, for offering their time to provide valuable guidance and inspiration to overcome various difficulties in the process of organizing the conference. We would like to take this opportunity to extend our heartfelt thanks to the honorary chair of this conference, Prof. Sankar Kumar Ghosh, Vice-Chancellor, University of Kalyani, India, for his active involvement from the very beginning until the end of the conference; without his support, this conference could never have assumed such a successful shape. Sincerest thanks are due to Prof. Bijay Baran Pal, University of Kalyani, and Prof. P. K. Roy, APIIT, India, for their valuable suggestions regarding the editorial review process. We express our sincere thanks to Prof. Samiran Chattopadhyay, Jadavpur University, for supporting us as in an important role in the Springer award committee. The editors also thank the other members of the award committee of CICBA 2018 for their efforts in selecting the best papers from of pool so many formidable accepted submissions.

Special words of appreciation are due to the Kalyani Government Engineering College, for coming forward to host to the conference, which incidentally was the second in the series. It was indeed heartening to note the enthusiasm of all the faculty, staff, and students of Kalyani Government Engineering College who organized the conference in a professional manner. The involvement of faculty coordinators and student volunteers is particularly praiseworthy in this regard. The editors leave no stone unturned and we the thank technical partners and sponsors for providing all the support and financial assistance.

It is needless to mention the role of the contributors. But for their active support and participation the question of organizing a conference is bound to fall through. The editors take this opportunity to thank the authors of all the papers submitted for their hard work, more so because all of them considered the conference as a viable platform to showcase some of their latest findings, not to mention their adherence to the deadlines and patience with the tedious review process. The quality of a refereed volume primarily depends on the expertise and dedication of the reviewers who volunteer with a smiling face. The editors are further indebted to the Technical Program Committee members and external reviewers who not only produced excellent reviews but also did these in short time frames, in spite of their very busy schedule. Because of their quality work, it has been possible to maintain the high academic standard of the proceedings.

The editors would like to thank the participants of the conference, who have considered the conference a befitting one in spite of all the hardships they had to undergo.

Last but not the least, the editors acknowledge all the volunteers for their tireless efforts in meeting the deadlines and arranging every minute detail meticulously to ensure that the conference achieved its goal, academic or otherwise. Happy Reading!

May 2019

J. K. Mandal
Somnath Mukhopadhyay
Paramartha Dutta
Kousik Dasgupta

Organization

Conference Tracks (Not Limited to)

Sushmitra Mitra	Indian Statistical Institute Kolkata, India
Shaikh Anowarul Fattah	BUET, Bangladesh
Biplab Sikdar	National University of Singapore, Singapore
Basabi Chakraborty	Iwate Prefectural University, Japan

General Chair

Xin Yao	Southern Univeristy of Science and Technology, Shenzhen, China
Carlos A. Coello Coello	Investigador Cinvestav 3F, CINVESTAV-IPN, México

Technical Program Committee Chairs

J. K. Mandal	University of Kalyani, India
Paramartha Dutta	Visva Bharati University, India
Somnath Mukhopadhyay	Assam University Silchar, India
Kousik Dasgupta	Kalyani Government Engineering College, India

Patron

Sourabh Kumar Das	Kalyani Government Engineering College, India

Conveners

Malay Kumar Pakhira	Kalyani Government Engineering College, India
Kousik Dasgupta	Kalyani Government Engineering College, India

Co-conveners

Swapan Kumar Mondal	Kalyani Government Engineering College, India
Shib Shankar Saha	Kalyani Government Engineering College, India

International Advisory Board

A. Damodaram	Jawaharlal Nehru Technological University, India
A. K. Nayak	Computer Society of India, India
A. Kaykobad	Bangladesh University of Engineering and Technology, Bangladesh
Amiya Nayak	Ottawa University, Canada

Anirban Basu	Computer Society of India, India
Arun Baran Samaddar	National Institute of Technology, Sikkim, India
Atal Chowdhury	Jadavpur University, India
Atulya Nagar	Liverpool Hope University, UK
Aynur Unal	Stanford University, USA
B. K. Panigrahi	Indian Institute of Technology Delhi, India
Barin Kumar De	Tripura University, India
Bidyut Baran Chaudhuri	Indian Statistical Institute Kolkata, India
Girijasankar Mallik	University of Western Sydney, Australia
Hyeona Lim	Mississippi State University, USA
K. V. Arya	Indian Institute of Information Technology and Management Gwalior, India
Millie Pant	Indian Institute of Technology Roorkee, India
Mrinal Kanti Naskar	Jadavpur University, India
Nandini Mukhopadhyay	Jadavpur University, India
Prith Banerjee	Schneider Electric, USA
Rahul Kala	Indian Institute of Information Technology Allahabad, India
Rajkumar Buyya	University of Melbourne, Australia
Sajal Das	University Texas at Arlington, USA
Santosh Mohanty	TCS Mumbai India
Shikharesh Majumdar	Carleton University, Canada
Somnath Mukhopadhay	Texas University, USA
Subarna Shakya	Tribhuvan University, Nepal
Subhansu Bandyopadhyay	Calcutta University, India
Vadim L. Stefanuk	Institute of Transmission Problems, Russia

Technical Program Committee

Arindam Pal	TCS Innovation Lab, India
A. C. Mondal	University of Burdwan, India
A. Chattopadhyay	Siliguri Institute of Technology, India
A. M. Sudhakara	University of Mysore, India
Abhishek Bhattacharya	Institute of Engineering and Management, India
Ajay K. Khan	Assam University Silchar, India
Alok Kumar Rastogi	Institute for Excellence in Higher Education Bhopal, India
Amiya Kumar Rath	Veer Surendra Sai University of Technology, India
Amlan Chakrabarti	Calcutta University, India
Andrew M. Lynn	Jawaharlal Nehru Technological University, India
Angshuman Bhttacharyya	National Institute of Technology Durgapur, India
Angsuman Sarkar	Kalyani Government Engineering College, India
Anindita Roy	BP Poddar Institute of Management and Technology, India
Anirban Guha	Jadavpur University, India
Anuradha Banerjee	Kalyani Government Engineering College, India

Arnab K. Laha	Indian Institute of Management Ahmedabad, India
Arpita Chakraborty	Techno India Salt Lake, India
Arundhati Bagchi Misra	Saginaw Valley State University, USA
Ashok Deshpande	University of California, USA
Ashok Kumar Rai	Gujarat University, India
Asif Ekbal	Indian Institute of Technology Patna, India
Asok Kumar	MCKV Institute of Engineering, India
Atanu Kundu	Heritage institute of Technology, India
Atta Ur Rehman Khan	COMSATS Institute of Information Technology Abbottabad, Iraq
Ayan Datta	IACS Kolkata, India
B. B. Pal	University of Kalyani, India
Balakrushna Tripathy	Vellore Institute of Technology, India
Bandana Barman	Kalyani Government Engineering College, India
Banshidhar Majhi	National Institute of Technology Rourkela, India
Bhaba R. Sarker	Louisiana State University, USA
Bhabani P. Sinha	Indian Statistical Institute Kolkata, India
Bhagvati Chakravarthy	University of Hyderabad, India
Bhaskar Sardar	Jadavpur University, India
Bibhas Chandra Dhara	Jadavpur University, India
Bijan Tadayon	Z Advanced Computing, Inc. (ZAC TM), USA
Bikash Patel	Kalyani Government Engineering College, India
Biplab K. Sikdar	Indian Institute of Engineering Science and Technology Shibpur, India
Brojo Kishore Mishra	C. V. Raman College of Engineering, India
Buddhadeb Manna	University of Calcutta, India
C. K. Chanda	Indian Institute of Engineering Science and Technology, India
C. Srinivas	Kakatiya Institute of Technology and Science, India
Carlos A. Bana e Costa	Universidade de Lisboa, Portugal
Celia Shahnaz	Bangladesh University of Engineering and Technology Dhaka, Bangladesh
Chandan Bhar	Indian School of Mines, India
Chandreyee Chowdhury	Jadavpur University, India
Chilukuri K. Mohan	Syracuse University, USA
Chintan Bhatt	Charotar University of Science and Technology Gujarat, India
Chintan Mandal	Jadavpur University, India
D. D. Sinha	Calcutta University, India
Dac-Nhuong Le	Haiphong University Haiphong, Vietnam
Dakshina Ranjan Kisku	National Institute of Technology Durgapur, India
Debashis De	Maulana Abul Kalam Azad University of Technology, India
Debasish Nandi	National Institute of Technology Durgapur, India
Debdatta Kandar	North East Hill University, India
Debesh Das	Jadavpur University, India

Debidas Ghosh	National Institute of Technology Durgapur, India
Debotosh Bhattacharjee	Jadavpur University, India
Deepak Khemani	Indian Institute of Technology Madras, India
Deepak Kumar	Amity University, India
Dhananjay Bhattacharyya	Saha Institute of Nuclear Physics Kolkata, India
Dhananjay Kumar Singh	Global ICT Standardization Forum for India (GISFI), India
Dharampal Singh	Namibia University, Namibia
Diganta Goswami	Indian Institute of Technology Guwahati, India
Dilip Kumar Pratihar	Indian Institute of Technology Kharagpur, India
Dipanwita Roychowdhury	Indian Institute of Technology Kharagpur, India
Dulal Acharjee	Purushottam Institute of Engineering and Technology, India
Durgesh Kumar Mishra	Computer Society of India, India
Esteban Alfaro Cortés	University of Castilla-La Mancha, Spain
Ganapati Panda	Indian Institute of Technology Bhubaneswar, India
Goutam Sanyal	National Institute of Technology Durgapur, India
Goutam Sarker	National Institute of Technology Durgapur, India
Govinda K.	Vellore Institute of Technology, India
Gunamani Jena	Roland Institute of Technology, India
H. S. Lalliel	University of Derby, UK
Hirak Maity	College of Engineering and Management Kolaghat, India
Indrajit Saha	National Institute of Tech. Teachers' Training and Research Kolkata, India
Irina Perfilieva	University of Ostrava, Czech Republic
J. V. R. Murthy	Jawaharlal Nehru Technological University Kakinada, India
Jimson Mathew	University of Bristol, UK
Jyoti Prakash Singh	National Institute of Technology Patna, India
K. Kannan	Nagaland University, India
K. Srujan Raju	CMR Group of Institutions, India
K. Suresh Basu	Jawaharlal Nehru Technological University, India
Kameswari Chebrolu	Indian Institute of Technology Bombay, India
Kamrul Alam Khan	Jagannath University, Bangladesh
Kandarpa Kumar Sarma	Gauhati University, India
Kartick Chandra Mandal	Jadavpur University, India
Kathleen Kramer	University of San Diego, USA
Kazumi Nakamatsu	University of Hyogo, Japan
Koushik Majumder	Maulana Abul Kalam Azad University of Technology, India
Krishnendu Chakraborty	Government College of Engineering and Ceramic Technology, India
Kui Yu	University of South Australia, Australia
Kunal Das	Narula Institute of Technology, India
Le Hoang Son	Vietnam National University, Vietnam

Lothar Thiele	Swiss Federal Institute of Technology Zurich, Switzerland
M. Ali Akber Dewan	Athabasca University, Canada
M. S. Prasad Babu	Andhra University, India
M. Sandirigama	University of Peradenia, Sri Lanka
Malay Bhattacharyya	Indian Institute of Engineering Science and Technology, India
Manas Kumar Bera	Haldia Institute of Technology, India
Manas Ranjan Senapati	Centurion University of Technology and Management, India
Manish Kumar Kakhani	Mody University, India
Massimo Pollifroni	University of Turin, Italy
M. Marjit Singh	North Eastern Regional Institute of Science & Technology, India
Md. Iftekhar Hussain	North East Hill University, India
Mohammad Ubadullah Bokhari	Aligarh Muslim University, India
Mohd Nazri Ismail	National Defence University of Malaysia (NDUM), Malaysia
N. V. Ramana Rao	Jawaharlal Nehru Technological University, India
Nabendu Chaki	Calcutta University, India
Nhu Nguyen	Duy Tan University, Vietnam
Nibaran Das	Jadavpur University Kolkata, India
Nilanjan Dey	Techno India College of Technology, India
Olema Vincent	University of Pretoria, South Africa
P. Premchand	Osmania University Hyderabad, India
P. S. Neelakanta	Florida Atlantic University, India
Parama Bhaumik	Jadavpur University, India
Partha Pratim Sahu	Tezpur University, India
Pawan Kumar Jha	Purbanchal University, Nepal
Pradosh K. Roy	Asia Pacific Institute of Information Technology, India
Pramod Kumar Meher	Nanyang Technological University, Singapore
Pranab K. Dan	Indian Institute of Technology Kharagpur, India
Prasanta K. Jana	Indian School of Mines Dhanbad, India
Prashant R. Nair	Computer Society of India, India
Pratyay Kuila	National Institute of Technology Sikkim, India
R. K. Jana	Indian Institute of Social Welfare and Business Management, India
R. Sankararama Krishnan	Indian Institute of Technology Kanpur, India
Rajeeb Dey	National Institute of Technology Silchar, India
Ram Sarkar	Jadavpur University, India
Rameshwar Dubey	Montpellier Business School, France
Ranjan Kumar Gupta	West Bengal State University, India
Ray Zhong	University of Auckland, New Zealand
Rober Hans	Tshwane University of Technology, South Africa
S. V. K. Bharathi	Symbiosis International University, India

S. A. Fattah	Bangladesh University of Engineering and Technology Dhaka, Bangladesh
S. D. Dewasurendra	University of Peradenia, Sri Lanka
S. K. Behera	National Institute of Technology Rourkela, India
S. P. Bhattacharyya	Texas A&M University, USA
S. G. Deshmukh	Indian Institute of Technology Mumbai, India
Saikat Chakrabarti	CSIR-IICB Kolkata, India
Samar Sen Sarma	University of Calcutta, India
Samiran Chattopadhyay	Jadavpur University, India
Sanchayan Mukherjee	Kalyani Government Engineering College, India
Sandip Rakshit	Kaziranga University, India
Sanjib K. Panda	Berkeley Education Alliance for Research in Singapore Ltd., Singapore
Sankar Chakraborty	Jadavpur University, India
Sankar Duraikannan	Asia Pacific University of Technology and Innovation, Malaysia
Santi P. Maity	Indian Institute of Engineering Science and Technology Shibpur, India
Sarbani Roy	Jadavpur University, India
Satish Narayana Srirama	University of Tartu, Estonia
Seba Maity	College of Engineering and Management Kolaghat, India
Shangping Ren	Illinois Institute of Technology Chicago, USA
Sheng-Lung Peng	National Dong Hwa University, Taiwan
Soma Barman	University of Calcutta, India
Soumya Pandit	University of Calcutta, India
Sripati Mukhopadhyay	Burdwan University, India
Sruti Gan Chaudhuri	Jadavpur University, India
Subhadip Basu	Jadavpur University, India
Subhranil Som	Amity University Noida, India
Subrata Banerjee	National Institute of Technology Durgapur, India
Sudhakar Sahoo	Institute of Mathematics and Applications, India
Sudhakar Tripathi	National Institute of Technology Patna, India
Sudip Kumar Adhikari	Cooch Behar Government Engineering College, India
Sudip Kumar Das	Calcutta University, India
Sudip Kundu	Calcutta University, India
Sudipta Roy	Assam University, India
Sukumar Nandi	Indian Institute of Technology Guwahati, India
Sumit Kundu	National Institute of Technology Durgapur, India
Sunita Sarkar	Assam University Silchar, India
Supratim Sengupta	Indian Institute of Engineering Science and Technology Shibpur, India
Sushmita Mitra	Indian Statistical Institute Kolkata, India
Swapan Kumar Mandal	Kalyani Government Engineering College, India
Syed Samsul Alam	Aliah University, India
T. K. Kaul	Sikkim University, India

Tamaghna Acharya	Indian Institute of Engineering Science and Technology, India
Tandra Pal	National Institute of Technology Durgapur, India
Tapan K. Ghosh	West Bengal University of Animal and Fishery Sciences, India
Tapas Halder	Kalyani Government Engineering College, India
Tridibesh Das	Kalyani Government Engineering College, India
Tushar Kanti Bera	Yonsei University, South Korea
U. Dinesh Kumar	Indian Institute of Management Bangalore, India
Utpal Biswas	University of Kalyani, India
V. Prithiviraj	Pondicherry Engineering College, India
Vincenzo Piuri	Università degli Studi di Milano, Italy
Vladimir A. Oleshchuk	University of Agder, Norway
Yoshihiro Kilho Shin	University of Hyogo, Japan
Zaigham Mahmood	University of Derby, UK
Arijit Chowdhury	TCS Innovation Lab, India
Hemanta Dey	Techno India College of Technology, India
Muheet Ahmed Butt	University of Kashmir, India
Samir Malakar	MCKV Institute of Engineering, Howrah, India
Snehasis Banerjee	TCS Innovation Lab, India
Tapodhir Acharjee	Assam University Silchar, India

Contents – Part I

Signal Processing and Communications

Microelectronics, Sensors, and Intelligent Networks

Contents – Part II

Intelligent Data Mining and Data Warehousing

Computational Forensics (Privacy and Security)

Computational Intelligence

Automatic Multiclass Classification of Foliar Leaf Diseases Using Statistical and Color Feature Extraction and Support Vector Machine

Aparajita Datta[1], Abhishek Dey[2($\boxtimes$)], and Kashi Nath Dey[3]

[1] Department of Computer Science and Engineering,
University of Calcutta, Kolkata, India
[2] Department of Computer Science, Bethune College,
University of Calcutta, Kolkata, India
abhishek7@gmail.com
[3] Department of Computer Science and Engineering,
DSCSDEC, JIS GROUP, Kolkata, India

Abstract. Disease detection in crops and plants is essential for production of good and improved quality of food, life and a stable agricultural economy. It becomes tedious and time consuming to observe the infected parts of plants manually. Recourses with proper expertise are also required to have continuous monitoring. Digital image processing along with computer vision techniques can be applied to automate early detection of plant diseases and it can save significant amount of resources. In this paper, an automated approach based on image processing and machine learning techniques is proposed which can detect three major kinds of diseases Downy Mildew, Frogeye Leaf Spot and Septoria Leaf Blight that affects apple, grapes, soybean, tomatoes and many other major plants of economic value. Generally, leaves are the most affected part of the plants. So, instead of the whole plant, concentration is given on the leaf. In this paper, image pre-processing methods like noise removal and contrast enhancement followed by colour space transformation and k-means clustering is used to segment affected parts of soybean leaves, after that both texture and colour features are extracted from segmented samples and Support Vector Machine (SVM) classification is used to separate three kinds of diseases mentioned previously.

Keywords: Foliar leaf disease · Machine learning · k-means clustering · Feature extraction · Support Vector Machine

1 Introduction

One of the major economical foundations of any country is agriculture and majority of population is actively or passively engaged in this profession. Effective growth of a plant and increase its yield is necessary to meet increasing demand in the agricultural industry. Therefore, constant monitoring of the plant is needed during its growth period and time of harvest. Plants are severely affected by diseases caused by fungus and bacteria. If plant diseases are not identified within a proper period of time it can spread rapidly and

© Springer Nature Singapore Pte Ltd. 2019
J. K. Mandal et al. (Eds.): CICBA 2018, CCIS 1030, pp. 3–15, 2019.
https://doi.org/10.1007/978-981-13-8578-0_1

cause a major damage in the agricultural output. Proper diagnosis of disease within a proper time can save lots of plants and can provide safety to the crop production. There are several control measures and strategic approaches once the disease is identified properly. Otherwise taking disease control measures without any prior identification can result in wastage of money, time and further crop loss [1].

About 80% to 90% of disease on the plant is on its leaves. So, instead of the whole plant, concentration is given on the leaf. Among many harmful diseases, Septoria Leaf Blight, Downy Mildew and Frogeye Leaf Spot are matters of concern in this paper. These diseases are observed in several plants like soybean, capsicum, capsicum annum, tomato, grapes, maize, rice, wheat etc.

In this paper, a novel method to automate classification of previously mentioned three diseases based on image processing and machine learning techniques is proposed. It is observed that, all of the plants show similar kind of symptoms when affected and after proper disease detection; all of the plants undergo similar kind of treatments. For example, the texture and color of leaf blight of tomato leaves are same as that of soybean leaves. The steps to classify these diseases remain same for other plants if classification is done for one plant. Hence, for experimental purpose affected soybean leaf samples are used in this paper. Soybean, which is economically one of the most important crops in the world, provides vegetable protein for millions of people and is used as a major ingredient for oil and several chemical products. Lower leaves are infected by Septoria Leaf Blight at early growth stage. Late in the growing season, infected leaves may turn yellow or rusty brown and drop prematurely. Frogeye Leaf Spot can occur at any stage of soybean development, the most common initial symptoms are tiny, yellow spots on the leaves [2]. These spots eventually enlarge and centers of these lesions become gray to brown and have reddish purple margins. Downy Mildew is a very common foliar disease of soybeans that forms yellow small spots at initial stage and in advanced stage spots become enlarged and coalesce to form larger yellow patches [2]. Later these lesions may turn into brown patches but a yellow border always exists at the boundary of the patches of the lesion. Hence, identification of these diseases is essential at early stage to maintain optimal production rate of soybean. Soybean leaves affected by these three diseases are shown in Fig. 1. Disease classification must be enough accurate to be reliable in real life work. Affected plant leaves must have visible symptoms of infection. Any detectable change in texture, color, shape can be considered as a symptom and can be used as a part of disease identification.

(a)   (b)   (c)

Fig. 1. (a) Septoria Leaf Blight, (b) Frogeye leaf spot, (c) Downy mildew

In recent years, quite a number of methods have been used to automate leaf disease detection in soybean leaves. [1] proposed a technique for detection of soybean damaged by insect using hyperspectral imaging. Detection of two common soybean diseases Frogeye and Brown Spot using shape features and k-nearest neighbor classifier is proposed in [3]. In [4], a method for soybean disease detection based on salient regions and k-means clustering is proposed. [5] introduced a method based on local descriptors (SIFT, DSIFT, SURF, PHOW) and Bag of Visual Words to detect soybean diseases. In our paper, main focus is on automated and accurate detection of Downy Mildew, Frogeye Leaf Spot and Septoria Leaf Blight independent of the plant so that these diseases can be identified at early stage. Soybean leaf samples affected with these three diseases are used only for experimental purpose.

The rest of the paper is organized as follows. The proposed methodology is explained in details in Sect. 2. Detailed experimental results and analysis are described in Sect. 3 and the conclusion is summed up in Sect. 4.

2 Methodology

The proposed method is comprised of four main phases; in the first phase, image sample of soybean leaves are pre-processed by applying noise removal and contrast enhancement techniques. In the second phase, a color transformation structure for the RGB leaf image sample is created and color space is converted to L*a*b* color space. Then, affected part of image is segmented using k-means clustering technique [8]. In the third phase, color and texture features for the segmented image sample are extracted from luminance and chrominance channels of the images respectively. Gray Level Co-occurrence Matrix (GLCM) is used for texture feature extraction [7]. Then, color and texture features are fused into a single feature matrix [10]. Finally, in the fourth phase the feature matrix obtained previously is passed as input to a Support Vector Machine (SVM) classifier for training purpose. A new set of affected leaf image samples are evaluated by the trained classifier for performance assessment. The proposed system is shown diagrammatically in Fig. 2.

2.1 Pre-processing

Pre-processing removes disease independent variations from the input image, enhances some image features or curbs unwanted distortions, thus making it suitable for further processing tasks like feature extraction and classification.

The input images are normalized in the range [0, 1] and resized to 256 × 256. The motivation of normalization is to achieve stable dynamic range for a set of images by changing range of pixel intensity values. Since the image acquisition is done without any prior criteria with respect to brightness or quality of image, image can be noisy, i.e. sudden random variation of brightness and color information can exist. So, the noise removal is an essential step but removal of noise must be done is such a way that original image remains unchanged [6]. In this paper, 2-D Gaussian filter is used for noise removal. The aim of contrast enhancement is to expand the dynamic range of

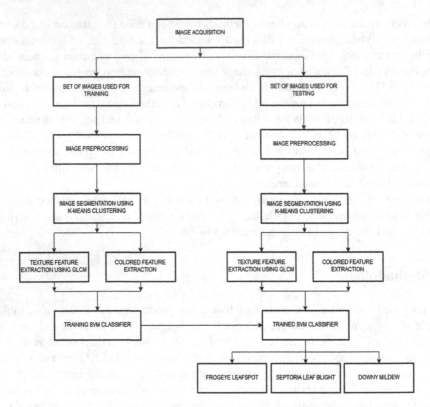

Fig. 2. Block diagram of the proposed system

gray levels in the image being processed. In this paper, contrast is enhanced using unsharp masking method. The pre-processing steps are shown in Fig. 3.

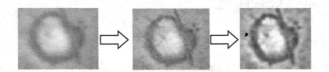

Fig. 3. (a) Normalized and resized leaf image sample, (b) Leaf image sample after noise removal, (c) Leaf image sample after contrast enhancement

2.2 Color Space Conversion and Segmentation

After pre-processing phase, Image segmentation using k-means clustering is used to find the affected portion of leaf image sample. In image segmentation, an image is partitioned into different groups or segments where the similarity between the elements of same group is higher than that of different groups. The goal of segmentation is to produce a simplified representation of an image thus making it easier to analyze [8].

In k-means clustering, n samples are grouped into k clusters such that each sample belongs to the cluster with the closest mean value, serving as prototype of that cluster. Mathematically, given a set of samples $(x_1, x_2 \ldots x_n)$, where each sample is a d-dimensional real vector, k-means clustering partitions the n samples into k ($\leq$ n) sets $S = \{S_1, S_2, \ldots, S_k\}$ in order to minimize the within-cluster sum of squares (WCSS) (sum of distance functions of each point in the cluster to the k centers) [11]. Therefore, the objective is to find: $arg_s \min \sum_{i=1}^{k} \sum_{x \in S_i} ||x - \mu_i||^2$

Here μ_i is the mean of points in S_i.

The main steps of k-means clustering algorithm used in this paper are shown below:

Step 1: Transform image from RGB to L*a*b* color space from RGB color space since it makes segments visually more differentiable.
Step 2: Classify colors using k-means clustering algorithm in 'a*b*' space since a*b space contains the color information.
Step 3: Label each pixel in the image from the results of k-Means algorithm.
Step 4: Generate images that segment the image by color.

Since k-means clustering for the entire image becomes time consuming the leaves are split into multiple quadrilateral sub-image samples and k-means clustering is done on those sub-images.

Selection of disease containing segment is the most vital issue in this context because in order to make the proposed method fully automated disease containing segment must be selected automatically without manual intervention. In this paper, k = 2 has been used so that two clusters are produced as output, one with the affected portion and the other with the unaffected portion of leaf image samples as shown in Fig. 4. It can be observed that, the entire affected portion of the leaves have colors ranging in red to yellow and the unaffected portions have color shades ranging within green to blue. Observing the scenario in an L*a*b* color space it can be noted that, since all the affected portions have colors ranging within red to yellow these pixels will have higher a* and b* values than that of unaffected green portions. It is obvious since both the red component and the yellow component has positive values and both green and blue components have negative values.

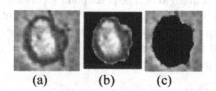

(a)   (b)   (c)

Fig. 4. (a) Pre-processed leaf image sample, (b) Cluster containing affected portion, (c) Cluster containing unaffected portion

As shown in Fig. 5, the affected portions of leaf samples can be plotted in the positive co-ordinates i.e. red to yellow ranges and the unaffected portions can be plotted in the negative co-ordinates i.e. green to blue ranges. Hence, the average of the color intensity has been taken of each segment and the highest one of them is considered as the affected segment. Using this logic, the affected segments, which actually contain disease information, are obtained for each image sample and saved for next phase feature extraction.

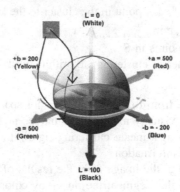

Fig. 5. Plot of affected and unaffected portions of leaf samples in L*a* b* color space (Color figure online)

2.3   Color and Texture Feature Extraction

The target of feature extraction is to decrease the original data by measuring some properties i.e. features that can distinguish one input object from another object. Image texture refers to the appearance, organization and structure of the parts of an object within the image [7].

In this paper, color space of the segmented image is changed to HSV in order to obtain three channels. Among them, one channel contains luminance information and other two channels contain information on chrominance [10]. Texture features are then extracted from the Value (V) channel that is the luminance or intensity of the image samples. Gray Level Co-occurrence Matrix (GLCM) is used for texture feature extraction purpose. GLCM signifies the spatial relationship between each intensity tone by calculating changes between grey levels i and j at a particular distance d and at a particular angle θ. After defining d and θ, pixel pairs separated by d, calculated across the direction defined by θ, are analyzed. After that, the number of pixel pairs that possess a given distribution of grey-level values is counted [10]. After obtaining GLCM of the segmented leaf image sample, $d = 1$ and $\theta = 0°$ are used for extracting following features from the matrix:

Entropy: $-\sum_{i=1}^{Ng} \sum_{j=1}^{Ng} P(i,j) \log(P(i,j))$, signifies the degree of disorder among pixels in the image

Contrast: $\sum_{n=0}^{Ng-1} |i-j|^2 \left\{ \sum_{i=1}^{Ng} \sum_{j=1}^{Ng} P(i,j) \right\}$, represents amount of local gray level variation in an image

Dissimilarity: $\sum_{n=0}^{Ng-1} |i-j| \left\{ \sum_{i=1}^{Ng} \sum_{j=1}^{Ng} P(i,j) \right\}$

Correlation: $\sum_{i=1}^{Ng} \sum_{j=1}^{Ng} \frac{ijP(i,j)-\mu_x\mu_y}{\sigma_x\sigma_y}$, signifies the linear dependency of gray levels on neighboring pixels

Variance: $\sum_{i=1}^{Ng} \sum_{j=1}^{Ng} (i-\mu)^2 P(i,j)$, signifies the dispersion (with regard to the mean) of the gray level distribution

Energy: $\sum_i \sum_j (P(i,j))^2$, signifies sum of squared elements in the GLCM

Inverse Difference Moment Normalized: $\sum_i \sum_j \frac{1}{1+(i-j)^2} P(i,j)$, signifies smoothness of image, it is expected to be high if the gray levels of the pixel are similar

Sum Average: $\sum_{i=2}^{2Ng} iP_{x+y}(i)$, signifies the mean of the gray level sum distribution of the image

Sum Entropy: $-\sum_{i=2}^{2Ng} P_{x+y}(i)\log\{P_{x+y}(i)\}$, signifies the disorder related to gray level sum distribution of the image

Sum Variance: $\sum_{i=2}^{2Ng} \left(i - \left[\sum_{i=2}^{2Ng} iP_{x+y}(i)\right]\right)^2$, signifies the dispersion (with regard to the mean) of the gray level sum distribution of the image

Difference Variance: $\sum_{i=2}^{2Ng} \left(i - \left[\sum_{i=2}^{2Ng} iP_{x-y}(i)\right]\right)^2$, signifies the dispersion (with regard to the mean) of the gray level difference distribution of the image

Difference Entropy: $-\sum_{i=0}^{Ng-1} i^2 P_{x-y}(i) \log\{P_{x-y}(i)\}$, signifies the disorder related to the gray level difference distribution of the image

Information measure of correlation 1: $\frac{HXY-HXY_1}{\max(HX,HY)}$, HX and HY are entropy of Px and Py

Information measure of correlation 2: $\sqrt{1 - e^{-(HXY2-HXY)}}$

Cluster Prominence: $\sum_i \sum_j (i+j-\mu_y-\mu_x)^4 P(i,j)$, signifies variation in gray-scales, low cluster Prominence signifies little variation in gray-scales

Cluster Shade: $\sum_i \sum_j (i+j-\mu_y-\mu_x)^3 P(i,j)$, signifies skewness of the matrix or lack of symmetry

Homogeneity: $\sum_{i=1}^{Ng} \sum_{j=1}^{Ng} \frac{P(i,j)}{1+(i-j)^2}$ signifies the closeness of the distribution of elements in the GLCM to the GLCM diagonal

In all equations, P(i, j) is the (i, j)-th entry of the normalized GLCM, that is, $P(i, j) = \sum_{i,j} P(i, j)/ij\, P(i, j)$, where P(i, j) is the (i, j)-th entry of the computed GLCM; Ng is the total number of gray levels in the image; and μ_y, μ_x and σ_x, σ_y denote the mean and SDs of the row and column sums of the GLCM, respectively. The gray level sum distribution is given by: $Px + y(k) = \sum_{\substack{i=1 \\ i+j=k}}^{Ng} \sum_{j=1}^{Ng} P(i, j)$, $k = 2, 3 \ldots 2Ng$; it is related to the distribution of the sum of co-occurring pixels in the image. The gray level difference distribution is given by: $Px - y(k) = \sum_{\substack{i=1 \\ |i-j|=k}}^{Ng} \sum_{j=1}^{Ng} P(i, j)$, $k = 0, 1, 2 \ldots, Ng - 1$; it is related to the distribution of the difference between co-occurring pixels in the image.

Hue (H) and Saturation (S) channels contain chrominance or color information [10]. H represents the wavelength of a color and S represents the amount of white color mixed with the monochromatic color. Therefore, the mean and standard deviation of both H channel and S channel are taken as features of the image. Then, all these colour and texture features are fused into a single feature matrix as shown in Fig. 6.

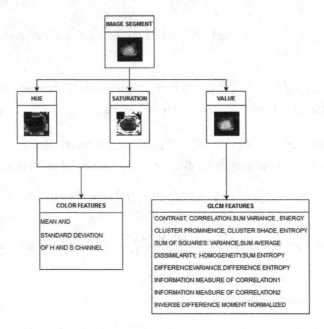

Fig. 6. Block diagram of texture and color feature extraction

2.4   Classification

In any classification method, input data is divided into training and testing sets. Each training set instance contains one target value (i.e. the class labels) and several attribute which are basically the features. In this paper, Support Vector Machine (SVM) classifier is used for classification purpose. SVM is a supervised model of learning that separates a set of training samples into two different classes, $(x_1, y_1), (x_2, y_2), \ldots (x_n, y_n)$ where $x_i \in R^d$, the d-dimensional feature space, and $y_i \in \{-1, +1\}$, the class label, with

$i = 1..n$. SVM computes the optimal hyper planes, which separates the classes, based on a kernel function (K). All samples, of which feature vector lies on one side of the hyper plane, belong to class -1 and the others are belong to class $+1$ [12].

In linear SVM, the training samples are linearly separable. A linear function of this form is shown below:

$$f(x) = w^T x + b \qquad (19)$$

such that for each training sample x_i the function results $f(x_i) > 0$ for $y_i = +1$, and $f(x_i) < 0$ for $y_i = -1$. In other words, training patterns of two different classes are separated by the hyperplane $f(x) = w^T x + b = 0$, where w is the weight vector and normal to hyperplane, b threshold or bias and x_i is the data point. In Fig. 7, linear SVM classification with a hyperplane that minimizes the separating margin between the two classes are indicated by data points by black and white circles. Support vectors are patterns of the training set that lie on the boundary hyperplane of the two classes [9].

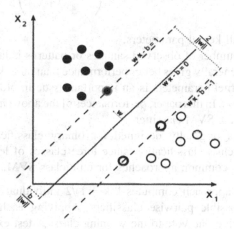

Fig. 7. Maximum-margin hyper plane and margins for a linear SVM trained with samples from two classes

If the data of the classes are non-separable, then non-linear SVM classifier is used [9]. Here, a nonlinear operator is used to map the input pattern x into a higher dimensional space H as shown in Fig. 8.

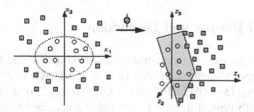

Fig. 8. Non-linear SVM classification

The nonlinear SVM classifier is defined as,

$$f(x) = w^T \phi(x) + b \tag{1}$$

The transformation from non-linear to linear separating hyperplane in higher dimensional feature space is obtained by taking help of kernel functions. A kernel function on two samples, represented as feature vectors in some input space, is defined as k(xi, xj) = ϕ(xi)T ϕ(xj), ϕ is the feature vector. Most commonly used kernels are:

$$\text{Linear kernel: } k(x_i, x_j) = x_i^T x_j \tag{2}$$

$$\text{Polynomial Kernel: } k(x_i, x_j) = (\gamma x_i^T x_j + r)^d, \gamma > 0 \tag{3}$$

$$\text{RBF Kernel: } k(x_i, x_j) = \exp\left(-\frac{\|x_i - x_j\|^2}{2\sigma^2}\right), \sigma > 0 \tag{4}$$

σ, γ, r and d are all kernel parameters.

In general, when number of observed samples or patterns is larger than number of features, RBF kernel generally gives better performance than other kernel functions [12]. Proper selection of kernel parameters is an important issue in order to gain very high accuracy of classification. In this paper, performances of the above mentioned kernels are compared for training the SVM classifier.

Though SVM was originally designed for binary classification, the proposed method requires multiclass classification since three classes of leaf diseases are considered. There are two common approaches for multiclass SVM:

(i) One against one approach computes k(k − 1)/2 individual binary classifiers by evaluating all possible pairwise classifiers. Applying each classifier to a test example would give one vote to the winning class. A test example is labelled to the class with the most votes [13].

(ii) One against all approach computes k separate binary classifiers for k-class classification. The nth binary classifier is trained using the data from the nth class as positive examples and the remaining (k − 1) classes as negative examples. During test, the class label is determined by the binary classifier that gives maximum output value [13].

In the proposed method, one-against-all method is used for multiclass classification.

3   Experimental Results and Discussion

All the image pre-processing, segmentation, feature extraction and SVM classification techniques in our proposed method are simulated in MATLAB version R2016a and run on a Intel(R) Core(TM) i3-4005U CPU with 4 GB memory. Total 1094 image samples of soybean leaves with typical disease symptoms are acquired from PlantVillage.org, including 373 image samples of Downy mildew, 380 images of Septoria Leaf Blight and 341 image samples of Frogeye Leaf Spot. Among 1094 samples, 794 samples are used for training purpose which consists of 273 samples of Downy mildew, 280 samples of Septoria Leaf Blight and 241 samples of Frogeye Leaf Spot. After pre-processing and segmentation steps, 17 texture features and 4 color features are extracted from these samples and a 794×21 feature matrix is formed as described in Sect. 2 and this feature matrix is fed into SVM classifier for training purpose.

Performance of the classifier are tested and evaluated by the following parameters: Accuracy = Correctly classified samples/Classified samples, Sensitivity = Correctly classified positive samples/True positive samples, Specificity = Correctly classified negative samples/True negative samples, Precision = Correctly classified positive samples/Positive classified samples

These parameters can be defined by using the following basic terms:

True positives (TP): It is the number of positive samples that are correctly labeled by the classifier, True negatives (TN): It is the number of negative samples that are correctly labeled by the classifier, False positives (FP): It is the number of negative samples that are incorrectly labeled as positive, False negatives (FN): It is the number of positive samples that are incorrectly labeled as negative.

Using the above mentioned terms the performance evaluation parameters can be defined as:

Accuracy = (TP + TN)/(TP + TN + FP +FN), Sensitivity= TP/(TP + FN), Specificity = TN/(TN + FP), Precision = TP/(TP + FP)

Multiclass SVM classifier is trained using different kernel functions as described in Sect. 2.4. It is clear from Table 1 that using Radial Basis Function (RBF) kernel, SVM classifier can achieve overall optimal accuracy after training. Trained SVM classifier is applied on five different test set of leaf image samples consisting of 300, 250, 200, 150 and 100 samples respectively which were not present in the trainset. It is also essential to analyze performance of classifier for three diseases separately for all the five cases.

Table 1. Performance comparison of kernel functions used in training the multiclass SVM classifier for five different test set of image samples

Kernel function	Accuracy for 300 image samples	Accuracy for 250 image samples	Accuracy for 200 image samples	Accuracy for 150 image samples	Accuracy for 100 image samples
Linear	97%	97%	98%	99%	98%
Polynomial	98%	94%	91%	92.5%	95.4%
RBF	96%	97%	97%	96%	98%

It can be observed from Tables 2, 3, 4, 5 and 6, much satisfactory result is obtained for all performance evaluation parameters by applying trained multiclass SVM classifier on five different test set of soybean leaf image samples. Hence, the proposed method in this paper can also be applied on other plants to classify Septoria Leaf Blight, Downy Mildew and Frogeye Leaf Spot diseases.

Table 2. Performance of SVM classifier (using RBF kernel) for 100 test samples of affected leaf image consisting of 34 Septoria Leaf Blight, 33 Downy Mildew and 33 Frogeye Leaf Spot

	TP	TN	FP	FN	Precision	Sensitivity	Specificity	Accuracy
Mildew	31	66	0	3	100%	91.1765%	100%	97%
Frogeye	32	65	3	0	91.4286%	100%	95.5882%	97%
Blight	34	66	0	0	100%	100%	100%	100%

Table 3. Performance of SVM classifier (using RBF kernel) for 150 test samples of affected leaf image consisting of 50 Septoria Leaf Blight, 50 Downy Mildew and 50 Frogeye Leaf Spot

	TP	TN	FP	FN	Precision	Sensitivity	Specificity	Accuracy
Mildew	50	99	1	0	98.0392%	100%	99%	99.3333%
Frogeye	49	100	0	1	100%	98%	100%	99.3333%
Blight	50	100	0	0	100%	100%	100%	100%

Table 4. Performance of SVM classifier (using RBF kernel) for 200 test samples of affected leaf image consisting of 65 Septoria Leaf Blight, 70 Downy Mildew and 65 Frogeye Leaf Spot

	TP	TN	FP	FN	Precision	Sensitivity	Specificity	Accuracy
Mildew	70	127	3	0	97.1429%	97.1429%	98.4615%	98%
Frogeye	62	135	0	3	96.9231%	96.9231%	98.5185%	98%
Blight	65	135	0	0	100%	100%	100%	100%

Table 5. Performance of SVM classifier (using RBF kernel) for 250 test samples of affected leaf image consisting of 87 Septoria Leaf Blight, 80 Downy Mildew and 83 Frogeye Leaf Spot

	TP	TN	FP	FN	Precision	Sensitivity	Specificity	Accuracy
Mildew	80	168	2	0	97.561%	100%	98.8095%	99.1935%
Frogeye	79	167	0	4	100%	95.1807%	100%	98.4%
Blight	87	161	2	0	97.7528%	100%	98.7578%	99.1935%

Table 6. Performance of SVM classifier (using RBF kernel) for 300 test samples of affected leaf image consisting of 100 Septoria Leaf Blight, 100 Downy Mildew and 100 Frogeye Leaf Spot

	TP	TN	FP	FN	Precision	Sensitivity	Specificity	Accuracy
Mildew	100	196	4	0	96.1538%	100%	97.9798%	98.6577%
Frogeye	94	200	0	6	100%	94%	100%	98%
Blight	100	198	2	0	98.0392%	100%	98.9796%	99.3243%

4 Conclusion

In this paper, we have developed a system which can automate classification of three harmful plant leaf affecting diseases namely Septoria Leaf Blight, Downy Mildew and Frogeye Leaf Spot. Our proposed method can be used on any plant affected by these three diseases. Manual intervention is totally eliminated by developing a new logic to automatically identify the segment containing disease information as explained in Methodology section. For classification purpose, multiclass SVM classifier is used which is much efficient than other classifiers in terms of computational overhead. Affected soybean leaf samples are used in experiment and performance is evaluated on different test set of samples. Experimental results of our method show that accuracy of disease detection is more than 95% in all cases. Hence, it can be concluded that the proposed method in this paper is very efficient and can be applied on any plant with leaves affected with three common but injurious plant leaf diseases.

References

1. Shrivastava, S., Hooda, D.S.: Automatic brown spot and frog eye detection from the image captured in the field. Am. J. Intell. Syst. **4**(4), 131–134 (2014)
2. Dongre, P., Verma, M.T.: A survey of identification of soybean crop diseases. Int. J. Adv. Res. Comput. Eng. Technol. **1**, 361–364 (2012)
3. Ma, Y., Huang, M., Yang, B., Zhu, Q.: Automatic threshold method and optimal wavelength selection for insect-damaged vegetable soybean detection using hyperspectral images. Comput. Electron. Agric. **106**, 102–110 (2014)
4. Gui, J., Hao, L., Zhang, Q., Bao, X.: A new method for soybean leaf disease detection based on modified salient regions. Int. J. Multimed. Ubiquitous Eng. **10**(6), 45–52 (2015)
5. Pires, R.D.L., et al.: Local descriptors for soybean disease recognition. Comput. Electron. Agric. **125**, 48–55 (2016)
6. Patil, A.B., Khirade, S.D.: Plant disease detection using image processing. In: International Conference on Computing Communication Control and Automation (2015)
7. Haralick, R.M., Shanmugam, K., Dinstein, I.: Textural features for image classification. IEEE Trans. Syst. Man Cybern. **SMC-3**(6), 610–621 (1973)
8. Dhanachandra, N., Manglem, K., Chanu, Y.J.: Image segmentation using k-means clustering algorithm and subtractive clustering algorithm. Procedia Comput. Sci. **54**, 764–771 (2015). Eleventh International Multi-Conference on Information Processing-2015 (IMCIP-2015)
9. Pujari, J.D., Yakkundimath, R., Byadgi, A.S.: Classification of fungal disease symptoms affected on cereals using color texture features. Int. J. Signal Process. Image Process. Pattern Recognit. **6**(6), 321–330 (2013). ISSN: 2005-4254
10. Arvis, V., Debain, C., Berducat, M., Benassi, A.: Generalization of the cooccurrence matrix for colour images: application to colour texture classification. Image Anal. Ster. **2004**(23), 63–72 (2004)
11. Hartigan, J.A., Wong, M.A.: A k-means clustering algorithm. J. R. Stat. Soc. Ser. C (Appl. Stat.) **28**(1), 100–108 (1979)
12. Hsu, C.-W., Chang, C.-C., Lin, C.-J.: A practical guide to support vector classification. Department of Computer Science National Taiwan University, Taipei 106, Taiwan
13. Hsu, C.-W., Lin, C.-J.: A comparison of methods for multi-class support vector machines. IEEE Trans. Neural Netw. **13**(2), 415–425 (2002)

Performance of Classifiers on MFCC-Based Phoneme Recognition for Language Identification

Himadri Mukherjee[1(✉)], Moumita Dutta[1], Sk Md Obaidullah[2],
K. C. Santosh[3], Teresa Gonçalves[2], Santanu Phadikar[4], and Kaushik Roy[1]

[1] Department of Computer Science, West Bengal State University, Kolkata, India
himadrim027@gmail.com, moumitadutta.email@gmail.com,
kaushik.mrg@gmail.com
[2] Department of Informatics, University of Evora, Evora, Portugal
sk.obaidullah@gmail.com, tcg@uevora.pt
[3] Department of Computer Science, The University of South Dakota,
Vermillion, SD, USA
santosh.kc@usd.edu
[4] Department of Computer Science and Engineering, Maulana Abul Kalam Azad
University of Technology, Kolkata, India
sphadikar@yahoo.com

Abstract. The automatic identification of language from voice clips is known as automatic language identification. It is very important for a multi lingual country like India where people use more than a single language while talking making speech recognition challenging. An automatic language identifier can help to invoke the language specific speech recognizers making voice interactive systems more user friendly and simplifying their implementation. Phonemes are unique atomic sounds which are combined to constitute the words of a language. In this paper, the performance of different classifiers is presented for the task of phoneme recognition to aid in automatic language identification as well as speech recognition. We have used Mel Frequency Cepstral Coefficient (MFCC) based features to characterize Bangla Swarabarna phonemes and obtained an accuracy of 98.17% on a database of 3710 utterances by 53 speakers.

Keywords: Automatic language identification · Speech recognition · Phoneme · MFCC

1 Introduction

Speech recognition based applications have developed significantly over the years facilitating the lives of the commoners. Though devices and applications have become more user friendly, residents of different multi-lingual countries like India have not been fully able to take advantage of them. They often use multiple languages while talking (which is perhaps one of the reasons for the limited success

© Springer Nature Singapore Pte Ltd. 2019
J. K. Mandal et al. (Eds.): CICBA 2018, CCIS 1030, pp. 16–26, 2019.
https://doi.org/10.1007/978-981-13-8578-0_2

of speech recognizers) in addition to the complexity of the Indic languages. A system which can determine the spoken language from voice signals can help in recognizing multilingual speech by helping to invoke language specific recognizers; this task of automatically determining the language from voice signals is termed as automatic language identification.

Every language has atomic and unique sounds known as phonemes; these phonemes are used in different combinations for constituting the words of that language. Identification of phonemes from voice signals can aid in language identification as presented in [1,3]. Vowel phonemes are an important aspect of a language playing a major role in the constitution of most of the words in it. Distinguishing phonemes of a single language is a crucial task prior to applying it in a multilingual scenario; it can also help in recognizing words and phrases from audio.

Hasanat et al. [5] distinguished Bangla phonemes with 13 reflection coefficients and autocorrelations; they used an Euclidean distance based technique for the classification of unknown phonemes obtaining an accuracy of 80%. Hybrid features were used by Kotwal et al. [7] for the classification of Bangla phonemes; they used a HMM based approach and obtained an accuracy of 58.53% when using train and test sets of 3000 and 1000 sentences, respectively. Hossain et al. [9] obtained accuracies of 93.66%, 93.33% and 92% with the help of Euclidean distance, hamming distance and artificial neural network, respectively, for classifying 10 phonemes out of which 6 were vowels and 4 were consonants. They used MFCC features in their experiments and tested their system on a database of 300 phonemes.

Zissman et al. [1] used a different approaches for language identification including a phoneme based approach and n-gram modelling. They experimented with the OGI multiple language telephonic speech corpus [2] and obtained an accuracy of 79.2% for 10 languages. They also carried out different experiments with 2 language closed sets like English-Japanese, Japanese-Spanish and English-Spanish which are detailed in [1]. Furthermore, Zissman [3] attempted at language identification with the help of phoneme recognition coupled with phonotactic language modelling obtaining accuracies of 89% and 98% for 11 languages and two language sets, respectively, from the OGI multi lingual telephonic speech corpus. Mohanty [6] used manner and place features coupled with a SVM based classifier for the task of language identification; experiments were performed for 4 different languages namely Hindi, Bangla, Oriya and Telugu on 500 words/language corpora producing an average word level accuracy of 89.75%.

Lamel et al. [8] performed different cross lingual experiments involving phone recognition; they obtained accuracies of 99% for language identification on clips of 2 s and 100% for sex as well as speaker identification. They had also obtained accuracies of 98.2% and 99.1% for speaker identification on the TIMIT and BREF datasets respectively with a single utterance per speaker. Koolagudi et al. [10] distinguished 15 different Indic languages with MFCC features and Gaussian Mixture Model; they used 300, 90 and 2 s of data per language for training, testing and validation respectively and obtained an accuracy of 88%. Berkling *et al.* [11] and Muthusamy *et al.* [12] have also employed and discussed different aspects of phoneme based techniques for language identification.

Bangla is not only one of the official languages of our country - India but also of our state - West Bengal. Moreover, based on the number of speakers, it is also among the top 3 and top 6 in India and the world respectively [4]. These factors inspired us to work with the same. In this paper, the performance of different classifiers for the task of Bangla vowel/swarabarna phonemes identification is presented. The adopted methodology is presented in Fig. 1. The clips were first pre processed and then subjected to feature extraction. The feature sets were then reduced using PCA. Both the reduced and non reduced feature sets were individually fed to different classifiers for performance analysis. The details of these steps is presented in the subsequent paragraphs. The remainder of the paper is organized as follows: Sect. 2 describes the datasets while Sect. 3 describes proposed methodology; the results are presented in Sect. 4 and the conclusion in Sect. 5.

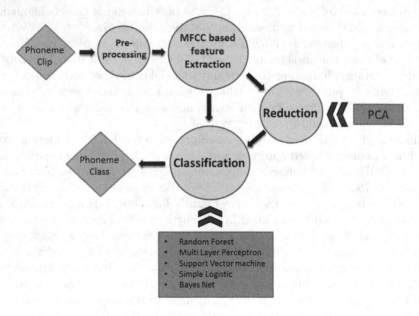

Fig. 1. Methodology of the proposed work.

2   Dataset

The quality of data is vital in an experiment. It needs to be ensured that inconsistencies are avoided during the data collection phase. We collected a dataset of Bangla swarabarna/vowel phonemes from 53 volunteers aged between 20–30 of whom 32 were male and 21 were female as we could not find any standard Bangla phoneme dataset available freely for research. The speakers uttered the 7 vowel phonemes (shown in Table 1) in one take; each of the volunteers repeated this 10 times. The 7 phonemes were recorded in a single take from the speakers in every iteration in order to get real life data as in terms of gushes of breath on the microphone, linked utterances, etc. The collected database of 3710 (10*7*53) phonemes were then segregated with a semi-supervised amplitude based technique.

Table 1. IPA symbols of the 7 swarabarna/vowel phonemes, their Bangla alphabetic representation and usage example.

IPA Symbol	ɔ	a	i	u	e	o	æ
Bangla Representation	অ	আ	ই, ঈ	উ, ঊ	এ	ও	অ্যা
Bangla Pronunciation as in	অমল	আশিষ	ছিলাম	মুল	ছেলে	ভোজ	নেড়া

Different local microphones were used for recording, including Frontech JIL-3442, to get variations as the microphones have disparate sensitivities helping to uphold real world characteristics; with the same purpose, the distance and angle of the microphones from the speakers were also varied in addition to different ambiences. The data was recorded in stereo mode with Audacity [13] in .wav format at a bitrate of 1411 kbps. Figure 2 present the waveform representation of a single channel clip of the 7 phonemes.

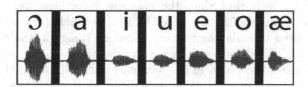

Fig. 2. Single channel waveform representation of the 7 phonemes.

3 Methodology

In the following sub-sections, the signal pre-processing (framing and windowing) and feature extraction are presented along with an introduction of the classification algorithms used.

3.1 Pre-processing

Framing. The spectral characteristics of an audio clip tend to show a lot of deviation through the entire length which complicates the task of analysis. In order to cope up with this, a clip is broken down into smaller parts termed as frames which ensures that the spectral characteristics are quasi stationary within each of such frames. As presented in Eq. (1), a clip having T samples can be subdivided into M frames, each of size G having O overlapping points.

$$M = \left\lceil \frac{T - G}{O} + 1 \right\rceil \tag{1}$$

In the present experiments, the frame size was chosen to be of 256 points and the overlap factor to be of 100 sample points in accordance with [14].

Windowing. The sample points at the start and end of a frame might not be aligned thereby disrupting the intra-frame continuity. These jitters interfere with the Fourier transformation for the spectrum based analysis in the form of spectral leakage. To tackle this problem, every frame is windowed. In our experiment, the hamming window was chosen in accordance with [14]. The hamming window A(n) is mathematically illustrated in Eq. (2) where, n ranges from start to end of a frame of size N.

$$A(n) = 0.54 - 0.46 \cos\left(\frac{2\pi n}{N - 1}\right), \tag{2}$$

3.2 Feature Extraction

Due to its utility as presented in [15], 19 standard MFCC features per frame were extracted for each clip. Since the phoneme recordings were of disparate lengths, different number of frames were obtained producing features of different dimensions. In order to make the feature dimension constant, the global highest and lowest of the MFCC values were used to define 18 equally spaced classes; the number of classes was set to 18 in accordance with [14]. Next, the occurrence of energy values in each of such classes was recorded; this was repeated for each of the 19 bands producing a dataset where each example is represented by 342 features.

In addition to this, the MFCC bands were also ordered in a descending manner using the band wise energy content and this sequence was added to the feature vector, producing a feature vector of 361 values. It was also observed that there were some classes (feature values) which did not have any energy value distributions; such feature values were identified to have similar values for all phoneme instances and were removed, ultimately producing a feature vector of 147 dimensions.

In order to observe the recognition performance using reduced features, the final feature vector was subjected to principal component analysis (PCA) following the work presented in [16]. This procedure produced a feature vector of 95 dimensions. The visual representation of the features for 7 phoneme classes for pre- and post-PCA reduction are presented in Figs. 3 and 4, respectively.

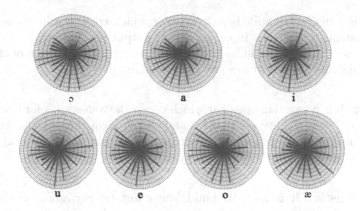

Fig. 3. Non reduced features for the 7 phonemes.

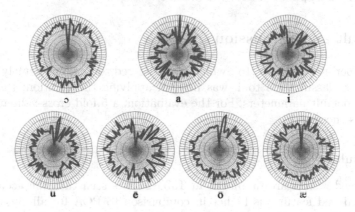

Fig. 4. PCA reduced features for the 7 phonemes.

3.3 Classification

Both the PCA reduced and non reduced feature sets were fed into various popular classifiers in pattern recognition problems. They were: Support Vector Machine (SVM), Random Forest (RF), Multi Layer Perceptron (MLP), BayesNet (BN) and Simple Logistic (SL). These algorithms are briefly outlined below.

SVM. It is a supervised learner which is used for classification as well as regression analysis. It generates an optimal hyperplane from a set of labelled instances provided at training time; for a 2D space, it finds a line which differentiates the instances based on their associated labels.

Random Forest. It is an ensemble learning based classifier which works with decision trees during training. It classifies an instance using the mode of the output of the individual decision trees.

MLP. It is a neural network based classifier which tries to mimic the human nervous system. It maps an input set to an output set and consists of nodes that are joined by means of links having different weights. It is one of the most popular classifiers in pattern recognition problems.

BayesNet. It is a bayesian classifier which uses a Bayes Network for learning by employing different quality parameters and search algorithms. Data structures consisting of conditional probability distributions, structure of network, etc. are provided by the base class.

Simple Logistic. It is used to build linear logistic regression models. The classifier uses LogitBoost as base learner and the number of iterations is further cross validated helping to select the attributes automatically.

4   Result and Discussion

For the experiments, Weka [16], which is considered to be an extremely popular open source classification tool, was used in applying the mentioned classifiers with their default parameters. For the evaluation, a 5 fold cross-validation procedure was chosen.

4.1   Results

The obtained results are tabulated in Table 2. It is seen that the accuracy for the non reduced features is higher in comparison to PCA for all classifiers. In the case of the non reduced sets the best performance was obtained with Random Forest while the worst was obtained using BayesNet; MLP, simple logistic and SVM obtained 2nd, 3rd and 4th ranks respectively. The ranks of the classifiers varied in the case of the PCA reduced set; similar to the non reduced set, BayesNet performed the worst; however, MLP generated the best result followed by Random Forest, SVM and simple logistic.

Table 2. Accuracy for different classifiers both on the non- reduced and reduced PCA feature sets.

	Without PCA	With PCA
RF	97.66	94.20
MLP	96.44	95.55
SVM	95.26	93.85
BN	90.62	82.67
SL	95.88	93.45

Since Random Forest produced the overall highest result using the non reduced feature set, we further fined tuned this algorithm's parameters.

First different number of cross validation folds were tested. The results are shown in Table 3 and it is seen that the highest accuracy was attained for both 15 as well as 20 cross-validation folds.

Table 3. Performance of Random forest for different number of folds of cross validation on the non reduced feature set.

Folds	5	10	15	20
Accuracy (%)	97.66	97.71	**97.84**	**97.84**

The number of training iterations using the default number of cross validation folds (5 in our experiment) was also tested, ranging from 100 to 500 iterations. The results are tabulated in Table 4 and it is observed that the highest accuracy (97.87%) was attained for 300 iterations.

Table 4. Performance of Random forest for different training iterations on the non reduced feature set.

Iterations	100	200	300	400	500
Accuracy (%)	97.66	97.60	**97.87**	97.66	97.57

Finally, for 15 folds of cross validation (chosen to be the best, even though the 20 folds also produced the same highest accuracy), a varying number of iterations was also tested. The obtained results are shown in Table 5 where it can be seen that an accuracy of 98.17% (highest) was attained for 400 training iterations, which is also the highest value obtained from all the experiments.

Table 5. Performance of Random forest for different training iterations and 15 fold cross validation on the non reduced feature set.

Iterations	100	200	300	400	500
Accuracy (%)	97.84	97.92	98.11	**98.17**	98.09

For this highest performing configuration, the confusion percentage among different phoneme pairs are presented in Table 6.

The 'u-o' phoneme pair created a total confusion of 9.05% (3.58 + 5.47), which is the highest in our experiment. One of the primary reasons for this result is that these 2 phonemes sound very close when pronounced separately and even closer when pronounced at a stretch. The same issue was observed

Table 6. Percentages of confusion for all phoneme pairs on the non reduced feature set using Random forest with 15 fold cross-validation and 400 training iterations.

	ɔ	a	i	u	e	o	æ
ɔ	-	0.94	0	0	0	0	0
a	1.32	-	0.19	0	0	0	0
i	0	0	-	0	0.38	0	0
u	0	0	0	-	0.38	5.47	0
e	0	0	0.19	0	-	0	0
o	0	0	0	3.58	0.19	-	0
æ	0	0	0	0	0.19	0	-

during the data collection phase as well. The phoneme pair 'ɔ-a' produced the next highest confusion with a value of 2.26%. It was observed that different speakers had extremely close pronunciations for these two phonemes which led to this confusion.

4.2 Statistical Significance Test

The non parametric Friedman test [17] was carried out on the non reduced dataset for checking the statistical significance. We divided the dataset into 5 parts (N) and used all the 5 classifiers (k) in the test. The obtained ranks and accuracies is presented in Table 7.

Table 7. Ranks and accuracies for different parts of the non reduced dataset on all classifiers.

Classifiers		Parts of the dataset					Mean rank
		1	2	3	4	5	
RF	A	96.77	99.19	98.65	97.98	98.52	1.9
	R	(1.0)	(1.0)	(1.0)	(3.0)	(3.5)	
BN	A	89.62	92.59	92.45	90.3	97.44	5.0
	R	(5.0)	(5.0)	(5.0)	(5.0)	(5.0)	
SL	A	95.01	96.9	97.71	97.3	99.06	3.2
	R	(3.0)	(4.0)	(4.0)	(4.0)	(1.0)	
SVM	A	94.88	97.98	97.98	98.38	98.52	2.7
	R	(4.0)	(2.0)	(3.0)	(1.0)	(3.5)	
MLP	A	96.5	97.71	98.11	98.25	98.79	2.2
	R	(2.0)	(3.0)	(2.0)	(2.0)	(2.0)	

The Friedman statistic (χ_F^2) [17] was calculated using these results with the help of Eq. (3), where R_j is the mean rank of the jth classifier.

$$\chi_F^2 = \frac{12N}{k(k+1)} \left[\sum_j R_j^2 - \frac{k(k+1)^2}{4} \right]. \tag{3}$$

The critical values at significance levels of 0.05 and 0.10 for the mentioned setup were found to be 9.448 and 7.779; we obtained a value of 11.96 for (χ_F^2) thereby rejecting the Null hypothesis, and demonstrating statistical significance.

5   Conclusion

The performance of different classifiers in the task of Bangla swarabarna phoneme identification is presented here; this can aid in language identification as well as speech recognition. Among different classifiers, the highest accuracy was obtained using Random Forest which demonstrated an average precision of 0.982.

In the future, we will experiment with other features in order to reduce the confusion between different phoneme pairs. We also plan to use other machine learning techniques like deep learning based approaches to obtain better results. Experiments will not only be performed on a larger Bangla phoneme dataset but also the same will be extended to other languages. The same will also be carried out by incorporating artificial noise in the datasets to make the system more robust. Experiments will also be done by integrating the phoneme identifier with a speech recognizer to observe both speech as well as language identification in real time.

References

1. Zissman, M.A., Singer, E.: Automatic language identification of telephone speech messages using phoneme recognition and n-gram modeling. In: Proceedings of ICASSP-94., vol. 1, p. I-305. IEEE (1994)
2. Muthusamy, Y.K., Cole, R.A., Oshika, B.T.: The OGI multi-language telephone speech corpus. In: Proceedings of ICSLP-92, pp. 895–898 (1992)
3. Zissman, M.A.: Language identification using phoneme recognition and phonotactic language modeling. In: Proceedings of ICASSP-95., vol. 5, pp. 3503–3506. IEEE (1995)
4. https://www.ethnologue.com/. Accessed 25 Mar 2018
5. Hasanat, A., Karim, M.R., Rahman, M.S., Iqbal, M.Z.: Recognition of spoken letters in Bangla. In: Proceedings of ICCIT (2002)
6. Mohanty, S.: Phonotactic model for spoken language identification in indian language perspective. Int. J. Comput. Appl. 19(9), 18–24 (2011)
7. Kotwal, M.R.A., Hossain, Md.S., Hassan, F., Muhammad, G., Huda, M.N., Rahman, C.M.: Bangla phoneme recognition using hybrid features. In: Proceedings of ICECE (2010)
8. Lamel, L.F., Gauvain, J.L.: Cross-lingual experiments with phone recognition. In: Proceedings of ICASSP-93., vol. 2, pp. 507–510. IEEE (1993)

9. Hossain, K.K., Hossain, Md.J., Ferdousi, A., Khan, Md.F.: Comparative study of recognition tools as back-ends for Bangla phoneme recognition. Int. J. Res. Comput. Appl. Robot. **2**(12), 36–40 (2014)
10. Koolagudi, S.G., Rastogi, D., Rao, K.S.: Identification of language using mel-frequency cepstral coefficients (MFCC). Procedia Eng. **38**, 3391–3398 (2012)
11. Berkling, K.M., Arai, T., Barnard, E.: Analysis of phoneme-based features for language identification. In: Proceedings of ICASSP-94., vol. 1, p. I-289. IEEE (1994)
12. Muthusamy, Y., Berkling, K., Arai, T., Cole, R., Barnard, E.: A comparison of approaches to automatic language identification using telephone speech. In: Proceedings of Eurospeech-93, pp. 1317–1310 (1993)
13. http://www.audacityteam.org/. Accessed 25 Mar 2018
14. Mukherjee, H., Dhar, A., Phadikar, S., Roy, K.: RECAL-A language identification system. In: Proceedings of ICSPC, pp. 300–304. IEEE (2017)
15. Mukherjee, H., Obaidullah, S.M., Phadikar, S., Roy, K.: SMIL - a musical instrument identification system. In: Mandal, J.K., Dutta, P., Mukhopadhyay, S. (eds.) CICBA 2017. CCIS, vol. 775, pp. 129–140. Springer, Singapore (2017). https://doi.org/10.1007/978-981-10-6427-2_11
16. Hall, M., Frank, E., Holmes, G., Pfahringer, B., Reutemann, P., Witten, I.H.: The WEKA data mining software: an update. ACM SIGKDD Explor. Newsl. **11**(1), 10–18 (2009)
17. Demšar, J.: Statistical comparisons of classifiers over multiple data sets. J. Mach. Learn. Res. **7**, 1–30 (2006)

On Developing Interval-Valued Dual Hesitant Fuzzy Bonferroni Mean Aggregation Operator and Their Application to Multicriteria Decision Making

Arun Sarkar[1] and Animesh Biswas[2(✉)]

[1] Department of Mathematics, Heramba Chandra College,
Kolkata 700029, India
asarkarmth@gmail.com

[2] Department of Mathematics, University of Kalyani,
Kalyani 741235, India
abiswaskln@rediffmail.com

Abstract. Main objective of this paper is to solve multicriteria decision making problems based on Bonferroni mean with interval-valued dual hesitant fuzzy (IVDHF) information. Firstly, the concept of IVDHF Bonferroni mean (IVDHFBM) operator is introduced. Some desirable properties of IVDHFBM are then investigated in detail. Further, IVDHF weighted Bonferroni mean (IVDHFWBM) operator is proposed considering different preference degrees of input arguments. Then the developed operators are then applied to multicriteria decision making for developing a method to solve models with interrelationship among the aggregated individual arguments. Finally, an illustrative example is given to demonstrate the applicability and effectiveness of the developed approach.

Keywords: Bonferroni mean · Interval-valued dual hesitant fuzzy set · Interval-valued dual hesitant fuzzy Bonferroni mean operator · Multi-criteria decision making

1 Introduction

Theory of Fuzzy sets (FSs) [1] and its extensions [2–5] are efficiently used in many areas of real life decision making problems [6–8] to deal with possibilistic imprecisions. Sometimes, decision makers (DMs) face difficulties to assign exact membership value corresponding to an element of a set for its belongingness due to some ambiguities raised due to a possible set of values. To overcome this problem, Torra and Narukawa [9] and Torra [10] proposed the concept of hesitant fuzzy set (HFS), which permits to assign membership degree of an element corresponding to a set of possible values between 0 and 1. Xia and Xu [11] developed hesitant fuzzy aggregation operators and applied them to multicriteria decision making (MCDM) under various circumstances. Gu et al. [12] introduced hesitant fuzzy weighted averaging (HFWA) operator to analyze evaluation model for risk investment with hesitant fuzzy information. Wei [13] defined hesitant fuzzy prioritized weighted average (HFPWA) operator and hesitant fuzzy prioritized weighted geometric (HFPWG) operator. However, HFSs ignores the fact that

© Springer Nature Singapore Pte Ltd. 2019
J. K. Mandal et al. (Eds.): CICBA 2018, CCIS 1030, pp. 27–46, 2019.
https://doi.org/10.1007/978-981-13-8578-0_3

the uncertainty of an element to a set exist commonly. To solve such case, Zhu et al. [14] proposed dual hesitant fuzzy (DHF) sets (DHFS). In DHFS the membership degree and non-membership degree are denoted by two sets of crisp values corresponding to an element to a given fixed set. DHFS is studied extensively and applied to many practical areas successfully within its short span after inception. Wang et al. [15] proposed some aggregation operators to aggregate DHF information, viz., DHF weighted average (DHFWA) operator, DHF weighted geometric (DHFWG) operator, DHF hybrid average (DHFHA) operator and DHF hybrid geometric (DHFHG) operator. Motivated by the idea of the Archimedean t-conorm and t-norm, Yu [16] introduced Archimedean t-conorm and t-norm in DHF environment and defined DHF aggregation operators, such as Archimedean t-conorm and t-norm operations based DHF weighted averaging (ADHFWA) operator and Archimedean t-conorm and t-norm operations based DHF weighted geometric (ADHFWG) operator.

Following the concepts of DHFSs and interval numbers, Ju et al. [17] extended fuzzy set to interval-valued dual DHF (IVDHF) set (IVDHFS) whose components are interval values rather than crisp values. The IVDHFS is more suitable to express the decision maker's hesitancy than the classical hesitant fuzzy set or its counterparts. They also developed some aggregation operators based on IVDHF elements (IVDHFEs), such as IVDHF weighted aggregation operators, IVDHF ordered weighted geometric operators, generalized IVDHF weighted aggregation operators, generalized IVDHF ordered weighted aggregation operators and IVDHF hybrid aggregation operators. Wei [18] also proposed some aggregation operator based of IVDHF uncertain linguistic information.

Although few efforts have been made to investigate IVDHF aggregation operators, all of them are based on the assumption that the aggregated arguments are independent. However, in many practical decision making problems, some situations are often encountered in which the attributes are interactive. To overcome such cases, Bonferroni [19] first defined the BM operator, which can capture the expressed interrelationship of the aggregated individual arguments.

The main purpose of this paper is to propose a series of IVDHF aggregation operators based on the BM and some of their interesting properties have also been investigated. The developed operators are then applied them to solve MCDM problems in IVDHF environments where the criteria are interactive. Finally, a practical example is considered and solved to illustrate the proposed method.

2 Preliminaries

Definition 1 [14]. Let X be a fixed set. Then a DHFS is defined as

$$\widetilde{D} = \left\{ \left\langle x, \widetilde{h}(x), \widetilde{g}(x) \right\rangle | x \in X \right\}$$

where $\widetilde{h}(x)$ and $\widetilde{g}(x)$ denote the membership degree and non-membership degree of the element $x \in X$ to the set D, respectively, with the conditions:

$0 \leq \gamma, \eta \leq 1, 0 \leq \gamma^+ + \eta^+ \leq 0$ where $\gamma \in \widetilde{h}(x)$, $\eta \in \widetilde{g}(x)$, $\gamma^+ = \bigcup_{\gamma \in \widetilde{h}(x)} \max\{\gamma\}$ and $\eta^+ = \bigcup_{\eta \in \widetilde{g}(x)} \max\{\eta\}$ for all $x \in X$.

DHFE is also introduced by Zhu et al. [11] and is expressed as $\tilde{d} = \left(\tilde{h}, \tilde{g}\right)$, where $\tilde{h}$ and $\tilde{g}$ are two hesitant fuzzy elements. The score function and accuracy function of DHFE $\tilde{d}$ are defined as

$$S\left(\tilde{d}\right) = \frac{1}{|\tilde{h}|} \sum_{\gamma \in \tilde{h}} \gamma - \frac{1}{|\tilde{g}|} \sum_{\eta \in \tilde{g}} \eta$$

$$A\left(\tilde{d}\right) = \frac{1}{|\tilde{h}|} \sum_{\gamma \in \tilde{h}} \gamma + \frac{1}{|\tilde{g}|} \sum_{\eta \in \tilde{g}} \eta$$

where $|\tilde{h}|$ and $|\tilde{g}|$ denote the crisp scalar cardinality of γ and η respectively.

For comparison of two DHFEs $\tilde{d}_1$ and $\tilde{d}_2$, the following conditions are to be satisfied.

Let $\tilde{d}_1$ and $\tilde{d}_2$. be two DHFEs

1. If $S\left(\tilde{d}_1\right) > S\left(\tilde{d}_2\right)$ then $\tilde{d}_1 > \tilde{d}_2$
2. If $S\left(\tilde{d}_1\right) = S\left(\tilde{d}_2\right)$ then

   if $A\left(\tilde{d}_1\right) > A\left(\tilde{d}_2\right)$ then $\tilde{d}_1 > \tilde{d}_2$; if $A\left(\tilde{d}_1\right) = A\left(\tilde{d}_2\right)$ then $\tilde{d}_1 = \tilde{d}_2$.

Definition 2 [17]. Let X be any universe of discourse. An IVDHFS $\tilde{K}$ on X is described as:

$$\tilde{K} = \left\{ \langle x, \tilde{h}(x), \tilde{g}(x) \rangle | x \in X \right\}$$

in which $\tilde{h}(x) = U_{[\gamma^l, \gamma^u] \in \tilde{h}(x)} \left\{ [\gamma^l, \gamma^u] \right\}$ and $\tilde{g}(x) = U_{[\eta^l, \eta^u] \in \tilde{g}(x)} \left\{ [\eta^l, \eta^u] \right\}$ are two set of interval values in $[0, 1]$, representing the possible membership degree and non-membership degree of the element $x \in X$ to the set $\tilde{K}$, respectively. With $[\gamma^l, \gamma^u], [\eta^l, \eta^u] \subset [0, 1]$ and $0 \le (\gamma^u)^+ + (\eta^u)^+ \le 1$, where $(\gamma^u)^+ = max\{\gamma^u\}$, and $(\eta^u)^+ = max\{\eta^u\}$ for all $x \in X$. For convenience Ju et al. [17] called the pair $\tilde{k}(x) = \left(\tilde{h}(x), \tilde{g}(x)\right)$ as an IVDHFE and is denoted by $\tilde{k} = \left(\tilde{h}, \tilde{g}\right)$ where $\tilde{K}$ is the set of all IVDHFEs.

To compare the IVDHFEs, Ju et al. [17] defined score function and accuracy function as follows.

Definition 3 [17]. Score function of IVDHFE $\tilde{k} = \left(\tilde{h}, \tilde{g}\right)$ is defined as

$$S\left(\tilde{k}\right) = \frac{1}{2} \left(\frac{1}{\Delta\tilde{h}} \sum_{[\gamma^l, \gamma^u] \in \tilde{h}} \left(\gamma^l + \gamma^u\right) - \frac{1}{\Delta\tilde{g}} \sum_{[\eta^l, \eta^u] \in \tilde{g}} \left(\eta^l + \eta^u\right) \right) \qquad (1)$$

where $\Delta\tilde{h}$ and $\Delta\tilde{g}$ is the number of intervals in $\tilde{h}$ and $\tilde{g}$ respectively.

Accuracy function of IVDHFE $\widetilde{k} = \left(\widetilde{h}, \widetilde{g}\right)$ is defined as

$$A\left(\widetilde{k}\right) = \frac{1}{2}\left(\frac{1}{\Delta\widetilde{h}}\sum_{[\gamma^l,\gamma^u]\in\widetilde{h}}\left(\gamma^l + \gamma^u\right) + \frac{1}{\Delta\widetilde{g}}\sum_{[\eta^l,\eta^u]\in\widetilde{g}}\left(\eta^l + \eta^u\right)\right)$$

Definition 4 [17]. Let $\tilde{\kappa}_1$ and $\tilde{\kappa}_2$ be any two IVDHFEs, then
If $S(\tilde{\kappa}_1) > S(\tilde{\kappa}_2)$ then $\tilde{\kappa}_1 > \tilde{\kappa}_2$

1. If $S(\tilde{\kappa}_1) = S(\tilde{\kappa}_2)$ then
2. if $A(\tilde{\kappa}_1) > A(\tilde{\kappa}_1)$ then $\tilde{\kappa}_1 > \tilde{\kappa}_2$; if $A(\tilde{\kappa}_1) = A(\tilde{\kappa}_2)$ then $\tilde{\kappa}_1 = \tilde{\kappa}_2$

Definition 5 [17]. Let $\widetilde{k}_i = \left(\widetilde{h}_i, \widetilde{g}_i\right)$ $(i = 1, 2)$ and $\widetilde{k} = \left(\widetilde{h}, \widetilde{g}\right)$ be any three IVDHFEs, then the operational laws of IVDHFEs as follows:

(i) $\widetilde{k}_1 \oplus \widetilde{k}_2 = \left(\bigcup_{[\gamma_1^l,\gamma_1^u]\in\widetilde{h}_1,[\gamma_2^l,\gamma_2^u]\in\widetilde{h}_2}\left\{\left[\gamma_1^l + \gamma_2^l - \gamma_1^l\gamma_2^l, \gamma_1^u + \gamma_2^u - \gamma_1^u\gamma_2^u\right]\right\}, \bigcup_{[\eta_1^l,\eta_1^u]\in\widetilde{g}_1,[\eta_2^l,\eta_2^u]\in\widetilde{g}_2}\left\{\left[\eta_1^l\eta_2^l, \eta_1^u\eta_2^u\right]\right\}\right)$

(ii) $\widetilde{k}_1 \otimes \widetilde{k}_2 = \left(\bigcup_{[\gamma_1^l,\gamma_1^u]\in\widetilde{h}_1,[\gamma_2^l,\gamma_2^u]\in\widetilde{h}_2}\left\{\left[\gamma_1^l\gamma_2^l, \gamma_1^u\gamma_2^u\right]\right\}, \bigcup_{[\eta_1^l,\eta_1^u]\in\widetilde{g}_1,[\eta_2^l,\eta_2^u]\in\widetilde{g}_2}\left\{\left[\eta_1^l + \eta_2^l - \eta_1^l\eta_2^l, \eta_1^u + \eta_2^u - \eta_1^u\eta_2^u\right]\right\}\right)$

(iii) $\lambda\widetilde{k} = \left(\bigcup_{[\gamma^l,\gamma^u]\in\widetilde{h}}\left\{\left[1 - (1 - \gamma^l)^\lambda, 1 - (1 - \gamma^u)^\lambda\right]\right\}, \bigcup_{[\eta^l,\eta^u]\in\widetilde{g}}\left\{\left[(\eta^l)^\lambda, (\eta^u)^\lambda\right]\right\}\right)$

(iv) $\widetilde{k}^\lambda = \left(\cup_{[\gamma^l,\gamma^u]\in\widetilde{h}}\left\{\left[(\gamma^l)^\lambda, (\gamma^u)^\lambda\right]\right\}, \cup_{[\eta^l,\eta^u]\in\widetilde{g}}\left\{\left[1 - (1 - \eta^l)^\lambda, 1 - (1 - \eta^u)^\lambda\right]\right\}\right)$

The BM was originally introduced by Bonferroni in [19], which is defined as follows:

Definition 6 [19]. Let $p, q \geq 0$ and a_i $i = 1, 2, \ldots, n$ be a collection of non-negative numbers, if

$$B^{p,q}(a_1, a_2, \ldots, a_n) = \left(\frac{1}{n(n-1)}\sum_{\substack{i,j = 1 \\ i \neq j}}^{n} a_i^p a_j^q\right)^{\frac{1}{p+q}} \tag{2}$$

Then B^{pq} is called the BM.
BM has the following properties [19]:

(i) $B^{p,q}(0, 0, \ldots, 0) = 0$
(ii) $B^{p,q}(a, a, \ldots, a) = a$
(iii) $B^{p,q}(a_1, a_2, \ldots, a_n) \geq B^{p,q}(d_1, d_2, \ldots, d_n)$ if $a_i \geq d_i$ for all i
(iv) $\min\{a_i\} \leq B^{p,q}(a_1, a_2, \ldots, a_n) \leq \max\{a_i\}$ for all i

3 Development of Interval-Valued Dual Hesitant Fuzzy Bonferroni Mean Operator

Definition 7. Let $\tilde{d}_i = \left(\tilde{h}_i, \tilde{g}_i\right)(i = 1, 2, \ldots, n)$ be a collection of IVDHFEs. Let $p, q > 0$

be any number. If $IVDHFBM^{p,q}\left(\tilde{d}_1, \tilde{d}_2, \ldots, \tilde{d}_n\right) = \left(\frac{1}{n(n-1)} \oplus_{\substack{i,j = 1 \\ i \neq j}}^{n} \left(\tilde{d}_i^p \otimes \tilde{d}_j^q\right)\right)^{\frac{1}{p+q}}$

then $IVDHFBM^{p,q}\left(\tilde{d}_1, \tilde{d}_2, \ldots, \tilde{d}_n\right)$ is called Interval-valued dual hesitant fuzzy Bonferroni mean (IVDHFBM) operator.

Theorem 1. Let $\tilde{d}_i = \left(\tilde{h}_i, \tilde{g}_i\right)(i = 1, 2, \ldots, n)$ be a collections of IVDHFEs and $p, q > 0$, then the aggregated value using IVDHFBM is also a *IVDHFE* and can be given as follows:

$$IVDHFBM^{p,q}\left(\tilde{d}_1, \tilde{d}_2, \ldots, \tilde{d}_n\right) = \left(\frac{1}{n(n-1)} \oplus_{\substack{i,j = 1 \\ i \neq j}}^{n} \left(\tilde{d}_i^p \otimes \tilde{d}_j^q\right)\right)^{\frac{1}{p+q}}$$

$$= \bigcup_{[\gamma_i^l, \gamma_i^u] \in \tilde{h}_i, [\gamma_j^l, \gamma_j^u] \in \tilde{h}_j} \left\{ \left[\left(1 - \prod_{\substack{i,j = 1 \\ i \neq j}}^{n} \left(1 - (\gamma_i^l)^p (\gamma_j^l)^q\right)^{\frac{1}{n(n-1)}}\right)^{\frac{1}{p+q}}, \right. \right.$$

$$\left(1 - \prod_{\substack{i,j = 1 \\ i \neq j}}^{n} \left(1 - (\gamma_i^u)^p (\gamma_j^u)^q\right)^{\frac{1}{n(n-1)}}\right)^{\frac{1}{p+q}} \right] \right\}, \qquad (3)$$

$$\bigcup_{[\eta_i^l, \eta_i^u] \in \tilde{g}_i, [\eta_j^l, \eta_j^u] \in \tilde{g}_j} \left\{ \left[1 - \left(1 - \prod_{\substack{i,j = 1 \\ i \neq j}}^{n} \left(1 - (1 - \eta_i^l)^p (1 - \eta_j^l)^q\right)^{\frac{1}{n(n-1)}}\right)^{\frac{1}{p+q}}, \right. \right.$$

$$1 - \left(1 - \prod_{\substack{i,j = 1 \\ i \neq j}}^{n} \left(1 - (1 - \eta_i^u)^p (1 - \eta_j^u)^q\right)^{\frac{1}{n(n-1)}}\right)^{\frac{1}{p+q}} \right] \right\} \right)$$

Proof. The proof would be performed through mathematical induction.
Here

$$\tilde{d}_i^p = \left(\bigcup_{[\gamma_i^l, \gamma_i^u] \in \tilde{h}_i} \left\{ \left[(\gamma_i^l)^p, (\gamma_i^u)^p\right] \right\}, \bigcup_{[\eta_i^l, \eta_i^u] \in \tilde{g}_i} \left\{ \left[1 - (1 - \eta_i^l)^p, 1 - (1 - \eta_i^u)^p\right] \right\} \right),$$

and

$$\tilde{d}_j^q = \left(\bigcup_{[\gamma_j^l,\gamma_j^u]\in \tilde{h}_j} \left\{ \left[\left(\gamma_j^l\right)^q, \left(\gamma_j^u\right)^q \right] \right\}, \bigcup_{[\eta_j^l,\eta_j^u]\in \tilde{g}_j} \left\{ \left[1 - \left(1-\eta_j^l\right)^q, 1 - \left(1-\eta_j^u\right)^q \right] \right\} \right)$$

Then

$$\tilde{d}_i^p \otimes \tilde{d}_j^q = \left(\bigcup_{[\gamma_i^l,\gamma_i^u]\in \tilde{h}_i, [\gamma_j^l,\gamma_j^u]\in \tilde{h}_j} \left\{ \left[\left(\gamma_i^l\right)^p \left(\gamma_j^l\right)^q, \left(\gamma_i^u\right)^p \left(\gamma_j^u\right)^q \right] \right\}, \right.$$

$$\left. \bigcup_{[\eta_i^l,\eta_i^u]\in \tilde{g}_i, [\eta_j^l,\eta_j^u]\in \tilde{g}_j} \left\{ \left[1 - \left(1-\eta_i^l\right)^p \left(1-\eta_j^l\right)^q, 1 - \left(1-\eta_i^u\right)^p \left(1-\eta_j^u\right)^q \right] \right\} \right)$$

Now for $n = 2$,

$$\left(\frac{1}{2} \oplus_{i,j=1 \atop i\neq j}^2 \left(\tilde{d}_i^p \otimes \tilde{d}_j^q \right) \right)^{\frac{1}{p+q}} = \left(\frac{1}{2} \left(\left(\bigcup_{[\gamma_1^l,\gamma_1^u]\in \tilde{h}_1, [\gamma_2^l,\gamma_2^u]\in \tilde{h}_2} \left\{ \left[\left(\gamma_1^l\right)^p \left(\gamma_2^l\right)^q, \left(\gamma_1^u\right)^p \left(\gamma_2^u\right)^q \right] \right\}, \right. \right. \right.$$

$$\bigcup_{[\eta_1^l,\eta_1^u]\in \tilde{g}_1, [\eta_2^l,\eta_2^u]\in \tilde{g}_2} \left\{ \left[1 - \left(1-\eta_1^l\right)^p \left(1-\eta_2^l\right)^q, 1 - \left(1-\eta_1^u\right)^p \left(1-\eta_2^u\right)^q \right] \right\} \right)$$

$$\oplus \left(\bigcup_{[\gamma_2^l,\gamma_2^u]\in \tilde{h}_1, [\gamma_2^l,\gamma_2^u]\in \tilde{h}_2} \left\{ \left[\left(\gamma_2^l\right)^p \left(\gamma_1^l\right)^q, \left(\gamma_2^u\right)^p \left(\gamma_1^u\right)^q \right] \right\}, \right.$$

$$\left. \left. \bigcup_{[\eta_1^l,\eta_1^u]\in \tilde{g}_1, [\eta_2^l,\eta_2^u]\in \tilde{g}_2} \left\{ \left[1 - \left(1-\eta_2^l\right)^p \left(1-\eta_1^l\right)^q, 1 - \left(1-\eta_2^u\right)^p \left(1-\eta_1^u\right)^q \right] \right\} \right) \right)^{\frac{1}{p+q}}$$

$$= \left(\bigcup_{[\gamma_1^l,\gamma_1^u]\in \tilde{h}_1, [\gamma_2^l,\gamma_2^u]\in \tilde{h}_2} \left\{ \left[\left(1 - \left(\prod_{i,j=1 \atop i\neq j}^2 \left(1 - \left(\gamma_i^l\right)^p \left(\gamma_j^l\right)^q \right) \right)^{\frac{1}{2}} \right)^{\frac{1}{p+q}}, \right. \right. \right.$$

$$\left. \left. \left. \left(1 - \left(\prod_{i,j=1 \atop i\neq j}^2 \left(1 - \left(\gamma_i^u\right)^p \left(\gamma_j^u\right)^q \right) \right)^{\frac{1}{2}} \right)^{\frac{1}{p+q}} \right] \right\}, \right.$$

$$\bigcup_{[\eta_1^l,\eta_1^u]\in \tilde{g}_1, [\eta_2^l,\eta_2^u]\in \tilde{g}_2} \left\{ \left[1 - \left(1 - \left(\prod_{i,j=1 \atop i\neq j}^2 \left(1 - \left(1-\eta_i^l\right)^p \left(1-\eta_j^l\right)^q \right) \right)^{\frac{1}{2}} \right)^{\frac{1}{p+q}}, \right. \right.$$

$$\left. \left. 1 - \left(1 - \left(\prod_{i,j=1 \atop i\neq j}^2 \left(1 - \left(1-\eta_i^u\right)^p \left(1-\eta_j^u\right)^q \right) \right)^{\frac{1}{2}} \right)^{\frac{1}{p+q}} \right] \right\} \right)$$

Thus it is true for $n = 2$.

Now it is to be proved that the following equality holds for all n.

$$\underset{\substack{i,j=1 \\ i \neq j}}{\overset{n}{\oplus}} \left(\tilde{d}_i^p \otimes \tilde{d}_j^q \right) = \left(\bigcup_{[\gamma_i^l,\gamma_i^u] \in \tilde{h}_i, [\gamma_j^l,\gamma_j^u] \in \tilde{h}_j} \left\{ \left[1 - \underset{\substack{i,j=1 \\ i \neq j}}{\overset{n}{\prod}} \left(1 - (\gamma_i^l)^p (\gamma_j^l)^q \right), \right. \right. \right.$$

$$\left. \left. 1 - \underset{\substack{i,j=1 \\ i \neq j}}{\overset{n}{\prod}} \left(1 - (\gamma_i^u)^p (\gamma_j^u)^q \right) \right] \right\},$$

$$\bigcup_{[\eta_i^l,\eta_i^u] \in \tilde{g}_i, [\eta_j^l,\eta_j^u] \in \tilde{g}_j} \left\{ \left[\underset{\substack{i,j=1 \\ i \neq j}}{\overset{n}{\prod}} \left(1 - (1 - \eta_i^l)^p (1 - \eta_j^l)^q \right), \right. \right.$$

$$\left. \left. \underset{\substack{i,j=1 \\ i \neq j}}{\overset{n}{\prod}} \left(1 - (1 - \eta_i^u)^p (1 - \eta_j^u)^q \right) \right] \right\} \right)$$

(4)

Let it be true for $n = k$. Then

$$\underset{\substack{i,j=1 \\ i \neq j}}{\overset{k+1}{\oplus}} \left(\tilde{d}_i^p \otimes \tilde{d}_j^q \right) = \underset{\substack{i,j=1 \\ i \neq j}}{\overset{k}{\oplus}} \left(\tilde{d}_i^p \otimes \tilde{d}_j^q \right) \oplus \left(\overset{k}{\underset{i=1}{\oplus}} \left(\tilde{d}_i^p \otimes \tilde{d}_{k+1}^q \right) \right)$$

$$\oplus \left(\overset{k}{\underset{j=1}{\oplus}} \left(\tilde{d}_{k+1}^p \otimes \tilde{d}_j^q \right) \right)$$

(5)

To prove (5) it is to be proved that

$$\overset{k}{\underset{i=1}{\oplus}} \left(\tilde{d}_i^p \otimes \tilde{d}_{k+1}^q \right) = \left(\bigcup_{[\gamma_i^l,\gamma_i^u] \in \tilde{h}_i, [\gamma_{k+1}^l,\gamma_{k+1}^u] \in \tilde{h}_{k+1}} \left\{ \left[1 - \overset{k}{\underset{i=1}{\prod}} \left(1 - (\gamma_i^l)^p (\gamma_{k+1}^l)^q \right), \right. \right. \right.$$

$$\left. \left. 1 - \overset{k}{\underset{i=1}{\prod}} \left(1 - (\gamma_i^u)^p (\gamma_{k+1}^u)^q \right) \right] \right\}, \bigcup_{[\eta_i^l,\eta_i^u] \in \tilde{g}_i, [\eta_{k+1}^l,\eta_{k+1}^u] \in \tilde{g}_{k+1}} \left\{ \left[\overset{k}{\underset{i=1}{\prod}} \left(1 - (1 - \eta_i^l)^p (1 - \right. \right. \right.$$ (6)

$$\left. \left. \left. \eta_{k+1}^l))^q, \overset{k}{\underset{i=1}{\prod}} \left(1 - (1 - \eta_i^u)^p (1 - \eta_{k+1}^u)^q \right) \right] \right\} \right)$$

It is obvious for $k = 2$ and let it is true for $k = m$.
Then for $k = m+1$,

$$\oplus_{i=1}^{m+1}\left(\tilde{d}_i^p\otimes\tilde{d}_{m+2}^q\right)=\left(\oplus_{i=1}^{m}\left(\tilde{d}_i^p\otimes\tilde{d}_{m+2}^q\right)\right)\oplus\left(\tilde{d}_{m+1}^p\otimes\tilde{d}_{m+2}^q\right)$$

$$=\left(\bigcup_{[\gamma_i^l,\gamma_i^u]\in\tilde{h}_i,[\gamma_{m+2}^l,\gamma_{m+2}^u]\in\tilde{h}_{m+2}}\left\{\left[1-\prod_{i=1}^{m}\left(1-(\gamma_i^l)^p(\gamma_{m+2}^l)^q\right),1-\prod_{i=1}^{m}\left(1-(\gamma_i^u)^p(\gamma_{m+2}^u)^q\right)\right]\right\},\right.$$

$$\left.\bigcup_{\substack{[\eta_i^l,\eta_i^u]\in\tilde{g}_i,\\ [\eta_{m+2}^l,\eta_{m+2}^u]\in\tilde{g}_{m+2}}}\left\{\left[\prod_{i=1}^{m}\left(1-(1-\eta_i^l)^p(1-\eta_{m+2}^l)^q\right),\prod_{i=1}^{m}\left(1-(1-\eta_i^u)^p(1-\eta_{m+2}^u)^q\right)\right]\right\}\right)$$

$$\oplus\left(\bigcup_{[\gamma_{m+1}^l,\gamma_{m+1}^u]\in\tilde{h}_{m+1},[\gamma_{m+2}^l,\gamma_{m+2}^u]\in\tilde{h}_{m+2}}\left\{\left[(\gamma_{m+1}^l)^p(\gamma_{m+2}^l)^q,(\gamma_{m+1}^u)^p(\gamma_{m+2}^u)^q\right]\right\},\right.$$

$$\left.\bigcup_{\substack{[\eta_{m+1}^l,\eta_{m+1}^u]\in\tilde{g}_{m+1},\\ [\eta_{m+2}^l,\eta_{m+2}^u]\in\tilde{g}_{m+2}}}\left\{\left[1-(1-\eta_{m+1}^l)^p(1-\eta_{m+2}^l)^q,1-(1-\eta_{m+1}^u)^p(1-\eta_{m+2}^u)^q\right]\right\}\right)$$

$$=\left(\bigcup_{[\gamma_i^l,\gamma_i^u]\in\tilde{h}_i,[\gamma_{m+2}^l,\gamma_{m+2}^u]\in\tilde{h}_{m+2}}\left\{\left[1-\prod_{i=1}^{m+1}\left(1-(\gamma_i^l)^p(\gamma_{m+2}^l)^q\right),1-\prod_{i=1}^{m+1}\left(1-(\gamma_i^u)^p(\gamma_{m+2}^u)^q\right)\right]\right\},\right.$$

$$\bigcup_{[\eta_i^l,\eta_i^u]\in\tilde{g}_i,[\eta_{m+2}^l,\eta_{m+2}^u]\in\tilde{g}_{m+2}}\left\{\left[\prod_{i=1}^{m+1}\left(1-(1-\eta_i^l)^p(1-\eta_{m+2}^l)^q\right),\right.\right.$$

$$\left.\left.\prod_{i=1}^{m+1}\left(1-(1-\eta_i^u)^p(1-\eta_{m+2}^u)^q\right)\right]\right\}\right)$$

i.e., (6) holds for $k=m+1$. Thus, (6) holds for all k.

Similarly, it can be proved that

$$\oplus_{j=1}^{k}\left(\tilde{d}_{k+1}^p\otimes\tilde{d}_j^q\right)=$$

$$\left(\bigcup_{[\gamma_{k+1}^l,\gamma_{k+1}^u]\in\tilde{h}_{k+1},[\gamma_j^l,\gamma_j^u]\in\tilde{h}_j}\left\{\left[1-\prod_{j=1}^{k}\left(1-(\gamma_{k+1}^l)^p\left(\gamma_j^l\right)^q\right),\right.\right.\right.$$

$$\left.\left.\left.1-\prod_{j=1}^{k}\left(1-(\gamma_{k+1}^u)^p\left(\gamma_j^u\right)^q\right),\right]\right\}\right)$$

$$\left(\bigcup_{[\eta_{k+1}^l,\eta_{k+1}^u]\in\tilde{g}_i,[\eta_j^l,\eta_j^u]\in\tilde{g}_j}\left\{\left[\prod_{j=1}^{k}\left(1-(1-\eta_{k+1}^l)^p\left(1-\eta_j^l\right)^q\right),\right.\right.\right.$$

$$\left.\left.\left.\prod_{j=1}^{k}\left(1-(1-\eta_{k+1}^u)^p\left(1-\eta_j^u\right)^q\right)\right]\right\}\right)$$

Now combining all the cases and using the operation $\oplus$ it can be easily be shown that the Eq. (4) holds for $n=k+1$. Thus (4) is true for all n.

Now, $\dfrac{1}{n(n-1)}\left(\oplus_{\substack{i,j=1\\ i\neq j}}^{n}\left(\tilde{d}_i^p\otimes\tilde{d}_j^q\right)\right)$

$$=\left(\bigcup_{[\gamma_i^l,\gamma_i^u]\in\tilde{h}_i,[\gamma_j^l,\gamma_j^u]\in\tilde{h}_j}\left\{\left[1-\prod_{\substack{i,j=1\\ i\neq j}}^{n}\left(1-(\gamma_i^l)^p\left(\gamma_j^l\right)^q\right)^{\frac{1}{n(n-1)}},\right.\right.\right.$$

$$\left.\left.\left.1-\prod_{\substack{i,j=1\\ i\neq j}}^{n}\left(1-(\gamma_i^u)^p\left(\gamma_j^u\right)^q\right)^{\frac{1}{n(n-1)}}\right]\right\}\right),$$

$$\cup_{[\eta_i^l,\eta_i^u]\in\widetilde{g}_i,[\eta_j^l,\eta_j^u]\in\widetilde{g}_j} \left\{ \left[\prod_{\substack{i,j=1\\i\neq j}}^{k} \left(1-(1-\eta_i^l)^p(1-\eta_j^l)^q\right)^{\frac{1}{n(n-1)}}, \right.\right.$$

$$\left.\left. \prod_{\substack{i,j=1\\i\neq j}}^{n} \left(1-(1-\eta_i^u)^p(1-\eta_j^u)^q\right)^{\frac{1}{n(n-1)}}\right]\right\}\right)$$

Then, $\text{IVDHFBM}^{p,q}\left(\tilde{d}_1,\tilde{d}_2,\ldots,\tilde{d}_n\right) = \left(\frac{1}{n(n-1)} \oplus_{\substack{i,j=1\\i\neq j}}^{n}\left(\tilde{d}_i^p \otimes \tilde{d}_j^q\right)\right)^{\frac{1}{p+q}}$

$$= \left(\cup_{[\gamma_i^l,\gamma_i^u]\in\widetilde{h}_i,[\gamma_j^l,\gamma_j^u]\in\widetilde{h}_j} \left\{ \left[\left(1-\prod_{\substack{i,j=1\\i\neq j}}^{n}\left(1-(\gamma_i^l)^p(\gamma_j^l)^q\right)^{\frac{1}{n(n-1)}}\right)^{\frac{1}{p+q}}, \right.\right.\right.$$

$$\left.\left. \left(1-\prod_{\substack{i,j=1\\i\neq j}}^{n}\left(1-(\gamma_i^u)^p(\gamma_j^u)^q\right)^{\frac{1}{n(n-1)}}\right)^{\frac{1}{p+q}}\right]\right\},$$

$$\cup_{[\eta_i^l,\eta_i^u]\in\widetilde{g}_i,[\eta_j^l,\eta_j^u]\in\widetilde{g}_j} \left\{ \left[1-\left(1-\prod_{\substack{i,j=1\\i\neq j}}^{n}\left(1-(1-\eta_i^l)^p(1-\eta_j^l)^q\right)^{\frac{1}{n(n-1)}}\right)^{\frac{1}{p+q}}, \right.\right.$$

$$\left.\left.\left. 1-\left(1-\prod_{\substack{i,j=1\\i\neq j}}^{n}\left(1-(1-\eta_i^u)^p(1-\eta_j^u)^q\right)^{\frac{1}{n(n-1)}}\right)^{\frac{1}{p+q}}\right]\right\}\right)$$

Theorem 2 (Idempotency). Let $\tilde{d}_i = \left(\tilde{h}_i,\tilde{g}_i\right)$ be a collection of IVDHFEs. If all $\tilde{d}_i(i=1,2,\ldots,n)$ are equal, i.e., $\tilde{d}_i = \tilde{d}$ for all i, then

$$\text{IVDHFB}^{p,q}\left(\tilde{d}_1,\tilde{d}_2,\ldots,\tilde{d}_n\right) = \tilde{d}$$

Proof: It is given that $\text{IVDHFB}^{p,q}\left(\tilde{d}_1,\tilde{d}_2,\ldots,\tilde{d}_n\right) = \text{IVDHFB}^{p,q}\left(\tilde{d},\tilde{d},\ldots,\tilde{d}\right)$

$$= \left(\frac{1}{n(n-1)} \oplus^{n}_{\substack{i,j=1 \\ i \neq j}} \left(\tilde{d}^p \otimes \tilde{d}^q \right) \right)^{\frac{1}{p+q}}$$

$$= \left(\bigcup_{[\gamma^l, \gamma^u] \tilde{\in} h} \left\{ \left[\left(1 - (1 - (\gamma^l)^p (\gamma^l)^q)^{\frac{1}{n(n-1)}} . (1 - (\gamma^l)^p (\gamma^l)^q)^{\frac{1}{n(n-1)}} . \dots n(n-1) \text{times} \right)^{\frac{1}{p+q}}, \right. \right. \right.$$

$$\left. \left(1 - (1 - (\gamma^u)^p (\gamma^u)^q)^{\frac{1}{n(n-1)}} . (1 - (\gamma^u)^p (\gamma^u)^q)^{\frac{1}{n(n-1)}} . \dots n(n-1) \text{times} \right)^{\frac{1}{p+q}} \right] \right\},$$

$$\bigcup_{[\eta^l, \eta^u] \tilde{\in} g} \left\{ \left[1 - \left(1 - n(n-1) \text{times product of term} (1 - (1 - \eta^l)^p (1 - \eta^l)^q)^{\frac{1}{n(n-1)}} \right)^{\frac{1}{p+q}}, \right. \right.$$

$$\left. \left. 1 - \left(1 - n(n-1) \text{times product of the term} (1 - (1 - \eta^u)^p (1 - \eta^u)^q)^{\frac{1}{n(n-1)}} \right)^{\frac{1}{p+q}} \right] \right\} \right)$$

$$= \left(\bigcup_{[\gamma^l, \gamma^u] \tilde{\in} h} \left\{ \left[(1 - (1 - (\gamma^l)^p (\gamma^l)^q))^{\frac{1}{p+q}}, (1 - (1 - (\gamma^u)^p (\gamma^u)^q))^{\frac{1}{p+q}} \right] \right\}, \right.$$

$$\bigcup_{[\eta^l, \eta^u] \tilde{\in} g} \left\{ \left[1 - (1 - (1 - (1 - \eta^l)^p (1 - \eta^l)^q))^{\frac{1}{p+q}}, \right. \right.$$

$$\left. \left. 1 - (1 - (1 - (1 - \eta^u)^p (1 - \eta^u)^q))^{\frac{1}{p+q}} \right] \right\} \right)$$

$$= \left(\bigcup_{[\gamma^l, \gamma^u] \tilde{\in} h} \left\{ \left[((\gamma^l)^{p+q})^{\frac{1}{p+q}}, ((\gamma^u)^{p+q})^{\frac{1}{p+q}} \right] \right\}, \right.$$

$$\bigcup_{[\eta^l, \eta^u] \tilde{\in} g} \left\{ \left[1 - ((1 - \eta^l)^{p+q})^{\frac{1}{p+q}}, 1 - ((1 - \eta^u)^{p+q})^{\frac{1}{p+q}} \right] \right\} \right)$$

$$= \left(\bigcup_{[\gamma^l, \gamma^u] \tilde{\in} h} \left\{ [\gamma^l, \gamma^u] \right\}, \bigcup_{[\eta^l, \eta^u] \tilde{\in} g} \left\{ [\eta^l, \eta^u] \right\} \right) = \tilde{d}$$

Hence the proof.

Theorem 3 (Monotonicity). Let $\tilde{d}_i = \left(\bigcup_{[\gamma^l_i, \gamma^u_i] \tilde{\in} h_i} \left\{ [\gamma^l_i, \gamma^u_i] \right\}, \bigcup_{[\eta^l_i, \eta^u_i] \tilde{\in} g_i} \left\{ [\eta^l_i, \eta^u_i] \right\} \right)$

$(i = 1, 2, \ldots, n)$ and $\tilde{d}^*_i = \left(\bigcup_{[\gamma^{*l}_i, \gamma^{*u}_i] \tilde{\in} h^*_i} \left\{ [\gamma^{*l}_i, \gamma^{*u}_i] \right\}, \bigcup_{[\eta^{*l}_i, \eta^{*u}_i] \tilde{\in} g^*_i} \left\{ [\eta^{*l}_i, \eta^{*u}_i] \right\} \right)$

$(i = 1, 2, \ldots, n)$ be two collections of IVDHFEs. If $\gamma^l_i \leq \gamma^{*l}_i$, $\gamma^u_i \leq \gamma^{*u}_i$ and $\eta^l_i \geq \eta^{*l}_i$, $\eta^u_i \geq \eta^{*u}_i$ for all $i = 1, 2, \ldots, n$. Then

$$IVDHFBM^{p,q} \left(\tilde{d}_1, \tilde{d}_2, \ldots, \tilde{d}_n \right) \leq IVDHFBM^{p,q} \left(\tilde{d}^*_1, \tilde{d}^*_2, \ldots, \tilde{d}^*_n \right)$$

Proof: Since $\gamma^l_i \leq \gamma^{*l}_i$, for all $i = 1, 2, \ldots, n$, then

$$1 - (\gamma^l_i)^p \left(\gamma^l_j \right)^q \geq 1 - (\gamma^{*l}_i)^p \left(\gamma^{*l}_j \right)^q \text{ for all } i, j$$

i.e., $\prod^n_{\substack{i,j=1 \\ i \neq j}} \left(1 - (\gamma^l_i)^p (\gamma^l_j)^q \right)^{\frac{1}{n(n-1)}} \geq \prod^n_{\substack{i,j=1 \\ i \neq j}} \left(1 - (\gamma^{*l}_i)^p (\gamma^{*l}_j)^q \right)^{\frac{1}{n(n-1)}}$ for all i, j

i.e., $\left(1-\prod_{\substack{i,j=1 \\ i \neq j}}^{n}\left(1-\left(\gamma_i^l\right)^p\left(\gamma_j^l\right)^q\right)^{\frac{1}{n(n-1)}}\right)^{\frac{1}{p+q}}$

$\leq \left(1-\prod_{\substack{i,j=1 \\ i \neq j}}^{n}\left(1-\left(\gamma_i^{*l}\right)^p\left(\gamma_j^{*l}\right)^q\right)^{\frac{1}{n(n-1)}}\right)^{\frac{1}{p+q}}$ for all i,j

(7)

Similarly,

$\left(1-\prod_{\substack{i,j=1 \\ i \neq j}}^{n}\left(1-\left(\gamma_i^u\right)^p\left(\gamma_j^u\right)^q\right)^{\frac{1}{n(n-1)}}\right)^{\frac{1}{p+q}}$

$\leq \left(1-\prod_{\substack{i,j=1 \\ i \neq j}}^{n}\left(1-\left(\gamma_i^{*u}\right)^p\left(\gamma_j^{*u}\right)^q\right)^{\frac{1}{n(n-1)}}\right)^{\frac{1}{p+q}}$

(8)

Now $\eta_i^l \geq \eta_i^{*l}$ for all i, then

$$\left(1-\left(1-\eta_i^l\right)^p\left(1-\eta_j^l\right)^q\right)^{\frac{1}{n(n-1)}} \geq \left(1-\left(1-\eta_i^{*l}\right)^p\left(1-\eta_j^{*l}\right)^q\right)^{\frac{1}{n(n-1)}}$$

i.e., $\left(1-\prod_{\substack{i,j=1 \\ i \neq j}}^{n}\left(1-\left(1-\eta_i^l\right)^p\left(1-\eta_j^l\right)^q\right)^{\frac{1}{n(n-1)}}\right)^{\frac{1}{p+q}}$

$\leq \left(1-\prod_{\substack{i,j=1 \\ i \neq j}}^{n}\left(1-\left(1-\eta_i^{*l}\right)^p\left(1-\eta_j^{*l}\right)^q\right)^{\frac{1}{n(n-1)}}\right)^{\frac{1}{p+q}}$

i.e., $1-\left(1-\prod_{\substack{i,j=1 \\ i \neq j}}^{n}\left(1-\left(1-\eta_i^l\right)^p\left(1-\eta_j^l\right)^q\right)^{\frac{1}{n(n-1)}}\right)^{\frac{1}{p+q}}$

$\geq 1-\left(1-\prod_{\substack{i,j=1 \\ i \neq j}}^{n}\left(1-\left(1-\eta_i^{*l}\right)^p\left(1-\eta_j^{*l}\right)^q\right)^{\frac{1}{n(n-1)}}\right)^{\frac{1}{p+q}}$

(9)

Similarly, it can be shown that

$$1 - \left(1 - \prod_{\substack{i,j=1 \\ i \neq j}}^{n} \left(1 - (1 - \eta_i^u)^p \left(1 - \eta_j^u\right)^q\right)^{\frac{1}{n(n-1)}}\right)^{\frac{1}{p+q}}$$

$$\geq 1 - \left(1 - \prod_{\substack{i,j=1 \\ i \neq j}}^{n} \left(1 - (1 - \eta_i^{*u})^p \left(1 - \eta_j^{*u}\right)^q\right)^{\frac{1}{n(n-1)}}\right)^{\frac{1}{p+q}} \tag{10}$$

Hence by the Eqs. (7–10)

$$S\left(IVDHFBM^{p,q}\left(\tilde{d}_1, \tilde{d}_2, \ldots, \tilde{d}_n\right)\right) \leq S\left(IVDHFBM^{p,q}\left(\tilde{d}_1^*, \tilde{d}_2^*, \ldots, \tilde{d}_n^*\right)\right)$$

Therefore using (1), get $IVDHFBM^{p,q}\left(\tilde{d}_1, \tilde{d}_2, \ldots, \tilde{d}_n\right) \leq IVDHFBM^{p,q}\left(\tilde{d}_1^*, \tilde{d}_2^*, \ldots, \tilde{d}_n^*\right)$
Hence the theorem.

Theorem 4 (Boundary). Let $\tilde{d}_i = \left(\tilde{h}_i, \tilde{g}_i\right)(i = 1, 2, \ldots, n)$ be a collection of IVDHFEs, and let for all $i = 1, 2, \ldots, n$,

$\gamma_{min}^l = min\left\{\gamma_{i_{min}}^l\right\}$ where $\gamma_{i_{min}}^l = min_{[\gamma_i^l, \gamma_i^u] \in \tilde{h}_i}\left\{\gamma_i^l\right\}$; $\gamma_{min}^u = min\left\{\gamma_{i_{min}}^u\right\}$ where

$\gamma_{i_{min}}^u = min_{[\gamma_i^l, \gamma_i^u] \in \tilde{h}_i}\left\{\gamma_i^u\right\}$; $\gamma_{max}^l = max\left\{\gamma_{i_{max}}^l\right\}$ where $\gamma_{i_{max}}^l = max_{[\gamma_i^l, \gamma_i^u] \in \tilde{h}_i}\left\{\gamma_i^l\right\}$; $\gamma_{max}^u = max\left\{\gamma_{i_{max}}^u\right\}$

where $\gamma_{i_{max}}^u = max_{[\gamma_i^l, \gamma_i^u] \in \tilde{h}_i}\left\{\gamma_i^u\right\}$; $\eta_{min}^l = min\left\{\eta_{i_{min}}^l\right\}$ where $\eta_{i_{min}}^l = min_{[\eta_i^l, \eta_i^u] \in \tilde{h}_i}\left\{\eta_i^l\right\}$; $\eta_{min}^u = min\left\{\eta_{i_{min}}^u\right\}$

where $\eta_{i_{min}}^u = min_{[\eta_i^l, \eta_i^u] \in \tilde{h}_i}\left\{\eta_i^u\right\}$; $\eta_{max}^l = max\left\{\eta_{i_{max}}^l\right\}$ where $\eta_{i_{max}}^l = max_{[\eta_i^l, \eta_i^u] \in \tilde{h}_i}\left\{\eta_i^l\right\}$;

$\eta_{max}^u = max\left\{\eta_{i_{max}}^u\right\}$ where $\eta_{i_{max}}^u = max_{[\eta_i^l, \eta_i^u] \in \tilde{h}_i}\left\{\eta_i^u\right\}$; and if $\tilde{d}_- = \left([\gamma_{min}^l, \gamma_{min}^u], [\eta_{max}^l, \eta_{max}^u]\right)$
and $\tilde{d}_+ = \left([\gamma_{max}^l, \gamma_{max}^u], [\eta_{min}^l, \eta_{min}^u]\right)$, then

$$\tilde{d}_- \leq IVDHFB^{p,q}\left(\tilde{d}_1, \tilde{d}_2, \ldots, \tilde{d}_n\right) \leq \tilde{d}_+ \tag{11}$$

Proof: For all $i = 1, 2, \ldots, n$, $\gamma_{min}^l \leq \gamma_i^l \leq \gamma_{max}^l$, and $\gamma_{min}^u \leq \gamma_i^u \leq \gamma_{max}^u$.
Thus $\left(\gamma_{min}^l\right)^p \leq \left(\gamma_i^l\right)^p \leq \left(\gamma_{max}^l\right)^p$ and $\left(\gamma_{min}^l\right)^q \leq \left(\gamma_j^l\right)^q \leq \left(\gamma_{max}^l\right)^q$.

i.e., $\left(\gamma_{min}^l\right)^p \left(\gamma_{min}^l\right)^q \leq \left(\gamma_i^l\right)^p \left(\gamma_j^l\right)^q \leq \left(\gamma_{max}^l\right)^p \left(\gamma_{max}^l\right)^q$ for all i, j

i.e., $\prod_{\substack{i,j=1 \\ i \neq j}}^{n} \left(1 - \left(\gamma_{min}^l\right)^p \left(\gamma_{min}^l\right)^q\right)^{\frac{1}{n(n-1)}} \geq \prod_{\substack{i,j=1 \\ i \neq j}}^{n} \left(1 - \left(\gamma_i^l\right)^p \left(\gamma_j^l\right)^q\right)^{\frac{1}{n(n-1)}}$

$$\geq \prod_{\substack{i,j=1 \\ i \neq j}}^{n} \left(1 - \left(\gamma_{max}^l\right)^p \left(\gamma_{max}^l\right)^q\right)^{\frac{1}{n(n-1)}}$$

i.e., $\left(1 - (\gamma_{min}^l)^{p+q}\right) \geq \prod_{\substack{i,j=1 \\ i \neq j}}^{n} \left(1 - (\gamma_i^l)^p (\gamma_j^l)^q\right)^{\frac{1}{n(n-1)}} \geq \left(1 - (\gamma_{max}^l)^{p+q}\right)$

i.e., $\left(1 - \left(1 - (\gamma_{min}^l)^{p+q}\right)\right)^{\frac{1}{p+q}} \leq \left(1 - \prod_{\substack{i,j=1 \\ i \neq j}}^{n} \left(1 - (\gamma_i^l)^p (\gamma_j^l)^q\right)^{\frac{1}{n(n-1)}}\right)^{\frac{1}{p+q}}$

$$\leq \left(1 - \left(1 - (\gamma_{max}^l)^{p+q}\right)\right)^{\frac{1}{p+q}}$$

i.e., $\gamma_{min}^l \leq \left(1 - \prod_{\substack{i,j=1 \\ i \neq j}}^{n} \left(1 - (\gamma_i^l)^p (\gamma_j^l)^q\right)^{\frac{1}{n(n-1)}}\right)^{\frac{1}{p+q}} \leq \gamma_{max}^l$ \hfill (12)

Similarly $\gamma_{min}^u \leq \left(1 - \prod_{\substack{i,j=1 \\ i \neq j}}^{n} \left(1 - (\gamma_i^u)^p (\gamma_j^u)^q\right)^{\frac{1}{n(n-1)}}\right)^{\frac{1}{p+q}} \leq \gamma_{max}^u$ for all i,j \hfill (13)

Again, since $\eta_{min}^l \leq \eta_i^l \leq \eta_{max}^l$ and $\eta_{min}^u \leq \eta_i^u \leq \eta_{max}^u$ For all $i = 1, 2, \ldots, n$, then $\left(1 - \eta_{min}^l\right)^p \geq \left(1 - \eta_i^l\right)^p \geq \left(1 - \eta_{max}^l\right)^p$ and $\left(1 - \eta_{min}^l\right)^q \geq \left(1 - \eta_j^l\right)^q \geq \left(1 - \eta_{max}^l\right)^q$ For all $i = 1, 2, \ldots, n$. Where $p, q > 0$.

i.e., $\prod_{\substack{i,j=1 \\ i \neq j}}^{n} \left(1 - (1 - \eta_{min}^l)^{p+q}\right)^{\frac{1}{n(n-1)}} \leq \prod_{\substack{i,j=1 \\ i \neq j}}^{n} \left(1 - (1 - \eta_i^l)^p (1 - \eta_j^l)^q\right)^{\frac{1}{n(n-1)}}$

$$\leq \prod_{\substack{i,j=1 \\ i \neq j}}^{n} \left(1 - (1 - \eta_{max}^l)^{p+q}\right)^{\frac{1}{n(n-1)}}$$

i.e., $\left(1 - \left(1 - (1 - \eta_{min}^l)^{p+q}\right)\right)^{\frac{1}{p+q}} \geq \left(1 - \prod_{\substack{i,j=1 \\ i \neq j}}^{n} \left(1 - (1 - \eta_i^l)^p (1 - \eta_j^l)^q\right)^{\frac{1}{n(n-1)}}\right)^{\frac{1}{p+q}}$

$$\geq \left(1 - \left(1 - (1 - \eta_{max}^l)^{p+q}\right)\right)^{\frac{1}{p+q}}$$

i.e., $\eta_{min}^l \leq 1 - \left(1 - \prod_{\substack{i,j=1 \\ i \neq j}}^{n} \left(1 - (1 - \eta_i^l)^p (1 - \eta_j^l)^q\right)^{\frac{1}{n(n-1)}}\right)^{\frac{1}{p+q}} \leq \eta_{max}^l$ \hfill (14)

Similarly, $\eta_{min}^u \leq 1 - \left(1 - \prod_{\substack{i,j=1 \\ i \neq j}}^{n} \left(1 - (1 - \eta_i^u)^p (1 - \eta_j^u)^q\right)^{\frac{1}{n(n-1)}}\right)^{\frac{1}{p+q}} \leq \eta_{max}^u$ \hfill (15)

From Eqs. (12–15), it is now clear that

$$S\left(\tilde{d}_-\right) \le S\left(IVDHFBM^{p,q}\left(\tilde{d}_1,\tilde{d}_2,\ldots,\tilde{d}_n\right)\right) \le S\left(\tilde{d}_+\right) \quad \text{and} \quad \text{hence} \quad \tilde{d}_- \le IVDHFB^{p,q}$$
$$\left(\tilde{d}_1,\tilde{d}_2,\ldots,\tilde{d}_n\right) \le \tilde{d}_+$$

Definition 8. Let $\tilde{d}_i$ $(i=1,2,\ldots,n)$ be a collection of IVDHFEs and let $\omega = (\omega_1,\omega_2,\ldots,\omega_n)^T$ be the weight vector with $\omega_i \in [0,1]$ and $\sum_{i=1}^n \omega_i = 1$. Let $p,q > 0$ be any numbers, If

$$IVDHFBM_\omega^{p,q}\left(\tilde{d}_1,\tilde{d}_2,\ldots,\tilde{d}_n\right) = \left(\frac{1}{n(n-1)} \oplus_{\substack{i,j=1 \\ i\neq j}}^n \left(\left(\omega_i\tilde{d}_i\right)^p \otimes \left(\omega_j\tilde{d}_j\right)^q\right)\right)^{\frac{1}{p+q}}$$

then $IVDHFBM_\omega^{p,q}\left(\tilde{d}_1,\tilde{d}_2,\ldots,\tilde{d}_n\right)$ is called Interval-valued dual hesitant fuzzy weighted Bonferroni mean (IVDHFWBM).

Theorem 5. Let $\tilde{d}_i = \left(\tilde{h}_i,\tilde{g}_i\right)$ $(i=1,2,\ldots,n)$ be a collections of IVDHFEs, whose weighted vector is $\omega = (\omega_1,\omega_2,\ldots,\omega_n)^T$, which satisfies $\omega_i \in [0,1]$ and $\sum_{i=1}^n \omega_i = 1$. Let $p,q > 0$ be any numbers. then the aggregated value by using IVDHFWBM is also a *IVDHFE* and

$$IVDHFWBM^{p,q}\left(\tilde{d}_1,\tilde{d}_2,\ldots,\tilde{d}_n\right) =$$

$$\left(\bigcup_{\substack{[\gamma_i^l,\gamma_i^u]\in\tilde{h}_i, \\ [\gamma_j^l,\gamma_j^u]\in\tilde{h}_j}} \left\{\left[\left(1-\prod_{\substack{i,j=1 \\ i\neq j}}^n \left(1-\left(1-(1-\gamma_i^l)^{\omega_i}\right)^p\left(1-\left(1-\gamma_j^l\right)^{\omega_j}\right)^q\right)^{\frac{1}{n(n-1)}}\right)^{\frac{1}{p+q}}, \right.\right.$$

$$\left.\left(1-\prod_{\substack{i,j=1 \\ i\neq j}}^n \left(1-(1-(1-\gamma_i^u)^{\omega_i})^p\left(1-\left(1-\gamma_j^u\right)^{\omega_j}\right)^q\right)^{\frac{1}{n(n-1)}}\right)^{\frac{1}{p+q}}\right]\right\},$$

$$\bigcup_{\substack{[\eta_i^l,\eta_i^u]\in\tilde{g}_i, \\ [\eta_j^l,\eta_j^u]\in\tilde{g}_j}} \left\{\left[1-\left(1-\prod_{\substack{i,j=1 \\ i\neq j}}^n \left(1-\left(1-(\eta_i^l)^{\omega_i}\right)^p\left(1-\left(\eta_j^l\right)^{\omega_j}\right)^q\right)^{\frac{1}{n(n-1)}}\right)^{\frac{1}{p+q}},\right.\right.$$

$$\left.\left.1-\left(1-\prod_{\substack{i,j=1 \\ i\neq j}}^n \left(1-(1-(\eta_i^u)^{\omega_i})^p\left(1-\left(\eta_j^u\right)^{\omega_j}\right)^q\right)^{\frac{1}{n(n-1)}}\right)^{\frac{1}{p+q}}\right]\right\}\right)$$

$$(16)$$

Proof: Similar proof as Theorem 1.

4 An Approach to Multi-criteria Decision Making with the Prioritization Among IVDHF Information

In this section, the proposed IVDHFWBM operators are used to develop an approach for MCDM under IVDHF environment. For a MCDM problem, let $X = \{x_1, x_2, \ldots, x_m\}$ be a set of alternatives to be selected. Also, let $C = \{C_1, C_2, \ldots, C_n\}$ be a collection of criteria with their weight vector $\omega = (\omega_1, \omega_2, \ldots, \omega_n)^T$ satisfying $\omega_j \in [0, 1]$ for $j = 1, 2, \ldots, n$, and $\sum_{j=1}^{n} \omega_j = 1$, where ω_j denotes the degree of importance of the criterion C_j. After evaluating the alternatives based on criteria a IVDHF decision matrix (IVDHFDM) $\widetilde{D} = \left(\widetilde{d}_{ij} \right)_{m \times n}$ is constructed by some decision maker. Two kinds of attributes may be associated with the problem. The benefit attributes, i.e., the bigger the attribute values, the better, and cost attributes, i.e., the smaller the attribute values, the better.

Now, in MCDM if the problem is associated with the later kind of attributes, then those cost attributes are required to be transformed into benefit attributes, i.e., transform the IVDHFDM $\widetilde{D} = \left(\widetilde{d}_{ij} \right)_{m \times n}$ into a normalized IVDHFDM $\widetilde{R} = \left(\widetilde{r}_{ij} \right)_{m \times n}$ where

$$\widetilde{r}_{ij} = \begin{cases} \widetilde{r}_{ij} \text{ for benefit attribute } C_j \\ \widetilde{r}_{ij}^c \text{ for cost attribute } C_j \end{cases} \tag{17}$$

$i = 1, 2, \ldots, \text{m}$ and $j = 1, 2, \ldots, \text{n}$.

Suppose that $\widetilde{R} = \left(\widetilde{r}_{ij} \right)_{m \times n}$ be a IVDHF decision matrix. Then, the developed IVDHFWBM operators are used to develop an approach for solving MCDM problems in a IVDHF environment. The proposed methodology is described through the following steps:

Step 1. Transform the IVDHF decision matrix $\widetilde{D} = \left(\widetilde{d}_{ij} \right)_{m \times n}$ into the normalized IVDHF decision matrix $\widetilde{R} = \left(\widetilde{r}_{ij} \right)_{m \times n}$ using Eq. (17).

Step 2. Aggregate the IVDHFEs $\widetilde{r}_{ij}$ for each alternative z_i using the *IVDHFWBM* operator as follows:

$$\widetilde{r}_i = IVDHFWBM^{p,q}(\widetilde{r}_{i1}, \widetilde{r}_{i2}, \ldots, \widetilde{r}_{in})$$

$$i = 1, 2, \ldots, m; j = 1, 2, \ldots, n.$$

Step 3. Finding score values using score function as defined in the Definition 3.

Step 4. The rank of all the alternatives is evaluated using Definition 4.

5   Illustrative Example

To establish the application potentiality of the developed methodology, a modified version of a practical problem adapted from an article published by Xu [20] is considered.

The problem is concerning of determining air-conditioning system for a municipal library. There are five feasible alternatives x_i $(i = 1, 2, \ldots, 5)$, and three criteria C_1 (economic), C_2 (functional), and C_3 (operational) are taken into consideration. The weight vector of the criteria C_j $(j = 1, 2, 3)$ is $\omega = (0.3, 0.5, 0.2)^T$. The characteristics of the alternatives x_i $(i = 1, 2, \ldots, 5)$ with respect to the criteria C_j $(j = 1, 2, 3)$ are represented using IVDHFEs $\tilde{d}_{ij} = \left(\tilde{h}_{ij}, \tilde{g}_{ij} \right)$, where $\tilde{h}_{ij}$ indicates the degree that the alternative x_i satisfies the criterion C_j and $\tilde{g}_{ij}$ indicates the degree that the alternative x_i does not satisfy the criterion C_j. The decision matrix $\tilde{D} = \left(\tilde{d}_{ij} \right)_{m \times n}$ is presented in Table 1 where the elements, $\tilde{r}_{ij}(i = 1, 2, \ldots, 5; j = 1, 2, 3)$ are in the form of IVDHFEs.

Table 1. .

	C_1	C_2	C_3
x_1	$\left(\begin{array}{c} \{[0.2,0.3],[0.3,0.4]\}, \\ \{[0.2,0.3],[0.4,0.5]\} \end{array} \right)$	$\left(\begin{array}{c} \{[0.6,0.8]\}, \\ \{[0.1,0.2]\} \end{array} \right)$	$\left(\begin{array}{c} \{[0.2,0.3],[0.4,0.6]\}, \\ \{[0.2,0.3]\} \end{array} \right)$
x_2	$\left(\begin{array}{c} \{[0.2,0.3],[0.4,0.5]\}, \\ \{[0.2,0.4]\} \end{array} \right)$	$\left(\begin{array}{c} \{[0.3,0.4],[0.4,0.7]\}, \\ \{[0.05,0.1],[0.1,0.2], \\ [0.2,0.3]\} \end{array} \right)$	$\left(\begin{array}{c} \{[0.5,0.7]\}, \\ \{[0,1,0.2],[0.2,0.3]\} \end{array} \right)$
x_3	$\left(\begin{array}{c} \{[0.3,0.5]\}, \\ \{[[0.3,0.4],[0.4,0.5]]\} \end{array} \right)$	$\left(\begin{array}{c} \{[0.5,0.6],[0.7,0.8]\}, \\ \{[0.1,0.2]\} \end{array} \right)$	$\left(\begin{array}{c} \{[0.2,0.3],[0.3,0.4]\}, \\ \{[0.4,0.5]\} \end{array} \right)$
x_4	$\left(\begin{array}{c} \{[0.1,0.2],[0.2,0.3]\}, \\ \{[0.5,0.7]\} \end{array} \right)$	$\left(\begin{array}{c} \{[0.7,0.8],[0.8,0.9]\}, \\ \{[0.01,0.1]\} \end{array} \right)$	$\left(\begin{array}{c} \{[0.6,0.7],[0.7,0.8]\}, \\ \{[0.01,0.1],[0.1,0.2]\} \end{array} \right)$
x_5	$\left(\begin{array}{c} \{[0.8,0.9]\}, \\ \{[0.01,0.1]\} \end{array} \right)$	$\left(\begin{array}{c} \{[0.4,0.6]\}, \\ \{[0.2,0.3],[0.3,0.4]\} \end{array} \right)$	$\left(\begin{array}{c} \{[0.2,0.3],[0.4,0.5]\}, \\ \{[0.3,0.5]\} \end{array} \right)$

Step 1. Considering all the criteria C_j $(j = 1, 2, 3)$ are the benefit criteria, the performance values of the alternatives x_i $(i = 1, 2, 3, 4, 5)$ do not need normalization.

Step 2. Utilize the aggregation operators IVDHFWBM as described in Eq. (16) (without loss of generality, suppose that $p = 1$ and $q = 1$) to aggregate all the preference values $\tilde{r}_{ij}$ for each alternative x_i and get r_i $(i = 1, 2, 3, 4, 5)$.

$x_1 = (\{[0.1194, 0.1842], [0.1194, 0.2361], [0.1194, 0.2063], [0.1194, 0.2558],$
$[0.1468, 0.1842], [0.1468, 0.2361], [0.1468, 0.2063], [0.1468, 0.2558],$
$[0.1391, 0.1842], [0.1391, 0.2361], [0.1391, 0.2063], [0.1391, 0.2558],$
$[0.1664, 0.1842], [0.1664, 0.2361], [0.1664, 0.2063], [0.1664, 0.2558]\},$
$\{[0.5668, 0.6566], [0.5668, 0.7033], [0.6243, 0.6566], [0.6243, 0.7033]\})$

$x_2 = (\{[0.1157, 0.1761], [0.1157, 0.2352], [0.1157, 0.2088], [0.1157, 0.2725],$
$[0.1320, 0.1761], [0.1320, 0.2352], [0.1320, 0.2088], [0.1320, 0.2725],$
$[0.1446, 0.1761], [0.1446, 0.2352], [0.1446, 0.2088], [0.1446, 0.2725],$
$[0.1629, 0.1761], [0.1629, 0.2352], [0.1629, 0.2088], [0.1629, 0.2725]\},$
$\{[0.5051, 0.6243], [0.5051, 0.6506], [0.5051, 0.6568], [0.5051, 0.6813],$
$[0.5051, 0.6836], [0.5051, 0.7068], [0.5425, 0.6243], [0.5425, 0.6506],$
$[0.5425, 0.6568], [0.5425, 0.6813], [0.5425, 0.6836], [0.5425, 0.7068],$
$[0.5306, 0.6243], [0.5306, 0.6506], [0.5306, 0.6568], [0.5306, 0.6813],$
$[0.5306, 0.6836], [0.5306, 0.7068], [0.5668, 0.6243], [0.5668, 0.6506],$
$[0.5668, 0.6568], [0.5668, 0.6813], [0.5668, 0.6836], [0.5668, 0.7068],$
$[0.5684, 0.6243], [0.5684, 0.6506], [0.5684, 0.6568], [0.5684, 0.6813],$
$[0.5684, 0.6836], [0.5684, 0.7068], [0.6031, 0.6243], [0.6031, 0.6506],$
$[0.6031, 0.6568], [0.6031, 0.6813], [0.6031, 0.6836], [0.6031, 0.7068]\})$

$x_3 = (\{[0.1253, 0.1899], [0.1253, 0.2030], [0.1253, 0.2289], [0.1253, 0.2434],$
$[0.1378, 0.1899], [0.1378, 0.2030], [0.1378, 0.2289], [0.1378, 0.2434],$
$[0.1533, 0.1899], [0.1533, 0.2030], [0.1533, 0.2289], [0.1533, 0.2434],$
$[0.1677, 0.1899], [0.1677, 0.2030], [0.1677, 0.2289], [0.1677, 0.2434]\},$
$\{[0.6442, 0.7181], [0.6442, 0.7409], [0.6717, 0.7181], [0.6717, 0.7409]\})$

$x_4 = (\{[0.1794, 0.2389], [0.1794, 0.2656], [0.1794, 0.2644], [0.1794, 0.2943],$
$[0.1794, 0.2574], [0.1794, 0.2834], [0.1794, 0.2839], [0.1794, 0.3127],$
$[0.2001, 0.2389], [0.2001, 0.2656], [0.2001, 0.2644], [0.2001, 0.2574],$
$[0.2001, 0.2834], [0.2001, 0.2839], [0.2001, 0.3127], [0.1978, 0.2389],$
$[0.1978, 0.2656], [0.2001, 0.2943], [0.1978, 0.2644], [0.1978, 0.2943],$
$[0.1978, 0.2574], [0.1978, 0.2834], [0.1978, 0.2839], [0.1978, 0.3127],$
$[0.2208, 0.2389], [0.2208, 0.2656], [0.2208, 0.2644], [0.2208, 0.2943],$
$[0.2208, 0.2574], [0.2208, 0.2834], [0.2208, 0.2839], [0.2208, 0.3127],$
$[0.1975, 0.2389], [0.1975, 0.2656], [0.1975, 0.2644], [0.1975, 0.2943],$
$[0.1975, 0.2574], [0.1975, 0.2834], [0.1975, 0.2839], [0.1975, 0.3127],$
$[0.2176, 0.2389], [0.2176, 0.2656], [0.2176, 0.2644], [0.2176, 0.2943],$
$[0.2176, 0.2574], [0.2176, 0.2834], [0.2176, 0.2839], [0.2176, 0.3127],$
$[0.2168, 0.2389], [0.2168, 0.2656], [0.2168, 0.2644], [0.2168, 0.2943],$
$[0.2168, 0.2574], [0.2168, 0.2834], [0.2168, 0.2839], [0.2168, 0.3127],$
$[0.2389, 0.2389], [0.2389, 0.2656], [0.2389, 0.2644], [0.2389, 0.2943],$
$[0.2389, 0.2574], [0.2389, 0.2834], [0.2389, 0.2839], [0.2389, 0.3127]\},$

$$\{[0.4491, 0.6463], [0.4491, 0.6873], [0.5554, 0.6463], [0.5554, 0.6873]\})$$
$$x_5 = (\{[0.1956, 0.2898], [0.1956, 0.3171], [0.2211, 0.2898], [0.2211, 0.3171]\},$$
$$\{[0.5071, 0.6539], [0.5071, 0.6829], [0.5467, 0.6539], [0.5467, 0.6829]\})$$

Step 3. The score value of $r_i (i = 1, 2, 3, 4, 5)$ for each candidate is evaluated using Definition 3. For $p = 1, q = 1$, score values are

$$S(x_1) = -0.4560, S(x_2) = -0.4290, S(x_3) = -0.5126, S(x_4) = -0.3427, S(x_5)$$
$$= -0.3418$$

Step 4. Because $S(r_5) > S(r_4) > S(r_2) > S(r_1) > S(r_3)$, the ranking of the alternatives x_i $(i = 1, 2, \ldots, 5)$ is determined as $x_5 \succ x_4 \succ x_2 \succ x_1 \succ x_3$ for $p = 1, q = 1$. Thus, the best alternative is found as x_5.

Again, if the values of P and q are taken in different such as $p = 2, q = 2$, then by the going through the similar steps the ranking of alternatives are as follows

$$x_4 \succ x_5 \succ x_2 \succ x_1 \succ x_3$$

For this case the best alternative is found as x_4.

This ranking result is marginally different from the ranking of alternatives as it reverses the best two alternatives keeping ranking of all the other alternatives as the same. It is to be noted here that the computational complexities increases with the increase of the parameter values of P and q. Again if at least one of the values among those two parameters is considered as zero the developed IVDHFWBM operator fails to capture interrelationship of the arguments. Thus to maintain interrelationship and less computational complexities, it is justified to consider the value of the parameters as $p = q = 1$.

6 Conclusions

In this article IVDHFWBM operator has been developed and applied to solve MCDM problems with IVDHF information. As like BM for aggregating crisp values, the developed IVDHFWBM operator can capture importance of each criterion and the interrelationship between criteria in MCDM. Also IVDHFNs can capture uncertainties in an efficient manner than other variants of HFNs. Thus combining BM with IVDHFNs appears as an innovative tool for capturing uncertainties in a significant way but also maintain interrelationship among the individual arguments. However, it is hoped that the develop method can extend the scope of solving MCDM problems in a better way.

References

1. Zadeh, L.A.: Fuzzy sets. Inf. Control **8**, 338–353 (1965)
2. Atanassov, K.T.: Intuitionistic fuzzy sets. Fuzzy Sets Syst. **20**(1), 87–96 (1986)
3. Biswas, A., Dewan, S.: Priority based fuzzy goal programming technique for solving fractional fuzzy goals by using dynamic programming. Fuzzy Inf. Eng. **4**, 165–180 (2012)
4. Biswas, A., Modak, N.: A fuzzy goal programming technique for multiobjective chance constrained programming with normally distributed fuzzy random variables and fuzzy numbers. Int. J. Math. Oper. Res. **5**, 551–570 (2013)
5. Biswas, A., Sarkar, B.: Pythagorean fuzzy multi-criteria group decision making through similarity measure based on point operators. Int. J. Intell. Syst. **33**, 1731–1744 (2018)
6. Biswas, A., Majumdar, D., Sahu, S.: Assessing morningness of a group of people by using fuzzy expert system and adaptive neuro fuzzy inference model. Commun. Comput. Inf. Sci. **140**, 47–56 (2011)
7. Biswas, A., et al.: Exploration of transcultural properties of the reduced version of the morningness-eveningness questionnaire (rMEQ) using adaptive neuro fuzzy inference system. Biol. Rhythm Res. **45**, 955–968 (2014)
8. Debnath, J., Biswas, A., Presobh, S., Sen, K.N., Sahu, S.: Fuzzy inference model for assessing occupational risks in construction sites. Int. J. Ind. Ergon. **55**, 114–128 (2016)
9. Torra, V., Narukawa, Y.: On hesitant fuzzy sets and decision. In: The 18th IEEE International Conference on Fuzzy Systems, Jeju Island, Korea, pp. 1378–1382 (2009)
10. Torra, V.: Hesitant fuzzy sets. Int. J. Intell. Syst. **25**, 529–539 (2010)
11. Xia, M.M., Xu, Z.S.: Hesitant fuzzy information aggregation in decision making. Int. J. Approximate Reasoning **52**, 395–407 (2011)
12. Gu, X., Wang, Y., Yang, B.: A method for hesitant fuzzy multiple attribute decision making and its application to risk investment. J. Convergence Inf. Technol. **6**(6), 282–287 (2011)
13. Wei, G.W.: Hesitant fuzzy prioritized operators and their application to multiple attribute decision making. Knowl. Based Syst. **31**, 176–182 (2012)
14. Zhu, B., Xu, Z.S., Xia, M.M.: Dual hesitant fuzzy sets. J. Appl. Math. 13 (2012). Article ID 879629. https://doi.org/10.1155/2012/879629
15. Wang, H.J., Zhao, X.F., Wei, G.W.: Dual hesitant fuzzy aggregation operators in multiple attribute decision making. J. Intell. Fuzzy Syst. **26**(5), 2281–2290 (2014)
16. Yu, D.: Archimedean aggregation operators based on dual hesitant fuzzy set and their application to GDM. Int. J. Uncertainty Fuzziness Knowl. Based Syst. **23**(5), 761–780 (2015)
17. Ju, Y., Liu, X., Yang, S.: Interval-valued dual hesitant fuzzy aggregation operators and their applications to multiple attribute decision making. J. Intell. Fuzzy Syst. **27**, 1203–1218 (2014)

18. Wei, G.: Interval-valued dual hesitant fuzzy uncertain linguistic aggregation operators in multiple attribute decision making. J. Intell. Fuzzy Syst. **33**, 1881–1893 (2017)
19. Bonferroni, C.: Sulle medie multiple di potenze. Bolletino Matematica Italiana **5**, 267–270 (1950)
20. Xu, Z.: Intuitionistic Fuzzy Bonferroni Means. IEEE Trans. Syst. Man Cybern. Part B **41**(2), 568–578 (2010)

Deep Convolutional Neural Network Based Facial Keypoints Detection

Madhuchhanda Dasgupta[1]([⊠]) and Jyotsna Kumar Mandal[2]

[1] Department of CSE, JIS College of Engineering, Kalyani, India
madhu.banik@gmail.com
[2] Department of CSE, Kalyani University, Kalyani, India
jkm.cse@gmail.com

Abstract. Facial keypoints (FKP) detection is considered as a challenging task in the field of computer vision, as facial features vary from individual to individual. It becomes a more challenging proposition as the same person facial image may also vary due to change in position, size, pose, expression etc. Some methods exist in literature for detection of FKPs. In this paper, a deep architecture is used to locate the keypoints on gray-scale images. As baseline method one hidden layer neural network and convolutional neural networks are built in the proposed work. Additionally, a block of pretrained Inception module is used to extract the intermediate features. Specifically, the sparse structure of Inception model reduces the computational cost of the proposed method significantly. The methods are evaluated on standard dataset and compared with existing state-of-the-art CNN based methods. The obtained results are promising and also bring out the efficiency of the proposed work.

Keywords: Facial keypoints · Convolutional neural network ·
Gray-scale image · Sparse structure · Inception model

1 Introduction

People usually do face recognition effortlessly without much consciousness but it remains a challenging task yet in the field of computer vision. Face recognition is identifying an individual from the face images. With technological improvement it has been widely applied in our daily life such as tracking faces in images, biometrics, information security, health care, access control, law enforcement and surveillance systems.

In face recognition, Facial keypoints (FKP) are used as a building block. This keypoints detection is to predict certain positions such as corners of the eyes, eyebrows, nose and mouth on face images. Over the last decade lots of work has been done in face detection and recognition. PCA, LDA, GABOR, LBP etc. are the traditional face recognition algorithms. Human neurons inspired artificial neural network is an adaptive system based on learning procedure that provides high accuracy. Convolutional Neural Networks (CNN) provides higher accuracy in computer vision field. Nowadays, CNN are the state-of-the-art performers for a wide variety of tasks. This model is also suitable for facial landmark detection with fast convergence and high accuracy.

© Springer Nature Singapore Pte Ltd. 2019
J. K. Mandal et al. (Eds.): CICBA 2018, CCIS 1030, pp. 47–56, 2019.
https://doi.org/10.1007/978-981-13-8578-0_4

In this paper, first Neural Network (NN) and then CNN based approaches are built as baseline methods to predict FKPs accurately and effectively.

In computation, efficient distribution of computing resources with finite computational budget is very necessary. To remove computational bottleneck and dimension reduction, Szegedy et al. [8] proposed Inception model which has low computational cost for its sparsely connected architecture. In proposed CNN this sparse architecture is added to reduce the number of computations effectively.

In the remaining part of the paper, literature review is provided in Sect. 2. In Sect. 3, proposed baseline methods are explained and experimental result analysis is given in Sect. 4. Section 5 concludes the document.

2 Related Work

With growing applications, huge work has been done in past on FKPs detection. Traditional methods have used feature extraction and different types of graphic models to detect facial keypoints. Vukadinovic [11] proposed Gabor feature based boosted classifiers to detect 20 different facial keypoints. Boosted regression and graph modes based method is presented by Valstar et al. [12]. Belhumeur et al. [14] used local detectors with a non-parametric set of global models for the part locations of faces. In some applications shape models and branch and bound are used for optimal landmark detection [13]. On the other hand, Wang et al. [4] addressed FKPs detection by applying histogram stretching for image contrast enhancement, followed by principal component analysis [5]. Cao et al. [26] proposed a generative Bayesian transfer learning algorithm for the face verification problem.

In the last few years, CNN has shown outstanding results and it also shows rapid advances in FKPs detection. Several papers propose CNN learning for FKPs detection [6, 7, 10, 21]. Deep neural network is used in face recognition [15, 25] as well. Shi [1] applied and discussed different algorithms starting from K Nearest Neighbours (KNN), linear regression, Decision tree to CNN for locating FKPs. Longpre, Sohmshetty [7] applied data augmentation techniques to expand the number of training examples to generalize the network for keypoints detection. Sun et al. [4] estimated FKPs by using three level convolutional neural network and outputs of multiple networks were merged for robust and correct estimation. They extracted high-level features over the whole face to locate high accuracy keypoints. Again the geometric ratios and constraints of keypoints are used to train the network to predict the keypoints simultaneously. Zhang and Meng [6] used a sparsely connected inception model to extract features and input those features to CNN to reduce computational complexity for detecting FKPs. In the proposed work similar approach is adopted for detection with enhancements.

3 Proposed Methods

3.1 Dataset

Dataset is provided by Dr. Yoshua Bengio, University of Montreal. Now this dataset is available in Kaggle open research dataset [2]. It has 7049 training data of gray-scale facial images and their corresponding 15 FKPs. Here, image dimension is 96 × 96 that is 9216 pixels and each pixel is represented by 8-bits. All 15 keypoints are in 2D images with [x, y] co-ordinates. So, 30 numerical values are to be predicted. The given dataset has 7049 rows with 31 columns where in each row first 30 columns represent 15 FKPs and last column has 9216 pixel values to represent one image. All 15 facial keypoints are shown in Fig. 1. Among the 7049 training images, there exist only 2140 training images which are completely and accurately labelled for all the 15 keypoints. To expand the training dataset, data augmentation technique is applied. 80% of the data is considered as training data and 20% data is used for validation purpose. The proposed model tested on 1783 test images.

Fig. 1. Augmented face with 15 facial keypoints

3.2 Data Augmentation

To train the convolutional neural networks, a large number of training samples are required to avoid over-fitting. Data Augmentation technique is applied to generate more image data to increase accurately labelled training dataset. Among most effective data augmentation techniques, horizontal reflection is one of them. It is quite straight forward technique in which the images are flipped horizontally with their keypoint labels and then remap the keypoint labels to their new representations so that left eye center becomes right eye center and vice versa. In this way, almost double amount of data are generated and creates augmented training dataset.

3.3   Network Architecture

Neural Network (NN)

Artificial neural networks are popular machine learning techniques [20]. As a baseline model a neural network is designed using Keras which is a Python based high-level neural network library. In the neural network, first reshape the input image of 96×96 into 9216×1 as the input of the network, then one hidden layer consists of 500 neurons and the output layer with 30 units as 15 sets of coordinates for 15 FKPs of facial images. The loss function is defined by mean square error (MSE) between the actual value and the obtained output from the keypoints vectors. To converge gradient descent faster, Nesterov momentum is used as an update rule. During the training phase, the network iterates for 400 epochs.

Convolutional Neural Network (CNN)

In the proposed work a convolutional neural network [23] is designed to achieve high accuracy. The main reason of popularity of CNN is its algorithm and improved network architecture. CNN has a typical structure – stacked convolutional layers followed by one or more fully connected layers [19]. In Convolutional layers feature maps are comprised of convolution operations followed by max pooling [9, 17]. The feature maps of CNN consists with only considering receptive fields so that smaller numbers of neurons are present in comparison with fully connected neural network and this is the unique property of CNN.

The proposed CNN architecture and hyper-parameters of it are given in Fig. 2 and Table 1 respectively. The layers of proposed CNN model are structured as following.

- As input size of the image is 96×96 and being a gray-scale image, the input layer size is $96 \times 96 \times 1$.
- First convolutional layer consists of 32 filters sized 3×3, stride 1 followed by max pooling of filter size 2×2 with stride 2.
- In second conv. layer 64 filters of size 3×3, stride 1 followed by max pooling 2×2 with stride 2.
- Third conv. layer consists of 128 filters of size 3×3, stride 1 and max pooling filter 2×2 with stride 2.
- The fourth conv. layer forms with 256 filters with dimension 3×3, stride 1 followed by max pooling 2×2 with stride 2.
- Next two fully connected layers consist with 256 and 128 hidden units respectively.

Finally output layer consists of 30 units. A set of coordinates [x, y] of 15 facial keypoints are stored on these 30 units [18].

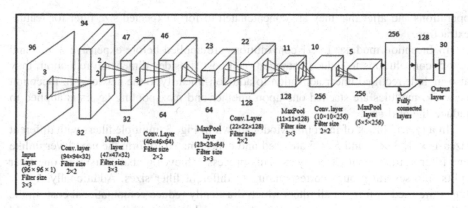

Fig. 2. Convolutional Neural Network architecture

Table 1. Hyper-parameters of CNN

	Convolution layer 1		Convolution layer 2		Convolution layer 3		Convolution layer 4	
	Conv	Pool	Conv	Pool	Conv	Pool	Conv	Pool
No. of filters	32	32	64	64	128	128	256	256
Filter size	3×3	2×2	3×3	2×2	3×3	2×2	3×3	2×2
Stride	1	2	1	2	1	2	1	2
Pad	0	0	0	0	0	0	0	0

The whole network is trained through backpropagation method and trying to minimize the error by using optimization algorithm. To evaluate the gradient of the error function initially high learning rate is set and gradually minimize the learning rate to get closer point of minimum loss to converge the model for an optimal set of weights. The network is tuned using different parameters and update rules [28] to make an optimal model. Deep networks with a large number of parameters are very powerful machine learning systems. But combining all parameters occurs overfitting which slow down the system. To address such problem dropout [16] is introduced which randomly drop units along with their connections from the neural network during training phase.

Inception Convolutional Neural Network (INCNN)
In multi-layer CNN architecture due to increased number of layers and parameters, the network is inclined to overfit and large numbers of computational resources are consumed. To overcome these, some adjustments are needed in the architecture level. Szegedy et al. [8] proposed Inception Model which considers sparsely connected architecture in the convolutions where lower dimension filters are used for convolution

operations and after that they are concatenated to form expected size filter for feature extraction.

In Inception module, 1 × 1 convolutions are applied before expensive 3 × 3 and 5 × 5 convolutions to reduce computational cost. Besides dimension reduction, they also include rectified linear activation to add non-linearity to the network. In Inception network, modules are stacked one upon another and max pooling layers is applied to reduce the grid size.

In a typical block of Inception Model shown in Fig. 3, multiple filters with different sizes 1 × 1, 3 × 3 and 5 × 5 are used and concatenated to form the next layer unlike one filter in traditional CNN layers. This process achieves global sparsity as one filter splits into several groups corresponding to different filter sizes. Additionally, 1 × 1 filters are used in front of all filters which drastically reduce computational cost. In the following experiments, pretrained Inception model is adopted to extract features and input these features into CNN architecture and this is named as INCNN in the proposed work.

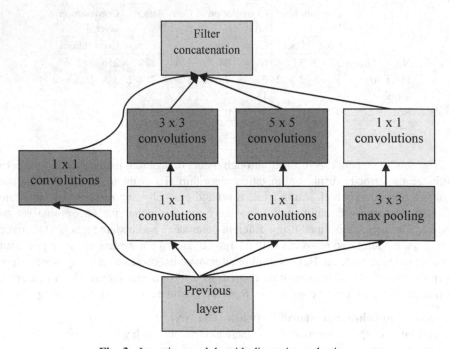

Fig. 3. Inception module with dimension reductions

4 Results

4.1 Experimental Setup

The experimental platform is Intel Core i5 Processor 2.2 GHz CPU plus 8 GB memory laptop. In the framework TensorFlow based model is used for building convolution neural network. In addition, the following packages are used in the proposed algorithm: Pandas, Numpy, Keras, Scikit, Matplotlib and main language Python is used for implementation of the algorithm.

4.2 Accuracy Detection

In this section, the performance of the proposed algorithm in terms of detection accuracy is discussed. Root Mean Square Error (RMSE) is an effective measure of the deviations in distances, has been used to compare accuracy measures of proposed method with other existing standard methods.

$$RMSE = \sqrt{\frac{1}{n}\sum_{i=1}^{n}(y_i - \hat{y}_i)^2}$$

Root Mean Square Error formula is shown above. The loss is calculated between the real and predicted FKPs. Here n = 30 given and y_i is the expected output and $\hat{y}_i$ is the predicted value of the i-th keypoint. Each model is evaluated with different update rules [22] and number of epochs and adjusts the hyper-parameters accordingly to achieve best possible RMSE.

A large learning rate caused loss to explode whereas too small learning rate showed a stagnant loss curve. Here 0.1 is chosen as initial learning rate and gradually decreases it to 0.001 for convergence of gradient descent [27]. To add non-linearity in the network Rectified Linear Unit (ReLU) activation function is used as it is observed that it works faster in deep convolutional neural network than equivalent tanh units [3]. Adam optimizer [24] is chosen for the network as in deep learning applications it performs best compared with other optimization algorithms. Batch size is set as 128 and epochs count set as 400 here. During experiment a large gap is observed in between training and validation errors. Regularization is added by using dropout value of 0.2 to minimize this gap.

Data augmentation technique is applied in the training dataset and shows a significant improvement in validation RMSE. In Table 2 training, validation losses are tabulated with epoch numbers in the form of mean square error (MSE).

Table 2. Training and validation loss in terms of MSE for NN, CNN, INCNN.

Epochs	NN		CNN		INCNN	
	Train loss	Validation loss	Train loss	Validation loss	Train loss	Validation loss
100	0.00567	0.00627	0.00222	0.00243	0.00129	0.00236
200	0.00423	0.00598	0.00179	0.00199	0.00078	0.00085
300	0.00376	0.00512	0.00132	0.00143	0.00060	0.00068
400	0.00291	0.00382	0.00124	0.00139	0.00038	0.00042

The target coordinates are divided by 48 to scale them in [−1, 1] and for that to find RMSE, RMSE = $\sqrt{MSE}$ * 48 is used here. Results have shown that INCNN has minimum loss and its validation RMSE value is 0.987.

Comparisons of proposed method with existing state-of-the art methods in terms of RMSE are shown in Table 3.

Table 3. Performance analysis in terms of RMSE

	RMSE
Shi [1] CNN model	1.874
LeNet [7]	1.349
NaimishNet [10]	1.03
Proposed method	0.987

The annotated faces with 15 keypoints of 3 individuals are shown in Fig. 4.

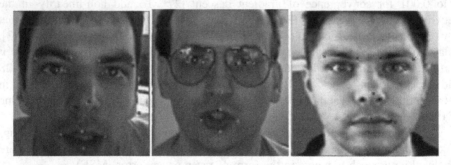

Fig. 4. Marked in blue for original and in red for predicted 15 facial keypoints. (Color figure online)

5 Conclusion

In the proposed work, one hidden layer neural network, convolutional neural network (CNN) and Inception model adopted convolutional neural network (INCNN) are designed for facial keypoints detection. It is observed from the performed experiments that applying CNN gives a more accurate result than simple NN. But after introducing the sparse architecture of INCNN, a far better accuracy with a very significant improvement in performance is achieved in facial keypoints prediction.

As a scope of future work, tuning the network by adjusting the hyper-parameters may improve the network performance. Again, applying more advanced image augmentation techniques to generalize the network and GPU implementation of the network for improved time complexity may be achieved.

References

1. Shi, S.: Facial Keypoints Detection, arXiv preprint arXiv:1710.05279, 15 October 2017
2. Kaggle dataset. https://www.kaggle.com/c/facial-keypoints-detection
3. Krizhevsky, A., Sutskever, I., Hinton, G.E.: Imagenet classification with deep convolutional neural networks. In: Advances in Neural Information Processing Systems, pp. 1097–1105 (2012)
4. Sun, Y., Wang, X., Tang, X.: Deep convolutional network cascade for facial point detection. In: Proceedings of the IEEE Conference on Computer Vision and Pattern Recognition, pp. 3476–3483 (2013)
5. Wang, Y., Song, Y.: Facial Keypoints Detection. Stanford University (2014)
6. Zhang, S., Meng, C.: Facial keypoints detection using neural network (2016)
7. Longpre, S., Sohmshetty, A.: Facial Keypoint Detection. Stanford University (2016)
8. Szegedy, C., et al.: Going deeper with convolutions. In: Proceedings of the IEEE Conference on Computer Vision and Pattern Recognition, pp. 1–9 (2015)
9. Lin, M., Chen, Q., Yan, S.: Network in network. arXiv preprint arXiv:1312.4400 (2013)
10. Agarwal, N., Krohn-Grimberghe, A., Vyas, R.: Facial Key points Detection using Deep convolutional Neural Network – NaimishNet (2017)
11. Vukadinovic, D., Pantic, M.: Fully automatic facial feature point detection using gabor feature based boosted classifiers. In: 2005 IEEE International Conference on Systems, Man and Cybernetics, vol. 2, pp. 1692–1698. IEEE (2005)
12. Valstar, M., Martinez, B., Binefa, X., Pantic, M.: Facial point detection using boosted regression and graph models. In: 2010 IEEE Conference on Computer Vision and Pattern Recognition (CVPR), pp. 2729–2736. IEEE (2010)
13. Amberg, B., Vetter, T.: Optimal landmark detection using shape models and branch and bound. In: 2011 IEEE International Conference on Computer Vision (ICCV). IEEE (2011)
14. Belhumeur, P.N., et al.: Localizing parts of faces using a consensus of exemplars. IEEE Trans. Pattern Anal. Mach. Intell. 35(12), 2930–2940 (2013)
15. Parkhi, O.M., Vedaldi, A., Zisserman, A.: Deep face recognition. In: BMVC, vol. 1, no. 3, p. 6 (2015)
16. Srivastava, N., Hinton, G., Krizhevsky, A., Sutskever, I., Salakhutdinov, R.: Dropout: a simple way to prevent neural networks from overfitting. J. Mach. Learn. Res. 15(1), 1929–1958 (2014)

17. Simonyan, K., Zisserman, A.: Very deep convolutional networks for large-scale image recognition. arXiv preprint arXiv:1409.1556 (2014)
18. Peter, S.: Detecting facial features using Deep Learning. https://towardsdatascience.com/detecting-facial-features-using-deep-learning-2e23c8660a7a
19. Zeiler, M.D., Fergus, R.: Visualizing and understanding convolutional networks. In: Fleet, D., Pajdla, T., Schiele, B., Tuytelaars, T. (eds.) ECCV 2014. LNCS, vol. 8689, pp. 818–833. Springer, Cham (2014). https://doi.org/10.1007/978-3-319-10590-1_53
20. Aggarwal, C.C.: Chapter 1 An Introduction to Neural Networks. Springer, Cham (2018). https://doi.org/10.1007/978-3-319-94463-0_8
21. Sun, Y., Wang, X., Tang, X.: Deep convolutional network cascade for facial point detection. In: IEEE Conference on Computer Vision and Pattern Recognition (CVPR) (2013)
22. Daniel Nouri's blog. http://danielnouri.org/notes/2014/12/17/using-convolutional-neural-nets-to-detect-facial-keypoints-tutorial/
23. Simonyan, K., Zisserman, A.: Very deep convolutional networks for largescale image recognition. arXiv preprint arXiv:1409.1556 (2014)
24. Kingma, D.P., Ba, J.: Adam: A method for stochastic optimization. arXiv preprint arXiv: 1412.6980 (2014)
25. Wang, W., Yang, J., Xiao, J., Li, S., Zhou, D.: Face recognition based on deep learning. In: Zu, Q., Hu, B., Gu, N., Seng, S. (eds.) HCC 2014. LNCS, vol. 8944, pp. 812–820. Springer, Cham (2015). https://doi.org/10.1007/978-3-319-15554-8_73
26. Cao, X., Wipf, D., Wen, F., Duan, G., Sun, J.: A practical transfer learning algorithm for face verification. In: Proceedings of the IEEE International Conference on Computer Vision, pp. 3208–3215 (2013)
27. Sutskever, I., Martens, J., Dahl, G.E., Hinton, G.E.: On the importance of initialization and momentum in deep learning. In: Proceedings of the 30th International Conference on Machine Learning ICML 2013, Atlanta, GA, USA, volume 28 of JMLR Proceedings, pp. 1139–1147, 16–21 June 2013
28. Glorot, X., Bengio, Y.: Understanding the difficulty of training deep feedforward neural networks. In: Proceedings of the 13th International Conference on Artificial Intelligence and Statistics (AISTATS) 2010, Chia Laguna Resort, Sardinia, Italy, volume 9 of J. Mach. Learn. Res. pp. 249–256 (2010)

A Frame Work for Detection of the Degree of Skin Disease Using Different Soft Computing Model

Manisha Barman[1(✉)], J. Paul Choudhury[2], and Susanta Biswas[3]

[1] Department of Information Technology,
Kalyani Government Engineering College, Kalyani, Nadia, WB, India
memanisha5@gmail.com
[2] Department of Information Technology,
Future Institute of Engineering and Management, Sonarpur, India
jnpcl93@yahoo.com
[3] Department of Engineering and Technological Studies, University of Kalyani,
Kalyani, Nadia 741235, India
biswas.su@gmail.com

Abstract. Health Informatics plays a great role in the recovery of disease. In health informatics system, the information regarding the conditions of various diseases and subsequent remedy regarding application of medicines have been stored in Computer memory. Based on the conditions of sickness of a particular organ of the patient, the status of the disease of that person can be ascertained using the stored information in the computer and accordingly certain measures are advised by the doctor to the patients with the help of a computer. In this paper skin disease detection technique is proposed using image processing techniques and soft computing models. The soft computing models include Fuzzy logic, Artificial Neural Network and Genetic algorithm. Initially image characteristics have been collected from digital images using image processing tools. Soft computing models viz using Fuzzy logic, Artificial Neural Network and Genetic algorithm have been applied on the image characteristics. Based on the minimum value of average error, the particular soft computing model has been selected to produce the estimated value of image characteristics. K means clustering algorithm has been applied to the estimated value of image characteristics to produce optimal number of clusters. Each cluster represents the degree of the disease. Then image processing tool has been applied to the unknown image of a patient to get image characteristics of new image. Now the selected soft computing tool has been applied on the image characteristics of new image to produce the estimated image characteristics. The estimated image characteristics has been compared with the cluster centre value of the clusters as formed based on Euclidian distance function. The cluster centre with minimum distance function value indicates the degree of disease of a patient.

Keywords: Digital image · Fuzzy logic · Artificial neural network · Genetic algorithm · K means clustering · Average error

© Springer Nature Singapore Pte Ltd. 2019
J. K. Mandal et al. (Eds.): CICBA 2018, CCIS 1030, pp. 57–66, 2019.
https://doi.org/10.1007/978-981-13-8578-0_5

1   Introduction

Skin diseases are the most common disease in human being. Most of the skin diseases are curable at initial stages but if it cannot be cured lastly it may go to skin cancer. So an early detection of skin disease can save the life of patient. With the advancement of computer technology, early detection of skin disease is possible. Texture analysis is one of the fundamental aspects of human vision by which surfaces and objects can be discriminated. Texture refers to the visual patterns or spatial arrangement of pixels which cannot be described by the intensity and color of that place.

1.1   Background Study

Mitra, Parekh [1] have used a multilayer perceptron neural network model for the diagnosis of skin disease from the available dataset. The available dataset as pixel values have been obtained after processing the available skin images. Initially the dataset have been partitioned into three classes, one class has been related to a topic dermaties, one related to Eczema and the third one to Urticaria. All these images are sealed to standard dimension of 100×100 which are stored in jpeg format. The resolution of these images are 72 pixel per inch. The used neural network architecture is 1-31-3 with 1 node as input layer, 31 nodes in hidden layer and 3 nodes in output layer. Log sigmoid activation function has been used for both the layers, it has been shown that the overall accuracy is 96.6% and 82.2% for two features respectively.

Lau, Al Jumaily [2] have used different types of neural network techniques for the diagnosis of skin cancers from the available dataset as pixel values of images. They have implemented using 3-layered back-propagation neural network classifier and auto-associative neural network. The author have shown that the accuracy is 89.9% for back propagation neural network and 80.8% for auto associative neural network. The image database including dermoscopy photo and digital photo have been used. Elgamal [3] has used hybrid techniques with wavelet transform, k nearest neighborhood algorithm and artificial neural network. The proposed hybrid techniques consists of three stages, namely, feature extraction, dimensionality reduction, and classification. In the first stage, the features have been related with images using discrete wavelet transformation. In the second stage, the features of skin images have been reduced using principle component analysis to form essential features. In the classification have been developed algorithm. The result has shown with a success of 95% and 97.5% for two feature respectively. The Author shown that the proposed hybrid techniques is robust and effective.

JaseemaYasmin, Mohamed Sadiq [4] have used an automated system for segmentation of colored skin images which has helped the early detection of malignant melanoma. Skin images have comprised of four major components: skin image acquisition, lesion segmentation, feature extraction, and lesion classification. Automatic segmentation of lesions in color skin images is the main focus of this paper This technique is one of the most important steps towards the automated analysis and evaluation of dermoscopy of images in the computer aided diagnosis of melanoma. The accuracy of segmentation is highly dependent on the success or failure of each computerized analysis procedure. An improved iterative segmentation algorithm using canny edge detector with iterative median filter is presented for border detection of real skin lesions, which has helped in early detection of malignant melanoma. Its performance is compared with the segmentation algorithm using canny detector. Finally authors have shown that their result was excellent.

Ercal et al. [5] have proposed, a simple and effective method to find the borders of tumors as an initial step towards the diagnosis of skin tumors from color images. The method has made use of an adaptive color metric from the red, green, and blue (RGB) planes that contain information to discriminate the tumor from the background. Using this suitable coordinate transformation, the image has been segmented. The tumor portion has been extracted from the segmented image and borders have been drawn. Garnavi et al. [6] have proposed a novel automatic segmentation algorithm using color space analysis and clustering-based histogram thresholding, which is able to find out the optimal color channel for segmentation of skin lesions.

The prediction of heart disease [6, 7] using various soft computing models v.i.z. fuzzy rule base, neural network, etc. have been worked on certain real parameter values i.e. blood pressure, cholesterol, fasting of blood sugar, maximum heart rate achieved, resting blood rate and predication has been made accordingly. The prediction disease using image processing tools along with soft computing models has been attempted by the authors [1–6]. They have worked on the images of skin. Segmentation of images have been done by [4, 6, 12, 13]. Neural network and classification techniques have been used in [2, 3, 4]. A lot of research work has been carried out using soft computing models in images have been attempted. But the evaluation on the performance of soft computing models on the images of defected organ has not been attempted [8, 9]. Prediction of degree of disease by analyzing digital images of defected organ has not been carried out earlier. That is the reason for the proposal of continuing the research work using image processing tools along with soft computing models in digital images in this proposed research work.

Here in this paper it has been proposed to develop an automated skin disease detection system for recognizing the disease conditions of human skin using the techniques of image processing and soft computing models. Here the texture features of skin images have been proposed to analyze using image processing tools. Under the domain of soft computing, the method of fuzzy logic, neural network and genetic algorithm have been used. Based on the minimum value of average error, the particular soft computing model has been chosen to produce the estimated value of image characteristics. K means clustering algorithm has been applied to the estimated value of image characteristics to produce optimal number of clusters. Each cluster represents the degree of the disease. Now image processing tool has been applied to the unknown image of a person to get image characteristics of new image. Now the selected soft computing tool has been applied on the image characteristics of new image to produce the estimated image characteristics. The estimated image characteristic has been compared based on Euclidian distance function with the cluster centre value of the clusters as formed. The cluster centre with minimum distance function value indicates the degree of disease of a person.

2 Methodology

2.1 Expert System

The knowledge base stores all relevant information, data, rules, cases, and relationships used by the expert system. A knowledge base can be formed by combining the knowledge of multiple human experts. A rule is a conditional statement that links given conditions to actions or outcomes. A frame is another approach used to capture and store knowledge in a knowledge base. It relates an object or item to various facts or values. A frame-based representation is ideally suited for object-oriented programming techniques. Expert systems making use of frames to store knowledge are also called frame-based expert systems.

2.2 Fuzzy Systems

The characteristic function of a crisp set assigns a value of either 1 or 0 to each individual in the universal set, thereby discriminating members and nonmembers of the crisp set under consideration. This function can be generalized such that the value assigned to the elements of the universal set fall within a specific range and indicate the membership grade of these elements in the set in question. Larger values denote higher degrees of set membership. Such a function is called a membership function and the set defined by it is a fuzzy set.

The range of values of membership function is the unit interval $[0, 1]$. Here each membership function maps the element of a given universal set X, which is always a crisp set, into real numbers in $[0, 1]$. The membership function of a fuzzy set A is defined by A, A: $X \longrightarrow [0, 1]$.

2.2.1 Fuzzy Time Series

Definition 1. Let $Y(t)$ $(t = ..., 0, 1, 2,.......)$, a subset of R', be the universe discourse on which fuzzy sets fi (t) $(i = 1, 2,........)$ are defined and $F(t)$ is a collection of $f_1(t), f_2(t),.......$ Then $F(t)$ is called a Fuzzy Time Series defined on $Y(t)$ $(t = ..., 0, 1, 2,......)$.

Definition 2. Suppose $F(t)$ is caused by $F(t-1)$ only i.e. $F(t-1) \longrightarrow F(t)$. Then this relation can be expressed as $F(t) = F(t-1). R(t, t-1)$ where $R(t, t-1)$ is the fuzzy relationship between $F(t-1)$ and $F(t)$ and $F(t) = F(t-1). R(t, t-1)$ is called the first order model of $F(t)$.

Definition 3. Suppose $R(t, t-1)$ is a first order model of $F(t)$. If for any t, $R(t, t-1)$ is independent of t i.e. for any t, $R(t, t-1) = R(t-1, t-2)$, then $F(t)$ is called a time variant fuzzy time series.

2.3   Artificial Neural Network

Neural networks are composed of simple elements operating in parallel. These elements are inspired by biological nervous systems.

As in nature, the network function is determined largely by the connections between elements. A neural network can be trained to perform a particular function by adjusting the values of the connections (weights) between elements. The components [10] of an artificial neural network have been furnished in Fig. 1.

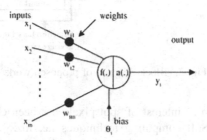

Fig. 1.   Artificial neural network

2.4   Genetic Algorithm

Genetic Algorithm is a method for solving both constrained and unconstrained optimization problems based on a natural selection process that mimics biological evolution. The algorithm repeatedly modifies a population of individual solutions. At each step, the genetic algorithm randomly selects individuals from the current population and uses them as parents to produce the children for the next generation. Over successive generations, the population "evolves" toward an optimal solution.

2.5   Error Analysis

$$\text{Estimated error} = |\text{estimated value actual value}|\text{actual value} \times 100$$

$$\text{Average error} = \sum \text{Estimated error}/\text{total number of data values}$$

3   Implementation

Step 1: Skin images have been collected from the DERMNET [11] which are used for research. Block diagram of Snap shot of the selected sample input images in the original RGB form, gray form and the corresponding the pixel value have been furnished in Fig. 2.

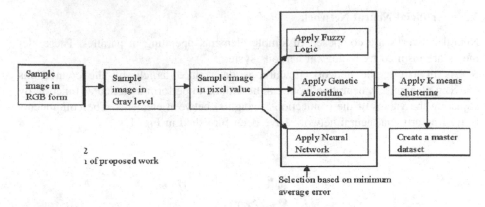

Fig. 2. Block diagram of proposed work

Step2: Initially region of interest of spot pixels has been chosen from 100 × 100 pixel based image. Soft computing techniques i.e. fuzzy logic, neural network, genetic algorithm have been applied on the selected pixel values of region of interest of the image.

3.1   Fuzzy Logic

Step 3: The available data are fuzzified based on gaussian function.

Step 4: Based on the available pixel values the universe of discourse U is defined within which the available data are and upon which the fuzzy sets will be defined. The universe of discourse is [50–100].

Step 5: The universe U is partitioned into five equal length intervals. The five intervals are chosen as [50–60], [61–70], [71–80], [81–90], [91–100] which have been assign as u_1, u_2, u_3, u_4 and u_5 respectively.

Step 6: Fuzzy sets are defined on the universe. First some linguistic values are determined. Second the fuzzy sets on U are defined. All the fuzzy sets will be labeled by the possible linguistic values. Let u_1, u_2,.......and u_5 are chosen as the elements of each fuzzy set. How well each u_k($k = 1, 2, \ldots\ldots, 5$) belonging to A_i determines the memberships of u_1, u_2, \ldots\ldots$u_6$ to each A_i($i = 1, 2, \ldots\ldots, 5$). If U_k completely belongs to A_i, the membership will be 1; if u_k does not belong to Ai at all, the membership will be zero; otherwise a number from (0, 1) is chosen as the degree to which u_k belongs to A_i. All the fuzzy sets A_i($i = 1, \ldots.., 6$) are expressed as follows:

$A_1 = \{u_1/1, u_2/0.5, u_3/0, u_4/0, u_5/0\}, A_2 = \{u_1/0.5, u_2/1, u_3/0.5, u_4/0, u_5/0\},$
$A_3 = \{u_1/0, u_2/0.5, u_3/1, u_4/0.5, u_5/0\}, A_4 = \{u_1/0, u_2/0, u_3/0.5, u_4/1, u_5/0.5\},$
$A_5 = \{u_1/0, u_2/0, u_3/0, u_4/0.5, u_5/1\}.$

where u_i($i = 1, \ldots.., 5$) is the element and the number below '/' is the membership of u_i to A_j($j = 1, \ldots\ldots 5$).

Step 7: The fuzzy logic relationships have been formed. The relationships are as follows.

$$R_1 = A_1^T \times A_1, R_2 = A_1^T \times A_2, R_3 = A_2^T \times A_2, R_4 = A_2^T \times A_3,$$

$$R_5 = A_3^T \times A_3, R_6 = A_3^T \times A_4, R_7 = A_4^T \times A_4, R_8 = A_4^T \times A_5, R_9 = A_5^T \times A_5.$$

Step 8: Using the individual fuzzy logic relationships, fuzzy logical matrix as R has been formed by summing all the relationships.

Step 9: The fuzzy output data has been formed using the relation $A_i = R \times A_{i-1}$ where A_{i-1} the fuzzy data for existing time occurrence and R is the fuzzy logic relationship matrix. Output data using defuzzification procedure is the fuzzy data for previous time occurrence, A_i is The fuzzy output data has been defuzzified into crisp.

Step 10: Error analysis has been made using the estimated data based on fuzzy logic with respect to original value to compute the estimated error and average error. The average error has been found as 3.559%.

3.2 Neural Network

Step 11: The fuzzified data as formed in step 6 has been fed into back propagation neural network to get the fuzzy estimated data based on neural network. The fuzzy output data has been formed based on the training and testing techniques of each interval.

Step 12: The fuzzy output data has been defuzzified into crisp output data using the method of defuzzification. Error analysis has been made using the estimated data based on neural network with respect to original data to compute the estimated error and average error. The average error has been found as 3.183%.

3.3 Genetic Algorithm

Step 13: The operators of genetic algorithm (reproduction, crossover, mutation) have been applied on the estimated data based on neural network as formed in step 12 to compute estimated data based on genetic algorithm.

Step 14: Error analysis has been made using the estimated data based on genetic algorithm with respect to original data to compute estimated error and average error. The average error has been found as 3.022%.

Step 15: A comparative study has been made on the basis of average error using three soft computing models viz fuzzy logic, neural network and genetic algorithm. The average error based on each model has been furnished in Table 1.

Table 1. Average error vs Soft computing Model

Soft computing model	Average error
Fuzzy logic	3.559%
Neural network	3.183%
Genetic algorithm	3.002%

Step 16: Since the average error based on Genetic algorithm is minimum value, the estimated data based on genetic algorithm has to be used for further processing in the detection of disease. Step 17: Kmeans clustering has been applied on the estimated data based on genetic algorithm to produce the optimal number of clusters. It has been observed that the optimal number of clusters as formed is 5 using the data elements. The cluster center value, the cluster number and the available data have been furnished in Table 2. This Table 2 has to be used to predict the degree of skin disease of new image belonging to a person having skin disease. Based on Doctor's advise it has been found that the center with cluster no 1 relates to degree massive disease, the cluster with cluster no 5 relates to no disease. The cluster with cluster no 2 relates to maximum disease, the cluster with cluster no 3, cluster no 4 relates to mild and little respectively. It can be mentioned that if the pixel value of new image can be placed to cluster no 1 the type of the image of skin relates the skin disease as massive. If the pixel value of new image can be placed to cluster no 2, the type of skin disease to be predicted is maximum. Accordingly the type of disease of skin can be predicted.

Table 2. Cluster centre and cluster value

Sl.no	Estimated data using GA	Cluster no	Cluster centre	Types of disease
1 2 3 4 5	55.6 55.124 56 56 59.486	11111	59.6000	Massive
6 7 8	62 67 72.773	222	79.3333	Maximum
9 10 11 12	76.967 76.967 89 90.382	3333	90.5000	Mild
13 14 15 16	89.5359 91.574 9494	4444	95.3333	Little
17 18 19 20	97 99.01299.0127999.011	5555	99.5000	No disease

Step 18: A new image (skin image) has been collected. The region of interest of new image has been chosen. The pixel values corresponding to the new image have been taken, which have to be used for processing.

Step 19: The genetic algorithm as selected in step 16 has been applied on the pixel values as obtained in step 18 to form the estimated value based on genetic algorithm.

Step20: The estimated value using genetic algorithm has been compared with the cluster center values as formed in step 17. Based on the minimum value of Euclidian distance function value from the cluster center, the cluster value has been chosen. Each cluster as formed in step 17 has represented the degree of disease. Therefore the cluster as selected signifies the degree of disease of the skin of the person whose image has been collected in the step 18. The estimated data based on genetic algorithm as against the selected cluster has been furnished in Table 3.

Step 21: The estimated data using Genetic algorithm for the data having serial no 1 is 55 which has a minimum distance from various cluster centers is 4.6. The nearest cluster is cluster 1. From Table 2 it is evident that the cluster no 1 relates to the skin

Table 3. Estimated data against selected cluster

Sl no	Estimated data	Cluster 1		Cluster2		Cluster 3		Cluster4		Cluster5		Selected cluster no	Types of disease
		Centre	Distance	Centre	Distance	Centre	Distance	Centre	Distance	Centre	Distance		
1	55	59.6	4.6	79.3	24.3	90.5	35.5	95.33	40.33	99.5	45.5	1	Massive
2	55	59.6	4.6	79.3	24.3	90.5	35.5	95.33	40.33	99.5	45.5	1	Massive
3	55.604	59.6	3.996	79.3	23.6	90.5	34.896	95.33	39.726	99.5	43.896	1	Massive
4	56	59.6	3.6	79.3	23.3	90.5	34.5	95.33	39.33	99.5	43.5	1	Massive
5	56	59.6	3.6	79.3	23.3	90.5	34.5	95.33	39.33	99.5	43.5	1	Massive
6	59.428	59.6	0.172	79.3	19.872	90.5	31.072	95.33	35.502	99.5	40.072	1	Massive
7	62.086	59.6	2.486	79.3	17.214	90.5	28.414	95.33	33.244	99.5	37.414	1	Massive
8	67	59.6	7.4	79.3	12.3	90.5	23.5	95.33	28.33	99.5	32.5	1	Massive
9	72.773	59.6	13.173	79.3	6.527	90.5	17.727	95.33	22.557	99.5	26.727	2	Maximum
10	76.971	59.6	17.371	79.3	2.329	90.5	13.529	95.33	18.359	99.5	22.529	2	Maximum
11	76.971	59.6	17.371	79.3	2.329	90.5	13.529	95.33	18.359	99.5	22.529	2	Maximum
12	89	59.6	29.4	79.3	9.7	90.5	1.5	95.33	6.33	99.5	10.5	3	Mild
13	90.382	59.6	30.782	79.3	11.082	90.5	0.118	95.33	4.948	99.5	9.118	3	Mild
14	89.53	59.6	29.93	79.3	10.23	90.5	0.97	95.33	5.8	99.5	9.97	3	Mild
15	91	59.6	31.4	79.3	11.7	90.5	0.50	95.33	4.33	99.5	8.5	3	Mild

disease type as massive. Therefore the degree of disease with respect to serial no 1 is massive. The estimated data using Genetic algorithm for the data having serial no 12 is 89. Minimum distance from various cluster centers is 1.5 the nearest cluster is cluster 3. From Table 2 the cluster no 3 represents the skin disease as mild. Thus the degree of disease with respect to serial no 12 is mild. The estimated data using Genetic algorithm for the data having serial no 17 is 94. Minimum distance from various cluster centers is 1.33 the nearest cluster is cluster 4. From Table 2 the cluster no 4 represents the skin disease as little. Thus the degree of disease with respect to serial no 17 is little. The estimated data using Genetic algorithm for the data having serial no 20 is 99, minimum distance from various cluster centers is 0.50 the nearest cluster is cluster 5. From Table 2 the cluster no 5 represents the skin disease as no disease. Thus the degree of disease with respect to serial no 20 is no disease accordingly any degree of disease of skin of a new person can be predicted.

4 Conclusion

Out of theses soft computing models, it has been observed that Genetic algorithm is the efficient soft computing algorithm for the detection of skin disease. The same technique can be used for the detection of heart disease and its degree and the disease of the other organs. In the existing manual system, personal error may occur in taking the manual measurements. But here in digital image processing system the probability of making manual error is less as compared to existing manual system.

References

1. Mitra, A.K., Parekh, R.: Automated detection of skin diseases using texture features. Int. J. Eng. Sci. Technol. (IJEST) **3**(6), 4801–4808 (2011). ISSN: 0975-5462
2. Lau, H.T., Al Jumaily, A.: Automatically early detection of skin cancer: study based on neural network classification. Int. J. Eng. Sci. Technol. (IJEST) **3**(6), 4801–4808 (2011). ISSN: 0975-5462
3. Elgamal, M.: Automatic skin cancer images classification. Int. J. Adv. Comput. Sci. Appl. **4**(3), 287–294 (2013)
4. JaseemaYasmin, J.H., Mohamed Sadiq, M.: An improved iterative segmentation algorithm using canny edge detector with iterative median filter for skin lesion border detection. Int. J. Comput. Appl. (IJCA) **50**(6), 37–42 (2012). ISSN: 0975-8887
5. Ercal, F., Moganti, M., Stoecker, W.V., Moss, R.H.: Detection of skin tumor boundaries in color images. IEEE Trans. Med. Imaging **12**(3), 1–8 (1993)
6. Garnavi, R., Aldeen, M., Emre Celebi, M., Bhuiyan, A., Dolianitis, C., Varigo, G.: Automatic segmentation of dermoscopy images using histogram thresholding on optimal color channels. Int. J. Biol. Life Sci. **8**(2), 100–109 (2012)
7. Barman, M., Paul Choudhury, J.: A fuzzy rule base system for the diagnosis of heart disease. Int. J. Comput. Appl. (0975–8887) **57**(7), 46–53 (2012)
8. Barman, M., Paul Choudhury, J.: A framework for selection of membership function using fuzzy rule base system for the diagnosis of heart disease. Int. J. Inf. Technol. Comput. Sci. **11**, 62–70(2013). Published Online October 2013 in MECS (http://www.mecs-press.org/). https://doi.org/10.5815/ijitcs.2013.11.07
9. Siler, W., Buckley, J.J.: Fuzzy Expert Systems and Fuzzy Reasoning, pp. 1–424. Wiley Interscience [11]. http://www.dermnet.com
10. Amaliah, B., Fatichah, C., Rahmat Widyanto, M.: ABCD feature extraction for melanoma skin cancer diagnosis. Int. J. Med. Imaging **3**(2), 1–8 (2010)
11. Nguyen, N.H., Lee, T.K., Stella Atkins, M.: Segmentation of light and dark hair in dermoscopic images: a hybrid approach using a universal kernel. Int. J. Comput. Technol. **7623**, 42–50 (2010). Proc. Of SPIN
12. Capdehourat, G., Corez, A., Bazzano, A., Muse, P.: Pigmented "skin lesions classification using dermatoscopic images". Int. J. Comput. Appl. **50**(6), 37–42 (2012)
13. Emre Celebi, M., Iyatomi, H., Schaefer, G., Stoecker, W.V.: Lesion border detection in dermoscopy images. Comput. Med. Imaging Graph. **33**, 148–153 (2009)

Load Balancing Strategy in Cloud Computing Using Simulated Annealing

Gopa Mandal[1]([✉]), Santanu Dam[2], Kousik Dasgupta[1],
and Paramartha Dutta[3]

[1] Kalyani Government Engineering College, Kalyani 741235, India
gopa.mandal@gmail.com
[2] Future Institute of Engineering and Management, Kolkata 700 150, India
sntndm@gmail.com
[3] Visva- Bharati University, Shantiniketan 731 235, India

Abstract. Cloud computing is an idea of diminution-based distributional model which depends on appropriate protocol over the internet. To meet the end user requirement here the resources like CPU, bandwidth and memory are provisioned and un-provisioned dynamically via an internet. To provide large scale computing infrastructure, these resources need to be scaled up and down dynamically on demand of the users in very flexible manner. The last decade records an aggressive growth in internet that is the reason cloud computing get a solid platform to expand its era. Though, it has a glorious future ahead but needs to resolve some problem. Load balancing is one of them. Load balancing is a mechanism to detect under loaded and overloaded node and distribute the load to balance them. To maintain the Quality of Service (QoS) cloud service provider (CSP) must have to satisfy the end users request on time for resources. For this reason, service providers must have to select a proper node that may complete user's task in between the deadline. So, providers must have to distribute a dynamic workload evenly across multiple nodes which ensure that no nodes are overloaded or under loaded which helps to reduce the average response time. It can be thought as an optimization problem and should have some adapting strategy to the changing needs. In this paper we propose a novel load balancing strategy to search under loaded node to balance load from overloaded one. Experimental results are really very encouraging of the sample application which is simulated by CloudAnalyst and the results of the proposed strategy are compared and outperformed the traditional strategy like First Come First Serve (FCFS), Round Robin (RR), local search algorithm like Stochastic Hill Climbing (SHC) and Genetic Algorithm (GA).

Keywords: Cloud computing · Load balancing · Simulated annealing · CloudAnalyst

1 Introduction

Cloud computing is a perfect example of distributed system, today is well known to all of us for its extensive use. To disburse job from resident to distant computer cluster it uses internet speed, which enables elasticity and scalability of computing resources like

© Springer Nature Singapore Pte Ltd. 2019
J. K. Mandal et al. (Eds.): CICBA 2018, CCIS 1030, pp. 67–81, 2019.
https://doi.org/10.1007/978-981-13-8578-0_6

networks, servers, storage moreover we can say cloud computing gaining popularity in industry and also in academia for its exclusive on requirement services offered by its providers like Google, Amazon [1]. In last decade cloud computing is become very popular alternative computing infrastructure due to aggressive growth of internet. in comparison of traditional one. This infrastructure is used by individual person or by any business to access their application from any corner of the world on demand [2]. Using Cloud services, it is possible to run an application without installation which is provided by cloud service provider as per their client request. Basically, the service providers provide CPU, memory and software "as a service". On demand services somehow reduced the capital cost of hardware and software [3]. It's also scalable that means wherewithal that needs to complete the end user's job that may be scale up and down as per the user's job size. It provides computing resources on rent to its end-users by the help of the virtual machine (VM's). The services of cloud are enabled using "pay-as-you go" or subscription basis. Users have to pay for cloud enable services as they pay for electricity or telephone services. Cloud services may be rented for an hour, or one day to next depends upon the need. This facility is very much appreciable if users need vary [4]. Cloud ensures resource whenever it is requested by its users within stipulated time. To ensure QoS cloud service providers, must manage the resources and make them available for their end users the providers also ensures that performance may be scaled up or keep it same [13]. Researchers found lots of possibility in it but still need to resolve some issue. Load balancing is identified as such a problem. So, it needs to dispense the total workload uniformly in the entire network. To make sure, at any moment all VM's in the environment does approximately same amount of work. It helps to restrain the situation of underloaded and overloaded nodes. A good load balancing (LB) algorithm's nature should be dynamic and adaptive to the situation [5]. Further load balancing algorithm broadly categorized and may be adapted depends upon their strategy as static algorithm and another should be dynamic algorithms. The Static algorithm is proffered in compatible and stable environments the researchers observed that the static algorithm produced well result especially in this environment. However, it has its own limitation due to inflexibility for this reason it can't be adapted in dynamic environment where dynamic changes to the attribute may happen at run time. A Dynamic algorithm in that situation are mostly preferred due to its flexible nature and take different attributes under consideration both prior or during run time [9]. A Dynamic algorithm is mostly preferred in dynamic heterogeneous environments. Depending upon the situation how the task is going to be allotted to the nodes or virtual machines and depending upon the current workload status on the specific nodes further dynamic algorithm can be categorize as centralized, decentralized and hierarchical.

(a) Centralized approach: In this approach one node act as central node which is responsible for managing, scheduling and distributing the entire workload into the networks. All information will be available to the central node before scheduling. For centralized algorithm, scheduling task is significantly optimal but not so scalable.

(b) Distributed approach: Every node in the network build a look up table which is called load vector based on current situation over the VMs. Load information consists the respective nodes assignment in term of jobs that are going to be executed. Decision to allocate a VM for the upcoming jobs is taken based on the condition of the local load vector. This approach shows significant advantage in widely distributed system and in dynamic environment. Where as compared to the centralized and distributed approach we can say in centralized approach global optimal scheduling policy adapted by every cloud cluster where more complex situations of multiple rooms, multiple cluster are handled via distributed load balancing strategy which often required more overhead and network overload.

(c) Hierarchical approach: In hierarchical scheduling strategy scheduler arrange resources hierarchically. In this approach higher level resources are arranged in higher level in comparison with the lower ones. This model can subsume the centralized and distributed method.

According to David Escalante et al. [10] basic objective of the algorithms to increase the throughput of the entire system by increasing system stability from single or multipoint failure also make system scalable to make available to all users. Prioritization of the resources in that way jobs with high priority gets maximum chance to execute their task [11, 15].

This paper tries to propose a basic Simulated annealing (SA) based load balancing strategy is introduced to balance entire system's load. Where initially VMs are allocated tasks using FCFS algorithm when the VM's are going to be exhausted then SA based strategy starts to find out the most appropriate host which can be used to provide the resources for next VM. CloudAnalyst [7] a CloudSim [6] based graphical interface used for simulation purpose. The result of the outcome of the experiment is really encouraging and balance the workload.

The paper is divided in six sections. Section 2 is the introduction of CloudAnalyst toolkit, Sect. 3 describes how the VM's Load Balancing are done by Simulated Annealing algorithm. We have given the description of the SA algorithm in Sect. 4. The Results obtained by simulation are furnished in Sect. 5. Section 6 is the final section containing the conclusion part.

2 CloudAnalyst

Infrastructures are distributed in cloud and also deployed geographic location wise. So, it need to take care of users and their request. Simultaneously we have to consider about the multiple parameters like depleted resources, required memory, bandwidth etc. and their impact on performance which cannot be predicted earlier. As a result, we found most difficult to get the real-world environment to check the performance of our propounded algorithm. In this consequence simulation of real world environment are most helpful for the researchers. Simulation enables partial feedback outwardly the real-world scenario divergently. By the use of the testbed we are trying to analyze the cloud environment from the user level and infrastructure level also. Different simulator is available today to adapt the scenario but here we have used the CloudAnalyst as a simulation environment. University of Melbourne first proposes this and the major objective of Cloud Analyst is to support the evaluation of social networks. It's a visual modeler developed on CloudSim which facilitate researchers to simulate programmatically [15]. A snapshot of the GUI of CloudAnalyst simulation toolkit is shown in Fig. 1(a) and its architecture is depicted in Fig. 1(b).

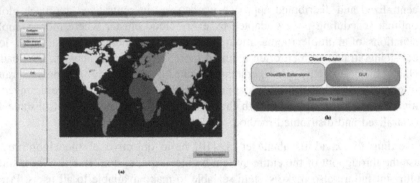

Fig. 1. Snapshot of CloudAnalyst (a) GUI of CloudAnalyst (b) Architecture of CloudAnalyst builds on CloudSim.

3   Simulated Annealing Algorithm for Load Balancing in Virtual Machines

Simulated annealing (SA) is a probabilistic method for finding best possible solution for any optimization problem proposed by Kirkpatric, Gelett and Vechhi [8]. The novelty of the method in finding out the global minimum of a cost function that may processes several local minima. It emulates the physical process of annealing of a solid to its base state which is the state where the minimum energy preserved. Proposed algorithm avoids to get arrested at local maxima that may be better than any others nearby solution but not the best one. The nature of any local search algorithm for any user's problem space say S, is that its starts with an initial configuration j which is $j \in S$. For a given specific related problem space say Sj if the current solution is j then we have to find the new value to replace the current value. This can be done by iterative improvement. The algorithm initiates its journey with a cost function along with a neighborhood structure. At the beginning of every iteration a configuration i which is required to generate configuration j by transition. Here $j \in p(i)$ that is the subset of configurations i.e. neighborhood of i, at any moment if algorithm found that $C(j) < C(i)$, then in the next iteration the start configuration will be 'j' otherwise it will be 'i'. More precisely we can say if i and $j \in p(i)$ are two configurations then algorithm consider j with a probability that can be obtain by min $\{1, \exp(-(C(j) - C(i)/c))\}$ where c is a positive control parameter here it's used as analogue of temperature which may varied in algorithm. If the transition generated by exhaustive analytical way, then the termination of the algorithm done by the definition of local minima.

3.1 Simulated Annealing to Balancing Load in Cloud

Any local search algorithm is defined more precisely with the specific problem. Therefore, the excellence of the algorithm is always related with the initial state and the definition of the field where it will be applied. The local search algorithm is best suited for local optimum but in case of global problem it is difficult to achieve the global optimal. For this reason, we have proposed to use simulated annealing as a global one.

The key idea behind simulated annealing is: a solid is heated until it meltdown and then it's cooled down slowly to solid the metal into regular crystal. Solid particles increase the internal energy when a fixed heating temperature is applied to the solid and get disordered, this process is called smelting. Internal energy is reduced if fixed temperature is not applied and finally it reached the ground state at normal temperature when cooling step applied. As a result, particles are ordered and solidified into a solid crystalline state. This process is called annealing. According to Metropolis criterion, when the particle temperature is T, the probability of particle balance is $\exp((-\Delta E)/KT)$. Where E is the internal energy at the temperature T and K is a Boltzmann constant. Internal energy E is modeled as an objective function, temperature T is modeled as control parameters, to formulate the algorithm which helps to solve the combinatorial optimization problem.

3.2 Problem Description

Typically cloud environment consists of a set of actual machines or host use to deploy virtual machines over those host. Let $J = \{1, 2, \ldots \ldots m\}$ is denoting the set of physical machines where $I = \{1, 2, \ldots n\}$ set of VMs need to be deployed over the available physical machines.

To simplify our system, we consider that the physical server or host environment is homogeneous or we can say it in same capacity. We also assume that physical server is quite enough to accumulate VM's. A resource monitoring module is used to collect the resource utilization of VMs. Each VMsi where $i \in I$ has a workload V_i here x_{ij} used to indicate ith VM deployed in jth physical host then we can say x_{ij} is equal to 1 or it will be 0 otherwise. We can define the current working load on the physical machine is

$$p_j = \sum_{i=1}^{m} V_i x_{ij} \tag{1}$$

Here V_i is the individual workload on the VMi. More precisely we can represent the workload as a job unit vector which is submitted by cloud users as a service request that may be Software, Infrastructure or Platform as a Service. Here we use Ti which represents the different type of service required by the end users. So, the attribute of the job unit vector (JUV) may be represented by Eq. 2.

$$JUV_i = f(T_i, NIC_i, AT_i, wc_i) \tag{2}$$

Here NIC_i is the number of instructions presents in the job, AT is the arrival time of the user's job and wc denotes worst case completion time of user's task. So, to avoid simulated annealing (SLA) violation we should make even the workload among the actual machines via VMs. To find out the current physical machine is capable to take more load we have to calculate the amount of available or residual resources on individual physical machine. For this reason, calculation of residual capacity is very much important. The residual capacity can be taken as load balancing metric. Let $rcap_j$ is the residual capacity of the physical machine j then we can conclude that if the load balancing factor (CPU_LB_i for VMi) collectively of all VMs is lesser than the residual capacity for that same host then the entire system load is balanced, otherwise we can say we have to initiate SLA. Here load balance factor on physical machine j for individual VM formulate in Eq. 3.

$$CPU\_LB_i = \frac{makespan}{average_{execution-time}} \tag{3}$$

In the makespan equation is related to the maximum completion time of the jth job which is assigned to VM$_i$and we can find the $average_{execution\_time}$ for the jobs which are dedicatedly assigned to a particular VM$_i$ is

$$average_{execution\_time} = \sum_{i=1}^{n} \left(\frac{Exec_{time}[J_i]}{Number\ of\ VMs} \right) \tag{4}$$

From Eq. 3 we can get the load balancing factor of an individual VM$_i$, Virtual machines are provisioned by the host which contains one or more physical machines, so we can conclude that if p_j be the load on the physical machine then the residual capacity is obtained from Eq. 5. Now if the residual capacity (r_{cap}) is less than the sum of all load balancing factor of the provisioned VMs obtained from Eq. 3, then we can say the entire load is balanced over the network. Otherwise we must initiate SLA.

$$r_{cap} = c - p_j \tag{5}$$

$$r_{cap} \leqslant \sum_{i=1}^{n} CPU\_LBi_i \tag{6}$$

But CSP needs to allocate these N number of jobs into M number of processors in such a way that cost function f(C) as indicated in Eq. 7 will be minimized.

$$f(C) = W_1 * ci(NIC \div MIPS) + W_2 * Dc \tag{7}$$

$$\Delta E = C(j) - C(i) \tag{8}$$

Where W_1 and W_2 are the control parameters. To set the value of the control parameter for obtaining the best result several test runs were performed over the testbed and finally we set the value of the $W_1 = 0.6$ and $W_2 = 0.4$ based on performance result. Preference or importance is given to user's task. In Eq. 7 c_i is the cost of execution and Dc defines delay cost that must be paid by the cloud service providers to his end user as penalty. If job completion time is more than the estimated completion time, then delay cost is applicable. The acceptance probability pr_{ij} as per SLA may be defined by.

$$pr_{ij} = min[1, exp(-(C(j) - C(i)/c))] \qquad (9)$$

The proposed algorithm is as follows.

4 Proposed Simulated Annealing Algorithm

Step 1: Create an index table that contains VM_{id} and their simultaneous requests.
Step 2: Schedule new job request of the users to VMs, in FCFS manner.
Step 3: Make necessary change in the index table.
Step 4: After allocation of the VMs in the most available host (supposing host as physical machine) h check the host's residual capacity as per Eq. 5.
  If residual capacity is greater than sum of CPU_LB_i (Eq. 6) then goto step 2.
  Else goto step 5: to initiate SLA
Step 5: A set of processing unit vector randomly initialize and tune the control parameter to a positive large value
Step 6: Do while the control parameter value reaches to minimum:
  Step 6-1: Create new cost function f(C') from f(C);
  Step 6-2: calculate ΔE using Eq. 8
  Step 6-3: If $\Delta E < 0$ or $exp\left(\frac{-(C(j) - C(i))}{C}\right)$ > random (0, 1) do f (C') = f(C);
 end if
  Step 6-4: decrease the temperature by a certain rate and iterate the loop until condition satisfied.
 end while
Step 7: and update index table globally with the current optimal solution.
Step 8: End

5 Simulation Results and Analysis

CloudAnalyst used for simulating the algorithm to counterfeit the situation they considered, social media like Facebook or other social media for configuration. Entire world is partitioned into six "Regions" as given in Table 1.

Table 1. Configuration of simulation environment

S. no.	User base	Region	Simultaneous online users during peak hrs	Simultaneous online users during off-peak hrs
1	UB1	0–N. America	4,70,000	80,000
2	UB2	1–S. America	6,00,000	1,10,000
3	UB3	2 – Europe	3,50,000	65,000
4	UB4	3 – Asia	8,00,000	1,25,000
5	UB5	4 – Africa	1,15,000	12,000
6	UB6	5 – Oceania	1,50,000	30,500

A single time zone is set for each user Base (UBs). We set the number of users during peak hours and off-peak hours. Simultaneously available users at the off hours considered only one tenth of the entire online user. Each DC has an amount of VMs to meet user's need. For simulation each machine considered of 4 GB of RAM, 100 GB of storage space and 1000 MB available bandwidth. Each DC contains 4 CPUs with 10000 MIPS capacity. Architecture followed by the host is X86 which is available in Linux operating system. Each users job needs 100 instructions to be executed. The proposed algorithm is executed into several separate set up to check the novelty of the proposed work. In Table 2 one DC is considered with 25, 50, 75 VMs later we increase the number of DCs. Later in 4, 5, 6 and 7 we considered two, three, four and five DC's. Now the performance is compared and analyzed with some existing system like. Genetic Algorithm (GA) [11], Stochastic Hill Climbing Algorithm (SHC) strategy [12] and First Come First Serve (FCFS). Figures 2, 3, 4, 5, 6 and 7 makes a comparative study of the proposed technique for the different scenarios to analyze the novelty of the work (Tables 3, 4, 5, 6 and 7).

Table 2. Simulation scenario and calculated overall average response time (RT) in (ms) using one DC

Sl. no.	Cloud configuration	Data center specification	RT in ms for proposed SA	RT in ms for GA	RT in ms for SHC	RT in ms for RR	RT in ms for FCFS
1	CC1	One DC with 25 VMs	326.86	329.01	329.02	330	330.11
2	CC2	One DC with 50 VMs	326.24	328.97	329.01	329.42	329.65
3	CC3	One DC with 75 VMs	235.46	244	329.34	329.67	329.44

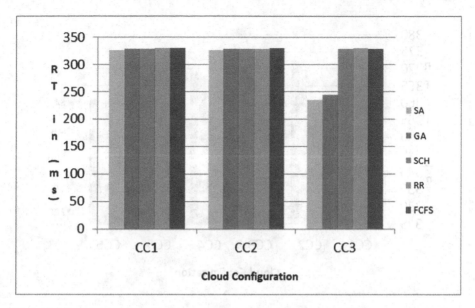

Fig. 2. Performance analysis of proposed ACO with GA, SHC and FCFS Result using one Datacenter.

Table 3. Simulation scenario and calculated overall average response time (RT) in (ms) using Two DC

Sl. no.	Cloud configuration	Data center specification	RT in ms for proposed SA	RT in ms for GA	RT in ms for SHC	RT in ms for RR	RT in ms for FCFS
1	CC1	Two DCs with 25 VMs each	352.31	360.77	365.44	376.27	376.34
2	CC2	Two DCs with 50 VMs each	347.51	355.72	360.15	372.49	372.52
3	CC3	Two DCs with 75 VMs each	346.05	355.32	359.73	369.48	370.56
4	CC4	Two DCs with 25, 50 VMs	345.21	350.58	356.72	367.91	368.87
5	CC5	Two DCs with 25, 75 VMs	345.52	351.56	357.23	369.45	367.23
6	CC6	Two DCs with 75, 50 VMs	344.86	352.01	357.04	356.01	361.01

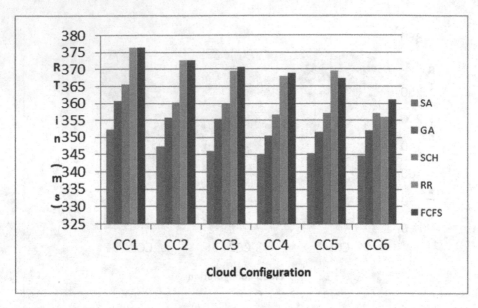

Fig. 3. Performance analysis of proposed SA with ACO, GA, SHC and FCFS Result using Two Datacenter.

Table 4. Simulation scenario and calculated overall average response time (RT) in (ms) result using Three Data Centers

Sl. no.	Cloud Configuration	Data Center specification	RT in ms for proposed SA	RT in ms for GA	RT in ms for SHC	RT in ms for RR	RT in ms for FCFS
1	CC1	Each with 25 VMs	342.13	350.32	356.82	366.17	363.34
2	CC2	Each with 50 VMs	340.86	350.19	355.25	363.52	363.52
3	CC3	Each with 75 VMs	338.34	346.01	350.73	360.18	361.56
4	CC4	Each with 25, 50, 75 VMs	336.89	345.98	350.01	361.21	360.87

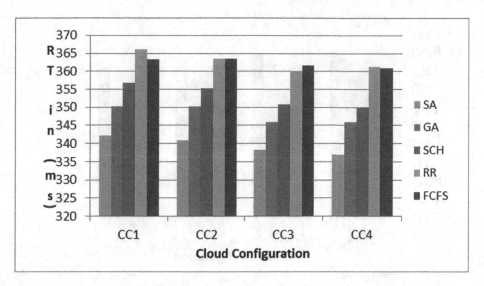

Fig. 4. Performance analysis of proposed SA with ACO, GA, SHC and FCFS Result using Three Datacenter.

Table 5. Simulation scenario and calculated overall average response time (RT) in (ms) result using Four Data Centers

Sl. no.	Cloud configuration	Data center specification	RT in ms for proposed SA	RT in ms for GA	RT in ms for SHC	RT in ms for RR	RT in ms for FCFS
1	CC1	Each with 25 VMs	336.89	348.85	354.35	359.35	360.95
2	CC2	Each with 50 VMs	337.25	345.54	350.71	356.93	359.97
3	CC3	Each with 75 VMs	332.32	340.65	346.46	352.09	358.44
4	CC4	Each with 25, 50, 75 VMs	331.23	337.88	344.31	351	355.94

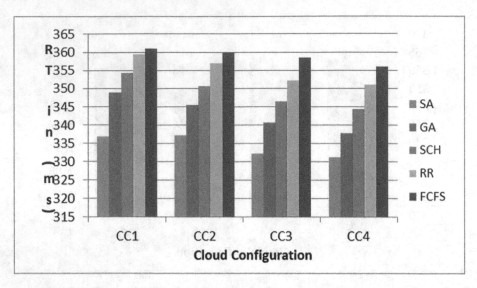

Fig. 5. Performance analysis of proposed SA with ACO, GA, SHC and FCFS Result using Four Datacenter.

Table 6. Simulation scenario and calculated overall average response time (RT) in (ms) result using Five Data Center

Sl. no.	Cloud configuration	Data center specification	RT in ms proposed SA	RT in ms for GA	RT in ms for SHC	RT in ms for RR	RT in ms for FCFS
1	CC1	Each with 25 VMs	329.02	335.64	342.86	348.57	352.05
2	CC2	Each with 50 VMs	318.45	326.02	332.84	339.76	345.44
3	CC3	Each with 75 VMs	317.2	322.93	329.46	335.88	342.79
4	CC4	Each with 25, 50, 75 VMs	314.24	319.98	326.64	334.01	338.01

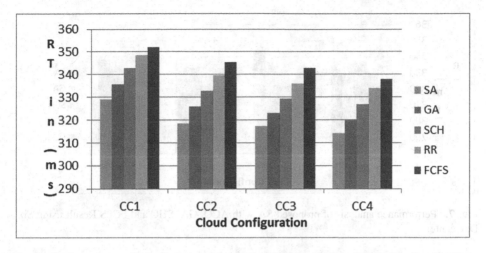

Fig. 6. Performance analysis of proposed SA with ACO, GA, SHC and FCFS Result using Five Datacenter

Table 7. Simulation scenario and calculated overall average response time (RT) in (ms) result using Six Data Center

Sl. no.	Cloud configuration	Data center specification	RT in ms for proposed SA	RT in ms GA	RT in ms SHC	RT in ms for RR	RT in ms FCFS
1	CC1	Each with 25 VMs	320.45	330.54	336.96	341.87	349.26
2	CC2	Each with 50 VMs	314.23	323.01	331.56	338.14	344.04
3	CC3	Each with 75 VMs	311.21	321.54	327.78	333.67	339.87
4	CC4	Each with 25, 50, 75 VMs	305.87	315.33	323.56	334.01	338.29

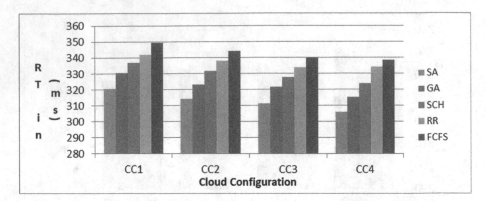

Fig. 7. Performance analysis of proposed SA with ACO, GA, SHC and FCFS Result using Six Datacenter.

6   Conclusion

Our proposed algorithm is compared with the state-of-the-art algorithm which helps to prove the novelty of the work as well as the efficiency of the algorithm by checking the feasibility and robustness. Rather than directly entering to the simulated annealing process our algorithm balances the load initially with the help of FCFS algorithm, which scrapes the run time to find the optimal node. It is not necessary that algorithm can find the global most optimal solution every time, but it can reach to optimal one. The efficiency of proposed algorithm depends upon the enough initial temperature annealing of slow speed with large number of iteration. Here we have considered all the jobs have the equal priority but the actual scenario may be different. Migration cost of user jobs from one host to another is not considered too. So variation of the simulated annealing or hybridization of the different soft computing approach need to take care which may produce better result are in anvil.

References

1. Buyya, R., Broberg, J., Goscinski, A.: Cloud Computing Principles and Paradigms. Wiley, Hoboken (2011)
2. Dasgupta, K., Mandal, B., Dutta, P., Mandal, J.K., Dam, S.: A genetic algorithm (GA) based load balancing strategy for cloud computing. In: International Conference on Computational Intelligence: Modelling Techniques and Applications (CIMTA). Procedia Technology, vol. 10, pp. 340–347 (2013)
3. Dikaiakos, M.D., Pallis, G., Katsa, D., Mehra, P., Vakali, A.: Cloud computing: distributed internet computing for IT and Scientific research. Proc. IEEE J. Internet Comput. **13**(5), 10–13 (2009)
4. Woodford, C.: Cloud computing, 23 March 2015. http://www.explainthatstuff.com/cloud-computing-introduction.html

5. Li, K., Xu, G., Zhao, G., Dong, Y., Wang, D.: Cloud task scheduling based on load balancing ant colony optimization. In: 2011 Sixth Annual ChinaGrid Conference. IEEE (2011). https://doi.org/10.1109/ChinaGrid.2011.17
6. Calheiros, R.N., Ranjan, R., Beloglazov, A., De Rose, C.A., Buyya, R.: CloudSim: a toolkit for modeling and simulation of cloud computing environments and evaluation of resource provisioning algorithms. Softw. Pract. Exp. **41**(1), 23–50 (2011)
7. Wickremasinghe, B., Calheiros, R.N., Buyya, R.: CloudAnalyst: a CloudSim-based visual modeler for analyzing cloud computing environments and applications. In: 2010 24th IEEE International Conference on Advanced Information Networking and Applications (AINA), pp. 446–452. IEEE, April 2010
8. Kirkpatrick, S., Gelatt Jr., C.D., Vecchi, M.P.: Science **220**, 671 (1983)
9. Rimal, B.P., Choi, E., Lumb, I.: A taxonomy and survey of cloud computing systems. In: Proceedings of the 5th International Joint Conference on INC, IMS and IDC. IEEE (2009)
10. Escalnte, D., Korty, A.J.: Cloud services: policy and assessment. Educ. Rev. **46**(4) (2011)
11. Ghomi, E.J., Rahmani, A.M., Qader, N.N.: Load-balancing algorithms in cloud computing: a survey. J. Netw. Comput. Appl. **88**, 50–71 (2017)
12. Mondal, B., Dasgupta, K., Dutta, P.: Load balancing in cloud computing using stochastic hill climbing-a soft computing approach. In: Proceedings of (C3IT-2012). Procedia Technology, vol. 4, pp. 783–789. Elsevier (2012)
13. Dam, S., Mandal, G., Dasgupta, K., Dutta, P.: An ant colony based load balancing strategy in cloud computing. In: Kumar Kundu, M., Mohapatra, D.P., Konar, A., Chakraborty, A. (eds.) Advanced Computing, Networking and Informatics - Volume 2. SIST, vol. 28, pp. 403–413. Springer, Cham (2014). https://doi.org/10.1007/978-3-319-07350-7_45
14. Dam, S., Mandal, G., Dasgupta, K., Dutta, P.: An ant-colony-based meta-heuristic approach for load balancing in cloud computing. In: Applied Computational Intelligence and Soft Computing in Engineering, p. 29 (2017). https://doi.org/10.4018/978-1-5225-3129-6.ch009
15. Aslam, S., Shah, M.A.: Load balancing algorithms in cloud computing: a survey of modern techniques. In: 2015 National Software Engineering Conference (NSEC), Rawalpindi, pp. 30–35 (2015)

An Advanced Particle Swarm Optimization Based Feature Selection Method for Tri-script Handwritten Digit Recognition

Suryadipto Sarkar[1]([✉]), Manosij Ghosh[2], Agneet Chatterjee[2],
Samir Malakar[3], and Ram Sarkar[2]

[1] Department of Electronics and Communication Engineering,
Manipal Institute of Technology, Manipal, Karnataka, India
ssarkarmanipal@gmail.com
[2] Department of Computer Science and Engineering, Jadavpur University,
Kolkata, India
manosij1996@gmail.com, agneet257@gmail.com,
raamsarkar@gmail.com
[3] Department of Computer Science, Asutosh College, Kolkata, India
malakarsamir@gmail.com

Abstract. Handwritten digit recognition is a well-studied pattern recognition problem. Most of the techniques, reported in the literature, have been concentrated on designing several feature vectors which represent the digits in a better way. But, at times, such attempt not only increases the dimensionality of extracted feature vector but also suffers from having irrelevant and/or redundant features. To address this, in the present work, a recently introduced Particle Swarm Optimization (PSO) based feature selection method has been applied with suitable modifications. For the course of this experiment, we have confined ourselves to a newly employed feature vector for handwritten digit recognition, namely DAISY feature descriptor. The proposed feature selection method is tested on three handwritten digit databases written in Bangla, Devanagari and Roman scripts. The experimental results show that significant amount of feature dimension is reduced without compromising on recognition accuracy. Comparison of the present feature selection method with two of its ancestors also reveals that the present method outperforms the others.

Keywords: Handwritten digit recognition · DAISY descriptor ·
Feature selection · Binary PSO · Bangla · Devanagari · Roman

1 Introduction

High variation in handwriting of different individuals is commonplace. This variation is also observed for a single individual when s/he writes the same text at different times. As a result, recognition of unconstrained handwriting becomes challenging and is still considered an open research topic to the document analysis community. These facts are equally applicable for handwritten digit recognition, which is considered as one of the classical pattern recognition problems. The reason behind this is the spectrum of utility

© Springer Nature Singapore Pte Ltd. 2019
J. K. Mandal et al. (Eds.): CICBA 2018, CCIS 1030, pp. 82–94, 2019.
https://doi.org/10.1007/978-981-13-8578-0_7

of the same, which ranges over tax form processing [1], license plate registration [2], postal code recognition [3], bank cheque recognition [4] etc. The aim of such recognition is to translate humanly understandable digits into machine-recognizable forms.

The challenges mostly faced in handwritten digit recognition involve digits being of varied dimensions and orientations due to the non-uniformity of handwritten texts reflected by the multi-faceted styles prevalent in human handwriting [5]. To handle such variations of handwriting, researchers have focused on generating new features which many a time result in producing large dimensional feature vectors. For example, authors have applied DAISY [5], Histogram of Oriented Gradients (HOG) [6], Local Binary Pattern (LBP) [7] and Mojette Transform [8] based feature vectors which are high dimensional.

In another direction of researches [9–16], many have either looked for different feature vectors while using simple classifiers like K-nearest Neighborhood (k-NN) [9], Random Forest (RF) [10], Rule based [11] and Multilayer Perceptron (MLP) [12], or deep learning based architectures like Convolutional Neural Network (CNN) [13] and Long Short-Term Memory (LSTM) [14] that work sans conventional feature extraction methods prior to classification. In the work [9], a feature vector which includes upper and lower profiles, vertical and horizontal projections and Discrete Cosine Transform (DCT) with standard deviation is used while grid based Hausdorff distance based features are extracted in [10] for feeding them to the respective classifiers. The authors in [11] have decomposed the digit image boundary into four salient visual primitives, namely closure, smooth curve, protrusion and straight segment, while the authors in [12] have relied on pixel intensity based feature vector for the same purpose.

Apart from these, several classifier combination methods have also been introduced in the literature for the said purpose. The authors in [15] have reported a correlation based classifier combination for handwritten digit recognition. In this work, eight different classifiers have been studied based on correlation among their recognition accuracies. On the other hand, feature to classifier based ensemble (i.e., single classifier and multiple feature vectors) has been described in [16]. Here, six categories of feature vectors (termed as structural, edge map, projection, zoning, concavity and gradient) are used while Multi-layer Perceptron (MLP) is the sole classifier. Also, the authors of work [17] have relied on a cascaded, classifier combination technique (i.e., a single feature vector and multiple classifiers) to perform handwritten digit recognition. In their work, three different versions of Artificial Neural Network (ANN) have been used with every single feature vector to improve recognition accuracy. Such architecture is employed on seven distinct feature vectors which lead to a cascaded classifier.

The highlighting point of the above discussion is that the researchers have mostly focused on designing more pattern representative feature vectors by introducing either new feature vector (e.g., [5–8]) or combining different existing feature vectors (e.g., [11, 16, 17]). As a result, the dimension of feature vector increases, which in turn affects computational cost of the recognition system. In addition, a feature vector generated in this way may contain conflicting information [18] and consequently misclassification would occur. To counter this problem, researchers have employed feature selection methods [17, 19–21] prior to the actual digit recognition process. Authors of the articles [17, 19, 20] have employed Genetic Algorithm (GA) for this purpose. In [21], performances of three swarm optimization algorithms, namely Binary

Fish School Search (BFSS), Advanced Binary Ant Colony Optimization (ABACO) and Binary Particle Swarm Optimization (BPSO), have been investigated. In the same paper, it has been shown that BPSO performs better than its counterparts.

Therefore, relying on the above discussion, we have used an advanced BPSO to optimize a *state-of-the-art* feature vector, called DAISY descriptor, for handwritten digit recognition. Also, the objective of the optimization of the feature vector involves an increase in recognition accuracy with a decreased feature vector size [22]. This requires us to perform the optimization in a multi-objective manner. To verify its robustness, it has been experimented over three digit databases written in Bangla, Devanagari and Roman scripts. Of these, the first database is an in-house database while the rest are standard databases. Here, an MLP-based classifier has been used for assessing performance of the digit recognition system.

In the following two sections, we briefly explain the DAISY descriptor (Sect. 2) and modified BPSO (Sect. 3). In Sect. 4, we first give a brief description of the databases used and then the performances of our feature selection method on these databases are reported. Finally, in Sect. 5, we conclude our paper, mentioning some possible directions of future research pertaining to this work.

2 DAISY Descriptor

DAISY descriptor, used in [5] for recognizing handwritten digits. This descriptor was designed to fuse the beneficial parts of Scale Invariant Feature Transform (SIFT) and Gradient Location Oriented Histogram (GLOH) descriptors, in order to enhance their computational efficiency. SIFT and GLOH descriptors essentially depend much on their use of gradient orientation histograms. But, DAISY descriptor is different from its precursors as it computes the histograms only once per region and then reuses it for all the neighboring pixels. The descriptor also takes less time to compute the feature vector than SIFT. This in turn facilitates a very efficient memory fetch pattern, and the early separation of the histogram layers greatly improve efficiency. In addition to these, it is devoid of distortions, scale change, contrast variation, and occlusions like its ancestors.

Firstly, in DAISY descriptor, a number of orientation maps, one for each quantized direction (say, $G_o(u, v)$ of the image gradient at point (u, v)) is calculated. These orientation maps, which depend upon the input image and the orientation of the derivative, are then convolved several times with varying sizes of Gaussian Kernels to obtain convolved orientation maps. Efficient implementation of such convolutions in this descriptor lessens the overall computational cost. The reason being that larger orientation maps can be computed easily as orientations with a large Gaussian kernel can be obtained from several consecutive convolutions with smaller kernels. The main parameters that control the shape of the descriptor are the radius of the outermost ring (r), the number of rings (R), the number of quantized histograms (h) and the number of orientations (o) per histogram. In addition, use of circular grids provides better positioning of features. These parameters have been tuned in [5] to obtain better descriptor points, which have been shown to describe the image more effectively while performing digit recognition. We follow process described in [5] for generating feature vector from handwritten digit images.

In the work [5], each digit image is described as a 3D feature map of size $a * b * c$, where a and b are the number of feature descriptor points along vertical and horizontal directions of the image respectively, whereas c represents the number of features extracted from individual descriptor points. In this work, for a digit image of size $H \times W$ the values are set as: $a = \left\lceil \frac{H - 2*r}{\Delta x} \right\rceil$, $b = \left\lceil \frac{W - 2*r}{\Delta y} \right\rceil$ and $c = (R * h + 1) * o$, where Δx and Δy are distances between descriptor sampling points along horizontal and vertical directions respectively. Also, the parameters R, h and o represent the number of circular rings per descriptor point, histograms sampled per ring and directional orientations per histogram respectively while the operator $\lceil . \rceil$ is defined as $\forall x \in \mathbb{R}, \lceil x \rceil = min\{n \in \mathbb{Z}\}, \forall n \geq x$.

As DAISY is a dense descriptor, it generates a relatively sizeable dimensional feature vector, which becomes computationally expensive for further processes. In [5], researchers introduce control parameters which limit the number of features extracted, but also ensure high recognition accuracy for this particular pattern recognition problem. In their work, the values of r, Δx and Δy determine the extent of pixels covered by the rings of the descriptor. These parameter values are fixed as $r = \left\lceil \frac{max\{H,W\}}{max\{a,b\}} \right\rceil$, $\Delta x = \left\lceil \frac{H}{(a+1)} - 1 \right\rceil$ and $\Delta y = \left\lceil \frac{W}{(b+1)} - 1 \right\rceil$. Figure 1(a–c) shows an illustration of the DAISY descriptor, generating points and rings on images taken from each script (Bangla, Devanagari and Roman) in our database. The image size is set to 200×200 with $a = b = 2$ for enhanced visualization.

3   Advanced BPSO

Particle Swarm Optimization (PSO) is an optimization algorithm based on the swarm behavior of birds, proposed by Ebelhart and Kennedy [23] in 1995. The utilization of the same for feature selection has been proposed in [24]. In this method, each feature vector is represented by a binary sequence of 0's and 1's. Here, '1' signifies that the corresponding feature value is selected while a '0' denotes the opposite. From a number of PSO schemes, we use the recently proposed version as reported in [25]. In this work, the classifier parameters have been included in the particles to allow for parameter optimization using PSO. In our work, to ensure classifier independence, the particles have been modified to include only the features. The parameter tunings of classifier is done in offline, which helps to reduce the computational complexity. We call this modified version advanced BPSO.

A set of m particles is created. These particles travel in the search space using PSO algorithm. Each particle x_j (refers to one feature) is an encoded binary sequence of size equal to the number of features in the original feature vector. A feature vector (here, j^{th}) of dimension n can be represented as:

$$x_j = \left\{ x_{j1}, x_{j2}, x_{j3}, \ldots, x_{jn} \right\} \tag{1}$$

In PSO, a global best (x_{ji}^{sb}) and a local best (x_{ji}^{pb}) for each particle are maintained and these parameters are used to direct the motion of a particle. If we have a particle which has a higher fitness value than its local or global best, then we substitute the local or global best by the current one.

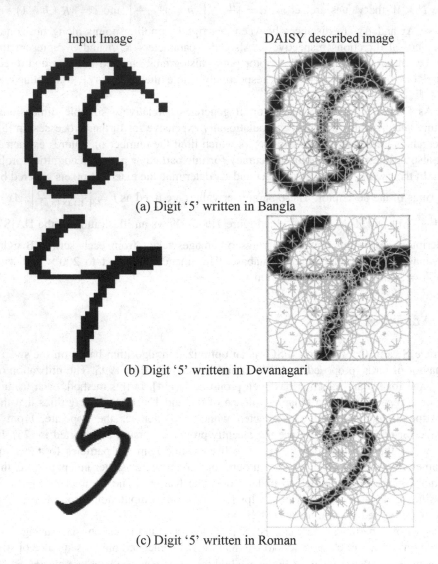

(a) Digit '5' written in Bangla

(b) Digit '5' written in Devanagari

(c) Digit '5' written in Roman

Fig. 1. Illustration of DAISY descriptor points (center of the red circular rings) and rings (light green) taking one sample digit image from each of the three said scripts. (Color figure online)

Fitness of a particle is determined using a classifier, which decides the ability of the selected features to classify the given patterns. The local and global updates are important parts of the PSO. Due to the problem of pre-mature convergence, a conditional *reset* mechanism is required. That is why, if for two consecutive iterations, there is no change in local or global best, then the same is reset to all zeros. The local best (if reset) is mutated with a probability of $(1/n)$, so that at least one of the points in local best becomes 1.

The value of velocity as in PSO is used to generate a probability for selecting or discarding a feature from the feature vector under consideration. For each feature of the feature vector, PSO assigns a velocity (v_{ji}) which changes as time (t) changes. The velocity of a particle is represented by Eq. 2. The variation in velocity is computed using the Eq. 3, where both r_1 and r_2 are random numbers while c_1 (cognitive component), c_2 (social component) are constants and $w = 0.5 + \tau/2$ (τ is a randomly generated scalar). Finally, conversion of velocity to probability is calculated using Eq. 4.

$$v_j = \{v_{j1}, v_{j2}, \ldots, v_{jn}\} \tag{2}$$

$$v_{ji}(t+1) = w * v_{ji}(t) + c_1 * r_1 * \left(x_{ji}^{pb} - x_{ji}\right) + c_2 * r_2 * \left(x_{ji}^{sb} - x_{ji}\right) \tag{3}$$

$$s\left(v_{ji}(t+1)\right) = \frac{a-1}{a + e^{-v_{ji}(t+1)}} + \frac{1}{2a}, a > 1 \tag{4}$$

In the function (refer to Eq. 4), value of 'a' is taken as 2.5 to bind the probability of selection of a feature value between 0.2 and 0.8. This bound is useful to prevent the premature convergence prevalent in PSO, where the particles get stuck in local optima. Incrementing the lower bound to 0.2 from 0 and decrementing the upper bound to 0.8 from 1 allows features with high velocity a slightly higher probability of being excluded and features with low velocity a slightly higher probability of inclusion. The particles are generated using a random number generator which gives the value of r. The value of x_{ji} at time $(t+1)$ is determined by Eq. 5.

$$x_{ji}(t+1) = \begin{cases} 0 & if\ r \geq \left(v_{ji}(t+1)\right) \\ 1 & otherwise \end{cases} \tag{5}$$

At each step, there is no mechanism to retain the best particles [23, 24]. This shortcoming is overcome by creating a memory of size twice the number of particles (m) used in PSO $(2 * m)$ in [25]. After every iteration, the particles in both memory and current population are combined and ranked using the score value of each solution which is calculated in Eq. 6.

$$score = w_1 * fitness(x_j) + w_2 * \frac{len(x_j)}{n} \tag{6}$$

Here, $len(x_j)$ indicates the number of feature values selected. The value of w_1 is taken as 100 and w_2 as 1. This allows us to retain the best particles in a multi-objective feature selection environment. The algorithm runs for a given number of iterations. The entire process is shown in Fig. 2.

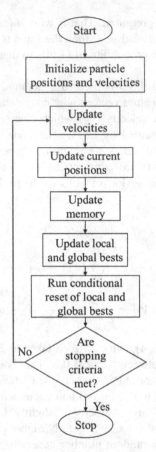

Fig. 2. Flowchart of present feature selection technique i.e., advanced BPSO

4   Result and Discussion

The present work investigates the effect of advanced BPSO based feature selection method in the domain of handwritten digit recognition. For recognition of digits, DAISY feature descriptor is extracted from each digit image of dimension 48×48. Inspired by the work described in [5], a feature vector of length 800 (considering $R = 3$, $h = 8$, $o = 8$ and $a = b = 2$) is generated from each of the input images. The extracted features are fed into BPSO for obtaining optimal set of features that provide admissible recognition accuracy. An MLP-based classifier has been used for the purpose of recognition. Recognition accuracy and number of features used at some instance, which are two attributes of the multi-objective function, have been made use of, here. In the following subsections, we first describe the databases used for the experiments, and then find the optimal number of hidden layer neurons for all the feature sets. Next, we report the performance of the advanced BPSO based feature selection method. And finally, we compare this method with two other feature selection methods.

4.1 Database Description

As mentioned earlier, the present feature selection technique has been experimented on three handwritten digit databases written in Bangla, Devanagari and Roman scripts. These are three most popularly used scripts in India. Of these, two are standard databases while the other one is an in-house database. For each script, the entire database is divided into two subsets, called *trainSet* and *testSet*. We place the first 20% samples of each digit class into *testSet* while the rest into *trainSet*. Description of the databases has been summarized is Table 1.

Table 1. Brief description of the databases used in the present work

Script	Source	Total number of samples (number of samples per class)	Number of samples per class	
			trainSet	testSet
Bangla	[in-house]	10000 (1000)	800	200
Devanagari[a]	Devanagari database [26]	5317 (459–635)	[367–508]	[91–127]
Roman	ICDAR-2013 competition [27]	35000 (3500)	2800	700

[a]Devanagari database contains unequal number of samples per class. It ranges from 459 to 635 samples per class

4.2 Selection of Optimal Number of Hidden Layer Neurons for MLP

The proposed feature selection technique aims at choosing the optimal number of features by hybridization of the concept of PSO and MLP-based classifier. Performance of MLP based classifier largely depends on the number of neurons in hidden layer and number of hidden layers used therein. For our experiment, we fix the number of hidden layers to one while we vary the number of neurons in the hidden layer from 50 to 125. The recognition accuracies (defined in Eq. 7) are depicted in Fig. 3(a–c). These figures show that the best accuracies for Bangla, Devanagari and Roman digit databases stand when the number of neurons in hidden layer are 90, 85 and 100 respectively. It is to be noted that during these experiments, default values of "nntool" of MATLAB [28] have been used for other parameters of MLP. Also, 15% of the *trainSet* images has been randomly selected as validation samples for MLP. The best case configuration has been used for the rest of the experiments.

$$Recognition\,Accuracy = \frac{Number\,of\,correctly\,classified\,Samples}{Total\,number\,of\,samples} * 100(\%) \quad (7)$$

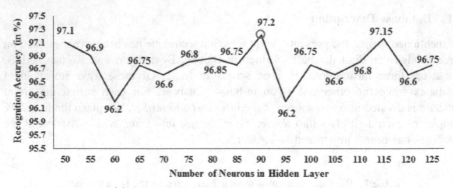

(a) Results on handwritten Bangla digit database

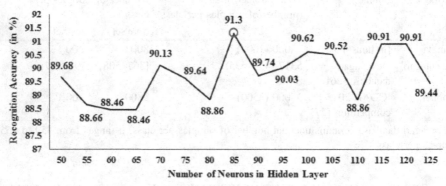

(b) Results on handwritten Devanagari digit database

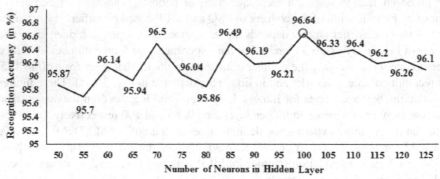

(c) Results on handwritten Roman digit database

Fig. 3. Recognition accuracies corresponding to different number of neurons in the hidden layer of MLP-based classifier for all the digit databases. The best recognition result in each case is marked using a red circle. (Color figure online)

4.3   Performance of Present Feature Selection Method

While using advanced PSO for selecting optimal set of features, 90, 85 and 100 number of neurons are used in the hidden layer of MLP for Bangla, Devanagari and Roman digit databases respectively. Top three results for each of the databases have been reported in Table 2. Considering the outcome of present technique, it can be stated that more than 50% of the features have been removed during the selection process without dipping the recognition accuracy.

Table 2. Recognition accuracies before and after applying advanced BPSO. Bold faced numbers indicate best score.

Script	Before feature selection		After feature selection		Increment in accuracy (%)	Reduction in feature size (%)
	Size of feature vector	Recognition accuracy (%)	Size of feature vector	Recognition accuracy (%)		
Bangla	800	97.20	373	97.50	**0.30**	53.38
			425	97.45	0.25	46.88
			334	97.40	0.20	**58.25**
Devanagari	800	91.30	429	91.69	**0.39**	46.38
			343	91.50	0.20	**57.13**
			380	91.50	0.20	52.50
Roman	800	96.64	409	96.78	**0.14**	48.88
			375	96.69	0.05	**53.13**
			375	96.69	0.01	46.13

4.4   Comparison with Other Feature Selection Methods

The present feature selection method has been compared with two other feature selection methods, namely basic BPSO [25] and Simulated Annealing [29]. For the purpose of comparison, we use MLP as the classifier (for configuration, see Sect. 4.2). The top performances, considering recognition accuracy, are reported in Table 3 along with the present one. These results show that a substantial reduction in the number of features has been achieved by basic BPSO, while compromising on the recognition ability. On the other hand, the present feature selection method shows almost similar feature reduction ability with respect to basic BPSO sans reducing the actual recognition accuracy. Hence, it can be inferred that the present feature selection method outperforms the others.

Table 3. Comparison of the present feature selection method with some other feature selection methods. Bold faced numbers indicate best score.

Script	Feature selection method	Recognition accuracy (in %) without feature selection	After feature selection	
			Size of feature vector	Recognition accuracy (in %)
Bangla	Basic BPSO	97.20	**348**	96.80
	Simulated annealing		400	96.45
	Present		373	**97.50**
Devanagari	Basic BPSO	91.30	**352**	89.14
	Simulated annealing		410	89.83
	Present		429	**91.69**
Roman	Basic BPSO	96.64	**374**	96.05
	Simulated annealing		381	96.00
	Present		409	**96.78**

5   Conclusion

In the present work, an advanced version of BPSO has been used for performing feature selection while recognizing handwritten digits using DAISY feature descriptor. The experiments have been conducted on three handwritten digit databases, and we witness a significant amount of reduction in feature dimension while the recognition accuracy is preserved. In spite of our effective endeavour in feature selection for this particular pattern recognition problem, there is still some room for improvement. First and foremost, more standard databases may be considered in future to prove the generalness of the feature selection method used here. In addition, use of some other *state-of-the-art* features for the aforementioned purpose would be another scope for future research. Last but not the least, applying local search method may improve the recognition accuracy further.

Acknowledgments. This work is partially supported by the CMATER research laboratory of the Computer Science and Engineering Department, Jadavpur University, India, and PURSE-II and UPE-II Jadavpur University projects. Ram Sarkar is partially funded by DST grant (EMR/2016/007213).

References

1. Ha, T.M., Bunke, H.: Off-line, handwritten numeral recognition by perturbation method. IEEE Trans. Pattern Anal. Mach. Intell. **19**(5), 535–539 (1997)
2. Naito, T., Tsukada, T., Yamada, K., Kozuka, K., Yamamoto, S.: Robust license-plate recognition method for passing vehicles under outside environment. IEEE Trans. Veh. Technol. **49**(6), 2309–2319 (2000)

3. Basu, S., Das, N., Sarkar, R., Kundu, M., Nasipuri, M., Basu, D.K.: Recognition of numeric postal codes from multi-script postal address blocks. In: Chaudhury, S., Mitra, S., Murthy, C.A., Sastry, P.S., Pal, S.K. (eds.) PReMI 2009. LNCS, vol. 5909, pp. 381–386. Springer, Heidelberg (2009). https://doi.org/10.1007/978-3-642-11164-8_62
4. Plamondon, R., Srihari, S.N.: Online and off-line handwriting recognition: a comprehensive survey. IEEE Trans. Pattern Anal. Mach. Intell. **22**(1), 63–84 (2000)
5. Chatterjee, A., Malakar, S., Sarkar, R., Nasipuri, M.: Handwritten digit recognition using daisy descriptor: a study. In: Proceedings of Fifth International Conference of Emerging Applications of Information Technology (EAIT). IEEE (2018)
6. Karthik, S., Murthy, K.S.: Handwritten Kannada numerals recognition using histogram of oriented gradient descriptors and support vector machines. In: Satapathy, S., Govardhan, A., Raju, K., Mandal, J. (eds.) Emerging ICT for Bridging the Future - Proceedings of the 49th Annual Convention of the Computer Society of India CSI Volume 2. AISC, vol. 338, pp. 51–57. Springer, Cham (2015). https://doi.org/10.1007/978-3-319-13731-5_7
7. Hassan, T., Khan, H.A.: Handwritten Bangla numeral recognition using local binary pattern. In: International Conference on Electrical Engineering and Information Communication Technology (ICEEICT), pp. 1–4. IEEE, May 2015
8. Singh, P.K., Das, S., Sarkar, R., Nasipuri, M.: Recognition of handwritten *Indic* script numerals using Mojette Transform. In: Mandal, J., Satapathy, S., Sanyal, M., Bhateja, V. (eds.) Proceedings of the First International Conference on Intelligent Computing and Communication. AISC, vol. 458, pp. 459–466. Springer, Singapore (2017). https://doi.org/10.1007/978-981-10-2035-3_47
9. Hassan, A.K.A.: Arabic (Indian) handwritten digits recognition using multi feature and KNN classifier. J. Univ. Babylon Pure Appl. Sci. **26**(4), 10–17 (2018)
10. Bhowmik, S., Sen, S., Hori, N., Sarkar, R., Nasipuri, M.: Handwritten Devanagari numerals recognition using grid based Hausdroff distance. In: Computer, Communication and Electrical Technology: Proceedings of the International Conference on Advancement of Computer Communication and Electrical Technology (ACCET 2016), West Bengal, India, 21–22 October 2016, p. 15. CRC Press, March 2017
11. Dash, K.S., Puhan, N.B., Panda, G.: Unconstrained handwritten digit recognition using perceptual shape primitives. Pattern Anal. Appl. **21**(2), 413–436 (2016)
12. Cireşan, D.C., Meier, U., Gambardella, L.M., Schmidhuber, J.: Deep big multilayer perceptrons for digit recognition. In: Montavon, G., Orr, G.B., Müller, K.-R. (eds.) Neural Networks: Tricks of the Trade. LNCS, vol. 7700, pp. 581–598. Springer, Heidelberg (2012). https://doi.org/10.1007/978-3-642-35289-8_31
13. Naz, S., Umar, A.I., Ahmad, R., Siddiqi, I., Ahmed, S.B., Razzak, M.I., Shafait, F.: Urdu Nastaliq recognition using convolutional–recursive deep learning. Neurocomputing **243**, 80–87 (2017)
14. Ahmed, M., Akhand, M.A.H., Rahman, M.H.: Handwritten Bangla numeral recognition using deep long short term memory. In: 6th International Conference on Information and Communication Technology for the Muslim World (ICT4M), pp. 310–315. IEEE, November 2016
15. Singh, P.K., Sarkar, R., Nasipuri, M.: Correlation-based classifier combination in the field of pattern recognition. Comput. Intell. **34**(3), 839–874 (2017)
16. Cruz, R.M., Cavalcanti, G.D., Ren, T.I.: Handwritten digit recognition using multiple feature extraction techniques and classifier ensemble. In: 17th International Conference on Systems, Signals and Image Processing, pp. 215–218, June 2010
17. Zhang, P., Bui, T.D., Suen, C.Y.: A novel cascade ensemble classifier system with a high recognition performance on handwritten digits. Pattern Recogn. **40**(12), 3415–3429 (2007)

18. Ghosh, M., Malakar, S., Bhowmik, S., Sarkar, R., Nasipuri, M.: Memetic algorithm based feature selection for handwritten city name recognition. In: Mandal, J.K., Dutta, P., Mukhopadhyay, S. (eds.) CICBA 2017. CCIS, vol. 776, pp. 599–613. Springer, Singapore (2017). https://doi.org/10.1007/978-981-10-6430-2_47

19. Ghosh, M., Guha, R., Mondal, R., Singh, P.K., Sarkar, R., Nasipuri, M.: Feature selection using histogram-based multi-objective GA for handwritten Devanagari numeral recognition. In: Bhateja, V., Coello Coello, C.A., Satapathy, S.C., Pattnaik, P.K. (eds.) Intelligent Engineering Informatics. AISC, vol. 695, pp. 471–479. Springer, Singapore (2018). https://doi.org/10.1007/978-981-10-7566-7_46

20. Chouaib, H., Cloppet, F., Vincent, N.: Fast feature selection for handwritten digit recognition. In: International Conference on Frontiers in Handwriting Recognition (ICFHR), pp. 485–490. IEEE, September 2012

21. Seijas, L.M., Carneiro, R.F., Santana, C.J., Soares, L.S., Bezerra, S.G., Bastos-Filho, C.J.: Metaheuristics for feature selection in handwritten digit recognition. In: Latin America Congress on Computational Intelligence (LA-CCI), pp. 1–6. IEEE, October 2015

22. Ghosh, M., Malakar, S., Bhowmik, S., Sarkar, R., Nasipuri, M.: Feature selection for handwritten word recognition using memetic algorithm. In: Mandal, J.K., Dutta, P., Mukhopadhyay, S. (eds.) Advances in Intelligent Computing. SCI, vol. 687, pp. 103–124. Springer, Singapore (2019). https://doi.org/10.1007/978-981-10-8974-9_6

23. Eberhart, R., Kennedy, J.: A new optimizer using particle swarm theory. In: Proceedings of the Sixth International Symposium on Micro Machine and Human Science, MHS 1995, pp. 39–43. IEEE, October 1995

24. Kennedy, J., Eberhart, R.C.: A discrete binary version of the particle swarm algorithm. In: IEEE International Conference on Systems, Man, and Cybernetics. Computational Cybernetics and Simulation, vol. 5, pp. 4104–4108. IEEE, October 1997

25. Wei, J., et al.: A BPSO-SVM algorithm based on memory renewal and enhanced mutation mechanisms for feature selection. Appl. Soft Comput. **58**, 176–192 (2017)

26. Dongre, V.J., Mankar, V.H.: Development of comprehensive Devnagari numeral and character database for offline handwritten character recognition. Appl. Comput. Intell. Soft Comput. **2012**, 29 (2012)

27. Diem, M., Fiel, S., Garz, A., Keglevic, M., Kleber, F., Sablatnig, R.: ICDAR 2013 competition on handwritten digit recognition (HDRC 2013). In: 12th International Conference on Document Analysis and Recognition (ICDAR), pp. 1422–1427. IEEE, August 2013

28. Beale, M.H., Hagan, M.T., Demuth, H.B.: Neural network toolbox™ user's guide. In: R2012a, The MathWorks, Inc., 3 Apple Hill Drive Natick, MA 01760-2098 (2012). www.mathworks.com

29. Lin, S.W., Lee, Z.J., Chen, S.C., Tseng, T.Y.: Parameter determination of support vector machine and feature selection using simulated annealing approach. Appl. Soft Comput. **8**(4), 1505–1512 (2008)

Gray Scale Image Segmentation with Vague Set

Ankita Bose[✉] and Kalyani Mali

Computer Science and Engineering, University of Kalyani,
Kalyani, West Bengal, India
boseankita8@gmail.com, kalyanimali1992@gmail.com

Abstract. Segmentation is no doubt a useful approach to solve an ambiguous situation. The domain of image segmentation deals with real life complexities. In this article we have proposed a new segmentation technique and named it as Vague Clustering Algorithm (VCA). Apart from the knowledge of fuzzy set this method is enriched with the concept of vague set. Fuzzy set theory treats the memberships in an exclusive way, so that the membership is a singleton, representing the fixed degree of belongings of an object to a cluster. The vague set represents the memberships in a different way, it defines the likelihood of belonging of an object to a cluster. Therefore, when fuzzy membership is represented by a single value between 0 and 1, the membership in a vague set is represented by a continuous sub interval of $[0, 1]$. In this article we have constructed a vague environment from the fuzzy environment which is followed by a type reduction. As vague set resembles an interval valued set, therefore type reduction essentially performs the defuzzification. We have compared the performance of our proposed VCA with the general Fuzzy C means (FCM) and Shadowed C means (SCM). To evaluate the performance, we choose different types of gray scale images and the experimental evidences prove the robustness of the proposed approach.

Keywords: Fuzzy set · Shadowed set · Vague set · Type reduction

1 Introduction

Image segmentation extracts objects by partitioning the image into separate regions. Therefore, making the representation easier to analyze. Numerous applications of image segmentation include the study of medical images for clinical analysis of the interior body, that helps in locating tumor, study of anatomical structure, measurement of tissue volume helps in well diagnosis to treat a disease. Other useful applications include object detection, pattern identification, processing of remote sensing images helps in detecting vegetation, water body, soil, etc. But the presence of noise, intensity overlaps, low resolution makes image segmentation a challenging task.

The era of fuzzy set theory begins with Zadeh [1]. The flexibility of fuzzy logic over the binary decision making of crisp set solves the real life ambiguity. But

© Springer Nature Singapore Pte Ltd. 2019
J. K. Mandal et al. (Eds.): CICBA 2018, CCIS 1030, pp. 95–105, 2019.
https://doi.org/10.1007/978-981-13-8578-0_8

in search of some more efficient approach that can lower down fuzzy complexity, there comes another set theoretic concepts [21].

One such approach is the Shadowed Set [2]. The introduction of shadowed set changes the concept of fuzzy set to some extent. In fuzzy set each object must be the part of one or more classes to some degree, but in shadowed set there can be some objects which may not be the part of any cluster and these objects are defined as shadow. The shadowed set supports the three valued logic, so that based on some predefined threshold, domain of membership is divided into three separate regions such as, 1 for the core objects that are definite members of a class, 0 for those which are not in the class and [0, 1] for the shadowed elements. Therefore the shadowed set reduces the computational burden by defining the problem domain that only concerns the shadowed region.

Another set theoretic approach is the Vague Set (VS) [3]. Vague set defines the likelihood of an element to a class [8]. More clearly a vague membership represents a continuous sub interval of [0, 1], it defines not only the membership of an object, but the amount of support it can have from that class depending on the evidences in favour or against of that object for that particular class. The membership interval is therefore bounded by a truth membership function (t_{vs}) representing the evidences in support and false membership function (f_{vs}) representing the evidences against an object in the vague set.

Shadowed set was proposed by W. Pedrcyz in 1998 [2], he further applied shadowed set in clustering in 2005 [4], in 2011 [5] Jie Zhou and W. Pedrcyz shows shadowed set in the characterization of rough- fuzzy clustering. S. Mitra and W. Pedrycz developed the Shadowed C means (SCM) clustering algorithm in 2010 [6,14]. Wen-Lung Gau in 1992 [3] first proposed the concept of vague set, in 2007 [7] Yang Q. et al. proposed Multi-criteria fuzzy clustering problems based on Vague set for statistical analysis, We have developed in 2016 [10] a clustering technique useful in real life data analysis, instead of direct approximation in this article we suggest a randomized way of exploring the search space [15].

In this article we have proposed Vague Clustering Algorithm (VCA), the motivation behind VCA is both the shadowed set and the vague set. As we have already stated that the introduction of shadowed set reduces the computational burden of the fuzzy set, therefore defining the appropriate membership to the shadowed elements of the shadowed set is the only important task. The increased fuzziness of the vague set helps us in extracting some more information from the shadowed region, another important issue is we need the objects to be in the vague environment from the fuzzy environment, which is solved with a positive order transformation, and the type reduction proposed by N.N. Karnik and J.M. Mendel in 2001 [16] helps in crisp decision making from the vague environment.

The rest of the paper is organized as follows. Section 2 gives a brief introduction of the background study, Sect. 3 describes the proposed VCA, Sect. 4 outlines a comparative study of the proposed VCA with the FCM and SCM, Sect. 5 is devoted to the conclusion and future scope.

2   Background Study

2.1   Shadowed Set

The mechanism behind three valued logic of the shadowed set is simply the mapping of fuzzy logic to shadowed environment. It can be defined as below.

$$S : U \rightarrow \{0, 1, [0, 1]\} \tag{1}$$

Here S represents the fuzzy set and U is the universe of discourse and $\forall\, u \in$ U, S(u) = 1 for the core elements, S(u) = 0 for the excluded elements which are not in the class and S(u) = [0, 1] represents the shadowed elements (Fig. 1).

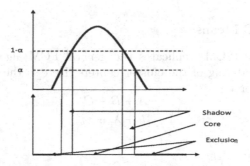

Fig. 1. Fuzzy set induces shadowed set via threshold α

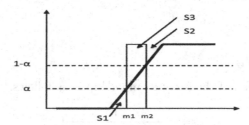

Fig. 2. Threshold α is calculated from Eq. 3

while defining the memberships, it is most likely to have a confusion around the membership of 0.5. Shadowed set bounds the uncertain region by defining a threshold (α). The memberships near 1 assigns the membership 1, the memberships near 0 assigns the memberships 0 and the memberships around 0.5 which is bounded by the threshold is defined by an interval [0, 1]. That means for the shadowed elements we can't define its membership exactly it can take any value between [0, 1]. In this way shadowed set reduces the uncertainty of the core and excluded region and that much uncertainty is induced in the shadowed region so that there will be a balance of uncertainty.

If we consider Fig. 2 balance of uncertainty can be defined as an optimization as in Eqs. 2 and 3.

$$J = \left| \int_{-\infty}^{m1} S(u)du + \int_{m2}^{\infty} (1 - S(u))du - \int_{m1}^{m2} du \right| \tag{2}$$

$$J = \left| \sum_{i:S(u_i)<\alpha} S(u_i) + \sum_{i:S(u_i)>1-\alpha} (1 - S(u_i)) - \mathbf{card}\,(u_i \in U | \alpha <= S(u) <= 1 - \alpha) \right| \tag{3}$$

Equation 2 when U represents the infinite universe and Eq. 3 when U represents the discrete universe.

2.2   Shadowed C Means

Shadowed C means (SCM) replicates the general FCM algorithm, with only difference in the updating of the cluster centers. Here is the representation of the i_{th} cluster center V_i.

$$V_i = \frac{A + B + C}{\beta_i + \lambda_i + \gamma_i} \tag{4}$$

where

$A = \sum_{u_j | x_{ij} > x_{imax} - \alpha_i} U_j$

$B = \sum_{u_j | \alpha_i < x_{ij} < (x_{imax} - \alpha_i)} (x_{ij})^m\, U_j$

$C = \sum_{u_j | x_{ij} < \alpha_i} ((x_{ij})^m)^m\, U_j$

$\beta_i = \mathbf{card}\,(U_j | \ x_{ij} >= x_{imax} - \alpha_i)$

$\lambda_i = \sum_{u_j | \alpha_i < x_{ij} < (x_{imax} - \alpha_i)} (x_{ij})^m$

and

$\gamma_i = \sum_{u_j | x_{ij} < \alpha_i} ((x_{ij})^m)^m$

The representation of the fuzzy membership is as follows.

$$x_{ij} = \frac{1}{\sum_{i=1}^{c} \left(\frac{d_{ij}}{d_{cj}} \right)^{\frac{2}{m-1}}} \tag{5}$$

As we are considering gray scale images for the application therefore the choice of α should be according to Eq. 3

2.3   Vague Set

The concept of vague set changes the concept of fuzzy set. In the vague environment each object is assigned a membership that is a sub interval of [0, 1]. Let X is the universe of discourse and $x_0 \in X$. If we define a vague set VS over X, it will

Algorithm 1. SCM

1.Assign initial cluster centers V_i, i=1,2...c. Set fuzzifier m and iteration counter T=1.
2.**Repeat**
3.Compute fuzzy membership x_{ij} from Eq. 5, for i=1,2..c clusters and j=1,2...N data objects
4.Compute threshold α_i using Eq. 3
5.Update center V_i with Eq. 4

be represented by a truth membership function (t_{VS}) and a false membership function (f_{VS}). Therefore, for some x_0 of VS, t_{x_0} is the lower bound of the vague environment derived form the evidences in support of x_0 and f_{x_0} is the upper bound of the vague environment derived from the evidences against x_0 [9]. So the general representation of the vague membership or the vague value is $[t_{VS}, 1 - f_{VS}]$, there are some other constraints that the vague set follows, these are 1. $t_{VS} <= u_F$, 2. $f_{VS} <= 1 - u_F$ and 3. $t_{VS} + f_{VS} = 1$, where u_F is the fuzzy membership. Figure 3 shows the vague set pictorially

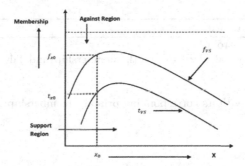

Fig. 3. Representation of Vague set

3   Proposed Vague Clustering Algorithm (VCA)

Our main purpose is to enhance the performance of shadowed set with the proper utilization of the vague environment. We have considered the shadowed region of the shadowed set as our problem domain. One important thing is, when we consider the shadowed set we are still considering the fuzzy membership, but to map shadowed elements from the shadowed set to vague set we need a transfer function, one such function that we have considered is the positive order transformation as shown below.

$$VS_i\left([t_{ij}, 1 - f_{ij}]\right) = \left[\frac{u_{ij}^P - u_{jmin}^P}{u_{jmax}^P - u_{jmin}^P}, 1 - \frac{u_{jmax} - u_{ij}}{u_{jmax} - u_{jmin}}\right] \quad (6)$$

In Eq. 6 u_{ij} is the fuzzy membership of the j_{th} object in the i_{th} cluster, u_{jmin} and u_{jmax} represents the minimum and maximum membership value of the i_{th} cluster. P represents the fuzzifire (we consider p = 2, as in FCM and SCM).

The algorithmic representation is here.

Algorithm 2. VCA

1. Initialize the cluster centers V_i randomly. Where i=1,2...c
2. Set fuzzifier p=2, iteration counter T=1
3. **Repeat**
4. Compute the fuzzy membership as in Eq. 5
5. Calculate α_i.
6. Obtain the objects of the shadowed region.
7. Compute t_{VS} and f_{VS} of the objects in the shadowed region.
8. Update prototype using KM type reduction(Algorithm: 3)
9. Increment T=T+1
10. **Untill** T<maxT and $V_{new}=V_{old}$

In Algorithm 3 we have considered the truth membership t_{VS} and false membership f_{VS} as the upper bound and lower bound of an interval valued set and the region in between, is the search space.

Algorithm 3. KM algorithm

1.Calculation of left centroid V_{iL}.
2.For each pattern X_k calculate the truth membership and false membership $[\overline{f_{ik}}, \underline{t_{ik}}]$.

3.Sort X_k and match with its corresponding primary membership;
4.Initialize w_{ik} by
$w_{ik} = \frac{\overline{f_{ik}} + \underline{t_{ik}}}{2}$
5.Compute centroid $V_i = \frac{\sum_{k=1}^{N} X_k w_{ik}}{\sum_{k=1}^{N} w_{ik}}$
6.Find a switch point γ ($1 \leq \gamma \leq$ N-1) such that $X_\gamma \leq V_i \leq X_{\gamma+1}$
7.Set

$$w_{ik} = \begin{cases} \overline{f_{ik}}, & \text{if } k \leq \gamma \\ \underline{t_{ik}}, & k > \gamma \end{cases}$$

8.Again compute new centroid $V_i' = \frac{\sum_{k=1}^{N} X_k w_{ik}}{\sum_{k=1}^{N} w_{ik}}$
check if $V_i'=V_i$, then stop and set $V_{iL}=V_i$. If not then go to step 6.
9. Calculation of right centroid V_{iR} is same but the only difference is in step 7.

$$w_{ik} = \begin{cases} \underline{t_{ik}}, & \text{if } k \leq \gamma \\ \overline{f_{ik}}, & k > \gamma \end{cases}$$

10. Finally the defuzzified crisp V_i can be represented as Crisp $V_i = \frac{V_{iL}+V_{iR}}{2}$

The KM algorithm is a type reduction technique, it helps in obtaining a crisp value from an interval valued representation. The search space bounded by truth membership function t_{VS} and false membership function f_{VS} actually represents the domain of uncertainty. So this is basically an interval bounded by upper bound and lower bound. Therefore instead of using traditional cluster center updation or any direct approximation, our suggested VCA chooses KM algorithm for center updation. The exponential convergence of KM algorithm increases the efficiency of VCA, reduces computational time and also explores the vagueness to reach to its optimum. Thereby not get influenced by the effect of initialization.

4   Experimental Analysis

For experimental analysis we have used MATLAB R2016b, Windows8 PC with CORE i5 processor and 4 GB RAM.

Overall experimental analysis is done over various gray scale images [18], we have considered some normal gray scale images, some texture images and medical CT scan image. We obtain the texture images from the Brodatz album [19] and we choose the CT scan [17] of a 35 year old woman with large tumor.

For all these gray scale images we have considered a fixed number of clusters and also performed multiple runs on each of them and then take the mean of the measured values.

We choose different validity indices such as Beta [13], Davies Bouldin [11] and Xei Beni [12] and Table 1 shows it clearly that VCA performs better over

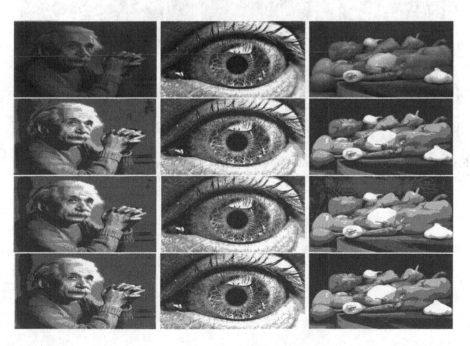

Fig. 4. Row1: Original gray scale images, Row2: Segmented images with FCM, Row3: Segmented images with SCM, Row4: Segmented images with VCA

Table 1. Validity indices measure of Figs. 4 and 5

Algorithm	Images	Beta	Davies-Bouldin	Xei-Beni
FCM	Figure 4	2.9196	1.0457	0.2752
	Figure 5	2.0341	0.8107	0.2903
SCM	Figure 4	3.1892	1.1273	0.1921
	Figure 5	1.9732	0.8232	0.2314
VCA	Figure 4	**3.6724**	**0.9085**	**0.15529**
	Figure 5	**2.2857**	**0.7693**	**0.1831**

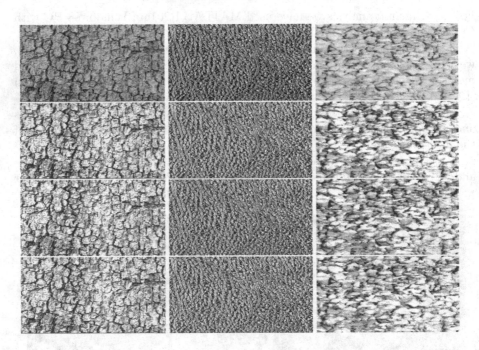

Fig. 5. Row1: Original gray scale texture images, Row2: Segmented images with FCM, Row3: Segmented images with SCM, Row4: Segmented images with VCA

Table 2. Measurement of volume error and accuracy % of Fig. 6

Algorithms	Volume error (V_E) %	Accuracy %
FCM	76 ± 2.5	66 ± 3.2
SCM	52 ± 5.3	74 ± 4.3
VCA	12 ± 3.2	86 ± 3

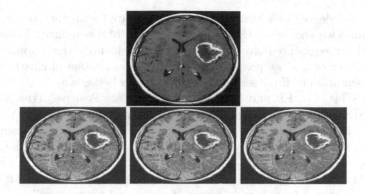

Fig. 6. Row1: Original CT scan images, Row2: Segmented images with FCM, Row3: Segmented images with SCM, Row4: Segmented images with VCA

Table 3. Measurement of CPU time and iteration

Algorithms	CPU time (s)	Iteration
FCM	32.21 ± 3.4	88 ± 1.7
SCM	46.33 ± 3.4	59 ± 2.4
VCA	22.92 ± 2.6	41.66 ± 2.2

FCM and SCM. With careful observation, we can see that for Fig. 4 images VCA efficiently extracts the objects from the background and for Fig. 5 images VCA can also segment the textures with good statistical measurement as shown in Table 1.

We process the CT scan image of Fig. 6 in a different way, as identification of the tumor is important than the overall segmentation. We obtain the ground truth information of the given CT scan image of Fig. 6 with the help of an interactive image segmentation tool [20]. Although it is not a very good way, but at least we can have some useful information. Depending on the ground truth of the original CT scan images and the segmented lesion we calculate the volume error (VE) that measures changes in the lesion size of the original image (V1) and lesion size of the segmented image (V2).

$$V_E = \frac{2 * abs(V1 - V2)}{V1 + V2} \tag{7}$$

$$Accuracy = \frac{TP + TN}{TP + FP + FN + TN} \tag{8}$$

In Eq. 7, we have calculated the volume error (VE) considering the concept behind Dice Similarity Coefficient (DSC). DSC measures the amount of similarity or overlap present between sets. If A and B represents two sets and l represents the amount of overlap, then the association of A and B is $\frac{l}{A}$ and $\frac{l}{B}$ respectively and value DSC is $\frac{l}{A} + \frac{l}{B} = \frac{2l}{A+B}$. Actually this quantitative measure represents the degree to which the sets are associated with each other. But in this literature we choose to determine the amount of dissimilarity between the actual and the segmented clusters so that we can identify the amount of mis-classification error and we pretend this as the representation of cluster volume. The representation of Eq. 7 serves this purpose in a better way.

In Eq. 8 TP, TN, FP and FN represents the True Positive, True Negative, False Positive and False Negative respectively. From Table 2 we can see that VCA shows very lesser volume error and highest accuracy and all the measurements of the form a ± b represents a as mean and b as the standard deviation.

For complexity analysis in terms of CPU time and iteration count we choose a set of 20 random images. The performance is enlisted in Table 3 and it ensures that VCA is robust in nature in terms of space and time as well as performs better over SCM and FCM.

5   Conclusion

A robust, flexible and efficient segmentation approach has been developed in this article. The performance of the shadowed set has been improved by removing the imprecision of the shadowed region. Transformation of the fuzzy environment to the vague environment not only increases the search space, but also increases the fuzziness and for some inexact information, the increased fuzziness helps us to correlate with the information in some logical way. From the comparative analysis of the proposed VCA with FCM and SCM it can be seen that VCA efficiently handles the uncertainty of the shadowed region and resulting in a decision making approach.

References

1. Zadeh, L.A.: Fuzzy sets. Inf. Control 8, 338–353 (1965)
2. Pedrycz, W.: Shadowed sets: representing and processing fuzzy sets. IEEE Trans. Syst. Man Cybern. B Cybern. 28, 103–109 (1998)
3. Gau, W.L., Daly, D.J.: Vague sets. IEEE Trans. Syst. Man Cybern. 23(2), 610–614 (1993)
4. Pedrycz, W.: Interpretation of clusters in the framework of shadowed sets. Pattern Recogn. Lett. 26, 2439–2449 (2005)
5. Zhou, J., Pedrycz, W.: Shadowed sets in the characterization of rough-fuzzy clustering. Pattern Recogn. 44, 1738–1749 (2011)
6. Mitra, S., Pedrycz, W., Barman, B.: Shadowed c-means: integrating fuzzy and rough clustering. Pattern Recogn. 43, 1282–1291 (2010)
7. Yang, Q., Li, J., Zhang, W., Gong, R.: Multi-criteria fuzzy clustering problems based on vague set theory. In: FSKD, pp. 196–200 (2007)
8. Li, G., Wang, H.X.: Constructing Vague environment, fuzzy information and engineering. In: AICS, vol. 78, pp. 711–715 (2010)
9. Xu, J., Liu, G.: Classification of electromagnetic targets based on Vague clustering. IEEE Trans. Inf. Technol. Comput. Sci. 2, 489–492 (2009)

10. Bose, A., Mali, K.: Clustering with Vague set. In: Second IEEE International Conference on Research in Computational Intelligence and Communication Networks, pp. 186–191 (2016)
11. Davies, D.L., Bouldin, D.W.: A cluster separation measure. IEEE Trans. Pattern Anal. Mach. Intell. **2**, 224–227 (1979)
12. Xie, X.L., Beni, G.: A validity measure for fuzzy clustering. IEEE Trans. Pattern Anal. Mach. Intell. **13**, 841–847 (1991)
13. Pal, S.K., Ghosh, A., Uma Shankar, B.: Segmentation with remotely sensed images with fuzzy thresholding, and quantitative evaluation. Int. J. Remote Sens. **21**(11), 2269–2300 (2000)
14. Mitra, S., Kundu, P.: Satellite image segmentation with shadowed c-means. Inform. Sci. **181**, 3601–3613 (2011)
15. Bose, A., Mali, K.: Fuzzy-based artificial bee colony optimization for gray image segmentation. SIViP **10**(6), 1089–1096 (2016)
16. Karnik, N.N., Mendel, J.M.: Centroid of a type-2 fuzzy set. Inf. Sci. **132**, 195–220 (2001)
17. http://cancergenome.nih.gov/
18. Base of 300 synthetic images. http://www.ensibourges.fr/LVR/SIV/
19. Brodatz, P.: Textures: A Photographic Album for Artists and Designers. Dover, New York (1966)
20. McGuinness, K., O'Connor, N.E.: A comparative evaluation of interactive segmentation algorithms. Pattern Recogn. **43**(2), 434–444 (2010)
21. Lu, A., Ng, W.: Vague sets or intuitionistic fuzzy sets for handling vague data: which one is better? In: Delcambre, L., Kop, C., Mayr, H.C., Mylopoulos, J., Pastor, O. (eds.) ER 2005. LNCS, vol. 3716, pp. 401–416. Springer, Heidelberg (2005). https://doi.org/10.1007/11568322_26

Geometrical Transformation Invariant Approach for Classification of Signatures Using k-NN Classifier

Chandrima Ganguly[1]([✉]), Susovan Jana[2], and Ranjan Parekh[1]

[1] School of Education Technology, Jadavpur University, Kolkata, India
cganguly.1992@gmail.com, rparekh@school.jdvu.ac.in
[2] Department of Production Engineering, Jadavpur University, Kolkata, India
jana.susovan2@gmail.com

Abstract. Signature-based authentication of human is still very popular approach. Manual checking is not always accurate and it depends on expertise. The need is an automated and accurate system for signature classification. The signatures do not necessarily comprise of well-formed letters. It can be a random combination of curves and lines. The written signature may be of variable sized, inclined in arbitrary angle or misplaced. This makes the classification task more challenging. This paper proposes an automated approach of handwritten signature classification addressing those problems. The binarized version of the input image is pre-processed in various ways to compensate translation, rotation and noise removal. The four features, which does not vary due to scaling, are selected from the pre-processed image for the classification using k-NN classifier. Overall system accuracy of the proposed approach is 92% on a dataset of 100 images.

Keywords: Signature classification · Gradient magnitude · Corner point ·
k-NN classifier

1 Introduction

Modern life is becoming more complex day by day. It requires countless daily transactions in various fields of work like financial, administrative, legal, social, political, economic, business and travel. The rapid growth in population has assumed utmost importance for protecting the identity of individuals and ensuring the security of documents involved. Conventionally, identification and security of paper documents have been ensured using a signature based system which has been mostly verified manually by humans with relevant experience. However since the world is becoming faster every day, cutting down on time and increasing the reliability of verification systems, have become an absolute necessity. People are therefore relying more on automated systems and machine intelligence to perform verification tasks. Image processing and pattern recognition techniques have been employed to perform verification tasks in an automated way by building data models of the signatures and using classifiers to segregate them into pre-defined classes.

© Springer Nature Singapore Pte Ltd. 2019
J. K. Mandal et al. (Eds.): CICBA 2018, CCIS 1030, pp. 106–120, 2019.
https://doi.org/10.1007/978-981-13-8578-0_9

The main challenges of a signature recognition system are two-fold: the first arises from the inherent variability of the signature itself. A signature does not necessarily comprise of a set of well-formed characters or alphabets, rather it is generally a combination of a set of lines and curves, intersecting or separate. Building a reliable data model of such an entity is difficult by itself. Moreover, two signatures are never identical as signatures written by the same person are bound to differ to some extent. Apart from the shape of the written signature, the size and orientation of the signatures are also liable to change. Given so much variability, it seems almost impossible to build a reliable recognition system, especially when it is also possible that others might be trying to purposely forge a valid signature. The second challenge arises from the variability introduced by an automated recognition system. These arise from the noises introduced by a data acquisition system, variation in lighting conditions and sensor characteristics, transformations like translation, rotation and scale of a scanned signature. An effective signature recognition system should be able to address both types of challenges. Such a system should also be efficient as most recognition tasks are expected in real time and should be done without much delay.

The rest of the paper is organized as follows: Sect. 2 includes a study of existing approaches, Sect. 3 outlines the proposed approach, Sect. 4 tabulates experimental results, Sect. 5 consists of an analysis of the current work side by side other works, and Sect. 6 brings up the conclusion and future scopes.

2   Literature Survey

A number of different approaches for signature recognition and classification have been proposed in existing literature. In the grid-based [1] the binary signature image was divided into horizontally and vertically 8×8 total 64 grids and calculate the features in four directions right to left, left to right, top to bottom and bottom to top respectively for each grid. The numbers of the white pixels are counted from the first white pixel to first black pixel and the number of the white pixel present between two black pixels present in each grid. The features were classified by using k-NN classifier and achieved 56% accuracy. A drawback of this approach is that the signature needs to be perfectly aligned to create horizontal and vertical grids; the technique fails for a rotated signature. A local binary pattern has been used in approach [2, 7, 11]. The center pixel works over a radius of 4.256 and generates a 64-bin histogram for each signature image and 10 nearest neighbors on the k-NN algorithm to classify the signatures. This method achieves an overall 70% accuracy. In paper [11] a local derivative pattern has been used. In paper [3] a grid feature [4, 9] and centroid feature are used. The system worked on 36 signatures of one writer and some forgery signatures. Then the signature image was divided into 10×10 grids in vertical as well as horizontal manner and then determines which grid contained more than 3 black pixels to save it as a feature. After generating the grid feature it segmented the image in regular 3 parts and calculates the distance between centroids of these three parts. The multiple global features, grid feature and SIFT feature have been used in a combined way in a different system [6]. Though the system used so many features to classify a signature still it has failed to generate a satisfactory accuracy and produced 88% overall accuracy. The system could not perform over signature position's variations. The pixel value defers when it is rotated or scaled in a different manner. To overcome this problem the introduced approach used the features which will not depend on the position of signature.

3 Proposed Approach

Most of the existing works on signature recognition focus on modeling the signature shapes using a variety of features, but these techniques usually do not work satisfactorily when the signatures are transformed using translation, rotation, and scaling. This paper utilizes a set of transformation invariant features to compensate for such transformation based variations. The system design in Fig. 1 outlines the procedure.

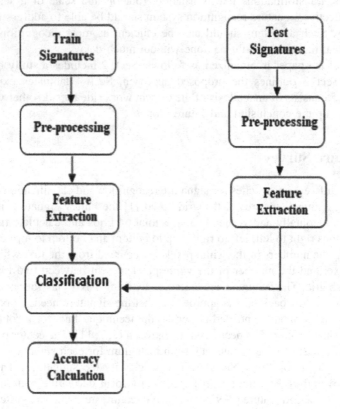

Fig. 1. System design of the proposed method

3.1 Image Pre-processing

This pre-processing step helps to improve scanned image's quality before features are extracted and to compensate for various geometrical transformations. There are lots of pre-processing steps i.e. Binarization, Compensating for rotation, Compensating for translation, and Noise Removal.

3.1.1 Binarization

The RGB image of the signature is converted to grayscale image (I_G) using the Eq. (1). In the second step, it is binarized using Otsu's algorithm [11]. The binary image is complemented to make the background black as shown in Fig. 2(d).

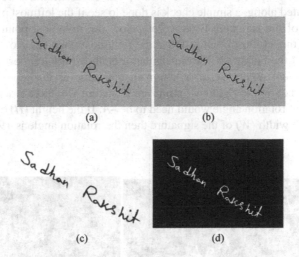

(a)   (b)

(c)   (d)

Fig. 2. (a) RGB image (b) Grayscale image (c) Binary image (d) Complemented binary image.

$$I_G = 0.2989 \times R + 0.5870 \times G + 0.1140 \times B \qquad (1)$$

3.1.2 Compensating for Rotation

In most cases, the signature is not exactly horizontal but inclined at a certain angle. What is more challenging is that the inclination angle would vary for the same person. For reliable recognition the system needs to compensate for the arbitrary inclination through a normalization step. In this work the bounding box of the signature is first determined by identifying the topmost *(T)*, leftmost *(L)*, bottommost *(B)* and rightmost *(R)* white pixels from the binary image. The width *(W)* and height *(H)* of the signature are now calculated:

$$W = R - L, H = B - T \qquad (2)$$

The length of the diagonal *(D)* and the angle *(A)* by which it is inclined to the horizontal are next determined:

$$D = \sqrt{W^2 + H^2} \qquad (3)$$

$$A = sin^{-1}\left(\frac{H}{D}\right) \qquad (4)$$

Assuming the signature would be oriented along the diagonal of the bounding box, it is then rotated by the angle A to make it horizontal. See Fig. 3. For the image shown the rotation angle would be positive i.e. counter-clockwise $(+A)$. On the other hand, if the signature was oriented along the other diagonal of the bounding box, then the rotation angle would be negative i.e. clockwise $(-A)$. To determine which diagonal the signature is oriented along, a simple check is done to see if the leftmost point (indicated by green mark) of the signature is above or below the rightmost point (indicated by yellow mark). If the leftmost point is above the rightmost point (as shown in Fig. 3(a)) and one-fourth of the height (H) of the signature is above the leftmost point then the rotation angle is $+A$, otherwise, it will remain the same as the input image. If the leftmost point is below the rightmost point the signature would be oriented along the other diagonal and rotation angle would need to be $-A$. If the height (H) of the signature is greater than the width (W) of the signature then the rotation angle is $+90$ as shown in Fig. 3(c).

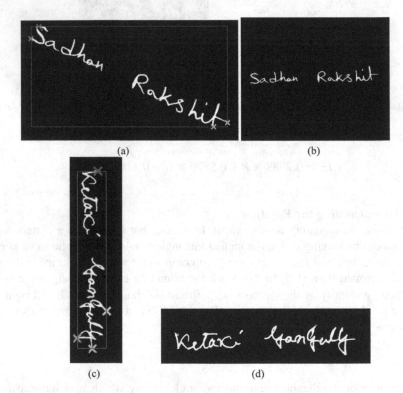

(a)   (b)   (c)   (d)

Fig. 3. (a), (c) Signatures before rotation (b), (d) Signatures after rotation (Color figure online)

3.1.3 Compensating for Translation

If the signature has a translation offset within the image, then there would be un-necessary borders around the signature which needs to be discarded, and the signature to be cropped as shown in Fig. 4.

Fig. 4. Cropped image

Cropping is done by calculating the boundaries [11] of the bounding box as done previously and keeping only the portion inside the box discarding all portions external to the box.

3.1.4   Noise Removal

In noise removal step, a filtered image is being generated by deleting all the extra pixels which are not part of the actual signature. It can be a spot of ink. To remove this noise the machine checks the generated area value of a signature and filter the image by using a minimum area value as a threshold which is fixed for each image.

The red boxes are denoting each area before removing the noise. In Fig. 5(a) the smallest red box points out one noise in this signature image and including it, total number of area boundary is 8. After applying the threshold in area value which is fixed for each image Fig. 5(b) is produced as a filtered image of the signature and the number of area boundary is 7.

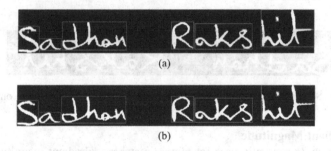

(a)

(b)

Fig. 5. (a) The image with noise (b) The filtered image (Color figure online)

3.2   Feature Extraction

Each person has a distinct signature style. To analyze the signatures correctly after placed it in a proper way, the following signature based features are estimated from the cropped image like Aspect Ratio *(AR)*, Number of Regions *(NR)*, Gradient Magnitude *(GM)* and Corner Points *(CP)*.

3.2.1   Aspect Ratio

The size of the signature may vary in time to time but the aspect ratio of the signature must be more or less same because if the height of the signature increases or decreases then the width will also increase or decrease for uniform scaling. The system extracts the four boundary pixel values to determine the aspect ratio of the signature. The four boundary pixels are *Top(x, y), Bottom(x, y), Right(x, y)* and *Left(x, y)*. The aspect ratio *(AR)* [4, 5, 8] can be measured by using Eq. (7).

$$Width = (Right\_x - Left\_x) \tag{5}$$

$$Height = (Bottom\_y - Top\_y) \tag{6}$$

$$AR = Height/Width \tag{7}$$

3.2.2 Number of Regions

Every person has a specific signature style. All the letters, lines and curves of the signature may not be connected always. The signature may contain more than one disconnected components. The number of disconnected components varies with the person. In the pre-processed version of signature, these disconnected components appear as distinct binary regions. These regions are not containing a similar number of pixels. The *NR* feature depicts the number of distinct regions. Refer to Eq. (8).

$$NR = Total\ number\ of\ binary\ regions \tag{8}$$

The red boxes in Fig. 6 are denoting each disconnected elements where the total number of the regions is 7.

Fig. 6. Showing disconnected components of a signature (Color figure online)

3.2.3 Gradient Magnitude

Gradient magnitude generally uses for texture matching. Gradient magnitude returned as a non-sparse matrix of the same size as input image as shown in Eq. (9), where $\frac{\partial f}{\partial y}$ is the gradient in x direction and $\frac{\partial f}{\partial y}$ is the gradient in y direction.

$$\nabla f = \begin{bmatrix} g_x \\ g_y \end{bmatrix} = \begin{bmatrix} \frac{\partial f}{\partial y} \\ \frac{\partial f}{\partial y} \end{bmatrix} \tag{9}$$

$$G_{xy} = \sqrt{g_y^2 - g_x^2} \tag{10}$$

Fig. 7. Gradient magnitude of a signature

Here the input images are pre-processed signature images. The resulting gradient magnitude matrix is processed by combining magnitudes in both x and y direction. Refer to Eq. (10). Gradient magnitude matrix can't be used as a classification feature. The mean value of this matrix used as a classification feature. Refer to Eq. (11). Figure 7 shows the gradient of a signature image.

$$GM = Mean(G_{xy}) \tag{11}$$

3.2.4 Corner Points
Corners of an image contain important features. The corner points [5, 8] of signatures are detected by using Harris corner detection method. It returns the coordinate values of the corner points. Here, total number of corner point used as classification feature CP. Figure 8 shows the corner points of a signature as blue markers.

$$CP = Total\ number\ of\ Corner\ points\ in\ the\ Signature \tag{12}$$

Fig. 8. Corner points of a signature (Color figure online)

3.2.5 Feature Vector
It is to be observed that each of the features does not depend on rotation, scaling and translation. The final feature vector (FV) is formed with the geometrical transformation independent features i.e. $AR, NR, GM, and\ CP$. Refer to Eq. (13).

$$FV = \{AR, NR, GM, CP\} \tag{13}$$

Figure 9 shows the scatter plot of features. 10 colors represent train samples of 10 distinct classes. This plot shows how the features are discriminating different classes of train data set.

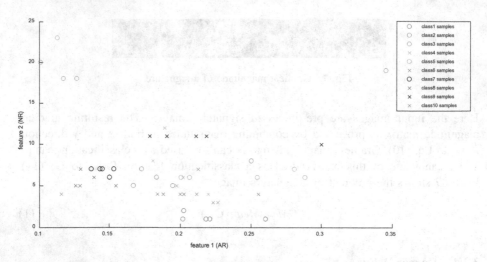

Fig. 9. Feature plot for different classes of train data set (Color figure online)

3.3 Classification

Each class *i* contains *n* number of train images and *m* number of test images. Here Euclidean distance (ED) classifier, k-NN classifier and Bayes classifier have been used. The signatures of individual writers are classified based on feature vector *FV*. Euclidean Distance (d) of two n-dimensional vectors, $p = \{p_1, p_2, ..., p_n\}$ and $q = \{q_1, q_2, ..., q_n\}$ is calculated using Eq. (14).

$$d(p,q) = \sqrt{(p_1 - q_1)^2 + (p_2 - q_2)^2 ... + (p_n - q_n)^2}$$
$$= \sqrt{\sum_{i=1}^{n}(p_i - q_i)^2} \tag{14}$$

Bayes classifier uses probability based on strong assumptions on features. It is able to classify a given sample x based on its n features but when the features contain a large amount of values the probabilistic classification becomes infeasible. Then it solves the problem using Eq. (15).

$$P(Ck \,|\, x) = P(Ck).(Ck)/P(x) \tag{15}$$

Where, Posterior denotes *P(Ck | x)*, Prior named as *P(Ck)*, Likelihood named as *P(x | Ck)* and Evidence state as *P(x)*.

k-Nearest Neighbours algorithm is used for classification in pattern recognition system. A signature is classified by its nearest neighbours and based on the similarity amongst them. This algorithm checks the features of a test signature and compares the same with the training samples. The class of the training sample, which is to the closest to the test signature, is selected as the class of test signature. Finally, the overall system accuracy is calculated using Eq. 16.

$$Accuracy = (No.\ of\ correctly\ classified\ Sample)/(Total\ no.\ of\ Sample) \qquad (16)$$

4 Experimental Results

The proposed approach is for offline signature [10] where the signatures to be collected using pen and paper. In this work, the system used total 100 signatures from 10 different persons. This dataset comprises 10 signatures from each individual, using blue or black ink on an A4 size page within a fixed size box where each page contains 10 signatures. The images have been scanned by using scanner application of smartphone. Each class contains total 10 signatures and they equally divided for train and test data. The signatures with different angle, different sizes have been used to determine the effectiveness of this approach. Figure 10 shows one sample of each class from the training dataset. Figure 11 shows one sample of each class from the testing dataset.

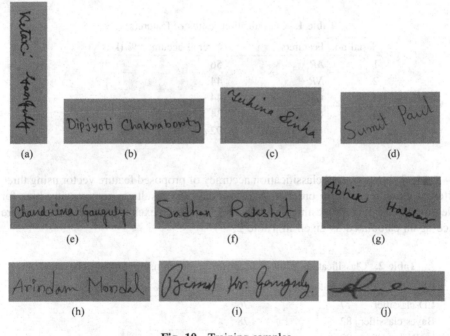

Fig. 10. Training samples

All four features are tested individually to see the classification ability of each feature. Finally, those four features are combined to get an improved accuracy. Table 1 depicts accuracy of individual features as well as combined features using k-NN classifier.

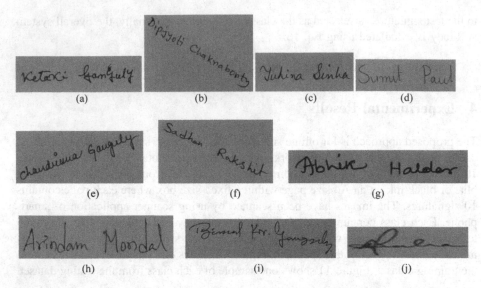

Fig. 11. Testing samples

Table 1. Classification results of feature(s)

Serial no.	Feature(s)	Overall accuracy % (k-NN)
1.	AR	56
2.	NR	44
3.	GM	44
4.	CP	34
5.	{AR, NR, GM, CP}	92

Table 2 shows overall classification accuracy of proposed feature vector using three different classifiers and in order to cross-validate the results to remove any bias for selecting the training and testing datasets, they have been exchanged and accuracies are once again calculated as given in Table 2.

Table 2. Classification result of proposed approach using different classifier

Classifier	Overall accuracy %	Overall accuracy % after exchanging data set
ED classifier	77	76
Bayes classifier	82	78
k-NN classifier	92	89

Figure 12 shows the distribution plot of each test sample based on their Euclidean Distance from each training sample of each class. The least distance value of each test sample determines the class of individuals. There are 10 classes and 50 test samples of 10 different color symbols to depict the result. The x-axis represents the classes and the y-axis represents the Euclidean Distance value of each sample. The red lines are samples of class 1. The green lines are samples of class 2 where two green samples are misclassified. The blue lines are samples of class 3. The cyan lines are samples of class 4 where two samples are misclassified. The magenta lines are samples of class 5. The yellow lines are samples of class 6. The black lines are samples of class 7. The red lines with the cross symbol are samples of class 8. The blue lines with the cross symbol are samples of class 9. The black lines with the cross symbol are samples of class 10.

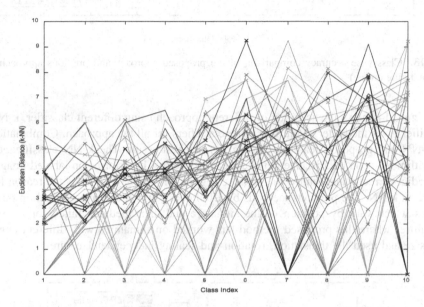

Fig. 12. Classification plot of each test sample (Color figure online)

5   Analysis

Table 3 shows the accuracy of two previous approaches on the same dataset using different classifier i.e. Euclidean Distance (ED) Classifier, Bayes Classifier, k-Nearest Neighbour (k-NN) classifier.

Table 3. Classification result of the previous approaches on the same dataset

Approach	Technique	ED classifier	Bayes classifier	k-NN classifier
Ubul et al.	Grid based	56	60	60
Ilmi et al.	LBP based	60	60	70

Figure 13 shows class wise accuracy comparison of the proposed approach and previous approaches. Redline depicts that proposed approach performs better than the previous approaches for most of the classes.

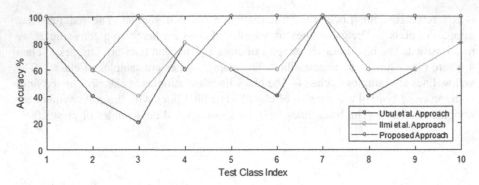

Fig. 13. Class wise accuracy comparison of the proposed approach and previous approaches (Color figure online)

Figure 14 shows the accuracy of different approach using different classifier. k-NN classifier gives the better result than other classifiers for all the approach. Combination of k-NN and proposed feature vector gives the best result. The k-NN classification algorithm relies on the distance between feature vectors. It performs on labeled images to predict correctly and returns the actual category for the image. This is the reason for selection k-NN. The previous methods by Ubul et al., Ilmi et al. have worked on pixel values which vary by position of the signature and their methods failed for rotated signatures where this proposed method has worked on signatures with different angle and size and used the translation, rotation and scaling independent features.

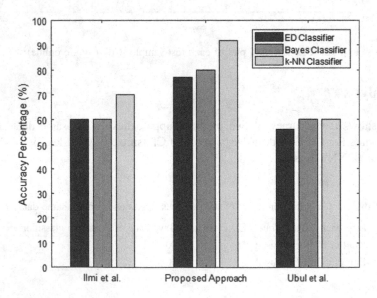

Fig. 14. Comparison of overall accuracy % using different classifier and different approaches

There are some systems where they used so many features to recognize and classify a signature which increases the computational time [6] but proposed system completes classification task within a fraction of a second.

6 Conclusion and Future Scope

Signature classification should be accurate because signature verification is a requirement for security purpose in daily life like in a bank, official purpose, forensic lab etc. In this paper, a transformation invariant method for signature recognition has been proposed. The input signature image is converted to a binary image. This binary image is pre-processed in different way to compensate translation, rotation and noise removal. The pre-processed image is used for feature extraction. Extracted features are Aspect ratio (AR), Number of regions (NR), Mean of gradient magnitude (GM) and Number of corner points (CP). These features are combined and used for classification of 10 signature classes. k-NN classifier gives the best result comparative to other classifiers used for experimentation. Overall classification accuracy is 92% using k-NN classifier.

The contributions of this paper are (a) prepared a ground truth handwritten signature dataset of 100 images (b) the signature classification technique is translation, rotation and uniform scaling independent. Extending the proposed technique to include images which are scaled non-uniformly and rotated by 180° may provide scopes for future research work.

References

1. Ubul, K., Adler, A., Abliz, G., Yasheng, M., Hamdulla, A.: Off-line Uyghur signature recognition based on modified grid information features. In: 11th International Conference on Information Science, Signal Processing and their Applications (ISSPA). IEEE (2012)
2. Ilmi, N., Budi, W.T.A., Nur, R.K.: Handwriting digit recognition using local binary pattern variance and K-Nearest neighbor classification. In: 4th International Conference on Information and Communication Technology (ICoICT). IEEE (2016)
3. Roy, S., Maheshkar, S.: Offline signature verification using grid based and centroid based approach. Int. J. Comput. Appl. **86** (2014)
4. Rathi, A., Rathi, D., Astya, A.: Offline handwritten signature verification by using pixel based method. Int. J. Eng. Res. Technol. (IJERT) **1** (2012)
5. Jana, R., Saha, R., Dutta, D.: Offline signature verification using Euclidian distance. Int. J. Comput. Sci. Inf. Technol. **5**, 707–710 (2014)
6. Marušić, T., Marušić, Ž., Šeremet, Ž.: Identification of authors of documents based on offline signature recognition. In: MIPRO, pp. 1144–1149, May 2015
7. Hiremath, G.: Verification of offline signature using local binary and directional pattern. Int. J. Innovative Sci. Eng. Technol. (IJISET) **3** (2016)
8. Panchal, T., Patel, H., Panchal, A.: License plate detection using Harris corner and character segmentation by integrated approach from an image. In: 7th International Conference on Communication, Computing and Virtualization, pp. 419–425 (2016)

9. Bisen, R., Mishra, A.: Offline signature verification with random and skilled forgery detection, using grid based feature extraction. Int. J. Electron. Electr. Comput. Syst. **5** (2016)
10. Yogesh, G., Patil, A.: Offline and Online Signature Verification Systems: A Survey. Int. J. Res. Eng. Technol. **3**, 328–332 (2014)
11. Kanetkar, S., Pathania, A., Venugopal, V., Sundaram, S.: Offline writer identification using local derivative pattern. In: 15th International Conference on Frontiers in Handwriting Recognition. IEEE (2016)

An Improved Technique for Modeling Fuzzy Time Series

Mahua Bose[✉] and Kalyani Mali

Department of Computer Science and Engineering, University of Kalyani,
Kalyani, India
e_cithi@yahoo.com, kalyanimali1992@gmail.com

Abstract. Fuzzy time series forecasting emerged as a new field of study during 1990s. In recent years it has become a popular research topic. In Fuzzy time series forecasting, performance of the model depends on two important steps: (1) Interval creation technique and (2) determination of fuzzy logical relationships (FLR) between past and present state. This paper presents a variable length data partitioning technique using Particle Swarm Optimization (PSO). Prediction is done by computing magnitude and direction of transition by simple mathematical operations. Novelty of this model is that it considers only the upward and the downward transitions while computing net variation. It does not take into consideration those cases where there is no change of states. In the iterative procedure, depending upon the position of cut points, lower bound and upper bound of the intervals (on which fuzzy sets are defined) are changed. This will in turn change the mid points of the interval which is used to measure variation of transition. This procedure is repeated until optimum positions of cuts corresponding to the lowest forecasting error are obtained. The experiment is carried out on standard datasets and results are compared with related models applied on the same dataset. Proposed idea outperforms others in terms of accuracy in prediction.

Keywords: Particle · Position · State · Transition · Variation

1 Introduction

Prediction about future event is always a crucial task. Advance knowledge about future is required for various activities like planning, management, production etc. Fuzzy Time Series forecasting differs from conventional forecasting in many ways. The basic difference is that, in Fuzzy Time Series models, data values are represented by fuzzy sets. It requires relatively small datasets for training also. Fuzzy Time Series model is used in many application areas like university enrollments, stock market, atmospheric science.

Theory of Fuzzy Time Series (FTS) is introduced by Song and Chissom [1–3]. Since then, notable research works have been done in this area. Basic model by Song and Chissom requires complex operations. Later a simple model has been developed by Chen [4] which is being followed by many researchers.

© Springer Nature Singapore Pte Ltd. 2019
J. K. Mandal et al. (Eds.): CICBA 2018, CCIS 1030, pp. 121–133, 2019.
https://doi.org/10.1007/978-981-13-8578-0_10

FTS algorithms usually partitions universe of discourse into intervals and fuzzy sets are defined on them. Number of intervals to be created and their lengths are central issue in Fuzzy Time series modeling. Work is on to improve accuracy of forecasting by adjusting intervals lengths. In order to create variable length partitions clustering algorithms [5–9] and Optimization based algorithms are employed. Particle swarm optimization technique [8, 10–15], has been applied for this purpose in most of the cases. In addition to that, Ant colony optimization [16], Genetic algorithms [17–19] have been utilized.

To determine fuzzy relationship between previous and current state mathematical models [20–23] and soft computing techniques have been applied. In this stage auto regression [16], support vector machine [12], neural network [9, 24–27] have been applied in the past.

Models using Optimization based algorithms for data partitioning used different algorithms in establishing fuzzy logical relationships for forecasting. Each model differs in the way the predicted value is computed. In this study we will also employ PSO [28] for data partitioning where each particle vector contains of a set cut points. Then the transition matrix is formed depending upon the position of cuts in each iteration (for each particle) and variation of transition and its direction is computed using simple arithmetic operations. Novelty of this work lies in the fact that the method considers only the upward and the downward transitions while computing net variation. It does not take into consideration those cases where there is no change of states. Net variation is used as predicted value. Optimal position of cuts yields minimum forecasting error.

This paper is divided into the following sections: Preliminary idea of FTS modeling is given in Sect. 2. Description of proposed forecasting model is given in Sect. 3. In Sect. 4, Comparative study of the proposed model with other FTS algorithms are shown. Conclusion is presented in Sect. 5.

2 Fuzzy Time Series

Let U be the Universe of discourse and $U = \{u_1, u_2, \ldots, u_k\}$. A fuzzy set [29, 30] Z on U is defined as follows:

$$Z = f_z(u_1)/u_1 + f_z(u_2)/u_2 + \ldots\ldots\ldots\ldots + f_z(u_k)/u_k$$

Where, membership value of u_i is denoted by $f_z(u_i)$ to the fuzzy set Z, and $1 \leq i \leq k$ and $0 \leq f_z(u_i) \leq 1$.

Let us consider, $X(t)(t = \ldots, 0, 1, 2, \ldots)$ is the universe of discourse and it is the subset of real time R_t. Fuzzy sets $f_k(t)(k = 1, 2, \ldots)$ are defined on X(t). Time(t) is called a fuzzy time series defined on X(t) if it is a collection of $f_1(t), f_2(t), \ldots$ [1–4, 31].

There are two types of fuzzy time series models: (1) first order model and (2) high order model. If the forecast k(t) is dependent on the previous state k(t − 1) only, then it is called first order model and is denoted by k(t − 1) -> k(t).

If the forecast k(t) is dependent on more than one past states k(t − 1), k(t − 2), …, k(t − n), then it is called high order model and is denoted by

$$k(t-n),\ldots\ldots\ldots k(t-2), k(t-1) -> k(t).$$

Basic Steps of a fuzzy time series forecasting model [4] are shown in Fig. 1.

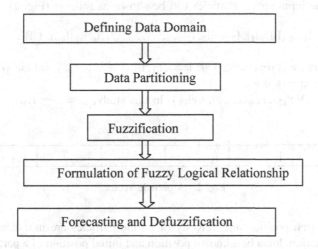

Fig. 1. Basic steps of a fuzzy time series forecasting model

3 Proposed Forecasting Technique

Phase 1: Data Preparation

Step 1. Compute the differences between each two consecutive observations at time t and t − 1 in actual time series.

Step 2. Add a positive (constant) value to the differences to make all of them positive.

Step 3. Define Data Domain D as follows:

$$D = [(D_{min} - Z_1) - (D_{max} - Z_2)]$$
$$LB = (D_{min} - Z_1)$$
$$UB = (D_{max} - Z_2)$$

Where, D_{min} is the minimum and and D_{max} is the maximum value in the difference series. Lower bound and upper bound of the data domain are LB and UB, respectively. Z_1 and Z_2 are two positive integers.

Illustration:

Let us consider TAIEX 1992 dataset. After execution of step 3 in phase1, $D_{min} = 4.07$, $D_{max} = 335.9$ and U = [0 − 350].

Phase 2: Designing the forecasting model

PSO [28] is utilised for optimizing the length of intervals by determining position of cut points. Let us consider that there are n intervals. A particle vector contains $n - 1$ cut points excluding LB and UB, i.e., $l_1, l_2, \ldots, l_{n-1}$, are the cut points between two adjacent intervals. Elements in each particle vector should be in ascending order within the range of the input space. Particles can be shown as follows (Fig. 2):

$$I_1 = [LB, l_1], I_2 = [l_1, l_2], \ldots\ldots\ldots\ldots I_n = [l_{n-1}, UB].$$

The i-th particle is represented as: $l_i = (l_{i1}, l_{i2}, \ldots\ldots\ldots, l_{im})$ and the velocity of the i-th particle is expressed as:
$Vel_i = (Vel_{i1}, Vel_{i2}, \ldots\ldots\ldots, Vel_{im})$. In this study, $m = n - 1$.

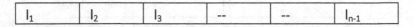

Fig. 2. A particle vector

Step 1. At first position and velocity of all the particles are initialized randomly. During initialisation, local best known position and initial position of a particle is same.

$$pbest_i = (pbest_{i1}, pbest_{i2}, \ldots\ldots\ldots.pbest_{im}).$$

Example: for the TAIEX 1992 dataset, initialization of the particle vector is shown in Table 1. Lower bound and upper bound of intervals created from the particle vector 1 is shown in Table 2.

Table 1. Initialisation of particles

Cut points	Particle 1	Particle 2	Particle 3	Particle 4	Particle 5
l_1	35	37	32	31	30
l_2	70	87	82	81	80
l_3	105	108	100	102	103
l_4	140	137	132	131	130
l_5	175	187	182	181	180
l_6	210	205	218	208	215
l_7	245	237	232	231	230
l_8	280	287	282	281	280
l_9	315	310	300	325	305

Table 2. Interval creation for particle 1

Interval no.	LB	UB	Middle point
1	0	35	17.5
2	35	70	52.5
3	70	105	87.5
4	105	140	122.5
5	140	175	157.5
6	175	210	192.5
7	210	245	227.5
8	245	280	262.5
9	280	315	297.5
10	315	350	332.5

Step 2. Initialize the iteration number to 1.

Step 3. For each particle, perform the steps 3.1 to 3.4 to calculate the fitness value.

Step 3.1. Based upon the position of cuts (in the particle vector) define fuzzy sets and fuzzify data values.

Suppose, the dataset is partitioned into n intervals ($I_1, I_2,\ldots\ldots I_n$) and fuzzy sets $A_1, A_2, \ldots\ldots\ldots\ldots, A_n$ are defined. Then,

$$A_1 = {}^1/_{I_1} + {}^{0.5}/_{I_2} + {}^0/_{I_3} + {}^0/_{I_4} \ldots\ldots\ldots\ldots\ldots\ldots. + {}^0/_{I_n}$$

$$A_2 = {}^{0.5}/_{I_1} + {}^1/_{I_2} + {}^{0.5}/_{I_3} + {}^0/_{I_4} \ldots\ldots\ldots\ldots\ldots\ldots. + {}^0/_{I_n}$$

$$\ldots\ldots\ldots\ldots\ldots\ldots\ldots\ldots\ldots\ldots\ldots\ldots\ldots\ldots\ldots\ldots$$

$$A_n = {}^0/_{I_1} + {}^0/_{I_2} + {}^0/_{I_3} + {}^0/_{I_4} \ldots\ldots\ldots\ldots\ldots\ldots. + {}^{0.5}/_{n-1} + {}^1/_{I_n}$$

Example: TAIEX dataset (1992) is partitioned into 10 intervals and fuzzy sets $A_1, A_2, \ldots\ldots\ldots\ldots, A_{10}$ are defined. Table 3 shows first few observations with fuzzified values and lower bound and upper bounds of intervals.

Step 3.2. a transition matrix and determine the magnitude and direction of transition as follows:

Example: In the transition matrix each row represents previous/current state p and each column represents the next state q. Number of occurrence of a FLR.

Table 3. Fuzzification of data

Data value	Fuzzified values	LB	UB	Mid value
259.2	A_8	245	280	262.5
206.64	A_6	175	210	192.5
233.8	A_7	210	245	227.5
210.9	A_7	210	245	227.5
159.31	A_5	140	175	157.5
254	A_8	245	280	262.5
227.61	A_7	210	245	227.5
222.73	A_7	210	245	227.5
171.91	A_5	140	175	157.5
263.89	A_8	245	280	262.5
202.98	A_6	175	210	192.5
98.28	A_3	70	105	87.5
318.42	A_{10}	315	350	332.5
212.71	A_7	210	245	227.5
176.07	A_6	175	210	192.5
170.59	A_5	140	175	157.5
301.59	A_9	280	315	297.5
235.39	A_7	210	245	227.5
222.5	A_7	210	245	227.5
–	–	–	–	–

$A_p \rightarrow A_q$ is represented by a cell (p, q) in the transition matrix. Based on Table 3, transition matrix for particle 1 is shown in Table 4.

Table 4. Transition matrix

t − 1	t									
	1	2	3	4	5	6	7	8	9	10
1	0	0	1	0	1	2	1	0	0	0
2	0	0	0	0	3	1	2	0	0	0
3	0	0	2	1	2	6	3	1	0	1
4	0	2	1	1	8	11	1	2	2	0
5	1	3	3	7	19	18	6	8	2	0
6	4	1	6	11	18	14	12	2	4	0
7	0	0	2	2	11	9	5	4	2	0
8	0	0	0	3	4	8	2	1	0	1
9	0	0	1	2	2	3	2	0	0	0
10	0	0	0	1	0	0	1	0	0	0

Step 3.3. Calculate predicted values.

Let us consider a fuzzy logical relationship: $A_p \rightarrow A_q \ A_r$

Where the fuzzified (difference) value between time 't − 1' and 't' is A_p. We have to find the predicted (difference) value between time 't + 1' and 't'. Now From the p-th row of the transition matrix, get the next possible states with the number of occurrences. From the relationship stated above, next states are A_q and A_r (where, $q \neq p$ and $r \neq p$) with the number of occurrences 'a' and 'b', respectively.

Let N_V be the Net variation. Then,

$$N\_V = ((a * (mid[q] - mid[p])) + (b * (mid[r] - mid[p])))/(a+b) \tag{1}$$

$$\text{Predicted value (P)} = (mid [p] + N\_V) \tag{2}$$

Example: First row of the Transition matrix establishes following relationship:

$$A_1 - > A_3 A_5 A_6 A_7$$

From the first row of the transition matrix, net variation will be computed as,
((87.5 − 17.5) + (122.5 − 17.5) + (2*(192.5 − 17.5)) + (227.5 − 17.5))/(1 + 1 +2 + 1) = 154

So, for any observation at time 't' with State A_1, the predicted value at time 't + 1' = 17.5 + 154 = 171.5.

Let us take another example. From the fifth row of the Transition matrix following relationship can be established:

$$A_5 - > A_1 A_2 A_3 A_4 A_5 A_6 A_7 A_8 A_9$$

In this case A_5 occurs 12 times in the right hand side. This observation is not taken into consideration while measuring variation. In this case net variation is calculated as above and the value is −32.59.

So, for any observation at time 't' with State A_5, the predicted value at time 't + 1' = 192.5 − 32.59 = 159.91.

Step 3.4. Compute the fitness value (Mean Square error) of the particle.

$$\text{Fitness} = \frac{\sum_{i=1}^{N}(\text{desired\_value} - \text{Predicted\_Value})^2}{N} \tag{3}$$

Step 4. Update the velocity and position of all particles.

The velocity and position update equations for the j-th dimension of the i-th particle in the swarm may be represented as:

$$V_{ij} = (\omega V_{ij} + c_1 (\text{pbest}_{ij} - l_{ij}) \text{rand1}() + c_2 (\text{gbest}_j - l_{ij}) \text{rand2}()) \tag{4}$$

$$l_{ij} = l_{ij} + V_{ij} \tag{5}$$

Where ω is the inertia weight; rand 1 and rand 2 are random positive numbers within the range {0, 1}.

Step 5. Update the personal best position vector (pbest), if its objective value at the current iteration is smaller than its objective value at the previous iteration.

Step 6. Choose the best particle among all particles.

Set local best known position with minimum MSE as Global best position $gbest_k$, (k = 1, 2, ..., m).

Step 7. Increment number of iterations by one.

Step 8. If iteration < MAX Limit, goto Step 3 else display the optimal position of cuts.

Phase 3: Adjusting the predicted value

Let Adj_P be the predicted value after adjustment. Then,

$$Adj\_P = (Predicted\ value\ (P) - Positive\ Constant\ (PC)) \tag{6}$$

This is the predicted difference value.

$$Forecast\ (t+1) = (Actual\ value\ (t) + Adj\_P) \tag{7}$$

4 Performance Evaluation

4.1 Datasets

Experiments are carried out using the following datasets.

(a) Daily stock price of Taiwan Stock Exchange Capitalization Weighted Stock Index (TAIEX) [32], Taipei, Taiwan (from 4.1.1992 to 29.12.1992). The dataset consists of 284 values (The minimum and the maximum of the time series are 3327.7 and 5391.6, respectively). First eleven months data are used for training and rest are used for testing.

(b) Civilian unemployment rates dataset [33], USA (from 1.1. 1948 to 1.12. 2013). The dataset consists of 792 observations, with minimum and the maximum of the time series are min = 2.5 and max = 10.8, respectively. Data values for the period 1.1. 1948−1.12. 2012 are used for training and the remaining data are used for testing.

4.2 Results and Discussion

For the execution of PSO algorithm, $\omega_{max} = 1.4$ and $\omega_{min} = 0.9$. Random positive numbers are: rand1 = 0.7 and rand2 = 1; Acceleration coefficients are: C1 = 2 and C2 = 2; maximum generation = 50; Number of particles = 5. Maximum and minimum velocities (for dataset 1) are +7 and −7, respectively. For the second dataset, maximum and minimum velocities are +1 and −1, respectively. Work is done using C++ language on Windows Environment.

In order to evaluate performance by the proposed method comparison is done with existing models, using different partitioning methods like equal sized partitioning [4], fuzzy c-means clustering [5], the Gath-GeVa clustering [6], PSO based partitioning [15] and interval information granular method [34]. Root Mean Square Error (RMSE) and Mean absolute percentage error (MAPE) are used to evaluate the forecasting performance. Results are analyzed using Tables 5, 6, 7, 8 and Figs. 3, 4.

Table 5. TAIEX forecasting

Date	Actual	Difference+PC	Predicted (P)	Adj_P	Final forecast
12/1/1992	3646.76	151.75	183.565	3.5647	3678.57
12/2/1992	3635.7	168.94	183.565	3.5647	3650.32
12/3/1992	3614.08	158.38	183.565	3.5647	3639.26
12/4/1992	3651.39	217.31	183.565	3.5647	3617.64
12/5/1992	3727.95	256.56	179.135	−0.865	3650.52
12/7/1992	3755.77	207.82	201.485	21.485	3749.44
12/8/1992	3761.01	185.24	179.135	−0.865	3754.9
12/9/1992	3776.55	195.54	157.642	−22.36	3738.65
12/10/1992	3746.75	150.2	157.642	−22.36	3754.19
12/11/1992	3734.3	167.55	183.565	3.5647	3750.31
12/12/1992	3742.61	188.31	183.565	3.5647	3737.86
12/14/1992	3696.76	134.15	157.642	−22.36	3720.25
12/15/1992	3688.26	171.5	176.691	−3.309	3693.45
12/16/1992	3674.92	166.66	183.565	3.5647	3691.82
12/17/1992	3668.67	173.75	183.565	3.5647	3678.48
12/18/1992	3657.99	169.32	157.642	−22.36	3646.31
12/21/1992	3576.09	98.1	183.565	3.5647	3661.55
12/22/1992	3579.97	183.88	201.725	21.725	3597.82
12/23/1992	3448.15	48.18	157.642	−22.36	3557.61
12/24/1992	3456	187.85	183.173	3.1727	3451.32
12/28/1992	3327.67	51.67	157.642	−22.36	3433.64
12/29/1992	3377.06	229.39	183.173	3.1727	3330.84

$$\text{RMSE} = \sqrt{\sum\nolimits_{i=1}^{n} ((\text{Actual} - \text{forecast}) * (\text{Actual} - \text{forecast}))/n} \qquad (8)$$

$$\text{MAPE} = \left(\sum\nolimits_{i=1}^{n} |\text{Actual} - \text{forecast}|/\text{forecast}\right) * 100/n \qquad (9)$$

Where n is the number of observations.

Table 6. Comparative study using TAIEX(1992) data

Methods	RMSE	MAPE
Equal length partitioning [4]	134.4	3.50
Fuzzy c-means clustering [5]	114.2	2.37
Gath-GeVa clustering [6]	107.2	2.09
PSO optimization based partitioning [15]	85.7	1.87
Information granules based model [34]	74.7	1.72
Proposed	45.19	0.89

Table 7. Unemployment forecasting

Date	Actual	Difference+PC	Predicted (P)	Adj_P	Final forecast
1/1/2013	7.9	1.5	1.48	−0.018	7.88
2/1/2013	7.7	1.3	1.48	−0.018	7.88
3/1/2013	7.5	1.3	1.48	−0.018	7.68
4/1/2013	7.5	1.5	1.48	−0.018	7.48
5/1/2013	7.5	1.5	1.48	−0.018	7.48
6/1/2013	7.5	1.5	1.48	−0.018	7.48
7/1/2013	7.3	1.3	1.48	−0.018	7.48
8/1/2013	7.2	1.4	1.48	−0.018	7.28
9/1/2013	7.2	1.5	1.48	−0.018	7.18
10/1/2013	7.2	1.5	1.48	−0.018	7.18
11/1/2013	7	1.3	1.48	−0.018	7.18
12/1/2013	6.7	1.2	1.48	−0.018	6.98

Table 8. Comparative study using unemployment data

Methods	RMSE	MAPE
Equal length partitioning [4]	0.26	2.75
Fuzzy c-means clustering [5]	0.24	2.78
Gath-GeVa clustering [6]	0.2	2.22
PSO optimization based partitioning [15]	0.19	2.17
Information granules based model [34]	0.18	2.14
Proposed	0.135	1.39

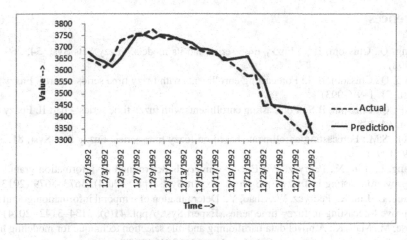

Fig. 3. TAIEX forecasting

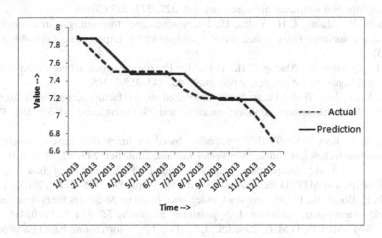

Fig. 4. Unemployment forecasting

5 Conclusion and Future Work

This study presents a simple mechanism to improve forecast accuracy of the Fuzzy Time Series model. To determine optimal interval length PSO is employed. Magnitude of the variation in transition is used to calculate the predicted value. It also acts as fitness evaluation function. Comparative study with other related methods on same dataset reveals that the proposed work shows highest forecast accuracy. At present this technique works for first order model. In future this technique can be extended for high order model.

References

1. Song, Q., Chissom, B.S.: Fuzzy time series and its models. Fuzzy Sets Syst. **54**, 269–277 (1993)
2. Song, Q., Chissom, B.S.: Forecasting enrollments with fuzzy time series – part I. Fuzzy Sets Syst. **54**, 1–9 (1993)
3. Song, Q., Chissom, B.S.: Forecasting enrollments with fuzzy time series – part II. Fuzzy Sets Syst. **64**, 1–8 (1994)
4. Chen, S.M.: Forecasting enrollments based on fuzzy time series. Fuzzy Sets Syst. **81**, 311–319 (1996)
5. Wang, L., Liu, X., Pedrycz, W.: Effective intervals determined by information granules to improve forecasting in fuzzy time series. Expert Syst. Appl. **40**(14), 5673–5679 (2013)
6. Wang, L., Liu, X., Pedrycz, W., Shao, Y.: Determination of temporal information granules to improve forecasting in fuzzy time series. Expert Syst. Appl. **41**(6), 3134–3142 (2014)
7. Bose, M., Mali, K.: A novel data partitioning and rule selection technique for modeling high-order fuzzy time series. Appl. Soft Comput. **63**, 87–96 (2018)
8. Cheng, S.-H., Chen, S.-M., Jian, W.-S.: Fuzzy time series forecasting based on fuzzy logical relationships and similarity measures. Inf. Sci. **327**, 272–287 (2016)
9. Egrioglu, E., Aladag, C.H., Yolcu, U.: Fuzzy time series forecasting with a novel hybrid approach combining fuzzy c-means and neural networks. Expert Syst. Appl. **40**, 854–857 (2013)
10. Bas, E., Egrioglu, E., Aladag, C.H., Yolcu, U.: Fuzzy-time-series network used to forecast linear and nonlinear time series. Appl. Intell. **43**, 343–355 (2015)
11. Chen, S.-M., Jian, W.-S.: Fuzzy forecasting based on two-factors second-order fuzzy-trend logical relationship groups, similarity measures and PSO techniques. Inf. Sci. **391–392**, 65–79 (2017)
12. Chen, S.M., Kao, P.Y.: TAIEX forecasting based on fuzzy time series, particle swarm optimization techniques and support vector machines. Inf. Sci. **247**, 62–71 (2013)
13. Hsu, L.-Y., et al.: Temperature prediction and TAIFEX forecasting based on fuzzy relationships and MTPSO techniques. Expert Syst. Appl. **37**, 2756–2770 (2010)
14. Singh, P., Borah, B.: Forecasting stock index price based on M-factors fuzzy time series and particle swarm optimization. Int. J. Approximate Reasoning **55**, 812–833 (2014)
15. Chen, S.M., Manalu, G.M.T., Pan, J.S., Liu, H.C.: Fuzzy forecasting based on two-factors second-order fuzzy-trend logical relationship groups and particle swarm optimization techniques. IEEE Trans. Cybern. **43**(3), 1102–1117 (2013)
16. Cai, Q., Zhang, D., Zheng, W., Leung, S.C.H.: A new fuzzy time series forecasting model combined with ant colony optimization and auto-regression. Knowl.-Based Syst. **74**, 61–68 (2015)
17. Cai, Q.S., Zhang, D.F., Leung, C.H., Wu, B.: A novel stock forecasting model based on fuzzy time series and genetic algorithm. Procedia Comput. Sci. **18**, 1155–1162 (2013)
18. Cheng, C.H., Chen, T.L., Wei, L.Y.: A hybrid model based on rough sets theory and genetic algorithms for stock price forecasting. Inf. Sci. **180**(9), 1610–1629 (2010)
19. Bas, E., Uslu, V.R., Yolcu, U., Egrioglu, E.: A modified genetic algorithm for forecasting fuzzy time series. Appl. Intell. **41**(2), 453–463 (2014)
20. Joshi, B.P., Kumar, S.: A computational method for fuzzy time series forecasting based on difference parameters. Int. J. Model. Simul. Sci. Comput. **4**(1), 1250023-1–1250023-12 (2013)
21. Kumar, S., Gangwar, S.S.: Partitions based computational method for high-order fuzzy time series forecasting. Expert Syst. Appl. **39**, 12158–12164 (2012)

22. Singh, S.R.: A computational method of forecasting based on high order fuzzy time series. Expert Syst. Appl. **36**, 10551–10559 (2009)
23. Bose, M., Mali, K.: High order time series forecasting using fuzzy discretization. Int. J. Fuzzy Syst. Appl. **5**(4), 147–164 (2016). https://doi.org/10.4018/IJFSA.2016100107
24. Aladag, C.H.: Using multiplicative neuron model to establish fuzzy logic relationships. Expert Syst. Appl. **40**(3), 850–853 (2013)
25. Singh, P., Borah, B.: High-order fuzzy-neuro expert system for daily temperature forecasting. Knowl.-Based Syst. **46**, 12–21 (2013)
26. Yu, T.H.-K., Huarng, K.: A neural network- based fuzzy time series model to improve forecasting. Expert Syst. Appl. **37**, 3366–3372 (2010)
27. Aladag, C.H., Basaran, M.A., Egrioglu, E.: A high order fuzzy time series forecasting model based on adaptive expectation and artificial neural networks. Math. Comput. Simul. **81**(4), 875–882 (2010)
28. Kennedy, J., Eberhart, R.: Particle swarm optimization. In: Proceedings of IEEE International Conference on Neural Networks, Piscataway, NJ, pp. 1942–1948 (1995)
29. Zadeh, L.A.: Fuzzy set. Inf. Control **8**, 338–353 (1965)
30. Zadeh, L.A.: The concept of a linguistic variable and its application to approximate reasoning – part I. Inf. Sci. **8**, 199–249 (1975)
31. Lee, L.W., Wang, L.H., Chen, S.M., Leu, Y.H.: Handling forecasting problems based on two-factors high-order fuzzy time series. IEEE Trans. Fuzzy Syst. **14**(3), 468–477 (2006)
32. Taiwan stock exchange capitalization weighted stock index. http://www.twse.com.tw/en/page/trading/exchange/FMTQIK.html
33. Civilian unemployment rates. www.forecasts.org/data/data/UNRATE.htm
34. Lu, W., Chen, X., Pedrycz, W., Liu, X., Yang, J.: Using interval information granules to improve forecasting in fuzzy time series. Int. J. Approximate Reasoning **57**, 1–18 (2015)

Classification of Skin Cancer: ANN Trained with Scaled Conjugate Gradient Algorithm

Kartik Sau[1(✉)] and Pallavi Saha[2(✉)]

[1] Department of Science and Humanities,
University of Engineering and Management, Kolkata 700-160, India
kartik_sau2001@yahoo.co.in
[2] Department of Computer Science and Engineering,
University of Engineering and Management, Kolkata 700-160, India
pallavisaha321@gmail.com

Abstract. Automatic detection and accurate classification of skin cancer has been achievable with the help of machine learning techniques. Now-a-days, skin cancer has posed to be a dreadful disease mostly seen in the western region of the world. The current work focuses on the automated identification of skin cancer. The proposed method initially deals with pre-processing steps like normalization and image enhancement. Texture based different features of the digital skin images are extracted by using Gray Level Co-occurrence Matrices (GLCM). Then classification is performed based on the extracted features using Support Vector Machine (SVM), Ensemble and Artificial Neural Network (ANN). To train the ANN, Scaled conjugate gradient (SCG) algorithm has been adopted. This paper compares the performance of these three classifiers in terms of some parameters namely accuracy, precision, recall and f-measure. The experimental results show the effectiveness of ANN-SCG classifier. The ANN-SCG model provides 84.21% accuracy, 83.33% precision, 71.42% f-measure and 76.91% recall which is superior to the SVM and Ensemble classifiers.

Keywords: ANN · SVM · Melanoma · Nevus · SCG

1 Introduction

In the western part of the world, mainly Europe, Australia and America, skin cancer is one of the most dreadful diseases among many white skinned people. The main reason behind it is ultraviolet light exposure, either from the sun or tanning beds. Every year approximately 4% skin cancer increases among the white skinned people. As a result, it spreads for all the white people after some particular time frame. The skin cancer Foundation mentions that everybody should examine his or her body on a monthly basis. So identification plays a crucial role in the detection of skin cancer. Therefore, automatic detection of skin cancer is essential to handle skin cancer among the white skinned people in monthly basis. Now-a-days, certain techniques are available to detect the skin cancer. Most of these techniques are well appreciated. In response to the demand almost every year, various types of techniques are introduced by different researchers. Still these techniques are not sufficient to meet the current requirement.

© Springer Nature Singapore Pte Ltd. 2019
J. K. Mandal et al. (Eds.): CICBA 2018, CCIS 1030, pp. 134–143, 2019.
https://doi.org/10.1007/978-981-13-8578-0_11

Under such circumstances, we performed the comparative study among SVM, Ensemble and ANN-SCG in terms of the different performance measuring metrics. The current paper is organized as follows. In Sect. 2 we have presented the different existing methods as a literature survey. In Sect. 3, we have presented the comparative study among SVM, Ensemble and ANN-SCG methods. The experimental results of these three methods along with conclusions are presented in Sects. 4 and 5 respectively.

2 Literature Survey

In 2012, Satheesha et al. [1] proposed a method to classify the melanoma skin cancer based on a novel hierarchical K- Nearest Neighbors (KNN) classifier. In this method, skin lesions are characterized by their color and as well as texture. Here for identification of skin cancer image acquisitions, pre-processing, Segmentation, feature extraction, classification is used. In 2013, J Abdul Jaleel proposed [2] Skin detection based on Maximum Entropy Threshold, feature extracted by using Gray Level Co-occurrence Matrix(GLCM), and classification using Back-Propagation Neural (BPN) Network is used for classification purpose. In 2014, Sarika Choudhuri et al. [3] proposed a method for skin cancer detection and classification based on Artificial Neural Network in their research work. In this paper, authors first try to remove hairs and noises by filtering techniques, and then segment the skin images by maximum entropy thresholding techniques. The different feature is extracted from it using grey level co-occurrence matrices GLCM and classification is performed using Artificial Neural Network (ANN). It classifies the given data set into cancerous or non-cancerous image. In 2015, Kaur et al. [4] proposed a method based on clustering based image thresholding, which can reduce the dark level image into binary image. In this method, images have two classes of pixels which computes the ideal limit isolates two classes for insignificant joined spread or proportionate, so that their between class difference is maximal. In 2016, Krishna [5] described a method for Skin Cancer Detection and Feature Extraction through Clustering Technique. In this technique, segmentation is done by various clustering techniques and feature is extracted using ABCD (Asymmetry Index Border, Colour Index, Diameter) method. In 2015, Gautam et al. [6] proposed for an automated method detection of skin cancer and classify between malignant and benign by using support vector machine. In this method dilation has been adopted to remove noise and then segmentation is performed on digital skin image. Features were extracted from the segmented portion of the skin image and were used to train SVM classifier. Jaleel et al. [4] designed a system for the classification of skin cancer based on Back propagation neural network. In this method first remove the noises and contrast of it is also adjusted by suitable method. 2D wavelet transform method is used to extract features from the image and then the extracted features are fed as input to the Back propagation neural network. In 2016, Fidan et al. [7] proposed a method to classify the skin cancer among normal, atypical and melanoma by using the concept of Artificial Neural Network. To improve the performance of these method Decision support Systems was also adapted. The experimental result shows the effectiveness of this method. Here abnormal and melanoma skin disease were classified with accuracy 93.3% where as normal skin lesion were correctly classified with accuracy 100%. In 2017, Sau et al. [8] proposed a method for pre processing of skin cancer using Anisotropic Diffusion and Sigmoid Function. In this method, authors critically normalized the skin lesion images followed by removing Gaussian noise and preserving some feature by anisotropic diffusion. For more improvement of it, authors applied sigmoid function in the spatial domain of the skin lesion image. Here, authors critically considered different parameters of anisotropic diffusion and sigmoid function. This innovative method has been successfully used in various low contrast affected skin lesion images. All most in all the cases, it gives the satisfactory results in terms of MSE PSNR, and SSIM values.

3 Methodology

3.1 Intensity of Normalization

Normalization technique enables us to achieve same intensity in the same regions of the digital skin image. It can be mathematically represented as follows.

$$I'(x,y) = \begin{cases} \phi_d + \lambda & \text{if} \quad I(x,y) \le \phi \\ \phi_d - \lambda & \text{if} \quad I(x,y) \ge \phi \end{cases} \tag{1}$$

$$where \ \lambda = \sqrt{\frac{\rho_d(I(x,y) - \phi)^2}{\rho}} \tag{2}$$

Here, $I'(x,y)$ stands for the normalized intensity; ϕ_d represents the average gray value of the desired image; ρ_d stands for the variance of intensity of the desired image; and ϕ signifies the average gray value of input images. ρ represents the variance of intensity of the skin image.

3.2 Image Enhancement

Image enhancement is one of the pre-processing techniques that are extensively used in image processing [11] to upgrade the visual information of the viewers. The contrast of the digital skin images has been adjusted by changing the values of intensity of the image. Each plane of color image (Red, Green and Blue) is adjusted by the following equations that always satisfying $0 = \text{fmin} \le g \le \text{fmax} = L - 1$

$$g = b\log(af + 1)$$

3.3 Feature Extraction Based on Texture

Textures are calculated from the skin images based on distribution of intensities at specified positions relative to each other from which different features are obtained. To calculate the texture different statistics are used; namely first order, second order and higher order statistics. The Gray Level Co-occurrence Matrix (GLCM) is a process to obtain texture based on second order statistical model [12]. The size of the Gray Level Co-occurrence Matrix (GLCM) is equal to the number of gray levels in the image. Let P_{ij} represent the Co-occurrence matrix and G represents the number of gray levels. Each of the element at position (i, j) in the matrix depicts the frequency by which pixel with gray level i is spatially related to pixel with gray level j. some of the texture features namely; entropy, energy, correlation, inverse difference moment (IDM), directional moment (DM), angular second moment (ASM), inertia and shade have been calculated from the GLCM. The formulas employed to compute the various features are depicted in Table 1 (Fig. 1).

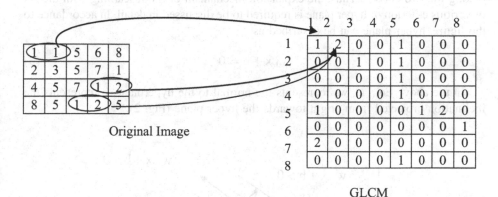

Fig. 1. GLCM calculation from the original image

Table 1. List of different features extracted from GLCM

Sl no.	GLCM feature	Formula
1	Entropy	$\text{Entropy} = -\sum_{i=0}^{G-1}\sum_{j=0}^{G-1} P(i,j) \times \log(P(i,j))$
2	Energy	$\sum_{i=0}^{G-1}\sum_{j=0}^{G-1} P(i,j)$
3	Correlation	$\sum_{i=0}^{G-1}\sum_{j=0}^{G-1} \frac{(i \times j) \times P(i,j) - \left(\mu_i \times \mu_j\right)}{\sigma_x \times \sigma_y}$
4	Angular second moment	$\sum_{i=0}^{G-1}\sum_{j=0}^{G-1} \{P(i,j)\}^2$
5	Inverse difference moment	$\text{IDM} = \sum_{i=0}^{G-1}\sum_{j=0}^{G-1} \frac{1}{1+(i-j)^2} P(i,j)$
6	Directional moment	$\text{DM} = \sum_{i=0}^{G-1}\sum_{j=0}^{G-1} P(i,j)|i-j|$
7	Inertia	$\text{Inertia} = \sum_{i=0}^{G-1}\sum_{j=0}^{G-1} \{i-j\}^2 \times P(i,j)$
8	Shade	$\text{Shade} = \sum_{i=0}^{G-1}\sum_{j=0}^{G-1} \{i+j-\mu_x-\mu_y\}^3 \times P(i,j)$

3.4 Classification Based on SVM, Ensemble and ANN Trained Classifier

3.4.1 Support Vector Machine

The Support Vector Machine (SVM) is a supervised training model used to classify some objects like to classify melanoma and nevus types skin cancer. In the current context SVM is performed between two classes, one is melanoma type's skin cancer and other is nevus types of skin cancer. The competence of SVM prevails in its capability to convert data in higher dimensional space where the mode of separation among the data is hyper plane. The best part of SVM is that by increasing the gap between two classes it enables the creation of best hyper plane which differentiate among the two classes. Thus, the expansion mechanism of SVM learning with the set of various criterion of hyper plane is required to be discussed in detail. In accordance to the figure, hyper plane can be described as

$$w_0.x + b = 0 \tag{3}$$

In the above Eq. (1), w_0 represents the normal to the hyperplane, b represents the inclination projected from origin towards the hyper plane (Fig. 2).

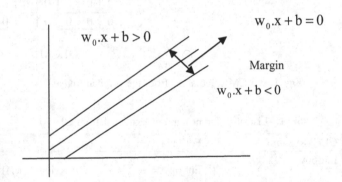

Fig. 2. Linear SVM classifier model

The point that resides on the hyper plane should meet the Eq. (1). Let us consider the training set comprises of (X_i, Y_i) where i = 1, ..., n feature vectors and Y =+ 1 are class labels. They must meet the following equations.

$$w_0.x + b > 0 \quad \text{if } Y_i = 1$$

$$w_0.x + b < 0 \quad \text{if } Y_i = -1$$

3.4.2 Ensemble

Ensemble method for classification is one of the most significant techniques in machine learning. There are different variety of ensemble method are available, they can give the different performance level. In the field of machine learning, ensemble learning engages different training algorithm to attain superior predictive performance which could not have been achieved if any one of the constituent algorithms is trained alone. Since ensemble can be skilled and applied for predictions, it is regarded as supervised learning algorithm. Ensemble tends to provide superior results whenever there is a prominent diversification among the different combined classification models. It integrates a set of skilled feeble classification model and data on which these models are trained. The three types of weak learners have been incorporated in the ensemble namely Discriminate (M_1), Decision Tree (M_2) and KNN (M_3). Ensemble helps to gain better predictive performance as compared to any single particular model. The main objective behind ensemble meta algorithms is to improve the accuracy of machine learning algorithms applied for classification as well as regression. Ensemble forecast response for new set of data (test data, D) by combining all the predictive outcomes from each of the weak learners. This aggregation of the outcomes of each weak learner to form the predictive response of the ensemble is carried out with the help of few methods viz. AdaBoostM1, LogitBoost, GentleBoost, RobustBoost, LPBoost, Total-Boost, RUSBoost, Subspace, and Bag (Fig. 3).

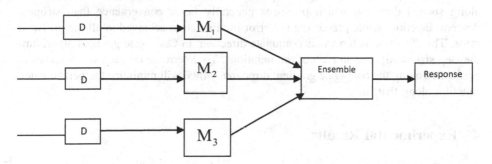

Fig. 3. Common workflow of ensemble classifier

3.4.3 Artificial Neural Networks

Artificial Neural Networks or Neural Networks (ANN) is calculating systems indistinctly motivated from the connectivity among the neurons in animal brains. ANN is basically a network comprising of several neurons, each of them is capable to transmit signal to another and receive signal from other. These neurons are arranged in layers. It is capable of memorizing complex designs and thereby able to predict some future value. In the training step, the different features extracted from the dataset are sent as input to train the ANN. In the testing phase an unknown set of data is fed as input to the ANN and response is recorded. In the current work, ANN has been trained by engaging scaled conjugate gradient algorithm (Fig. 4).

Input   Hidden   Output

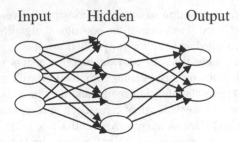

Fig. 4. A typical architecture of ANN.

3.4.4   Scaled Conjugate Gradient

The weights of the fundamental back propagation algorithm are adjusted in the steepest descent direction (i.e. the most negative of the gradient). In the steepest descent algorithm the performance function is decreasing more drastically, this does not necessarily produce the fastest convergence (Hagan et al. 1996). For faster convergence; the conjugate gradient algorithm is applied. In this algorithm, search is carried out along such a direction which produces generally faster convergence than steepest descent direction, while preserving the error minimization achieved in all the previous steps. This direction is termed as conjugate direction. In Conjugate gradient algorithm, the step size is adjusted in each of the iterations. To determine the step size a search is performed along the conjugate gradient direction, which will minimize the performance function along that line.

4   Experimental Results

To evaluate the performance of these three methods, we have collected some skin cancer images from Department of Dermatology of the University Medical Center Groningen (UMCG). These images are different in size, color as well as contrast. Also, surrounding has some unwanted artifacts. The proposed method is applied in a Matlab 2015 environment, which was installed in processor i5 of the standard machine with 8 GB RAM. Initially, the input image has been normalized and then contrast has been adjusted. Figure 5.a represents the input Melanoma Cancer Image skin. Figure 5.b depicts the normalized Melanoma Cancer image and Fig. 5.c represents the enhanced Melanoma Cancer image. The different output of Melanocytic nevus Image as presented in Fig. 6. Here we extract eight features based on texture for a set of enhanced skin image are tabulated in Table 2. The efficiency of the three different classification models have been estimated on the basis of performance measuring metrics such as; accuracy, precision, recall and f-measure. They are defined in the following equations; here, t_p represents true positive, t_n represents true negative, f_p represents false positive and f_n represents false negative.

$$\text{Accuracy} = \frac{tp + tn}{tp + fp + fn + tn} \quad \text{Precision} = \frac{tp}{tp + fp}$$

$$\text{Recall} = \frac{tp}{tp + fn} \quad \text{F-measure} = 2 * \frac{\text{Recall} * \text{Precision}}{\text{Recall} + \text{Precision}}$$

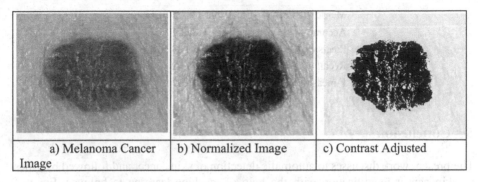

| a) Melanoma Cancer Image | b) Normalized Image | c) Contrast Adjusted |

Fig. 5. (a) Melanoma Cancer Image (b) normalized image (c) contrast adjusted

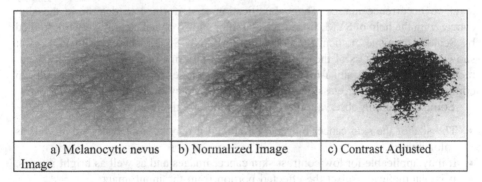

| a) Melanocytic nevus Image | b) Normalized Image | c) Contrast Adjusted |

Fig. 6. (a) Melanocytic nevus Image (b) normalized image (c) contrast adjusted

Table 2. Value of different features computed by using GLCM from the enhanced skin image.

Sl No	Entropy	ASM	DM	Shade	Prominence	Inertia	Energy	Homogeneity
1	7.3716	167165	54318371	375535	−1.86E+28	8.9274E+35	4071435	92677
2	6.3224	167668	1699300000	565242	−3.4631E+28	2.0471E+36	33005968	100980
3	4.6313	177000	6853000000	452071	−4.9749E+28	3.2588E+36	9435373	126890

Simulation results of the different classification models have been depicted in Table 3. It has been observed that SVM achieves accuracy of 73.33%, precision of 66.66%, recall of 66.66% and f-measure 66.66%. Moreover, ANN-SCG reflects better results in comparison to other classifiers by attaining an accuracy of 84.21%, precision of 83.33%, recall of 71.42% and f-measure of 76.91%.

Table 3. Experimental result of ANN-SCG with other tested classifiers (in percentage)

Metric	SVM	Ensemble	ANN-SCG
Accuracy	73.33	83.33	84.21
Precision	66.66	66.66	83.33
Recall	66.66	80	71.42
F-measure	66.66	72.72	76.91

5 Conclusion

The present work discusses to automatic detection of skin cancer and followed by types of skin cancer identification with the help of machine learning techniques. For this initially preprocessing is carried out by normalization and enhanced techniques. The features of the skin cancer are extracted from the image on the basis of texture by Gray level co occurrence matrix. Then classification is performed to determine the skin cancer with the help of SVM, Ensemble classifier and Artificial Neural Network trained by Scaled conjugate gradient (SCG) algorithm (ANN-SCG). The experimental result shows the effectiveness of these three techniques in terms of parameter namely accuracy, precision, recall and f-measure. ANN-SCG model provides superior results in comparison to the other classifiers reflecting an accuracy of 84.21%.

Some concluding observations from the study are given below.

- The size of the skin cancer may be varied and it may be gray scale and as well as color images.
- It may applicable for low contrast skin cancer images and as well as bright images.
- It is automatically select the effected portion from the input image.
- The quality of the output images is good enough, so it helps to find different feature via feature extraction.
- It can be applicable for different medical science along with various industrial applications also.

References

1. Satheesha, T.Y., Narayana, D., Giriprasad, M.: Review on early detection of melanoma SITU. Int. J. Adv. Technol. Eng. Res. (2012). National Conference on Emerging Trends in Technology (NCET-Tech)
2. Jaleel, J.A., Salim, S., Aswin, R.B.: Artificial neural network based detection of skin cancer. Int. J. Adv. Res. Electr. Electron. Instrum. Eng. **1**(3), 200–205 (2012)

3. Choudhari, S., Biday, S.: Artificial neural network for skin cancer detection. Int. J. Emerg. Trends Technol. Comput. Sci. **3**(5), 147–153 (2014)
4. Kaur, H., Singh, A.: Enhanced skin cancer detection techniques using Otsu segmentation method. Int. J. Adv. Res. Comput. Sci. Softw. Eng. **5**(5) (2015)
5. Krishna, M.C., Ranganayakulu, S.: Skin cancer detection and feature extraction through clustering technique. Int. J. Innov. Res. Comput. Commun. Eng. **4**(3) (2016)
6. Gautam, D., Ahmed, M.: Melanoma detection and classification using SVM based decision support system. In: 2015 Annual IEEE India Conference (INDICON) (2015)
7. Fidan, U., Sarl, I., Kumrular, R.K.: Classification of skin lesions using ANN. In: Medical Technologies National Congress (TIPTEKNO) (2016)
8. Sau, K., Maiti, A., Ghosh, A.: Preprocessing of skin cancer using anisotropic diffusion and sigmoid function. In: Bhattacharyya, S., Chaki, N., Konar, D., Chakraborty, Udit Kr., Singh, C.T. (eds.) Advanced Computational and Communication Paradigms. AISC, vol. 706, pp. 51–61. Springer, Singapore (2018). https://doi.org/10.1007/978-981-10-8237-5_6
9. Moller, M.F.: A scaled conjugate gradient algorithm for fast supervised learning. Neural Netw. **6**(4), 525–533 (1993)
10. Yuan, X., Yang, Z., Zouridakis, G.: SVM-based texture classification and application to early melanoma detection. In: 28th Annual International Conference of the IEEE Engineering in Medicine and Biology Society, EMBS 2006 (2006)
11. Maglogiannis, I., Zafiropoulos, E., Anagnostopoulos, I.: An intelligent system for automated breast cancer diagnosis and prognosis using SVM based classifiers. Appl. Intell. **30**(1), 24–36 (2009)
12. Farooq, M.A., Azhar, M.A.M., Raza, R.H.: Automatic Lesion Detection System (ALDS) for skin cancer classification using SVM and neural classifiers. In: 2016 IEEE 16th International Conference on Bioinformatics and Bioengineering (BIBE) (2016)
13. Hagan, M.T., Demuth, H.B., Beale, M.H.: Neural Network Design. Pws, Boston (1996)

An Algorithm for Selecting Optimal Trust Path in Online Social Networks Using Particle Swarm Optimization

Munmun Bhattacharya[✉] and Debanjana Ghosh

Department of Information Technology, Jadavpur University, Kolkata, India
munmunds@gmail.com, dghosh2992@gmail.com

Abstract. In this decade online social networks (OSNs) become very popular and it attracts millions of people. Everyday a set of the new users are joining on different social networking sites. Sometimes one user needs to communicate with a totally unknown user for several purposes. If two unknown participants wish to communicate with each other, the evaluation of their trustworthiness along a certain trust path between them within the social network is required. But trustworthiness is a subjective parameter and it depends on the role that the participants play within the network. One end user can measure the trustworthiness of its own single hops connections. But when they need to know the authenticity of a user who is not directly connected with them, then the requirement of multi-hop trust path arise. In a social network graph, multiple trust paths are possible [4] between two users. In this paper we have tried to describe an optimal trust path selection algorithm using Particle swarm intelligence technique; so that one end user can conclude the trustworthiness of another end user, even they are totally unknown to each other. We have tested our algorithm using some real-world datasets.

Keywords: Social network · Local trust · Trusted path · Trustworthy · PSO

1 Introduction

With the emergence of the online social network, every day huge amount of data, in form of picture, text, and video are uploaded to the network. For different reasons, people need to share their personal or confidential information with other users of the network. That's why it becomes a very important issue to recognize trustworthiness [3, 14] of a user inside the network. In the real world, if anyone needs to know trustworthiness of an unknown person, they can ask the where about of that person to their friend or familiar. But in the online network, as it is a virtual world, it is not so easy to find the trustworthiness of a stranger. Moreover, there are many services oriented platform available on the internet where the requester and the service provider both trustor and trustee wants to know the trustworthiness and the quality of the services [13, 15]. In a social network graph if a participant wants to know the trustworthiness between two nodes, then it is required to establish a distributed trust mechanism, to find an optimal trust path [6–10, 12] between them.

© Springer Nature Singapore Pte Ltd. 2019
J. K. Mandal et al. (Eds.): CICBA 2018, CCIS 1030, pp. 144–154, 2019.
https://doi.org/10.1007/978-981-13-8578-0_12

A number of algorithms such as Bellman-Ford dynamic algorithm, Dijkstra's algorithm [1] can be used for finding optimal trust path between two pairs of the node. But these traditional algorithms have some shortcomings; firstly, they are only appropriate for the graph without negative edge weights. Another problem with these algorithms is they can search only for the most optimal route. They cannot determine any other similar/non-similar optimal trust routes. Moreover, they are very efficient for static networks, in the dynamic network environment; their computational complexity goes very high.

With Artificial neural network (ANN) we can get the optimal route [2] very fast. But the problem is with increasing number of network nodes complexity of the hardware increases considerably and the reliability of the solution decreases. It is less adaptable in the dynamic network graph, including the weight of the edges. ANNs also find the most optimal path, without considering sub-optimal paths [11].

The rest of the paper is organized as follows: next section outlines the literature review of previous works. Section 3 describes the problem formulation. In Sect. 4, the proposed algorithm is discussed. The implementation, details of experimental results and analysis is given in Sect. 5. Conclusion and future works are presented in Sect. 6.

2 Literature Review

2.1 A Basic Overview of PSO

Particle Swarm Optimization (PSO) [5] is a computational method that optimizes a problem by iteratively trying to improve a candidate solution with regard to a given measure of quality. It solves a problem by having a population of candidate solutions, here dubbed particles, and moving these particles around in the search-space according to simple mathematical formulae over the particle's position and velocity. Each particle's movement is influenced by its local best-known position, and also guided toward the best-known positions in the search-space, which are updated as better positions are found by other particles. This is expected to move the swarm toward the best solutions.

Particle swarm optimization, a population-based stochastic optimization technique which is inspired by the social behavior of birds flock and fish school etc., was developed by Kennedy and Eberhart [5]. Particle swarm optimization has roots in two main component methodologies. Perhaps more obvious are its ties to artificial life in general and to bird flocking, fish schooling, and swarming theory in particular. It is also related to evolutionary computation, and has ties to both genetic algorithms and evolutionary programming [5].

The initial idea of particle swarms was developed by Kennedy, a social psychologist, and Eberhart, an electrical engineer, which was essentially aimed at producing computational intelligence by exploiting simple analogs of social interaction, rather than purely individual cognitive abilities. The first simulations [5] were influenced by Heppner and Grenander's work [16] and involved analogs of bird flocks searching for corn. These ideas soon developed into a powerful optimization method, called as Particle Swarm Optimization (PSO).

The algorithmic flow in PSO starts with a population of particles whose positions, that represent the potential solutions for the studied problem, and velocities are randomly initialized in the search space. The search for the optimal position (solution) is performed by updating the particle velocities, hence positions, in each iteration or generation in a specific manner as follows.

In every iteration, the fitness of each particle's position is determined by some defined fitness measure and the velocity of each particle is updated by keeping track of two "best" positions. The first one is the best position (solution) a particle has traversed so far. This value is called pBest. Another "best" value is the best position (solution) that any neighbor of a particle has traversed so far. This best value is a neighborhood best and is called nBest. When a particle takes the whole population as its neighborhood, the neighborhood best becomes the global best and is called as gBest accordingly. A particle's velocity and position are updated as follows.

$$v_{id} = v_{id} + c_1 r_1 (p_{id} - x_{id}) + c_2 r_2 (g_{id} - x_{id}); \tag{1}$$

$$x_{id} = x_{id} + v_{id} \tag{2}$$

Where,
$i = 1, 2, \ldots\ldots, N$ and
$d = 1, 2, \ldots\ldots, D$
c_1 and c_2 are positive constants, called acceleration coefficients,
N is the total number of particles in the swarm,
D is the dimension of problem search space, i.e. number of parameters of the function being optimized,
r_1 and r_2 are two independently generated random numbers in the range[0,1].

The other vectors are defined as:

$x_i = [x_{i1}, x_{i2}, \ldots\ldots, x_{iD}]$ is the position of ith particle;
$v_i = [v_{i1}, v_{i2}, \ldots\ldots, v_{iD}]$ is the velocity of ith particle;
$p_i = [p_{i1}, p_{i2}, \ldots\ldots, p_{iD}]$ is the best position of the ith particle or pBest$_i$;
$g_i = [g_{i1}, g_{i2}, \ldots\ldots, g_{iD}]$ is the best position found by the neighborhood of the particle i or gBest$_i$.

Equation (1) calculates a new velocity for each particle by using its previous velocity, the particle's position at which the best possible fitness has been achieved so far, and the neighbors' best position achieved. Equation (2) updates each particle's position in the solution hyperspace. Here, c1 and c2 are two learning factors, which control the influence of pBest and gBest on the search process. In all initial studies of PSO, both c1 and c2 are taken to be 2.0 yielding good results [5]. However, in most cases, the velocities quickly attain very large values, especially for particles far from their global best. As a result, particles have larger position updates with particles leaving boundary of the search space. As a result, particles have larger position updates with particles leaving boundary of the search space. To control the increase in velocity,

velocity clamping is used in Eq. (1). Thus, if the right side of Eq. (1) exceeds a specified maximum value V_{max}, then the velocity on that dimension is clamped to V_{max}.

2.2 Overview of Online Social Network

Online social networking sites in the Internet have the same common goal [15]; the service providers manage an online virtual community wherein users are free to create their profiles and share their profiles, common interests and behavior with other people.

3 Problem Formulation

A social network graph can be defined as $G\ (V,\ E,\ T_{ij})$ where V is the set of vertices $\{v_i\}$, and each vertex represents an individual in the social network. $E \subseteq V \times V$ is the set of edges (relationships) between vertices; T_{ij} is a non-negative number representing trust value between vertex v_i to v_j. Though trust is a very subjective parameter and it can vary from individual to individual. Trust value from vertex v_i to v_j may not be the same as v_j to v_i ($T_{ij} \neq T_{ji}$). But for simplicity in this paper, we use only undirected graph so we use $G\ (V,\ E)$ to define a social network graph. We use vertex and node interchangeably throughout the paper.

An optimal trust path is a path from vertex v_i to vertex v_j. A path is a sequence vertex (v_i, v_k, v_l, ..., v_j) with edges where one vertex will appear only once. The optimal trust path problem is to select a path between two nodes having maximum trust value with the minimum number of hops.

3.1 Path Finding Algorithm

For finding optimal trust path, we incorporated a method that at each step we choose the edge with the highest trust value but the path will be with the minimum number of hop. To achieve this target, instead of all original trust values in the trust graph, are replaced by their reciprocals. Then we use the particle swarm optimization algorithm for finding the shortest path, where we actually get the most trusted path with the minimum number of hops [12].

For an original graph G_{uv} where u and v are directly connected node with trust value T_{uv}; another graph G'_{uv} is constructed as

$$G'_{uv} = \begin{cases} \frac{1}{T_{uv}} \ if\ T_{uv}! = 0 \\ 0 \ \ otherwise \end{cases}$$

The idea is to make the smaller trust value larger and larger value smaller. To understand the design, suppose for a given set of three ratings: 2, 4, and 5.

Ratings: 2, 4, 5 (Ascending order)
Reciprocals: $\frac{1}{2}, \frac{1}{4}, \frac{1}{5}$ (Descending order $\sim$0.5, 0.25, 0.2)

Thus we see how the highest rating 5 became the smallest trust rating 0.2 and the smallest value 2 becomes the largest element 0.5. For clear explanation of our algorithm, w take a synthetic graph in Fig. 1 with original trust rating, then we replace the edge weight with their reciprocals in Fig. 2. Now if we apply Dijkstra's Shortest Path Algorithm in the second graph, we can easily get the shortest path from the resultant matrix. Suppose, if we want to know the most trusted path from Node 5 to Node 6. There is more than one alternate trusted path from the source to the destination. But our target is to select the path [5-1-6], which is actually most trusted path with least minimum hops. For getting this result we use Particle Swarm Optimization.

Instead of PSO algorithm, Dijkstra's algorithm can be used. But Dijkstra's algorithm has some drawback; firstly, it can be applicable for the graph without negative edge weights, but in reality trust rating may be neagative. Another problem with this algorithm is it can search only for the most optimal route. It cannot determine any other similar/non-similar optimal routes. Finally, it is very efficient for static graphs, but real trust graphs are dynamic in nature, where the computational complexity of the algorithm is relatively very high.

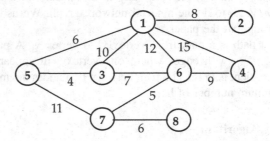

Fig. 1. A sample graph with original trust rating

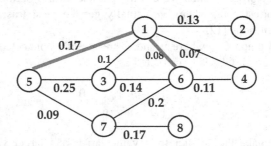

Fig. 2. After modifying trust rating of the graph of Fig. 1

4 Proposed Algorithm

After modifying the graph weight, we use the particle swarm optimization algorithm to select the most optimal shortest path. For our specified problem, we decode the PSO parameter with the graph parameter in the following way:

Particle(i) = a path from the initial node to the destination node
Cost of the Particle = 1/weight
Initial velocity of a particle = zero.

Then in each iteration, the velocity of the particles gets updated according the following equation (which is corresponding equation of Eq. 1):

$$\text{particle(i).Velocity} = w^*\text{particle(i).Velocity} + c1^*\text{rand}^*(\text{particle(i).Best.Position} - \text{particle(i).Position}) + c2^*\text{rand}^*(\text{GlobalBest.Position} - \text{particle(i).Position}) \tag{3}$$

where, i = 0 to maximum number of particle
particle(i).Best.Position = the pBest or the best position of that particular particle. It is calculated in terms of particle cost. The lesser is the cost; the better is the position of the particle.
GlobalBest.Position = the gBest or the position of the particle who has the best position among all other particles.
Acceleration coefficients c1 and c2 are set to 2 as the values of c1 and c2 are suggested as 2 in PSO literature.

Initial particle position is taken as random. Then in each iteration, position of the particle gets updated according to the following equation:

$$\text{particle(i).Best.Position} = \text{particle(i).Position} + \text{particle(i).Velocity} \tag{4}$$

$$\text{particle(i).Position} = \text{unifrnd(VarMin, VarMax, VarSize)} \tag{5}$$

where, particle(i).Velocity is calculated according to Eq. (3).
particle(i).Position gets updated according to the Eq. (5).
Velocity bound: The velocity is bounded in between $-V\text{max}$ to $+V\text{max}$.
VarMin = $-V\text{max}$
VarMax = $+V\text{max}$.

Decode(particle)
Particle = a path from the initial node (s) to the destination node (t), the edges are appended into the path consecutively.

Repeat this step until a particle is formed.

Step 1: First the initial node is selected.

Step 2: Then next node (node$_j$) is selected from the nodes having direct links with the current node such that the corresponding edge weight is minimum, that is,

$$j = \min\{T_{ij} \mid (i, j) \in E\}.$$

Step 3: Repeat step 2 until the destination node (t) is reached.

Optimum Trust Path Selection Algorithm

Input:

    n← number of nodes in the network

    G ← Adjacency list with trust value Tij

    where i, j are directly connected neighbours

    s ←source node

    t ← target node

    Population_size← total number of particle

    Iteration ← Maximum iteration the algorithm will execute

Algorithm:

    Repeat the following steps until termination condition holds:

    for i = 0 to population_size

    {

        Path=decode(particle)   // Find the optimal path

        Trust=cost(Path)   //calculate trust value of ith particle

        if the Trust of ith paricle > Trust of pBest

        {

            pBest = position of ith particle

            VpBest = Velocity of ith particle

        }

        choose the Particle with the best trust value of all particle as gBest

        for i = 0 to population_size

        {

            calculate new velocity of ith particle according to (1)

            calculate new position of ith particle according to (2)

        }

Output:

    Particle having minimum path weight is selected.

    Actually this is the optimal trust path with minimum number of hops.

5   Implementation Results and Analysis

5.1   Experimental Design

For trying to measure the performance of our algorithm, we simulate a computer environment in Windows 7 and design a software program using Python, where we store the online social graphs information in the text file and the graphs will form in our program at the time of execution as an adjacency list representation. Next, we implement the decoding part of the particle where a full path from source to destination may be existing or non-existing. Then the algorithm gets executed and finds the particle with minimum value, which is actually the shortest path.

5.2   Results and Analysis

Our main target in this paper was the algorithm is working correctly or not. Moreover can we get the optimal trust path or not? Using a several no of test cases (Demonstrated in Table 1), we have tried to find out that we are getting actual shortest path or not and the corresponding execution time. We execute our algorithm and the particle that is selected as optimal one, for accuracy we compared the path with Dijkstra's algorithm to known the path is exactly shortest or not.

Table 1. Different testing environment with no of Particle 50, 60, 70, 90, 130, 150, 200

Dataset	Number of users	No of Edges	No of Iteration
Zachary	34	78	50/100/200
Freeman	48	347	50/100/200
Advogato	6542	32608	50/100/200

In Table 2, we have demonstrated the accuracy of our algorithm. As the Iteration number and particle size is fixed, execution will going on until the total number of iteration is over even if the optimal result is reached. Different execution time is shown in Table 3 and the data is also represented in graphical view in Figs. 3, 4 and 5.

Table 2. Frequency for obtaining Optimal Trust Path

Dataset	Number of users	Our Algorithm
Zachary	34	99%
Freeman	47	98.5%
Advogato	6542	98%

Table 3. Execution time in millisecond with different test environment

No of	Iteration = 50			Iteration = 100			Iteration = 200		
particle	Advogato	Freeman	Zachary	Advogato2	Freeman2	Zachary2	Advogato22	Freeman22	Zachary23
50	37.537	0.411	0.169	110.891	0.514	0.322	215.928	0.811	0.809
60	44.7065	0.288	0.35	104.91	0.496	0.454	220.002	0.911	1.5
70	53.5778	0.256	0.379	110.356	0.682	0.682	178.435	1.2911	1.222
90	105.016	0.34	0.3685	117.747	0.81	0.893	352.046	1.697	1.697
130	113.035	0.505	0.447	130.035	0.69	0.625	342.226	1.957	1.904
150	141.393	0.686	0.738	186.587	1.116	0.856	438.267	1.076	2.12
190	144.711	1.988	0.757	208.077	1.591	1.725	673.443	2.372	2.678
200	163.4988	1.67	0.634	236.377	1.336	1.218	628.544	5.261	2.672

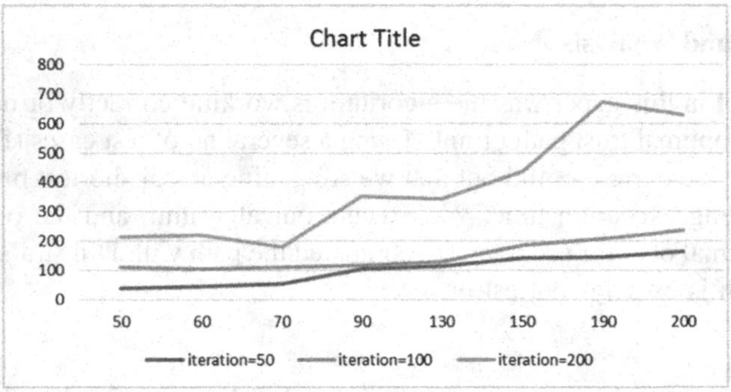

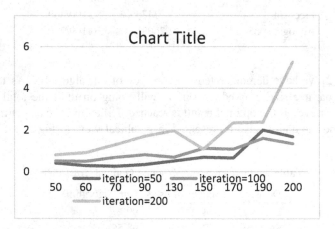

Fig. 3. Result on Advogato graph start_node = 2, end_node = 3000 (Time in millisecond)

Fig. 4. Result on Freeman data, start_node = 1, end_node = 37 (Time in millisecond)

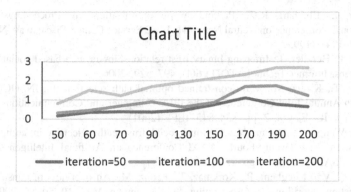

Fig. 5. Result on Zachary Club data, start_node = 2, end_node = 16, no_of_node = 35 (Time in millisecond)

6 Conclusion

Before involving a new relationships or sharing personal information, recognizing the trustworthiness of the people is a primary concern in online social networks. To address these issues, we have tried to present an algorithm for finding optimal and reliable trust path in large online social networks. In trust rating estimation accuracy is very much depended on the length of the path. With experimental evaluation; we have tried to determine that our algorithm is very efficient to find the trust path. We use some small world real datasets for algorithmic analysis. Finally, some statistical results of the experimental research were presented and interpreted.

We only tried to propose an algorithm for finding shortest and more trusted path here. We have not fully compared this algorithm with other existing algorithm. For small graph still Dijkstra's algorithm takes less time than our algorithm. In near future we would like to invent more prominent algorithm to gain improved accuracy using less runtime. Performance and execution time fully depends on no of iteration and no of particle we have taken for the execution. There is no such ideal condition to address the optimization.

References

1. Lawler, E.L.: Combinatorial Optimization: Networks and Matroids, pp. 59–108. Holt, Rinehart, and Winston, New York (1976)
2. Ali, M.K.M., Kamoun, F.: Neural networks for shortest path computation and routing in computer networks. IEEE Trans. Neural Networks **4**(6), 941–954 (1993)
3. Grabner-Kräuter, S., Bitter, S.: Trust in online social networks: a multifaceted perspective. Forum Soc. Econ. **44**(1), 48–68 (2015)
4. Mohemmed, A.W., Sahoo, N.C.: Efficient computation of shortest paths in networks using particle swarm optimization and noising metaheuristics. Discrete Dyn. Nat. Soc. **2007**, 25 (2007)

5. Kennedy, J., Eberhart, R.C.: Particle swarm optimization. In: Proceedings of IEEE International Conference on Neural Networks, IEEE Service Center, Piscataway, NJ, vol. IV, pp. 1942–1948 (1995)
6. Golbeck, J., Hendler, J.: Inferring binary trust relationships in web-based social networks. ACM Trans. Internet Technol. (TOIT) 6(4), 497–529 (2006)
7. Korkmaz, T., Krunz, M.: Multi-constrained optimal path selection. In: INFOCOM 2001. Twentieth Annual Joint Conference of the IEEE Computer and Communications Societies. Proceedings. IEEE, Vol. 2, pp. 834–843. IEEE (2001)
8. Liu, G., Wang, Y., Orgun, M.: Optimal social trust path selection in complex social networks. In: The Twenty-Fourth AAAI Conference on Artificial Intelligence, Atlanta, Georgia, USA, 11–15 July, pp. 1391–1398 (2010)
9. Kuipers, F., Van Mieghem, P., Korkmaz, T., Krunz, M.: An overview of constraint-based path selection algorithms for QoS routing. IEEE Commun. Mag. 40, 50–55 (2002)
10. Zeng, Z., Gao, Y., Chen, Z., Deng, X.: Trust path-searching algorithm based on PSO. In: The 9th International Conference for Young Computer Scientists, pp. 1975–1979 (2008)
11. Xu, G., Xu, C., Tian, X., Zhang, L., Li, X., Li, W.: PSO-TPS: an optimal trust path selection algorithm based on particle swarm optimization in small world network. In: Proceedings of 2nd International Conference on Cloud Green Computing, pp. 594–600, November 2012
12. Bhattacharya, M., Nesa, N.: An algorithm for predicting local trust based on trust propagation in online social networks. IJCA (0975– 8887) 156(7), 8–15 (2016)
13. Hang, C.-W., Wang, Y., Singh, M.P.: Operators for propagating trust and their evaluation in social networks. In: Proceedings of the 8th International Conference on Autonomous Agents and Multiagent Systems. International Foundation for Autonomous Agents and Multiagent Systems, vol. 2, pp. 1025–1032 (2009)
14. Abdul-Rahman, A., Hailes, S.: Supporting trust in virtual communities. In: Proceedings of the 33rd Annual Hawaii International Conference on System Sciences, 2000, pp. 9–pp. IEEE (2000)
15. Zhang, Z.: Feeling the sense of community in social networking usage. IEEE Trans. Eng. Manage. 57(2), 225–239 (2010)
16. Heppner, F., Grenander, U.: A stochastic nonlinear model for coordinated bird flocks. In: The Ubiquity of Chaos, pp. 233–238 (1990)

Different Schemes for Improving Fuzzy Clustering Through Supervised Learning

Anup Kumar Mallick[1]([✉]) and Anirban Mukhopadhyay[2]([✉])

[1] Department of Electronics and Communication Engineering,
Kalyani Government Engineering College, Kalyani 741235, India
anupratan@gmail.com
[2] Department of Computer Science and Engineering, University of Kalyani,
Kalyani 741235, India
anirban@klyuniv.ac.in

Abstract. Clustering is an important unsupervised learning tool to find natural grouping of instances from a given unlabeled data based on some similarity/dissimilarity measures. However, clustering the data points at the boundary of multiple overlapping clusters is really a challenge. The challenge also lies in many real life applications where the boundaries among clusters are not rigid and clear. There are several hard and soft clustering algorithms which attempt to address these challenges. Hard clustering algorithms though perform well in the presence of well separated clusters, it shows poor performance in presence of such difficulties mentioned above. Researchers have recommended several soft clustering algorithms for handling such dilemma. In this article, we have proposed different schemes toward improvement of Fuzzy clustering employing supervised classification. The superiority of our prescribed schemes are demonstrated by comparing its performance with that of Fuzzy c-means clustering. The comparison has also been made among different schemes we have proposed in this article.

Keywords: Fuzzy c-means algorithm · K-means algorithm ·
K-nearest neighbors classifier · Cluster validity indices

1 Introduction

The interest in clustering has been growing rapidly in the last few decades. There is no universally accepted definition for clustering [1,2]. In simple words the purpose of clustering is to group similar objects in the same cluster and dissimilar objects in different clusters. Clustering algorithms can broadly be categorized into hard and soft clustering algorithms. The hard clustering algorithm like K-means [3,4] assign each object to a particular cluster. However, these classical hard clustering algorithms many a times miss-cluster real-life applications where overlapping clusters, objects on boundary of clusters are found. The soft clustering provide soft boundaries to incorporate objects on the boundary of clusters.

© Springer Nature Singapore Pte Ltd. 2019
J. K. Mandal et al. (Eds.): CICBA 2018, CCIS 1030, pp. 155–164, 2019.
https://doi.org/10.1007/978-981-13-8578-0_13

One of the most popular soft computing algorithms is Fuzzy c-means (FCM) clustering algorithm [5] where each object is assigned with certain membership value [0,1] to each cluster.

By this time, several modifications in different approaches were recommended to improve the performance of fuzzy clustering. Maji *et al.* [6–8] integrated the principle of Rough and Fuzzy sets to incorporate both the probalistic and possibilitic membership simultaneously for reducing noise sensitivity of FCM and coincident clusters of PCM (Possibilistic c-means). Pedrycz [9] coined the concept of collaborative fuzzy clustering where several subsets of patterns were processed together with an objective to find a structure that is common to all and this approach was refined later by Shen and Pedrycz [10]. However, the present work is improvement of fuzzy clustering using supervised learning and it was mainly inspired by the following two modifications [11,12]. Mukhopadhyay and Maulik [11] proposed to train Support Vector Machine based classifier by the data points having higher membership degree to the clusters and the class labels of the remaining data points are predicted by the trained classifier. But, the sizes of training and testing data points were not specifically fixed, rather they took the size iteratively from a predefined lower and upper value. Attempt was also made by Bandhopahyay, Mukhopadhyay and Maulik [12] to consider the data points having the difference between the highest membership value and the next highest membership value higher than a certain tuning parameter as the training data points. In that article also the tuning parameter was not specifically fixed. The last two approaches motivated to find a specific threshold point. In this article, we have proposed four schemes to set the threshold. For easy discussion, the data points crossing the threshold have been termed as core data points and the others as boundary data points. Here, we have employed weighted K-nn classifier to be trained by the core data points and the class labels of the boundary data points have been predicted by this trained classifier. The superiority of our schemes was checked by comparing the performance of our proposed schemes with that of traditional FCM algorithm. The comparison among our different proposed schemes were also done.

The rest of this article is arranged as follows: the next section describes the Fuzzy c-means clustering algorithm. In Sect. 3 weighted K-nearest neighbors classifier has been discussed. Section 4 describes our proposed clustering schemes. Data Set and performance metrics we have used have been illustrated in Sect. 5. In Sect. 6 the performance of our proposed algorithm has been evaluated and compared with existing clustering algorithms. Finally we conclude the article in Sect. 7.

2   Fuzzy C-Means Clustering Algorithm

FCM is a popular soft clustering method developed by Dunn in 1973 and later improved by Bezdek in 1981 [5]. The aim of the algorithm is to partition a given data set into a set of c fuzzy partitions. It allows each data point to belong to two or more clusters with certain membership degrees [0,1] such that the sum of the memberships of any data point to all the clusters is 1. It is based on minimizing the following objective function:

$$J_m = \sum_{i=1}^{n}\sum_{k=1}^{c} u_{ki}^m \|z_k - x_i\|^2, \tag{1}$$

where n is the number of objects, c is the number of clusters, u_{ki} denotes the fuzzy membership degree of point i to cluster k and m indicates the fuzzy control exponent and it is any real number greater than 1. In our article we have set m as 2. Here, z_k denotes the center of the kth cluster, x_i is the ith data point and $\|.\|$ means inner product induced norm. FCM algorithm attempts to optimize the position of the cluster centers iteratively. It returns with finite number of cluster centers and a partition matrix in which each element has degree of membership to each cluster. It starts with initializing the cluster centers and then at each iteration the fuzzy membership of each data point to each cluster is calculated using the formula given in the following Eq. (2)

$$u_{ki} = \frac{1}{\sum_{j=1}^{c}\left(\frac{\|z_k - x_i\|}{\|z_j - x_i\|}\right)^{\frac{2}{m-1}}} \quad \text{for } 1 \le k \le c \text{ and } 1 \le i \le n. \tag{2}$$

Clearly, more the data point is close to a cluster center more is its membership to that cluster. Then the cluster centers are updated or recomputed using the following Eq. (3)

$$z_k = \frac{\sum_{i=1}^{n} u_{ki}^m . x_i}{\sum_{i=1}^{n} u_{ki}^m}. \tag{3}$$

The algorithm stops when there is no more significant displacement of cluster centers. Finally each data point is assigned to the cluster in which it has the maximum membership. Though it is one of the most popular soft clustering techniques it is prone to getting trapped at some suboptimal point [13].

3   Weighted K-nearest neighbors classifier

The power of neighbors in classification was proposed in 1967 by Cover and Hant in their paper [14] where they claim that half the classification information in an infinite sample set is contained in the nearest neighbors. Thereafter several efforts were put forwarded toward development of K-nearest neighbors (K-nn) algorithm for classification and regression. K-nn is a popular, nonparametric and instance based technique used for classification and regression. It is nonparametric [15] in the sense that it does not make any assumption on the underlying data distribution and instance-based means the prediction of output class depends solely on the training data set of that particular instance. K-nn classifier has no model other than storing the entire data set, so no learning is required. It finds k nearest neighbors of the test data point from the training data points. To determine which k objects are nearest a distance measure is used. K-nn classifier deploys different techniques to calculate the distance namely Euclidean distance, Manhattan distance, Minkowski distance, Hamming distance and Cosine distance etc.. Once the k nearest neighbors of the test object is selected, the output class is predicted with the highest frequency from the k-most similar instances. Each instance in essence vote for their class with most voted class is considered as prediction. By this time Several variations and modifications of K-nn classifier like distance weighted K-nn classifier [16] have been proposed. In distance weighted K-nn classifier each k neighbors is assigned with a weight depending on the distance of the neighboring points from the data point whose class is to be predicted. The philosophy behind weighted K-nn is that one is more influenced by closer neighborhood than that of farther neighborhood. There exists different weighing methods like inverse, squared inverse or self defined. When tie occurs due to equal numbers of votes to multiple classes, it is resolved by considering one of the class randomly or by the nearest or by the smallest class between the equally voted class.

4   Proposed Clustering Techniques

This section illustrate our proposed schemes for improvement of clustering algorithm. At first we have executed the classical FCM Algorithm for clustering a data set. Thereafter the decision of core data and boundary data has been taken. In the second stage the weighted K-nn classifier has been trained by the core data points and finally the boundary points have been assigned to their respective clusters by the trained classifier.

4.1   First Stage: Selection of Core Data

Initially, the given data set has been clustered by classical fuzzy c-means clustering algorithm which provides cluster centers and fuzzy membership grades to which data points belong to each cluster. Suppose, the highest membership of data point x_i is denoted by u_{hi}, next highest membership by u_{nhi} and the difference between the highest membership u_{hi} and the next highest membership u_{nhi} is denoted by Δu_i and is expressed by $\Delta u_i = u_{hi} - u_{nhi}$. This difference between the highest membership and the next highest membership has a significant importance. It is obvious that more the membership difference of a data point, the higher will be its chance to be nearer the cluster center or in the core region of a cluster and in its contrary a less membership difference indicates the data point to be on the boundary of multiple clusters. Selecting a threshold of membership difference above which data points will be treated as core data decide the performance of the clustering algorithm. A large value of threshold allows only a few data points to the core thereby missing incorporation of several core data points, whereas a small value of threshold permits more data points to the core set though some of them are on or close to the boundary of different clusters. Therefore, in rest of the subsection we have discussed our four different proposed schemes to judiciously select this threshold.

In **Single mean** scheme the mean value of membership difference Δu_i for all the data points is selected as threshold, here denoted by $\Delta u_{threshold}$ written in Eq. 4.

$$\Delta u_{threshold} = \frac{1}{n}\sum_{i=1}^{n}\Delta u_i, \qquad (4)$$

here n is the number of data points. Thus the data points which have the membership value Δu_i greater than the threshold given by Eq. 4 will be put in the core set, otherwise in the boundary set. Essentially, as the decision regarding the selection of core data points and boundary data points has been taken by a single mean, we have named this scheme as single mean scheme.

In **Single median** scheme the membership difference of all data points is sorted in ascending order and is kept in a vector U_{srtd}. Here the median of sorted membership vector U_{srtd} is selected as threshold $\Delta u_{threshold}$ and is given by Eq. 5.

$$\Delta u_{threshold} = \begin{cases} U_{srtd}\left(\frac{n+1}{2}\right), & \text{if n is odd} \\ \frac{U_{srtd}\left(\frac{n}{2}\right)+U_{srtd}\left(\frac{n}{2}+1\right)}{2}, & \text{if n is even} \end{cases} \qquad (5)$$

Here $U_{srtd}(i)$ denotes the ith term of the vector U_{srtd}. These two schemes do not ensure selection of data points from each cluster of data set. Another two schemes named by us as *Clusterwise mean* and *Clusterwise median* aim to select core data points from each cluster. Thus threshold is selected for each cluster. In **Clusterwise mean** the threshold of a cluster j is the mean value of membership differences Δu_i of the data points belonging to that particular cluster and is given in Eq. 6.

$$\Delta u_{threshold}(j) = \frac{1}{n_j}\sum_{p\in C_j}\Delta u_p. \qquad (6)$$

Here C_j denotes the jth cluster, n_j is the number of data points in j^{th} cluster, p is the index of data points belonging to j^{th} cluster and is subset of $i(p \sqsubseteq i)$, where i is a set given by 1,2,3,...,n and n is the number of whole data points. The objects having membership difference Δu_i greater than the threshold $\Delta u_{threshold}$ of that cluster is regarded as core data. The core data set is the collection of data points having membership difference more than that their respective cluster threshold. The similar approach is taken in **Clusterwise median** scheme where membership difference of a cluster is sorted in ascending order and the median of this sorted membership difference is selected as the threshold for that cluster given in Eq. 7.

$$\Delta u_{threshold}(j) = \begin{cases} U_{srt}^{j}\left(\frac{n_j+1}{2}\right), & \text{if } n_j \text{ is odd} \\ \frac{U_{srt}^{j}\left(\frac{n_j}{2}\right)+U_{srt}^{j}\left(\frac{n_j}{2}+1\right)}{2}, & \text{if } n_j \text{ is even} \end{cases} \qquad (7)$$

Here U_{srt}^{j} is the vector consisting of the sorted membership differences in ascending order of the data points belonging to the jth cluster, n_j is the number of data points in the jth cluster and $U_{srt}^{j}(i)$ is the ith term of U_{srt}^{j}. Similar to

Clusterwise mean here also the whole core data set is formed by picking data points crossing their respective cluster threshold.

4.2 Second Stage: Assignment of Boundary Points

The core data points are more confident regarding clustering as they are closer to the cluster centers than the boundary data points. This motivated to deploy a classifier for training by the core data points. Thus after the first stage the core objects were fed to a weighted K-nn classifier which returned the predicted class levels of boundary data points.

5 Experimental Results

The performance of the proposed algorithm has been checked on different synthetic data sets (Data 1, Data 2, Data 3) and real-life data sets (Iris, Zoo, Thyroid). The proposed schemes have been compared with themselves and with that of fuzzy clustering using different cluster validity indices i.e., Adjusted Rand Index and Minkowski Score.

5.1 Synthetic Data Sets

Data 1: This data set has been generated artificially. This data set has 500 objects each with 20 features and the number of clusters is 5.
Data 2: Data 2 is an another synthetic data set which also consists of 500 objects but have 30 attributes in each data. This data set is divided into 5 clusters.
Data 3: This data set is bigger one, having 1200 data points with 30 features partitioned in 6 clusters.

5.2 Real-Life Data Sets

Iris: It is one of the most popular data sets in clustering. The data set consists of 150 data of flowers with 4 attributes length and width of sepals and petals. The flowers belong to three different classes namely iris setosa, iris virginica and iris versicolor.

Zoo: This data set consists of 101 data of different types of animal. Each data point consists of 17 features where the first attribute is animal name which has been ignored here. There are 15 boolean attributes corresponding to hair, features, eggs, milk, airbone, aquatic, predator, toothed, backbone, breathes, venomous, fins, tail, domestice and catsize, and a set of values: {0,2,4,5,6,8} corresponding to the attribute - legs. The data set contains 7 different classes of animals.

Thyroid: It has 215 data points which is divided into 3 classes. Each data point is consist of 5 features and these are T-3 resin uptake test(a percentage), Total Serum thyroxin as measured by the isotopic displacement method, Total serum triiodothyronine as measured by radioimmuno assay, basal thyroid-stimulating hormone (TSH) as measured by radioimmuno assay, maximal absolute difference of TSH value after injection of 200 micro grams of thyrotropin-releasing hormone as compared to the basal value.

The real life data sets have been collected from UCI Machine Learning Repository (https://archive.ics.uci.edu/ml/index.php).

5.3 Performance Metrics

There are some indices to verify one's claim of superiority in clustering outcome to the others outcomes these are termed as performance metrics or cluster validity indices. Here we have used Adjusted rand index and Minkowski score for evaluation of different schemes. The indices are discussed below.

Adjusted rand index: The Adjusted Rand index (ARI) [17] is a measure of how much a clustering algorithm has achieved the true clustering or the known ground truth. Suppose T is the true clustering known from the domain knowledge and C is the result obtained from some clustering algorithm. Let a be the number of data pairs belonging to same cluster in both T and C, while b denotes the number of data pairs belonging to same cluster in T but to different clusters in C, the number of pairs belonging to different clusters in T but to the same cluster in C is denoted by c and d represents the number of pairs belonging to different clusters in both T and C. Then the Adjusted rand index is defined [18] as follows in Eq. 8.

$$ARI(T,C) = \frac{2(ad - bc)}{(a+b)(b+d) + (a+c)(c+d)}. \tag{8}$$

The value of Adjusted rand index ranges between 0 and 1. A higher value of ARI indicates closeness of the result to the true clustering.

Minkowski score: The Minkowski score [19] is an another important cluster validity index evaluated by normalized difference of true clustering matrix T and derived clustering matrix C. The score is calculated by the following Eq. 9.

$$MS(T,C) = \frac{\|T - C\|}{\|T\|}. \tag{9}$$

Here $\|C\| = \sqrt{\sum\sum C_{ij}}$ and $\|T\| = \sqrt{\sum\sum T_{ij}}$

C_{ij} is 1 if the data points i and j belong to same cluster in clustering C and 0 if they belong to different clusters. The Minkowski score ranges from 0 to infinity. Lower the value of the score better is the clustering.

5.4 Input Parameters

The parameters of the weighted K-nn classifier are selected by hit and trial method to obtain the best result. The number of neighboring points k is selected as 5 and distance measure is *cosine*. The weights of the neighboring points are set as squared-inverse to the distance between the test point and the neighboring point given in the following Eq. 10.

$$w_i = \frac{1}{d^2(x_p - x_i)}. \tag{10}$$

Here w_i is the weight of the ith neighbor x_i, x_p is the point whose class is to be predicted and d is the distance notion. The ties in weighted K-nn classifier are resolved by considering the nearest class in data sets between the equally voted classes.

Table 1. Average values of Adjusted Rand index and Minkowski score produced for proposed clustering algorithms over 10 runs comparing with FCM and among themselves

Data sets	Measure indices	FCM	Single mean	Single median	Clusterwise mean	Clusterwise median
Data 1	ARI	0.7607	0.5265	0.7264	0.8475	**0.8486**
	MS	0.4951	0.9356	0.5524	0.3556	**0.3541**
Data 2	ARI	0.5063	0.5213	0.5670	**0.7008**	0.6813
	MS	0.9484	0.9935	0.9273	**0.7306**	0.7529
Data 3	ARI	0.4218	0.5601	0.5604	**0.6220**	0.6104
	MS	1.0405	0.9467	0.9289	**0.8305**	0.8414
Iris	ARI	0.7330	**0.9418**	0.9232	**0.9418**	**0.9418**
	MS	0.5987	**0.2786**	0.3200	**0.2786**	**0.2786**
Zoo	ARI	0.5424	0.5652	0.5652	0.5866	**0.7858**
	MS	0.7835	0.7813	0.7813	0.7486	**0.5548**
Thyroid	ARI	0.4430	0.5197	0.5366	0.6504	**0.7180**
	MS	0.7258	0.6676	0.6542	0.5734	**0.5150**

6   Performance Evaluation

The average value of performance indices obtained by 10 consecutive iterations has been shown in Table 1. From the mentioned table, it is evident that the *Single mean* and *Single median* scheme outperforms FCM in the datasets *Data2*, *Data3*, *Iris*, *Zoo* and in *Thyroid*, whereas both the *Clusterwise mean* and *Clusterwise median* outperform FCM for all the data sets. The relatively poor performance of *Single mean* and *single median* schemes comes from the fact that if the data set is so distributed that data points from some particular clusters are only selected to core due to their higher value of difference of membership(Δu_i) and they are sent to the classifier, as a consequence the trained classifier assign the boundary points to that particular clusters thereby miss their actual cluster belongings.

This challenge motivated the authors to propose the other two schemes i.e., *Clusterwise mean* schemes and *Clusterwise median* schemes where some of the objects from each cluster essentially be selected as core and fed to the classifier for training. This ensures the improvement of the algorithm which is also evident from the result Table 1. *Clusterwise mean* is providing the best result for the data sets *Data1*, *Data2*, and*Data3* and *Clusterwise median* for the data sets *Zoo* and *Thyroid*. Besides *Clusterwise mean* and *Clusterwise median, Single mean* is also providing the best result for *Iris* Data set.

7   Conclusion

In this article, different algorithms for improvement of fuzzy clustering has been proposed. The performance of the proposed algorithms have been evaluated and compared. Clusterwise mean scheme or Clusterwise median scheme consistently outperforming fuzzy c-means algorithm and giving the best results for all the data sets used. Thus the authors recommend to apply **Clusterwise mean** scheme or **Clusterwise median** scheme to fetch best result.

In future the performance of the proposed algorithms may be improved by deploying other classifiers in place of weighted K-nn classifier as it's performance decreases with the increase in dimensionality(generally for more than 10)[20] of the data sets. The betterment can also be achieved by fine tuning the percentage of core and neighboring objects by exploiting the nature of the data distribution.

References

1. Hansen, P., Jaumard, B.: Cluster analysis and mathematical programming. Math. Program. **79**(1–3), 191–215 (1997)
2. Jain, A.K., Dubes, R.C.: Algorithms for Clustering Data. Prentice-Hall Inc., Upper Saddle River (1988)
3. Kanungo, T., Mount, D.M., Netanyahu, N.S., Piatko, C.D., Silverman, R., Wu, A.Y.: An efficient k-means clustering algorithm: analysis and implementation. IEEE Trans. Pattern Anal. Mach. Intell. **24**(7), 881–892 (2002)
4. Likas, A., Vlassis, N., Verbeek, J.J.: The global k-means clustering algorithm. Pattern Recogn. **36**(2), 451–461 (2003)
5. Bezdek, J.C.: Pattern Recognition with Fuzzy Objective Function Algorithms. Kluwer Academic Publishers, Norwell (1981)
6. Maji, P., Paul, S.: Robust rough-fuzzy c-means algorithm: design and applications in coding and non-coding RNA expression data clustering. Fundam. Inf. **124**, 153–174 (2013)
7. Maji, P., Pal, S.K.: Rough set based generalized fuzzy c -means algorithm and quantitative indices. IEEE Trans. Syst. Man Cybern. Part B Cybern. **37**(6), 1529–1540 (2007)
8. Maji, P., Roy, S.: Rough-fuzzy clustering and multiresolution image analysis for text-graphics segmentation. Appl. Soft Comput. **30**, 705–721 (2015)
9. Pedrycz, W.: Collaborative fuzzy clustering. Pattern Recogn. Lett. **23**, 1675–1686 (2002)

10. Shen, Y., Pedrycz, W.: Collaborative fuzzy clustering algorithm: some refinements. Int. J. Approximate Reasoning **86**, 41–61 (2017)
11. Mukhopadhyay, A., Maulik, U.: Towards improving fuzzy clustering using support vector machine: application to gene expression data. Pattern Recogn. **42**(11), 2744–2763 (2009)
12. Bandyopadhyay, S., Mukhopadhyay, A., Maulik, U.: An improved algorithm for clustering gene expression data. Bioinformatics **23**(21), 2859–2865 (2007)
13. Groll, L., Jakel, J.: A new convergence proof of fuzzy c-means. IEEE Trans. Fuzzy Syst. **13**(5), 717–720 (2005)
14. Cover, T., Hart, P.: Nearest neighbor pattern classification. IEEE Trans. Inf. Theory **13**(1), 21–27 (1967)
15. Altman, N.S.: An introduction to kernel and nearest-neighbor nonparametric regression. Taylor and Francis **46**(3), 175–185 (1992)
16. Samworth, R.J.: Optimal weighted nearest neighbour classifiers. Ann. Stat. **40**(5), 2733–2763 (2012)
17. Yeung, K.Y., Ruzzo, W.: Details of the adjusted rand index and clustering algorithms supplement to the paper (an emperical study on principal component analysis for clustering gene expression data). Bioinformatics **17**(3), 763–774 (2001)
18. Maulik, U., Mukhopadhyay, A., Bandyopadhyay, S.: Efficient clustering with multiclass point identification. J. 3D Images **17**, 763–774 (2001)
19. Saha, I., Mukhopadhyay, A.: Improved crisp and fuzzy clustering techniques for categorical data. IAENG Int. J. Comput. Sci. **35**(1), 438–450 (2008)
20. Beyer, K., Goldstein, J., Ramakrishnan, R., Shaft, U.: When is "nearest neighbor" meaningful? In: Beeri, C., Buneman, P. (eds.) ICDT 1999. LNCS, vol. 1540, pp. 217–235. Springer, Heidelberg (1999). https://doi.org/10.1007/3-540-49257-7_15

A Hybrid Model for Optimal Pseudorandom Bit Sequence Generation

Ramen Pal[1](✉) and Somnath Mukhopadhyay[2](✉)

[1] Department of Computer Science and Engineering, University of Kalyani,
Kalyani, India
ramen.pal673@gmail.com
[2] Department of Computer Science and Engineering, Assam University, Silchar, India
som.cse@live.com

Abstract. Chaotic map gained its importance in the field of cryptography, due to its properties like, randomness, unpredictability, sensitivity on initial condition, aperiodicity, which is used to generate pseudorandom bit streams. In this paper the optimal values of chaos parameters are generated through Real Coded Genetic Algorithm (RCGA), which is optimal, unpredictable, and optimally sensitive. Here, a non-deterministic RCGA based optimal pseudo-random bit sequence generator based on Chaotic maps, such as Logistic Chaotic map, Skew Tent Chaotic map, Cross Coupled Logistic Chaotic map, Cross Coupled Skew Tent Chaotic map is proposed. A real coded crossover and mutation technique is proposed for RCGA. Seed values for chaotic map have been optimized by using all sub-functions of GA (RCGA). These seed values are used to generate optimal pseudorandom bit stream of finite length. The randomness of the bit stream is tested by using *NIST statistical test suit*.

Keywords: Real coded genetic algorithm · Logistic Chaotic Map ·
Skewtent chaotic map · Cross Coupled Logistic Chaotic Map ·
Cross coupled skewtent chaotic map · NIST

1 Introduction

The tool is used to generate a random sequence is called Random Number Generator or RNG. RNG can be divided in two classes, viz, Pseudo Random Number Generator (PRNG) and Truly Random Number Generator (TRNG) [2]. PRNG algorithms are deterministic in nature [6], the input to this type of algorithm is called seed and the output of this type of algorithm is a pseudorandom bit sequence [1]. The deterministic nature of the aforementioned algorithm is useful to generate same bit sequence for a same seed multiple times.

Chaotic maps are evolution functions. In the domain of mathematics a chaotic map can be used to produce chaotic and unpredictable number sequence, for its deterministic simplicity and chaotic behavior. In last two decades it is seen that Chaotic map can be used to design deterministic random numbers generators or

J. K. Mandal et al. (Eds.): CICBA 2018, CCIS 1030, pp. 165–179, 2019.
https://doi.org/10.1007/978-981-13-8578-0_14

PRNG [21]. In 2013, Hu et al. proposed a Pseudorandom bit sequence generator(PRBG) based on Chen chaotic system [10]. In 2015 Martinez and Canton proposed a PRBG based on K-model maps [9]. In 2015 Sadkhan and Mohammad proposed a PRBG based on Unified chaotic map [19]. In 2014 Akhshani et al. proposed a PRBG based on Quantum chaotic map, and it showed that the output chaotic sequence is non-periodic [2]. In 2014 Francois et al. proposed a Secure PRNG three-mix, from where it is seen that rather than using a single chaotic map, mixing of several chaotic maps for designing a PRNG can be done [13]. In 2016, Liu et al. proposed a PRNG based on new multi-delayed Chebyshev map [11]. From the aforementioned PRNGs, it has been observed that these PRNGs generate a random bit sequence of finite length by using chaotic map. The main inputs to these PRNGs are the optimal seed values of the chaotic map, but it does not optimized the seed values for the respective chaotic map and the optimality should be checked mathematically. This task is difficult to perform for each execution to get a random bit sequence. So, they must rely on a set of optimal seed values. A predefined optimal seed value or a set of optimal seed values will not only degrade the security, but also not generate a unique bit sequence in each and every execution of a PRNG. In this research it has been established that the seed values for a chaotic map can be optimized by using evolutionary search algorithms like GA, and this optimized seed will generate a pseudorandom, unique and optimal bit sequence.

GA is a metaheuristic search algorithm. It works on randomly taken initial population of chromosomes. Each chromosome from the population is associated with a fitness value. The fitness value is calculated by using a fitness calculation strategy. GA uses the Darwin principle of natural selection and applies genetic operations, like Elitism, Crossover, Mutation, etc. in an ordered way. It is an iterating process, i.e. aforementioned genetic operations are performed iteratively until a predefined termination condition is achieved [8,14,15,18,20]. In recent years RCGA gains significant importance over the Binary Coded Genetic Algorithms or BCGA due to its properties like, fast execution rate, efficiency and straightforwardness.

In this paper a RCGA has been proposed to find the optimal values of Chaos parameters, Sect. 2 of the paper considers to obtain optimal seed values of chaotic map using various chaotic equation like Logistic, Skew-tent and Cross-coupled version of each of them. Also these optimal system parameters have been used to generate a pseudorandom bit sequence, and NIST specified tests are performed to conform the randomness. Results are discussed in Sect. 3. Conclusion and future scope is given in Sect. 4 and references are provided in the end.

2 Proposed Method for Pseudo-random Bit-Stream Generation

The propose technique consists of a three-step process. In the first step, an initial population of size n is encoded. Here n is the number of chromosomes. In the second step, different chaotic maps are considered separately. The system parameters of one of these chaotic maps are optimized by using genetic algorithm. In the third step, these optimized system parameters are used to generate a pseudorandom bit sequence by using the respective chaotic map equation. The randomness of the generated bit sequence is tested using NIST statistical test suit for randomness.

This proposed method considers Logistic, Skew tent, Cross coupled Logistic and Cross Coupled Skew tent map equations. One of these equation can be used for the generation of pseudorandom bit sequence. A seed is combination of μ and X_0, where μ is the system or control parameter and X_0 is the initial population value.

Logistic map shows complex chaotic behavior, i.e. Population values in each time step will be different [3,12,22]. The logistic map equation is presented in Eq. 1.

$$X_{i+1} = F(X_i, \mu) = \mu X_i (1 - X_i) \tag{1}$$

Skew tent chaotic map is a one dimensional chaotic map. This map is ergodic and also shows complex chaotic behavior [11,16]. The skew tent map equation is presented in Eq. 2.

$$X_{i+1} = G(X_i, \mu) = \begin{cases} \frac{X_i}{\mu} & \text{where, } 0 \leq X_i \leq \mu \\ \frac{1-X_i}{1-\mu} & \text{where, } \mu \leq X_i \leq 1 \end{cases} \tag{2}$$

The pseudorandom bit sequence for the logistic map or the skew tent map is generated by using Eq. 3.

$$P(i) = \begin{cases} 0 & \text{if, } X_i \leq mean(X_i) \\ 1 & \text{Otherwise} \end{cases} \quad \text{where, } 0 \leq i \leq n \tag{3}$$

Two chaotic maps are called cross coupled, if they have the same number time step, i.e. same in population size, and shares the values of each other's population. This paper shows that the proposed method has successfully been able to generate an optimal pseudorandom bit sequence by using cross coupled logistic map or cross coupled skew tent map. The cross coupled logistic map equation is presented in 4–5 and the cross coupled skew tent map equation is presented in 6–7.

$$X_{i+1} = F_1(X_i, \mu_1) \tag{4}$$

$$X_{j+1} = F_2(X_j, \mu_2) \tag{5}$$

$$X_{i+1} = G_1(X_i, \mu_1) \quad \text{where, } 0 \leq i \leq n \tag{6}$$

$$X_{j+1} = G_2(X_j, \mu_2) \quad \text{where, } 0 \leq j \leq n \tag{7}$$

The pseudorandom bit sequence for the cross coupled maps are generated by using 8.

$$P(i) = \begin{cases} 0 & \text{if, } X_i < X_j \\ 1 & \text{Otherwise} \end{cases} \quad \text{where, } 0 \leq i \leq n \qquad (8)$$

The length of the pseudorandom bit sequence and n are taken as a user input. A seed is constituted by using two parameters X and μ of a chaotic map. So, the length of the chromosomes is 2. The propose method assumes the values of P_c and P_m are 0.9 and 0.1 respectively. The value of P_c and P_m can also be taken as user input, but it has to keep in mind that P_c must be a very high probabilistic value and P_m must be a very low probabilistic value. Total number of generations is 200. The proposed algorithm is presented in Algorithm 1.

Algorithm 1. Proposed method for Pseudorandom Bit stream Generation

---

Input: Number of chromosomes n, Length of the pseudorandom bit sequence is q
Output: Optimized seed for chaos and pseudorandom bit stream
1: **begin**
2: Initial population encoding, where each chromosome is the seed for chaos and its real coded
3: Optimal seed value for chaotic map optimization by using RCGA
4: Optimal pseudorandom bit sequence generation.
5: **end**

Section 2.1 considers the initial encoding process. Section 2.2 considers the optimization of seed values. Section 2.3 considers the pseudorandom bit sequence generation process.

2.1   Initial Population Encoding

Initial mating pool or population has n number of chromosomes. Each chromosome is real coded and it represents a seed of a chaotic map. The first value and second value of a seed are X_0 and μ. The value of X_0 should be in the range 0 to 1, and it is chosen randomly. The value of μ is different for different chaotic maps. For Eq. 1 and for Eqs. 4–5, the value of μ should be in the range 3 to 4, and for the Eq. 2 and Eqs. 6–7, the value of μ should be in the range 0 to 1.

2.2   Optimal Seed Value for Chaos Optimization

Optimal seed values for chaos are optimized by using a RCGA. This method is presented in Algorithm 2. Here the fitness value of each chromosome is calculated first. It generates a bit sequence of size 128 bit for each chromosome by using a chaotic map. After this the randomness of the bit sequence corresponding to each chromosome, is tested by using Poker test. The result of the poker test is a chi-square value χ^2 which is also the fitness value for a chromosome. The proposed method considers this Poker test function, i.e. Eq. 9 as the objective function to minimize the χ^2 value in each generation. In a poker test for a $k-$bit of bit-stream, a positive integer q is selected in such a way that $\frac{k}{q} \geq 5 \times 2^q$. After that $z = \frac{k}{q}$ is calculated. After that the bit sequence is divided into z non-overlapping sub blocks, each of which is q bit of length. k_i is the count of the ith type of occurrences in q bit sub blocks [1,16]. The calculation of χ^2 value can be expressed mathematically in Eq. 9.

$$\chi^2 = \frac{2^q}{z}(\sum_{i=1}^{2^q} k_i{}^2) - k \qquad (9)$$

Elitism is performed by comparing the fitness value of the fittest chromosome X from the previous generation with the fitness value of the weakest chromosome Y from the current generation, i.e. if $fitness(X) > fitness(Y)$, then Y is replaced by the X in the output mating pool, otherwise Y survives in that generation, the selection is done by using Binary Tournament Selection(BTS) process. BTS is easy to implement and it is also efficient. BTS can avoid the premature convergence, because it gives the chance for selection to each and every chromosome, and that can degrade the convergence [7,17]. In BTS two chromosomes are selected randomly and after comparing their fitness values, the fittest chromosome survives in the mating pool [8]. The size of the mating pool is n.

Algorithm 2. Optimal seed value for chaotic map optimization

Input: n, Initial population
Output: Optimized seed for chaos
 1: **begin**
 2: **for** gen= 1 to 200 **do**   ▷ Number of Generations
 3:     **for** each chromosome from the mating pool **do**
 4:         By using chromosome as a seed and the objective function, generate a pseudorandom bit sequence X.
 5:         Compute the fitness value, by applying the Poker test of randomness on X.
 6:     **end for**
 7:     **for** i= 1 to n **do**   ▷ Elitism operation is done here
 8:         Select the weakest chromosome Y from the current generation.
 9:         Select the fittest chromosome Z from the previous generation.
10:         Compute the fitness values of Y and Z. Keep the fittest chromosome in the current generation and discard the other one.
11:     **end for**
12:     Create a mating pool of size N by using BTS.
13:     Perform Crossover operation on the mating pool of real coded chromosomes.
14:     Perform Mutation operation on the mating pool of real coded chromosomes.
15: **end for**
16: **end**

The next operation is crossover. Proposed crossover technique on real coded chromosomes is presented in Algorithm 3. This method minimizes the χ^2 value of a bit sequence of size *128* bit for a seed value of a chaotic map by using the objective function 9. In this method, two chromosomes are selected from the mating pool and copied to variables randomly. Then a crossover probabilistic value $Cross_{prob}$ is also chosen within the range *0 to 1*. Then this $Cross_{prob}$ is compared with the P_c. If it is greater than the P_c, then these chromosomes are copied directly to the output mating pool, otherwise crossover operation is performed on them. In a crossover operation, first the values of X_0 and μ are subtracted and the absolute results are stored in variables $temp_1$ and $temp_2$ respectively. Then some amount of values, i.e. a and b are taken randomly from $temp_1$ and $temp_2$ within the range *0 to $temp_1$* and *0 to $temp_2$* respectively. Then one of the following set of operation is performed over them. The first set

---

Algorithm 3. Proposed crossover technique on real coded chromosomes

---

Input: Mating pool, n, P_c
Output: Mating pool contains offspring
1: **begin**
2: **for** i=1 to $n/2$ **do**
3:      Select two chromosomes X_1 and X_2 randomly from the mating pool.
4:      Copy X_1 and X_2 randomly in two variables $chrom_1$ and $chrom_2$.
5:      Select a crossover probability $Cross_{prob}$ within the range *0 to 1*.
6:      **if** $Cross_{prob} \leq P_c$ **then**
7:          Compute the absolute difference of μ's of $chrom_1$ and $chrom_1$, i.e. $temp1 = |$ $\mu_{chrom1} - \mu_{chrom2}|$
8:          Compute the absolute difference of X_0's of $chrom_1$ and $chrom_2$, i.e. $temp2 = | X_{0_{chrom1}} - X_{0_{chrom2}}|$
9:          Select two random values a and b within the range *0 to $temp_1$* and *0 to $temp_2$* respectively.
10:          Select an integer value *Choice* randomly, within the range *1 to 2*.
11:          **if** *Choice* = 1 **then**
12:              Add μ with A and X_0 with B of the $chrom_1$
13:              Subtract μ with A and X_0 with B of the $chrom_2$
14:          **else**
15:              Subtract μ with A and X_0 with b of the $chrom_1$
16:              Add μ with A and X_0 with B of the $chrom_2$
17:          **end if**
18:          Boundary restriction is performed here
19:      **end if**
20:      $chrom_1$ and $chrom_2$ are copied back to their respective positions in the resultant mating pool
21: **end for**
22: **end**

---

of operation is *Addition then Subtraction*, i.e. a and b are added with X_0 and μ of the first chromosome, and a and b are subtracted with X_0 and μ of the second chromosome. The second set of operation is *Subtraction then Addition*, i.e. a and b are subtracted with X_0 and μ of the first chromosome, and a and b are added with X_0 and μ of the second chromosome. The set of operation is also chosen randomly. The output of this procedure is the offspring, which is then copied to the mating pool.

After that mutation is executed over the mating pool. Proposed mutation technique on real coded chromosomes is presented in Algorithm 4. In this technique, one chromosome from the mating pool is selected randomly. Then a mutation probabilistic value $Mute_{prob}$ is chosen randomly within the range 0 to 1. Then $Mute_{prob}$ is compared with the P_m. If it is greater than P_m, then this selected chromosome is copied directly to the output mating pool, otherwise it gets mutated. In mutation operation the integer part of the μ is neglected here, thus the X_0 and the fractional part of μ are copied in two separate variables, $temp_1$ and $temp_2$ respectively. Like crossover, here two set of operations are also present and the set of operation is also chosen randomly. In first set of operation X is calculated, where $X = temp2 \times Mute_{prob}$. Then, this X is added with $temp_1$ and subtracted with $temp_2$. In second set of operation X is also calculated, where $X = temp1 \times Mute_{prob}$. Then, this X is subtracted with $temp_1$ and

---

Algorithm 4. Proposed mutation technique on real coded chromosomes

Input: Mating pool, n, P_m
Output: Mating pool contains offspring
  1: **begin**
  2: **for** i=1 to $n/2$ **do**
  3:     Select one chromosome *chrom* randomly from the mating pool
  4:     **if** $Mute_{prob} \leq P_m$ **then**
  5:         Copy the X_0 and the fractional part of μ of *chrom* in $temp1$ and $temp2$ respectively
  6:         Select a integer value *Choice* randomly, within the range *1 to 2*
  7:         **if** $Choice = 1$ **then**
  8:             Take $(Mute_{prob} * 100)\%$ amount of value X from $temp_2$. Add X to $temp_1$ and subtract X from $temp_2$
  9:         **else**
 10:             Take $(Mute_{prob} * 100)\%$ amount of value X from $temp_1$. Add X to $temp_2$ and subtract X from $temp_1$
 11:         **end if**
 12:         Boundary restriction is performed here
 13:     **end if**
 14:     Update μ of *chrom* by adding the previously discarded integer part of μ with $temp_2$. $temp_1$ will be the updated X_0 of *chrom*
 15:     *chrom* is copied to the resultant mating pool in the same position, where it was during the selection
 16: **end for**
 17: **end**

---

added with $temp_2$. Finally the integer part of μ, which was neglected previously, is added with current $temp_1$ to get the updated μ. The $temp_2$ is copied to X_0. The resultant seed is the offspring, which is then copied to the resultant mating pool.

2.3   Optimal Pseudorandom Bit Sequence Generation

q bit optimal pseudorandom bit sequence can be generated by using the same objective function, that was used in Sect. 2.2. The optimal seed value which is the output of the Sect. 2.2 is used here as a seed for the aforementioned objective function on chaotic map.

3   Result and Analysis

The randomness of the optimal pseudorandom bit sequence is tested by using NIST statistical test suit. This test determines the unpredictability of a Pseudo Random Number Generator (PRNG). In recent years NIST becomes the industry norm for the randomness testing and it is the most stringent test suit. It contains 15 nearly independent statistical tests, which is focused on finding all possible types of non-randomness pattern that could exist in a pseudorandom bit sequence. If any type of non-randomness pattern is found by any of this test, then the sequence is declared as non-random, otherwise it is declared as random [4]. The results of these tests are represented by *P-values*. *P-value* is the probabilistic value. If the output *P-value* of a test is greater than or equal to *0.01*, then PRNG will pass that test for randomness with a *99%* confidence. NIST specified tests are performed to conform the randomness of the result of the proposed algorithm with different chaotic map functions. The results are shown in Tables 1, 2, 3 and 4.

Table 1 represent the *P-value* and *Result* of each test, which is present in NIST test suit. A pseudorandom bit sequence of finite length is the input for each test. This bit sequence is generated by using the proposed method where Logistic map equation is taken into consideration. Obtained *P-value* for a test, if greater than or equal to *0.01*, then it can be concluded that this proposed method has passed the particular test. For the each sub test of Random Excursion and the Random Excursion Variant test, if $P-value \geq 0.01$, then the sequence will be random, otherwise it will be non-random. From this table it can be clearly observed that all the P-values are greater than or equal *0.01*. So, it can conclude that this proposed method will generate pseudorandom bit sequence by using Logistic chaotic map.

Table 1. NIST test for the proposed method with logistic chaotic map

Index	Test index	P-value	Result
1	Frequency	0.9005	Pass
2	Block frequency	0.5681	Pass
3	Runs	0.1849	Pass
4	Longest-run-of-ones	0.4746	Pass
5	Binary matrix rank	0.2701	Pass
6	DFT(Spectral)	0.8711	Pass
7	Non overlapping template matching	0.9907	Pass
8	Overlapping template matching	0.2610	Pass
9	Maurers *universal statistical*	0.9673	Pass
10	Linear complexity	0.9856	Pass
11	Serial 1	0.3644	Pass
	Serial 2	0.9231	Pass
12	Approximation entropy	0.0607	Pass
13	Cumulative sums (Cusums)	0.9555	Pass
14	Random excursion		
	-4	0.3965	Random
	-3	0.2284	Random
	-2	0.9058	Random
	-1	0.2670	Random
	1	0.9478	Random
	2	0.5497	Random
	3	0.5385	Random
	4	0.0399	Random
15	Random Excursions Variant		
	-9	0.3965	Random
	-8	0.2284	Random
	-7	0.9058	Random
	-6	0.2670	Random
	-5	0.3965	Random
	-4	0.3965	Random
	-3	0.2284	Random
	-2	0.9058	Random
	-1	0.2670	Random
	1	0.9478	Random
	2	0.5497	Random
	3	0.5385	Random
	4	0.0399	Random
	5	0.9478	Random
	6	0.5497	Random
	7	0.5385	Random
	8	0.0399	Random
	9	0.0399	Random

Table 2. NIST test for the proposed method with skew tent chaotic map

Index	Test index	P-value	Result
1	Frequency	0.1336	Pass
2	Block frequency	0.7178	Pass
3	Runs	0.5949	Pass
4	Longest-run-of-ones	0.1767	Pass
5	Binary matrix rank	0.2159	Pass
6	DFT(Spectral)	0.8711	Pass
7	Non overlapping template matching	0.2769	Pass
8	Overlapping template matching	0.9156	Pass
9	Maurers *universal statistical*	0.9272	Pass
10	Linear complexity	0.8685	Pass
11	Serial 1	0.3449	Pass
	Serial 2	0.1249	Pass
12	Approximation entropy	0.0141	Pass
13	Cumulative sums (Cusums)	0.8690	Pass
14	Random excursion		
	−4	0.0166	Random
	−3	0.7985	Random
	−2	0.8221	Random
	−1	0.0572	Random
	1	0.3503	Random
	2	0.4405	Random
	3	0.5228	Random
	4	0.4966	Random
15	Random excursions variant		
	−9	0.5211	Random
	−8	0.5259	Random
	−7	0.5294	Random
	−6	0.6485	Random
	−5	0.7055	Random
	−4	0.7210	Random
	−3	0.9326	Random
	−2	0.8273	Random
	−1	0.3447	Random
	1	0.0890	Random
	2	0.2752	Random
	3	0.3525	Random
	4	0.3531	Random
	5	0.3778	Random
	6	0.4250	Random
	7	0.4631	Random
	8	0.4945	Random
	9	0.5211	Random

Table 2 shows that all the *P-values* are greater than or equal *0.01*. So, it can be concluded that this proposed method will generate Pseudorandom bit sequence by using Skew tent chaotic map.

Table 3. NIST test for the proposed method with cross coupled logistic chaotic map

Index	Test index	P-value	Result
1	Frequency	0.8231	Pass
2	Block frequency	0.9665	Pass
3	Runs	0.0903	Pass
4	Longest-run-of-ones	0.0799	Pass
5	Binary matrix rank	0.1285	Pass
6	DFT(Spectral)	0.1443	Pass
7	Non overlapping template matching	0.6161	Pass
8	Overlapping template matching	0.0205	Pass
9	Maurers *universal statistical*	0.9616	Pass
10	Linear complexity	0.4232	Pass
11	Serial 1	0.0338	Pass
	Serial 2	0.7023	Pass
12	Approximation entropy	0.1435	Pass
13	Cumulative sums (Cusums)	0.9555	Pass
14	Random excursion		
	−4	0.1027	Random
	−3	0.1201	Random
	−2	0.3130	Random
	−1	0.7576	Random
	1	0.4629	Random
	2	0.4499	Random
	3	0.5671	Random
	4	0.5281	Random
15	Random excursions variant		
	−9	0.3960	Random
	−8	0.6056	Random
	−7	0.8352	Random
	−6	0.4739	Random
	−5	0.5320	Random
	−4	0.3447	Random
	−3	0.2404	Random
	−2	0.2199	Random
	−1	0.0801	Random
	1	0.3173	Random
	2	0.5637	Random
	3	0.4674	Random
	4	0.5083	Random
	5	0.5320	Random
	6	0.3657	Random
	7	0.2983	Random
	8	0.3017	Random
	9	0.3320	Random

Table 3 shows that all the *P-values* are greater than or equal *0.01*. So, it can be concluded that this proposed method will generate Pseudorandom bit sequence by using Cross coupled Logistic chaotic map.

Table 4. NIST test for the proposed method with cross coupled skew tent chaotic map

Index	Test index	P-value	Result
1	Frequency	0.4952	Pass
2	Block frequency	0.9918	Pass
3	Runs	0.0133	Pass
4	Longest-run-of-ones	0.1381	Pass
5	Binary matrix rank	0.6420	Pass
6	DFT(Spectral)	0.1443	Pass
7	Non overlapping template matching	0.6410	Pass
8	Overlapping template matching	0.0528	Pass
9	Maurers *universal statistical*	0.9822	Pass
10	Linear complexity	0.6767	Pass
11	Serial 1	0.0112	Pass
	Serial 2	0.8521	Pass
12	Approximation entropy	0.2402	Pass
13	Cumulative sums (Cusums)	0.9642	Pass
14	Random excursion		
	−4	0.3898	Random
	−3	0.9593	Random
	−2	0.8101	Random
	−1	0.8366	Random
	1	0.7274	Random
	2	0.8700	Random
	3	0.4736	Random
	4	0.9253	Random
15	Random excursions variant		
	−9	0.5695	Random
	−8	0.5448	Random
	−7	0.5154	Random
	−6	0.4795	Random
	−5	0.4344	Random
	−4	0.4203	Random
	−3	0.5673	Random
	−2	0.9020	Random
	−1	0.8312	Random
	1	0.6698	Random
	2	0.8055	Random
	3	0.5673	Random
	4	0.8090	Random
	5	0.6698	Random
	6	0.5629	Random
	7	0.5154	Random
	8	0.5448	Random
	9	0.5695	Random

Table 4 shows that all the *P-values* are greater than or equal *0.01*. So, it can be concluded that this proposed method will generate Pseudorandom bit sequence by using Cross coupled skew tent chaotic map.

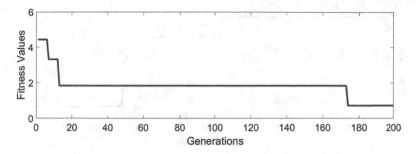

Fig. 1. Bar diagram showing minimization of fitness values in 200 iteration with logistic chaotic map

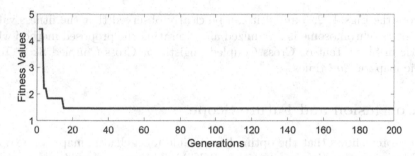

Fig. 2. Bar diagram showing minimization of fitness values in 200 iterations, with skew tent chaotic map

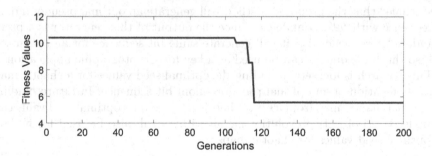

Fig. 3. Bar diagram showing minimization of fitness values in 200 iterations, with cross coupled logistic chaotic map

The generation wise growth in fitness values for *200* generations by using different type of chaotic map functions are shown as a bar diagram in Figs. 1, 2, 3 and 4. The X-axis of the graph represents the number of generations and the Y-axis represents the fitness values of the fittest chromosome in each generation.

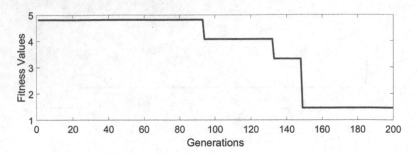

Fig. 4. Bar diagram showing minimization of fitness values in 200 iterations, with cross coupled skew tent chaotic map

From the Figs. 1, 2, 3 and 4 it can be clearly observed that the fitness value of the fittest chromosome is minimized after iterating the proposed method with Logistic or Skew Tent or Cross Coupled Logistic or Cross Coupled Skew Tent chaotic map for *200* times.

4   Conclusion and Future Scope

This research shows that the optimal seed value for a chaotic map can be optimized by using evolutionary algorithm(RCGA). This optimal seed values can be used to generate an optimal pseudorandom bit sequence. This paper proposes a RCGA enabled pseudorandom bit sequence generator, which passes all the statistical tests of NIST, by using four different types of chaotic maps. So, it can be concluded that the proposed method will generate an optimal pseudorandom bit sequence with *99%* confidence. Since the output of this generator is a pseudorandom bit sequence, i.e. it will generate same bit sequence for an optimized seed, so this bit sequence can be used as a key for Cryptographic applications.

This research is focused on finding the optimal seed values for a chaotic map for the generation of an optimal pseudorandom bit sequence. In future, finding the optimal chaotic map from a set of chaotic maps and its optimal seed value can be made. Multi-objective evolutionary algorithms will also be used for finding the optimal seed values for chaotic maps.

References

1. Menezes, A., van Oorschot, P., Vanstone, S.: Handbook of Applied Cryptography. CRC Press, Boca Raton (1996)
2. Akhshani, A., Akhavan, A., Mobaraki, A., Lim, S.C., Hassan, Z.: Pseudo random number generator based on quantum chaotic map. Commun. Nonlinear Sci. Numer. Simul. **19**(1), 101–111 (2014)
3. Bandyopadhyay, D., et al.: A novel secure image steganography method based on chaos theory in spatial domain. Int. J. Secur. Priv. Trust Manage. (IJSPTM) **3**(1), 11–22 (2014)

4. Bassham, L.E., et al.: SP 800–22 rev. 1a. A statistical test suite for random and pseudorandom number generators for cryptographic applications. National Institute of Standards & Technology, April 2010
5. Bhoskar, T., et al.: Genetic algorithm and its applications to mechanical engineering: a review. In: 4th International Conference on Materials Processing and Characterization, vol. 2, no. (4–5), pp. 2624–2630, July 2015
6. Barangi, M., Chang, J.S., Mazumder, P.: Straintronics-based true random number generator for high speed and energy-limited applications. IEEE Trans. Magn. **52**(1), 1–9 (2016)
7. Goldberg, D.E., Deb, K.: A comparative analysis of selection schemes used in genetic algorithms. Found. Genet. Algorithms **1**, 69–93 (1991)
8. Goldberg, D.E.: Genetic Algorithm in Search, Optimization and Machine Learning. Addison- Wesley, Boston (1989)
9. Garca-Martnez, M., Campos-Cantn, E.: Pseudo-random bit generator based on multi-modal maps. Nonlinear Dyn. **82**(4), 2119–2131 (2015)
10. Hu, H., Liu, L., Ding, N.: Pseudorandom sequence generator based on the chen chaotic system. Comput. Phys. Commun. **184**(3), 765–768 (2013)
11. Liu, L., Miao, S., Cheng, M., Gao, X.: A pseudorandom bit generator based on new multi-delayed Chebyshev map. Inf. Process. Lett. **116**(11), 674–681 (2016)
12. Lorenz, E.N.: The Essence of Chaos, 3rd edn. CRC Press, New York (1995)
13. François, M., Grosges, T., Barchiesi, D., Erra, R.: Pseudo-random number generator based on mixing of three chaotic maps. Commun. Nonlinear Sci. Numer. Simul. **19**(4), 887–895 (2014)
14. Mukhopadhyay, S., Mandal, J.K.: Denoising of digital images through PSO based pixel classification. Cent. Eur. J. Comput. Sci. **3**(4), 158–172 (2013)
15. Mukhopadhyay, S., Mandal, J.K.: A fuzzy switching median filter of impulses in digital imagery (FSMF). Circ. Syst. Sig. Process. **33**(7), 2193–2216 (2014). https://doi.org/10.1007/s00034-014-9739-z
16. Pareek, N.K., Patidar, V., Sud, K.K.: A random bit generator using chaotic maps. Int. J. Netw. Secur. **10**(1), 32–38 (2010)
17. Razali, N.M., Geraghty, J.: Genetic algorithm performance with different selection strategies in solving TSP. In: Proceedings of the World Congress on Engineering, IAENG II, pp. 1134–1139, July 2011
18. Sanjib Ganguly, D.S.: Distributed generation allocation on radial distribution networks under uncertainties of load and generation using genetic algorithm. IEEE Trans. Sustain. Energ. **6**(3), 688–697 (2015)
19. Sattar, B., Sadkhan, R.S.M.: Proposed random unified chaotic map as PRBG for voice encryption in wireless communication. In: International Conference on Communication, Management and Information Technology, vol. 65, no. 6, pp. 314–323, September 2015
20. Mukhopadhyay, S., Chaudhuri, T.D., Mandal, J.K.: A hybrid PSO-fuzzy based algorithm for clustering Indian stock market data. In: Mandal, J.K., Dutta, P., Mukhopadhyay, S. (eds.) CICBA 2017. CCIS, vol. 776, pp. 475–487. Springer, Singapore (2017). https://doi.org/10.1007/978-981-10-6430-2_37
21. Stoyanov, B., Kordov, K.: Novel secure pseudo-random number generation scheme based on two tinkerbell maps. Adv. Stud. Theor. Phys. **9**(9), 411–421 (2015)
22. Patidar, V., Sud, K.K., Pareek, N.K.: A pseudo random bit generator based on chaotic logistic map and it's statistical testing. Informatica **33**(4), 441–452 (2009)

Analysis and Categorization of Human Facial Emotion Using PCA and Artificial Neural Network

Md. Iqbal Quraishi[1(✉)], Jyoti Prakash Jodder[2], J. Paul Chaudhury[1,2], and Mallika De[1,2]

[1] Department of Information Technology,
Kalyani Government Engineering College, Kalyani, Nadia, India
iqbalqu@gmail.com
[2] Department of Computer Science and Engineering,
Kalyani Government Engineering College, Kalyani, Nadia, India
jyotiprakashjodder@gmail.com

Abstract. The research on human facial emotions started with Darwin in 1965 [1]. Now it becomes one of the interesting research areas of computer science. In this paper we propose a very simple but effective way to classify emotions from human facial image. We work with seven emotions: Neutral, Angry, Fearful, Disgust, Happy, Sad, Surprise and ten different human face images in each emotion for our experiment. Our work is based on Edge detection, Segmentation, Gabor transformation and GLCM calculation. Canny edge detection technique is used for edge detection and morphological segmentation technique is used for segmentation. We use Principal component analysis (PCA) for dimension reduction of our dataset. A neural network is used to classify emotions. Finally a comparison has been made with some existing methods which prove the effectiveness of our proposed system final output in the form of emotions.

Keywords: Canny edge detection · Morphological segmentation · Gabor transformation · Gray level co-occurrence matrix (GLCM)

1 Introduction

Clustering Emotion is a strong feeling deriving from one's circumstances, mood, or relationships with others. Nonverbal communication plays a vital role in human communications [2] and it also helps in smooth interaction between human and computer in human machine interface. Emotion classification through computer system can be used in many applications such as human behavior understanding, perceptual user interfaces, and interactive computer games [3].

So, facial emotion classification is become more and more important in the intelligent communication between human and computer [4]. American psychologist Dr. Paul Ekman is a pioneer of emotion study and their relation to facial expressions [5]. He concluded there are six basic emotions [6]: anger, disgust, fear, happiness, sadness,

© Springer Nature Singapore Pte Ltd. 2019
J. K. Mandal et al. (Eds.): CICBA 2018, CCIS 1030, pp. 180–205, 2019.
https://doi.org/10.1007/978-981-13-8578-0_15

and surprise [7]. Here is the description of the facial expressions (Table 1) based on features bound to face components [8].

Table 1. Description of human facial emotions.

Emotion Type	Sample Image	Description
Angry		Eyebrows are pulled down; wrinkles between eyebrows, the lips are stressed.
Disgust		Upper lip is pulled up, bottom lip is either pulled down or pulled up and the nose is turned up.
Fearful		Eyes are widely opened, mouth is opened, and both eyebrows are pulled up.
Happy		Mouth sides are pulled up, the mouth is either slightly opened or closed.
Neutral		Facial muscles are relaxed and wrinkles are minimal.
Sad		The inner side of eyebrows is pulled up and mouth sides are pulled down.
Surprise		Eyes are widely opened. Mouth is opened, wrinkles on top of the eyebrows.

Our work is aimed to classify the seven emotions with the basis of above characteristics of facial expressions.

2 Related Work

Emotion study is a popular research area of computer science as well as Artificial intelligence. In last few decades many research have been done on this area.

Ilbeygi et al. [9] proposed a new method using fuzzy inference system (FIS) to recognize six basic emotions (Anger, Disgust, Fear, Happiness, Sadness and Surprise) which is also applicable for partial occluded images. Their average precision rate is 93.96%. Sengupta et al. [10] designed a hybrid approach of Neural Networks (NNs) combined with Hidden Markov Models (HMMs) for facial emotion classification. They used Multilayer perceptron (MLP) as NN and work with four emotions: Anger, Dislike, Joy, and Surprise. Nagpal et al. [11] proposed a novel approach for the detection of four emotions (Angry, Happy, Fair and Normal) They use Mutation Bacteria Foraging optimization (MBFO) and Adaptive Median Filter (AMF) for removal of noise from the image. Hong et al. [12] proposed a component approach to classify the Seven facial expressions of Emotion (happy, sad, surprised, fearful, disgusted, angry and neutral). They use grayscale, Local Binary Patterns, Sobel and Canny edge detection techniques for preprocessing the input image. Finally the facial emotions are classified using a Support Vector Machine (SVM) and a pairwise adaptive SVM (pa-SVM). Their classification rate is 98.57%. Lin et al. [13] proposed a new facial expression recognition scheme, which involve a statistical synthesis of hierarchical classifiers. The input images are first decomposed by a multi-scale Gabor-filter, and encoded using radial grids. They work with seven emotions Happy, Sad, Surprise, Disgusted, Angry, Scared, Neutral and two databases CK and JAFFE. Axel et al. [14] proposed Optical flow based analyses to detect emotions. They use a feature point tracking technique to capture basic emotions (happy, sad, angry, surprise, fear and disgust). They deal with five facial image regions (eyebrows, eyes and mouth) form human facial image dataset contains different genders and nationality. Habibizad et al. [15] proposed a new algorithm to recognize human face emotions (Natural, Fear, Happy, Sad, Angry, Dislike and Surprise). Their method involves three stages: pre-processing, feature extraction and classification with filtering, adjusting contrast, edge detection segmentation and Second particle swarm optimization (PSO) technique. Lee [16] present and implement an automatic extraction and recognition technique of facial emotions. They use color feature-map for detecting facial region and Bezier curve for classify the emotions. Success rate of this system is 78.8%. Amir et al. [58] used fuzzy clustering technique to classify emotions. They used Fuzzy C-Means (FCM) for clustering and construct a classification system to simulate communication between human to human. Tsai and Jan [48] used subspace model analysis for analyze data, PCA technique and multilayered perceptron (MLP) to classify emotions. They worked with the JAFFE database. Rizon et al. [59] worked with only lip feature. They used genetic algorithm to recognize six basic emotions and JAFFE database as face image database.

3 Tools and Materials Used

3.1 Facial Expression Database

In our experiments the Japanese Female Facial Expression (JAFFE) Database [17] is used as facial expression database which is extracted from ATR Media Information Science Labs [18, 19]. It consists of 213 grayscale images of ten Japanese women (Fig. 14) with seven facial expressions: happy, sad, surprise, anger, disgust, fear and neutral (6 basic emotions [6] + neutral) (Figs. 16, 17, 18, 19, 20, 21 and 22). Each person has two to four images (Fig. 15) for each of seven expressions [3]. The photos were taken in Kyushu University at the Psychology Department [17]. This database is very popular and used in many research works related to emotions [20–23].

3.2 Canny Edge Detection

The Canny edge detector, also known as optimal edge detection method, is an edge detection operator that uses a multi-stage algorithm to detect the edges in an image [24]. It was developed by Canny in 1986 [25]. Canny's edge detection algorithm [25] has three main principles: low error rate, well localization of edge points and one response to a single edge. Canny proposed two new techniques: no maximum suppression and double thresholding to enhance the older edge detection methods [26].

The Canny edge detector is widely used in image processing to find object boundaries in an image and to locate sharp intensity changes. The Canny edge detector consider a pixel as an edge when gradient magnitude of the pixel is larger than its neighbor pixels in the direction of maximum intensity change [27].

3.3 Morphological Segmentation

Image segmentation is the technique of partitioning a digitized image into multiple segments. The goal of segmentation is to simplify an image so that it becomes more meaningful and easier to analyze [28, 29]. Image segmentation is mainly used to locate boundaries and objects in images. The output of image segmentation process is a set of image segments that collectively cover the entire input image [30]. Image segmentation is an important step to understand the content of an image.

Morphological segmentation is one of the image segmentation techniques. For morphological segmentation, erosion and dilation are the two basic operators [31].

3.4 Grey Level Co-occurrence Matrices (GLCM)

Texture is an important characteristics used to identify region of interest in an image [32]. Grey Level Co-occurrence Matrices (GLCM), which is also known as gray-level spatial dependence matrix [33], is one of the earliest methods for second order statistical texture features extraction proposed by Haralick et al. [34] in 1973. In short GLCM is a matrix where the number of rows and columns is equal to the number of gray levels in the image. GLCM contains the second-order statistical information of neighboring pixels of an image. Textural properties can be calculated from GLCM to understand the details about the image content [35]. GLCM measures how often pairs of pixel with a specified spatial relationship and specific values occur in an image [33]. GLCM contains the information about the positions of neighbor pixel with similar gray level values [36]. The first pixel is known as reference and the second pixel is known as neighbor pixel [37].

The co-occurrence matrix is useful in image analysis applications, such as in remote sensing, biomedical, industrial defect detection systems and a number of applications related with image processing [38–44].

After creating the GLCMs, we can derive several statistical features from it. This gives information about the texture of an image. The following table (Table 2) shows the statistical features.

Table 2. Description of statistical features obtained from GLCM.

Statistical features	Description
Contrast	Measures the local variations in the gray-level co-occurrence matrix
Correlation	Measures the joint probability occurrence of the specified pixel pairs
Energy	Provides the sum of squared elements in the GLCM. Also known as uniformity or the angular second moment
Homogeneity	Measures the closeness of the distribution of elements in the GLCM to the GLCM diagonal

The following figure (Fig. 1) shows how first three values in a GLCM calculated by the graycomatrix method. GLCM (1,1) contains the value 1 because there is only one occurrence of two horizontally adjacent pixels having values 1 and 1 respectively in the input image. Element of GLCM (1,2) contains the value 2 because there are two occurrence of two horizontally adjacent pixels having values 1 and 2. Element of GLCM (1,3) contains the value 0, as there are no occurrence of adjacent pixels with the values 1 and 3.

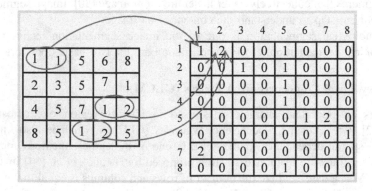

Fig. 1. Process used to create the GLCM

3.5   Gabor Transformation

The Gabor transformation, named after Dennis Gabor, is a special case of Fourier transformation which is used to determine sinusoidal frequency and phase content of a signal as it changes with time. The function is transformed with a Fourier transform after multiplied by a Gaussian function to derive the time-frequency analysis [45].

A 2D Gabor function consists of a sinusoidal wave of a certain frequency and orientation modulated by a Gaussian envelope. It is given by

$$f(x,y) = exp\left(-\frac{1}{2}[\frac{x^2}{\sigma_x^2} + \frac{y^2}{\sigma_y^2}]\right)\cos\left(2\pi u_0 x + \emptyset\right) \qquad (1)$$

Where,

$\emptyset$ and u_0 are the phase and frequency of the sinusoidal wave. The values σ_x and σ_y are the sizes of the Gaussian envelope in the x and y directions, respectively [46].

From the Gabor transformation we can extract several features from an image. The following table (Table 3) shows some features and its description.

Table 3. Description of features obtained from Gabor transformation.

Features	Description
Gabor mean	Returns the mean values of the elements along different dimensions of an array containing two-dimensional convolution of double image and Gabor transformed image
Gabor standard deviation	Computes the standard deviation of the convoluted Gabor transformed image

3.6   Principal Component Analysis (PCA)

Principal component analysis (PCA) is a statistical procedure which was invented in 1901 by Karl Pearson [47], that used in classical feature extraction and data representation technique also known as Karhunen-Loeve Expansion. It is a linear method that projects the high dimensional data onto a lower dimensional space [48].

3.6.1   Steps for Calculating PCA
The steps to calculate PCA are shown below [60].

Step 1: Take a dataset as input data.
Step 2: Subtract the mean value from each of the data dimensions.
Step 3: Construct the covariance matrix.
Step 4: Measure the eigenvectors & eigenvalues from covariance matrix.
Step 5: Select components and make a feature vector.
Step 6: Derive the new data set.

3.7 Artificial Neural Network (ANN)

An Artificial Neural Network (ANN) is a biologically inspired mathematical or computational model that is capable of machine learning and pattern recognition.

Artificial neural networks are represented by a set of nodes arranged in layers, and a set of weighted directed links connecting them. The nodes and the links are equivalent to the neurons (information processing unit) and the synapses (communicating media) of a biological nerves system respectively. Artificial neural networks consist of three parts: input layer, one or more hidden layers and output layer. Artificial neural networks are widely used to solve a variety of tasks that are very hard to solve by ordinary rule-based programming [49–53].

3.7.1 Basic Structure of Artificial Neuron

The first artificial neuron based on biological model was proposed by Warren McCulloch and Walter Pitts in 1943 [61]. The architecture of MaCulloh Pitts neuron model is shown in Fig. 2.

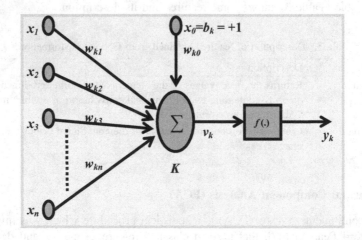

Fig. 2. MaCulloh Pitts neuron model

Here,

K is the MaCulloh Pitts neuron,
$x_1, x_2 \ldots\ldots x_n$ are the input signals to the neuron.
$w_{k1}, w_{k2} \ldots\ldots w_{kn}$ are the weights of the input signals.
x_0 is the bias input (b_k) which value is assigned +1.
w_{k0} is the weight of bias input.
$v_k = u_k + b_k.$
[Where $u_k = x_1 w_{k1} + x_2 w_{k2} + x_3 w_{k3} + \ldots + x_n w_{kn}$]
$y_k = f(v_k).$
$f(.)$ is called activation function or threshold function.

3.7.2   Back Propagation Algorithm

Back Propagation is a supervised learning algorithm proposed by Rumelhart et al. [54]. It is one of the famous and important learning algorithms among ANNs. In the learning process the gradient-decent search method is used to adjust the connection weights for reducing the inaccuracy of ANNs. The neural networks made by back propagation learning algorithm are called back propagation learning networks (BPNs) [55].

3.7.3   Feed-Forward Neural Networks (FNN)

Feed-forward neural networks (FNN) are one of the popular and simple structures among artificial neural networks. In this network the information flow moves in only forward direction (Fig. 3). The information from the input nodes to the output nodes goes through the hidden nodes (if any). Feed-forward neural networks are used to solve problems by modeling complex input-output relationships [56, 57].

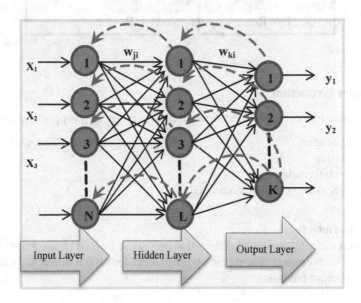

Fig. 3. Feed forward back propagation neural network

4   Proposed System

4.1   ROI Selection

Take a human facial image as input in matlab. Select and crop the region of interest (ROI). We select eye and lip region for our region of interest (ROI) (Fig. 4).

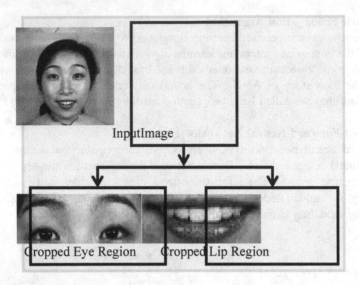

Fig. 4. ROI selection

4.2 Feature Extraction

After ROI selection we apply four separate processes on the cropped image:

  i. Edge detection;
 ii. Segmentation.
iii. Gabor transformation
 iv. Gray level co-occurrence matrix (GLCM)

4.2.1 Edge Detection

In this section we apply canny edge detection on gray scale ROI image and extract total no. of Edge Pixels from it. We repeat above process for all ten different facial images and seven different emotions.

4.2.2 Segmentation

In this section morphological segmentation is applied to the gray scale ROI image and No. of Pixels is extracted from it. After that only one eye is cropped and features: No of Pixels in an Eye, Length of an Eye and Width of an Eye are extracted.

4.2.3 Gabor Transformation

In this section Gabor transformation is used on ROI image to extract features Gabor mean and Gabor standard deviation in 5 orientations with 6 different scales. We use the Eq. (1)

$$f(x, y) = exp\left(-\frac{1}{2}[\frac{x^2}{\sigma_x^2} + \frac{y^2}{\sigma_y^2}]\right)cos(2\pi u_0 x + \emptyset) \tag{1}$$

Where,

$u_0 = 1/(\gamma * \delta)$
Here $\gamma = [0.5, 1.5, 2.5, 3.5, 4.5, 5.5]$ and $\delta = [4, 8, 12, 16, 20, 24]$, the values are chosen randomly.

$x = a\cos\theta + b\sin\theta$

and $y = -a\sin\theta + b\cos\theta$

The values of a and b lies between the available range of x and y coordinate.

The following table (Table 4) shows the Gabor transformation of ROI image in 5 orientations and 6 different scales of Pixels in an Eye, Length of an Eye and Width of an Eye are extracted.

Table 4. Gabor transformation of ROI image in different orientations and different scales.

Scale	Orientations				
	0°	15°	30°	45°	60°
1 $\gamma=0.5$ $\delta=4$					
2 $\gamma=1.5$ $\delta=8$					
3 $\gamma=2.5$ $\delta=12$					
4 $\gamma=3.5$ $\delta=16$					
5 $\gamma=4.5$ $\delta=20$					
6 $\gamma=5.5$ $\delta=24$					

4.2.4 Gray Level Co-occurrence Matrix (GLCM)

In this section a Gray level co-occurrence matrix (GLCM) prepared from the ROI image and features: Contrast, Homogeneity, Energy and Correlation are extracted from it.

GLCM measurements are made for pixel distances d = 1 and angles θ = 0, π/4, π/2 and 3 π/4 radians. The angles are represented as offset (Fig. 5). The following table (Table 5) shows the offset values of specified angles.

Table 5. Offset values of specified angles for GLCM measurements.

Angles in radian	Angles in degree	Offset values
0	0°	[0 1]
π/4	45°	[–1 1]
π/2	90°	[–1 0]
3 π/4	135°	[–1–1]

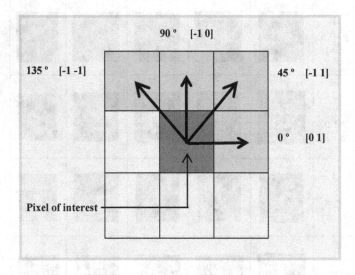

Fig. 5. Geometry for measurement of GLCM for unit distance (d) and 4 angles (θ).

After Canny edge detection, Morphological segmentation, Gabor transformation and Gray level co-occurrence matrix (GLCM) calculation with the help of extracted features a dataset is prepared. A neural network will be trained with the help of that dataset to get desired output. After that we will test all dataset for emotion classification. The flowchart human emotion classification system is shown below (Fig. 6).

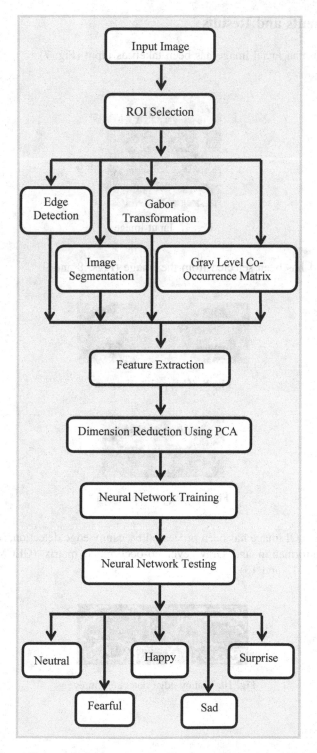

Fig. 6. Flow chart of human facial emotion classification system using artificial neural network (ANN) volunteer

5   Experiments and Results

Step1: A human facial image has been taken as input (Fig. 7)

Fig. 7. Input image

Step 2: ROI has been selected from the image (Figs. 8 and 9)

Fig. 8. Cropped eye region

Fig. 9. Cropped lip region

Step 3: The ROI image has been processed by canny edge detection, segmentation, Gabor transformation and Gray level co-occurrence matrix (GLCM) technique (Figs. 10, 11, 12 and 13).

Fig. 10. Canny edge detection on eye

Fig. 11. Canny edge detection on lip

Fig. 12. Segmentation on eye

Fig. 13. Segmentation on lip

Step 4: After some calculation features has been extracted from ROI image and prepared a dataset (Tables 6, 7, 8 and 9.).

Table 6. Features extracted from edge detection.

Experiment no.	Number of edge pixel in eyes	Number of edge pixel in lips
1	484	256
2	495	274
3	483	236
4	549	187
5	447	184
6	439	195
7	458	186

Table 7. Features extracted from segmentation.

Experiment no.	No. of pixels in eyes	No. of pixels in an eyes	Width of an eye	Length of an eye	No. of pixels in lips	Width of lips	Length of lips
1	1120	364	40	13	948	57	27
2	1119	342	33	15	895	50	26
3	1103	372	40	16	927	57	25
4	921	328	30	15	982	54	24
5	828	349	43	16	798	58	19
6	851	330	41	16	843	57	20
7	807	350	42	18	859	58	20

194   Md. I. Quraishi et al.

Table 8. Some features extracted from Gabor transformation.

Experiment no.	Gabor mean (scale:1 orientation:1)	Gabor mean (scale:1 orientation:2)	Gabor standard deviation (scale:1 orientation:1)	Gabor standard deviation (scale:1 orientation:2)
1	4.28E-06	2.05E-09	0.6702075	0.1854291
2	4.19E-06	2.00E-09	0.6910024	0.1312587
3	4.13E-06	1.98E-09	0.6862336	0.1243167
4	3.61E-06	1.73E-09	0.6231442	0.1275396
5	4.21E-06	2.01E-09	0.6301300	0.1266880
6	4.28E-06	2.05E-09	0.6244349	0.1281803
7	4.20E-06	2.01E-09	0.6944172	0.1264241

Table 9. Some features extracted from Gray level co-occurrence matrix (GLCM).

Experiment no.	Contrast (angle = 0°)	Homogeneity (angle = 0°)	Energy (angle = 0°)	Correlation (angle = 0°)
1	0.510491	0.8324479	0.089946	0.932895
2	0.527008	0.8319531	0.086575	0.928894
3	0.502455	0.8360714	0.089922	0.929460
4	0.457812	0.8378571	0.088750	0.927238
5	0.434598	0.8403236	0.105406	0.932005
6	0.389508	0.8431026	0.113946	0.932309
7	0.393303	0.8501897	0.112771	0.934252

Step 6: Step 1 to 4 repeated for ten different human face images (Fig. 14) where each person has two to four images (Fig. 15) for each of seven expressions (Figs. 16, 17, 18, 19, 20, 21 and 22).

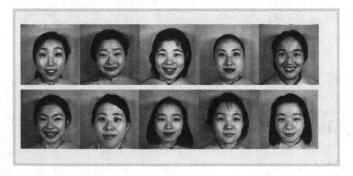

Fig. 14. Ten different human face images.

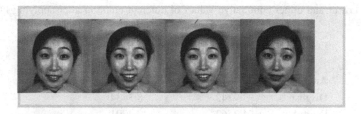

Fig. 15. Different images of a model with happy emotion.

Step 7: The above process (step 1 to step 6) has been executed with seven different human facial emotions: Neutral (Fig. 16), Fearful (Fig. 17), Disgust (Fig. 18), Happy (Fig. 19), Sad (Fig. 20), Surprise (Fig. 21) and Angry (Fig. 22). **St-**
ep

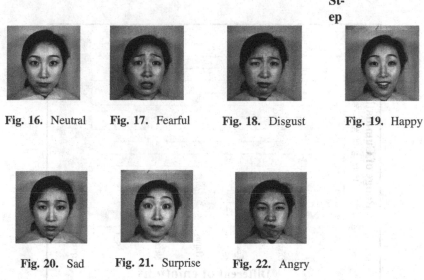

Fig. 16. Neutral   **Fig. 17.** Fearful   **Fig. 18.** Disgust   **Fig. 19.** Happy

Fig. 20. Sad   **Fig. 21.** Surprise   **Fig. 22.** Angry

8: Principal compo-   nent analysis (PCA) has been applied for
                                                           dimension reduction of our dataset. The
following table (Table 10), figures shows the lower and upper values of PCA for different emotions (Fig. 23) and Graphical representation of cumulative values with respect to different experiments for several emotion (Figs. 24, 25, 26, 27, 28, 29, 30, 31 and 32).

Table 10. Lower and upper cumulative values of different emotion after applying PCA to the dataset.

Emotion name	Range of cumulative values	
	Lower value (x 10^7)	Upper value (x 10^7)
Angry	3.3011	6.4089
Disgust	3.9242	8.3434
Fearful	4.2562	7.4791
Happy	7.097	18.782
Neutral	1.9740	2.8181
Sad	2.2967	6.7767
Surprise	21.112	80.023

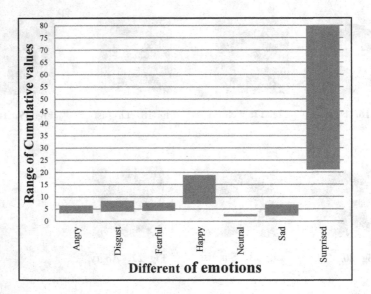

Fig. 23. Graphical representation of cumulative values of different emotions.

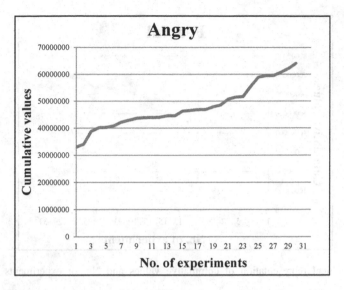

Fig. 24. Graphical representation of cumulative values and No. of experiments for Angry emotion.

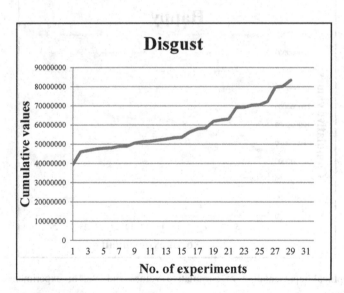

Fig. 25. Graphical representation of cumulative values and No. of experiments for Disgust emotion.

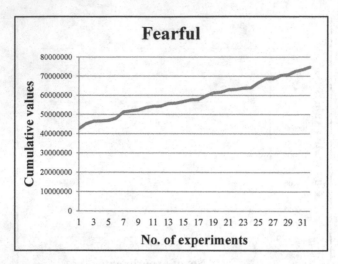

Fig. 26. Graphical representation of cumulative values and No. of experiments for Fearful emotion.

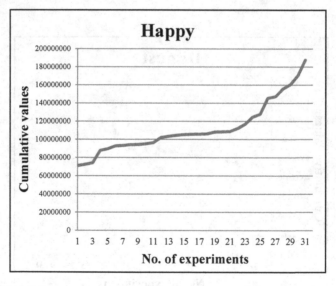

Fig. 27. Graphical representation of cumulative values and No. of experiments for Happy emotion.database.

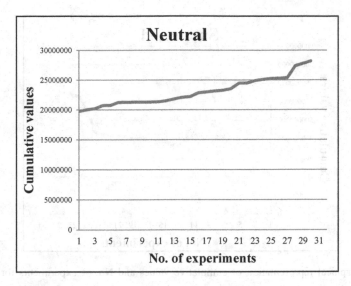

Fig. 28. Graphical representation of cumulative values and No. of experiments for Natural emotion.

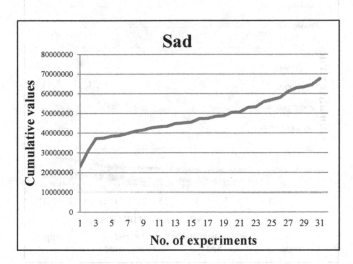

Fig. 29. Graphical representation of cumulative values and No. of experiments for Sad emotion.

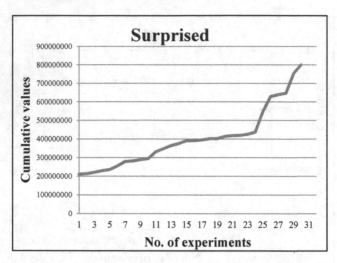

Fig. 30. Graphical representation of cumulative values and No. of experiments for Surprised emotion.

Fig. 31. Graphical representation of cumulative values and No. of experiments for seven different emotions.

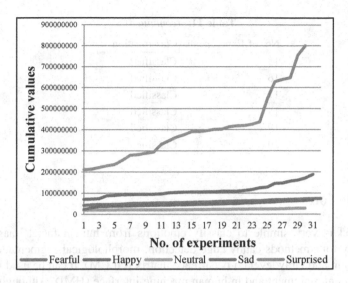

Fig. 32. Graphical representation of cumulative values and No. of experiments for five concluded emotions.

Step 9: A Back Propagation Feed Forward Neural Network has been used for training the input data. The input data has been taken form cumulative values after applying PCA on the dataset. The system has been trained with 150 samples and tested with 100 samples. It has been found that the system miss classify 5 samples and observed that 95 samples are classified successfully. The system produces 95% accuracy to classify emotions. The following table (Table 11) shows 20 experimental results out of 100 for simplicity.

Table 11. Emotion classification status of our proposed system

No. of Experiments	Classification status
1	Classified
2	Classified
3	Classified
4	Classified
5	Not classified
6	Classified
7	Classified
8	Classified
9	Classified
10	Classified
11	Classified
12	Classified
13	Not classified
14	Classified

(*continued*)

Table 11. (*continued*)

No. of Experiments	Classification status
15	Classified
16	Classified
17	Classified
18	Classified
19	Classified
20	Classified

6 Conclusion

This method is very simple to classify emotions from human facial images which include only four methods canny edge detection, morphological segmentation, Gabor transformation and Gray level co-occurrence matrix (GLCM). It can be used in security purpose, for entertainment and in human machine interface (HMI). Although we faced some difficulties through this work, at first features were extracted from pixel values directly but it was unable to give satisfactory results, after this failure we apply Fast Fourier Transform (FFT), Discrete Cosine Transform (DCT), Fan-beam Transform, Radon Transform and Hough Transform separately ROI images but it also become useless. With the basis of the data from Table 10 obtained from PCA, we can see that the range (lower and upper value) of emotion Angry and Disgust completely over-lapped with PCA range of emotion Fearful and Sad. So, we are able to classify only 5 emotions (Fearful, Happy, Neutral, Sad and Surprise) from all 7 emotions.

7 Future Work

In future we want to find some new features which can classify all seven taken emotions and work with other facial databases because here we use only JAFFE database as facial emotion database and able to classify only five facial emotions. We can use neuro-fuzzy system to classify human facial emotions.

References

1. Darwin, C.: The expression of emotions in man and animals. In: Murray, J. (ed.). Chicago Press, Chicago (1965)
2. Aishah, A.R., Komiya, R.: A preliminary study of emotion extraction from voice. In: National Conference on Computer Graphics and Multimedia (CoGRAMM 2002), Malacca (2002)
3. Guo, G., Dyer, C.R.: Learning from examples in the small sample case: face expression recognition. IEEE Trans. Syst. Man Cybern. Part B Cybern. **35**(3), 477–488 (2005)
4. Song, M., Bu, J., Chen, C.: Expression recognition from video using a coupled hidden Markov model (2004). 0-7803-8560 8/04/$20.00©2004IEEE

5. http://en.wikipedia.org/wiki/Paul_Ekman
6. Ekman, P.: Facial expression and emotion. Am. Psychol. **48**, 384–392 (1993)
7. Ekman, P.: An argument for basic emotions. Cogn. Emot. **6**(3/4), 169–200 (1992)
8. Di Gesù, V., Zavidovique, B., Tabacchi, M.E.: Face expression recognition through broken symmetries. In: Sixth Indian Conference on Computer Vision, Graphics & Image Processing (2008). 978-0-7695-3476-3/08 $25.00 © 2008 IEEE https://doi.org/10.1109/icvgip.2008
9. Ilbeygi, M., Shah-Hosseini, H.: A novel fuzzy facial expression recognition system based on facial feature extraction from colour face images. Eng. Appl. Artif. Intell. **25**, 130–146 (2012)
10. Hu, T., De Silva, L.C., Sengupta, K.: A hybrid approach of NN and HMM for facial emotion classification. Pattern Recogn. Lett. **23**, 1303–1310 (2002)
11. Nagpal, R., Nagpal, P., Kaur, S.: Hybrid technique for human face emotion detection. Int. J. Adv. Comput. Sci. Appl. (IJACSA) **1**(6), 91–101 (2010)
12. Hong, K., Chalup, S.K., King, R.A.R.: A Component Based Approach for Classifying the Seven Universal Facial Expressions of Emotion (2013). 978-1-4673-6010-4/13/$31.00c 2013 IEEE
13. Gu, W., Xiang, C., Venkatesh, Y.V., Huang, D., Lin, H.: Facial expression recognition using radial encoding of local Gabor features and classifier synthesis. Pattern Recognit. **45**, 80–91 (2012)
14. Besinger, A., et al.: Optical flow based analyses to detect emotion from human facial image data. Expert Syst. Appl. **37**, 8897–8902 (2010)
15. Habibizad navin, A., Kamal Mirnia, M.: A new algorithm to classify face emotions through eye and lip features by using particle swarm optimization. In: 2012 4th International Conference on Computer Modeling and Simulation (ICCMS 2012) IPCSIT, vol. 22. IACSIT Press, Singapore (2012). © (2012)
16. Lee, Y.-H.: Detection and recognition of facial emotion using Bezier curves. IT CoNvergence PRActice (INPRA) **1**(2), 11–19 (2013)
17. www.kasrl.org/jaffe.html
18. J. database. Kyoto, Japan.: ATR Media Information Science Labs
19. Lyons, M.J., Akamatsu, S., Kamachi, M., Gyoba, J.: Coding facial expressions with Gabor wavelets. In: Proceedings of 3rd IEEE International Conference Automatic Face and Gesture Recognition, pp. 200–205 (1998)
20. Lyons, M.J., Budynek, J., Akamatsu, S.: Automatic classification of single facial images. IEEE Trans. Pattern Anal. Mach. Intell. **21**(12), 1357–1362 (1999)
21. Zhang, Z., Lyons, M., Schuster, M., Akamatsu, S.: Comparison between geometry-based and Gabor-wavelets-based facial expression recognition using multi-layer perceptron. In: Proceedings of 3rd IEEE International Conference Automatic Face and Gesture Recognition, pp. 454–459 (1998)
22. Zhang, Z.: Feature-based facial expression recognition: Sensitivity analysis and experiments with a multi-layer perceptron. Int. J. Pattern Recognit. Artif. Intell. **13**(6), 893–911 (1999)
23. Dailey, M.N., et al.: Evidence and a computational explanation of cultural differences in facial expression recognition. In: Emotion, vol. 10, no. 6, pp. 874–893, December 2010
24. http://en.wikipedia.org/wiki/Canny_edge_detector
25. Canny, J.: A computational approach to edge detection. IEEE Trans. Pattern Anal. Mach. Intell. **8**(6), 679–698 (1986)
26. Biswas, R., Sil, J.: An Improved Canny Edge Detection Algorithm Based on Type-2 Fuzzy Sets. Elsevier Ltd. (2012). https://doi.org/10.1016/j.protcy.2012.05.134
27. Ding, Lijun, Goshtasby, Ardeshir: On the canny edge detector. Pattern Recogn. **34**, 721–725 (2001)

28. Shapiro, L.G., Stockman, G.C.: Computer Vision, pp 279-325. New Jersey, Prentice-Hall (2001). ISBN 0-13-030796-3
29. Barghout, L., Lee, L.W.: Perceptual information processing system. Paravue Inc. U.S. Patent Application 10/618,543, filed 11 July 2003
30. http://en.wikipedia.org/wiki/Category:Image_segmentation
31. Su, T.-C., Yang, M.-D., Wu, T.-C., Lin, J.-Y.: Morphological segmentation based on edge detection for sewer pipe defects on CCTV images. Expert Syst. Appl. **38**, 13094–13114 (2011)
32. Sebastian, B., Unnikrishnan, A., Balakrishnan, K.: Grey level co-occurrence matrices: generalisation and some new features. Int. J. Comput. Sci. Eng. Inf. Technol. (IJCSEIT) **2** (2), 151–157 (2012)
33. http://www.mathworks.in/help/images/analyzing-the-texture-of-an-image.html#f11-29651
34. Haralick, R.M., Shanmugam, K., Dinstein, I.: Textural features for image classification. IEEE Trans. Syst. Man Cybern. **SMC-3**, 610–621 (1973)
35. Hikawa, H.: Implementation of simplified multilayer neural network with on-chip learning. In: Proceedings of the IEEE International Conference on Neural Networks (Part 4), vol. 4, pp. 1633–1637 (1999)
36. Harshavardhan, M., Visweswara Rao, S.: GLCM architecture for image extraction. Int. J. Adv. Res. Electron. Commun. Eng. (IJARECE) **3**(1) 75–82 (2014)
37. Heikkinen, K., Vuorimaa, P.: Computation of two texture features in hardware. In: Proceedings of the 10th International Conference on Image Analysis and Processing, Venice, Italy, pp. 125–129, 27–29 September 1999
38. Conners, R.W., Harlow, C.A.: A theoretical comparison of texture algorithms. IEEE Trans. Pattern Anal. Machine Intell. **PAMI-2**, 204–222 (1980)
39. Conners, R.W., Trivedi, M.M., Harlow, C.A.: Segmentation of a high-resolution urban scene using texture operators. Comput. Vis. Graph. Image Process. **25**, 273–310 (1984)
40. Haralick, R.M., Shanmugam, K.: Computer classification of reservoir sandstones. IEEE Trans. Geo. Eng. **GE-11**, 171–177 (1973)
41. He, D.C., Wang, L., Juibert, J.: Texture feature extraction. Pattern Recogn. Lett. **6**, 269–273 (1987)
42. Iizulca, M.: Quantitative evaluation of similar images with quasi-gray levels. Comput. Vis. Graph. Image Process. **38**, 342–360 (1987)
43. Siew, L.H., Hodgson, R.H., Wood, E.J.: Texture measures for carpet wear asessment. IEEE Trans. Pattern Anal. Mach. Intell. **PAMI-10**, 92–105 (1988)
44. Weszka, J.S., Dyer, C.R., Rosenfeld, A.: A comparative study of texture measures for terrain classification. IEEE Trans. Syst. Man Cybern. **SMC-6**, 269–285 (1976)
45. http://en.wikipedia.org/wiki/Gabor_transform
46. Chen, C.H., Pau, L.F., Wang, P.S.P. (eds.) The Handbook of Pattern Recognition and Computer Vision, 2nd Edn. pp. 207–248, World Scientific Publishing Co., Singapore (1998)
47. Pearson, K.: On lines and planes of closest fit to systems of points in space (PDF). Phil. Mag. **2**(11), 559–572 (1901)
48. Tsai, P.H., Jan, T.: Expression-invariant face recognition system using subspace model analysis. In: IEEE International Conference on Systems, Man and Cybernetics, vol. 2, pp. 1712–1717 (2005)
49. Shao, Y.E., Hsu, B.S.: Determining the contributors for a multivariate SPC chart signal using artificial neural networks and support vector machine. Int. J. Innovative Comput. Inf. Control **5**(12(B)), 4899–4906 (2009)
50. Chou, P.H., Hsu, C.H., Wu, C.F., Li, P.H., Wu, M.J.: Application of back-propagation neural network for e-commerce customers patterning. ICIC Express Lett. **3**(3 (B)), 775–785 (2009)

51. He, C., Li, H., Wang, H., Yu, W., Liang, X.: Prediction of compressive yield load for metal hollow sphere with crack based on artificial neural network. ICIC Express Lett. **3**(4 (B)), 1263–1268 (2009)

52. Wu, J.K., Kang, J., Chen, M.H., Chen, G.T.: Fuzzy neural network model based on particle swarm optimization for short-term load forecasting. Proc. CSU-EPSA **19**(1), 63–67 (2007)

53. Li, D.K., Zhang, H.X., Li, S.A.: Development cost estimation of aircraft frame based on BP neural networks. Fire Control Command Control **31**(9), 27–29 (2006)

54. Rumelhart, D.E., Hinton, G.E., Williams, R.J.: Learning representations by back-propagating errors. Nature **323**(6088), 533–536 (1986)

55. Sivanandam, S.N., Deepa, S.N.: Principle of Soft Computing, pp. 74–83. Wiley India Edition (1993)

56. Karimi, B., Menhaj, M.B., Saboori, I.: Multilayer feed forward neural networks for controlling de-centralized large-scale non-affine nonlinear systems with guaranteed stability. Int. J. Innovative Comput. Inf. Control **6**(11), 4825–4841 (2010)

57. ZareNezhad, B., Aminian, A.: A multi-layer feed forward neural network model for accurate prediction of flue gas sulfuric acid dew points in process industries. Appl. Therm. Eng. **30**(6-7), 692–696 (2010)

58. Jamshidnejad, A., Jamshidined, A.: Facial emotion recognition for human computer interaction using a fuzzy model in the e-business. In: Conference on Innovative Technologies in Intelligent Systems and Industrial Applications (CITISIA 2009) (2009). 978-1-4244-2887-8/09/$25.00 ©2009 IEEE

59. Rizon, M., Karthigayan, M., Yaacob, S., Nagarajan, R.: Japanese face emotions classification using lip features. In: Geometric Modelling and Imaging (GMAI 2007) (2007). 0-7695-2901-1/07 $20.00 © 2007 IEEE

60. http://www.cs.otago.ac.nz/cosc453/student_tutorials/principal_components.pdf

61. McCulloch, W., Pitts, W.: A logical calculus of the ideas immanent in nervous activity. Bull. Math. Biophys. **7**, 115–133 (1943)

A Time Efficient Threshold Based Ant Colony System for Cloud Load Balancing

Chandan Banerjee[✉], Abhishek Roy, Alokananda Roy, Anisha Saha,
and Arnab Kumar De

Department of Information Technology,
Netaji Subhash Engineering College, Kolkata 700152, India
chandanbanerjeel@gmail.com,
abhishek.roy281996@gmail.com,
march.riverine@gmail.com,
anishasaha58@gmail.com, arnabde49@gmail.com

Abstract. To enhance the speed of data transfer and remote server working performances, the suggested algorithm accomplishes load balancing in virtual machines by maintaining high availability and avoiding downtime issues when a datacenter experiences heavy traffic. This result has been obtained through minimizing the average response time and datacenter processing time by decently scheduling the requests and balancing the incoming load between the VMs. To achieve so, a combination of two scheduling techniques, Ant Colony Optimization System coupled with Threshold implemented Load Balancer algorithm has been designed. This paper also brings up comparisons among various cloud task scheduling algorithms such as Round-Robin (RR) and Active VM Load Balancer with the proposed technique. All algorithms have been simulated using Cloud Analyst toolkit package. Experimental results showed that the proposed Threshold based ACO system outperformed other stated algorithms.

Keywords: Load balancing · Task scheduler · Virtual machine ·
Ant Colony Optimization · Threshold · Datacenter controller · Cloud-analyst

1 Introduction

An important aspects of cloud computing is virtualization [1] which makes use of virtual devices by segregating it from the physical device. It increases scalability of resources and decreases the cost, improving infrastructure utilization by creating a system of independent computing devices where the idle jobs are being allotted and the workload across the computing resources are evenly distributed. But it becomes difficult to allot the incoming jobs or tasks manually when thousands of VM are in use [2]. That's why we require an algorithm which can efficiently allocate tasks to respective VMs. Autonomic computing mechanizes the procedure through which the client can arrange assets on-request. By limiting client contribution, it accelerates the procedure, diminishes work costs and decreases the likelihood of human mistakes [3].

© Springer Nature Singapore Pte Ltd. 2019
J. K. Mandal et al. (Eds.): CICBA 2018, CCIS 1030, pp. 206–219, 2019.
https://doi.org/10.1007/978-981-13-8578-0_16

An efficient task scheduler and load balancer ought to adjust its scheduling strategy. A dynamic scheduling algorithm, Ant Colony Optimization known can be implemented with the datacenter controller, to achieve this.

2 Related Work

Techniques inspired by swarm intelligence like honeybee foraging system [4] have taken place in the area of load balancing and task scheduling research. Also, a random search algorithm known as the Ant Colony Optimization system emulates the behavior of real ant colonies. Initially, ants start searching their foods randomly and depositing a chemical known as pheromone laid on paths travelled. Each line of a pheromone table speaks of the probabilistic directing inclination for every destination and every column speaks of the likelihood of picking a neighbor as the following jump. The forthcoming ants follow the trail and refresh the pheromone table of a hub. As this proceeds, a large portion of the ants draw in to pick the briefest way as there has been an immense measure of pheromones collected on this way [5]. The conduct of the ants is utilized for searching closest answers for discrete and constant advancement issues, directing and stack load balancing [6].

A multi-target improvement planning technique [7] considers make-span and the client's spending costs as imperatives of the issue and accomplishing multi-target enhancement of both execution and cost, understood by utilizing ACO.

In a hybrid cloud condition, multi-objective scheduling technique in light of Ant Colony optimization (MOSACO) [8] streamlines the limited pool of open and private registering assets considering the deadline and cost requirements, limiting job execution time and costs utilizing time-first and cost-first advancement systems, separately.

Max-Min, another variant of Ant System [9], exploits the stagnation stage, making all edges get instated to τmax and reinitialized to τmin. It can be connected to distinguish potential arrangements in the pursuit space utilizing pheromone trail and make new encouraging introductory solution for localized search.

The heuristic data esteems in the directing tables of AntNet [10] adaptation indicates that forward ants pick the following bounce haphazardly but are changed over to the regressive ants when they touch base at the last destination. The retrogressive ant heads out back to the source through the turnaround course, discharging pheromones on each connection cruised by it.

Transformative processing is connected to Virtual Machine Placement [11] to limit the quantity of dynamic physical servers, in order to use under-stacked servers to spare vitality when Ant Colony System combined with the order and exchange migration (OEM) local search technique, called OEMACS, through pheromone affidavit.

3 Proposed Work

An integration of two main sections, dealing with the organized management of the requested jobs has been aimed for implementation.

In order to determine the closest VM, ACO system has been taken into consideration over other techniques for a handful of reasons. ACO finds its objective as to the look for a minimum value path during a graph. The algorithm possesses positive feedback mechanism, hence producing well structured solutions rapidly. It also helps in achieving intrinsic parallelism and finds its utmost usefulness in dynamic applications. The disadvantages are overhead and the stagnation phenomenon making the algorithm converge to local optimal solution [5].

The datacenter controller handles some quintillion bytes of requests generated every day, also housing an enormous amount of digital information that are requested to be processed. It manages and ensures the systematic execution of requests. Each VM in the VM list is associated with a Threshold which refers to the number of task that can be executed by a particular VM in one unit time (capacity of a VM). Once the VM closest is determined using the general ACO algorithm, the task is then allocated to the chosen VM if and only if the number of tasks being currently executed by the VM is less than its own Threshold value. If not, the modified ACO datacenter calls for the general ACO system to search for the next nearest VM corresponding to the user base requesting for the execution of the task. The mentioned process goes on and on until the system finds appropriate VM that abides by all criteria and conditions.

Decreasing the overall response time and the data center processing time are the ultimate goal of the proposed method.

1. *General ACO Problem Representation:* The ants are being initially placed in a random manner on the starting VMs. During an iteration, the ants travel from one VM to the other and while doing, they develop the solution to the cloud scheduling problem.
2. *Heuristic Desirability:* A simple heuristic of the inverse of expected execution time of the task of a VM is used.
3. *General ACO Constraint Satisfaction:* The method is implemented as a simple, short-term memory of the visited VM, in order to, avoid visiting a VM more than once in one ACO procedure and minimize time of the assigned couplings (task and VM).
4. *Pheromone Updating Rule:* Pheromone evaporates on all edges and new pheromone is deposited by all ants on visited edges; its value is proportional to the quality of the solution built by the ants [12].
5. *Probabilistic Transition Rule:* While in the process of the ants marking their journey over the considered graph and a solution being developed, every node obtains a probabilistic verdict. The probabilistic transition rule, called random proportional, is the one typical of ant system [15].
6. *Fitness function:* This analyses similarity or closeness of a considered resolution with the ideal resolution of a required problem. In other words, it determines the extent of practicability or how realistic the solution is.
7. *Threshold Implemented Modified ACO Datacenter Controller Problem Representation:* In this problem, it is to be determined whether the closest VM as per ACO system is fit for allocation of a task, following the rule of not exceeding the threshold concept.

8. *Threshold implemented modified ACO Datacenter Controller Constraint Satisfaction:* The factor is accomplished by using two parameter list- the threshold of each VM and the number of task(s) being executed by the concerned VM. While the threshold parameter remains constant throughout the execution of the program, the number of task(s) being executed by the concerned VM is susceptible to change or rather get updated.

9. *Final VM allocation rule:* The system decides a particular VM for a concerned task based on the algorithm constrains being satisfied. If the chosen VM fails to do so, the general ACO system has to get executed to find the next nearest VM (Fig. 1).

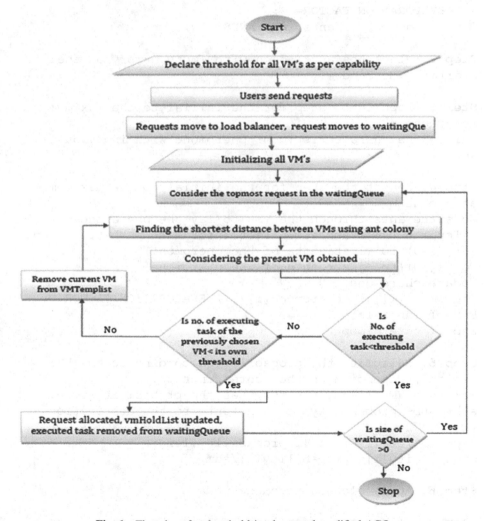

Fig. 1. Flowchart for threshold implemented modified ACO

3.1   Algorithm 1. Ant Colony VM Load Balancer

Input: Tasks List and VM list
Output: The best solution for tasks allocation on VMs.

Step 1. Initialize:
Set constant **alpha**= 1;
Set constant **beta**= 1;
Set **ONE_UNIT_PHEROMONE**= 1;
Set **EVAPORATION_FACTOR**= 2;
Set the number of ants, **NUM_ANTS**= 10;

Step 2. Place the ants, each with empty memory on the starting VMs randomly.

Step 3. Repeat the step for the initial to the maximum ant-count -
Relate the characteristic of pheromone with individual ants.

Step 4. Repeat the step for the initial to the maximum ant-count -
Move the ants through the VMs to lay the pheromone.
Calculate the evaporation factor for each path travelled.
For (i=0) to (i<strength of the pheromone)
For (j=0) to (j<strength of the pheromone)
Update pheromone.
pheromone[i][j]= pheromone[i][j]/ EVAPORATION_FACTOR
End of inner loop
End of outer loop

Step 5. Calculate the probability according to the VMs visited, depending on the score function.
For each VM already visited, set the probability to 0.
sum= sum+ probability of each route to the destination VM.
Repeat, for (i=0) to (i<probability.length)
probability[i]= probability[i]/sum

Step 6. Apply global pheromone update.

Step 7. Select the under-load VM from the highest probability from the value of the pheromone.

Step 8. End.

3.2   Algorithm 2. Threshold Implemented Modified Load Balancer

Input: Closest VM obtained from previous algorithm.
Output: Task allocated to the appropriate VM and system waiting for new task.

Steps 1. Initialize the each VM and the VM list.
Declare and initialize the virtual machine threshold list (denotes the capacity of each VM).
Declare and initialize the virtual machine holding list (denotes how much task each VM is presently executing).
Declare the temporary VM list.
Set nextAvailVMprev= -1;

Step 2. Place any approaching tasks in waitingQueue arranged by their arriving time.

Step 3. Perform Modified Ant Colony optimization while Cloudlet List not empty or there are more incoming Cloudlets.
Get the nearest VM by calculating the shortest distance.

Step 4. For each task to be allocated, initialize the temporary VM list (copy of original VM list).

Step 5. If there is still task present in the waitingQueue which is yet to be performed and the number of task being presently executed by the VM is less than the threshold of that VM,
allocate the task to the considered VM.
Otherwise, go to the next step.

Step 6. If one or more task is still present in the waitingQueue which are yet to be performed but the number of task being presently executed by thc VM is not less than the threshold of that VM, check whether the previously considered VM (nextAvailVMprev) is a valid VM and whether the number of tasks executed by the that VM has dropped from its own threshold value by now or not.
If yes, move to step 8, else go to step 7.

Step 7. Set nextAvailVMprev = nextAvailVM.
Remove the presently considered VM from the temporary VM list.
Call function submitWaitingCloudlet() and find the next nearest VM to the corresponding user base from which the task is demanded to be performed.

Step 8. Allocate the task to the particular VM which has satisfied the conditions in the previous step.

Step 9. End.

4 Experimental Results

4.1 Simulation Configuration

5 User Bases (UB) and 2 data centers (DC) are considered for all input parameters. Table 1 represents input configurations.

Table 1. Input configuration

Entity type	Parameters	Value
User Base	Number of user bases	5
	Requests per hour	60
	Data Size per request	100 (bytes)
	Average peak users	17020
VMs	Number of VMs	25 per datacenter
	Memory	1024 (first 25) 512 (second 25)
	Bandwidth	1000
Data centers	Number of data centers	2
User grouping factor	Number	1000
Request grouping factor	Number	250
Executable instruction length per request	Number	1000

4.2 Comparison of Proposed ACO with Round Robin and Active VM Monitoring

The proposed Threshold implemented ACO has been compared with the other algorithms against each three service broker policies on the basis of average response time and average datacenter processing time.

4.2.1 Average Response Time for Optimize Response Time Service Broker Policy

It is observed by comparing Tables 2, 3 and 4 and from Fig. 2, that the proposed algorithm yields better response time than the other two.

Table 2. Response time by region of Active VM Load Balancing

Userbase	Avg (ms)	Min (ms)	Max (ms)
UB1	529.56	75.42	911.18
UB2	272.22	78.87	370.11
UB3	660.99	320.34	1199.77
UB4	603.57	449.37	1239.39
UB5	662.00	438.94	1339.47

Table 3. Response time by region of Round Robin

Userbase	Avg (ms)	Min (ms)	Max (ms)
UB1	522.92	140.20	922.67
UB2	270.51	83.57	369.43
UB3	657.85	334.43	1161.08
UB4	589.47	449.37	1116.89
UB5	639.30	439.41	1321.18

Table 4. Response time by region of Threshold based modified ACO Load Balancer

Userbase	Avg (ms)	Min (ms)	Max (ms)
UB1	438.60	64.89	1120.88
UB2	270.87	83.70	520.02
UB3	590.56	327.16	1427.90
UB4	600.30	446.92	1239.39
UB5	651.11	439.03	1142.09

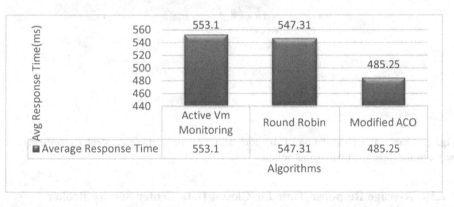

Fig. 2. Graphical representation of the comparison of the average response time between the three load balancing policies.

4.2.2   Average Data Center Processing Time for Optimize Response Time Service Broker Policy

It is observed by comparing Tables 5, 6 and 7 and from Fig. 3, that the proposed algorithm yields better datacenter processing time than the other two.

Table 5. Datacenter request servicing time of Active VM Load Balancing

Data center	Avg (ms)	Min (ms)	Max (ms)
DC1	375.34	15.23	857.08
DC2	280.95	31.58	656.10

Table 6. Datacenter request servicing time of Round Robin

Data center	Avg (ms)	Min (ms)	Max (ms)
DC1	360. 68	15.37	870.08
DC2	302.12	31.29	649.28

Table 7. Datacenter request servicing time of Threshold based modified ACO Load Balancer

Data center	Avg (ms)	Min (ms)	Max (ms)
DC1	296.02	15.46	1115.20
DC2	260.91	31.25	779.82

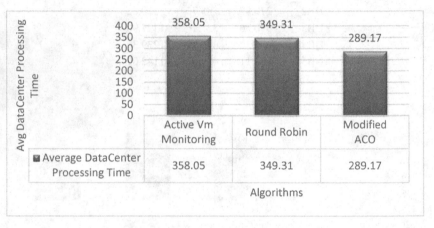

Fig. 3. Graphical representation of the comparison of the average datacenter processing time between the three load balancing policies.

4.2.3 Average Response Time for Closest Data Center Service Broker Policy

It is observed by comparing Tables 8, 9 and 10 and from Fig. 4, that the proposed algorithm yields better response time than the other two.

Table 8. Response time by region of Active VM Load Balancing

Userbase	Avg (ms)	Min (ms)	Max (ms)
UB1	534.39	129.17	923.17
UB2	300.69	105.07	367.81
UB3	643.90	309.22	1182.10
UB4	562.08	430.69	880.32
UB5	601.93	467.26	1321.79

Table 9. Response time by region of Round Robin

Userbase	Avg (ms)	Min (ms)	Max (ms)
UB1	531.03	129.17	924.48
UB2	300.42	105.07	368.08
UB3	648.91	305.93	1179.78
UB4	562.05	479.02	895.32
UB5	602.51	466.01	1318.65

Table 10. Response time by region of Threshold based modified ACO Load Balancer

Userbase	Avg (ms)	Min (ms)	Max (ms)
UB1	443.07	82.42	994.56
UB2	276.44	109.87	678.14
UB3	549.15	332.35	1199.73
UB4	557.09	480.69	783.49
UB5	601.26	467.26	1348.47

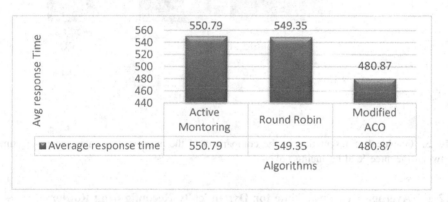

Fig. 4. Graphical representation of the comparison of the average response time between the three load balancing policies.

4.2.4 Average Data Center Processing Time for Closest Data Center Service Broker Policy

It is observed by comparing Tables 11, 12 and 13 and from Fig. 5, that the proposed algorithm yields better datacenter processing time than the other two.

Table 11. Datacenter request servicing time of Active VM Load Balancing

Data center	Avg (ms)	Min (ms)	Max (ms)
DC1	395.28	15.39	872.87
DC2	250.12	58.79	315.90

Table 12. Datacenter request servicing time of Round Robin

Data center	Avg (ms)	Min (ms)	Max (ms)
DC1	320.63	15.38	943.08
DC2	225.87	61.83	625.02

Table 13. Datacenter request servicing time of Threshold based modified ACO Load Balancer

Data center	Avg (ms)	Min (ms)	Max (ms)
DCl	393.44	15.41	873.87
DC2	249.87	58.79	312.86

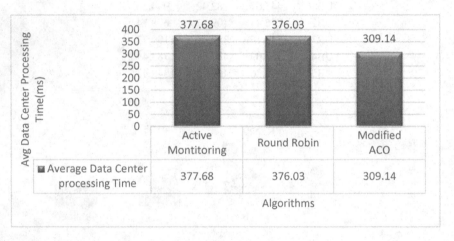

Fig. 5. Graphical representation of the comparison of the average datacenter processing time between the three load balancing policies.

4.2.5 Average Response Time for Dynamically Reconfiguring Routers Service Broker Policy

It is observed by comparing Tables 14, 15 and 16 and from Fig. 6, that the proposed algorithm yields better response time than the other two.

Table 14. Response time by region of Active VM Load Balancing

Userbase	Avg (ms)	Min (ms)	Max (ms)
UB1	2794.88	130.62	39756.97
UB2	1662.00	118.04	69051.40
UB3	2563.80	310.25	58390.72
UB4	678.90	486.89	2497.47
UB5	635.00	473.07	1284.29

Table 15. Response time by region of Round Robin

Userbase	Avg (ms)	Min (ms)	Max (ms)
UB1	2978.96	130.62	27885.73
UB2	1660.75	89.33	9660.57
UB3	3510.52	320.07	58390.85
UB4	969.02	486.89	4494.18
UB5	948.62	473.29	10099.54

Table 16. Response time by region of Threshold based modified ACO Load Balancer

Userbase	Avg (ms)	Min (ms)	Max (ms)
UB1	705.29	122.48	22346.91
UB2	811.71	104.72	67243.62
UB3	885.12	320.09	15376.60
UB4	927.38	482.48	4625.74
UB5	660.25	453.10	1990.51

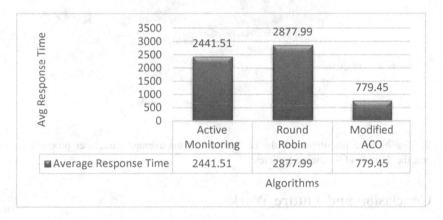

Fig. 6. Graphical representation of the comparison of the average response time between the three load balancing policies.

4.2.6 Average Data Center Processing Time for Dynamically Reconfiguring Routers Service Broker Policy

It is observed in Fig. 7, that the proposed algorithm yields better datacenter processing time than the other two (Tables 17, 18 and 19).

Table 17. Datacenter request servicing time of Active VM Load Balancing

Data center	Avg (ms)	Min (ms)	Max (ms)
DC1	2328.53	16.26	58066.62
DC2	1611.54	62.53	68997.86

218   C. Banerjee et al.

Table 18. Datacenter request servicing time of Round Robin

Data center	Avg (ms)	Min (ms)	Max (ms)
DC1	2824.39	16.26	58069.66
DC2	1610.42	34.54	9609.25

Table 19. Datacenter request servicing time of Threshold based modified ACO Load Balancer

Data center	Avg (ms)	Min (ms)	Max (ms)
DCl	587.08	16.26	22299.55
DC2	761.22	58.44	67193.54

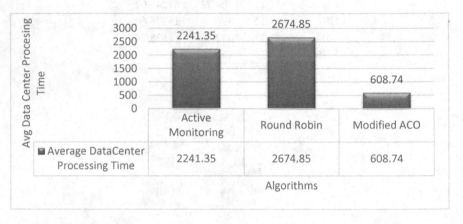

Fig. 7. Graphical representation of the comparison of the average datacenter processing time between the three load balancing policies.

5   Conclusion and Future Work

It is to be concluded from the experimental results that the proposed modified Ant Colony Optimization with threshold performs better than Round Robin and Active VM Load Balancer for the all the three service broker policies based on the Optimized Response Time and Closest Data Center Processing Time. The average response time and the average data center processing time is less than that of the round robin and active VM load balancing algorithms.

In future work the impact of priority amongst tasks and load adjusting would be taken into consideration. Likewise, the correlation between the proposed approach and other metaheuristics methodologies will be performed. This method does not consider the blame tolerance issues. Analysts can continue to incorporate the adaptation to non-critical failure issues in their future inquires about.

References

1. Gao, Y., Guan, H., Qi, Z., Hou, Y., Liu, L.: A multi-objective ant colony system algorithm for virtual machine placement in cloud computing. J. Comput. Syst. Sci. **79**(8), 1230–1242 (2013)
2. Qiyi, H., Tinglei, H.: An optimistic job scheduling strategy based on QoS for cloud computing. In: Proceedings of the IEEE International Conference on Intelligent Computing and Integrated Systems, Guilin, China, pp. 673–675 (2010)
3. Hamdaqa, M.: Cloud computing uncovered: a research landscape, pp. 41–85. Elsevier Press (2012). ISBN 0-12-396535-7
4. Mishra, R., Jaiswal, A.: Ant colony optimization: a solution of load balancing in cloud. Int. J. Web Semant. Technol. (IJWesT) **3**(2), 33 (2012). https://doi.org/10.5121/ijwest.2012.3203
5. Bonabeau, E., Dorigo, M., Theraulaz, G.: Swarm Intelligence: From Natural to Artificial Intelligence. Oxford University Press, New York (1999)
6. Blum, C.: Ant colony optimization: introduction and recent trends. ALBCOM, LSI, Universitat Politècnica de Catalunya, Jordi Girona 1-3, Campus Nord, 08034 Barcelona, Spain. Accepted 11 October 2005
7. Zuo, L., Shu, L., Dong, S., Zhu, C., Hara, T.: A multi-objective optimization scheduling method based on the ant colony algorithm in cloud computing. https://doi.org/10.1109/ACCESS.2015.2508940
8. Zuo, L., Shu, L., Dong, S., Chen, Y., Yan, L.: A multi-objective hybrid cloud resource scheduling method based on deadline and cost constraints. IEEE Access. https://doi.org/10.1109/access.2016.2633288
9. Stützle, T., Hoos, H.H.: MAX-MIN ant system. Future Gener. Comput. Syst. **16**(8), 889–914 (2000)
10. Di Caro, G., Dorigo, M.: AntNet: distributed stigmergetic control for communications networks. J. Artif. Intell. Res. **9**(3), 317–365 (1998)
11. Liu, X.-F., Zhan, Z.-H., Deng, J.D., Li, Y., Gu, T., Zhang, J.: An energy efficient ant colony system for virtual machine placement in cloud computing. IEEE. https://doi.org/10.1109/tevc.2016.2623803
12. Dorigo, M., Gambardella, L.M.: Ant colony system: a cooperative learning approach to the traveling salesman problem. IEEE Trans. Evol. Comput. **1**(1), 53–66 (1997)

Signal Processing and Communications

Design of Synthetic 3-D Pulmonary Phantoms Using 2-D Graphical User Interface

Arijit De[1], Nirmal Das[1], Ram Sarkar[1], Punam Kumar Saha[2],
and Subhadip Basu[1(✉)]

[1] Department of Computer Science and Engineering, Jadavpur University,
Kolkata 700032, India
subhadip@cse.jdvu.ac.in
[2] Department of ECE and Radiology, University of Iowa,
Iowa City, IA 52242, USA

Abstract. Analysis of pulmonary artery or vein tree has utmost importance in the study and clinical diagnosis of Chronic Obstructive Pulmonary Diseases (COPD). Due to difficulty in acquiring real life patient data and highly complex structure of artery/vein tree, design of imitated/approximate digital pulmonary phantoms for experimental purposes is an active research area. In this work, we discuss theory and methods of designing 3-D mathematical phantoms based on real pulmonary data using a custom made Graphical User Interface (GUI). These approximate phantoms are made using 3-D spheres as the basic unit which are placed in 3-D space using cubic Bezier curves. Results and design steps are explained using appropriate 3-D rendering of digital phantoms developed by our GUI.

Keywords: Human pulmonary vasculature · 3-D rendering · Digital phantom ·
Mathematical modeling · COPD · Artery · Vein

1 Introduction

Respiration is an essential process for the survival of living organisms. In case of human beings, it is performed collectively by the nose, nasal cavities, pharynx, larynx, and trachea that divide into bronchi and enters the lungs where it further subdivides into bronchioles and finally alveoli. Exchange of gases (Oxygen and Carbon dioxide) with the blood vessels takes place in the alveoli of the lungs. The alveoli are tiny air sacs within the lungs where the exchange of oxygen and carbon dioxide takes place.

The pulmonary artery and pulmonary veins carry deoxygenated and oxygenated blood respectively and form a separate circuit through the heart and lungs only. These arteries and veins are intertwined along the air ways and branches successively until they form capillaries in the alveolar region.

The airways keep on branching until very fine alveoli are formed. This branching has an order of 17 according to [1] and the lowest order has endings in the order of 10^8. Pulmonary arteries and veins run along the surface of these fine structures. All these give us an idea of the complexity of the artery/vein (A/V) network in human lungs.

© Springer Nature Singapore Pte Ltd. 2019
J. K. Mandal et al. (Eds.): CICBA 2018, CCIS 1030, pp. 223–233, 2019.
https://doi.org/10.1007/978-981-13-8578-0_17

Analysis of pulmonary vessel network is very important for diagnosis of several diseases related to lungs. Chronic Obstructive Pulmonary Diseases (COPD) are a group of diseases that blocks airflow inside the lungs and make it difficult to breathe [2]. Emphysema and chronic bronchitis are the most common conditions that make up COPD. Pulmonary Embolism (PE) is another disease in which one or more arteries/veins in the lungs get blocked. In most cases, PE is caused by blood clots that travel to the lungs from the legs or, rarely, from other parts of the body (deep vein thrombosis). The symptoms include difficulty in breathing, chest pain and cough (sometimes accompanied by blood) [3].

With the help of clearly distinct artery and vein regions in 3-D images of pulmonary vessels, diagnosis on patients will be more efficient and fast as embolisms or any unusual structures can be accurately identified.

Segmented pulmonary arteries and veins from patients' *in-vivo* chest images (CT Scan/Ultrasound etc.) have useful clinical applications in COPD [4]. It is the first step towards further analysis like flow analysis [5] of the vessel network for detection of any obstruction (in case of PE).

Due to high branching factor and large number of bifurcated or intertwined vessels, *in-vivo* analysis of pulmonary A/V tree is a complex and time-consuming process and needs to be handled by domain experts. Also, to get different kinds of real data, many human patients are required but the repeated exposure to CT scan/MRI is harmful. Hence, the need to have *prototype* or *synthetic* structures arises as this will reduce the dependency on participation of patients during diagnosis. These synthetic structures generated mathematically are called *phantoms* which are smaller and relatively simpler than real pulmonary A/V trees, while maintaining the same structural features like bifurcations, intertwinements and conjointness. This type of phantoms is called approximate phantoms. There are two types of phantoms in general – (1) physical and (2) digital. Physical phantoms are created by casting a replica of actual vasculature. For example, pig lung cast phantom is generated by injecting a rapid hardening compound into the pulmonary vasculature extracted by performing pneumonectomy on the ensanguined pig. Then the vessel cast is digitized using a CT scanner. Both synthetic and physical phantoms were used in [6–9] for experimentation and analysis. Digital phantoms are made by creating multiple tubular structures of varying geometry and various scales of overlap and attaching them at desired points to mimic the actual structure. Both types of phantoms are used for assessing performance of segmentation of pulmonary A/V tree, qualitatively and quantitatively. Different types of physical vessel phantoms are in use, for quantitative assessment of mean differences between the clinical studies and the phantom-based experiments as stated in [10–12].

In many theoretical studies, physical phantoms are not essential rather approximate digital phantoms fulfill the basic purposes. Hence, several researchers have paid attention to the development of synthetic vascular phantoms. To efficiently test new algorithms and experiment on pulmonary data, the size and complexity of the data can be reduced keeping the structural features like branching angle, width of vessels intact or scaled to a lower resolution for fast computation.

The main purpose of our work is to recreate the vascular structures in the digital space, using mathematical curve generation techniques and 3-D graphical rendering. In contemporary literature, a number of research articles are available on digital phantom generation [10–13] and computational analysis of blood vessels [14–16]. Most of the research works conducted previously focuses on coronary arteries and myocardial infarction as seen in [10, 12]. But substantial work on digital phantom generation of pulmonary vasculature is not available yet, hence our work is focused on pulmonary A/V which have a higher degree of complexity due to repeated bifurcations. A different approach in phantom generation is shown in [13] that applies computer generated 3-D mesh for creating vascular structures. But in this present work, we have used 3-D spheres as the building blocks of vessels. The works in [14, 15] focuses on centrelines of carotid arteries.

From the above discussion, the importance of mathematically generated synthetic 3D phantoms have been clearly established. The phantom generation method of the present work is aligned with the work [17, 18] but the previous methods concentrated on generating cerebrovascular phantom.

The present work aims to discuss about generation of approximate mathematical phantom mimicking real pulmonary A/V network (conjointness of artery-vein at varying scale) and reconstructing accurate pulmonary phantom with the help of a custom-developed GUI. In this GUI, we can select points from a real lung image data and create small portions of the entire lung network having similar curvature and width. This tool will also be useful to the research community to prepare ground truth images of pulmonary data.

The paper is organized as follows. Section 2 describes the theory of 3-D digital images and the fundamentals of phantom generation. Section 3 contains experimental results of phantoms generated using the theory explained in Sect. 2. Finally, the conclusions are drawn in Sect. 4.

2 Theory and Method

A 3-D cubic grid is expressed by $\{\mathcal{Z}^3 | \mathcal{Z} \text{ is the set of positive integers}\}$. A point on the grid, which is frequently referred as a voxel, is a member of $\mathcal{Z}^3$ and is denoted by a triplet of integer coordinates. Each voxel has 26 adjacent voxels, i.e. two voxels $A = (x_1, x_2, x_3)$ and $B = (y_1, y_2, y_3) \in \mathcal{Z}^3$ are adjacent if and only if

$$\{\max(|x_i - y_i|) \leq 1 | 1 \leq i \leq 3\},$$

where $| \cdot |$ means the absolute value. Two adjacent points in a cubic grid are often referred to as neighbors of each other. All 26 neighbors of a voxel $\mathcal{V}$ omitting itself are symbolized as $\mathcal{N}^*(\mathcal{V})$.

2.1 Distance Transform

The distance transform (DT) is an algorithm generally applied to binary images. The output of this algorithm is same as the input image except that the values of each foreground points of the image are changed to the distance to the nearest background from that point. Numerous DT algorithms have been developed both in 2-D and 3-D

[19–22] in the past. If $P = (x_1, x_2, x_3)$ is a point in a 3-D image, then DT value of that point will be,

$$DT(P) = \begin{cases} DT(Q_i) + d_k, & |DT(Q_i) + d_k < DT(P) \\ DT(P), & otherwise \end{cases} \quad (1)$$

where, Q_i is the neighbor of P, $i =1, 2, ..., 26$ and $d_{k=1,2,3}$ is the approximate Euclidean distance from three different kinds of neighbor. Distance transform performs very well in case of binary images.

2.2 Phantom Generation

We now define a sphere $\mathcal{S}(o, r)$, with the center o having coordinates (x_c, y_c, z_c) and radius r is the locus of all points (x, y, z) in $\mathcal{Z}^3$ such that

$$(x + x_c)^2 + (y + y_c)^2 + (z + z_c)^2 = r^2 \quad (2)$$

The points on the sphere with radius r can be parameterized via, $x = x_0 + r cos\theta sin\gamma$, $y = y_0 + r cos\theta sin\gamma$, $z = z_0 + r cos\gamma$, where $0 \le \theta \le 2\pi$ and $0 \le \gamma \le \pi$.

Two points p_1 and p_2 in $\mathcal{Z}^3$ may be connected by a set of adjacent points $\{p_1, p_2, ..., p_i, p_{i+1}, ..., p_n\}$. Then a tubular structure $T(p_1, p_n)$ in $\mathcal{Z}^3$ having uniform radius r may be defined as a collection of spheres $\mathcal{S}_1, ... \mathcal{S}_i, \mathcal{S}_{i+1}, ..., \mathcal{S}_n$ having radius r and the set of adjacent center points, $C = \{p_1, p_2, ..., p_i, p_{i+1}, ..., p_n\}$ respectively. When the points p_1 and p_n are connected through a digital straight line then the corresponding tubular structure forms a simple tubular structure or *pipe* as shown in Fig. 1(a). One or more *pipes* may be joined together to form other shapes as shown in Fig. 1(b) and (c).

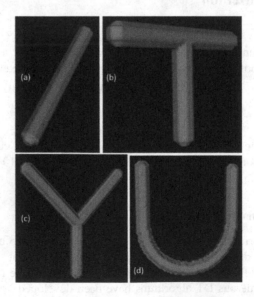

Fig. 1. 3-D rendering of some basic shapes like (a) straight tube, (b) T-Shape, (c) Y-Shape and (d) U-Shape

The T-Shape, which is shown in Fig. 1(b), is generated by first creating a straight tube as shown in Fig. 1(a) and then placing equal number of spheres from one end of the tube extending at right angle to the first tube. The Y-Shape, which is shown in Fig. 1(c), is created by joining three simple straight tubes at a common end keeping two of them at 135° from the vertical tube. The U-Shape, as shown in Fig. 1(d), is prepared by first creating two parallel straight tubes at a known distance from each other. Then, a half-circle is created using the general equation of a circle and placing the sphere centers in the locus of the equation in such a way such that the ends of the half-circle coincide with the ends of the tubes.

For phantom design in this work, piecewise linear interpolation technique using cubic *Bézier curves* has been used. To develop pulmonary A/V trees, multiple tubular structures are generated branching at various locations. A *Bezier curve* is a parametric curve that uses *Bernstein Polynomial* as a basis function [23]. A Bézier curve of degree n (order n + 1) is represented by $\mathcal{R}(t) = \sum_{i=0}^{n} b_i \mathcal{B}_{i,n}(t), 0 \leq t \leq 1$. The coefficients b_i, called the control points or Bezier points, together with the basis function $\mathcal{B}_{i,n}(t) = \sum_{i=0}^{n} {}_{i}^{n}C(1-t)^{n-i} t^i b_i$ determine the shape of the curve.

Two tubular structures $T_1(u_1, u_n); u_1, u_n \in C_1$ and $T_2(v_1, v_m); v_1, v_m \in C_2$ in $\mathcal{Z}^3$, may be connected to each other when, $C_1 \cap C_2 \neq \varnothing$.

An example of a conjoint structure made of two curved tubular structures which is a common case in real pulmonary artery/vein tree is given in Fig. 2(a). The cross section at the conjoint region which depicts the degree of conjointness is shown in Fig. 2(b).

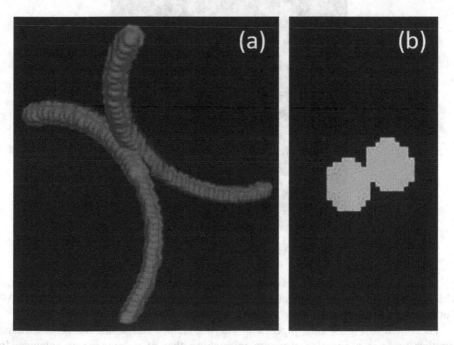

Fig. 2. (a) 3-D rendered diagram of two curved pipes joined together, (b) Cross section at the conjoint region

In tubular structure $T(p_1, p_n)$ in $\mathcal{Z}^3$, the spheres at the endpoints may have different radii which are calculated by the Euclidean distance transform (DT) value of the image as it approximately represents the distance of the voxel from the surface of the object. The radius of the spheres is gradually decreased from r_1 to r_n by the following methodology. We define *range* as the number of centre points. We define another variable *step* as

$$step = range \div (r_1 - r_n) \tag{3}$$

The radius decreases by 1 after every *step* iterations until its value becomes r_n. An illustration of the said concept is shown in Fig. 3.

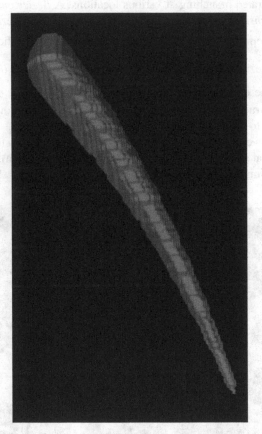

Fig. 3. A curved pipe with varying diameter

In this work, the phantoms have been designed and saved in analyze image formats which are widely used in medical imaging field and easily visualized using itk-SNAP Version 3.6.0 [24, 25].

As shown in Fig. 3, such pipes with varying shapes and scales can be assembled together to form a complex structure mimicking that of pulmonary vasculature. In general, the scale varies from thicker vessels which gradually change to thinner vessels as the length increases. The vessels are mostly attached together in higher scale, i.e., when they are thick. Some vessels may overlap one another or meet at lower scale but two or more vessels are not attached at the end. Some complex shapes created based on the said theories are shown in Fig. 4.

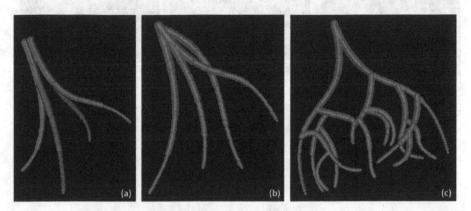

Fig. 4. 3-D rendering of complex structures created by joining pipes mathematically generated using *Bézier curves*. (a) a structure made of 4 curved pipes joined at one end. (b) are for pipes of varying radii emanating from one point. (c) structure made of several pipes of varying sizes and diameters joined at several points.

3   Experimental Outcomes

We have developed a custom GUI using Qt version 5 [26] which is an open source cross-platform application development framework based on C++ language. It is widely used to develop GUI based applications and also for mobile applications. The output of the generated phantom is shown using itk-SNAP [24, 25] which has impressive 3-D rendering capability.

In this work, we have taken a physical pig lung phantom and generated a digital phantom by replicating a very small portion of the original phantom. It is done by loading the original phantom image in the custom-made GUI and selecting points from the top, front and side view images of the phantom. For each curve, exactly four points need to be selected as we have used cubic Bézier curves which has one start point, one end point and two control points.

Experts can select regions of interest from the original data which can then be mimicked as a mathematically generated digital phantom using the developed software on which various analysis and experiments can be performed. Figure 5 shows a screenshot of the developed GUI in which the DT of the image is visible, and a point is selected.

The curves are generated step by step by adding four points of each curve. The user can generate output at any time and check if the desired phantom is achieved or not. More curves can be added to the current phantom being generated until the desired output is observed. Figure 6(a–g) shows 12 steps of the pig lung phantom being generated.

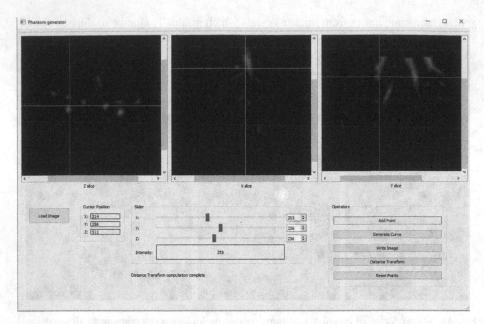

Fig. 5. Screenshot of the developed GUI showing basic functionalities like calculating DT, adding points for curve, generating and finally writing the output to disk.

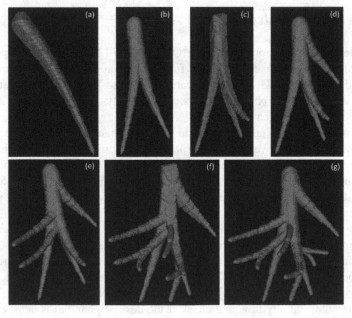

Fig. 6. Steps of phantom generation - (a) Step 1, (b) Step 2, (c) Step 3, (d) Step 4, (e) Step 6, (f) Step 10, (g) Step 12

The final phantom which is generated after adding subsequent curves to the phantom in Fig. 6(g), is shown in Fig. 7(b). The region in the physical pig lung phantom, from which the digital phantom is generated is displayed in Fig. 7(a).

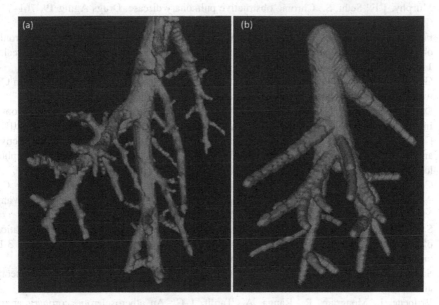

Fig. 7. (a) A small region of physical pig lung phantom, (b) digital phantom of the same region generated by our method

4 Conclusion

In this work, we have generated a near accurate phantom by selecting points from the original data with a user-friendly GUI. As discussed earlier, the purpose of this work is to provide aid in research efforts towards developing digital pulmonary phantoms. This type of digital pulmonary phantoms can be used for analysis of pulmonary lung diseases where segmentation of pulmonary arteries and veins are required.

As these phantoms are smaller in size but structurally similar to real data, results obtained by using these digital phantoms will be very similar or even completely accurate to those obtained using real pulmonary data. Our method requires user intervention for selecting 4 points for each curve which may become a lengthy task in case of generating a complex phantom with many tubes. In the future, automatic detection and segmentation of pulmonary arteries and veins of varying scale can be facilitated using phantoms developed by our method.

Acknowledgement. This project is partially supported by the CMATER research laboratory of the Computer Science and Engineering Department, Jadavpur University, India, DST PURSE-II and UPE-II project and Research Award (F.30-31/2016(SA-II)) from UGC, Government of India and CSIR-HRDG, Government of India.

References

1. Singhal, S., Henderson, R., Horsfield, K., Harding, K., Cumming, G.: Morphometry of the human pulmonary arterial tree. Circ. Res. **33**, 190–197 (1973)
2. Murphy, T.F., Sethi, S.: Chronic obstructive pulmonary disease. Drugs Aging **19**, 761–775 (2002)
3. Fletcher, M., et al.: COPD uncovered: an international survey on the impact of chronic obstructive pulmonary disease [COPD] on a working age population. BMC Public Health **11**, 1–13 (2011)
4. Gurney, J.W., et al.: Regional distribution of emphysema: correlation of high-resolution CT with pulmonary function tests in unselected smokers. Radiology **183**, 457–463 (1992)
5. Das, N., Rakshit, P., Nasipuri, M., Basu, S.: 3-D digital flows in cerebrovascular phantoms. In: 9th International Conference on Pattern Recognition, ICAPR 2017, ISI, Bangalore (2011)
6. Gao, Z., Grout, R.W., Holtze, C., Hoffman, E.A., Saha, P.: A new paradigm of interactive artery/vein separation in noncontrast pulmonary CT imaging using multiscale topomorphologic opening. IEEE Trans. Biomed. Eng. **59**, 3016–3027 (2012)
7. Cai, Z., Bai, E.: A Dynamic Arterial Tree Phantom for studies of bolus chasing CT Angiography Robert McCabe CIRS Tissue Simulation and Phantom Technology. Ge Wang Madhavan Lakshmi Raghavan and Jarin Kratzberg **4**, 88–100 (2010)
8. Saha, P.K., Gao, Z., Alford, S.K., Sonka, M., Hoffman, E.A.: Topomorphologic separation of fused isointensity objects via multiscale opening: separating arteries and veins in 3-D pulmonary CT. IEEE Trans. Med. Imaging **29**, 840–851 (2010)
9. Saha, P.K., Basu, S., Hoffman, E.A.: Multiscale opening of conjoined fuzzy objects: theory and applications. IEEE Trans. Fuzzy Syst. **24**, 1121–1133 (2016)
10. Brunette, J., Mongrain, R., Ranga, A., Tardif, J.-C.: An atherosclerotic coronary artery phantom for particle image velocimetry. Proc. Can. Eng. Educ. Assoc. **2**(2) (2011)
11. Le Floc'h, S., Cloutier, G., Finet, G., Tracqui, P., Pettigrew, R.I., Ohayon, J.: On the potential of a new IVUS elasticity modulus imaging approach for detecting vulnerable atherosclerotic coronary plaques: in vitro vessel phantom study. Phys. Med. Biol. **55**, 5701–5721 (2010)
12. Hansen, H.H.G., Lopata, R.G.P., De Korte, C.L.: Noninvasive carotid strain imaging using angular compounding at large beam steered angles: validation in vessel phantoms. IEEE Trans. Med. Imaging **28**, 872–880 (2009)
13. De Santis, G., De Beule, M., Van Canneyt, K., Segers, P., Verdonck, P., Verhegghe, B.: Full-hexahedral structured meshing for image-based computational vascular modeling. Med. Eng. Phys. **33**, 1318–1325 (2011)
14. Piccinelli, M., Veneziani, A., Steinman, D.A., Remuzzi, A., Antiga, L.: A framework for geometric analysis of vascular structures: application to cerebral aneurysms. IEEE Trans. Med. Imaging **28**, 1141–1155 (2009)
15. Antiga, L., Piccinelli, M., Botti, L., Ene-Iordache, B., Remuzzi, A., Steinman, D.A.: An image-based modeling framework for patient-specific computational hemodynamics. Med. Biol. Eng. Comput. **46**, 1097–1112 (2008)
16. Zhu, H., Ding, Z., Piana, R.N., Gehrig, T.R., Friedman, M.H.: Cataloguing the geometry of the human coronary arteries: a potential tool for predicting risk of coronary artery disease. Int. J. Cardiol. **135**, 43–52 (2009)
17. Banerjee, A., Dey, S., Parui, S., Nasipuri, M., Basu, S.: Design of 3-D phantoms for human carotid vasculature. In: Proceedings of the 2013 3rd International Conference on Advances in Computing and Communications, ICACC 2013, pp. 347–350 (2013)

18. Banerjee, A., Dey, S., Parui, S., Nasipuri, M., Basu, S.: Synthetic reconstruction of human carotid vasculature using a 2-D/3-D interface. In: ICACCI, pp. 60–65 (2013)
19. Borgefors, G.: Distance transformations in digital images. Comput. Vis. Graph. Image Process. **34**, 344–371 (1986)
20. Borgefors, G.: Distance transformations in arbitrary dimensions. Comput. Vis. Graph. Image Process. **27**, 321–345 (1984)
21. Danielsson, P.E.: Euclidean distance mapping. Comput. Graph. Image Process. **14**, 227–248 (1980)
22. Cuisenaire, O., Macq, B.: Fast Euclidean distance transformation by propagation using multiple neighborhoods. Comput. Vis. Image Underst. **76**, 163–172 (1999)
23. Abrahamsen, A.: Cubic Bézier curves. In: Control, pp. 1–4 (2000)
24. itk-SNAP Homepage. http://www.itksnap.org/pmwiki/pmwiki.php. Accessed 07 Apr 2018
25. Yushkevich, P.A., et al.: User-guided 3D active contour segmentation of anatomical structures: significantly improved efficiency and reliability. Neuroimage **31**, 1116–1128 (2006)
26. Qt Homepage. https://www.qt.io. Accessed 03 Apr 2018

Multi-lingual Scene Text Detection by Local Histogram Analysis and Selection of Optimal Area for MSER

Neelotpal Chakraborty[1]([⊠]), Saikat Biswas[2], Ayatullah Faruk Mollah[3], Subhadip Basu[1], and Ram Sarkar[1]

[1] Computer Science and Engineering Department, Jadavpur University, Kolkata, India
neelotpal_chakraborty@yahoo.com,
subhadip@cse.jdvu.ac.in, raamsarkar@gmail.com
[2] Computer Science and Engineering Department, Meghnad Saha Institute of Technology, Kolkata, India
saikat.sb4@gmail.com
[3] Computer Science and Engineering Department, Aliah University, Kolkata, India
afmollah@aliah.ac.in

Abstract. The problem of scene text detection has been quite intriguing for the research fraternity due to wide scope of applications. In recent times, some robust technique like Maximally Stable Extremal Region (MSER) has been developed and have gained immense popularity in detection and localization of text components in the wild. However, the problem of an optimal threshold and range of area in MSER has been addressed by very few researchers. In this work, we address this problem by dynamic thresholding through local histogram analysis and formulating a generalized range of the area for the MSER function. The detected MSERs are then analyzed by observing their region properties to distinguish text components from non-text ones and finally bounding the text components. The proposed technique is evaluated on a set of 200 images with multi-lingual text comprising English, Bangla, Hindi and Oriya languages.

Keywords: Multi-lingual text detection · Scene text · Text localization · MSER · Dynamic thresholding · Optimal area range

1 Introduction

Scene text detection [1] is a domain widely explored by researchers due to its applications in several areas like tourist and traveller assistance, forensics, information retrieval via search engines, unnoticed text detection in the wild, image to text conversions, etc. This wide scope of applications for meeting human necessities has led to the development of many robust techniques. Recent techniques based on Maximally Stable Extremal Regions (MSERs) [2], have become successful to a great extent in scene text detection and localization [3] in complex wild images, with additionally achieving a significant degree of language independence [7].

© Springer Nature Singapore Pte Ltd. 2019
J. K. Mandal et al. (Eds.): CICBA 2018, CCIS 1030, pp. 234–242, 2019.
https://doi.org/10.1007/978-981-13-8578-0_18

MSER method has been subjected to immense modifications either individually or in combination with other techniques, to address challenges like motion blur, perceptive distortions, warping, complex heterogeneous image textures, uneven shapes and orientations [9], etc. and yielded significantly improved results. However, the problem of deciding an optimal threshold and region area range in MSER approach is rarely considered, although a fixed threshold value and area range are sensitive to tremendous variation in texture properties among images and may not be suitable enough to capture significant amount of text regions.

This growing need for dynamism has led us to perform local histogram analysis to automatically determine threshold for MSER with a dynamic area range selection in a particular input image. Finally analysis of the regional properties is made on the detected MSERs to filter out the non-text regions and generating bounding boxes around the multi-lingual text regions having words in English/Bangla/Hindi/Oriya in the image.

2 Literature Survey

Foreground detection in any natural image has become relatively simplified by the method of MSER. Ever since its inception in the work [1], this technique has gained immense popularity in scene text detection field.

Due to the limitations of MSER against blurred regions, the method proposed in [2] makes MSER detection edge-based and stroke width transform is applied to the detected regions for filtering out the non-text regions. In the work [3], the extremal regions are determined in an image without considering region stability and applying a sequential classifier to localize the text regions. The method proposed in [4] enhances image contrast and then applies MSER method in combination with stroke width features for detecting text. Certain prominent text features have been used to detect text regions in the work [5]. MSER method has been used to detect multi-lingual scene texts in the works [7–10] and multi-oriented scene texts in the work [11].

Latest works have also relied on MSER technique to initially detect the probable text regions. In the work [12], MSERs are determined for multiple resolutions in multiple channels and finally these regions are cascaded to localize the text regions. Other techniques such as the work [13] explores ring radius transform and similarity based region grouping is applied in [14] to perform text detection. The work in [15] analyses the homogeneity of the foreground by binning process and extracts the multi-lingual text regions based on their stability and pixel density.

3 Proposed Method

Initially we formulate an optimal window size in order to capture the local histogram characteristics for dynamically deciding a threshold. The sharp peaks of a histogram usually represents the background in case of a homogenous image which leads us to calculate the sharp peaks from the histogram of the local region by using the method in [6] for which the algorithm is given in Sect. 3.1.

3.1 Local Histogram Analysis

An image of size W × H is taken as input (sample image is shown in Fig. 1), and the sharp peaks of histogram of the image region within the window of size localW × localH, is determined using Algorithm 1 below:

```
Algorithm 1:
1. [W,H] = size(image);
```

(Due to bitwise representation of pixels we extract the logarithmic values with base 2.)

```
2. localW = round(W/log₂W);
3. localH = round(H/log₂H);
```

4. Select local regions of size localW×localH and determine sharp peaks from histogram.

Fig. 1. An input image of size 2322 × 4128 with presence of multi-lingual text. The top part of the text region is in English followed by Oriya, Bangla, Hindi and again English.

3.2 MSER Detection

First introduced in the work [2], the idea of MSER is based on taking regions where intensities stay nearly the same through a wide range of thresholds and used for blob detection in images where a number of co-variant regions are extracted. In other words, an MSER is a stable connected component of some gray-level sets of the image. The MSER algorithm used in text detection in the work [1] combines MSER with Canny edges to help overcome limitations against blur to a certain extent.

The threshold value is determined by taking the mean of the sharp peaks obtained from each locality and after this the MSER function is applied to the gray scale image by selecting the area range from the Eq. 1 using window size information from Algorithm 1 as follows:

$$\text{Area Range} = [\text{minimum area, maximum area}]. \tag{1}$$

Where minimum area is calculated as: $W \times H/localW \times localH$ and maximum area is calculated as: $\log_2(\text{color in bit depth}) \times winW \times winH$. The detected MSERs after local histogram analysis and automatic area selection is depicted in Fig. 2.

Fig. 2. The MSERs detected on the basis of local histogram analysis and dynamic region area selection.

Here we achieve dynamism in the overall MSER detection process by solving both the threshold and ORAR selection for MSER function.

3.3   Region Property Analysis

After detecting the MSERs, we observe that certain non-text regions get captured. In order to eliminate such regions significantly, their properties are explored which helps in distinguishing the text MSERs from the non-text ones as shown in Fig. 3. However, it is to be noted that while enforcing conditions to eliminate non-text regions, the text regions cannot be compromised. Hence, we set only two region properties [5]: Eccentricity and Solidity.

Eccentricity. It is the ratio between the distance between the foci of an ellipse and its major axis length. The value is between 0 which represents a circle, and 1 which represents a line segment. The proposed method filters out any component having an eccentricity greater than 0.9 since with this threshold except the English letters 'I' and 'l', no other letters among the considered languages are represented by a single line segment.

Fig. 3. Text MSERs after reducing non-text regions based on region property analysis.

Solidity. It is the ratio between the area of the detected MSER and the area in the convex hull of the region. The proposed method retains the MSERs having solidity greater than 0.3 which has been calculated after experimentation on several images.

Thus, the final text components so obtained are represented in white, while the remaining parts of the image are projected as black as illustrated in Fig. 4.

Fig. 4. Text components depicted as white and remaining parts of the image as black. An admissible amount of false positives is present in the final output.

4 Experimental Results and Discussion

The proposed method is evaluated on 200 smartphone camera captured images containing multi-lingual and multi-oriented texts [15]. Since the words in the text region may vary language-wise, hence the ground truth is prepared at word level where each true positive corresponds to a word in the image as shown in Fig. 5.

Fig. 5. Bounded words in the sample input image are considered as true positives. Some false positives are also bounded. No false negative occurs in this case.

Some of the sample output images with bounding boxes are illustrated in Fig. 6.

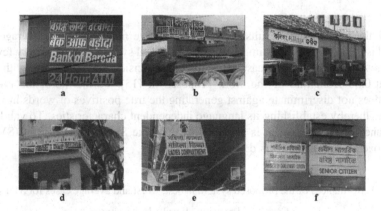

Fig. 6. Sample images with outputs depicted in bounding boxes with both true and false positives.

From the generated output images we observe that very few words fall into false negative class as given in Fig. 6(a). The false positives generated are relatively low. Even very small-sized text regions are detected by the proposed system (sample is given in Fig. 6(c)). However, the system faces a few failure cases as given in Fig. 7, either due to failure in generating a suitable threshold that may. be too high to capture any text (Fig. 7(a)) or due to high presence of noise and blur (Fig. 7(b)).

a   b

Fig. 7. Some failure cases where few or no true positives are generated.

The performances of the proposed technique are evaluated in best, worst and average cases as given in Table 1, where the best case denotes presence of heavy text and worst case denotes presence of very low text or noisy or blur images.

Table 1. Performances of the proposed system in best, worst and average cases for in-house multi-lingual dataset.

Case	Precision	Recall	F-measure
Best	0.85	1.00	0.88
Worst	0.33	0.33	0.33
Average	0.59	0.84	0.68

From the performance results in Table 1, we have noticed that the average recall achieved is 0.84 which is a testimony that the proposed system generated very few false negatives. Also we see an increase in the average precision and F-measure with values 0.59 and 0.68 from that of the work proposed in [15]. Furthermore, the proposed method does not discriminate against generating the true positives of words in varying languages thereby establishing its language independent characteristics. To validate the performance of our system, it is also evaluated on the Street-View dataset (SVT) [3] and the overall performance is depicted in Table 2.

Table 2. Performances of the proposed system in best, worst and average cases for SVT dataset.

Case	Precision	Recall	F-measure
Best	0.31	1.00	0.47
Worst	0.08	0.33	0.14
Average	0.19	0.66	0.29

The tabulated results from Table 2 gives us a clear picture that the average recall 66% is very high compared to that in [3] having 32.9% which is slightly lower than recall in the worst case for our system. The poor precision and f-measure are attributed to selective text tagging in SVT annotation, as a result some untagged texts detected by the proposed method gets recognized as false positive. Some of the successfully detected scene text results and failure cases for SVT are illustrated in Fig. 8.

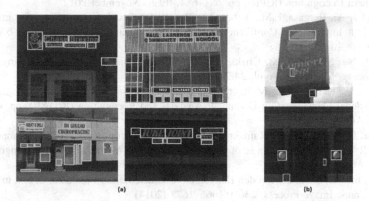

Fig. 8. Sample images from SVT dataset with outputs depicted in bounding boxes with both true and false positives. (a) Successful text localization (b) Failure cases

5 Conclusion

The proposed technique attempts to make the MSER thresholding and area selection more dynamic on the basis of local histogram analysis and achieves reasonably good recall and F-measure. This method offers a way for scene text localization in multi-lingual and multi-oriented environment. However, there is a need to address limitations like presence of high noise and blur towards which the method is sensitive. In future, we plan to bring about more robustness and dynamism into the method so that it becomes invariant to size of the images across multiple image datasets.

Acknowledgments. This work is partially supported by the CMATER research laboratory of the Computer Science and Engineering Department, Jadavpur University, India, PURSE-II and UPE-II, project. SB is partially funded by DBT grant (BT/PR16356/BID/7/596/2016) and UGC Research Award (F.30-31/2016(SA-II)). RS, SB and AFM are partially funded by DST grant (EMR/2016/007213).

References

1. Chen, H., Tsai, S.S., Schroth, G., Chen, D.M., Grzeszczuk, R., Girod, B.: Robust text detection in natural images with edge-enhanced maximally stable extremal regions. In: 2011 18th IEEE International Conference on Image Processing (ICIP), pp. 2609–2612. IEEE, September 2011
2. Matas, J., Chum, O., Urban, M., Pajdla, T.: Robust wide-baseline stereo from maximally stable extremal regions. Image Vis. Comput. **22**(10), 761–767 (2004)

3. Neumann, L., Matas, J.: Real-time scene text localization and recognition. In: 2012 IEEE Conference on Computer Vision and Pattern Recognition (CVPR), pp. 3538–3545. IEEE, June 2012

4. Li, Y., Lu, H.: Scene text detection via stroke width. In: 2012 21st International Conference on Pattern Recognition (ICPR), pp. 681–684. IEEE, November 2012

5. Gonzalez, A., Bergasa, L.M., Yebes, J.J., Bronte, S.: Text location in complex images. In: 2012 21st International Conference on Pattern Recognition (ICPR), pp. 617–620. IEEE, November 2012

6. Shaikh, S.H., Maiti, A.K., Chaki, N.: A new image binarization method using iterative partitioning. Mach. Vis. Appl. **24**(2), 337–350 (2013)

7. Gomez, L., Karatzas, D.: Multi-script text extraction from natural scenes. In: 2013 12th International Conference on Document Analysis and Recognition (ICDAR), pp. 467–471. IEEE, August 2013

8. Kumar, D., Prasad, M.N., Ramakrishnan, A.G.: Multi-script robust reading competition in ICDAR 2013. In: Proceedings of the 4th International Workshop on Multilingual OCR, p. 14. ACM, August 2013

9. Li, Y., Jia, W., Shen, C., van den Hengel, A.: Characterness: an indicator of text in the wild. IEEE Trans. Image Process. **23**(4), 1666–1677 (2014)

10. Bosamiya, J.H., Agrawal, P., Roy, P.P., Balasubramanian, R.: Script independent scene text segmentation using fast stroke width transform and GrabCut. In: 2015 3rd IAPR Asian Conference on Pattern Recognition (ACPR), pp. 151–155. IEEE, November 2015

11. Yin, X.C., Pei, W.Y., Zhang, J., Hao, H.W.: Multi-orientation scene text detection with adaptive clustering. IEEE Trans. Pattern Anal. Mach. Intell. **37**(9), 1930–1937 (2015)

12. Tian, C., Xia, Y., Zhang, X., Gao, X.: Natural scene text detection with MC–MR candidate extraction and coarse-to-fine filtering. Neurocomputing **260**, 112–122 (2017)

13. Dey, S., et al.: Script independent approach for multi-oriented text detection in scene image. Neurocomputing **242**, 96–112 (2017)

14. Gómez, L., Karatzas, D.: Textproposals: a text-specific selective search algorithm for word spotting in the wild. Pattern Recogn. **70**, 60–74 (2017)

15. Dutta, I.N., Chakraborty, N., Mollah, A.F., Basu, S., Sarkar, R.: Multi-lingual text localization from camera captured images based on foreground homogenity analysis. In: Kalita, J., Balas, V., Borah, S., Pradhan, R. (eds.) Recent Developments in Machine Learning and Data Analytics. AISC, vol. 740, pp. 149–158. Springer, Singapore (2019). https://doi.org/10.1007/978-981-13-1280-9_15

Implementing Dial-On-Demand Technique for Inter and Intra Cluster Communication in Energy Conserving Postbox Delay Tolerant Networks

Priyanka Das[1(✉)], Biplav Chakraborty[1], Gourav Sarkar[1], Suman Sen[1], Archan Mukherjee[1], and Tanmay De[2]

[1] Department of Computer Science and Engineering, NSHM Knowledge Campus, Durgapur, India
priyanka.das.2206@gmail.com
[2] Department of Computer Science and Engineering, National Institute of Technology, Durgapur, Durgapur, India

Abstract. The Delay Tolerant Network (DTN) was designed first as a means to communicate between interplanetary bodies in space. Gradually the concept gave way to a terrestrial DTN that was to cement the communication gaps in networks that were heterogeneous and resource challenged in nature. Due to unavailability of end-to-end routing paths, energy exhausted nodes and unreliable communication resources, traditional routing strategies failed to connect, resulting in a plethora of research work for DTN protocols. The Postbox DTN is a variant of the classical DTN wherein there are always ON persistent nodes called Postboxes in a cluster via which all other nodes communicate. The Energy Conserving Postbox (ECOP) DTN uses a trio of time-multiplexed ECOPs in a bid to reduce energy consumption and overhead for the Postboxes. This paper proposes an approach for intra cluster communication using ECOPs that aims to further lower the energy consumption and the chances of single-point-of-failure in the network. We also devise the very first energy efficient inter cluster communication algorithm for Postbox DTN. For the said purpose we utilize the technology of Dial-On-Demand routing wherein a communication channel is only activated when a request to do so arrives. Apart from energy this also saves network bandwidth. This postulate is also seconded by simulation results.

Keywords: Message priority · Bandwidth usage · Postmaster · Scheduled power ON/OFF · Energy drainage · Time-to-live

1 Introduction

DTN gained widespread popularity during the mid 2000's when Kevin Fall proposed the network as an answer to the challenged networks that the TCP/IP

© Springer Nature Singapore Pte Ltd. 2019
J. K. Mandal et al. (Eds.): CICBA 2018, CCIS 1030, pp. 243–256, 2019.
https://doi.org/10.1007/978-981-13-8578-0_19

was unable to connect. Kevin Fall was associated with the IPN project that created the concept of DTN for space communication in order to build the first ever Solar System Internet (which eventually happened in 2016). The similarities between communication in space and that in terrestrial challenged networks like the marine networks, sensor networks, military networks etcetera, suggested that the same theology can be applied to these earthly networks. Likewise a new layer was added on top of network specific transport layers known as the bundle layer which made it possible to apply DTN procedures to existing networks. This bundle layer acted as a bridge between heterogeneous and intermittently connected networks by translating, storing, forwarding and 'tolerating' delay of messages between them. Apart from the obvious routing issues, these networks are almost always energy drained due to their vigorous neighbour searching, remote locations and uneven recharge opportunities. As such routing mechanisms need to be energy efficient to actually benefit these networks. For the past decade and a half research in this domain has sped up impressively. Few variants of this classical model of DTN has been put forward along the way that customize the network for a particular kind of communication. The Postbox DTN is one such network. This network, as the name suggests, has a single always ON Postbox node that, like a real life one, acts as a message repository. Nodes wanting to receive/send messages try to establish a connection with the Postbox and pick-up/leave their respective messages from/to this Postbox. This type of layout is suitable for sensor networks where the base station can act as a Postbox. It can also be a more cost effective alternative to nanosatellites [18] in rural networks, with the Postbox acting as a kiosk. One big advantage with this structure is that the nodes do not need to worry about connecting to each other for message sharing. The Postbox becomes the single-point-of-contact of all the nodes present in the cluster. Though simple and effective, this mode of communication is not devoid of problems. Most importantly an always ON Postbox consumes a lot of energy and this single Postbox structure gives way to the single-point-of-failure scenario, and might create heat islands. ECOPs presented a solution to both the above problems [5]. ECOPs are a collection of Postboxes (usually 3) that work in tandem with each other using a time-shared Scheduled ON/OFF routine. These are energy saving cost effective devices that are not as power consuming as the original Postbox. In this paper we propose a novel energy efficient inter cluster communication mechanism between ECOPs. To the best of our knowledge no such solution has yet been proposed for inter cluster Postbox communication. We also combine this with two different ways of communicating within (intra) a cluster. The rest of the paper is divided into sections that first discusses some related work in this genre, with the section after it explaining the proposed schemes. A complete analysis of the simulation results is presented before ending the paper with the conclusion.

2   Related Work

As mentioned earlier, the concept for a Delay/Disruption Tolerant Network was inspired from the one that was being created for Interplanetary communication [3]. This research group was headed by Internet pioneer Vint Cerf. Since Kevin Fall mapped those space oriented approaches to terrestrial applications in his path breaking paper [11] in $SIGCOMM'03$, the research community has lapped up the idea and consequently proposed many solutions and variants to the original idea. Let us discuss some of those noteworthy contributions.

Routing and Energy Studies in Generic DTN: Perhaps the first routing protocol that could be applied to terrestrial DTN was the epidemic routing [25], which though was initially designed for vehicular networks. The epidemic routing is a oracle-less flooding based protocol that replicates and shares messages to every node which does not possess a copy of that message. Though good in small, sparse and low traffic networks it starts to deteriorate once these assumptions change. Spray and Wait [22] and Spray and Focus [22] are another set of oracle-less flooding based protocol that replicate a message to only a predefined L number of neighbours in their first (spray) phase. In their second phase they either forward the message to only the destination or use an utility function to decide the next move. More such oracle-less flooding algorithms are Credit Based Routing [6] and Spraying [19], Practical routing [14], Conditional shortest path routing [2] etc. Another set of DTN protocols use network oracle to make forwarding decisions and instead of flooding the network they do selective forwarding of messages. Some of them are Seek and Focus [23], Mobispace [16] and Utility based routing [10]. The work in [21] uses acknowledgements for opportunistic contacts equipped with network coding to increase reliability in mobile DTNs.

Energy efficient mechanisms in DTN rely on either intelligent energy saving mode shifting, data compression or employ special auxiliary energy efficient nodes in the network. The Data Compression Algorithm for energy constrained Devices [20] uses data compression as a means to reduce energy usage, stating that the size of data becomes is proportional to the overall network energy usage. The paper [17] introduces a continuous-time Markov framework to model the message dissemination in DTN using which they formulate the optimization problem of opportunistic forwarding. This they do with the constraint of energy consumed for both two-hop and epidemic forwarding message deliveries and then design different kinds of forwarding policies such as static and dynamic policies. The threshold dynamic policy is considered optimal among these policies, for both two-hop and epidemic forwarding. The work in paper [24] discusses Power Saving Management (PSM). Here a node transmitting or receiving a DTO (Data Transfer Object) is in the transmitting or receiving state after which it switches to a PSM mode which consists of switching between sleeping and search states (wireless interface states). Optimal Energy Aware Epidemic routing [15] has a energy conscious rule for transmission of messages between non destination nodes. The rule states that two such nodes can only share messages if they have a predefined amount of energy (T for the transmitter and r for the receiver) left in them. There are few researchers who believe in employing inexpensive, battery-powered, stationary nodes with radio and storage called throwboxes [1] to save energy. According to them, when two nodes pass by the same location at different times, the throwbox creates a new contact opportunity by acting as a router, significantly increasing the delivery rate. Nevertheless they might increase the cost of maintenance and installation, consume additional energy and might even be not possible for all networks to employ them.

Homing Pigeon Based DTN: The Homing Pigeon Based Delay Tolerant Network (HoP-DTN) [12] is a variant of the vanilla DTN. Here the network is made of almost static nodes which are actually clusters who are represented by respective cluster heads. Communication to and from these nodes is done in a proactive manner i.e. auxiliary nodes are employed, known as pigeons, dedicated to each node. These pigeons carry messages in bulk from their home nodes and move around the network relegating them to respective destination nodes before returning to its abode (hence the befitting name). Routing in HoP-DTN is a Traveling Salesman Problem which some researchers have dealt by using the Ant Colony Optimization technique. Since scheduling of pigeons is of paramount concern here, many efficient approaches have been proposed [7,8,13] though the domain lacks any dedicated solution for energy efficiency (to the best of our knowledge).

Postbox DTN: As has already been introduced in Sect. 1, this DTN has a single persistent node in every cluster that is always UP/ON. Routing of messages is done via the Postbox itself where every node has to make a connection to the Postbox to collect or send its messages [9]. In terms of energy usage this model of operation at one hand reduced the energy consumption as nodes did not have to frantically invest energy in neighbour searching, but on the other hand the always ON Postbox did use a lot of energy coupled with the threat of single-point-of-failure that could potentially disrupt communication in the whole network. Whether in use or not, an always ON Postbox consumed energy and had the threat of building heat islands around it [4]. To deal with this problem ECOPs (Energy Conserving Postboxes) were introduced [5]. Here the single large Postbox in each cluster is replaced by a group of energy efficient Postboxes, i.e ECOPs, that are connected to each other. These nodes will have scheduled contacts with each other as well as a definite time for being ON/UP, all the while time sharing the responsibilities. To all other nodes in the network they will appear as a single Postbox, hiding all their working and splitting of responsibility. We split the original Postbox into 3 ECOPs, all of equal buffer size, numbered as ECOP1, ECOP2 and ECOP3. Initially only ECOP1 is active and the other two are in sleep mode. At first ECOP1 is ON for 1 h. Then ECOP2 is switched ON for the last 20 min of ECOP1 being ON (i.e. when ECOP1 has been ON for 40 min). The same is followed for ECOP3, and the job cycle continues.

3 Objectives

The biggest advantage to go for a structure like that of Postbox DTN is that in any other cluster based topology, the cluster heads (CH) are burdened with extra duties though they have almost the same qualities and deficiencies of a normal node. This further drains their resources. Furthermore in DTN we cannot expect a normal node to be always UP/ON even if it is a CH. Thus creating special nodes, that act like a real life Postbox, with special hardware capabilities will not victimize an arbitrary normal node. As routing of messages is done by direct-contact-with-destination-only mechanism, we eliminate any case of retransmission-to-the-same-node-it-came-from scenario. The Postbox does not have to do any node-searching and the other nodes too do not have to do any neighbour searching (other than Postbox-searching), thereby reducing energy usage. Hence Postbox DTN is our choice of model. From the literature study of existing mechanisms we have analyzed and come to agree that our proposed work should have the following objectives:

1. The proposed scheme must be energy efficient.
2. It should eliminate the problem of single-point-of-failure that is present in classical Postbox DTN.
3. The scheme must be easy to deploy and not require expensive topological changes.
4. It must act differently towards high priority messages.
5. It must optimize the use of network bandwidth.

4   Proposed Approach

There are multiple ECOPs scattered over the network. Ideally they must all be connected to each other at all times. That though is an energy rich prerogative. A more energy conscious solution would be to have connections among these ECOPs based on Dial-On-Demand. Therefore we are creating a network of ECOPs based on DoD, but other nodes are oblivious to the existence of such a network. There though is one democratically anointed head ECOP known as Postmaster. The Postmaster is that ECOP which collects and relegates all foreign-cluster bound messages.

Before explaining the new ECOP architecture, let us first explain what is Dial-On-Demand (DoD) routing. Dial on Demand Routing is a routing method where a network connection to a remote site is established only when needed. In other words, if the router attempts to send out data and the connection is off, then the router will automatically set up a connection, send the information, and impendent the connection when no more data needs to be sent. DoD is preferred for organizations that must pay per minute for a WAN setup, where a connection is always set up. Invariant connections can become needlessly pricey if the organization does not require a constant internet connection.

4.1   Intra Cluster Communication

In this section we propose two new approaches for intra cluster communication. The first method is suitable for clusters that are large in size i.e. geographically widespread with more number of cluster members. The second method applies to those clusters that are relatively more compact.

Method 1: The Close Friends Technique. Clusters that are large in size and (or) are sparse in nature, i.e. covering a considerable amount of geographical region cannot do with one central static Postbox as faraway nodes find it difficult to frequently communicate with the one stationary Postbox in the cluster. For such cases we design a Postbox cluster which has more than one ECOP scattered around the cluster network (let the number of ECOPs in a cluster be denoted by N_{ECOP}). Between them they have DoD connections. Other nodes try to connect with any one of these ECOPs in order to send/receive messages. We call this strategy the Intra cluster communication mechanism using ECOPs with Close Friends Technique (or ECOP_CF). Figure 1 shows a diagrammatic representation of the concept.

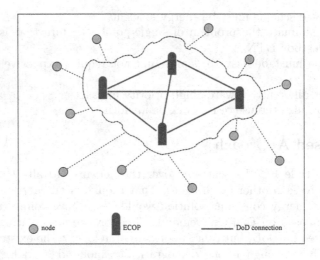

○ node   ▮ ECOP   ——— DoD connection

Fig. 1. An Energy Conserving Postbox DTN using the Close Friends technique with Dial-On-Demand connection

Each ECOP maintains the complete list of nodes in the cluster network. Each node is assigned a value known as the Closeness Factor (CF).

$$CF = \frac{1}{\phi_A} + \gamma_A \text{ where,}$$

$$\phi_A = \frac{1}{nd} \sum_{i=0}^{nd} \phi_i$$

$$\gamma_A = \frac{1}{nc} \sum_{i=0}^{nc} \gamma_i$$

where ϕ is the inter connectivity time period, γ is the connectivity time period, nd is the number of disconnections and nc is the number of connections all with respect to the ECOP and a node A. Every node in the list has their corresponding

CF value for that ECOP. This list will be updated at particular predefined intervals. A sample list is shown in Table 1.

Table 1. Sample list with an ECOP containing nodal Closeness Factor

Node ID	Closeness Factor (CF)
#1	2.500
#2	5.050
#3	1.034
...	...
#n	0.045

When message m for node B arrives from node A to ECOP1, them m is shared with s (or N_{ECOP}, whichever is less) other ECOPs. These s ECOPs are those who have the s highest CF values for node B, where

$$s = (P - p_m) + 1$$

where P is the lowest value of priority that any message can have in the network and p_m is the priority of message m (considering priority of value 1 is the highest). To ensure delivery we also consider a threshold value of message time-to-live (ttl), called ϵ which is the network decided percentage of remaining time-to-live of any message which should be treated as the danger line. When ttl of m (ttl_m) reaches ϵ then m should be passed onto all ECOPs (if not already done so). This value is represented as:

$$ttl_m^c = \frac{\text{current value of } ttl_m}{\text{initial value of } ttl_m} \times 100$$

Algorithm 1 elucidates the process more clearly.

Accordingly messages could be passed among ECOPs to reach the destination quicker. (To be noted is the fact that a ECOP never connects to a node, a node does. So if the local ECOP has a copy of the message intended for this node, it is more likely to reach the destination quicker). The best feature of this type or architecture is the disintegration of power. So there is no one man (Postbox in this case) rule. If one ECOP goes down there are others to fill in for it. Its more like a democratic structure of ECOPs, with each having and exercising equal capabilities. Naturally we can completely eliminate the single-point-of-failure scenario here. Just like the nodes of this cluster, the ECOPs of the other cluster are oblivious to this group ECOP structure. This scheme does smart utilization of ECOP buffer. Also the nodes waste less energy scanning for (or moving towards) the Postbox due to a local ECOP nearby.

Algorithm 1. AtEachECOP_Intra_CF

---

1 **for** *each node A in the cluster* **do**
2      $\phi_A = \frac{1}{\eta d} \sum_{i=0}^{nd} \phi_i$
3      $\gamma_A = \frac{1}{nc} \sum_{i=0}^{nc} \gamma_i$
4      $CF_A = \frac{1}{\phi_A} + \gamma_A$
5 **if** *message m for node B arrives at this ECOP* **then**
6      $s = (P - p_m) + 1$
7   check for s nodes with top values of CF_B
8   **if** $N_{ECOP} <= s$ **then**
9   send copies of message m to N_{ECOP} ECOPs
10   **else**
11   send copies of message m to the s ECOPs selected
12   **if** $ttl_m^c <= \epsilon$ **then**
13   send copies of message m to the rest of the $(N_{ECOP} - s)$ ECOPs

---

Method 2: The DoD Technique. In this method we would be using the trio of ECOP concept earlier presented in [5] but in a more energy conscious way. We call this strategy the Intra cluster communication mechanism using ECOPs using Dial-on-Demand Technique (or ECOP_DoD, see Fig. 2). This scheme uses not one but four threshold values τ_1, τ_2, τ_3 and τ_4 where τ_1 and τ_2 work in the same periphery. τ_1 is the smaller of the two thresholds and is used to check the requirement for ECOP2 and τ_2 is used to check that of ECOP3. The thresholds work on a value (δ) which is dependent on the network traffic inflow and outflow from the ECOP and its percentage of remaining energy, i.e.

$$\delta = \alpha_1 b + \alpha_2 r$$

where α_1 and α_2 are network decided impact factors and b is the percentage of bandwidth usage at ECOP, while r is the percentage of energy used up. The mechanism works in the following way:

1. initially only ECOP1 is active and the other two are in sleep mode.
2. if $\delta > \tau_1$ and $\delta <= \tau_2$ then establish DoD connection with ECOP2 and now both ECOP1 and ECOP2 are active.
3. if $\delta > \tau_1$ and $\delta > \tau_2$ then establish DoD connection with ECOP3 and now all the ECOPs are active.
4. if all ECOPs are active and $\delta <= \tau_2$ and $\delta > \tau_1$ for time τ_4 then close DoD connection to ECOP3 and switch it to sleep mode.
5. if all ECOPs (or ECOP1 and ECOP2) are active and $\delta <= \tau_1$ for time τ_4 then close DoD connection to ECOP2 (and ECOP3 if it is active) and switch it to sleep mode.
6. if $\delta <= \tau_1$ and $r > \tau_3$ then activate ECOP2 while switching ECOP1 to sleep mode until further recharging. Repeat this process using a Round Robin scheduling.

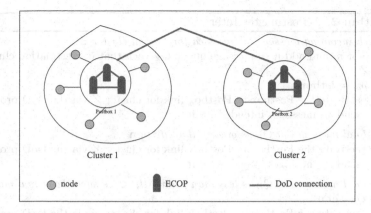

Fig. 2. An Inter and Intra cluster Energy Conserving Postbox-DTN using the DoD connection

This model differs from classical ECOP as it is not a periodic distribution of duties like in the previous case but only a demand based one. Hence if the network is receiving low traffic for quite a bit of time then ECOP DoD would waste lesser energy than normal ECOP, as it will not be unnecessarily shifting between ECOPs transferring data and control each and every time due to its fixed schedule. Thus apart from cashing on in the advantage of the normal ECOP of consuming less energy than classical Postbox model, it improves it by removing the unnecessary context switching. When a connection is set up a message is transferred from the ECOP to the destination thus employing a one hop transfer keeping in congruence with the Postbox Based Routing Protocol [9].

4.2   Inter Cluster Communication

For communicating with foreign clusters, ideally bulk messaging should be done. Regardless of what mechanism is used for intra cluster communication, there would be a single Postbox (or the one active in case of Time scheduled ECOP) that has been elected as the head ECOP. Messages destined for foreign clusters would be collected at the head ECOP known as Postmaster. If number of messages at Postmaster is more than threshold μ then the Postbox-to-Postbox link would be activated via the Dial-On-Demand protocol. If though number of messages is less than μ, and a message's ttl equals ϵ, the link should be activated even then. If any message of utmost priority arrives, then the link is activated then and there. The complete procedure is explained in Algorithm 2 (also see Fig. 2). A thing to be noted is that the value of ϵ should not be too low as the message reaching the foreign Postmaster is only half the journey done (if message is not meant for the foreign Postmaster itself) as after that it needs to be forwarded to its nodal recipient.

Algorithm 2. AtPostmaster_Inter

---

1 **for** *each incoming message m intended for foreign cluster* **do**
2   accept m and add it to message queue Q_Z such that its destination cluster is Z
3   **if** $p_m = 1$ **then**
4   activate the Postbox-to-Postbox link for cluster Z via the DoD protocol
5   send all messages intended for it
6   **if** *total messages at Q_Z is greater than μ* **then**
7   activate the Postbox-to-Postbox link for cluster Z via the DoD protocol
8   send all messages intended for it
9   **if** *total messages at Q_Z is less than μ and $ttl_i^c <= \epsilon$ such that i is a message in Q_Z* **then**
10   activate the Postbox-to-Postbox link for cluster Z via the DoD protocol
11   send all messages intended for it

---

5 Performance Analysis

5.1 Simulation Analysis

For simulation purposes, we have considered that there are a total of randomly switching from ON to OFF state 30 nodes in a cluster (in case of sparse network we have decreased the number of connections to central Postbox) and for Inter cluster communication, there are 30 such clusters. The simulation scenario has been created using the C programming language. One unit of simulation time is equivalent to 1 min. The buffer capacity of classical Postbox is of 300 units, the ECOPs in ECOP_DoD are 100 each and that of ECOP_CF (there are 6 in a cluster) are of 50 each. Energy consumption has been considered at 1 unit each at message forward/receive, 0.01 units per unit size of the Postboxes (maintenance purposes) and total initial energy is 300 units. The energy consumption due to other peripheral causes, being same in all cases, have not been taken into consideration. The plots that have been depicted here in this paper have the following values of the threshold and impact factors: the value of P is 3, ϵ (intra) is 40%, τ_1 is 60%, τ_2 is 80%, τ_3 is 70%, τ_4 is 30 min, α_1 is 0.4, α_2 is 0.6, μ is 5 messages and ϵ (inter) is 50%. We have compared our algorithms with the existing mechanisms in Postbox DTN like ECOP (the scheduled ON/OFF trio of ECOPs) and the traditional classic Postbox (referred to as simply Postbox). For inter cluster communication as there are no previous mechanisms apart from the original Postbox (vanilla version), we compared it with our proposed scheme that we have referred here as simply Postmaster.

Energy Consumption. Figures 3 and 4 shows the comparison between ECOP_CF, ECOP_DoD, ECOP and Classical Postbox on the basis of Average Percentage of Remaining energy with respect to (w.r.t.) increasing time, while the Message Traffic from all nodes is kept at a constant of 50. From results

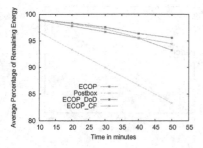

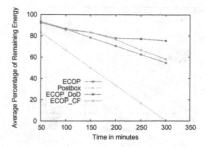

Fig. 3. Energy consumption when message traffic is 50, w.r.t. time

Fig. 4. Energy consumption when message traffic is 150, w.r.t. time

it can be statistically stated that ECOP_CF conserves 7.85% and 106.2% more energy than Postbox when the time is varied till 50 and 300 min respectively and 0.51% more energy than ECOP when the time is varied till 50 and 300 min respectively. ECOP_DoD uses 1.01% and 13.34% less energy than ECOP when the time is varied till 50 and 300 min respectively and 8.4% and 117.56% less than Postbox when the time is varied till 50 and 300 min respectively. On comparing each other, ECOP_DoD uses 4.27% less energy than ECOP_CF. When examining the inter cluster communication mechanisms, Postmaster conserves 14.21% and 237.37% more energy than the traditional Postbox when the time is varied till 50 and 300 min respectively.

Delivery Capability. Simply conserving energy is not enough, as the main purpose of any network is to deliver messages before their time-to-live expires. Likewise we did a simulation to test the mechanisms on the basis of message delivery capability. To showcase the robustness of our proposed schemes we have introduced random Postbox (or ECOP) failure scenarios. Figures 5 and 6 show the results of such experiments. If we compare ECOP_DoD and ECOP, when a huge message traffic is created within a short span of time during network initialization (within the first 40 min, see Fig. 5), then the performance of ECOP tends to degrade. This is so because the message traffic exceeds the buffer size of the lone ECOP when the second ECOP is yet to be active according to the time schedule. Our new ECOP_DoD scheme is safe from any such degradation as the instant it requires help it sends a DoD signal to the other ECOPs to back it up. To sum it up, ECOP_DoD delivers 27.3% and 0.64% more messages than ECOP and 1.63% and 0.57% more than Postbox w.r.t. simulation time period of 20 and 200 min respectively. ECOP_CF delivers 45.46% and 19.3% more messages than ECOP and 17.76% and 19.2% more than Postbox w.r.t. simulation time period of 20 and 200 min respectively. When the network considered is sparse, the results are a bit different as expected (see Figs. 7 and 8). In sparse network, ECOP_DoD delivers 7.38% and 5.25% more messages than ECOP and 11.34% and 4.57% more than Postbox w.r.t. simulation time period of 20 and 200 min respectively. Similarly ECOP_CF delivers 108.35% and 79.3% more messages than ECOP

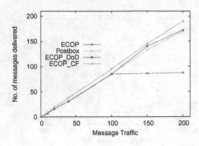

Fig. 5. Delivery capability (Time constant at 20 min)

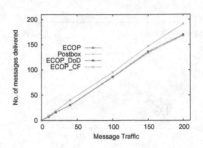

Fig. 6. Delivery capability (Time constant at 200 min)

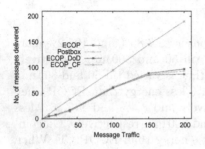

Fig. 7. Delivery capability (Time constant at 20 min) in a sparse network

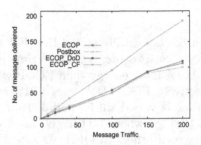

Fig. 8. Delivery capability (Time constant at 200 min) in a sparse network

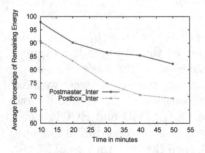

Fig. 9. Comparing energy consumption with respect to time (message traffic constant at 50) for inter cluster communication

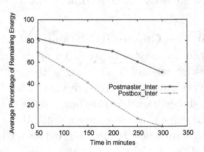

Fig. 10. Comparing energy consumption with respect to time (message traffic constant at 150) for inter cluster communication

and 116.8% and 62.5% more than Postbox w.r.t. simulation time period of 20 and 200 min respectively. When compared amongst themselves, ECOP_CF on an average delivers 17.27% and 81.45% more messages than ECOP_DoD in a normal and a sparse network respectively. For inter cluster communication the two protocols perform more or less similar and it only differs when the single-Postbox failure occurs (Figs. 9 and 10).

6   Conclusion

In today's era everything we use needs to be energy efficient. The applications in Postbox DTN are also hit by the "energy drainage" issue that has handicapped other variants of the DTN. In this work we have proposed two such energy conscious mechanisms for intra cluster communication and another one for inter cluster communication in Postbox DTN. We have, in both our intra and inter cluster communication mechanisms, inculcated all the requisite parameters that are paramount to network performance like inter connectivity time, connectivity time period, number of disconnections between a node and an ECOP in a definite time period, number of connections between a node and an ECOP in a definite time period, percentage of bandwidth usage, remaining energy levels of ECOPs, priority of a message, its remaining time-to-live and number of messages waiting in a queue at Postmaster. Applying proper thresholds and impact factors on these attributes enhances the workability and performance of our system. All together they strive to achieve the best solution possible, the consensus of which is also proven via the simulation results where we have compared these mechanisms with existing ones. Hence finally we can claim that we have achieved all the objectives that we had set out to achieve for this work.

References

1. Banerjee, N., Corner, M.D., Levine, B.N.: An energy-efficient architecture for DTN throwboxes. In: Proceedings of the 26th IEEE International Conference on Computer Communications (INFOCOM 2007), pp. 776–784 (2007)
2. Bulut, E., Geyik, S.C., Szymanski, B.K.: Conditional shortest path routing in DTNs. In: WOWMOM, pp. 1–6 (2010)
3. Burleigh, S., et al.: Delay-tolerant networking: an approach to interplanetary Internet. IEEE Commun. Mag. **41**(6), 128–136 (2003)
4. Choi, J.: Virtual machine placement algorithm for energy saving and reliability of servers in cloud data centers. J. Netw. Syst. Manage. (2018)
5. Das, P., De, T.: ECOP: energy conserving postboxes in postbox delay tolerant networks. Procedia Comput. Sci. **57**, 952–959 (2015)
6. Das, P., Dubey, K., De, T.: Credit based routing in delay tolerant networks. In: Proceedings of the 2nd IEEE International Conference on Parallel, Distributed and Grid Computing (PDGC), pp. 158–163. IEEE (2012)
7. Das, P., Dubey, K., De, T.: Threshold triplet incorporated scheduling of storage based pigeons in homing-pigeon-based delay tolerant networks. In: Proceedings of the 5th International Conference on Computers and Devices for Communication (CODEC). IEEE (2012)
8. Das, P., Dubey, K., De, T.: Priority aided scheduling of pigeons in homing-pigeon-based delay tolerant networks. In: Proceedings of the 3rd IEEE International Advance Computing Conference (IACC), pp. 212–217. IEEE (2013)
9. Dubey, K., Das, P., De, T.: Postbox DTN: it's modeling and routing analysis. In: Proceedings of the 2nd IEEE International Conference on Parallel, Distributed and Grid Computing (PDGC), pp. 343–348. IEEE (2012)

10. Dubois-Ferriere, H., Grossglauser, M., Vetterli, M.: Age matters: efficient route discovery in mobile ad hoc networks using encounter ages. In: Proceedings of the 4th ACM International Symposium on MobiHoc, pp. 257–266. ACM (2003)
11. Fall, K.: A delay-tolerant network architecture for challenged internets. Technical report, Intel Research (2003)
12. Guo, H., Li, J., Qian, Y.: HoP-DTN: modeling and evaluation of homing-pigeon based delay tolerant networks. IEEE Trans. Veh. Technol. **59**(2) (2010)
13. Guo, H., Li, J., Qian, Y.: Modeling and evaluation of homing-pigeon based delay tolerant networks with periodic scheduling. In: Proceedings of IEEE International Conference on Communications, ICC 2009, pp. 4988–4992. IEEE Press, Piscataway (2009)
14. Jones, E.P.C.: Practical routing in delay-tolerant networks. In: Proceedings of the WDTN, pp. 237–243. ACM Press (2005)
15. Khouzani, M., Eshghi, S., Sarkar, S., Venkatesh, S.S., Shroff, N.B.: Optimal energy-aware epidemic routing in DTNs. In: Proceedings of MobiHoc (2012)
16. Leguay, J., Friedman, T., Conan, V.: DTN routing in a mobility pattern space. In: Proceedings of the ACM SIGCOMM Workshop on Delay-Tolerant Networking, WDTN, pp. 276–283 (2005)
17. Li, Y., Jiang, Y., Jin, D., Su, L., Zeng, L., Wu, D.O.: Energy-efficient optimal opportunistic forwarding for delay-tolerant networks. IEEE Trans. Veh. Technol. **59**(9), 4500–4512 (2010)
18. Marchese, M., Patrone, F., Cello, M.: DTN-based nanosatellite architecture and hot spot selection algorithm for remote areas connection. IEEE Trans. Veh. Technol. **67**(1), 689–702 (2018)
19. Das, P., Dubey, K., De, T.: Routing in delay tolerant networks using credit based spraying. In: Proceedings of the 3rd IEEE International Advance Computing Conference (IACC), pp. 218–223. IEEE (2013)
20. Sadler, C.M., Martonosi, M.: Data compression algorithms for energy-constrained devices in delay tolerant networks. In: Proceedings of SenSys (2006)
21. Sassatelli, L., Ali, A., Panda, M., Chahed, T., Altman, E.: Reliable transport in delay-tolerant networks with opportunistic routing. IEEE Trans. Wireless Commun. **13**(10), 5546–5557 (2014)
22. Spyropoulos, T., Psounis, K., Raghavendra, C.S.: Spray and wait: an efficient routing scheme for intermittently connected mobile networks. In: Proceedings of the SIGCOMM Workshop on Delay-Tolerant Networking, WDTN, pp. 252–259. ACM (2005)
23. Spyropoulos, T., Psounis, K., Raghavendra, C.S.: Efficient routing in intermittently connected mobile networks: the single-copy case. IEEE/ACM Trans. Netw. **16**(1), 63–76 (2008)
24. Trullols-Cruces, O., Morillo-Pozo, J., Barcelo-Ordinas, J.M., Garcia-Vidal, J.: Power saving trade-offs in delay/disruptive tolerant networks. In: Proceedings of IEEE (2011)
25. Vahdat, A., Becker, D.: Epidemic routing for partially connected ad hoc networks. Technical report, CS-200006, Duke University (2000)

Compare Speckle Denoising Models Based on Total Variation and Filtering Methods

Arundhati Bagchi Misra[1]($\boxtimes$) and Hyeona Lim[2]

[1] Department of Mathematical Sciences, Saginaw Valley State University,
University Center, MI 48710, USA
abmisra@svsu.edu
[2] Department of Mathematics and Statistics, Mississippi State University,
Mississippi State, MS 39762, USA
hlim@math.msstate.edu

Abstract. Image denoising is among the most fundamental problems
in image processing. A large range of methods covering various fields of
mathematics are available for denoising an image. The initial denoising
models are derived from energy minimization using nonlinear partial differential equations (PDEs). These methods are very fast and removes
noise very well. The filtering based models have also been used for quite
a long time where the denoising is done by smoothing operators. The
most successful method among them was the nonlocal means proposed
by Buades, Coll and Morel in 2005. Though the method is very accurate in removing noise, it is very slow and hence quite impractical. In
2008, Gilboa and Osher extended some known PDE and variational techniques in image processing to the nonlocal framework. The motivation
behind this was to make any point interact with any other point in the
image. Using nonlocal PDE operators, they proposed the nonlocal total
variation method for Gaussian noise. Based on this, a nonlocal PDE
based speckle denoising model has been developed. The model is faster
than nonlocal means but still much slower than the total variation based
models. Additionally in 2005 Mahmoudi and Sapiro improve the existing non local means model by using similar neighborhoods. In this paper,
we compare the nonlocal tv based model with the faster nonlocal means
model for removing speckle noise from images. We compare these models
and try to find the better one.

Keywords: Image denoising · Speckle denoising models ·
Nonlocal means · Nonlocal PDE · Nonlocal TV ·
Faster non local means

1 Introduction

Image restoration is a very important process and is often necessary as a pre-
processing for other imaging techniques such as segmentation and compression.

© Springer Nature Singapore Pte Ltd. 2019
J. K. Mandal et al. (Eds.): CICBA 2018, CCIS 1030, pp. 257–270, 2019.
https://doi.org/10.1007/978-981-13-8578-0_20

In general, an observed image f is represented by the equation

$$f = u + n, \tag{1}$$

where u is the original noise free image, f is the observed noisy image and n is the Gaussian noise. Here $u, f : \Omega \subset \mathbb{R}^2 \to \mathbb{R}$. For any denoising model, the main objective is to reconstruct u from an observed image f.

The noise represented in the above equation is additive or Gaussian noise. Several partial differential equation (pde) based models are developed to remove Gaussian noise. The initial model developed by Rudin, Osher and Fatemi [12] is the starting point of our paper. Later filtering based non local means method also provided remarkable results [2,3]. But these models were slow compared to pde based models. In 2008 Gilboa and Osher combined the pde and filtering models to obtain non local total variation model [4]. They provided good results and were faster than non local means, but still slower than pde models. In 2005, Mahmoudi and Sapiro [9] proposed ways to fasten non local means method. They proposed to improve the non local means method by restricting the comparisons only for similar neighbourhood chosen by certain criteria.

All methods described above are meant for Gaussian noise images. These do not work well on speckle noise images found in widely used ultrasound images. Ultrasound images provide low cost images that are extremely helpful for clinical diagnosis. But the process results in images corrupted with speckle noise. Speckle noise is granular in nature and it exists inherently in the image. Unlike Gaussian noise, which affects single pixels of an image, speckle noise affects multiple pixels. The speckle noise model is given by

$$f = u + \sqrt{u}n, \tag{2}$$

where u is the desired image to find, n is Gaussian noise and f denotes the observed image. Hence it is not possible to remove speckle noise with the traditional PDE based Gaussian denoising models. In 2005 Krissian, Kikinis, Westin and Vosburgh first developed a pde based denoising model to remove speckle noise from ultrasound images [7]. In [10,11] non local total variation based methods have been developed for speckle noise images which are based on the initial speckle model. In this paper we compare the non local TV based method with the faster non local means method.

2   Preliminaries

In this section we discuss about the preliminary models of image denoising and also the models that have been compared in this paper. We first talk about the initial denoising model based on partial differential equations [12]. This model was mainly developed for Gaussian noise. We then introduce the initial denoising model for speckle noise images [7,8]. Next we focus on filtering based nonlocal means method [2,3]. The nonlocal means method was also developed for Gaussian noise images. The model takes advantage of high redundancy present in any image and compares neighboorhood pixels to measure similarity and remove unwanted noise. This model provides very good results but takes a very long time. So, a faster alternative is proposed by Mahmoudi and Sapiro [9] based on similar neighborhoods. In our model we try to combine the positive aspects of both total variation model and nonlocal means model to obtain faster model with high quality denoising. For that we rely on the non local total variation model proposed by Gilboa and Osher [4]. They developed nonlocal versions of classical derivatives and used it to redefine required operators.

2.1 Total Variation Denoising Model

In 1992 Rudin Osher and Fatemi [12] proposed the total variation (TV) denoising model as the minimization problem:

$$\min_u \int_\Omega |\nabla u| \ \mathrm{d}\boldsymbol{x} \tag{3}$$

subject to the constraints,

$$\int_\Omega f \ \mathrm{d}\boldsymbol{x} = \int_\Omega u \ \mathrm{d}\boldsymbol{x} \tag{4}$$

$$\text{and } \int_\Omega \frac{1}{2}(f-u)^2 \ \mathrm{d}\boldsymbol{x} = \sigma^2, \tag{5}$$

where σ is the standard deviation of the noise n. The first constraint (4) signifies the fact that the noise in (1) is of zero mean and the second constraint (5) states that the standard deviation of the noise is σ. These constraints ensure that the resulting image and the observed images are quite close to each other.

Combining the above constraints the TV functional is obtained by

$$F(u) = \int_\Omega |\nabla u| \ \mathrm{d}\boldsymbol{x} + \frac{\lambda}{2} \int_\Omega (f-u)^2 \ \mathrm{d}\boldsymbol{x}. \tag{6}$$

Here λ is a constraint parameter. The equivalent Euler-Lagrange equation gives the TV denoising model as

$$\frac{\partial u}{\partial t} - \nabla \cdot \left(\frac{\nabla u}{|\nabla u|}\right) = \lambda(f-u). \tag{7}$$

To avoid singularities, it was regularized by using $|\nabla u| \approx |\nabla^\varepsilon u| = (u_x^2 + u_y^2 + \epsilon^2)^{1/2}$.

2.2 Speckle Denoising Model

In 2005 Krissian, Kikinis, Westin and Vosburgh [7] considered the speckle noise model by

$$f = u + \sqrt{u}n, \tag{8}$$

where u is the desired image to find, n is Gaussian noise and f denotes the observed image. Thus, we have $n = \frac{f-u}{\sqrt{u}}$. Then replacing $f-u$ in (6) with the new expression for n, the minimization functional for speckle denoising is given by

$$F(u) = \int_\Omega \left[|\nabla u| + \frac{\lambda}{2}\left(\frac{f-u}{\sqrt{u}} \right)^2 \right] \, d\boldsymbol{x}. \tag{9}$$

From energy minimization of this functional, the TV-based speckle denoising model can be derived as:

$$\frac{\partial u}{\partial t} - \frac{u^2}{f+u}|\nabla^\epsilon u| \nabla \cdot \left(\frac{\nabla u}{|\nabla^\epsilon u|} \right) = \lambda |\nabla^\epsilon u| (f - u). \tag{10}$$

2.3   Nonlocal Means Method

In 2005 Buades, Coll and Morel proposed the new state of art image denoising algorithm known as nonlocal means algorithm [2]. The algorithm is given by the formula

$$NL[u](\boldsymbol{x}) = \frac{1}{C(\boldsymbol{x})} \int_\Omega e^{-\frac{(G_a * |u(\boldsymbol{x}+\cdot) - u(\boldsymbol{y}+\cdot)|^2)(0)}{h^2}} u(\boldsymbol{y}) \, d\boldsymbol{y}, \tag{11}$$

where $C(\boldsymbol{x}) = \int_\Omega e^{-\frac{(G_a * |u(\boldsymbol{x}+\cdot) - u(\boldsymbol{z}+\cdot)|^2)(0)}{h^2}} \, d\boldsymbol{z}$. Here G_a is the Gaussian kernel with standard deviation a, h is a filtering parameter and $u(\boldsymbol{x} + \cdot)$ denotes the neighborhood of the pixel $\boldsymbol{x}$. Here each pixel value is denoised using the weighted average of all the pixels in the image. Thus for a given discrete noisy image $u = \{u(i) : i \in I\}$, the estimated value $NL[u](i)$, for a pixel i, is computed as

$$NL[u](i) = \sum_{j \in I} w(i, j) u(j), \tag{12}$$

where the weight $w(i, j)$ depends on the similarity of the i and j pixels and satisfies the conditions $0 \le w(i, j) \le 1$ and $\sum_j w(i, j) = 1$. In this paper the authors measured the similarity of a square neighborhood $\mathcal{N}_i$ of a fixed size at each pixel i as a decreasing function of the weighted Euclidean distance, $||u(\mathcal{N}_i) - u(\mathcal{N}_j)||_{2,a}^2$, where $j \in I$ and $a > 0$ is the standard deviation of the Gaussian kernel. The weight function is defined as

$$w(i, j) = \frac{1}{C(i)} e^{-\frac{||u(\mathcal{N}_i)-u(\mathcal{N}_j)||_{2,a}^2}{h^2}}, \tag{13}$$

where $C(i)$ is the normalizing constant given by

$$C(i) = \sum_j e^{-\frac{||u(\mathcal{N}_i)-u(\mathcal{N}_j)||_{2,a}^2}{h^2}}. \tag{14}$$

The similar neighborhoods have a very small Euclidean distance which in turn results in larger weight. The authors used Fig. 1 to illustrate the weight function values for different neighborhoods [2]. From Fig. 1 we can see that $w(p, q_1)$ and $w(p, q_2)$ will have much higher values than $w(p, q_3)$. The pixels p and q_3 have the same grey level value, but since the neighborhood is much different the weight $w(p, q_3)$ will be very close to zero. Thus nonlocal means offers a very robust pixel comparison. Since the nonlocal means uses the similarity neighbourhood for denoising, it works really well for periodic or patterned textured cases. But though the method is very good in removing noise, it is very slow and hence quite impractical.

Fig. 1. Nonlocal means neighborhood comparison

2.4   Faster Nonlocal Means of Similar Neighborhoods

As we see the non local means method takes longer than the total variation model. So, even though it is effective it is not practical due to the computation time. A faster model was proposed by Mahmoudi and Sapiro in 2005 [9]. They classified the image blocks based on their average gray values and gradient orientation. Only similar blocks are used for weight computation. The total number of weight computations are hence reduced and computational complexity is improved. This restriction in neighborhoods resulted in a faster model.

2.5   Nonlocal TV Model

In 2008, Gilboa and Osher extended some known PDE and variational techniques in image processing to the nonlocal framework [4]. The motivation behind this was to make any point interact with any other point in the image. Since the classical derivatives were local operators, they had to redefine the required operators in [4] following the ideas of Zhou and Scholkopf [13,14]. Gilboa and Osher proposed the nonlocal TV (NLTV) model based on the NLTV operator $(\int_{\Omega} |\nabla_{\mathrm{NL}} u|)$, as follows:

Fig. 2. Results comparison for Gaussian noise images

$$\frac{\partial u}{\partial t} = \kappa_{\mathrm{NL}}(u) - \lambda(u - f)$$

$$= \int_{\Omega} w(x,y)(u(y) - u(x))(|\nabla_{\mathrm{NL}} u|^{-1}(x) + |\nabla_{\mathrm{NL}} u|^{-1}(y)) \, dy - \lambda(u - f), \tag{15}$$

where $\nabla_{\mathrm{NL}}(\cdot) =$ nonlocal gradient, $\mathrm{div}_{\mathrm{NL}}(\cdot) =$ nonlocal divergence and $\kappa_{\mathrm{NL}}(\cdot) = \mathrm{div}_{\mathrm{NL}} \frac{\nabla_{\mathrm{NL}}}{|\nabla_{\mathrm{NL}}|}$ denotes the nonlocal curvature. Since the steepest descent scheme (15) is very slow, a faster numerical scheme was introduced by Bresson in [1]. The scheme is based on the Split Bregman method introduced in [5]. It was proved to be very fast for regular TV. It also provided faster results for speckle noise images in [10].

3   Compare Speckle Denoising Models

We now present the comparison of the nonlocal tv based model and the faster nonlocal means model for speckle noise images. We would like to see that if we can obtain better results by combining both nonlocal means and total variation methods or if we can do so just by developing models based entirely on filtering based models.

3.1   Nonlocal Total Variation Based Model for Speckle Noise Images

This model is described in [10]. Hereo the authors extended the idea presented in [4] and developed the following nonlocal TV based speckle denoising model:

$$\min_{u} F(u), \quad F(u) = \int_{\Omega} \left[|\nabla_{\mathrm{NL}} u| + \lambda \left(\frac{f - u}{\sqrt{u}} \right)^2 \right] dx \tag{16}$$

where ∇_{NL} is a nonlocal gradient defined in [4]. For faster computation, the Split Bregman scheme [5] was used for finding a solution to (16). The Split Bregman functional is of the form

$$\min_{u} F(u), \quad F(u) = \int_{\Omega} |d| + \lambda \frac{(f - u)^2}{u} + \frac{\beta}{2} \|d - \nabla_{\mathrm{NL}} u - b\|_2^2. \tag{17}$$

Then the optimality condition for u gives us the equation

$$\left(\lambda - \beta \frac{u^2}{u + f} \Delta_{\mathrm{NL}} \right) u = \lambda f - \beta \frac{u^2}{u + f} \mathrm{div}_{\mathrm{NL}}(d - b). \tag{18}$$

Denoting the discretized points $x, y \in \Omega \times \Omega$ by i and j, and using the discrete definition for $\mathrm{div}_{\mathrm{NL}}$ and $\Delta_{\mathrm{NL}}[1,4]$, the discrete minimization scheme was given as:

$$\lambda u_i - \beta \frac{u_i^2}{u_i + f_i} \left(\sum_j w_{ij}(u_j - u_i) \right)$$

$$= \lambda f_i - \beta \frac{u_i^2}{u_i + f_i} \left(\sum_j \sqrt{w_{ij}}(d_{ij} - d_{ji} - b_{ij} + b_{ji}) \right). \tag{19}$$

Hence, the iteration steps are:

$$u_i^{k+1} = \frac{1}{\lambda + \beta \frac{u_i^2}{u_i + f_i} \sum_j w_{ij}} \left[\beta \frac{u_i^2}{u_i + f_i} \sum_j w_{ij} u_j^k + \lambda f_i \right.$$

$$\left. - \beta \frac{u_i^2}{u_i + f_i} \left(\sum_j \sqrt{w_{ij}} (d_{ij} - d_{ji} - b_{ij} + b_{ji}) \right) \right], \tag{20}$$

$$d_{ij}^{k+1} = \frac{\sqrt{w_{ij}}(u_j^{k+1} - u_i^{k+1}) + b_{ij}^k}{\sqrt{\sum_j w_{ij}(u_j^{k+1} - u_i^{k+1})^2 + b_{ij}^{k}{}^2}} \max \left(\sqrt{\sum_j w_{ij}(u_j^{k+1} - u_i^{k+1})^2 + b_{ij}^{k}{}^2} - \frac{1}{\beta}, 0 \right), \tag{21}$$

$$b_{ij}^{k+1} = b_{ij}^k + \sqrt{w_{ij}}(u_j^{k+1} - u_i^{k+1}) - d_{ij}^{k+1}. \tag{22}$$

It was shown in [10], that (20)–(22) provides a fast and accurate nonlocal scheme for TV based speckle denoising model.

3.2   Faster Non Local Means Method for Speckle Noise Images

Our second model was the one described in [9]. The authors provided a method to make the non local means model work faster. In the original nonlocal means model [2, 3] each pixel is compared with every other pixel in the image to measure similarity. To reduce computational complexity, the authors compared each pixel with a neighborhood of pixels present in a predefined smaller window in the image. But still the model was extremely slow. In [9] the authors restricted the comparison to only similar neighborhoods and used only the similar blocks for weight comparison, thus reducing the computational time.

The authors suggested two filters to classify image blocks: Average gray value and average gradient.

Average Gray Value Method: Based on the assumption of zero mean additive noise, similar neighborhoods should have similar average gray values. For each pixel i, maximum $2n + 1$ weights $w(i, j)$ are calculated for pixels j with closest neighborhood. Additionally, $w(i, j)$ is considered if $\eta_1 < \frac{\overline{v}(i)}{\overline{v}(j)} < \eta_2$, where $\overline{v}(i), \overline{v}(j)$ = average gray values in the neighborhood of i, j, $\eta_1 < 1, \eta_2 > 1$ are constants close to one.

Average Gradient Method: The average gradient in the neighborhood of pixel i is defined as $\overline{\nabla v}(i) = (\overline{v_x}(i), \overline{v_y}(i))$, where $\overline{v_x}(i), \overline{v_y}(i)$ = average horizontal and vertical derivatives in the neighborhood of pixel i.

The average gradient orientation is used instead of gradient magnitude. For two similar blocks, average gradient magnitude might differ a lot for additive

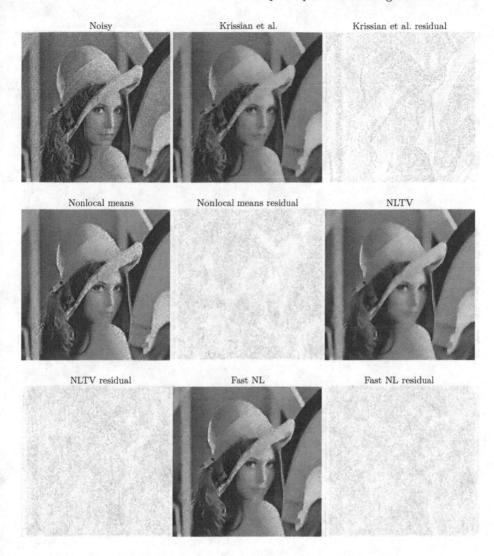

Fig. 3. Synthetic image result (Lenna) with absolute residual

noise but the orientation must be similar. The average gradient orientation difference is same as the angle between the average gradient directions of i, j and is given as

$$\theta(i,j) = \angle\left(\overline{\nabla v}(i), \overline{\nabla v}(j)\right)$$

For small gradient magnitude, only orientation is not a reliable measure. For blocks with similar averages, $w(i,j)$ is computed if the gradients in pixel i or j are small or $\theta(i,j)$ is small enough. The gradient and orientation thresholds(σ_∇ and

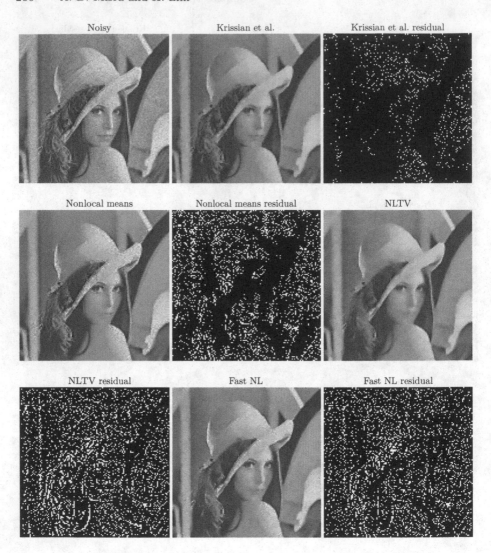

Fig. 4. Synthetic image result (Lenna) with speckle noise residual

σ_θ) are calculated using robust statistics. The weight function is thus defined as:

$$
w(i,j) = \begin{cases} \frac{1}{Z(i)} e^{-\frac{\|v(N_i)-v(N_j)\|_{2,a}^2}{h^2}}, & \Big[(\|\nabla v(i)\| < \sigma_\nabla \\ & \text{or } (\|\nabla v(j)\| < \sigma_\nabla \\ & \text{or } (|\theta(i,j)| < \sigma_\theta)\Big] \\ & \text{and}(\eta_1 < \frac{\bar{v}(i)}{\bar{v}(j)} < \eta_2) \\ 0, & \text{otherwise.} \end{cases}
$$

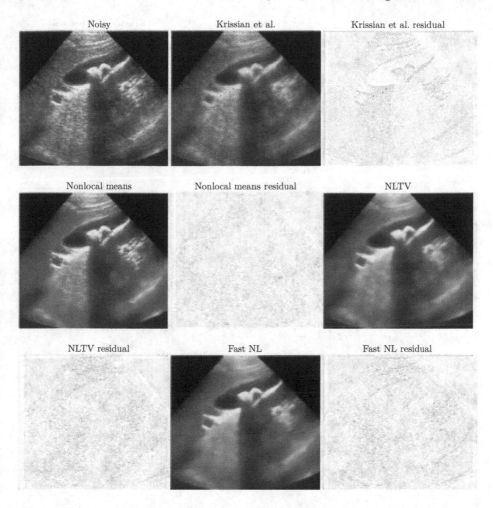

Fig. 5. Ultrasound image result (Gallstones)) with absolute residual

4   Numerical Results

The numerical results are displayed in the next pages. We have considered the images of size 128×128 and the summary of results are in Table 1. Other than the visual results, we have used peak-signal-to-noise ratio (PSNR) for synthetic images, which was mentioned in [6], to measure the efficiency of the models. A cleaner image provides a higher PSNR value. We have provided the absolute residual ($|f - u|$) and the speckle noise residual ($n = \frac{f-u}{\sqrt{u}}$) for all images. The results of the two main models are presented along with the TV based initial speckle noise model [7] and the original non local means model.

It is evident from the visual results that the fast non local means method is working and is also quite comparable to the nonlocal tv model. The non local

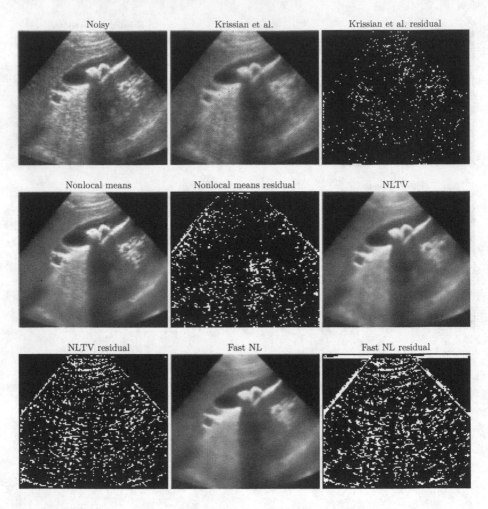

Fig. 6. Ultrasound image result (Gallstones) with speckle noise residual

Table 1. Summary of numerical results

	Krissian		Nonlocal		NLTV		Fast NL	
Images	Time(secs)	PSNR	Time(secs)	PSNR	Time(secs)	PSNR	Time(secs)	PSNR
Lenna (PSNR = 24.51)	0.72	26.39	11.46	28.21	4.67	29.10	4.57	29.09
Gallstones	0.59	–	11.95	–	4.62	–	4.81	–

tv model is slightly faster than the faster non local means model and PSNR is also slightly higher. So, both of them are equally good for denoising speckle noise images. But still both these methods are slower than the original tv based model(Krissian). It appears from these results that we can combine these two methods to develop a faster and efficient denoising model.

5   Conclusion

In this paper we have compared four existing models with speckle noise images. The PDE based TV model [12] is very fast but has a blurring effect. Nonlocal means [2] has very effective denoising properties but it is very slow. We have compared them with non local tv model [10] and with a faster non local means model [9]. It appears the last two models are providing quite comparable results. The PSNR values are close and the timings are very similar. But still they are much slower than the initial tv based speckle denoising (Krissian) model.

The results of these paper are quite encouraging and would help us to design a new denoising model. Our next plan is to develop a non local total variation based model with the similar neighborhood approach. We hope to get efficient result with faster computation time. Since both non local tv and faster nonlocal means have very close results, we hope to obtain some good results by combining these two. The solution can be obtained by using Split Bregman method. We plan to develop the new method for speckle noise images.

References

1. Bresson, X.: A short note for nonlocal tv minimization. Technical report (2009)
2. Buades, A., Coll, B., Morel, J.M.: A non-local algorithm for image denoising. In: 2005 IEEE Computer Society Conference on Computer Vision and Pattern Recognition, CVPR 2005, vol. 2, pp. 60–65, June 2005
3. Buades, A., Coll, B., Morel, J.M.: On image denoising methods. Technical report, Technical Note, CMLA (Centre de Mathematiques et de Leurs Applications) (2004)
4. Gilboa, G., Osher, S.: Nonlocal operators with applications to image processing. Multiscale Model. Simul. **7**(3), 1005–1028 (2008). http://dblp.uni-trier.de/db/journals/mmas/mmas7.html#GilboaO08
5. Goldstein, T., Osher, S.: The split Bregman method for L1-regularized problems. SIAM J. Img. Sci. **2**, 323–343 (2009). http://portal.acm.org/citation.cfm?id=1658384.1658386
6. Kim, S., Lim, H.: A non-convex diffusion model for simultaneous image denoising and edge enhancement. Electron. J. Differ. Equ. Conf. **15**, 175–192 (2007)
7. Krissian, K., Kikinis, R., Westin, C.F., Vosburgh, K.: Speckle-constrained filtering of ultrasound images. In: Proceedings of the 2005 IEEE Computer Society Conference on Computer Vision and Pattern Recognition (CVPR 2005), CVPR 2005, vol. 2, pp. 547–552. IEEE Computer Society, Washington, DC (2005)
8. Krissian, K., Vosburgh, K., Kikinis, R., Westin, C.F.: Anisotropic diffusion of ultrasound constrained by speckle noise model. Technical report 0004, Department of Radiology, Brigham and Women's Hospital, Harvard Medical School, Laboratory of Mathematics in Imaging, October 2004. ISSN
9. Mahmoudi, M., Sapiro, G.: Fast image and video denoising via nonlocal means of similar neighborhoods. IEEE Signal Process. Lett. **12**, 839–842 (2005)
10. Misra, A.B., Lim, H.: Nonlocal total variation based speckle denoising model. In: Mohan, S., Suresh Kumar, S. (eds.) ICSIP 2012. Lecture Notes in Electrical Engineering, vol. 221. Springer, India (2013). https://doi.org/10.1007/978-81-322-0997-3_46

11. Misra, A.B., Lim, H.: Nonlocal speckle denoising model based on non-linear partial differential equations. In: Mandal, J.K., Satapathy, S.C., Sanyal, M.K., Sarkar, P.P., Mukhopadhyay, A. (eds.) Information Systems Design and Intelligent Applications. AISC, vol. 340, pp. 165–176. Springer, New Delhi (2015). https://doi.org/10.1007/978-81-322-2247-7_18
12. Rudin, L.I., Osher, S., Fatemi, E.: Nonlinear total variation based noise removal algorithms. Phys. D: Nonlinear Phenom. **60**(1–4), 259–268 (1992)
13. Zhou, D., Schölkopf, B.: A regularization framework for learning from graph data. In: ICML Workshop on Statistical Relational Learning, pp. 132–137 (2004)
14. Zhou, D., Schölkopf, B.: Regularization on discrete spaces. In: Kropatsch, W.G., Sablatnig, R., Hanbury, A. (eds.) DAGM 2005. LNCS, vol. 3663, pp. 361–368. Springer, Heidelberg (2005). https://doi.org/10.1007/11550518_45

Using Probabilistic Optimization Algorithms to Reduce PAPR in OFDM System

Ashim Kumar Mahato[1](✉) (iD), Shoiab Naafi[2] (iD), and Debaprasad Das[2] (iD)

[1] Department of Computer Science and Engineering, Assam University,
Silchar 788011, Assam, India
ashim.cse.2005@gmail.com

[2] Department of Electronics and Communication Engineering, Assam University,
Silchar 788011, Assam, India

Abstract. Orthogonal frequency division multiplexing (OFDM) is a swiftly growing multi-carrier modulation technique. OFDM gives high data rate for transmission of information from one location to another. Peak to average power ratio (PAPR) has been a constraining component of OFDM. Various techniques have been proposed to reduce PAPR. Partial Transmit Sequence (PTS) is a distortion less technique that improves PAPR performance. The PTS technique reduces PAPR by a fair margin. However, the major drawback of PTS is that for large number of IFFT calculations the computational complexity increases. Various optimization techniques have been implemented to reduce the complexity in PTS technique. In this paper, we propose an Ant Colony Optimization (ACO) based PTS technique to achieve least PAPR in OFDM. The simulation results confirm that the proposed technique can accomplish the noteworthy PAPR diminishment with less computational complexity.

Keywords: Orthogonal frequency division multiplexing (OFDM) ·
Particle Swarm Optimization (PSO) ·
Partial Transmit Sequence (PTS) ·
Peak to average power ratio (PAPR) · Ant Colony Optimization (ACO)

1 Introduction

In recent years with the interest for higher information rates, a multicarrier modulation technique has got a noteworthy consideration called OFDM. OFDM technique diminish the impact of the noise and interferences productively. It also reduces inter symbol interference (ISI). One of the principal downside of OFDM system is large PAPR. When several sinusoidal get added orderly in inverse fast Fourier transform (IFFT) at a particular instant, high PAPR occurs then. Different techniques are being introduced to diminish high PAPR of the OFDM system [1]. Clipping and filtering technique uses linear amplifiers to transmit data in OFDM system. The clipping uses an ideal low-pass filter which increases

© Springer Nature Singapore Pte Ltd. 2019
J. K. Mandal et al. (Eds.): CICBA 2018, CCIS 1030, pp. 271–279, 2019.
https://doi.org/10.1007/978-981-13-8578-0_21

the PAPR of the OFDM signal [2]. Pamungkasari et al. [3] proposed selected mapping (SLM) which is one of the simplest technique among the other techniques used to reduce PAPR. The SLM has high computational complexity as a result of large number of IFFT blocks.

In PTS technique, data blocks are divided into various disjoint sub-blocks. Then, phase of each sub-blocks are modified by a set rotation factors to obtain lowest PAPR value. However, with the increase in number of sub-blocks, computational complexity also increases [4]. In [5] the tone rejection technique provides better PAPR reduction while using optimized peak reduction tone (PRT) positions. The performance deteriorates for non-optimal PRT positions. In coding technique few bits of the codeword is used to upgrade BER, and also used to reduce PAPR [6].

In [7], a partial transmit sequence using the real-valued genetic algorithm (RVGA) has been proposed which reduces the PAPR along with reducing the computational complexity. Wang et al. [8] proposed a modified artificial bee colony (ABC-PTS) algorithm to search the better blend of phase factors. It essentially decreases the computational complexity for bigger PTS sub-block while keeping down the PAPR.

In [9], Liang et al. proposed a PAPR reduction method by modifying the genetic algorithm. It reduces PAPR along with computational complexity.

Jiang et al. [10] introduced a nonlinear optimization approach called simulated annealing (SA). This method provides less complexity by finding the best blend of phase factors. It is suitable for transmission of data at high data rate.

In 2017, Joshi et al. [11] proposed a modified genetic algorithm for PTS by using a novel octagonal geometry for constellation extension purpose. The upside of this strategy is that, it does not require to transmit the side data unlike the other PTS techniques, which in turn decreases the quantity of search.

This paper is organized as follows. In Sect. 2, definition of PAPR of OFDM signal and CCDF are introduced. In Sect. 3, we have described the principle of PTS technique. In Sect. 4, we have presented minimization of PAPR using probabilistic optimization algorithms. Next, the results are discussed in Sect. 5. The conclusions are presented in the Sect. 6.

2   OFDM System and PAPR

The OFDM signal sequence in discrete time domain is expressed as

$$x(n) = \frac{1}{\sqrt{N}} \sum_{n=0}^{N-1} X_k e^{\frac{j2\pi nkt}{LN}}, \qquad k = 0, 1, \dots LN - 1. \tag{1}$$

Therefore, the PAPR of OFDM signal $x(n)$ is given by [8]

$$PAPR(x(n)) = 10 \log_{10} \frac{\max_{0 \le n \le NT} |x(n)^2|}{E\left[|x(n)^2|\right]} \qquad (dB) \tag{2}$$

The PAPR reduction is evaluated by CCDF. Probability of the PAPR of an OFDM signal is greater than the given threshold $PAPR_0$, which is expressed as [14]

$$CCDF = Pr(PAPR > PAPR_0). \tag{3}$$

3   Partial Transmit Sequence (PTS) Technique

In the PTS technique, an input symbol sequence X is divided into M disjoint symbol sequences, as $x_m = [x_{m,1}, x_{m,2}, ..., x_{m,N}]$, $0 \leq m \leq (M-1)$, which can be represented as [15]

$$X = \sum_{m=1}^{M} x_m. \tag{4}$$

At that point the IFFT activities perform for each sub-square x_m, $0 \leq m \leq (M-1)$, and weighted by a phase factor $b_m = e^{j\Theta_m}$, where $\Theta_m \in [0, 2\pi]$ for $m = 1, 2, ..., M$. The principle objective is to choose an arrangement of phase factors that gives the most minimal PAPR when combined with time domain signal, where x is defined as [15]

$$x = \sum_{m=1}^{M-1} b_m x_m. \tag{5}$$

In PTS, when the number of sub blocks is larger then PAPR reduction is better. However, the issue is that computational complexity increments exponentially with the quantity of sub blocks. Figure 1 shows a block diagram of PTS technique.

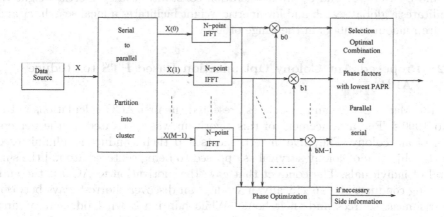

Fig. 1. Block diagram of PTS technique [10].

4   Minimization of PAPR Using Probabilistic Optimization Algorithms

In this section, an existing PAPR minimization technique is compared with our proposed PAPR reduction technique.

4.1   Particle Swarm Optimization Based PTS to Reduce PAPR

Particle Swarm Optimization (PSO) was presented in 1995 by Eberhart and Kennedy [16], based on the social behavior of bird flocking or fish schooling. The PSO technique is mainly used to find the optimum solution in a swarm which consists of many particles. The position and velocity is updated frequently based on the local best value *pbest* and global best value *gbest*.

The population is called the swarm and individuals are called particles. As indicated by the particle's own particular flying background and the flying knowledge of the best particle among the swarm, the position of the swarm is refreshed. The local best and global best particles are represented by w_i^p and w_i^g respectively. Hung et al. [12] have shown how the position can be updated by the following equation.

$$w_i(t+1) = w_1(t) + v_i(t+1) \qquad (6)$$

The velocity can be updated by

$$v_i(t+1) = Wv_i(t) + c_1r_1[w_i^p(t) - w_i(t)] + c_2r_2[w_i^g(t) - w_i(t)] \qquad (7)$$

The value of the new velocity depends upon the old velocity weighted by W and furthermore connected with the particle and the global best by factor c_1 and c_2. Here, c_1 and c_2 are acceleration constant. A large inertia weight W facilitates a global search and low inertia weight facilitates a local search. r_1 and r_2 are random numbers in the range of [0,1].

4.2   Proposed Ant Colony Optimization Based PTS to Reduce PAPR

In [13], Marco Dorigo and associates presented the first ACO calculations in the mid 1990's. The advancement of this algorithm was motivated by the perception of ant colony. They live in settlements and their conduct is administered by the objective of colony survival as opposed to being centered around the survival of individuals. The conduct that gave the motivation to ACO is the ants foraging conduct, and specifically, how ants can discover shortest ways between nourishment sources and their home. While hunting down food, ants at first investigate the region encompassing their home in an arbitrary way. Ants leave a pheromone trail on the ground. Ants can only smell pheromone. They choose their path that has strong pheromone concentrations. At the point when a subterranean ant finds a sustenance source, it surveys the amount and nature of the nourishment source and passes on it back to the home. The pheromone trails will guide different ants to the food source.

In ACO based PTS technique, each potential solution is represented as an ant with position vector X, assigned as phase weighting factor.

The method of ACO based PTS technique is given below:

Step 1: Initialize a population of ants with arbitrary positions, where each ant contains k variable. Define the maximum number of iterations T, the pheromone evaporation factor (ρ) and transfer probability constant(P_0).

Step 2: Assess fitness function for every ant. Let τ_{best} and its objective value equal to the position and the objective value of the best initial ant.

Step 3: Calculate the state transition probability of each ant given by the equation

$$P_{ij} = (\tau_{best} - \tau_{i,j})/\tau_{best} \qquad (8)$$

Step 4: If the state transition probability ($P_{i,j}$) is less then transfer probability constant (P_0) then perform local search, otherwise perform global search.

Step 5: For every ant compare its current object value with the object value of τ_{best}, If the current value is better, then update the τ_{best} and its object value with the current position and its object value.

Step 6: Update the pheromone value using the equation

$$\tau_{ij} = (1 - \rho)\tau_{ij} + \Delta\tau_{ij} \qquad (9)$$

where, $\Delta\tau_{ij}$ is the left amount of information in the path.

Step 7: Termination criteria: If the maximum number of iteration achieved then stop.

Table 1. Simulation parameters.

Sl.no	Parameters	Values
1	Number of subcarriers	$N = 128$
2	Modulation technique	16-QAM
3	Number of sub blocks	$M = 4$
4	Number of phase factor	$W = 4$
5	Random OFDM symbol generated	1000
6	Number of iterations	30

5   Results

The simulation parameters are shown in Table 1. Here, the numbers of subcarriers $N = 128$ and number of sub-blocks $M = 4$. 16-QAM modulation technique is used with oversampling factor 4. To measure the performance of the proposed algorithm, we have considered 1000 OFDM symbols. There are four phase factors (W) which are denoted as $\{+1, -1, +j, -j\}$.

Figure 2 shows the CCDFs of the PAPR of the conventional OFDM, PTS and PSO-PTS based OFDM systems. Here, we have considered acceleration constant $c_1 = c_2 = 2$ and inertia weighting factor $w = 0.9$. When, $CCDF = 10^{-3}$, the PAPR is reduced to 8.68 dB from 11.35 dB in conventional OFDM system using PSO-PTS.

Figure 3 shows the CCDFs of the PAPR of the conventional OFDM, PTS and proposed ACO-PTS based OFDM systems. Here, we have considered the pheromone evaporation factor $\rho = 0.8$, the transfer probability constant $P_0 = 0.2$. When, $CCDF = 10^{-3}$, proposed ACO-PTS based OFDM system provides a PAPR reduction of 3.06 dB from 11.35 dB of the conventional OFDM system.

Figure 4 shows the CCDFs of the PAPR of the conventional OFDM, PTS, PSO-PTS and proposed ACO-PTS based OFDM systems. When, $CCDF = 10^{-3}$, the PAPR values of the system are 11.35 dB, 7.15 dB, 8.68 dB and 8.29 dB, respectively. The proposed ACO-PTS based OFDM system gives a better PAPR reduction of 0.39 dB compared to the existing PSO-PTS based OFDM system.

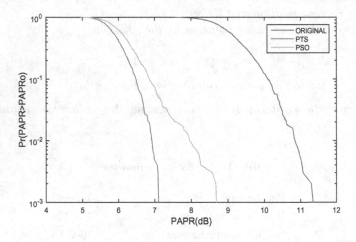

Fig. 2. PAPR comparison of PSO-PTS and PTS for N = 128 and 16-QAM modulation.

Table 2 presents the comparative analysis of the PAPR performance of the proposed technique with the existing techniques.

Table 2. Comparison the PAPR performance.

Sl.no	Technique	PAPR performance
1	Original OFDM	11.35 dB
2	PTS	7.15 dB
3	PSO-PTS	8.68 dB
4	Proposed ACO-PTS	8.29 dB

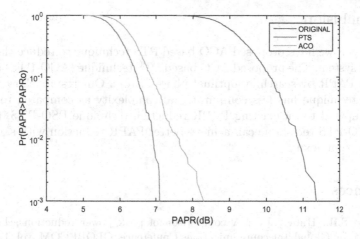

Fig. 3. PAPR comparison of ACO-PTS and PTS for N = 128 and 16-QAM modulation.

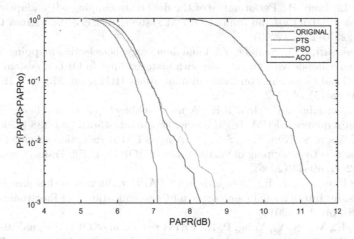

Fig. 4. PAPR comparison of ACO-PTS, PSO-PTS and PTS for N = 128 and 16-QAM modulation.

Table 3. The computational complexity of PTS, PSO-PTS and ACO-PTS techniques, size of population/particles S = P = 4

Methods	Number of subcarrier	Number of iteration (I)	Computational complexity
PTS	128	-	$W^M = 4^4 = 256$
PSO-PTS	128	30	$PI = 4 \times 30 = 120$
ACO-PTS	128	30	$SI = 4 \times 30 = 120$

Complexity analysis of the PTS, PSO-PTS, and proposed ACO-PTS techniques are presented in Table 3.

6 Conclusion

In this paper, we have proposed ACO based PTS technique to reduce the PAPR of OFDM system. The proposed ACO based PTS technique (ACO-PTS) achieves minimum PAPR by searching optimal phase factors. Our results show that the proposed technique has less computational complexity as compared to that of PTS. Compared to an existing PAPR reduction technique PSO-PTS, the proposed ACO-PTS technique can achieve better PAPR reduction with same computational complexity.

References

1. Muller, S.H., Huber, J.B.: A comparison of peak power reduction schemes for OFDM. In: Global Telecommunications Conference, GLOBECOM, vol. 1, pp. 1–5. IEEE (1997)
2. Ochiai, H., Imai, H.: Performance of the deliberate clipping with adaptive symbol selection for strictly band-limited OFDM systems. IEEE J. Sel. Areas Commun. 18(11), 2270–2277 (2000)
3. Pamungkasari, P.D., Sanada, Y.: Time domain cyclic-selective mapping for PAPR reduction using delayed correlation with matched filter in OFDM system. In: 22nd International Conference on Telecommunications (ICT), pp. 373–377. IEEE, Sydney, AU (2015)
4. Kang, S.G., Kim, J.G., Joo, E.K.: A novel subblock partition scheme for partial transmit sequence OFDM. IEEE Trans. Broadcast. 45(3), 333–338 (1999)
5. Yoo, S., Yoon, S., Kim, S.Y., Song, I.: A novel PAPR reduction scheme for OFDM systems: selective mapping of partial tones (SMOPT). IEEE Trans. Consum. Electron. 52(1), 40–43 (2006)
6. Ann, P.P. and Jose, R.: Comparison of PAPR reduction techniques in OFDM systems. In: International Conference on Communication and Electronics Systems (ICCES), pp. 1–5 (2016)
7. Lain, J.-K., Wu, S.-Y., Yang, P.-H.: PAPR reduction of OFDM signals using PTS: a real-valued genetic approach. EURASIP J. Wirel. Commun. Netw. 2011(16), 126 (2011)
8. Wang, Y., Chen, W., Tellambura, C.: A PAPR reduction method based on artificial bee colony algorithm for OFDM signals. IEEE Trans. Wirel. Commun. 9(110), 2994–2999 (2010)
9. Liang, H., Chen, Y.R., Huang, Y.F., Cheng, C.H.: A modified genetic algorithm PTS technique for PAPR reduction in OFDM systems. In: 15th Asia-Pacific Conference on Communications, APCC 2009, pp. 182–185 (2009)
10. Jiang, T., Xiang, W., Richardson, P.C., Guo, J., Zhu, G.: PAPR reduction of OFDM signals using partial transmit sequences with low computational complexity. IEEE Trans. Broadcast. 53(3), 719–724 (2007)
11. Joshi, A., Saini, D.S.: GA-PTS using novel mapping scheme for PAPR reduction of OFDM signals without SI. Wirel. Pers. Commun. 92(2), 639–651 (2017)
12. Hung, H.-L., Huang, Y.-F., Yeh, C.-M., Tan, T.-H.: Performance of particle swarm optimization techniques on PAPR reduction for OFDM systems. In: IEEE International Conference on Systems, Man and Cybernetics, SMC 2008, pp. 2390–2395 (2008)

13. Dorigo, M., Maniezzo, V., Colorni, A.: Ant system: optimization by a colony of cooperating agents. IEEE Trans. Syst. Man Cybern. Part B (Cybern.) **26**(1), 29–41 (1996)
14. Kermani, E.M., Salehinejad, H., Talebi, S.: PAPR reduction of OFDM signals using harmony search algorithm. In: 18th International Conference on Telecommunications (ICT), pp. 90–94 (2011)
15. Muller, S.H., Huber, J.B.: OFDM with reduced peak-to-average power ratio by optimum combination of partial transmit sequences. Electron. Lett. **33**(5), 368–369 (1997)
16. Shi, Y., et al.: Particle swarm optimization: developments, applications and resources. In: Proceedings of the 2001 Congress on Evolutionary Computation, vol. 1, pp. 81–86. IEEE (2001)

DDOS Attack on Software-Defined Networks and Its Mitigation Techniques

Raktim Deb[✉] and Sudipta Roy

Department of Computer Science and Engineering,
Triguna Sen School of Technology, Assam University, Silchar 788011, India
debraktim@gmail.com, sudipta.it@gmail.com

Abstract. The emergence of promising Software Defined Networks to be exact SDN has been a center of attraction for the researchers as well as industry for its capability of network management in terms of simplicity, elasticity, and programmability. Despite all these promising opportunities; due to the introduction of various architectural entities of SDN poses new security threats and vulnerabilities, which leads an agenda for attackers. There are several possible attacks in SDN among them this paper prioritizes the impact of the DDoS attack on SDN and existing mitigation techniques.

Keywords: Software Defined Network · OpenFlow · DDoS attack · Mitigation techniques

1 Introduction

Software Defined Networking (SDN) is the biggest development in today's networking environment. This latest development brings many problems with this new technology. The basic idea of this environment is to strike out the control logic from the network nodes and form a centralized logical control to guide the network traffic [1,2]. This idea helps SDN to manage network traffic freely and without changing underneath topology by means of software programming. Moreover, it is a convenient and promising idea to manage huge network traffic in current trends where network traffic increasing day by day. But this promising idea also comes with a threat of making centralized function unavailable by exhausting computing or memory resources; which leads the network in single point failure or denial of services. Denial of service attack is one of the severe threats of SDN at present as it is able to break down a controller and may disrupt a whole network [3]. The DDoS attack in SDN means that an attacker may generate the huge flow of traffic to the centralized control of SDN and be making it busy to do some specific tasks. Thus, DDoS attack and its mitigation are one of the priority concerns in SDN as well as our discussion topic for this paper. The remainder of this paper is organized as follows. Section 2 presents a conceptual view of SDN architecture to provide fundamental background. In

J. K. Mandal et al. (Eds.): CICBA 2018, CCIS 1030, pp. 280–292, 2019.
https://doi.org/10.1007/978-981-13-8578-0_22

Sect. 3, some fundamental discussions are presented about OpenFlow protocol, which will give a better understanding about of DDoS attack in SDN and in Sect. 4 we have discussed regarding the DDoS attack and a comparative idea about its existing countermeasures followed by a conclusion in the last section.

2   A Conceptual View of SDN Architecture

This section provides a glimpse of fundamental concepts of SDN architecture. Before going into an in-depth discussion of SDN architecture, we must have to understand the conceptual differences of SDN with the present networking system and working procedure of its nodes (router/switch). A network node is tightly coupled with two components popularly known as control plane and data plane as shown in Fig. 1.

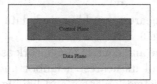

Fig. 1. Traditional switch

The responsibility of the control plane is to manage the network traffic and based its decision on the data plane is responsible for moving/dropping the network traffic. The first conceptual difference begins here, in SDN these two components are not being tightly coupled; they are an individual entity as depicted in Fig. 2.

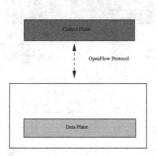

Fig. 2. OpenFlow switch

The second conceptual difference comes from the working procedure of the networking system. In a traditional network, the nodes are aware of its nearest neighbor. Whenever a network packet arrives at a node, the control plane makes

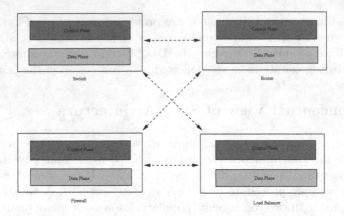

Fig. 3. Traditional networking

the decision to select the nearest neighbor and data plane moves that packet accordingly as shown in Fig. 3.

But in SDN as data plane and control plane work as an individual entity [2,4]; the data plane is unaware of its nearest neighbor and the control plane forms a centralized point of the network system and having the image of underneath topology. Thus, data plane works as a simple forwarding device and control plane works as a decision maker of the entire network. Whenever a network packet arrives at the data plane, it simply forwards that packet to the control plane. The control plane takes the decision about making a motion (forward/drop) of that packet and instruct data plane accordingly. After getting the instruction from the control plane only, data plane makes the movement of that incoming packet as described in Fig. 4.

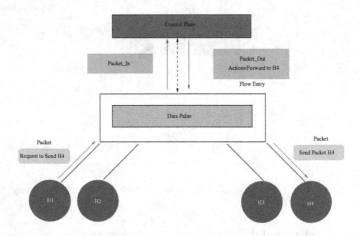

Fig. 4. Working procedure of SDN

The concept of centralized control provides SDN architecture list of additional benefits compared to the traditional network. First, It makes network policy management easy and simple. Moreover, the policy can be maintained dynamically. As SDN control plane has global knowledge of network topology and more and more sophisticated network provisions can be implemented. The backbone of SDN is OpenFlow specification which is discussed in Sect. 3.

For these dynamic capabilities of SDN, more industry people are growing their interest in shifting to SDN.

3   OpenFlow

OpenFlow specification [1] is considered one of the first standards in SDN architecture. This specification basically builds up with two components which are OpenFlow enabled switch and a communication protocol namely OpenFlow protocol. The OpenFlow protocol is implemented on both sides of SDN architecture and this protocol is responsible for making communication between the control plane and data plane. This protocol is made up of the concept of flows to determine network traffic based on predefined/dynamically defined rules [4]. The OpenFlow enabled switch consists of the number of tables containing the number of packet movement (forward/drop) rules. Each and every rule agrees with a subset of network traffic and takes some action on it.

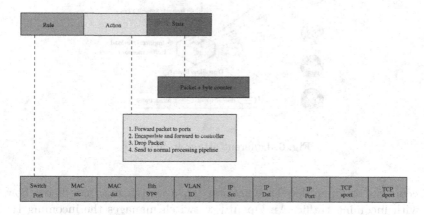

Fig. 5. OpenFlow protocol

Figure 5 shows the components of OpenFlow protocol. The responsibility of the centralized control plane is to install the flow rules into the flow table of an OpenFlow switch based on some incoming network traffic. Thus OpenFlow protocol is the key enabler for SDN that allows direct manipulation of OpenFlow switch. Whenever a switch receives a new packet, it looks into the flow table to determine the destination path. If the packet mismatches with an existing entry in the flow table, a message (PacketIn) is forwarded to the controller to an inquiry about new flow. The control plane determines the new routing path and sends a message (PacketOut) to the switch to install the rule for new flow then only a switch to act accordingly. Each flow entry has its own strict lifetime after which switch mechanically deletes the entry. Due to this working procedure in SDN architecture, DoS attacks have the serious impacts on the proper functioning of the network.

4   DDoS Attack and Its Impact in SDN

Distributed denial of service attack is the subclass of denial of service (DoS) attacks. A DDoS attack passes off when an attacker, or attackers, attempts to make it impossible for a service to be delivered by exhausting computing resources.

The fundamental concept of SDN architecture [5,6] and the implementation of rule-based communication make SDN more vulnerable to Denial of service attack as sown in Fig. 6.

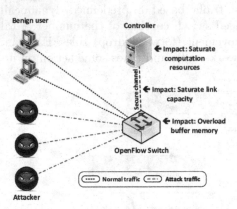

Fig. 6. Different attack in SDN [7]

According to OpenFlow specification [1], a switch does not know how to deal with incoming traffic. An OpenFlow switch manages the incoming traffic by means of sending PacketIn and receives PacketOut messages. Which means, there is certain involvement of a control plane for every new incoming traffic. This certain involvement of control plane is the root cause of the threat of DoS attack. By any means along with normal traffic, if an attacker is able to generate a vast amount of new traffic to the control plane, then only it is possible to exhaust the computational resources of the controller, which leads to a denial of service to the normal traffic. Such scenario drastically reduces the performance of the network or it may sometimes lead to complete failure of whole networking as the only control knows the underneath topology. In next very section, some popularly used mitigation techniques of DDoS attack in SDN are discussed

5   DDoS Attack Mitigation Techniques

5.1   AVANT-GUARD:

AVANT-GUARD was proposed by Shin et al. in 2013 [8]. In this mitigation technique, they address two kinds of challenges in SDN network. The first challenge is to moderate the control plane saturation attack: bottleneck that emerges during the communication between data plane and control plane. The second challenge is to generate quick response about network status and payload information from the data plane to control plane. To meet these challenges, they suggest two new modules: a connection migration module and an actuating module. The objective of the first module is to send flow requests to the control plane only for those sources that are completed TCP connection between sources to data plane and restrict if not completed. The responsibility of the actuating trigger module is accelerating the information about network status to the control plane. With the help of this module, the control plane is able to define traffic statistics and install proper condition to the data plane. Similarly, data plane inspects the condition against the collected packet; if the condition is matched, then either it installs the flow rules for the collections or sends a callback message to the control plane indicating the condition is met. To meet these challenges, they made a slight modification in the OpenFlow switch architecture shown in Fig. 7.

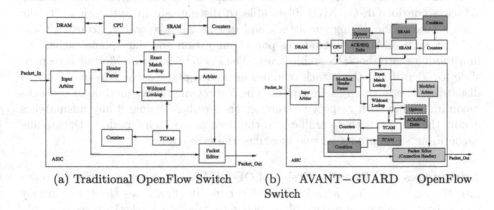

(a) Traditional OpenFlow Switch   (b)   AVANT–GUARD   OpenFlow Switch

Fig. 7. Comparative view of two Architectures

To implement the connection migration module, the header parser and the arbiter of OpenFlow Switch have been modified. The header parser is adjusted same as TCP flags and the arbiter is altered to constrain the packet editor to initialize connection migration or reply with TCP ACK/SYN packet. Also, two data structures being introduced in the AVANT-GUARD embedded OpenFlow switch which is ACK/SEQ delta structure and optional structure. The first data structure maintains the SEQ number of SYN of connection initiator and the optional data structure maintains TCP options like the timestamp. For implementing actuating trigger, all condition fields are being attached with TCAM and SRAM storage collectively labeled as Condition.

Advantages and Pitfalls: It reduces the burden of control plane as less number of packets are sent to the control plane for decision making and most importantly, packet filtering is imposed in data plane only. The problem with AVANT-GUARD is that it is able to mitigate only TCP-based DoS attack but fails to defend any other protocol based DoS attack. Moreover, AVANT-GUARD modifies the switch architecture which simply means that all switches must be equipped with AVANT-GUARD otherwise entire network will be vulnerable. AVANT-GUARD also suffers from delay in imposing extra data structure to implement connection migration module and actuating the trigger.

5.2   OF-GUARD

During DoS Attack, an attacker is able to generate a large number of fake network traffic along with a small number of normal traffic. For all unidentified traffic, OpenFlow switch sends PacketIn messages to control plane and it has to decide how to deal with this unidentified traffic. Which means, as much as unidentified traffic increases the workload of control plane will be increased. For such reason control plane may exhaust computational resources during a DoS attack scenario. OF-GUARD [9] is able to distinguish an authenticate traffic from a fake traffic during the attack and discard all fake traffic. To reach these objectives OF-GAURD introduces packet migration and data plane cache, two new modules into the SDN architecture. The Packet Migration Module is responsible for identifying the attack scenario and data plane cache is responsible for discarding the incoming fake traffic. The Packet migration module also checks incoming traffic with respect to some given threshold value; if any mismatches occur, then it sends those traffic into the data plane cache module. Data plane cache using some proactive rule identifies the fake traffic.

Advantages and Pitfalls: Design of OF-GUARD is attack-driven as it comes into the act only when attack scenario occurs. It guarantees the transparency to the control plane as a data plane needs to generate PacketIn messages only for the filtered packets. But, this technique is also having some loopholes similar to AVANT-GUARD. All the OpenFlow switch needs to be equipped with OF-GAURD otherwise entire network will be vulnerable which is very hard to implement. Not only that, in an attack scenario if all the OpenFlow switch of a network itself compromised then it will impossible to OF-GUARD to detect DoS attack.

5.3   FlowRanger

In SDN 1.4 standard [1], the control plane can arrange a flow parameter on OpenFlow switches to constrain the forwarding rate from each OpenFlow switch, but this constraint causes some legitimate packets to be dropped at a prior stage. It is additionally not clear how to set an optimum transmitting rate to restrain for each OpenFlow switch in arrange to have optimum performance. Due availability of this constraint in SDN, the standard DOS attack causes dropping of legitimate packets. To illuminate this problem FlowRanger [10] introduces job prioritization process based on the attacking threats of the source. The FlowRanger comprises three components among them first component is trust management, the second one is queuing management and the last component is the request scheduling. At any point when the controller gets a new PacketIn request, the first components come into action. The responsibility of the trust management component is to track the trust values of request users in SDN network. In FlowRanger, control plane maintains the record of trust users. If a user uses SDN during normal time, then the trust value increases for that user otherwise decreases. For a user, if trust value is lower than given threshold value, the controller notifies the user as an attacker. Next, the second component (queuing management) based on the trust regard of sender maps the request to a comparing priority queue. Finally, the request scheduling component determines the preparing arrange of all requests in distinctive need queues.

Advantages and Pitfalls: The FlowRanger improves the overall performance of SDN as because of job prioritization. Due to this prioritization concept, the service quality of any rightful hosts will not be degraded during a DoS attack in SDN. One downside of FlowRanger is that a non-active user will assign lower priority which may lead to network delay. The FlowRanger does not react to the peak loads attack or controller attack instantaneously. The enhancements are not worth mentioning after two queues since two queues can be adequate to supply detection between standard network activity and gigantic traffic during the attack. But two queues may cause long service time and slower processing for the control plane, which might lead to the dismissal of both demands.

5.4 IP Filtering

Dao et al. proposed IP Filtering [11] that analyzes user traffic behavior. For estimating traffic behavior, they address four parameters: The counter of IP address, the minimum amount of packets for each connection, the mean connections of frequent users and the statistic counter of IP address. The working procedure of IP Filtering such as whenever a counter IP address is reached average connection of frequent user, it checks data traffic characteristic by requesting the statistic counter. If statistic counter of an IP address is less than the minimum number of per traffic, this means malicious traffic and then control plane dispatches a dropped rule for the address to the OpenFlow switch.

Advantages and Pitfalls: This technique is advantageous as malicious traffic can be removed quickly from the CAM tables, but if flow duration is greater than the predefined timeout, then it sends a PacketIn message to the control plane which may lead extra burden to the control plane. Since by convention IP Filtering technique drops all malicious packets, IP Filtering is not able to judge false positive flows and mistakenly drop those packets.

5.5 Self-management Scheme

Sahay et al. aim to create an autonomic DDoS mitigation framework [12] by utilizing SDN advances. The thought behind this framework is to preserve the inclusion of ISPs and their clients to moderate DDoS attacks established in the instant communication between DDoS monitoring, analysis, detection, and response modules. The proposed disseminated, collaborative framework grants the clients to inquire DDoS mitigation service from ISPs. Consequent to request, ISP's can alter the name of the odd activity and redirect them to secure middle-boxes, while attack discovery and analysis modules are sent at the customer end, evading security spillage and other lawful concerns. More precisely, the ISP is responsible for collecting the threat data given by clients in order to execute security policies and alter flow table within the SDN subsequently. In case the flow is considered as a legitimate flow by the client at that point the as it were an ISP control plane will tag it with a rich priority value for which it can able to take a path with higher quality. Something else, an ISP control plane will assign a very low priority and designated as a noxious flow.

Advantages and Pitfalls: The self - management scheme is an on-demand lightweight process so it reduces the burden of control plane and balances the load across the different path. This scheme can only manage link state flooding, but not able to deal with flooding in flow tables in the switch or control plane overloading.

5.6 FLOOD-GUARD

Wang et al. Proposed FLOOD-GUARD [13] a lightweight, adaptable, and a proficient, protocol-independent framework during 2015. This framework is utilized for mitigating data plane to control plane saturation attack in SDN. To reach the objective, Flood-Guard comprises two new modules among them the first module is the proactive flow rule analyzer and the second module is packet migration. The proactive flow rules are the compelling and time-sensitive data plane flow rules which can be produced by an application based on present control plane state. The analyzer module comprises of the utmost use of the network architecture during the event of saturation attack. This module implemented in control plane as a control plane application. The packet migration module having two components: the first one is migration agent and second one named as data plane cache. The migration agent actualizes in control plane as a control plane application. The data plane cache element works as an interface for the control plane and data plane. The packet migration module passes on the network flows to the OpenFlow control plane without over-burdening it. An intangible architecture of FLOOD-GUARD is shown in Fig. 8.

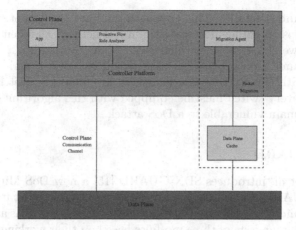

Fig. 8. Architecture of FLOOD-GUARD

Advantages and Pitfalls: FLOOD-GUARD is a light weighted scalable framework. It represents a more generic algorithm to detect any protocol based attack without modifying the basic architecture of SDN. FLOOD-GUARD is able to dispatch dynamic flow rules which are very efficient during attack scenario. But to maintain dynamicity to the flow rules, it has to implement a complex data structure proactive flow dispatcher. This dispatcher takes more time to explore the patch condition which leads an overhead to the system. It brings the high accuracy of the system as it updates the rules each and every time after a change, but it reduces the performance of the system. Moreover, FLOOD-GUARD is implemented in switch also, which means each and every switch must be FLOOD-GUARD equipped otherwise the system remains vulnerable.

5.7   Entropy-Based Mitigation Techniques

In 2015 Wang et al. introduces an entropy-based [14] lightweight DDoS attack mitigation technique. The proposed model is implemented in OpenFlow switch. An OpenFlow switch is able to identify its local topology, but unable to differentiate whether the IP address falls within the local network or not. Moreover, It also lacks in retaining information about the packet number for a specific flow during certain intervals. This approach modifies Counters field of the OpenFlow table and introduces a new component RPLocal alongside with Received Packet. The RPLocal keeps track of the flow entry of the local network. This approach mitigates DoS attack by identifying the differences between the mean entropy of flow entries of a node with flow entropy of a node and then it is compared with the threshold value. Due to dynamic traffic in a network the mean entropy and threshold are implemented as adaptive by nature, i.e. there is no fixed value for the mean entropy and threshold.

Advantages and Pitfalls: This approach modifies the Counter field of flow table which helps to gather flow statistic in the network. The entropy calculation is a light weighted process which reduces the overloading problem of the frequent communication process between OpenFlow switch and control plane. The problem with this that it is implemented in OpenFlow switch. For that in SDN network, every switch must be equipped with this algorithm otherwise the network will remain vulnerable to a DoS attack.

5.8 SDN-GUARD

In 2016 Dridi et al. introduces SDN-GUARD [15] a new DoS Mitigation Technique. SDN-GUARD try to mitigate all the loopholes that exist in the previous mitigation techniques as discussed earlier. SDN-GUARD works as a control plane application and it consists of three modules based on their working functionality which are named as flow management module, rule aggregation module, and monitoring module. The first module identifies the routing path for the flow entries. To moderate the impact of DoS attack flow management module is also responsible for identifying the threat probability of each and every flow entry and assign hard timeout to the corresponding entries. To determine the threat probability SDN-GUARD introduces Intrusion Detection System (IDS). The second module aggregates the malicious flows and restricts the insertion of flow entries into the switches TCAMs. The responsibility of the third module is to collect the flow statistics like flow throughput, the bandwidth of a link and switch bandwidth for the other two modules of the SDN-GUARD. The implementation overview of SDN-GUARD is shown in Fig. 9.

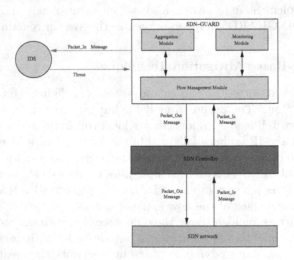

Fig. 9. Architecture of SDN-GUARD

Advantages and Pitfalls: SDN suffers from several kinds of DoS attack like control plane overloading problem, exhausting the switch to control plane bandwidth and switch TCAM memory overflow. The design of SDN-GUARD can able to mitigate all these existing problems dynamically by managing path flow, rule entry timeouts and aggregating the flow rule entries based on threat probability. The SDN-GUARD is implemented in control plane as a control plane application so there is no need of making each and every switch to be SDN-GUARD equipped. But to compute the threat probability each and every time SDN-GUARD must need to communicate with IDS which leads an extra burden on the control plane. SDN-GUARD self-balanced the throughput to the unutilized link which is considered as an additional benefit of this technique.

6 Summary

The intention of every mitigation technique is to secure SDN from DDoS attack as well as maintaining the performance of SDN during the attack scenario. The table represents the targeted performance at the time of the DDoS attack, types of packets it is able to deal with, implementation side and time efficiency of the approach.

Table 1. Comparison between different parameters of Mitigation Techniques

Approaches	Implementation side	Controller workload	Control plane bandwidth	Flow table uses	Network bandwidth	Dealing packets	Time efficiency
AVANT-GUARD	Data plane	Yes	Yes	Yes	Yes	Only TCP	Moderate
OF-GUARD	Data plane	Yes	Yes	Yes	Yes	All	Moderate
Flow ranger	Control plane	Yes	No	No	No	All	No
IP filtering	Control plane	Yes	Yes	Yes	Yes	All	No
Self-management	Control plane	No	No	No	Yes	All	No
FLOOD-GUARD	Both Data plane and Control plane	Yes	No	Yes	Yes	All	Moderate
Entropy-based	Data plane	Yes	Yes	Yes	Yes	All	Yes
SDN-GUARD	Control plane	Yes	Yes	Yes	Yes	All	Moderate

7 Conclusion

In this paper, a conceptual view of SND architecture is presented along with concise descriptions of OpenFlow specification. The security issue of SDN is the highest concern and DDoS attack security is one of the major issues in SDN. We explained DDoS attack and its impingement on Software Defined Network. Then we have discussed different mitigation which is implemented in SDN architecture to prevent the DDoS attack. The advantages and disadvantages of those techniques are presented. Table 1 gives us a glimpse of overall discussion and finding throughout the research study.

References

1. Open Networking Foundation. https://www.opennetworking.org/
2. Kreutz, D., Ramos, F.M.V., Paulo, E.V., Christian, E.R., Azodolmoky, S.: Software-defined networking: a comprehensive survey. Proc. IEEE. **103**(1), 14–76 (2015)
3. Akhunzada, A., Ahened, E., Gani, A., Khan, M.K., Imran, M., Guizani, S.: Securing software defined networks: taxonomy, requirements, and open issues. IEEE Commun. Mag. **53**, 36–43 (2015)
4. Jarraya, Y., Madi, T., Debbabi, M.: A survey and a layered taxonomy of software-defined networking. IEEE Commun. Surv. Tutor. **6**(4), 1955–1977 (2014)
5. Shu, Z., Wan, J., Li, D., Lin, J., Vasilakos, A.V., Imran, M.: Security in software-defined networking: threats and countermeasures. Mobile Netw. Appl. **21**, 764–776 (2016)
6. Kreutz, D., Ramos, F.M.V., Verissimo, P.: Towards secure and dependable software-defined networks. In: ACM SIGCOMM Workshop on Hot Topics in Software Defined Networking (2013)
7. ResearchGate. https://www.researchgate.net/figure/Impact-of-DDoS-attack-in-SDN_fig2_318858825
8. Shin, S., Yegneswaran, V., Porras, P., Gu, G.: AVANT-GUARD: scalable and vigilant switch flow management in software-defined networks. In: ACM Conference on Computer and Communications Security, pp. 413–424 (2013)
9. Wang, H., Xu, L., GU, G.: OF-GUARD: a DoS attack prevention extension in software-defined networks. In: Open Networking Summit 2014, Poster Session. USENIX (2014)
10. Wei, L., Fung, C.: Flow-Ranger: a request prioritizing algorithm for controller Dos Attack in SDN. In: IEEE International Conference on Communications (ICC), pp. 5254–5259 (2015)
11. Dao, N.N., Park, J., Cho, S.: A feasible method to combat against DDoS attack in SDN network. In: International Conference on Information Networking (ICOIN), pp. 309–311 (2015)
12. Sahay, R., Blanc, G., Zhang, Z., Debar, H.: Towards autonomic DDoS mitigation using software defined networking. In: Network and Distributed System Security (NDSS) Symposium, pp. 1–7 (2015)
13. Wang, H., Xu, L., Gu, G.: FloodGuard: a DoS attack prevention extension in software-defined networks. In: International Conference on Dependable Systems and Networks, pp. 239–250 (2015)
14. Wang, R., Jia, Z., Ju, L.: An entropy-based distributed DDoS detection mechanism in software-defined networking. In: IEEE Trustcom, pp. 310–317 (2015)
15. Dridi, L., Zhani, M.F.: SDN-GUARD: DoS attacks mitigation in SDN networks. In: International Conference on Cloud Networking, pp. 212–217 (2015)

A New Wide Range Voltage Gain DC/DC Converter for SPV Water Pumping System

Amit Samanta[1]([✉]), Ananta Pal[2], and Shib Sankar Saha[1]

[1] Department of Electrical Engineering,
Kalyani Government Engineering College, Kalyani, Nadia, West Bengal, India
amtsmnta@gmail.com
[2] Department of Electrical Engineering, Netaji Subhash Engineering College,
Garia, West Bengal, India

Abstract. A non-isolated dc-dc buck-boost converter with wide range of voltage gain is proposed in this paper. The proposed converter uses an active clamp circuit incorporated in a simple circuit of classical buck-boost converter. The proposed structure is capable to achieve extreme high step-up voltage gain even with a duty ratio within acceptable range for practical applications. However, the proposed converter can also operate as conventional buck-boost converter without activating the clamp circuit for step-down operation and step-up operation with moderate voltage gain, thereby omitting both switching and conduction losses of the clamp circuit. Performance of the proposed converter has been verified through computer simulation with MATLAB Simulink for nominal 24 V input voltage, 6 V–400 V output voltage, 500 W output power and switching frequency of 40 kHz. The simulated results were found to be in close agreement to the predicted behavior of the proposed converter.

Keywords: Buck-boost converter · Wide range voltage gain ·
Non-isolated DC-DC converter · Solar photo-voltaic (SPV) pumping system

1 Introduction

Since the industrial revolution in 17th century, uncontrolled use of conventional energy sources like coal, petroleum natural gas has caused depletion of fossil fuel reserved in earth. It is estimated that, the total reserve of fossil fuel can meet the energy demand of the world for at most 100 years at present rate of reserve to production ratio. But, the world's energy demand is increasing day by day with the increase in population and advancement of living standard of developed as well as developing countries. Moreover, use of conventional energy sources cause emission of greenhouse gases to the environment with the ultimate effect of ozone layer depletion, climate change, global warming, loss of biodiversity etc. Therefore, to meet future energy demand as well as to minimize further environmental degradation, the world is gradually leaning towards more and more use of renewable or green energy sources like, solar, wind, geothermal, tidal etc.

Water pumping worldwide is generally dependent on conventional electricity or diesel generated electricity [1]. With the steep rise of energy pricing and recent

© Springer Nature Singapore Pte Ltd. 2019
J. K. Mandal et al. (Eds.): CICBA 2018, CCIS 1030, pp. 293–306, 2019.
https://doi.org/10.1007/978-981-13-8578-0_23

development of economically affordable solar photovoltaic (SPV) arrays, great attention is being paid towards more and more use of SPV energy sources in various industrial, residential, agricultural and commercial applications. Photovoltaic (PV) water pumping is one such promising application, which can replace conventional pumps to meet the need of community water supplies and irrigation, especially in rural areas prone to frequent power disruption or areas without grid power. In Indian scenario, out of total 26 million agricultural pumps, nearly 7 million pumps are diesel based and remaining are grid connected. However, due to unreliable grid supply and increasing diesel prices, solar water pumping systems are getting immense popularity in recent years. According to a recent survey study [2, 3] the Indian market of solar water pumping system is projected to grow at a compound annual growth rate (CAGR) of 18.7% during FY 2017–22 [4]. The Ministry of New and Renewable Energy (MNRE), Govt. of India has set an ambitious target to install at least one million solar water pumping systems at various locations for irrigation and supply of drinking water by the year 2020–21.

In conventional solar water pumping system, as shown in Fig. 1, the d.c. voltage generated by SPV array is processed by suitable dc/dc converters depending on the voltage rating of the PV array [5]. A maximum power point tracking (MPPT) controller is used to enable the dc/dc converter to draw maximum power from the solar SPV array. This stage is followed by a single phase inverter to feed single phase induction motor of the pump. In order to generate 230 V a.c. power as suitable for single phase induction motor drives, conventional solar water pumping systems use two different configurations of power processing schemes, with their own merits and demerits. In the first scheme, the dc/dc converter generates 24 V or 48 V d.c. to produce low voltage a.c., which is stepped up to 230 V a.c. by single phase transformers. The electrical power generated by SPV array being inconsistent in nature, 24 V/48 V battery banks are used as an intermediate storage system to get un-interrupted supply of electrical power even in absence of sufficient solar irradiation. In the second scheme, the cost and power loss of the single phase transformer is avoided, by generating 400 V d.c. bus using a dc/dc boost converter and 230 V single phase a.c. supply is directly generated from the 400 V d.c. bus. However, if an intermediate storage as power back up is required, then the battery banks are to be maintained at 400 V, which increases overall cost of the SPV system by many fold.

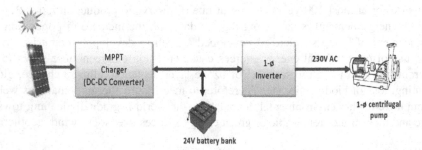

Fig. 1. Conventional solar water pumping system.

In conventional solar water pumping systems, if the motor is started with full supply voltage, then the motor draws 4 to 10 times of full load current from the SPV array through the dc/dc converter and the inverter [3]. Thus, the current rating and hence the cost of the power converters are increased considerably. In order to avoid this, electro-mechanical starters like auto-transformer starter, star-delta starter etc. are used to obtain reduced voltage starting, thereby maintain low starting current. The low starting torque developed by the induction motor due to low working flux at reduced starting voltage is sufficient to meet starting load torque demand of the pump, as the load torque of pump varies as square of its speed. These starters can limit the starting current to the acceptable limit. However, large size and high cost of these starters hinder its popularity in modern applications. In recent years, PWM inverters are being used for smooth variation of supply voltage applied to the induction motor for speed control as well as to limit the starting current. But, the minimum on-time requirement of semiconductor switches does not allow the duty ratio to reduce below 15 to 20% of switching time period. Thus, the starting voltage at motor terminals can't be reduced to well acceptable limit. An alternative solution, to obtain reduced voltage at motor terminals is to modulate the dc bus voltage of the inverter without modulating the pulse-width of semiconductor switches of the inverter.

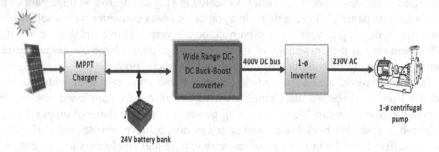

Fig. 2. Drive train architecture of proposed SPV water pumping system.

The drive train architecture of proposed SPV water pumping system is shown in Fig. 2. Primarily, the dc-dc converter is to regulate the dc bus voltage of the inverter over a wide range, such that, in addition smooth variation of speed, soft starting of the pump can be achieved with the system. Theoretically, any dc-dc converter with buck-boost characteristics, like classical buck-boost converter, Cuk converter, zeta converter or sepic converter can be used for such system. Voltage gain of these converters is given by,

$$\text{Voltage Gain} = V_o/V_s = \delta/(1-\delta) \tag{1}$$

Theoritically, the voltage gain of these converters can be varied from zero to infinite by varying the duty ratio from 0 to 1. But, an extremely low duty ratio (less than 0.2) or an extremely large duty ratio (greater than 0.8) may lead to large current stress of semiconductor devices, reverse-recovery problem of the diode, large amount of power loss in power switches, rectifier diodes, the equivalent series resistances (ESR) of inductors and capacitors. Isolated dc-dc converters such as, fly-back converter, forward converter, half bridge or full bridge converter use high frequency transformer as a link between the input and output side. High voltage gain of these dc-dc converters can be achieved by adjusting the turns-ratio of the transformer. However, the leakage inductance of the transformer results in high voltage spikes on semiconductor devices and large EMI/RFI. Many new structures of dc-dc converters have been proposed by power electronics engineers, in recent years, to achieve high voltage gain with duty ratio within acceptable range.

A high gain boost converter using diodes and coupled windings instead of active switches have been presented in [6]. Paper [7] presents a new circuit with steep step-up ratio by integrating a switched-capacitor circuit within a boost converter. A new step-up structure is realized in [8] by splitting the output capacitor of a basic boost converter and combining it with the main switch in the form of a switched-capacitor circuit. In the model presented in [9], a coupled inductor and a clamped capacitor have been used in a boost converter to achieve high voltage gain. An inductor and a transformer have been combined in [10] to increase the voltage gain of a dc-dc converter. In the boost converter presented in [11], two identical inductors are charged in parallel but discharged in series to achieve high voltage gain. Multilevel voltage multiplier cells have been used in the dc-dc boost converter presented in [12] to improve voltage gain of the converter. The paper [13] presents an integration of boost converter with a self-lift cuk converter to develop a high voltage-gain dc-dc converter. However, these converters suffer from one of the drawbacks of more component count, large circulating current loss or requirement of complicated control and drive circuitry.

In present work, a non-isolated dc-dc buck-boost converter with wide range of voltage gain, is proposed alleviating most of the problems mentioned above. The proposed converter is capable of delivering power over a wide range of output voltage. Although, a cascaded buck-boost converter can also achieve a wide range of voltage gain, it suffers from the drawbacks of more switching and conduction loss due to two-stage power conversion. But in the proposed converter, the power is processed in two stages only when step-up operation with an extremely large voltage gain is to be achieved. However, for step-down operation and step-up operation with moderate voltage gain, it works as a conventional buck-boost converter with single stage power conversion, thereby avoiding the problems of excess switching and conduction loss.

2   The Proposed Converter

The structure of the proposed converter as shown in Fig. 3 has been derived from a classical buck-boost converter. The proposed converter uses an active voltage clamp circuit in addition to the basic components required by a classical buck-boost converter. The active voltage clamp circuit comprises of a semiconductor switch (S_2), an inductor (L_1) and a clamping capacitor (C_c). A diode (D_1) is also used in the buck-boost converter to prevent discharging of the clamping capacitor (C_c), when the active clamp switch (S_2) is turned ON. For step-down operation and step-up operation with moderate voltage gain, the proposed converter operates in the same way to a classical buck-boost converter without any clamp circuit. The clamp circuit is activated, only when an extremely high voltage step-up gain is to be achieved. The active voltage clamp circuit basically shifts upward the positive rail of d.c. source applied to the input of the buck-boost converter.

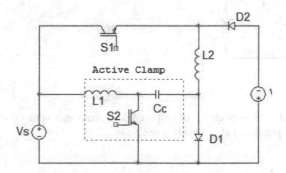

Fig. 3. Circuit of proposed buck-boost converter

3 Operation and Analysis of Proposed DC-DC Converter

For simplification of analysis, operating conditions of the proposed converter are discussed with following assumptions:

(i)   All semiconductor switches and power diodes are ideal and loss free.
(ii) The inductances are ideal and loss free.
(iii) The clamping capacitor (C_c) is large enough, such that voltage (V_{cc}) across it is maintained constant during a switching cycle.
(iv) Similarly, the output filter capacitor (C_o) is large enough to maintain the output voltage (V_o) constant during a switching cycle.

The converter is operated in continuous conduction mode (CCM).

3.1 Operation of Proposed Converter Without Active Voltage Clamp Circuit

The proposed converter is operated without active voltage clamp circuit, while performing voltage step-down or for performing step-up with a voltage gain up to 5. The operation of the proposed converter without active voltage clamp circuit is identical to that of conventional buck-boost converter. Under steady-state conditions, the operation of the converter can be divided into two modes. The topological equivalent circuits and key waveforms during mode 1 and mode 2 operations are given in Figs. 4 and 5 respectively. Before starting of mode 1, let the inductor current (i_{L2}) was maintained through the diode (D_2) thereby transferring its energy to the load.

Mode 1 $(t_o - t_1)$**:** Mode 1 operation of starts, as soon as, the switch (S_1) is turned ON and the diode (D_2) stops conduction as it gets reversed biased by the source voltage (Vs) and load voltage (Vo). The current through inductor (L_2) now increases linearly

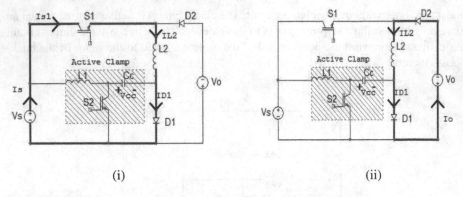

(i)   (ii)

Fig. 4. Topological equivalent circuit of proposed dc/dc converter without active clamp circuit during (i) mode 1 operation and (ii) mode 2 operation.

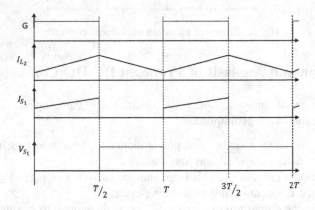

Fig. 5. Key waveforms of proposed dc/dc converter without active clamp circuit.

from its initial value of (I_1). This is the active mode of the buck-boost converter. The state equation during this mode is given by,

$$i_{L_2} = I_1 + \frac{V_s}{L_2}(t - t_0) \tag{2}$$

This mode ends, when the switch (S_1) is turned OFF after a time of t_{ON}. At the end of this mode, the current through the inductor is given by,

$$I_2 = I_1 + \frac{V_s}{L_2}.t_{ON}; \quad \text{where } t_{ON} = t_1 - t_0 \tag{3}$$

Mode 2 ($t_1 - t_2$): As soon as the switch (S_1) is turned OFF, the inductor current is maintained through the diode (D_2) and the load. Thus, energy stored in the inductor is transferred to the load and hence the inductor current is linearly decreased from its initial value (I_2). This is the passive mode of the buck-boost converter. The state equations during this mode is given by,

$$i_{L_2} = I_1 - \frac{V_o}{L_2}(t - t_1) \qquad (4)$$

This mode ends, when the switch, (S_1) is turned ON again after a tine of t_{OFF}. At the end of this mode, the current through the inductor is given by,

$$I_1 = I_2 - \frac{V_o}{L_2}.t_{OFF}; \qquad \text{where } t_{OFF} = t_2 - t_1 \qquad (5)$$

Thus, by volt-sec balance of the inductor (L_2), the voltage gain of the converter is obtained as,

$$\frac{V_o}{V_s} = \frac{\delta}{(1 - \delta)} \qquad (6)$$

3.2 Operation of Proposed Converter with Active Voltage Clamp Circuit

Whenever, a step-up voltage gain above 3 is required to be obtained, the active voltage clamp circuit of the proposed converter is also activated along with the conventional buck-boost part. Under steady-state conditions also, the operation of the converter with the active voltage clamp circuit can be divided into two modes. The topological equivalent circuits and key waveforms during these two modes are given in Figs. 6 and 7 respectively. Before starting of mode 3, let the current (i_{L_2}) of inductor (L_2) was maintained through the diode (D_2 and D_1) thereby transferring its energy to the load.

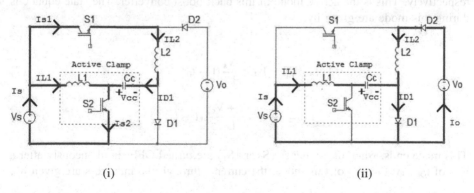

Fig. 6. Topological equivalent circuit of proposed dc/dc converter with active clamp circuit during (i) mode 1 operation and (ii) mode 2 operation.

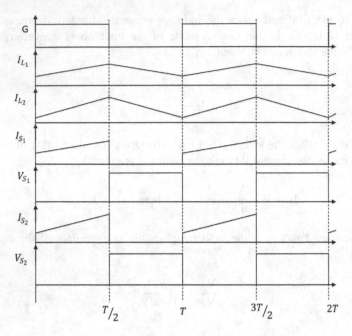

Fig. 7. Key waveforms of proposed dc/dc converter with active clamp circuit.

Similarly, the current (i_{L_1}) of inductor (L_1) was maintained through the diodes (D_1) and the clamping capacitor (C_c), thereby transferring its energy to the clamping capacitor.

Mode 1 ($t_o - t_1$): Mode 1 operation of starts, as soon as the switches (S_2 and S_1) are turned ON simultaneously. Now, the diodes (D_2 and D_1) stop conduction as diode (D_2) gets reversed biased by the source and load voltage and diode (D_1) gets reversed biased by the clamping capacitor voltage. The current (i_{L_1}) of inductor (L_1) and the current (i_{L_2}) of inductor (L_2) now increase linearly from their initial values of I_{11} and I_{21} respectively. This is the active mode of this buck-boost converter. The state equations during this mode are given by,

$$i_{L_1} = I_{11} + \frac{V_s}{L_1}(t - t_0) \tag{7}$$

$$i_{L_2} = I_{21} + \frac{V_s + V_{cc}}{L_2}(t - t_0) \tag{8}$$

This mode ends, when the switches (S_2 and S_1) are turned OFF simultaneously after a tine of t_{ON}. At the end of this mode, the currents through the inductors are given by,

$$I_{12} = I_{11} + \frac{V_s}{L_1}.t_{ON} \tag{9}$$

$$I_{22} = I_{21} + \frac{V_s + V_{cc}}{L_2}.t_{ON} \tag{10}$$

$$\text{where, } t_{ON} = t_1 - t_0 \tag{11}$$

Mode 2 ($t_1 - t_2$): As soon as, the switches (S_2 and S_1) are turned OFF, the inductor current (i_{L_1}) is maintained through the diode (D_1) and the clamping capacitor (C_c). Similarly, the inductor current (i_{L_2}) is maintained through the diodes (D_2 and D_1) and the load. Thus, energy stored in inductor (L_1) is transferred to the clamping capacitor (C_c) and the energy stored in inductor (L_2) is transferred to the load. This causes the currents (i_{L_1} and i_{L_2}) to decrease linearly from their initial values of (I_{12} and I_{22}) respectively. This is the passive mode of the buck-boost converter. The state equations during this mode are given by,

$$i_{L_1} = I_{12} - \frac{V_{cc}}{L_1}(t - t_1) \tag{12}$$

$$\text{and } i_{L_2} = I_{22} - \frac{V_o}{L_2}(t - t_1) \tag{13}$$

This mode ends, when the switches (S_2 and S_1) are turned ON again after a time of t_{OFF}. At the end of this mode, the currents through the inductors are given by,

$$I_{11} = I_{12} - \frac{V_{cc}}{L_1}.t_{OFF} \tag{14}$$

$$\text{and } I_{21} = I_{22} - \frac{V_o}{L_2}.t_{OFF} \tag{15}$$

$$\text{where, } t_{OFF} = t_2 - t_1 \tag{16}$$

Thus, by volt-sec balance of the inductors (L_1 and L_2), the voltage gain of the converter is obtained as,

$$\text{Voltage Gain, } \frac{V_o}{V_s} = \frac{\delta(2 - \delta)}{(1 - \delta)^2} \tag{17}$$

4 Design and Simulation of Proposed DC/DC Converter

In present work, a new wide range voltage gain dc-dc converter working on proposed topology is developed for the applications of SPV water pumping systems. The design expressions of the passive components $(L_1, L_2, C_c$ and $C_o)$ for the proposed converter have been derived from the equations governing its operation during different topological modes as stated in Sect. 3 and detailed as below.

$$L_1 = \frac{V_s . \delta}{f_{sw} . \Delta I_{L1}} \tag{18}$$

$$L_2 = \frac{V_o . (1 - \delta)}{f_{sw} . \Delta I_{L2}} \tag{19}$$

$$C_c = \frac{I_{L1} . (1 - \delta)}{f_{sw} . \Delta V_{cc}} \tag{20}$$

$$C_o = \frac{I_o . \delta}{f_{sw} . \Delta V_{co}} \tag{21}$$

Where,

δ is the operating duty ratio
f_{sw} is the switching frequency
ΔI_{L1} is the permissible current ripple through L_1
ΔI_{L2} is the permissible current ripple through L_2
ΔV_{cc} is the permissible voltage ripple across clamping capacitor C_c
ΔV_{co} is the permissible voltage ripple at the output and
I_o is the load current.

Based on the design guidelines mentioned above, the active and passive components of the proposed converter have been selected for given specifications and detailed in Table 1

Table 1. Specification and major components of proposed soft-switched coupled-inductor boost converter

Specifications	Major components
Rated i/p voltage supply: 21.6 V–27.6 V	Inductor(L_1): 220 µH
Rated output voltage: 400 V	Inductor(L_2): 5600 µH
Rated output power: 500 W	Clamping capacitor(C_c): 220 µH, 450 V
Switching frequency: 40 kHz	Filter capacitor(C_o): 220 µH, 800 V
	Main Switch(S_1): IRG4PH40K (1200 V, 15 A)
	Diode(D_2 and D_1): RHRP30120 (1200 V, 30 A)
	Clamp Circuit Switch(S_2): IRG4PC50UD (600V, 27 A)

5 Simulation and Performance Analysis of Proposed DC/DC Converter

In order to test the validity of proposed converter, a prototype model of the proposed dc-dc converter with given specifications and designed components as detailed in Table 1, was prepared and simulated with MATLAB Simulink. The prototype converter was tested for rated input voltage with different duty ratio under different load conditions. Important results are presented in this section. Figure 8 shows the waveforms of main switch gate pulse, input voltage, output voltage and inductor current of proposed dc-dc converter without active clamp circuit with 20% duty ratio. Here, an output voltage of 6 V was obtained with an input voltage of 24 V. Figure 9 shows the waveforms of main switch and clamp switch gate pulse, input voltage, output voltage, clamp capacitor voltage and inductor currents of proposed dc-dc converter with active clamp circuit with 80% duty ratio. It is observed that, an output voltage of 576 V was obtained for an input voltage of 24 V. At last, Fig. 10 shows waveforms of main switch and clamp switch gate pulse, input voltage, output voltage, clamp capacitor voltage and inductor currents of proposed dc-dc converter with active clamp circuit with 76% duty ratio. From this figure, it is evident that, 400 V rated voltage was obtained with 76% duty ratio for an input voltage of 24 V. Thus, the proposed converter can produce an wide range of output voltage of 6 V–400 V for an input voltage of 24 V although the duty ratio was maintained within practical limits of 20% to 80%.

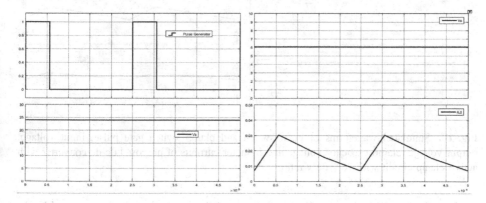

Fig. 8. Simulated waveforms of main switch gate pulse, input voltage, output voltage and inductor current of proposed dc-dc converter without active clamp circuit with 20% duty ratio.

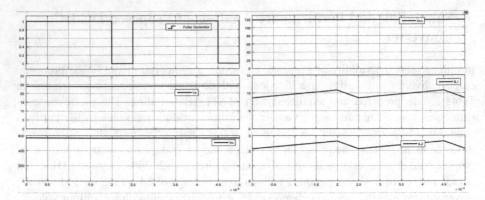

Fig. 9. Simulated waveforms of main switch and clamp switch gate pulse, input voltage, output voltage, clamp capacitor voltage and inductor currents of proposed dc-dc converter with active clamp circuit with 80% duty ratio.

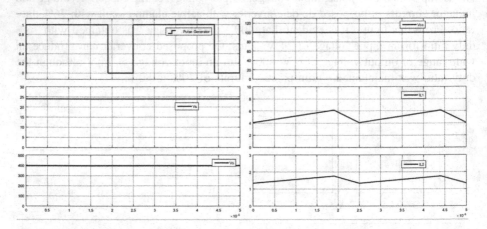

Fig. 10. Simulated waveforms of main switch and clamp switch gate pulse, input voltage, output voltage, clamp capacitor voltage and inductor currents of proposed dc-dc converter with active clamp circuit with 76% duty ratio.

In order to verify the superiority of proposed dc-dc converter over cascaded buck-boost converter for the same specifications, a prototype model of cascaded buck-boost converter was prepared and simulated with MATLAB Simulink. The gain-duty ratio plot of proposed prototype converter and cascaded buck-boost converter is depicted in Fig. 11. It is evident that, the proposed converter can provide higher voltage gain than cascaded buck-boost converter for the same duty ratio.

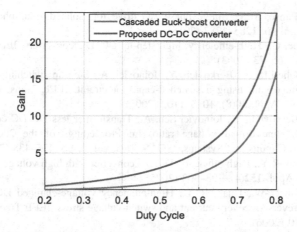

Fig. 11. Gain comparison of proposed dc-dc converter and cascaded buck-boost converter.

6 Conclusion

A non-isolated dc-dc buck-boost converter with wide range voltage gain is proposed in this work for wide applications in SPV water pumping systems. The proposed converter can achieve extreme high step-up voltage gain even with a duty ratio within acceptable range for practical applications through two-stage power conversion. But, it works as conventional buck-boost converter for step-down operation and step-up operation with moderate voltage gain. Thus, both switching and conduction losses are minimized. Performance of the proposed converter has been verified through computer simulation with MATLAB Simulink for nominal 24 V input voltage, 6 V–400 V output voltage, 500 W output power and switching frequency of 40 kHz. The simulated results were found to be in close agreement to the predicted behavior of the proposed converter.

Acknowledgement. The authors would like to acknowledge Department of Science and Technology, Govt. of West Bengal for financial assistance under WBDST-FIST Programme to carry out this work.

References

1. Foster, R., Majid, G., Cota, A.: A test book of solar energy. Renew. Energy Environ. (2014)
2. Rohit, K.B., Karve, G., Khatri, M.: Solar water pumping system. Int. J. Emerg. Tech. Adv. Eng. **3**, 225–259 (2013)
3. Chandel, S.S., Naik, M.N.: Review of solar photo voltaic water pumping system technology for irrigation and community drinking water supplies. Sci. Direct Comput. Electr. Eng. **45**, 14–28 (2015)
4. Indian Power Sector analysis report, January 2018. https://www.ibef.org/industry/power-sector-india.aspx

5. Ugale, J.H., Panse, M.S.: Single phase AC drive for isolated solar photovoltaic water pumping system, pp. 1285–1287 (2015)
6. Fred, Q.Z., Lee, C.: High-efficiency, high step-up DC–DC converters. IEEE Trans. Power Electron. **18**(1), 65–73 (2003)
7. Abutbul, O., Gherlitz, A., Berkovich, Y., Ioinovici, A.: Step-up switching-mode converter with high voltage gain using a switched-capacitor circuit. IEEE Trans. Circuits Syst. I: Fundam. Theory Appl. **50**(8), 1098–1102 (2003)
8. Axelrod, B., Berkovich, Y., Ioinovici Sen, A.: Transformer less DC-DC converters with a very high DC line-to-load voltage ratio. In: Proceedings of the 2003 International Symposium on Circuits and Systems, ISCAS 2003, vol. 3, pp. 435–438 (2003)
9. Wai, R.J., Duan, R.Y.: High-efficiency DC/DC converter with high voltage gain. IEE Proc.-Electr. Power Appl. **152**(4), 793–802 (2005)
10. Wai, R.-J., Liu, L.-W., Duan, R.-Y.: High-efficiency voltage-clamped DC–DC converter with reduced reverse-recovery current and switch-voltage stress. IEEE Trans. Ind. Electron. **53**(1), 272–280 (2006)
11. Lung-Sheng Yang and Tsrong-Juuliang: Transformer less DC-DC converters with high step-up voltage gain. IEEE Trans. Ind. Electron. **56**(8), 3144–3152 (2009)
12. Trazamni, H., Babari, E., Sabahi, M.: Full soft-switching high step-up DC-DC converter based on active resonant cell. IET Power Electron. **10**(13), 1729–1739 (2017)
13. Pires, V.F., Foito, D., Silva, J.F.: A single switch hybrid DC/DC converter with extended static gain for photovoltaic applications. Electr. Power Syst. Res. **146**, 228–235 (2017)

Fault Analysis and Trend Prediction in Telecommunication Using Pattern Detection: Architecture, Case Study and Experimentation

Kartick Chandra Mondal[1](✉) and Hrishav Bakul Barua[2](✉)

[1] Department of Information Technology, Jadavpur University, Kolkata, India
kartickjgec@gmail.com
[2] TCS Research and Innovation Lab, Kolkata, India
hrishav.smit5@gmail.com

Abstract. In recent years, almost every industry especially digital, e-commerce and telecommunication experienced exponential growth of data. Harvesting knowledge in these highly dynamic databases and finding closed patterns to analyze modern trends attracted considerable interest in this decade. To group similar types of data object or identify regions where data density is high in a dataset and forming clusters is the birds eye of researchers. Data mining and Business analytics have became an integral part of Telecommunication industry for extracting usage patterns of new as well as profiled customers and retaining them in competitive market. Providing better services without interruption is an essential aspect as this gains the confidence of the customers. In this paper, we have stated various challenges faced by the industry and have proposed a unified architecture for Telecom data analytics. Case studies have been put forward for Customer usage pattern detection and Network fault analysis using clustering and bi-clustering techniques to group and segment customer for business predictions as well as to identify faulty nodes in the network and predict network failures.

Keywords: Fault analysis · Telecommunication data · Clustering · Association rule-mining · Bi-clustering

1 Introduction

The constantly growing telecommunication industry implements many innovative ideas for betterment and business expansion. Smart phones and broadband services become essential part of the society and drive new trends such as Internet banking, video streaming, mobile payments and IoT devices. The industry engenders substantial amount of data daily in terms of Call Detail Records (CDRs), i.e. calling pattern of a customer (the source, destination, duration of call and others), data flows through wire-line for land-line communication

© Springer Nature Singapore Pte Ltd. 2019
J. K. Mandal et al. (Eds.): CICBA 2018, CCIS 1030, pp. 307–320, 2019.
https://doi.org/10.1007/978-981-13-8578-0_24

or wireless network that is also known as network data. Due to the competition between Telecom providers, customers switch between providers to get new and better facilities and services. Customers compare Telecom service providers very thoroughly and choose the most suitable provider as per their needs. So, providers must carry out business analysis and prediction for customers and find meaningful and interesting patterns to facilitate customer needs in a better way and avoid losing customers. Retaining a valued customer is much cheaper and easier than adding a new good customer. So, giving importance to existing customers and providing better services to them through customer data analysis is an indispensable task in telecom industry.

Data growth is very high in telecommunication industry and there is more scope to analyze and discover information from this data. There are many challenges associated with mining telecommunication data as well. Telecommunication companies maintain call details in CDR format which is kept in production databases for several months. CDR contains descriptive information and billions of call detail records (of customers) are readily available for mining. Call detail record is very important for marketing and to identify fraudulent activity as well. Telecommunication companies also maintain detailed customer information, such as billing, plans used, address as well as information obtained from third parties, such as credit score, mode of payment, customer satisfaction rate etc. CDR data can be inspected to find odd or abnormal calling behaviors of customers. The likelihood of fraud is predicted using a customer's credit score which is often incorporated into the analysis phase of the data. It helps in determining if a fraud is actually taking place or not. Telecommunications providers also generate and store large amount of data related to the network operations. This is because the network elements such as switches and routers in these large telecommunication networks have some self-diagnostic features that permit them to produce both alarm messages and status. These messages can be mined in order to support network management functions namely fault isolation and prediction.

There are several data mining challenges faced by the telecommunication industry.

- The first issue is the volume of the telecommunication data.
- The second is that, raw telecommunication data is not suitable for data analysis. Data preprocessing is necessary.
- The real time data mining needs to be applied for fraud detection. Learned protocol and rules need to be applied in real-time.

Winter Corporation conducted a survey on 2003 [2] that revealed that the three largest databases in industry sector belong to telecommunication companies (France Telecom having 29 Terabytes, AT&T having 26 Terabytes, and SBC having 25 Terabytes) [1]. Thus, the scalability is a key concern of data mining methods. Secondly, the format of telecommunication data is not readily suitable for mining semantic information. The transactions or events needs to be transformed into appropriate format before data analysis. For example, one typically wants to mine call detail data at the customer (i.e. phone-line) level but the raw data represents individual phone calls. Thus, it is often necessary to aggregate data to the appropriate semantic level [31] before mining the data. "An alternative is to utilize a data mining method that can operate on the transactional data directly and extract sequential or temporal patterns" [32,33]. If we deal with these issues then the efficiency of data mining will definitely increase.

Motivation: Business analytics and intelligence are coming into focus these days and for only good reasons. All the industries are heavily dependent on data and decisions on the data trends to predict business and retain market hold. Telecom industry has grown to prominence as the earth is getting more and more connected day by day as we have targeted telecom data for our cases. Telecom industry business heavily relies on networks and customer satisfaction. So, the main focus of the data generated for customer's call details and network elements needs to be analyzed for decision making and business predictions. We intend to propose a unified architecture for analytics and mining of telecom data for customer trend prediction and network fault analysis. The proposed architecture can be modified as per industry needs and type of analytic task to be done.

Organization of the Paper: The Sect. 2 surveys the major clustering techniques and use of data mining in Telecommunication. The Sect. 3 discusses the datasets used for pattern detection and business analysis. Section 4 discusses the proposed architecture for data mining and trend prediction. The Sect. 5 shows the experimentations in two cases (using clustering in customer data and FIST in network data) where it has been discussed how data mining and its application helps Telecommunication industry in various aspects. Section 6 is the concluding section of the paper.

2   A Literature Survey on Data Mining and Telecommunication

This section places a systematic survey of some of the pioneering as well as recent data mining algorithms in cluster analysis and bi-clustering. A brief survey on the use of data mining in telecommunication has also been discussed. The main techniques in data mining are Clustering, Classification and Association Rule mining [3]. Mostly Clustering is being used in Telecom data for various trend analysis and customer segmentation on various factors. Clustering technique can be implemented using partitioning, hierarchical, density-based and grid-based methods. The most popular are the partitioning methods. Partitioning techniques has K-means [31] as a pioneering algorithm. CHAMELEON [10] and BIRCH [9] are famous hierarchical approach algorithms. The famous algorithms in density-based approach are DBSCAN [4] and OPTICS [32]. Grid-based approaches mainly used are [5–8]. Some other specialized algorithms for performing clustering in multi-density and variable-density spaces are TDCT [11], 3D-CATD [12] and Soft TDCT [33].

Data mining plays a key role in analysis of various types of data to make strategic decision in Telecom [20–23]. These companies also face a number of data mining challenges due to the enormous size of their data sets, the sequential and temporal aspects of their data, and the need to predict very rare events such as customer fraud and network failures in real-time. In last few years telecommunication sector changed rapidly. As market is almost saturated in terms of getting new customers now a days, now in the smart phone era where 3G and 4G network taken the space of Telecom sector major focus shifted on keeping their valued customers and providing better service. Every telecom providers want to create a customer baseline and focus on churn management.

Some applications of data mining in telecommunication industry.

- Identification of Fraud
- Improving marketing efforts
- Fault isolation and prediction
- Profit Optimization
- Churn Management

Fraud is very serious issue that the telecommunication industry faces since it leads Revenue leakage. "It estimated that the industry is losing $46.3 billion per year from fraud, increasing at a rate of 15% from 2011. This amounts to 2.09% of revenue" [13]. Different types of frauds are: Roaming Fraud, Premium Rate Service Fraud, Abuse or Arbitrage Fraud, International Revenue Share Fraud (IRSF), Domestic Revenue Share Fraud (DRSF), Call and SMS Spamming, Subscription Fraud, Wangiri Fraud, SMS Phishing/Pharming and Private Branch Exchange (PBX) Fraud [15–18,34]. Use of Data mining for Telecom sector are stated in [14,19]. The main use of data mining in Telecom are surveyed to be Marketing, Fault Isolation and Prediction [24,25], Profit Optimization [29], Churn Management [22,26–29].

3   Datasets

Understanding the various types of data generated in telecommunication industry is very important before we can discover knowledge from that data. Useful knowledge cannot be generated until and unless one can understand the behavior of the raw data. The various kinds of data generated in this industry can be grouped in three different types. These three datasets are explained in details in next three subsequent subsections.

3.1   General Customer Data of Any Telecom Industry

Customer belongs to different region in the world even though service providers mainly focused on city region. The first contact point between service provider and a customer is Customer Relationship Management (CRM) counter or exchange where customer applies for a new connection with their identification, address details. Customer's calling or usage patterns analysis helps to identify fraudulent activity. For example, when suddenly a customer started ISD call and crossed the credit limit, it is a matter to be taken seriously and investigated. So, we can assume that may be the customer is at risk and check his network activity to solve the matter. Information about the customer includes the following fields in general.

- Name of the Customer - Title, First Name (Forename), Last Name (Surname), Designatory letters, etc.
- Person Information Date of Birth, Gender, etc.
- Billing and Installation address Building Number, Building Name, Address Lines, Town, County, Postal/Zip Code, Country, etc.
- Payment history Cash, Cheque, ECS, debit/credit card etc.
- Service plan Number of products purchased, actual products purchased, Order/Subscription Value, Order/Renewal dates
- Customer Services Information Complaint details, customer query details, etc.
- Transactional Information calling pattern, voice, data, internet etc.

3.2 Call Detail Record (CDR) Data

The CDR dataset actually holds the information about the call which is stored as the call detail record of a customer. The number of call detail records generated is huge since whenever a call is placed on the network the corresponding details are stored in a CDR. Call detail record includes information like originating and terminating phone numbers, date, time and duration of call. Usually these call detail records are not directly used for Data Mining. A typical CDR structure of Electronic Worldwide Switch Digital (EWSD Switch) and its field have been shown in Fig. 1 and discussed in Table 1. A sample call detail record has been shown in Listing 1.1. We have generated a dataset of 8000 records that is similar to any standard Telecom industry customer data.

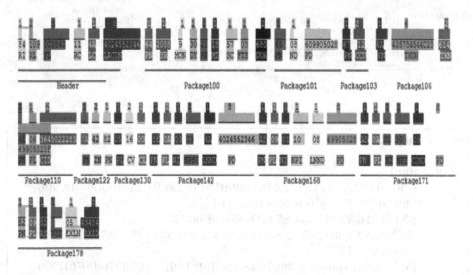

Fig. 1. Outgoing CDR structure of EWSD Switch.

Table 1. Details of CRD data structure.

Section Name	Field Name	Field Detail	Section Name	Field Name	Field Detail
Header	RI	Record Identifier		PN	Package Number
	RL	RecordLength		YR	Year
	FL	Flags		MON	Month
	RC	Record Sequence & Charge Status		DY	Day
	LO	LAC Length & Owner ID Length	Package 100	HR	Hour
	LACDN	Local Area Code & Directory Number		MI	Minutes
Package101	PN	Package Number		SC	Seconds
	ND	Number of Digits		FTS	Flags Tenths of Seconds
	PD	Packed Digits		DUR	Duration
Package103	PN	Package Number		PN	Package Number
	CCU	Call Charge Units	Package106	TKGN	Trunk Group Number
Package110	PN	Package Number		TKN	Trunk Number
	PL	Package Length	Package122	PN	Package Number
	CID	Connection ID		ZN	Zone
Package130	PN	Package Number		PN	Package Number
	PL	Package Length		PL	Package Length
	CV	Cause Value	Package142	NI	Nature of Address Indicator
	CL	Coding Standard		NPSI	Numbering Plan Indicator & Presentation Indicator)& Screening Indicator
	PN	Package Number		LNND	Local Area Code Length & Number of Digits
Package168	PL	Package Length		PD	Packed Digits
	NI	Nature of Address Indicator		PN	Package Number
	NPI	Numbering Plan Indicator	Package171	PL	Package Length
	LNND	Local Area Code Length & Number of Digits		NI	Nature of Address Indicator
	PD	Packed Digits		NPI	Numbering Plan Indicator
Package178	PN	Package Number		CDND	Number of Carrier Access Code Digits & Number of Digits
	PL	Package Length		PD	Packed Digits
	RS	Reserved			
	VID	Version ID			
	EXLN	Exchange ID Length			
	EXID	Exchange ID			

Listing 1.1. CDR Example

```
1 Sample CDR:
2
3 8484000
      C0040110A8411277547640809191107260B6B0000650A996
      3697048670200006953465441 4
      E3131016A4343534A544D6E016E06  2478
      C0A97A2A0082051000048E0A03130A8411277547990B02100B9
        963697048
      F0A80A01100A9963697048AB0B01100B9963697048F0B209
```

3.3   Network Data

The first step is the acquisition and preparation of data. It is difficult for researchers to acquire the actual data set from telecom industries. This is because customers private details may be misused. The network dataset for this paper is generated considering standard Telecom data for any industry. The actual data can be retrieved from network log generated from circuit switch.

Data Preparation. In the data preparation phase, data is collected, integrated and cleaned. Integration of data may require extraction of data from multiple sources. Then, cleaning of data takes place to resolve any ambiguous and erroneous data. Full characterization of data is performed after arranging in tabular form. Also, redundant and problematic data items are to be removed at this stage. Not all fields of the database are always suitable. Fields with unique values, like IP addresses or personal unlock codes are need not be used. These do not have predictive value as they uniquely identify each row. Also, fields with only one value are left out, as these represent a negligible part of the data. Finally, fields with too many null values are also excluded. These has formed the data preprocessing and cleaning stage.

Variables Obtained from Raw Dataset. Variables are extracted from actual dataset are divided into two categories. Useful variable are those which are used for experiment and non-useful variables are those which are unique or constant across column values.

Useful Variables. Before discussing about the data-field/variable, its important to know how this data has been generated. All these alarm messages has been generated by HP based product, OpenView Operations (OVO) agents which are installed in every node (switch & router) in the network. This agent constantly sense response from connected nodes and generates alarm if anything goes wrong.

EVENT_UUID. This is the uniquely defined message number identified by agent displayed on the message properties screen. Five field separated by - (hyphen character). Sample data: 61b5ab34-f88d-71e5-019f-0ac7d0a30000

EVENT_TIMESTAMP. Time-stamp of the occurrence of the event.

CATEGORY. Category of the node.

NODENAME. Name of the Node.

Example - OR-BLS-RTR-BDK-CDOT.zone.company.co.in In the above example first two digits represents circle code unique for each circle. OR is Orissa circle, WB is West Bengal Circle etc. Next three digits is the SSA code. SSA is secondary switching area where main locality switch is present. Next is the exact location of node and connection between them, it may be three nodes connected together then it will be XXX-XXX-XXX- or for two connecting node XXX-XXX- as per above example it is the sub-locality area between RTR-BDK- and the suffix part separated by . is the switch type and domain name. Center for Development of Telematics, C-DOT is the type of switch and zone.company.co.in is company domain of eastern region of company EAST zone.

MESSAGE. Represents whether a node is up or down.

SEVERITY. Based on severity value, it has been defined how critical a event is and accordingly color code can be defined as shown in Table 2

EVENT_OID. Event object Id

OV_OBJECTID. OVO Agent object id

PID. Process Id of the demon constantly up and running.

EVENT_TIME. Time of the event

NUMBER_VARBINDS. Number of bind variables.

Non-useful Variables. These have been removed from final dataset.

IP Address. The IP address of the data collection switch, Removed for security reason.

Application. Field contains null/zero

PROTOCOL. The field contains names of the event type, two types Canonical (generic)-event & SNMPv1-event.

TRAPSOURCE. If any line has been trapped then this field represents IP address of the trap source, removed for security reason. Field contains mainly null values as trapping is a rare event.

TRAP_NAME. It is the Exchange name or SSA (Secondary Switching Area) name where trapping is done.

FORWARD_ADDRESS. This address contains value if any external service providers network used during disaster such as earthquake flood etc. Removed as this is very rare event and field contains null/zero value.

EVENT_SOURCE. Only Internet Protocol is being used as event source. So the field contains static value.

EVENT_TYPE. This field contains Identical data as in EVENT_OID column only difference is one '.' (dot character) is prefixed with the value, hence the field has been removed.

Table 2. Detail severity value with corresponding color.

Severity	Color	Description
1	Red	Critical
2	Orange	Major
3	Yellow	Minor
4	Cyan	Warning
5	Green	Normal
6	Dark Blue	Unknown
7	Pink	Owned
8	Beige	Owned by some other operator

4   Proposed Architecture

Telecom industry generates huge amount of data daily. It includes customer data, billing data, provisioning data, connection data and much more. All the categories of data are generally kept in different databases such as customer database, billing database and provisioning database. Customer database holds all the customer information and details. Billing database holds the billing related data for each customer and provisioning database holds the details about the plans and provisions held by each customer. To predict trends and analyze the future business trends out of these data, we have to aggregate, segregate and summarize these data. The network related data can be achieved from network logs in network switches of Telecom industries.

The proposed architecture is a general unified one which we propose and apply, in two cases, on standard Telecom data for pattern prediction in customer call related data and network fault analysis. We have chosen these two cases as these are the most sought after data for higher management to take technical and managerial decisions.

The architecture is shown in Fig. 2. We have defined the architecture in 6 layers.

- Database Layer - Constitutes the major databases in a standard Telecom industry
- Switch Layer - Contains the network switches from which we get the network logs for fault analysis
- Data pruning/cleaning and Data Warehousing Layer - This layer has the methods of cleaning the data, pruning it and make it suitable for analysis and mining. Also, data from different tables are aggregated, segregated and

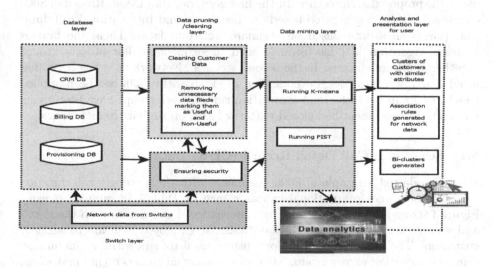

Fig. 2. Proposed data-mining architecture for Telecom

joined to form summary data and transforming relevant data into suitable form is done.
- Security Layer - This layer ensures that customer data is not accessed without proper permission and authentication. Protect the private data from being accessed by other applications and anonymization of data before mining.
- Data mining Layer - The main data mining engine is in this layer. We have implemented K-means [31] and FIST [30] algorithms for pattern analysis and trend prediction and network fault detection. Other data mining methods, approaches and techniques can be added in this layer as added features if required for any applications.
- Analysis and Presentation Layer - This layer has the front end applications to generate clusters, bi-clusters and other analytic reports for end users to view the final outcome of data mining.

In Fig. 2, the black arrows signifies flow of data and information between the layers and the brown lines and arrows in Database Layer signifies aggregation, joining and transformation of data from the databases into useful forms for business analytics and mining.

This architecture can be modified to work in scalable cloud computing environment and this remains a prospect for future work along with integration of other data mining tools and techniques in the existing base architecture. We also intend to introduce approximate or energy efficient computing [35] into such architecture for gaining speedup and saving energy in huge data mining tasks.

5   Experiment, Results and Analysis

Two scenarios have been experimented on our prepared telecommunication data using the proposed architecture. In the first scenario, Call Detail Record of 8000 customers has been generated based on their Local and International call duration (anonymous data based on standard Telecom data). Then, the famous k-means algorithm [31] has been applied to segment similar objects groups together and form clusters. In the second scenario, Network data has been analyzed based on the message events. The FIST algorithm [30] has been applied which results in bi-cluster and association rule. Closed groups have been taken for discussion and identified closed patterns based on similar characteristics.

5.1   Scenario I: Call Detail Record (CDR) Data

We have selected a sample of 8000 customers with their average call duration for both local and international call as shown in Table 3 (8 samples shown). Figure 3 shows the graph with average international call duration on the x axis and average local call duration on the y axis. We employed K-means to segment customers. The Fig. 3 shows 6 major clusters of customers with maximum customers in lower left corner group. That means many customers do not make local as well as international calls for long durations. Similarly, we can make out the trends in other figures. Figures 3 and 5 have 6 clusters and Figs. 4 and 6 have 9 major clusters. We experimented with 6 and 9 cluster formations using K-means in these cases. From the cluster results it is seen that the dataset used for this segmentation has customers in all the combinations of local and international call durations. The customers are evenly distributed into all class. The results can be used to target customers with low local and international call durations and give them lucrative offers so that they increases their call durations.

5.2   Scenario II: Network Data

We have used our own FIST algorithm [30] on our prepared dataset. FIST will generate condensed representation of association rules and bi-clusters. Example of the extracted association rules and bi-cluster is represented in Listing 1.2. After generating the rules and bi-clusters, We can decode them to extract useful knowledge. For example, the bi-cluster mentioned in the Listing 1.2, one can easily find that Node STATE-EXCHANGE-RTR-CR.zone.service-provider.co.in was in unresponsive state on 02-04-2016 between 10:12 AM to 10:18 AM. From the result set Alive (up) and Unresponsive (down) of the nodes can be grouped which can be identified by the bi-cluster. Appropriate action can be taken on

Table 3. Sample of Call Detail Record Data Set.

Customer number	Average local call duration	Average international call duration
1	2	2
2	1	2
3	1	3
4	3	2
5	4	5
6	4	4
7	5	5
8	6	5

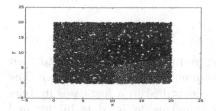

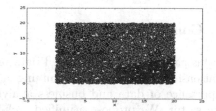

Fig. 3. Clusters with k=6 for average local vs international call duration.

Fig. 4. Clusters with k=9 for average local vs international call duration.

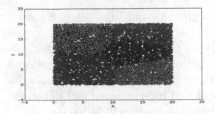 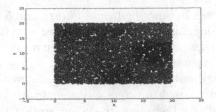

Fig. 5. Clusters with k=6 for average local vs international call duration.

Fig. 6. Clusters with k=9 for average local vs international call duration.

the network elements which are in faulty state or those can be isolated from network if the duration is more. Similar decoding can be done using association rules and we can get important useful information regarding the fault detection on network data.

Listing 1.2. Example of association rule and bicluster generated from network data.

```
 1 Sample of Exact Association Rule with minimum support = 5%
 2 ─────────────────────────────────────────────────────────
 3 [Anticedent]   [Consequent]   [Support]      [Confidence]   [ObjectList]
 4 [OV_OBJECTID=62662, SEVERITY=1]      [NODENAME=WB-CAL-RTR-CR.zone.
     company.co.in, CATEGORY=13, EVENT_OID
     =1.3.6.1.4.1.11.2.17.1.0.58916866, PID=13063, NUMBER_VARBINDS
     =18]   [19]    [1.0]    [5, 13, 19, 21, 39, 45, 48, 67, 81, 82, 95,
     107, 120, 137, 171, 173, 180, 189, 195]
 5
 6 Sample of Approximate Association Rule with minimum support = 5% and
     minimum confidence = 10%
 7 ─────────────────────────────────────────────────────────
 8 [Anticedent]   [Consequent]   [Support]      [Confidence]   [ObjectList]
 9 [NODENAME=NEI-MGH-RTR-AR.zone.company.co.in, OV_OBJECTID=89518]
             [EVENT_TIME=4/2/2016 10:13]  11        0.37931034      [11, 12,
          18, 22, 28, 29, 30, 36, 40, 47, 49]
10
11 Sample of Bicluster Example
12 ─────────────────────────────────────────────────────────
13 [ClosedSet]    [Support]      {Object List}
14 [MESSAGE=WB-CAL-RTR-CR.zone.company.co.in: IF E1 1/3/6 of the node
     WB-CAL-RTR-CR.zone.company.co.in is Down , NODENAME=WB-CAL-RTR-
     CR.zone.company.co.in, OV_OBJECTID=62662, CATEGORY=13, EVENT_OID
     =1.3.6.1.4.1.11.2.17.1.0.58916867, SEVERITY=5, PID=13063,
     NUMBER_VARBINDS=18] [15]    {6, 14, 31, 41, 55, 68, 85, 96, 108,
     123, 139, 174, 185, 190, 196}
```

6   Conclusion

In this paper, we have surveyed data mining and telecommunication and their relationships. The use of data mining in telecommunication sector is shown. The importance of data and business analytics is identified in a few cases in Telecom sector. We propose a unified architecture and model for data mining and analysis from telecom databases using clustering, bi-clustering and rule mining to address customer segmentation, churn management and network fault detection problems. We have also shown that this architecture is efficient in finding the desired patterns and information when used effectively on telecom data. Decision making and business intelligence are well supported by this architecture. In future, we intend to enhance the architecture by adding more data mining tools and algorithmic paradigms into it and also a scope for cloud data mining and analytics is envisioned. Also we have intended to introduce energy efficiency and good enough speedup in such architectures using approximate data mining and analytics for huge data.

References

1. https://books.google.co.in/books?isbn=1605669873
2. https://www.kdnuggets.com
3. Han, J., Kamber, M.: Data Mining: Concepts and Techniques. Morgan Kaufmann Publishers, San Francisco (2004)
4. Ester, M., Kriegel, H.P., Sander, J., Xu, X.: A density-based algorithm for discovering clusters in large spatial databases with noise. In: International Conference on Knowledge Discovery in Databases and Data Mining, pp. 226–231 (1996)
5. Hsu, C.-M., Chen, M.-S.: Subspace clustering of high dimensional spatial data with noises. In: Dai, H., Srikant, R., Zhang, C. (eds.) PAKDD 2004. LNCS (LNAI), vol. 3056, pp. 31–40. Springer, Heidelberg (2004). https://doi.org/10.1007/978-3-540-24775-3_6
6. Wang, W., Yang, J., Muntz, R.R.: STING: a statistical information grid approach to spatial data mining. In: Proceedings of 23rd International Conference on Very Large Databases, pp. 186–195. Morgan Kaufmann Publishers (1997)
7. Sheikholeslami, G., Chatterjee, S., Zhang, A.: WaveCluster: a multi-resolution clustering approach for very large spatial database. In: SIGMOD (1998)
8. Agrawal, R., Gehrke, J., Gunopulos, D., Raghavan, P.: Automatic subspace clustering of high dimensional data for data mining applications. ACM SIGMOD Rec. **27**, 94–105 (1998). ACM Special Interest Group on Management of Data
9. Zhang, T., Ramakrishnan, R., Livny, M.: BIRCH: an efficient data clustering method for very large databases. In: Proceeding of SIGMOD 1996, pp. 103–114. ACM, New York (1996)
10. Ertoz, L., Steinbach, M., Kumar, V.: Finding clusters of different sizes, shapes, and densities in noisy, high dimensional data. In: SIAM International Conference on Data Mining (2003)
11. Barua, H.B., Das, D.K., Sarmah, S.J.: A density based clustering technique for large spatial data using polygon approach. IOSRJCE **3**(6), 1–10 (2012). ISSN: 2278-0661, TDCT
12. Barua, H.B., Sarmah, S.J.: An extended density based clustering algorithm for large spatial 3D data using polyhedron approach (3D-CATD). Int. J. Comput. Appl. **58**(2), 4–15 (2012)
13. Nadaf, M., Kandam, V.: Data mining in telecommunication. Int. J. Adv. Comp. Theory Engg. **2**(3), 92–96 (2013). ISSN (Print) : 2319-2526
14. Marwaha, R.: Data mining techniques and applications in telecommunication industry. Int. J. Adv. Res. Comput. Sci. Softw. Eng. **4**(9), 430–433 (2014)
15. Howells, I., Scharf-Katz, V., Stapleton, P.: Fraud Types, Fraud Methods, & Fraud Technology. TELECOM FRAUD 101 (2013)
16. Fawcett, T., Provost, F.: Fraud Detection: Handbook of Data Mining and Knowledge Discovery, pp. 726–731. Oxford University Press, Oxford (2002)

17. Shortland, R., Scarfe, R.: Data mining applications in BI. In: BT Technology Journal, vol. 25, Nos. 3&4, July/October 2007
18. Rosset, S., Murad, U., Neumann, E., Idan, Y., Gadi, P.: Discovery of fraud rules for telecommunications: challenges and solutions. In: Proceedings of the 5th ACM SIGKDD, pp. 409–413. ACM Press (1999)
19. Weiss, G.M.: Data Mining in the Telecommunication Industry, pp. 486–491. Fordham University, USA (2009)
20. Joseph, M.V.: Data mining and business intelligence application in telecommunication industry. Int. J. Eng. Adv. Technol. (IJEAT) 2(3), 525–528 (2013). ISSN: 2249-8958
21. Camilovic, D.: Data mining and CRM in telecommunications. Serb. J. Manag. 3(1), 61–72 (2008)
22. Umayaparvathi, V., Iyakutti, K.: Applications of data mining techniques in telecom Churn prediction. Int. J. Comput. Appl. 42(20), 5–9 (2012)
23. Sasisekharan, R., Seshadri, V., Weiss, S.: Data mining and forecasting in large-scale telecommunication networks. IEEE Expert 11(1), 37–43 (1996)
24. Klemettinen, M., Mannila, H., Toivonen, H.: Rule discovery in telecommunication alarm data. J. Netw. Syst. Manag. 7(4), 395–423 (1999)
25. Weiss, G., Hirsh, H.: Learning to predict rare events in event sequences. In: Proceeding of the 4th International Conference on Knowledge Discovery and Data Mining, pp. 359–363. AAAI Press (1998)
26. Chang, Y.-T.: Applying data mining to telecom churn management. IJRIC, 67–77 (2009)
27. Zhang, Y., Liang, R., Li, Y., Zheng, Y., Berry, M.: Behavior-based telecommunication churn prediction with neural network approach. In: ISCCS, pp. 307–310 (2011)
28. Balle, B., Casas, B., Catarineu, A., Gavald, R., Manzano-Macho, D.: The architecture of a churn prediction system based on stream mining. In: Proceedings of the 16th International Conference of the Catalan Association for Artificial Intelligence, vol. 256, p. 157 (2013)
29. Berson, A., Smith, S., Thearling, K.: Building Data Mining Applications for CRM. McGraw-Hill, New York (1999)
30. Mondal, K.C., Pasquier, N., Mukhopadhyay, A., Maulik, U., Bandhopadyay, S.: A new approach for association rule mining and bi-clustering using formal concept analysis. In: Perner, P. (ed.) MLDM 2012. LNCS (LNAI), vol. 7376, pp. 86–101. Springer, Heidelberg (2012). https://doi.org/10.1007/978-3-642-31537-4_8
31. MacQueen, J.: Some methods for classification and analysis of multivariate observations. In: Proceedings of the Fifth Berkeley Symposium on Mathematical Statistics and Probability, vol. 1(14), pp. 281–297, June 1967
32. Ankerst, M., Breunig, M.M., Kriegel, H.P., Sander, J.: OPTICS: ordering points to identify the clustering structure. ACM SIGMOD Rec. 28(2), 49–60 (1999)
33. Barua, H.B., Sarmah, S., Biswas, M.: Soft TDCT: a fuzzy approach towards triangle density based clustering. Int. J. Comput. Appl. 90(8), 7–14 (2014)
34. http://docplayer.net/13751535-Telecom-fraud-101-fraud-types-fraud-methods-fraud-technology-authored-by-dr-ian-howells-dr-volkmar-scharf-katz-and-padraig-stapleton.html
35. Mittal, S.: A survey of techniques for approximate computing. ACM Comput. Surv. (CSUR) 48(4), 62 (2016)

A Review on Image Defogging Techniques Based on Dark Channel Prior

Tannistha Pal$^{(\boxtimes)}$, Arghadeep Datta, Taniya Das, Ipsita Das,
and Dipa Chakma

Department of Computer Science and Engineering,
National Institute of Technology, Agartala, Barjala, Jirania 799055, India
tannisthapaul@gmail.com, argha.dutt96@gmail.com,
tinni.taniya@gmail.com, dasips200616@gmail.com,
dipachakma96@gmail.com

Abstract. Images captured in adverse weather condition critically degrade the quality of an image and thereby reduces the visibility of an image. This, in turn, affects several computer vision applications like visual surveillance detection, intelligent vehicles, remote sensing, etc. Thus acquiring the clear vision is the prime requirement of any image. In the last few years, many approaches have been made towards solving this problem. In this paper, a comparative analysis also has been made on different existing image defogging algorithms. And a defogging technique called Dark Channel Prior Technique on images has been implemented. We perform a in depth study of this technique and establish its pseudo code which is the contribution of the paper. Experimental results show that the used method shows efficient results by significantly improving the visual effects of the image in foggy weather but this method has some limitations too for the images containing sky region. We have also performed some objective measurement on the images to determine the technique used. Finally, we conclude the whole work with its relative advantages and shortcomings.

Keywords: Visibility · Dark Channel Prior · Objective measurement · Image dehazing

1 Introduction

Images of outdoor scenes are usually degraded due to various atmospheric factors like scattering of large number of suspended aerosol particles in the atmosphere resulting in poor visibility of image [1, 2, 11–13]. In last decade, many techniques have evolved to solve this problem, and many researchers come with different ideas. These techniques can be classified as physics based approach, dark channel approach, filtering approach etc. Furthermore, we made a comparative analysis of all three techniques along with their advantages and shortcomings over dark channel prior.

The remainder of this paper is organized as follows. Section 2 discusses some state of art methods on image dehazing techniques along with their relative advantages and disadvantages. Section 3 focuses on the methodology of Dark Channel Prior dehazing algorithm along with its pseudo code. Section 4 deals with result and discussion and also

J. K. Mandal et al. (Eds.): CICBA 2018, CCIS 1030, pp. 321–332, 2019.
https://doi.org/10.1007/978-981-13-8578-0_25

presented some objective measurements to evaluate the dehazing performance of Dark Channel Prior Technique. Section 5 concludes this paper and indicates some future work.

2 Literature Review

Hazy or foggy images are never desired ones. But in reality, we do face situations where picture quality is degraded due to bad weather conditions.

In this paper, we thoroughly get a rundown on some existing defogging techniques proposed by Nayar et al. [1], Al-Zubaidy et al. [2], Oakley et al. [3], Tan [4], He et al. [5], Wang et al. [6], Chen et al. [7] and Xu et al. [8].

In [1, 2], the proposed method in this paper is a weather condition based method. It tried to recover scene structure from one or two images without prior knowledge of atmospheric conditions.

Oakley et al. [3] technique is mainly concerned with correction of simple contrast loss due to added airlight in an image which is often caused by optical scattering of light due to fog or mist. First of all, for detecting the presence of airlight in an arbitrary image, a statistical model is formulated. It provides an algorithm to estimate the level of airlight in an image, assuming airlight to be constant throughout the image. It is based on finding the minimum of a global cost function, applicable to both monochrome and color images. After estimating airlight, image correction is performed.

In [4], we come across a method where a single image is taken as input and haze is removed by maximizing the local contrast of the restored image. At first estimation of atmospheric light and light chromaticity is done. Using it, removal of light chromaticity is done, then using the chromaticity, removal of light color from the input image is done and delta cost, smoothness cost for every pixel is evaluated. This further leads to an estimation of airlight and thus finally computation of direct attenuation is done which enhances the visibility. This method solely works on enhancing the contrast.

In [5–8], dark channel prior statistics is used to remove haze from outdoor hazy images which is more efficient than previous state of art methods. It is based on the observation that local patches in outdoor haze free images contain pixels which have very low intensity in at least one color channel and this method is efficient than other existing defogging approaches. The summarization of different researchers on Image Dehazing Technique along with their advantages and shortcomings is depicted in Table 1.

Table 1. Summarization of different researchers on image dehazing techniques

Method	Author/Year	Advantages	Shortcomings	Application
Physical-based model [1, 2]	(1) S.K Nayar (2) Y. Al-Zubaidy	3D structure recovered from this algorithm	Assumptions that are taken in consideration are not practically possible. Like here, it is assumed that reflected ray travels to an observer without attenuation, which is impossible	Used in earlier days of dehazing

(*continued*)

Table 1. (*continued*)

Method	Author/Year	Advantages	Shortcomings	Application
Correction of simple contrast loss [3]	(1) John P. Oakley	(1) applicable to both black and white images and color images	Images generated in mid and far IR bands does not give the desired result	Can be used in continuous processing, i.e., video
Contrast maximization [4]	(1) R. Tan	Enhances visibility of the image	The method does not physically improve brightness or depth of the image	It is helpful in smoothing the quality of an image
Using dark channel prior [5–8]	(1) Kaiming He (2) J. Wang (3) J. Chen (4) H. Xu	(1) only single image is required (2) transmission map is estimated accurately	(1) For airlight estimate assumption is required that only 0.1% brightest pixels are taken (2) Method becomes invalid when scene object is similar to airlight like car headlights, snowy ground, etc.	It is simpler but more effective dehazing method

3 Implementation of Dark Channel Prior Technique on Images

Images in the outdoor environment sometimes are captured hazy by the camera due to the presence of aerosol particles in the environment which causes the light to scatter. The incoming airlight blending with the scene radiance also poses a problem. A major problem is posed by the unknown depth as haze depends on this factor.

After analyzing procedure used in [5] Dark channel prior, we get the following output mentioned below. Every parameter and constraints mentioned in [5] are kept same here. Assumptions too are being kept same.

This paper deeply analyzes Dark Channel Prior Technique. The DCP technique for image dehazing is done through the following steps.

Formation of hazy images can be described by the following model:-

$$I(x) = J(x)t(x) + A(1 - t(x)) \tag{1}$$

Where I, is the observed intensity, J is the scene radiance, t is the transmission medium defined by the light that is not scattered and reaches the camera, A is the atmospheric or global light. The term $J(x)t(x)$ defines the direct attenuation and $A(1 - t(x))$ defines the airlight.

The transmission, 't' can be expressed in the form of the following formula

$$t(x) = e^{-\beta d(x)} \tag{2}$$

Where β is the scattering coefficient of the atmosphere and d is the scene depth.

Geometrically, the haze imaging Eq. (1) means that in RGB color space, the vectors A, I(x), and J(x) are coplanar, and their end points are collinear. The transmission t is the ratio of two line segments:

$$t(x) = \frac{A^c - I^c(x)}{A^c - J^c(x)} \tag{3}$$

1. Estimating the transmission – We assume that atmospheric light A is given. Normalizing Eq. (1), gives us:

$$\frac{I^c(x)}{A^c} = t(x)\frac{J^c(x)}{A^c} + 1 - t(x) \tag{4}$$

Applying dark channel prior to it (4) we get:

$$\min_{y \in \Omega(x)}\left(\min_c \frac{I^c(y)}{A^c}\right) = t(x)\min_{y \in \Omega(x)}\left(\min_c \frac{J^c(y)}{A^c}\right) + 1 - t(x) \tag{5}$$

A^c is always positive which means

$$\min_{y \in \Omega(x)}\left(\min_c \frac{J^c(y)}{A^c}\right) = 0 \tag{6}$$

From (4) & (5) we get:

$$t(x) = 1 - \min_{y \in \Omega(x)}\left(\min_c \frac{I^c(y)}{A^c}\right) \tag{7}$$

We have noticed that dark channel prior is not a good prior for sky region but fortunately, the color of the sky in a hazy image I is very similar to the atmospheric light A.

$$\min_{y \in \Omega(x)}\left(\min_c \frac{I^c(y)}{A^c}\right) -> 1 \tag{8}$$

(8) gives t(x) -> 0 which is true because the sky is indefinitely distant.

We optionally keep a small amount of haze for perceiving the depth of distant object by introducing a constant parameter ω which is set to 0.95 for this paper. The equation now becomes

$$t(x) = 1 - \omega \min_{y \in \Omega(x)}\left(\min_c \frac{I^c(y)}{A^c}\right) \tag{9}$$

Therefore, a more generalized formula can be written as

$$I(x) = J(x)t_1(x) + A(1 - t_2(x)) \tag{10}$$

As we can find the additive term using (8), so the problem is now only left for the multiplicative term $J(x)t_1(x)$.

Problem: As the transmission maps are not constant in a patch, it results in distortion of the image in the form of block artifacts.

Solution: Refine transmission maps by applying soft matting.

2. Soft Matting – (1) has a similar form as the image matting equation

$$I = F\alpha + B(1 - \alpha) \tag{11}$$

Where F and B are foregrounds, and background colors.
α is the foreground opacity. As the transmission map in the haze imaging equation is exactly an alpha map, we can apply a closed-form framework of matting to refine the transmission.

$$E(t) = t^T L t + \lambda(t - \tilde{t})^T (t - \tilde{t}) \tag{12}$$

Here the first term is a smoothness term and the second term is a data term with a weight λ. The matrix L is called the Laplacian matrix.

$$(L + \lambda U)t = \lambda \tilde{t} \tag{13}$$

Where U is an identity matrix of the same size as L.

3. Estimating the atmospheric light – Contrary to the method of assuming that the atmospheric light is known, now we will try to find out the most-haze opaque region. With reference to Tan's work, the brightest region is assumed to be the most-haze opaque region which is true only when the weather is overcast and sunlight can be affectedly ignored. In this case, the atmospheric light is the only source of light. So, the scene radiance of each color channel can be represented as

$$J(x) = R(x)A \tag{14}$$

Where $R \leq 1$ is the reflectance of the scene points. The haze imaging model can now be written as

$$I(x) = R(x)At(x) + (1 - t(x))A \leq A \tag{15}$$

But for practical purposes, we cannot ignore sunlight, so the equation becomes

$$I(x) = R(x)St(x) + R(x)At(x) + (1 - t(x))A \tag{16}$$

From this equation, we can conclude that the brightest pixel in the image can be brighter than the atmospheric light.

Problem: The brightest pixels in an image can be brighter than atmospheric light.

Solution: Using dark channel method for finding the most haze opaque region in the image and then selecting top 0.1 percent brightest pixels in dark channel for improving estimation of atmospheric light.

4. Recovering Scene Radiance – We can recover the scene radiance according to (1) by using estimated atmospheric light and the transmission map.

Problem: When the transmission t(x) is close to zero, J(x)t(x) can be very close to zero causing directly recovered scene radiance to be noisy.
Solution: Providing a lower bound t_0 (typical value = 0.1) to the transmission, t(x).

Therefore, final scene radiance is J(x) is recovered by

$$J(x) = \frac{I(x) - A}{\max(t(x), t_0)} + A \tag{17}$$

We increase the exposure in the final recovered image since the haze-free image has lower scene radiance.

5. Size of the patch – Patch size of 15 × 15 is taken here. This paper establishes the pseudocode of DCP Technique which is described below.

Dark Channel Prior Pseudocode:
MAIN()
Input – A single hazy image $I(x) = J(x)t(x) + A(1 - t(x))$.
Output – A de-hazed image.
Initialization –

1. Select a hazy image and read the image into a variable imageRGB.
2. Resize the image with scaling factor 0.1.
3. Find dark channel of the image using darkchannel(imageRGB) function and store into variable 'JDark'.
   (3.1) Select a JDark zero matrix.
   (3.2) Select patch size as 15 and pad size as half of patch size i.e. 7.
   (3.3) Let height be height of imageRGB and width be width of imageRGB.
   (3.4) For j = 1 to height
   (3.5) For i = 1 to width
   (3.6) Patch = J(j : j + patchsize − 1), i : (i + patchsize − 1), :)
   (3.7) JDark = min(patch(:))
   (3.8) End For
   (3.9) End For
   (3.10) Return JDark.
4. Find atmospheric light using atmLight(imageRGB, JDark) function and store into variable 'atmospheric.'

(4.1) Create a vector of pixels of JDark in JDarkVec and vector of pixels of original image in imageRGBVec.

(4.2) Sort the JDarkVec.

(4.3) Store the last few indices of JDarkVec as those indices will have pixel value close to 1.

(4.4) Let numpx be size of image by 1000.

(4.5) Let atm be a zero matrix of size 1×3.

(4.6) For i = 1 to numpx

(4.7) atm = atm + imageRGBVec(indices(i), :)

(4.8) End For

(4.9) Return atmospheric = atm/numpx.

5. Find transmission light using transmissionEstimation(imageRGB, atmospheric) and store into variable transmission.

(5.1) Take amount of haze we are keeping into a variable omega = 0.95.

(5.2) For i = 1 to 3

(5.3) im(:, :, i) = imageRGB(:, :, ind)./atmospheric(i)

(5.4) End For

(5.5) Return transmission = 1 − omega * darkChannel(im)

6. Apply soft matting to the image using matte(imageRGB, transmission) function and store into a variable refinedTransmission.

(6.1) Take epsilon = 10^4 and lambda = 10^4.

(6.2) Let matrix mattingLaplacian = sparse matrix with rows and columns as number of pixels of imageRGB.

(6.3) For row = 2 to size of imageRGB(1) − 1

(6.4) For col = 2 to size of imageRGB(2) − 1

(6.5) Take matrix windowIndices with 4 elements row − 1, col − 1, row + 1, col + 1 and reshape imageRGB into window matrix using windowIndices. size.

(6.6) Find covariance of mean of the matrix window.

(6.7) Take inverse of the matrix window.

(6.8) For firstRow = windowIndices(1) : windowIndices(3)

(6.9) For firstCol = windowIndices(2) : windowIndices(4)

(6.10) mattingLaplacianRow = ((firstRow − 1) * imageSize(2)) + firstCol;

(6.11) For secondRow = windowIndices(1) : windowIndices(3)

(6.12) For secondCol = windowIndices(2) : windowIndices(4))

(6.13) mattingLaplacianCol = ((secondRow − 1) * imageSize(2)) + secondCol;

(6.14) If(mattingLaplacianRow == mattingLaplacianCol) then

(6.15) kroneckerDelta = 1;

(6.16) Else then

(6.17) kroneckerDelta = 0;

(6.18) End If

(6.19) Set mattingLaplacian = mattingLaplacian + (kroneckerDelta − windowInv NumPixels * (1 + transpose(rowPixelVariance)/windowInvCovarianceIdentity * colPixelVariance));

(6.20) End For.

(6.21) End For.

T. Pal et al.

(6.22) End For.
(6.23) End For.
(6.24) End For.
(6.25) End For.
(6.26) Return refinedTransmission = transpose of matting Laplacian + lambda product of transimission divided by lambda product of the number of pixels in imageRGB.
7. Find scene radiance using getRadiance(atmospheric, imageRGB, refinedTransmission) and store into dehazedImage.
(7.1) Take lower bound of transmission light, t0 = 0.1.
(7.2) For i = 1 to 3
(7.3) DehazedImage(:, :, i) = atmospheric(i) + (imageRGB(:, :, i) − atmospheric (i))./max(refinedTransmission, t0)
(7.4) End For.
(7.5) Return DehazedImage = DehazedImage./max(max(max(DehazedImage)))
8. dehazedImage is the desired output

4 Result and Discussion

Original and processed images have been implemented on Benchmark images [2–5] and some real time images collected from different sources [14]. Both sets of real time data set and bench mark data set are being implemented by the dark channel prior algorithm that has been depicted in Fig. 1. From Fig. 1, it is understood that although this technique produces good results in hazy or fog degraded images but if the image consists of sky region, the algorithm fails to produce a good quality image.

The next stage of the experiment demonstrates a qualitative assessment evaluation or performance evaluation based on reference and non-reference strategies on the fog degraded images to examine the efficiency of the technique used.

4.1 Performance Evaluation

Performance Evaluation is conducted based on non-reference methods and reference methods, and it has been observed that using these methods the quality of the restored image is much effective than the original fog degraded image. We have implemented these assessment techniques on the color images of size 300 * 300.

4.1.1 Non-reference Methods

Non-reference Methods are some methods used for evaluation of restored images where no reference image is available for the input/degraded image. Generally, the non reference methods that are used for evaluating the haze free output image is determined by three parameters e, r and σ. Any better enhancement technique should have higher values of e, r and lower values for σ [9]. Figure 2 depicts the performance evaluation on sample image 4 based on non reference strategy.

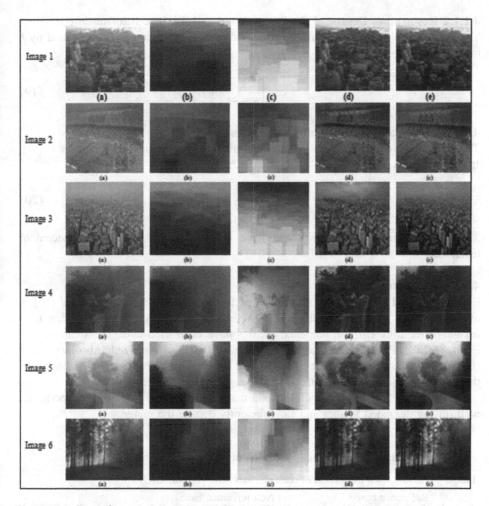

Fig. 1. (a) Input hazy image collected from different sources [2–4], (b) Dark channel, (c) Transmission map, (d) Radiance, (e) Output image

4.1.1.1 Increased Rate of Visible Edges
The increased rate of visible edges is determined by e metrices
It is represented as:

$$e = \frac{n_r - n_0}{n_0} \tag{18}$$

Here n_r and n_0 are cardinal no. image of edges in original and contrast image. It depicts no of new edges that occur in the restored images.

4.1.1.2 Restoration Degree of the Image Edge and Texture Information
The Restoration degree of the image edge and texture information is determined by $\bar{r}$ metrics. It is represented as:

$$\bar{r} = \exp\left[\frac{1}{n_r}\sum \log r_i\right] \tag{19}$$

4.1.1.3 Percentage of the Number of Saturated Pixels
The Percentage of the Number of Saturated pixels is represented as σ metrics. It is represented as:

$$\sigma_y = \frac{n}{M*N}*100 \tag{20}$$

It shows the no of pixels those have been saturated after the enhancement technique.

4.1.2 Reference Methods
Reference-based parametric evaluation is performed when a reference image [10] is available. Here we have considered the reference image as original fog degraded image. Three different non reference metrics have been used here, i.e. Mean Square Error (MSE), Peak Signal to Noise Ratio (PSNR), Normalized Absolute Error (NAE) and MD. A higher value of PSNR and lower value of MSE and NAE indicates that the restoration efficacy of the output image produces better results.

From Table 2, it is clearly understood that Dark Channel Prior method performs well on fog degraded images and can efficiently dehaze the image.

Table 2. Performance evaluation of dark channel prior technique

Image	Performance evaluation of dark channel prior techniques							
	Reference based			Non-reference based				
	MSE	PSNR	NAE	e	σ	r	Visible edges in the original image	Visible edges in the restored image
Image 1	3.2899e+03	12.9590	0.3819	0.09936	0.001	0.86224	33353	36667
Image 2	2.2991e+03	14.5153	0.3324	5.8848	0.044	2.0083	1936	13329
Image 3	7.1176e+03	9.6075	1.4194	0.00976	0	1.323	31040	30737
Image 4	2.4213e+03	14.2902	0.5013	1.1322	0	1.3025	10564	22525
Image 5	3.4438e+03	12.7604	0.3066	11.9503	3.4556	1.3437	604	7822
Image 6	786.3512	19.1746	0.2860	0.62424	1.5089	1.2438	13796	22408

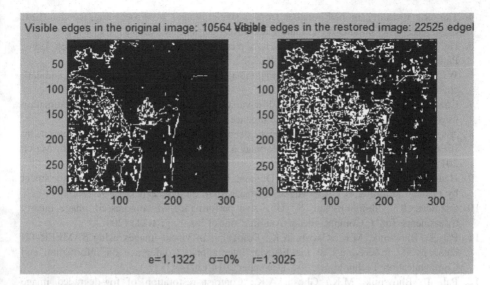

Fig. 2. Performance evaluation on sample Image 4 based on non reference strategy

5 Conclusion and Future Work

The problem of degradation in outdoor images because of poor atmospheric environment is a serious issue in computer vision-based applications. Images acquired by a visual system are severely degraded under the hazy and foggy weather, which will affect several computer vision based applications. Therefore, restoring the degraded image to its clear form is of great significance. The paper investigated many approaches about image dehazing algorithms. This paper performed an in-depth study of Dark Channel Prior Technique and implemented it on real time and benchmark dataset, and a comparative analysis is also being done. This paper also establishes the pseudocode of this dark channel prior technique. Finally, to evaluate the effectiveness of the technique used, different performance evaluation is carried out based on reference and non reference strategies. Experimental results demonstrate that the used methods show good results for fog degraded visual images but this technique has some disadvantage too. If the image consists of sky region, the algorithm fails to produce a good quality image and this problem need to be addressed.

References

1. Nayar, S.K., Narasimhan, S.G.: Vision in bad weather. In: Proceedings of the Seventh IEEE International Conference on Computer Vision, vol. 2, pp. 820–827 (1999)
2. Al-Zubaidy, Y., Salam, R.A.: Removal of atmospheric particles in poor visibility outdoor images. Telkomnika **11**(8), 4244–4250 (2013)
3. Oakley, J.P., Bu, H.: Correction of simple contrast loss in color images. IEEE Trans. Image Process. **16**(2), 511 (2007)

4. Tan, R.: Visibility in bad weather from a single image. In: Proceedings of the IEEE Conference on Computer Vision and Pattern Recognition, June 2008
5. He, K., Sun, J., Tang, X.: Single image haze removal using dark channel prior. IEEE Trans. Pattern Anal. Mach. Intell. **33**(12), 2341–2353 (2011)
6. Wang, J., He, N., Zhang, L., Lu, K.: Single image dehazing with a physical model and dark channel prior (2015)
7. Chen, J., Chau, L.: An enhanced window-variant dark channel prior for depth estimation using single foggy image. In: IEEE Conference (2014)
8. Xu, H., Guo, J., Liu, Q., Ye, L.: Fast image dehazing using improved dark channel prior. In: IEEE International Conference on Information Science and Technology, 23–25th March 2012 (2012)
9. Hautiere, N., Tarel, J.-P., Aubert, D., Dumont, E.: Blind contrast enhancement assessment by gradient rationing at visible edges. J. Image Anal. Stereol. **27**(2), 87–95 (2008)
10. Sakuldee, R., Udomhunsakul, S.: Objective performance of compressed image quality assessments. Int. J. Comput. Electr. Autom. Control Inf. Eng. **1**(11) (2007)
11. Pal, T., Bhowmik, M.K., Ghosh, A.K.: Defogging of visual images using SAMEER-TU database. In: Proceedings of the Elsevier International Conference on Information and Communication Technologies, 3–5 December 2014 (2014)
12. Pal, T., Bhowmik, M.K., Ghosh, A.K.: Contrast restoration of fog-degraded image sequences. In: Das, K.N., Deep, K., Pant, M., Bansal, J.C., Nagar, A. (eds.) Proceedings of Fourth International Conference on Soft Computing for Problem Solving. AISC, vol. 335, pp. 325–338. Springer, New Delhi (2015). https://doi.org/10.1007/978-81-322-2217-0_28
13. Pal, T., Bhowmik, M.K., Bhattacharjee, D., Ghosh, A.K.: Visibility enhancement techniques for fog degraded images: a comparative analysis with performance evaluation. In: 26th IEEE Conferencce on TENCON on Technologies for Smart Nation, Marina Bay Sands, Singapore (2016)
14. https://unsplash.com/search/photos/mist

Brain Tumor Detection by Wavelet Based Fusion Technique

Tejal Kothari[1], Ankita Pramanik[1(✉)], and Santi P. Maity[2]

[1] Department of Electronics and Telecommunication Engineering, IIEST,
Shibpur, Howrah, West Bengal, India
kothari.tejal17@gmail.com,
ankita@telecom.iiests.ac.in
[2] Department of Information Technology, IIEST, Shibpur, Howrah,
West Bengal, India
santipmaity@it.iiests.ac.in

Abstract. The present work aims to improve accuracy in computer aided diagnosis on brain tumor detection. To improve the segmentation process, a novel wavelet based fusion technique to combine two different segmentation techniques-absorbing Markov chain (AMC) and k-means clustering, is proposed here. The efficacy of the presented segmentation algorithm is demonstrated on the BRATS-2012 dataset containing ground truth images of MRI brain tumor images of T2 modality. A dice coefficient of $\sim 78\%$ on an average for the images is achieved against $\sim 67\%$ and $\sim 72.9\%$ dice values in the existing works. The present work also uses the support vector machine to classify the brain tumor as benign or malignant.

Keywords: Brain tumor · Wavelet based fusion · k-means clustering · Absorbing Markov chain · Support vector machine

1 Introduction

Brain tumor is an uncontrolled growth of brain cells. It can be classified as benign or malignant. Most brain and spinal cord tumors develop from glial cells i.e., the supporting cells of the brain, referred to as glioma [1]. Gliomas can be classified as low grade and high grade. High grade gliomas (HGGs) are deadly and hard to operate on. Gliomas accounts for about 33% of all brain and CNS (central nervous system) tumors, and 80% of all the brain tumors classified as malignant [2]. The incidence of CNS tumors in India ranges from 5 to 10 per 100,000 populations with an increasing trend and accounts for 2% of malignancies [3]. In spite of prominent advancements being made in research of glioma, the diagnosis of patient is still poor.

The time factor is a crucial step towards the [4] discovery of the disease in the patient, especially in brain tumor. These days computer aided diagnosis (CAD) methods are widely used in several medical areas for improving the detection at an early stage. It is worth mentioning that CAD is not a competitive method, instead a complete, sometimes a parallel method. The use of CAD methods in pathology [5] can extensively enhance the efficiency and accuracy of pathologists' decisions. The various

© Springer Nature Singapore Pte Ltd. 2019
J. K. Mandal et al. (Eds.): CICBA 2018, CCIS 1030, pp. 333–343, 2019.
https://doi.org/10.1007/978-981-13-8578-0_26

imaging diagnostic methods for tumor include positron emission tomography (PET), computed tomography (CT), magnetic resonance imaging (MRI) [6] etc. Each imaging modality offers certain advantages and disadvantages. For tumor detection, MRI is widely used as it gives better contrast and resolution for the soft tissues and gives detailed information about tumor.

Detection of cancer in early stage is the key to increasing the chance of patients' survival. However, in developing countries there is a shortage of trained medical persons. Hence, automatic brain tumor detection is essential. Thus, development of appropriate segmentation technique for tumor detection has become necessary. So, quite a large amount of research activities on MRI brain tumor detection of different modalities is being carried out.

The rest of the paper is organized as follows: Sect. 2 provides the literature review with the scope and contributions of the present work. The existing tools and techniques used in this paper are discussed in Sect. 3. Section 4 presents the proposed methodology. The results and discussions are presented in Sect. 5. Finally, the conclusions and future scope of works are given in Sect. 6.

2 Literature Review

Few existing works on MRI image uses red, green, blue (RGB) colour space or some alternate colour model to improve the efficacy of the segmentation algorithm. The work in [7] converts the RGB image to the hue, saturation, value (HSV) color model. It then applies the watershed algorithm followed by Canny edge detection on the output image for tumor extraction.

Pre-processing plays an important role in improvement of the overall segmentation process. In [8], pre-processing on MRI brain images is done using sharpening and median filters. Then, the resultant image is enhanced by histogram equalization, followed by segmentation through thresholding. On the segmented image, morphological operations are performed. Finally, through image subtraction approach, the tumor region is obtained.

The work in [9] uses Sobel operator as a pre-processing method and the technique of equalisation of histogram for image enhancement. After this, thresholding is done followed by segmentation using morphological operators. The work also analyzes the tumour by calculating its area and perimeter.

The performance of the different algorithms can get seriously hampered due to presence of noise in an image. So, many a works introduce a noise cleaning procedure. In [11], the median filter and bilateral filter are used to remove the noise from the MRI images and the best image out of both is selected based on performance evaluation. Then, watershed segmentation is applied and tumor is extracted through connected component labelling.

In recent times, super-pixels are also being used to improve the segmentation process [12]. The work in [12] gives the outline of simple linear iterative clustering version 0 (SLICO) based segmentation for brain tumor CT images. The clustered images are then grouped together using region merging algorithm. The use of SLICO however leads to over-segmentation of images. Also, SLICO does not work well with different images.

Few recent works also uses principal component analysis (PCA) and k-means clustering method in combination for segmentation [10]. PCA is used for feature dimensionality reduction and formation of precise number of cluster to increase the accuracy. Then, the tumor boundary is highlighted through k-means clustering.

Some works uses fuzzy c-means (FCM) method for better segmentation [13]. In [13], T1-contrast MRI modality images are used. First, the images are N3 corrected, then, anisotropic diffusion filtering and unsharp masking is applied for pre-processing of images. Segmentation and labeling of the images are done by FCM. The work uses unsharp masking method which may amplify noise. Also, FCM used requires initialization of the 'c' clusters which is a time consuming process.

The use of FCM in [13] increases the computational complexity and also requires pre-initialization of 'c' clusters. The proposed work mainly focuses on automation of the whole process with reduction in elapsed time for detection of tumor.

From the above discussions it can be inferred that segmentation plays a crucial role on the accuracy of the image analysis.

2.1 Scope and Contributions of the Present Work

The existing methods use various segmentation techniques, all of which come with their own advantages and disadvantages. The problem of over-segmentation encountered in segmentation by super-pixel method [12] is tackled here by proposing absorbing Markov chain (AMC) based segmentation. To the best of the authors' knowledge, the proposed work is the first work using AMC for brain tumor segmentation. The proposed work also uses Otsu and k-means method in combination, to automate the process as the Otsu method automatically determines the number of clusters, thus, dealing with the initialization problem of [13]. The use of k-means ensures low computational complexity, therefore lesser elapsed time than any hierarchical clustering methods like FCM. The existing techniques are fused so as to maximize the benefits. It has been seen that wavelets allow the decomposition of images at different scales and decomposed images can be reconstructed subsequently with high precision. This work is based on HGGs of T2 modality of MRI. T2 images are chosen as they have higher contrast than any other modalities. The present work not only improves the segmentation process but also classifies the segmented tumor as benign or cancerous. The present work's contributions can be recapitulated as follows:

(i)   AMC based segmentation to overcome the problems of over-segmentation introduced by the best known SLICO method.
(ii) Segmentation in two parallel arms using AMC and k-means clustering are coupled through wavelet based fusion technique to improve segmentation performance.
(iii) Incorporation of noise cleaning operation before segmentation process.
(iv) Tumor's classification as benign or malignant.

The efficacy of the segmentation and classification process is also presented by carrying out extensive simulations.

3 Existing Tools and Techniques

The present work uses AMC and k-means clustering for segmentation of the tumor. It then identifies the features from this segmented image to classify the tumor. The existing tools and techniques are discussed below.

3.1 k-means Method

k-means clustering is a type of unsupervised learning algorithm which enables the grouping of unlabeled data points, i.e., the data points without defined categories or groups. For an image, each pixel value is considered as the data point. The Euclidean distance metric is used in this paper. The process starts by picking k, the number of clusters. At first, this algorithm randomly assigns the centroid (based on number of clusters k chosen), since it does not know where the centroids of each cluster is. Then, it goes through all data points and assign them to the centroid it is closest to, i.e. the data points closest to one of the centroid is assigned under one label. After the assignment of all points, the centroids locations of the k clusters are updated. The process repeats until the convergence is achieved. Convergence here means: when the points does not move between the clusters and the centroids become stable.

The algorithm aims at minimizing within-cluster sum of squares given by:

$$A = \sum_{i=1}^{n} \sum_{j=1}^{n_i} \left(\|u_i - v_j\| \right)^2 \tag{1}$$

where,

$\|u_i - v_j\|$' is the Euclidean distance between u_i and v_j.

'n_i' represents data points' number in i^{th} cluster.

'n' is the number of cluster centers.

3.2 AMC

An AMC is a semi supervised method, defined by the m x m transition matrix V, on a set of states given as C = {$c_1, c_2, c_3, \ldots \ldots \ldots c_m$}. The probability p_{jk}, often referred to as transition probability, is the probability of moving from state c_j to state c_k. The chain starts in some state and move successively from one state to another with this probability being independent of the state it was in before the current state.

A state is said to be absorbing if once a certain state is reached, it is impossible to leave that state. The absorbing states signify nodes with no children. If $p_{jj} = 1$, i.e. $p_{jk} = 0$ for all $j \neq k$, the process is said to be an AMC. A non-absorbing state is known as transient. Let an AMC has 'a' absorbing states and 'b' transient states. For the process to be absorbed in AMC, the probability should be 1. The canonical form for the transition matrix V is given as below,

$$V \longrightarrow \begin{pmatrix} A & B \\ 0 & I \end{pmatrix} \tag{2}$$

where, A is a b × b matrix which contains probabilities of entering absorbing states, B is a b × a matrix containing probability values of entering other states. 0 is a zero matrix of size a × b and I refers to the a × a identity matrix. '0' and 'I' states have no chance of leaving absorbing states. The fundamental matrix F is equal to $(I - B)^{-1}$. It tells us about the average number of states to absorption. The simple solution matrix FA shows that there is no chance of ending up in a non-absorbing state. In AMC, for an image, the entire boundary and other nodes are referred to as absorbing or transient nodes respectively.

For each transient state, the absorbed time is defined mathematically as:

$$y = N x d \tag{3}$$

Here, 'd' is a b dimensional column vector with all elements as 1.

3.3 Area

In this step, the area of the tumor is calculated from the binary image. Here, JPEG image of size 256 × 256 is used. Mathematically, the summation of total number of white and black pixels represents a binary image. The white tumor area is calculated in millimeter square (mm^2).

3.4 Entropy

Image entropy is a quantity which is used to describe the amount of information an image contains. A higher value of entropy is an indication of the fused image containing more information than the segmented images. It is measured by the formula:

$$E = -\sum_0^{L-1} P_i \log_2 P_i \tag{4}$$

3.5 Dice Similarity Coefficient

Dice similarity coefficient (DSC) is a measure used for comparing the similarity of two images i.e., the final segmented image with the ground truth image. The formula used in this paper for dice coefficient calculation is given by:

$$\text{Dice} = 2 \times (|P \cap Q|)/(|P| + |Q|) \tag{5}$$

where P is the segmented tumor region and Q is the ground truth tumor region. The proposed algorithm is elaborated in the next section.

4 Proposed Methodology

Most of the current research is targeted at semiautomatic segmentation of brain tumors to minimize human interaction and thus the errors [14]. This section proposes a tumor detection algorithm with this aim. The input to the proposed system is MRI image of brain taken from BRATS 2012 dataset [15]. The block diagram of the proposed method is given in Fig. 1. The various steps of the algorithm are described below.

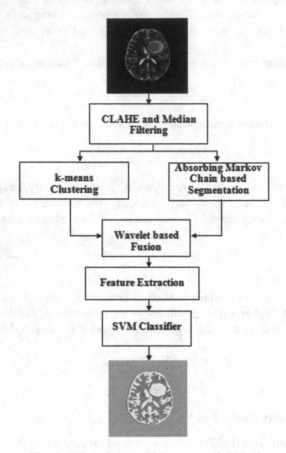

Fig. 1. Block diagram of the proposed method

In the first step of the algorithm, pre-processing of the MRI image is done by contrast limited adaptive histogram equalization (CLAHE) method. CLAHE works on tiles of the image thus, enhancing the contrast of each tile separately. Through CLAHE, hidden finer details can be displayed which is an important aspect for tumor images. Since, CLAHE can lead to artifacts and degraded edges, therefore the pre-processing is followed by median filtering. Median filtering is proposed to be used as it can remove different noises like Gaussian noise, salt and pepper noise etc. while retaining the edges.

This is followed by segmentation. It is the process of subdividing an image into different regions and labeling the regions with similar characteristics, such as color, intensity, texture etc., under one group. To make the best use of the advantages of the various segmentation algorithms, the present work proposes the segmentation to be done in two parallel arms, in one by k-means clustering and in the other arm by AMC. In k-means, the algorithm requires an initialization of 'k' values according to which the centroids are randomly assigned because the knowledge of the centre of each cluster is not definite. The wrong selection of 'k' can lead to several iterations, hence consumes more time. So, selection of the centroids is critical to the overall performance of the algorithm. Hence, the present work proposes to use Otsu method so that its local maxima can act as the value of cluster. The use of Otsu segmentation also automatizes the algorithm.

The AMC method has been used in making medical decisions, saliency detection [16] etc. But it has not been used for segmentation of brain tumor. This is the first work to make use of AMC for brain tumor segmentation. A graph is constructed for an image expressed as a Markov chain with the super pixels as its nodes and the link between two nodes as edges. When the absorbing state is reached, there is no movement from one state to the other and thus the region is segmented.

The results obtained by the two algorithms are fused by wavelet based technique. A combination of significant information from two or more images into a single image is known as image fusion. The main advantages of performing fusion are: (1) It provides more information (2) It improves the quality of the image (3) It helps in removing noise (4) It helps in enhancing some features which are not visible in any of the image. Many fusion techniques such as averaging method, selecting the maxima or minima, Laplacian pyramid method etc., are available. But as the wavelets exists for a finite duration and can show abrupt changes in images, the wavelet based fusion technique is proposed to be used. The Coiflets wavelet based fusion is used in this paper as it gives good peak signal to noise ratio (PSNR) and high entropy values compared to other methods. In this method, discrete wavelet transform (DWT) is applied to both the segmented image to get the decomposed coefficients. These coefficients are merged through a fusion rule of maximum so that a sharper and brighter image is achieved.

In the next step, the fused image is acquired through inverse DWT. After the fusion process, features like area of the extracted tumor, entropy of the ground truth and fused image and the dice coefficient are calculated for each image. These features are then passed onto a support vector machine (SVM) classifier to detect the tumor to be benign or malignant. SVM is all about selecting the best decision boundary that can separate different classes. However, the SVM needs to be trained which time is consuming. To remove this shortcoming, the proposed work uses the centroids obtained from k-means clustering to train the SVM classifier to achieve overall automation of the proposed work. The performances of the proposed algorithm are presented in the next section.

5 Results and Discussions

The experimental output of the proposed methodology on the BRATS dataset is discussed here. However, due to paucity of space, output of various stages for two test images only is shown in Figs. 2 and 3 and with the corresponding extracted features in Tables 1 and 2.

The efficacy of the proposed algorithm is also demonstrated here. The comparison of the proposed method with the existing works is shown in Table 3. The average dice

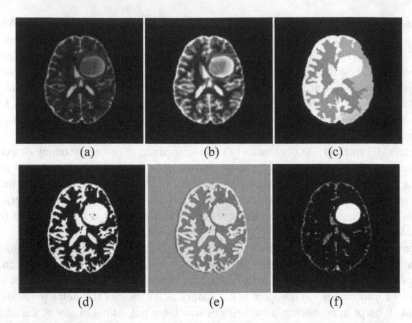

Fig. 2. For Patient 1 (a) Original image (b) Median filtered image (c) AMC (d) k-means (e) Fused image (f) Ground truth image

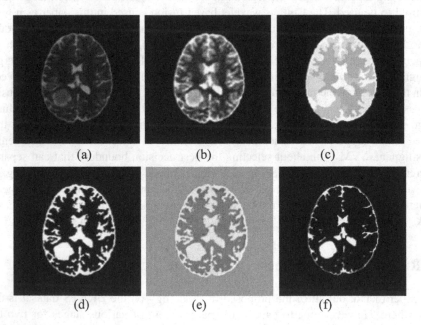

Fig. 3. For Patient 2 (a) Original image (b) Median filtered image (c) AMC (d) k-means (e) Fused image (f) Ground truth image

Table 1. Features for patient 1

Sr. no.	Parameter	Value
1.	Area of ground truth image (mm^2)	1723
2.	Area of segmented image (mm^2)	1850
3.	Entropy of segmented image (dB)	6.87
4.	DSC	91.40

Table 2. Features for patient 2

Sr. no.	Parameter	Value
1.	Area of ground truth image (mm^2)	956
2.	Area of segmented image (mm^2)	1032
3.	Entropy of segmented image (dB)	4.35
4.	DSC	87.12

score of all the images is $\sim$78%, with the highest value being $\sim$93.89% and the lowest being $\sim$70.84%. The average DSC obtained by the work in [12] and [13] is $\sim$67% and $\sim$72.9%, respectively against the DSC of $\sim$78% achieved by the proposed method. Thus it can be seen from Table 3 that the proposed algorithm gives improved results.

Table 3. Comparison with existing papers

Sr. no.	Paper	DSC
1.	[12]	67%
2.	[13]	72.9%
3.	Proposed method	78%

After the segmentation, the SVM classifier is applied on the images. In the presented cases, SVM categorizes the entire tumor as malignant as is the actual case. Thus, reliable results can be obtained by the SVM classifier. The overall execution time in MATLAB using Intel Corei3 processor with 16 GB RAM and 4 GHz speed is 1.402784 s.

6 Conclusions and Future Works

In this work, a semi-automatic method of segmentation is proposed. The presented algorithm is simple to use and is much efficient compared to the existing works. The computation time is also an important aspect apart from obtaining accurate tumor segmentation. The overall execution time of segmenting all the images is $\sim$1.402784 s. Also, a higher DSC value of $\sim$78% is achieved by the proposed algorithm against ∼72.9% achieved by FCM method. Furthermore, the area of extracted tumor is close to that of the ground truth image.

The future work includes attainment of improved DSC value. The work can be further advanced to 3D images. Other fusion techniques, to improve the overall performance, may be explored in the future. The efficacy of the present segmentation algorithm can be tested on tumors in other regions of the body.

References

1. Goodenberger, M.L., Jenkins, R.B.: Genetics of adult glioma. Cancer Genet. **205**(12), 613–621 (2012)
2. Johns Hopkins Medicine Health Library. http://www.hopkinsmedicine.org/healthlibrary. Accessed 19 Apr 2018
3. Dasgupta, A., Gupta, T., Jalali, R.: Indian data on central nervous tumors: a summary of published work. South Asian J. Cancer **5**(3), 147–153 (2016)
4. Jamaludin, A., Kadir, T., Zisserman, A.: Automatic modic changes classification in spinal MRI. In: Vrtovec, T., et al. (eds.) CSI 2015. LNCS, vol. 9402, pp. 14–26. Springer, Cham (2016). https://doi.org/10.1007/978-3-319-41827-8_2
5. El-Dahshan, E.-S.A., Mohsen, H.M., Revett, K., Salem, A.-B.M.: Computer-aided diagnosis of human brain tumor through MRI: a survey and a new algorithm. Expert Syst. Appl. **41**(11), 5526–5545 (2014)
6. Kharrat, A., Benamrane, N., Messaud Mohamed, B., Abid, M.: Detection of brain tumor in medical images. In: 3rd International Conference on Signals, Circuits and Systems (SCS), pp. 1–6. IEEE, Medenine (2009)
7. Maiti, I., Chakraborty, M.: A new method for brain tumor segmentation based on watershed and edge detection algorithms in HSV colour model. In: National Conference on Computing and Communication Systems (NCCCS), pp. 1–6. IEEE, Durgapur (2012)
8. Natarajan, P., Krishnan, N., Kenkre, N.S., Nancy, S., Singh, B.P.: Tumor detection using threshold operation in MRI brain images. In: IEEE International Conference on Computational Intelligence & Computing Research (ICCIC), pp. 1–4. IEEE, Coimbatore (2012)
9. Murthy, T.S.D., Sadashivappa, G.: Brain tumor segmentation using thresholding, morphological operations and extraction of features of tumor. In: International Conference on Advances in Electronics, Computers and Communications (ICAECC), pp. 1–6. IEEE, Bangalore (2014)
10. Katkar, J., Baraskar, T., Mankar, V.R.: A novel approach for medical image segmentation using PCA and k-means clustering. In: International Conference on Applied and Theoretical Computing and Communication Technology (ICATCCT), pp. 430–435. IEEE, Davangere (2015)
11. Dhage, P., Phegade, M.R., Shah, S.K.: Watershed segmentation brain tumor detection. In: International Conference on Pervasive Computing (ICPC), pp. 1–5. IEEE, Pune (2015)
12. Wang, X., Ma, P., Zhao, J.: Brain tumor CT image segmentation based on SLIC0 superpixels. In: International Congress on Image and Signal Processing, BioMedical Engineering and Informatics (CISP-BMEI), pp. 427–431. IEEE, Datong (2016)
13. Sehgal, A., Goel, S., Mangipudi, P., Mehra, A., Tyagi, D.: Automatic brain tumor segmentation and extraction in MR images. In: Conference on Advances in Signal Processing (CASP), pp. 104–107. IEEE, Pune (2016)
14. Gordillo, N., Montseny, E., Sobrevilla, P.: State of the art survey on MRI brain tumor segmentation. Magn. Reson. Imaging **31**(8), 1426–1438 (2013)

15. Menze, B.H.: The multimodal brain tumor image segmentation benchmark (BRATS). IEEE
Trans. Med. Imaging **34**(10), 1993–2024 (2015)
16. Jiang, B., Zhang, L., Lu, H., Yang, C., Yang, M.-H.: Saliency detection via absorbing
Markov chain. In: IEEE International Conference on Computer Vision (ICCV), pp. 1665–
1672. IEEE, Sydney (2013)

An Approach Towards Analyzing Various VM Allocation Policies in the Domain of Cloud Computing

Debashis Das[1(✉)], Pramit Brata Chanda[1], Samit Biswas[2], and Sourav Banerjee[1]

[1] Kalyani Government Engineering College, Nadia, Kalyani 741235, West Bengal, India
debashis2124@gmail.com, souravacademia@gmail.com
[2] IIEST Shibpur, Botanic Garden, Howrah 711103, West Bengal, India

Abstract. Cloud Computing has become a new age technology that has got the high degree of potency nowadays. Cloud Computing uses the concept of virtualization. It also provides resources to applications by allocating virtual machines to specific application. Optimizing resources in the cloud environment is more beneficial, minimizing allocation cost and satisfying client requests are the main purpose of working with VM allocation strategy. So, the resource allocation policies play crucial role for allocating and controlling the resources among several applications in cloud computing environment. This paper illustrates a comparative study on various VM allocation policies. The study and performance analysis of these algorithms are done on the basis of total allocation cost in between VM to Host considering different attributes and different service level agreements (SLA) in the domain of cloud computing.

Keywords: Cloud computing · Service level agreements (SLA) · Virtual Machine (VM) · VM allocation strategy (VAS)

1 Introduction

Cloud computing [10] is an imitation for validating convenient, on-demand web ingress to shared puddle of configurable computing assets (e.g., applications, services, servers) that can be swiftly distributed and delivered with minimum management strive or service provider dealings. Cloud computing presents a compelling solution for software evolution and ingress of data with transparency. The Cloud stage is generally sliced up of various datacenters and consumers have entrance to only a computational ability over a scalable network. The disposition of these computational assets is organize by a provider, and assets are allocated in a workable way, as per customer demands. The way to employ cloud stage for running software is thoroughly disparate thing than conventional implementations, where software runs atop infrastructures normally measure following

© Springer Nature Singapore Pte Ltd. 2019
J. K. Mandal et al. (Eds.): CICBA 2018, CCIS 1030, pp. 344–351, 2019.
https://doi.org/10.1007/978-981-13-8578-0_27

Table 1. Allocation cost

Virtual Machine	Host	
	H_1	H_2
VM_1	5	10
VM_2	2	8
VM_3	4	4
VM_4	6	3
VM_5	5	2
VM_6	6	4

to the worst occurrence. To adjust unexpected requests on the infrastructures in a flexible procedure, the procedure of allocation and reallocation should be dynamic in cloud environment. Another fundamental feature of the resource allocation techniques in cloud computing is to assurance that the demands of all applications are appropriately met. Datacenter Resources are not only geographically distributed but also resource demand can modify dynamically by the customers at the moment of run time. So the resource allocation in such a large-scale distributed system is a vastly challenging task. Managing of resources are a main role of any dynamic systems, it also requires some involve policies and conclusions for the organizing of dynamic objective as for examples CPU. In cloud computing VM (Virtual Machine) allocation problem in datacenters is an exacting topic. VM allocation issue can be noticed in two ways - 1. static and 2. dynamic. A VM allocation points to map each VM to host a given objective role for optimization. The objective role can be minimizing for execution time, maximizing utilization or providers profit. The VM allocation policy [12] assists in creating an instance of VM to a host inside a datacenter. The allocation of VM can produce of higher quality utilization of hosts processing ability. Also, it may assist in minimizing makespan of cloudlets and the total completion time. Designing a superior VM allocation policy is a difficult task in the domain of cloud computing We have considered three VM allocation policies which are 1. Serial VM Allocation Policy [1] 2. Optimal VM Allocation policy [1] and GS VM Allocation Policy [2] for Vm Allocation. Using these policies we have computed total allocation cost (cost means execution time) of VMs for allocating to the host. After computing the results we have seen which algorithm is most appropriate to reach our objective means calculating the VM allocation cost for each algorithm and comparing with each other. Table 1 represent the allocation cost to allocate each VM to the each host. As for examples Time require for allocate VM_1 to H_1 and H_2 are 5 and 10 respectively.

2   Related Work

Virtual Machine [12] is a crucial module which is controlled by Virtual Machine Monitor (VMM) or hypervisor such as VMware, XEN, KVN etc. The Cloud users submit a job into the datacenter through the cloudlet. Cloudlet is a collection of jobs to employing for services. The service appeals of the cloudlets are completed by the VMs. The correspondence between VMs and Cloudlet is controlled by a broker policy [14,15] which is called DatacenterBroker [16]. Each datacenter subsists of physical nodes which are called hosts. The VMs are appraised as logical machines which can execute some specific operations. The VMs are allocated into the hosts. The VM allocation [17] into the hosts are handled by VM allocation policy [14]. The VM allocation approach selects hosts from a datacenter that fulfills the VMs requirement. The VM Scheduler [14] is responsible for allocating hosts processing cores to the VMs either in time-share or in space-shared approach. Tziritas et al. [7] proposes network load minimization and energy efficiency. The authors propose algorithms are for application aware workload consolidation, considering both separately as well as together. But the authors consider a cloud domain with an initial placement. Then attempt to optimize the VM allocation by migration for attaining network load minimization and energy efficiency. Cura [4] allocates previously clustered VMs for MapReduce cluster. However, in this case the problem is over-provisioning of the resources. Exactly Equal no of VMs may not be accessible for clustering for all the time. This over-provisioning can lead to starvation of other requests. Shabeera and Kumar [9] proposed algorithms to allocate VM in MapReduce cloud. They suggested PAM, Greedy and random based algorithms to allocate VM into the host. They are not examining the data arrangement. CAM [5] uses a min-cost flow model for VM and data arrangement by reviewing storage utilization, modifying load of CPU and link of network capacities. This proposal considers both delay scheduling and VM migration. But the problems of these techniques are append additional overhead to the system. He et al. [8] proposes VM consolidation for energy saving by considering VMs as moldable. Moldable VMs can modify their resource capacities in the time of consolidation moment without jeopardizing QoS. Alicherry and Lakshman [6] proposed an algorithm for resource allocation in distributed cloud system. The authors examine the allocation of VMs only. They want to show approximation algorithm for allocating VMs in nearest data centers. Alicherry and Lakshman [3] proposed algorithms of placing VMs in cloud system for optimizing data entrance latencies. The data location is already accessible and they also attempt to minimize the distance of inter-VM and distances of VM-data node. But without optimizing arrangement of data, VM placement optimization may not provide a superior outcome.

3   Experimental Results and Performance Analysis

In this section we have describe three different virtual machine allocation policies and shown the procedure of the allocation of VM into the host. For experiment all the algorithms we have taken six VM VM_1, VM_2, VM_3, VM_5, VM_5 and VM_6 and two host H_1 and H_2. Allocation cost for each VM to allocate into the different host are showing Table 1. We have also taken C_{ij} (i denotes as VMs number and j is denotes as hosts number) as a parameter to compute the allocation cost for particular algorithms. Using all the C_{ij}s value we have calculate the C_{TOTAL} to compute the allocation cost for each algorithms. We have optimized the VM allocation cost after computing total allocation cost for each algorithm.

3.1 Serial VM Allocation Policy

In this policy we used Seiral Task Assignment Approach (STAA) algorithm for allocation of VMs. First some VM allocate to H_1, next to H_2 and so on. So in this policy VM must be allocated to the host serially. In this approach we have seen first 3 VM allocated to H_1 and next 3 VM allocated to H_2. Using this approach We have shown the allocation of VMs to the host in Table 2. Here total allocation cost $C_{TOTAL} = C_{11} + C_{21} + C_{31} + C_{42} + C_{52} + C_{62} = (5 + 2 + 4 + 3 + 2 + 4) = 20$.

Table 2. Serial VM allocation

Virtual Machine	Host
VM_1	H_1
VM_2	H_1
VM_3	H_1
VM_4	H_2
VM_5	H_2
VM_6	H_2

3.2 Optimal VM Allocation Policy

In this policy we used Optimal Task Assignment Approach (OTTA) algorithm for allocating VM into the host. Here each VMs must be allocated to every host to diminish total allocation cost. We have shown in Table 3 how to allocate VMs into the host using OTTA algorithm. In this policy first 5 VM allocated to H_1 and next 1 allocated to H_2. We have calculated total VM allocation cost using this algorithm and here total allocation cost is $C_{TOTAL} = C_{11} + C_{21} + C_{31} + C_{41} + C_{51} + C_{62} = (5 + 2 + 4 + 6 + 5 + 4) = 26$.

3.3 GS VM Allocation Policy

We have computed VM allocation policy using Gale/Shapley (GS) algorithm [11,13]. Purpose of this algorithm pair each VM to each host and get stable matching. We have selected VM and host preference list depending upon which VMs allocation cost to the particular host should have minimum allocation cost. Here a host can be hold more no of VMs. We have shown the VM allocation to the host in Table 4 using this algorithm. We have calculated the allocation cost using each VMs allocation cost for particular host form Table 1. Total allocation cost is $C_{TOTAL} = C_{11} + C_{21} + C_{32} + C_{42} + C_{52} + C_{61} = 5 + 2 + 4 + 3 + 2 + 6 = 22$.

Table 3. Optimal VM allocation

Virtual Machine	Host
VM_1	H_1
VM_2	H_1
VM_3	H_1
VM_4	H_1
VM_5	H_1
VM_6	H_2

Table 4. GS VM allocation

Virtual Machine	Host
VM_1	H_1
VM_2	H_1
VM_3	H_2
VM_4	H_2
VM_5	H_2
VM_6	H_1

4   Comparison and Analysis

We have analyzed the performance of VM allocation cost using three algorithms (STAA, OTTA and GS). After computing we have seen that STAA algorithm results minimum allocation cost and more details are showing in Table 5. Different allocation cost has shown using graphical view in Fig. 1 and easily we can differentiate which algorithms are better for VM allocation. Seeing at the Table 5 we can easily said that serial VM Allocation Policy have taken minimum cost for allocating VMs into the host. We have also calculated AVMUTR (Average Virtual Machine Utilization Rate) for all policies particularly. AVMUTR is better in Optimal VM Allocation Policy. The Different AVMUTR of these policies have shown in Fig. 2 and also Table 6.

Table 5. Allocation cost comparison

Sl. no.	Policy	Allocation cost
1	Serial VM Allocation Policy	20
2	Optimal VM Allocation Policy	26
3	GS VM Allocation Policy	22

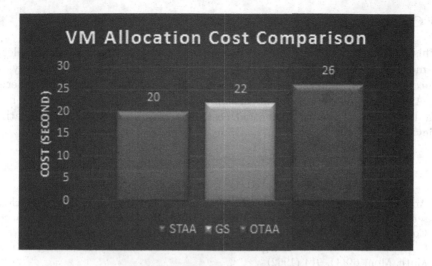

Fig. 1. Comparison of VM allocation cost

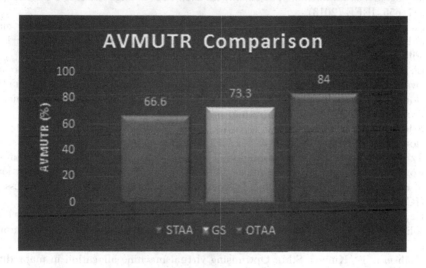

Fig. 2. Comparison of AVMUTR

Table 6. AVMUTR comparison

Sl. no.	Policy	AVMUTR (%)
1	Serial VM Allocation Policy	66.6
2	Optimal VM Allocation Policy	84
3	GS VM Allocation Policy	73.3

5   Conclusion and Future Work

In this paper, we present VM allocation policies for cloud computing. By selecting more number of VM allocation policies, allocation cost can probably be reduced. From all studies and comparison analysis, we can decided that Serial VM Allocation policy is better allocation policy for VM allocation into the host as it has taken minimum Allocation cost. Selecting an appropriate allocation policy will have enduring profits continue to enhance future.

References

1. Adhikari, M., Banerjee, S., Biswas, U.: Smart task assignment model for cloud service provider. ACCTHPCA **5**, 43–46 (2012). IJCA Special Issue on Advanced Computing and Communication Technologies for HPC Applications
2. Gale, D., Shapley, L.S.: College admissions and the stability of marriage. Amer. Math. Mon. **69**(1), 914 (1962)
3. Alicherry, M., Lakshman, T.: Optimizing data access latencies in cloud systems by intelligent virtual machine placement. In: 2013 Proceedings IEEE INFOCOM, pp. 647–655. IEEE (2013)
4. Palanisamy, B., Singh, A., Langston, B.: Cura: a cost-optimized model for map reduce in a cloud. In: IEEE 27th International Symposium on Parallel & Distributed Processing (IPDPS), pp. 1275–1286. IEEE (2013)
5. Li, M., Subhraveti, D., Butt, A.R., Khasymski, A., Sarkar, P.: CAM: a topology aware minimum cost flow based resource manager for mapreduce applications in the cloud. In: Proceedings of the 21st International Symposium on High-Performance Parallel and Distributed Computing, pp. 211–222. ACM (2012)
6. Alicherry, M., Lakshman, T.: Network aware resource allocation in distributed clouds. In: INFOCOM, pp. 963–971. IEEE (2012)
7. Tziritas, N., Xu, C.Z., Loukopoulos, T., Khan, S.U., Yu, Z.: Application-aware workload consolidation to minimize both energy consumption and network load in cloud environments. In: 42nd International Conference on Parallel Processing (ICPP), pp. 449–457. IEEE (2013)
8. He, L., Zou, D., Zhang, Z., Chen, C., Jin, H., Jarvis, S.A.: Developing resource consolidation frameworks for moldable virtual machines in clouds. Fut. Gen. Comput. Syst. **32**, 69–81 (2014)
9. Shabeera, T., Kumar, S.M.: Optimising virtual machine allocation in mapreduce cloud for improved data locality. Int. J. Big Data Intell. **2**(1), 2–8 (2015)
10. Khara, S.: A survey on virtual machine allocation and security in cloud. Int. J. Innov. Res. Technol. (IJIRT) **2**(7), 817–821 (2015). ISSN: 2349–6002
11. Xu, H., Li, B.: Egalitarian stable matching for VM migration in cloud computing. In: 2011 IEEE Conference on Computer Communications Workshops (INFOCOM WKSHPS), Shanghai, pp. 631–636 (2011)
12. Banerjee, S., Mandal, R., Biswas, U.: Wireless Pers. Commun. **98**(2), 1799–1820 (2018). https://doi.org/10.1007/s11277-017-4946-0. ISSN 0929-6212
13. Xu, H., Li, B.: Seen as stable marriages. In: Proceedings of the INFOCOM (2011)
14. Calheiros, R.N., Ranjan, R., De Rose, C.A.F., Buyya, R.: CloudSim: a novel framework for modelling and simulation of cloud computing infrastructures and services, p. 1. Technical report, GRIDSTR- 2009–1, Grid Computing and Distributed Systems Laboratory. The University of Melbourne. Australia (2009)

15. Chatterjee, T., Ojha, V.K., Adhikari, M., Banerjee, S., Biswas, U., Snášel, V.: Design and implementation of an improved datacenter broker policy to improve the QoS of a cloud. In: Kömer, P., Abraham, A., Snášel, V. (eds.) Proceedings of the Fifth International Conference on Innovations in Bio-Inspired Computing and Applications IBICA 2014. AISC, vol. 303, pp. 281–290. Springer, Cham (2014). https://doi.org/10.1007/978-3-319-08156-4_28
16. Banerjee, S., Adhikari, M., Kar, S., Biswas, U.: Development and analysis of a new cloudlet allocation strategy for QoS improvement in cloud. Arabian J. Sci. Eng. 40(5), 1409–1425 (2015)
17. Quiroz, A., Kim, H., Parashar, M., Gnanasambandam, N., Sharma, N.: Towards autonomic workload provisioning for enterprise grids and clouds. In: 10th IEEE/ACM International Conference on Grid Computing, pp. 50–57. IEEE (2009)

Blueshift of Optical Signal in PhC Based Butterworth Filter Due to Joule Heat Dissipation

Arpan Deyasi[1(✉)] and Angsuman Sarkar[2]

[1] Department of Electronics and Communication Engineering,
RCC Institute of Information Technology, Kolkata, India
deyasi_arpan@yahoo.co.in
[2] Department of Electronics and Communication Engineering,
Kalyani Government Engineering College, Kolkata, India
angsumansarkar@ieee.org

Abstract. Filters in all-optical circuit have the potential advantage over that of optoelectronic circuits because of very high SNR, thanks to the reduced scattering between photons instead of electron-electron collisions. This property makes the PhC based filters as the blue-eyed candidate for optical signal processing in photonic circuits. Semiconductor heterostructures are in general the constituent element of photonic crystal (PhC) based devices, whose performance is characterized by passband width at the desired frequency of communication spectrum, along with magnitude of ripple in that region of interest. The present paper shows that effect of device temperature has a great deal of influence on the performance parameters of the filter, under different polarized conditions and different magnitudes of structural parameters within physically realizable limit. But modulation of bandwidth is negligibly small as observed from simulated results within the choice of temperature range. Results are critically constructive for inclusion of this filter in optical integrated circuit.

Keywords: Device temperature · Ripple · Passband · Butterworth filter · Photonic crystal · Polarized incidence

1 Introduction

Research in the domain of optical signal processing initiated a long ago, and made significant progress after the invention of photonic crystal [1], which reformed the scenario of optical communication [2, 3]. Photonic crystal (PhC) has the distinctive characteristic of blocking electromagnetic wave propagation in desired wavelength region [4] and also allowing the signals in other spectra. This feature is inevitably used for physical realization of optical filter [5], along with transmitter [6], receiver [7], sensor [8], switch [9], and moreover, photonic crystal fiber [10]. Filter is the most significant discovery as concerned by researchers using PhC, as it can effectively controls the passage of optical signal, and more precisely, choice of structural parameters [11], angle of incidence of input wave [12], material constitutions [13] makes possible shift of passband in order to increase SNR. This design is possible in

© Springer Nature Singapore Pte Ltd. 2019
J. K. Mandal et al. (Eds.): CICBA 2018, CCIS 1030, pp. 352–360, 2019.
https://doi.org/10.1007/978-981-13-8578-0_28

MHz region for use of mobile communication [14], as well as in beyond THz for optical communication [15, 16].

Based on 2D PhC, optical transmission system is proposed by Kawanishi [17] in the IP and FTTH regions. This concept is extended by a group of workers for reservoir computing to solve pattern recognition problems [18] using semiconductor optical amplifiers. Ultra-fast optical signal processing concept is introduced by Konishi [19], and for that purpose, nanowire PhC based switch is designed [20]. Different semiconductor materials and cavity design techniques [21] are later proposed to reduce pulse broadening effect in switches. Nonlinear mixing techniques are realized to achieve better correlation [22], which is essential in signal processing. Digital gates are recently proposed [23] which explores a new possibility of optical communication. But all these works are carried out for room temperature and temperature dependence of these features are yet to be explored. For long-time operation of all-optical circuit, generated joule heat causes rise in temperature, which, in turn, modulates device performance. This phenomenon has a serious effect in conventional Si-air based PhC, as higher temperature causes increase in dielectric property of Si, which degrades the optical performance. Semiconductor heterostructures in this context works as the suitable alternative which is first reported by Martelli et al. [24]. Its effect is evaluated for sensor application [25], and waveguide [26]. Effect of temperature on polarization-dependent PCF is experimentally analyzed in recent past [27].

In present optical signal processing, spectrum shape and its region of interest plays a crucial role, as optimized bandwidth and lowering of ripple are the two major criteria for achieving higher SNR. Therefore, THz signal processing requires analysis of the external condition at the time of operation, precisely for operation during longer periods. The circuit temperature at certain times may become extremely high, and performance of the filter at that condition requires a through inspection. This idea is the backbone of the present work, where redshift/blueshift of the filter passband is analytically computed for semiconductor based PhC over a wide range of temperature, and corresponding ripple is calculated in the passband region. In presence of different polarized incidence of e.m wave, filter spectrum is designed for different structural parameters and angle of incidences nearby the spectrum of 1550 nm central wavelength. Findings are perilously imperative for setting up the working boundaries of all-optical circuits considering the Joule heat dissipation.

2 Mathematical Formulation

For p-polarized electromagnetic wave incident on the first layer of the structure at angle θ_i, reflectivities at the interface may be put into the following form

$$r_{12} = -r_{21} = \frac{n_1 \cos(\theta_t) - n_2 \cos(\theta_i)}{n_1 \cos(\theta_t) + n_2 \cos(\theta_i)} \tag{1}$$

Similarly, for s-polarized incident wave,

$$r_{12} = -r_{21} = \frac{n_1 \cos(\theta_i) - n_2 \cos(\theta_t)}{n_1 \cos(\theta_i) + n_2 \cos(\theta_t)} \tag{2}$$

where n_1 and n_2 are the refractive indices of the layers of the unit cell. Hence, transfer matrix at any arbitrary interface

$$M_{1,2}^T = \frac{1}{t} \begin{pmatrix} 1 & r_{21(12)} \\ r_{21(12)} & 1 \end{pmatrix} \tag{3}$$

Introducing phase factor of the e.m field, propagation matrix can be represented as

$$W_{1,2} = \begin{pmatrix} \exp[j\beta_{1,2}l_{1,2}] & 0 \\ 0 & -\exp[j\beta_{1,2}l_{1,2}] \end{pmatrix} \tag{4}$$

where 'l_i' is the length of the ith layer where the electromagnetic wave propagated, and 'β_i' is considered as wavevector of this i^{th} layer. So for a unit cell with only two layers with length 'l_1' and 'l_2', corresponding refractive indices are 'n_1' and 'n_2'.

Diagram of the unit cell is given below (Fig. 1):

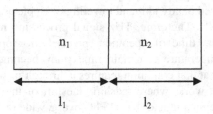

Fig. 1. Unit cell for the proposed filter

Taking into account these factors, we can evaluate the transfer matrix of the fundamental cell constituted by the ith and j^{th} layers. This value is represented by

$$J = J_1^{Tr} W_1 J_2^{Tr} W_2 \tag{5}$$

If the structure has 'Z' number of layers, then total transfer matrix

$$J_{tot} = J^Z \tag{6}$$

Transmission coefficient is given by

$$T = \frac{1}{[J_{11}(tot)]^2} \tag{7}$$

The temperature variation of refractive indices is considered as per the Adachi's model [28], and is therefore incorporated inside Eq. (7).

3 Results and Discussions

Using Eq. (7) along with Adachi's model, transmittivity of the 1D PhC is computed for different polarization conditions at different device temperatures. Figure 2 shows the bandwidth variation for 'p' and 's' polarized incidences only having $Al_xGa_{1-x}N/GaN$ compositon. In Fig. 2a, As temperature is slowly deviated (increased) and assuming the layer dimensions and material constitution are remained intact, the notch of the transmittivity profile along −ve Y axis (negative due to the fact that highest value of transmittivity is taken as 0 dB and set as reference) is getting increased. Thus a conclusive statement may be raised that rejection of noise capability becomes better with enhancement of chip temperature. Considering the desired bandpass region, we can found that the profile looks asymmetric i.e. rejection or filtration of noise is weaker as shorter value of transmittance speaks about lower SNR. In accordance with if we look inside the passband, we will find that magnitude of ripple is growing. Thus with increase in temperature, the conventional characteristics of Butterworth property starts deviating. It is observed that the whole spectrum is slowly shifted towards lower wavelength magnitude i.e. we can summarize this shift as blueshift of the passband spectrum. With decrease in the value of l_1, the notch length is increasing i.e. better noise rejection. Similar observations are made for s-polarized incidence, depicted in Fig. 2b.

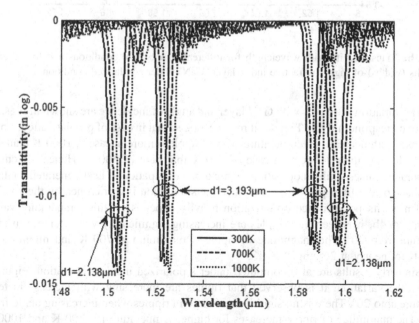

Fig. 2a. Transmittivity with wavelength for different device temperature conditions and for different lengths (widths) of higher refractive index layer (GaN) under p-polarized condition

From Fig. 3, it is shown that ripples are decreasing with increasing temperature in very slight manner. So, we can work on long range of temperature variation. Also the spectrum is shifted towards left with decreasing temperature, i.e., blueshift occurs. Moreover the notch length is enhanced with higher value of temperature. This ensures improvement of filter characteristics through higher noise rejection level.

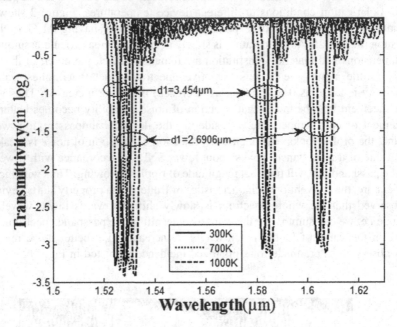

Fig. 2b. Transmittivity with wavelength for different temperature conditions and for different lengths (widths) of higher refractive index layer (GaN) under s-polarized condition

The variation of ripples with GaN layer and angle of incidence are shown in Figs. 4a and 4b correspondingly. In Fig. 4a, it may be looked that in case of p-polarization, ripple increases with decrease in temperature. That is ripple is more in case of 1000 K than that of 700 K and ripple is more in case of 700 K than that of 300 K. Hence the circuit temperature raises while in operation owing to the dissipation of heat generated controls the shape of the filter passband, and since the simulation is carried nearby the zone of 1550 n, so its performance optimization heavily depends on this temperature value. From Fig. 4b, it is seen that ripples are increasing significantly with increase in temperature from 20°. The magnitude of ripple is maximum at 700 K and minimum at 300 K for nearly at 26° angle.

Similarly results are also computed under s-polarized incident condition. Figure 5 shows the variation. It is observed that ripples are increasing with increase in temperature upto 20°. There is no significant change in ripples when increasing angle from 20°. The magnitude of ripple increases for higher temperature i.e. 700 K and 1000 K for the particular angle 16°.

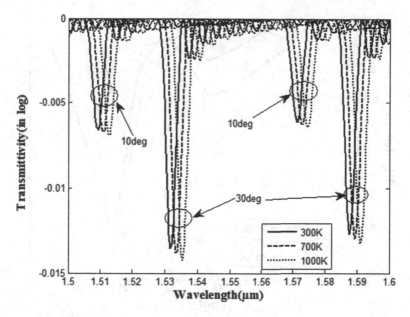

Fig. 3. Transmittivity under p-polarized wave incidence for the AlGaN/GaN structure with different angle of incidences

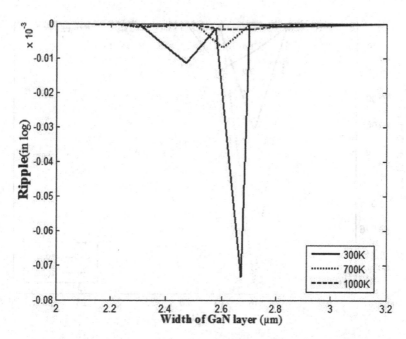

Fig. 4a. Ripple at passband with thickness of GaN layer under for p-polarized condition for different device temperatures

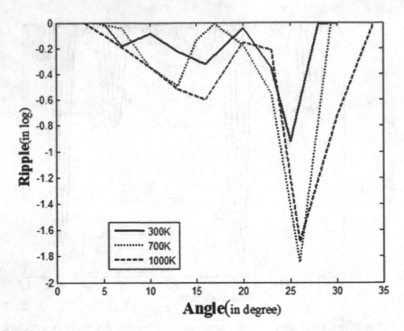

Fig. 4b. Ripple with angle of incidence for different temperatures under p-polarized condition

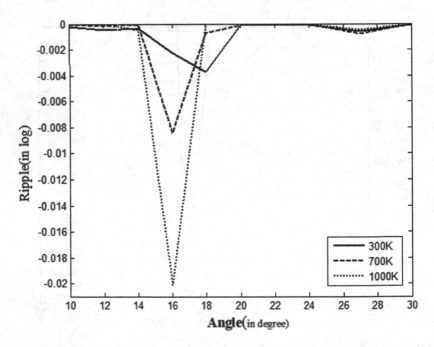

Fig. 5. Ripple with changing value of incidence angle for different temperatures for s-polarized wave

4   Conclusion

Through this simulation work, circuit temperature effect on the filter profile is theoretically analyzed and calculated in the 1550 nm spectra zone as this region is considered best for optical communication. In all-photonic circuit, realization of filter is essential from communication point of view, and Butterworth characteristic is mostly preferred for optical signal processing. Also it is customary to investigate the oblique incidence effect on the SNR performance as normal incidence is the near ideal phenomenon, and in the chip, electromagnetic wave incidence can't be externally controlled. Thus notch length in the two sides of the passband and ripple in side passband are simultaneously computed for performance evaluation, and dependence on dimensions of different layers and angle of incidence are varied along with possible rise of circuit temperature within feasible limit for optimized output. Results suggest that the optical filter can work upto a tolerable range of 1000 K without very much performance deviation, which is excellent considering the present progress of research in all-photonic IC replacing its optoelectronic complement. All the simulations are carried in such a way that bandwidth of the structure remains almost constant which is one of the elementary aims of filter design. This result will be experimentally realized in connection with Bragg grating based sensor fabrication.

References

1. Yablonovitch, E.: Inhibited spontaneous emission in solid-state physics and electronics. Phys. Rev. Lett. **58**, 2059–2061 (1987)
2. Zhang, C., Zhang, Z., Xu, X., Cai, W.: Thermally optimized polarization-maintaining photonic crystal fiber and its FOG application. Sensors **18**(2), 567 (2018)
3. Cavanna, A., Jiang, X., Taheri, M., Leuchs, G., Chekhova, M.V., Joly, N.Y.: Photonic crystal fiber designs for third-harmonic and photon triplet generation. In: Nonlinear Optics, OSA Technical Digest, paper NTh2A.7 (2017)
4. Moloudian, G., Sabbaghi-Nadooshan, R., Hassangholizadeh-Kashtiban, M.: Design of all-optical tunable filter based on two-dimensional photonic crystals for WDM (wave division multiplexing) applications. J. Chin. Inst. Eng. **39**(8), 971–976 (2016)
5. Saravi, S., Pertsch, T., Setzpfandt, F.: Photonic crystal waveguides as integrated sources of counterpropagating factorizable photon pairs. In: Conference on Lasers and Electro-Optics, OSA Technical Digest, paper FTh1G.2 (2018)
6. Salomoni, M., Pots, R., Auffray, E., Lecoq, P.: Enhancing light extraction of inorganic scintillators using photonic crystals. Crystals **8**(2), 78 (2018)
7. Nozaki, K., et al.: Forward-biased photonic crystal photodetector towards amplifier-free bias-free receiver. In: Conference on Lasers and Electro-Optics, OSA Technical Digest, paper STh4 N.1 (2017)
8. Zhu, E.Y., Rewcastle, C., Gad, R., Qian, L., Levi, O.: Ultrasound sensing with a photonic crystal slab. In: Conference on Lasers and Electro-Optics, OSA Technical Digest, paper JTh2A.98 (2018)
9. Iman, O., Rafah, N.: Ultralow-power all optical switch based on hybrid nonlinear photonic crystals. Sens. Lett. **15**(4), 315–319 (2017)

10. Xing, S., Kharitonov, S., Hu, J., Brès, C.: Fiber fuse in GeAsSe photonic crystal fiber and its impact on undamaged segment. In: Conference on Lasers and Electro-Optics, OSA Technical Digest, paper JTh2A.93 (2018)

11. Zhao, X., Yang, Y., Chen, Z., Wang, Y., Fei, H., Deng, X.: Ultra-wide tuning single channel filter based on one-dimensional photonic crystal with an air cavity. J. Semicond. **38**(2), 023004 (2017)

12. Liu, Y., Wang, S., Zhao, D., Zhou, W., Sun, Y.: High quality factor photonic crystal filter at $k \approx 0$ and its application for refractive index sensing. Opt. Express **25**, 10536–10545 (2017)

13. Kumar, S., Das, R.: Refractive index sensing with 1D photonic crystal. In: Frontiers in Optics, paper LTh2F.3 (2017)

14. Shams, H., Seeds, A.: Photonics, fiber and THz wireless communication. Opt. Photonics News **28**(3), 24–31 (2017)

15. Xu, X., Song, N., Zhang, Z., Cai, W., Gao, F.: High precision photonic crystal fiber optic gyroscope for space application. In: Asia Communications and Photonics Conference, paper Su1A.3 (2017)

16. Wang, B.L., Hsu, J.M.: Broadband dispersion compensating photonic crystal fiber with a high compensation ratio. In: International Conference on Advanced Materials for Science and Engineering (2016)

17. Kawanishi, S.: Optical signal processing in photonic crystal structures for high-speed optical transmission. In: Lasers and Electro-Optics - Pacific Rim (2007)

18. Vandoorne, K., et al.: Toward optical signal processing using Photonic Reservoir Computing. Opt. Express **16**(15), 11182–11192 (2008)

19. Konishi, T.: Diversity of optical signal processing led by optical signal form conversion. J. Phys: Conf. Ser. **206**(1), 012013 (2010)

20. Alipour-Banaei, H., Tabrizi, A.A.: Design and analysis of all optical switch based on photonic crystal microcavity. In: International Conference on Nanotechnology and Biosensors, pp. 33–37 (2010)

21. Yu, Y., et al.: All-optical signal processing using InP photonic-crystal nanocavity switches. In: 16th International Conference on Transparent Optical Networks (2014)

22. Kibria, R., Austin, M.W.: All optical signal-processing techniques utilizing four-wave mixing. Photonics **2**, 200–213 (2015)

23. Serajmohammadi, S., Absalan, H.: All optical NAND gate based on nonlinear photonic crystal ring resonator. Inf. Process. Agric. **3**(2), 119–123 (2016)

24. Martelli, C., Canning, J., Groothoff, N., Lyytikainen, K.: Strain and temperature characterization of photonic crystal fiber Bragg gratings. Opt. Lett. **30**, 1785–1787 (2005)

25. Yu, Y., et al.: Some features of the photonic crystal fiber temperature sensor with liquid ethanol filling. Opt. Express **18**, 15383–15388 (2010)

26. Lang, B., Oulton, R., Beggs, D.M.: Optimised photonic crystal waveguide for chiral light-matter interactions. J. Opt. **19**, 045001 (2017)

27. Kim, Y.H., Song, K.Y.: Characterization of nonlinear temperature dependence of Brillouin dynamic grating spectra in polarization-maintaining fibers. J. Lightwave Technol. **33**, 4922–4927 (2015)

28. Adachi, S.: GaAs, AlAs, and AlxGa1-xAs: material parameters for use in research and device applications. J. Appl. Phys. **58**, R1–R29 (1985)

A Propose System of an Efficient Power Regeneration Technique in Automobile Using Arduino UNO

Debabrata Chowdhury[✉], Sudipta Paul, Rohan Ghosh,
Anusree Kundu, and Tamoghna Ghosh

Department of Information Technology,
Kalyani Government Engineering College, Kalyani, West Bengal, India
debabrata.chowdhury@gmail.com

Abstract. Studies on alternative methods of fuel for Vehicles has become need of hour due to limitations of fuel based energy, price of fuel and global warming. One of the alternative that has already gained importance is electric vehicle. Research fraternity have already started working on development of fuel efficient hybrid electrical vehicles. The current generation of electrical vehicle runs on a battery that needs to be charged frequently in either charging stations or home before they can be used. The major components of any electric vehicles are battery technology, charger design, motor, steering, braking etc. One of the major disadvantage is that the power generation in electric vehicle is nil and hence the travelling distance shortens for these type of vehicles. This again is a cause of concern as electric as an energy is also reducing and causing global warming in general. This paper proposes a system for design of a power regeneration system for the electric vehicles. The proposed approach will not only increase the range of the travelling distance of an electric vehicle but also become fuel efficient. Another motive is to make an automatic vehicle power management system which will run without the human intervention using Arduino. The work is tested in different scenarios and results reported.

Keywords: Electrical vehicles · Power regeneration · Arduino UNO · Automobile system

1 Introduction

Electrical Vehicles (EVs) first came into existence in the middle of 19th century, when electricity was among the preferred methods for motor vehicle propulsion, to provide more comfortable and easy operation better than the cars run by bio fuel. Modern internal combustion engines are supplying power to motor vehicles for around 100 years, but electric power is also being used in nowadays in vehicles, like trains and smaller vehicles of all types [1]. In the 21st century, EVs and HEVs saw reappearance due to technological developments and an increased focus on renewable energy [2]. In United States and European countries, the popularity of EV is increasing rapidly as a result of direct or indirect Government support. Meanwhile, high fuel duty taxes and

© Springer Nature Singapore Pte Ltd. 2019
J. K. Mandal et al. (Eds.): CICBA 2018, CCIS 1030, pp. 361–377, 2019.
https://doi.org/10.1007/978-981-13-8578-0_29

higher crude oil prices has also compelled automobile companies to develop EV so that there is less emission and provide higher fuel economy.

Road EVs are generally vehicles that involves electric propulsion [3–5]. EVs can be broadly classified into three types: pure electric vehicles (PEVs), hybrid electric vehicles (HEVs), and fuel cell electric vehicles (FCEVs). Literature survey suggests that field-oriented control (FOC) and variable-voltage variable frequency (VVVF) are adopted widely. However, the initial cost of battery and its management create bottleneck in PEVs though it has considerable less amount emission. The HEVs are considered as the interim solution and FCEV has long-term potential for future main stream vehicles [6–11]. In case of Hybrid Electric Vehicle (HEV) or Electric Vehicles (EV) it is found that though it is efficient in fuel but it has very less or almost zero ability of power regeneration. Further efficient energy management system (EMS) is being used to perform the monitoring work of power flows from source to destination. It is also being used as a tool for minimize the energy consumption. Here, Arduino has an important role to play for controlling the system to manage the power utilization strategy, in specially for parallel HEVs and EVs. The Arduino controller are mainly used to monitor and control the energy generation and consumption of the system [12]. This paper mainly focuses at using and modifying the current EVs to increase the range of the travelling distance by reducing energy wastage using Arduino.

The rest of the paper is organized as follows: Sect. 2 provides an overview of electrical vehicles and its working principle. Section 3 in general discusses the basic units for finding battery performance and characterization. The architecture of the proposed system is detailed in Sect. 4. This section also shows the formulation for finding out the total time taken for charging. Section 5 gives the different components of the proposed system with a discussion of the its implementation using Arduino UNO in Sect. 6. The results and performance measure of the proposed prototype is detailed in Sect. 7, which is followed by conclusion in Sect. 8.

2 The Electric Vehicle

An electric vehicle uses one or more electric motors for propulsion. Its source of power may be a collector system by electricity from off-vehicle sources, or may be self-contained with a battery, solar panels or an electric generator that converts fuel to electricity [1]. EVs can be seen in the form of road and rail vehicles, surface and underwater vessels, electric aircraft and electric spacecraft. The next section details the different components of an Electric vehicle.

2.1 Components of an Electric Vehicle

2.1.1 The Battery

Batteries are the power source of most electric vehicles [8]. The batteries are charged and then used to drive the vehicle. There are different kinds of batteries that can be used in EVs, such as Lead Acid, lithium ion, Solid state, aluminum ion, lithium sulfur, and metal-air etc.

2.1.2 The Motor Controller
This monitors the power distribution. It also governs the operation of motors, batteries, accelerator pedal etc. It has microprocessor that controls the current to the motors that helps to change the driving style.

2.1.3 The Electric Engine
It is the power house of the electric car. It can be operated on either AC or DC current. AC motors are less expensive and lighter than DC engines. AC engines are more common and it has reduced number of moving parts, may suffer from less mechanical wear and tear. AC technology requires a more sophisticated controller.

2.1.4 Regenerative Braking
To enhance the range of vehicles, the regenerative braking system has become very popular today in EV. Here the energy produced while applying the brake, is reused to reduce the wastage of energy [3]. When the user applies the brake, the electric motor goes into reverse mode, allowing the motor itself to do most of the "braking" and thus prevent more kinetic energy from being lost. In the conventional system the energy is wasted due to friction between brake and wheel.

2.1.5 The Drive System
The drive system's function is to transfer mechanical energy to the traction wheels, generating motion. In that case different types of arrangement may be done depending upon the components and the use [19]. For example, a large electric motor may be coupled to the rear wheels using a differential housing. In some designs, multiple smaller motors power each wheel individually.

2.2 Energy Efficiency and Environmental Impact

The main benefit of electric vehicle is its impact on environment is very less compared to conventional fuel run vehicles. As the EVs don't have any kind of emission, the pollution caused by them is negligible. The electric vehicles are eco-friendly [22]. Besides, use of EVs may reduce the use of bio fuels which are non-renewable. The EVs are energy efficient; the power can be turned off when the car is idle, which is not suitable for conventional cars.

2.3 The Working of Electric Car

Electric car is given power form the rechargeable batteries installed inside the car. These batteries are also used for the functioning of wipers and lights. Electric cars also lacks exhaust system. They don't have any gas tank, as they do not use fuel for locomotion or propelling the engines. The battery packs are the same kind of batteries that are commonly used to start a gasoline engine. The only difference is, they also store energy that is used in powering the vehicle [6]. A regulator on the batteries to ensure energy amount produced and that which is consumed by the car is constant.

One of the major differences is the electric motor. There are three types of them available in the market: DC brushless with top speed, AC induction with the best acceleration and permanent magnet motor. These motors are used in creating an electric vehicle.

The three main components of electric car are:- Electric motor, Controller and Battery. When the switch is on, the current is passed from the battery. The controller takes power from the battery and passes it on to the electric motor. Before that, the controller converts the 300 V DC into a maximum of 240 V AC, 2 phase power which is suitable for motor. After getting current, the electric motor converts electrical energy to mechanical energy [4]. The mechanical energy helps to move the vehicle forward. There are some Variable potentiometers connected between accelerator and the controller. These potentiometers tell the controller how much power it is supposed to deliver. When the accelerator is released it delivers 0 V and when they are fully pressed, it gives maximum output.

3   Basic Units for Battery Performance and Characterization

An EV may have more than one pack of battery situated in a different location in the car. The basic terms for battery performance and characterization are as given below.

3.1   Ampere-hour Capacity

Ampere-hour (Ah) capacity is the total charge that can be discharged from a fully charged battery under specified conditions. The conditions are predefined by the manufacturer. A nominal condition, for example, can be defined as 20 °C and discharging at 1/20 C-rate. To represent a battery capacity, Wh (or kWh) capacity is also used. The rated Wh capacity is defined as:

$$Rated\ Wh\ Capacity = Rated\ Ah\ Capacity * Rated\ Battery\ Voltage \qquad (1)$$

3.2   C-rate

C(nominal C-rate) is used to represent a charge or discharge rate equal to the capacity of a battery in one hour. For a 1.6 Ah battery, C is equal to charge or discharge the battery at 1.6 A.

3.3   Internal Resistance

Internal resistance is the overall equivalent resistance within the battery. It is different for charging and discharging and may vary as the operating condition changes.

3.4 Peak Power

According to the U.S. Advanced Battery Consortium (USABC)'s definition, the peak power is defined as

$$P = \frac{2V^2oc}{9R} \tag{2}$$

Where, Voc is the open-circuit voltage and R is the internal resistance of battery. The peak power is actually defined at the condition when the terminal voltage is 2/3 of the open-circuit voltage.

3.5 Cut-off Voltage

Cut-off voltage is the minimum allowable voltage defined by the manufacturer. It can be interpreted as the "empty" state of the battery.

3.6 State of Charge (SOC)

SOC is defined as the remaining capacity of a battery and it is affected by its operating conditions such as load current and temperature.

$$\text{SOC} = \text{Remaining Capacity/Rated Capacity} \tag{3}$$

If the Ah capacity is used, the change of SOC can be expressed as

$$\Delta \text{SOC} = \text{SOC(t)} - \text{SOC}(t_0) \tag{4}$$

SOC is a critical condition parameter for battery management. Accurate gauging of SOC is very challenging, but the key to the healthy and safe operation of batteries.

3.7 Depth of Discharge (DOD)

DOD is used to indicate the percentage of the total battery capacity that has been discharged. For deep-cycle batteries, they can be discharged to 80% or higher of DOD.

$$\text{DOD} = 1 - \text{SOC} \tag{5}$$

3.8 Cycle Life (Number of Cycles)

Cycle life is the number of discharge–charge cycles the battery can handle at a specific DOD (normally 80%) before it fails to meet specific performance criteria. The actual operating life of the battery is affected by the charging and discharging rates, DOD, and other conditions such as temperature. The higher the DOD, the shorter the cycle life. To achieve a higher cycle life, a larger battery can be used for a lower DOD during normal operations.

4 Architecture of the Proposed Power Regeneration System

A complete solution for designing energy efficient smart car is given in this paper. To reduce the wastage of energy we need to modify the self-generation technique of producing energy in vehicle. In the vehicle considered for the experimental setup as given in Fig. 1, there are two batteries (b_1, b_2) to supply power and two motors (m_1, m_2) are attached to rear wheels. Battery b_1 will run motor m_1 and b_2 runs motor m_2. The motors m_1 and m_2 are coupled together using a connector. The batteries, motors and the sensors will be controlled by a microcontroller, called Arduino which will be installed in the car. The next section details the basic methodology of the proposed system.

4.1 Basic Methodology

The two motors are connected or joined to each other with the help of connector as in the Fig. 1 below. At a time only one battery will supply power to one motor that will help the vehicle to run. The main concept is when one battery (b_1) supplies power to a motor (m_1), it runs the vehicle as well as rotates shaft of the other motor (motor 2) connected with it. Then the motor (m_2) acts like a generator and converts mechanical energy to electrical energy that charges the battery (b_2) connected to the generator (m_2). In this case, it can be observed that current flows from b_1 to b_2. In this scenario, b_1 is discharged and b_2 is charged, m_1 is acting like a motor, while m_2 is acting like a generator. This system is depicted in the Fig. 1 below:

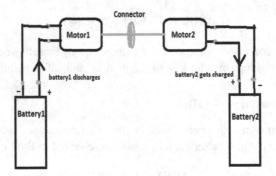

Fig. 1. Discharging of battery1 and charging of battery2

After a certain amount of time when the charge level or SOC of battery1 (b_1) comes to a particular level, battery1 (b_1) is stopped discharging and battery 2 (b_2) is allowed to discharge. That means, now the battery2 will supply current to motor2 resulting the rotation of motor2 shaft which in turn, will help to move the car and will rotate the shaft of motor1. Now, motor1 acts like a generator and converts mechanical energy to electrical energy that charges the battery1. At this stage, it can be observed current flows from battery2 to battery1. This system is showed in this Fig. 2 below.

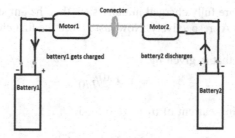

Fig. 2. Discharging of battery2 and charging of battery1

Again when the SOC of battery2 reaches a particular level, the battery1 again is allowed to enter the discharging state whereas battery2 enters the charging state. Thus a charging and discharging cycle is formed. This charging and discharging cycle continues until the batteries reach to a certain amount of charge level or to a no. of charging and discharging cycles. After that, both the batteries supply power to motors individually until they are drained completely. The main fact is that, the vehicle runs continuously as at any instant either one of those motors gets power from battery.

It can be seen from Figs. 1 and 2 that there will be two different electrical circuits. The first one consists of battery1 and motor1 and the second one consists of battery2 and motor2. These two circuits can be controlled by a switch. The change of direction of current flow in the circuits is done with the help of a switching device called 2 channel Relay module that is controlled by Arduino Uno microcontroller. To control the switch and its timing, a program is written and uploaded to the Arduino.

4.2   Formulation the Total Charging Time of the Proposed System

This section formulates the total charging time of the proposed system. For finding the total charging time first we need to understand the battery charging and discharging time.

Battery Charging Time: Charging time of a battery is given the proportionate of battery ampere hour (Ah) and charging current as given in equation below:

$$Tc = \frac{Ah}{Ic} \tag{6}$$

Battery Discharging Time: Similarly, battery discharge time is given by proportionate of battery ampere hour (Ah) and discharging charging current as given in equation below:

$$Tc = \frac{Ah}{Id} \tag{7}$$

Let both the batteries are fully charged initially such that the ampere hour of battery b_1 is A_1 and battery b2 is A_2 respectively. Now just before the first charge of b_1 is reduced by $x_0\%$.

So time taken for that is given by:

$$t_1 = A_1 * {}^{x0}\!/\!_{Id0} \tag{8}$$

where, I_{d0} = discharging current of b_1 at zero load.

$$\text{So charge level of } b_1 \text{ is } A_1 = A_1 * (1 - x_0) \tag{9}$$

From the next cycle the charging and discharging cycle start. Now b2 is discharged by $x_1\%$.

$$\text{So time taken to discharge } (t_2) = A_2 * x_1/i_{d2} \tag{10}$$

where I_{d2} = discharging current of b_2 when m1 and m2 are connected.

$$\text{So charge level of } b_2 \text{ is } A_2 = A_2 * (1 - x_1) \tag{11}$$

Now it will charge b_1 by t_2 time.
So charge level of b_1 is

$$\begin{aligned} A_1 &= A_1 * (1 - x_1) + t_2 * I_c, \\ &= A_1 * (1 - x_1) + (A_2 * x_1/I_{d2}) * i_c \end{aligned} \quad \text{[derived from by (10)]} \tag{12}$$

where, I_c = charging current generated by m1 for b1.
After that, b1 will again discharged by $x_2\%$.

$$\text{So time taken to discharge } (t_3) = A_1 * x_2/i_{d1} \tag{13}$$

where i_{d1} = discharging current of b1 when m1 and m2 are connected.

$$\text{Thus, } (t_3) = A_1 * (1 - x_2) * x_2/i_{d1} \quad \text{[derived from (9)]} \tag{14}$$

By this time b2 will be charged for time amount t3.
So now charge of b2 will be

$$\begin{aligned} A_2 &= A_2 + t_3 * i_{c2} \\ &= A_2 * (1 - x) + (A_1 * (1 - x) * x/id_1) * ic_2 \end{aligned} \quad \text{[derived from by (10), (13)]} \tag{15}$$

where, i_{c2} = charging current generated by m2 for b2.
Thus the first cycle of charging and discharging completes. Now the total amount of time elapsed so far from the above is

$$t = t_1 + t_2 + t_3 \tag{16}$$

This cycle will be repeated until the batteries reach a definite charge level (say n). The value of x considered here is 1%, this value has been obtained empirically by experiment. An experiment is performed taking x = 1% and the results are reported in Sect. 7.

4.3 Comparison Between Existing Power Regeneration System with Proposed System

Recently different types of electric vehicle power regeneration systems are there. In these all system mainly researchers are focusing on regeneration from regenerative braking system. Some limitations are to regeneration, it mainly depends upon the braking frequency as well as braking inertia of the vehicle. It is mainly converts some part of kinetic energy to electric energy while decelerating. So number of braking is the regeneration source of electric [13, 14]. In proposed system there is a scope to regeneration while system is in running condition and it will be optimized the power regeneration automatically. Electric Vehicle Energy Harvesting/Regeneration is the another key factor in research field. There are several way to power harvesting from uncommon sources like Electrodynamics, Photovoltaic, Turboelectric, Dielectric Elastomer Generator etc. It is shown how some are being proved in applications such as wave power but vehicle applications are in the roadmaps such as tires, sails, boat hulls and airship fabric that generate electricity and how many will combine into structural electronics. Components-in-a-box gives way to more reliable, more compact, lighter weight smart structural materials. It is all here. Electric vehicles are creating more and more of their own electricity from daylight, wind and other sources including regeneration. So in common way there are lot of limitations are found [5, 6]. In proposed system we are regenerating power in day-night session or independent factors of wind and others existing regenerating methods.

5 Components of the Proposed System

The lists of components with its detail, that are required to make this system prototype are described below.

5.1 Hardware Used

In this section, we will discuss about the different hardware used in the proposed system:

5.1.1 Model Car

The Model Car is a small representation of an automobile. Basically, the lower portion of the model car is needed for our project. The base of the car is used to install all the hardware elements of the project. The two back wheels is powered by motors.

5.1.2   Motor

Two motors are needed in our project. The motors are connected to separate batteries. These motors are also a main part of the "Dynamo process" of our project.

5.1.3   Gear System

The gear system is installed in our system to transmit power from motor to wheels. Two motors are coupled to each other using a pulley. When one battery is giving power to its particular motor, through the system the other motor is rotated, that recharges the other battery.

5.1.4   Rechargeable Batteries

Two rechargeable batteries are required in this project. The batteries are used to give power to their corresponding motors. While one battery is discharging, the other one is getting charged at the same time. For our project, we will be using two 4 V Lead Acid batteries.

5.1.5   Arduino Uno

Arduino is a microcontroller. It can be used to control electrical and electronic devices by sending digital or analog inputs to the devices. We are using the Arduino Uno board as the main controller of our project. Until now, the board is used to control the motors through "2 channel Relay", an obstacle sensor to detect any obstacle and for voltage sensing of batteries.

5.1.6   2-Channel Relay Module

Basically it is used as a switch that can control high voltage as well as low voltage circuits. Here we have used a 5 V, 10 A 2-Channel Relay interface board. It can be controlled directly with 3.3 V or 5 V logic signals from a microcontroller like Arduino Uno.

5.1.7   A Set of Resistances

It is the opposition to the flow of electric current. It is represented by the uppercase letter R. The standard unit of resistance is the ohm, and symbol is the omega (Ω).

5.2   Software Used

This section details the different software used in the design of the proposed system:

5.2.1   Arduino Sketch

A sketch is the name that Arduino uses for a program. It's the unit of code that is uploaded to and run on an Arduino board. Arduino consists of both a physical programmable circuit board (microcontroller) and a piece of software, or IDE (Integrated Development Environment) that runs on computer, used to write and upload computer code to the physical board.

5.2.2   Dev C++ Compiler

It is a free full-featured integrated development environment (IDE) for programming in C and C++. We have used this IDE to perform some calculations.

5.2.3   Windows 8.1 Operating System

It is the OS of the host computer of the Arduino Sketch.

6   Implementation Using Arduino UNO

The implementation of the proposed system using Arduino UNO is detailed in this section. The system has a motor channel with 2-relay module and.

6.1   Motor Control with 2-Channel Relay Module

This relay module has 4 inputs, Vcc, Gnd, IN1 and IN2. Vcc is connected to 5 V of Arduino Uno and Gnd pin is connected to Gnd pin of Arduino Uno. IN1 and IN2 are connected to analog pin 7 and 8 of Arduino Uno. Arduino feeds digital input HIGH or LOW (form its analog pin 7 & 8) to the relay through IN1 and IN2 to turn off and on the 2 channels. Apart from that each channel has three (3) pins, NO (normally open), COM (common), NC (normally closed). By default NC and COM are connected and when an input LOW is given from Arduino through input pin IN1 or IN2, the connection between COM and NC is lost and NO gets connection with COM. Again on the input HIGH through input pin IN1 or IN2 from Arduino, the connection between NC and COM is established and COM is disconnected from NO as detailed in Fig. 3. Thus the relay can be used as a switch to control any other circuit. For each channel the battery positive line is connected to NO, one of the motor pin is connected to COM and the other motor pin is connected to battery negative line. In this way the battery will be discharged.

Again to charge the batteries, the NC pin of each channel is connected to the positive line of each battery, through a p-n junction diode. The diodes will prevent the batteries from discharging through the NC pins as they are connected to the batteries in reverse bias. The diodes will allow flow of current from channel's NC pins to batteries. This way the battery will be charged as given in Fig. 3.

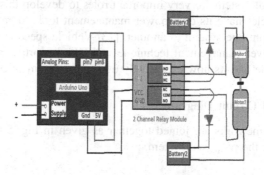

Fig. 3. Motor control with relay using Arduino Uno

6.2   Voltage Measurement

The voltages of the batteries have to be measured regularly to perform, the switching operation between the circuits. Arduino analog inputs are used to measure DC voltage between 0 and 5 V. But the voltage level above 5 V can't be measured by arduino directly. So to measure more than 5 V the concept of voltage divider is used. The voltage divider reduces the voltage to a level that arduino can measure. As depicted in Fig. 4. Then a calculation is performed in the code for the voltage measurement in arduino to have the actual voltage. This allows voltages greater than 5 V to be measured. Since we are using two 4 V batteries so we directly measuring voltage of them by connecting the +ve side of battery to the Analog pin of arduino and −ve pin to the ground of arduino.

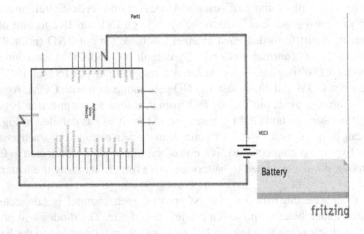

Fig. 4. Circuit for battery voltage sensing using Arduino Uno

Design and implementation of a battery monitoring system as well as power management control system are very important roles to develop this proposed system. Many hybrid vehicles have its own power management tools to get optimized power while switching from one system to another. [23] Vehicle speed and load are another factor to when power management technique will take important role. Arduino controller does this role and its now extensively used in power management tool.

6.3   The Overall Circuit Diagram

The above two frameworks are joined together as given in Fig. 5 to give the overall circuit diagram for the proposed system.

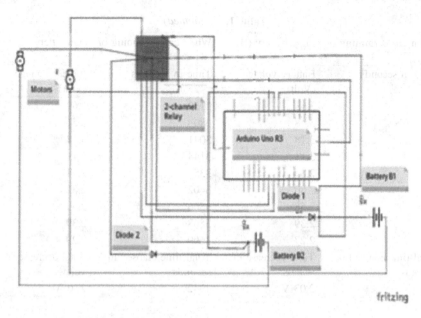

Fig. 5. Circuit diagram integrating all the components of the car

7 Results and Performance Comparison

The performance of the proposed system is found out using several set of experimentation and reported as given in Tables 1 and 2. The discharge graph of battery when only battery b_1 is used and when both batteries b_1 and b_2 are used is shown in Fig. 6.

Table 1. Experimental values of battery b1 discharging time

When car is running on single battery (B1)		When car is running on both battery (B1 & B2)	
Time in seconds	Battery voltage (Volt)	Time in seconds	Battery voltage (Volt)
5	4.30	2267	4.30
35	4.20	2473	4.20
70	4.14	2535	4.16
95	4.13	2577	4.13
125	4.06	2628	4.06
155	4.03	2649	4.02
185	3.93	2680	3.92
215	3.91	2690	3.89
245	3.81	2711	3.82

(*continued*)

Table 1. (*continued*)

When car is running on single battery (B1)		When car is running on both battery (B1 & B2)	
Time in seconds	Battery voltage (Volt)	Time in seconds	Battery voltage (Volt)
275	3.68	2752	3.69
305	3.48	2804	3.51
335	3.18	3041	3.18
365	3.11	3144	3.11
395	2.83	3351	2.94
425	2.80	3402	2.82
455	2.58	3506	2.59
485	2.39	3568	2.39
515	2.27	3609	2.29
Total time elapsed in seconds	Total decrease in voltage	Total time elapsed in seconds	Total decrease in voltage
510	2.03 V	1342	2.01 V

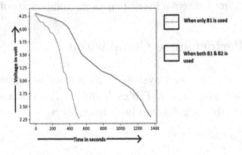

Fig. 6. Discharge graph of battery b_1

Table 2. Experimental values of battery b2 discharging time

When car is running on single battery (B2)		When car is running on both battery (B1 & B2)	
Time in seconds	Battery voltage (Volt)	Time in seconds	Battery voltage (Volt)
5	4.30	2260	4.30
35	4.20	2470	4.20
70	4.14	2538	4.16
95	4.12	2579	4.13
125	4.06	2626	4.06
155	4.03	2638	4.02
185	3.92	2718	3.92

(*continued*)

Table 2. (*continued*)

When car is running on single battery (B2)		When car is running on both battery (B1 & B2)	
Time in seconds	Battery voltage (Volt)	Time in seconds	Battery voltage (Volt)
215	3.91	2696	3.89
245	3.81	2716	3.82
275	3.68	2757	3.69
305	3.47	2800	3.51
335	3.18	3046	3.18
365	3.11	3144	3.11
395	2.81	3354	2.94
425	2.80	3406	2.82
455	2.56	3505	2.59
485	2.35	3569	2.39
515	2.28	3630	2.29
Total time elapsed in seconds	Total decrease in voltage	Total time elapsed in seconds	Total decrease in voltage
510	2.02 V	1370	2.01 V

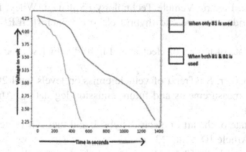

Fig. 7. Discharge graph of battery b_2

From the above Tables 1 and 2 and graphs of Figs. 6 and 7 it is clearly visible that when both batteries b_1 and b_2 are used in the way described in the power generation section to drive the car, then it takes more time to decrease the same amount of voltage of the batteries than that of the system when b_1 and b_2 are used separately. So the car having the system will cover more distance. Thus the aforementioned system is efficient with respect to energy and travelling distance covered.

8   Conclusion

The advent of the all-electric vehicle is destined to have a significant impact on the future not only of road transport but also to the motor industry itself. It will change the structure of the car-production supply chain and the ratio of semiconductor components to purely mechanical parts. The traditional design pattern of the conventional car with an internal combustion engine, gear box and heavy mechanical power distribution to the front and/or rear wheels will become obsolete. Proposed system is definitely a new concept to regeneration of power without braking condition or day-night variable factors. The technology or prototype put forward in this paper proves that by using same charge, batteries car traverses more distance than using single battery one after one. Electric vehicles represent a major part of this change and the achievement of its objectives will mark a milestone in the history vehicle. These EVs are definitely more environmentally friendly than internal-combustion vehicles and hybrid vehicles. Batteries are being engineered to have a long life. As the electric cars use become more widespread, battery recycling will become economically more feasible. Research into other energy sources such as fuel cells and renewable energy like solar cell makes the future look brighter for electric vehicles.

References

1. James, L., John, L.: Electric Vehicle Technology Explained. Wiley, England (2003)
2. Jones, W.D.: Hybrids to the rescue [hybrid electric vehicles]. IEEE Spectr. **40**(1), 70–71 (2003)
3. Chan, C.C.: The state of the art of electric and hybrid vehicles. Proc. IEEE **90**(2), 247–275 (2002)
4. Rexeis, M., Hausberger, S.: Trend of vehicle emission levels until 2020—prognosis based on current vehicle measurements and future emission legislation. Atmos. Environ. **43**(31), 4689–4698 (2009)
5. Chan, C.C.: The state of the art of electric, hybrid, and fuel cell vehicles. Proc. IEEE **95**(4), 704–718 (2007). Article ID 4168013
6. Chan, C.C., Bouscayrol, A., Chen, K.: Electric, hybrid, and fuel-cell vehicles: architectures and modeling. IEEE Trans. Veh. Technol. **59**(2), 589–598 (2010). Article ID 5276874
7. Chan, C.C., Wong, Y.S.: Electric vehicles charge forward. IEEE Power Energ. Mag. **2**(6), 24–33 (2004)
8. Campanari, S., Manzolini, G., Garcia de la Iglesia, F.: Energy analysis of electric vehicles using batteries or fuel cells through well-to-wheel driving cycle simulations. J. Power Sources **186**(2), 464–477 (2009)
9. Sandy Thomas, C.E.: Transportation options in a carbon-constrained world: hybrids, plug-in hybrids, biofuels, fuel cell electric vehicles, and battery electric vehicles. Int. J. Hydrogen Energy **34**(23), 9279–9296 (2009)
10. Eaves, S., Eaves, J.: A cost comparison of fuel-cell and battery electric vehicles. J. Power Sources **130**(1–2), 208–212 (2004)
11. Offer, G.J., Howey, D., Contestabile, M., Clague, R., Brandon, N.P.: Comparative analysis of battery electric, hydrogen fuel cell and hybrid vehicles in a future sustainable road transport system. Energy Policy **38**(1), 24–29 (2010)

12. Scharich, N., et al.: Battery management system using Arduino. In: 2017 IEEE Technology & Engineering Management Conference (TEMSCON). IEEE (2017)

13. Nagalakshmi, S., et al.: Design and implementation of Aurdino based smart home energy management system using renewable energy resources. Int. J. ChemTech Res. CODEN (USA) 10(6), 696–701 (2017). ISSN 0974-4290. ISSN (Online) 2455-9555

14. Moreno, J., Ortúzar, M.E., Dixon, J.W.: Energy-management system for a hybrid electric vehicle, using ultracapacitors and neural networks. IEEE Trans. Industr. Electron. 53(2), 614–623 (2006)

15. Patil, S.K.: Regenerative braking system in automobiles. Int. J. Res. Mech. Eng. Technol. 2, 45–46 (2012)

16. Allan, R.: Energy harvesting and regeneration embraced by auto industry (2018). Electronic Design. http://www.electronicdesign.com/automotive/energy-harvesting-and-regeneration-embraced-auto-industry. Accessed 28 Apr 2018

17. IDTechEx Ltd. Electric Vehicle Energy Harvesting/Regeneration 2017–2037. https://www.idtechex.com/research/reports/electric-vehicle-energy-harvesting-regeneration-2017-2037-000495.asp. Accessed 28 Apr 2018

18. Elsaed, Y., et al.: Development of a robust hybrid vehicle power management control system. Int. J. Eng. Tech. Res. V4 (2015). https://doi.org/10.17577/ijertv4is030651

19. Tie, S.F., Tan, C.W.: A review of power and energy management strategies in electric vehicles. In: 2012 4th International Conference on Intelligent and Advanced Systems (ICIAS2012), pp. 412–417 (2012)

20. Chen, H., Lu, F., Guo, F.: Power management system design for small size solar-electric vehicle. In: 2012 IEEE 7th International Power Electronics and Motion Control Conference-ECCE Asia, pp. 2658–2662 (2012)

21. Ganji, B., Kouzani, A.Z.: A study on look-ahead control and energy management strategies in hybrid electric vehicles. In: 2010 8th IEEE International Conference on Control and Automation (ICCA), pp. 388–392 (2010)

22. Kebriaei, M., Niasar, A.H., Asaei, B.: Hybrid electric vehicles: an overview. In: 2015 International Conference on Connected Vehicles and Expo (ICCVE). IEEE (2015)

23. Model car. https://en.wikipedia.org/wiki/Model_car. Accessed 28 Apr 2018

24. Arduino Uno. https://en.wikipedia.org/wiki/Arduino_Uno. Accessed 28 Apr 2018

25. Arduino - Sketch (n.d.). https://www.arduino.cc/en/Tutorial/Sketch. Accessed 28 Apr 2018

26. Electric Motor. https://en.wikipedia.org/wiki/Electric_motor. Accessed 28 Apr 2018

27. Regenerative brake. https://en.wikipedia.org/wiki/Regenerative_brake. Accessed 28 Apr 2018

28. Young, K., Wang, C., Wang, L.Y., Strunz, K.: Electric vehicle battery technologies. In: Garcia-Valle, R., Peças Lopes, J. (eds.) Electric Vehicle Integration into Modern. PEPS, pp. 15–56. Springer, New York (2013). https://doi.org/10.1007/978-1-4614-0134-6_2

Microelectronics, Sensors, and Intelligent Networks

Quantum Inspired Genetic Algorithm for Relay Node Placement in Cluster Based Wireless Sensor Networks

Gopendra Vikram Singh, Subash Harizan, and Pratyay Kuila[✉]

Department of Computer Science and Engineering,
National Institute of Technology, Ravangla 737139, Sikkim, India
gopendra.99@gmail.com, subashharizan@gmail.com, pratyay_kuila@yahoo.com

Abstract. Efficient deployment of relay nodes with coverage of all the sensor nodes along with connectivity is very challenging for cluster based wireless sensor networks (WSNs). In this paper, we have proposed a Quantum-Inspired Genetic Algorithm (QIGA) based relay node placement for cluster based WSNs. The algorithm places minimum number of relay nodes to coverage of all the sensor nodes by the placed relay nodes or cluster heads (CHs) and simultaneously, connectivity amongst the relay nodes is also ensured. We have also formulated Linear programming (LP) for the problem. A suitable quantum-chromosome representation and efficient derivation of fitness is given. We perform extensive simulation on the proposed algorithm and obtained results show better performance.

Keywords: Wireless sensor networks ·
Quantum inspired genetic algorithm (QIGA) · Cluster heads (CHs) ·
Coverage and connectivity

1 Introduction

Nowadays, wireless sensor networks (WSNs) have become very popular for their tremendous role in real-life applications such as environmental monitoring, military surveillance, health care, disaster management, etc. [1]. WSNs consist of large number of sensor nodes that can sense the target/region and forward the sensed data to the base station (BS) directly or via other sensor nodes. In most of the large applications, the large number of deployed sensor nodes are grouped into clusters [2,3]. Each cluster consists of a leader node or cluster head (CH) and member sensor nodes. The CHs collect the data from their member sensor nodes, aggregate the data and transmitting it to the base station (BS) directly or via other CHs. Due to the energy constraints of the sensor nodes and extra work load of the CHs, many researchers have suggested to use some less energy-constrained node, relay nodes or gateways to act as CH [4–8]. Note that the sensor nodes have also limited communication and sensing range. Therefore, coverage of the sensor nodes by the placed relay nodes or gateways is very important for proper

© Springer Nature Singapore Pte Ltd. 2019
J. K. Mandal et al. (Eds.): CICBA 2018, CCIS 1030, pp. 381–391, 2019.
https://doi.org/10.1007/978-981-13-8578-0_30

functioning of the network. Moreover, the relay nodes have also limited communication range and thereby communication between the placed relay nodes is also essential for data communication with the BS.

It is noteworthy that, the relay node placement problem with clustering in WSNs is NP-hard [9]. Therefore, contrary to the traditional heuristic algorithm, a meta-heuristic approach can provide better solution with reasonable time. Moreover, with the expansion of quantum computation, quantum-inspired evolutionary algorithms [10] have been given more importance by the research communities. Quantum-inspired genetic algorithms (QIGA) [11–13] is a combination of evolutionary algorithm and quantum principles. With the help of quantum principles, these evolutionary algorithms provide better result with less computational complexity. Population size has a very huge impact on computational complexity in evolutionary algorithms. With a very small population size, QIGA provides a reasonable solution with reduced computational cost in lesser time.

In this paper, we have employed quantum-inspired genetic algorithm (QIGA) to solve the above multi-objectives clustering problem in WSNs. The performance of the proposed algorithm is found to be very effective. Our main contributions in this paper are summarized as follows:

- We form the Linear Programming (LP) formulation for the deployment of minimum number of CHs.
- QIGA based algorithm is applied to solve the following objectives, (i) placement of minimum number of relay nodes, (ii) ensure full coverage of all the sensor nodes, (iii) ensure connectivity between the placed relay nodes along with BS.
- We perform the extensive simulation of the proposed algorithm.

Rest of the paper is organized as follows. Survey of literatures relevant to our work is given in Sect. 2. The Sect. 3 briefly explains the system model, problem formulation and terminologies. Section 4 provides an overview of QIGA. To evaluate the proposed work, Sect. 6 shows the simulation results. Finally, the paper is concluded in Sect. 7.

2   Related Works

Mina et al. [14] have proposed Quantum inspired gravitational search algorithm (QIGSA) to find the adaptive design of WSN to enhance the energy consumption to increase the life span of the network. Here, limitation of communication range was taken as the constraint of the problem. The proposed QIGSA was found to be very effective is shown in their work where they compare QIGSA with other existing algorithms. Minimization of number of cluster heads is not consider in their problem.

In [12], have proposed QIGA to solve the multi-hop energy balanced for unequal clustering in WSNs to maximizing the life span of the network. Here, authors have not considered the communication between the cluster heads which is essential for the routing. Chun et al. [13] presented a hybrid clustering algorithm where LEACH and QEA are integrated to solve the selection of cluster head more effectively and efficiently. Energy consumption of sensor nodes are consumed to extend the network life span. Connectivity amongst the cluster heads along with base station which is necessary for the data transmission is not considered. In [15], authors have proposed a particle swarm optimization (PSO) for an energy efficient clustering and routing algorithm. Here, load balancing of the clusters are also taken in account for prolonging the network life span. Efficient particle encoding scheme and multi-objective fitness function are presented for the routing algorithm. Authors compared the proposed algorithm with existing algorithm and found to be more superior.

NSGA-II based approach was proposed by Jia et al. [16] to select the optimal number of sensor nodes out of large number of sensor nodes to preserved the coverage of the whole area. Here, connectivity is ensure by considering the communication range of sensor nodes as twice the sensing range [17]. But this assumption is not suitable for the target based WSN.

Bari et al. [18] formulates the relay node placement problem in terms of Integer Liner Programming (ILP). Here, the main objective is to minimize the number of selected potential positions for relay node placement with taking care of the $k_s(k_s \geq 1)$ and $k_r(k_r \geq 1)$ survivability of the sensor nodes and relay nodes respectively. GA based relay node placement algorithm have been proposed by Gupta et al. [19]. Here, the objective is to deploy minimum number relay nodes to the predefine given positions such that the relay nodes must be k-connected with the deployed sensor nodes. Connectivity among the relay nodes is not taken into account which may hamper the multi-hop routing of the valuable data. Then the work is extended in [20] by considering the connectivity too. In the fitness function, authors have considered three conflicting objectives: k-coverage and m-connectivity with minimum number of sensor nodes. Although the problem is a multi-objective optimization problem in nature, authors have not used any multi-objective evolutionary algorithms.

3   System Model and Problem Formulation

3.1   Network Model

We assume a WSN in which N number of sensor nodes are deployed in a two dimensional large area to sense the targeted region. We also assume that the proposed algorithm places some relay nodes or gateways to be acted as cluster head (CH) in the given number of potential positions. The sensor nodes sense the targeted area and transmit the data to their corresponding CH, i.e., a relay node or gateway. After collecting the sensed data from the member sensor nodes, the CHs aggregate it and forward the aggregated data to the base station directly or through other CHs. A sensor node can join a CH as a member, only if the CH is within the communication range (R_{sen}) of the sensor node. The communication link is established between two CHs only if they are within the communication range (R_{CH}) of each other.

3.2   Problem Formulation and Terminologies

Problem Formulation: Given a set of N number of sensor nodes and M number of predefine set of potential positions, we have to select the minimum number of potential positions to place the CHs such that the each sensor node is within the communication range of at-least one CH and simultaneously connectivity amongst the placed CHs along with BS must also be preserved.

The following terminologies are used to describe the proposed algorithm.

- $S = \{s_1, s_2, \dots, s_N\}$ denotes the set of sensor nodes.
- $T = \{\eta_1, \eta_2, \dots, \eta_M\}$ is the set of potential positions.
- Let the proposed algorithm selects P number of potential positions to place the relay nodes. $C = \{c_1, c_2, \dots, c_P\}$ denotes the set of CHs or relay nodes to be placed on selected potential positions, $P < M$.
- R_{sen} and R_{CH} denote the communication range of sensor nodes and CHs respectively, $R_{CH} > R_{sen}$.
- $Dist(s_i, c_j)$ represents the distance between s_i and c_j.
- BS denotes the base station.
- $COV(s_i)$ denotes the set of CHs that are within the communication range (R_{sen}) of s_i. It is represented as:

$$COV(s_i) = \{c_j | Dist(s_i, c_j) \leq R_{sen}, \forall c_j \in C\} \tag{1}$$

- $COM(c_j)$ denotes th set of CHs that are within the communication range of c_j and it is represented as:

$$COM(c_j) = \{c_i | Dist(c_i, c_j) \leq R_{CH}, \forall c_i \in C\} \tag{2}$$

Now, we form the above problem in terms of Linear Programming Problem (LPP). Let ρ_i, γ_{ij} and δ_i be the Boolean variables that can be define as follows:

$$\rho_i = \begin{cases} 1, & \text{if } \eta_i \text{ is selected for} \\ & \text{placement of CH.} \\ 0, & \text{otherwise.} \end{cases} \tag{3}$$

$$\gamma_{ij} = \begin{cases} 1, & \text{if } s_i \text{ is a cluster} \\ & \text{member of } c_j \\ 0, & \text{otherwise.} \end{cases} \tag{4}$$

$$\delta_i = \begin{cases} 1, & \text{if BS is within communication} \\ & \text{range } (R_{CH}) \text{ of } c_i \\ 0, & \text{otherwise.} \end{cases} \tag{5}$$

The LPP can be formulated as to:

$$\text{Minimize } F = \sum_{i=1}^{M} \rho_i \tag{6}$$

Subject to

$$|COV(s_i)| \geq 1, \forall s_i \in S \tag{7}$$

$$\sum_{j=1}^{P} \gamma_{ij} = 1, \forall s_i \in S \tag{8}$$

$$|COM(c_i)| + \delta_i \geq 1, \forall c_i \in C \tag{9}$$

Here, the constraint (7) ensures coverage of all the sensor nodes by the placed CHs. The constraint (8) implies that each sensor nodes can only join a single CH to form a cluster. Connectivity between the placed CHs and the base station is ensured by constraint (9).

4   An Overview of QIGA

The Quantum-Inspired Genetic Algorithm (QIGA) [10–13] is a novel combination of quantum computation and evolutionary computation. Similar to the conventional GA, the QIGA has the common phases of genetic operations like initialization of the population, selection, crossover, mutation and evaluation of fitness. Contrary to the GA, QIGA has some extra features as quantum interference and measurement. QIGA is built on the concept of quantum bit (qubit) and superposition of states of quantum mechanics. The qubit or gene of chromosome is defined as the smallest unit of information that can represent the two state of quantum computer simultaneously. The state of the qubit is either '0' or '1' or linear superposition of both '0' and '1'. $|\alpha|^2$ and $|\beta|^2$ are the probability of the amplitude which can specifies the state, where, $|\alpha|^2 + |\beta|^2 = 1$. The probability of having the state '1' is specifies by the $|\alpha|^2$ and the state '0' is specifies by the $|\beta|^2$. Linear combination of qubit (superposition) coefficient for $|0\rangle$ is α and $|1\rangle$ is β are also called amplitudes. A qubit state can be represented as $|\psi\rangle = \alpha|0\rangle + \beta|1\rangle$. The pseudo-code of QIGA is given in Algorithm 1.

5   Proposed QIGA Based Approach

Various variants of QIGA are there in the literature [11]. Here we have employed QIGA with crossover and mutation operators.

5.1   Quantum Chromosome Representation

A quantum chromosome q_i^t is an array of M number of qubits. It can be represented as:

$$q_i^t = \begin{bmatrix} \alpha_{i1}^t | \alpha_{i2}^t | \dots | \alpha_{iM}^t \\ \beta_{i1}^t | \beta_{i2}^t | \dots | \beta_{iM}^t \end{bmatrix} \tag{10}$$

Algorithm 1. Pseudocode of QIGA

1: Initialize $t = 0$.
2: Initialize $Q(t)$.   /* $Q(t)$ be the initial Quantum population*/
3: Produce $P(t)$ by observing the states of $Q(t)$.
4: Evaluate $P(t)$ using the fitness function.
5: Store the best solution among $P(t)$ in b.
6: **while** !$Terminate$ **do**
7:     $t = t + 1$.
8:     Update $Q(t)$ using $Q(t-1)$ and quantum gates.
9:     Produce $P(t)$ by observing the states of $Q(t)$
10:    Evaluate $P(t)$.
11:    Store the best solution among $P(t)$ in b.
12:    Quantum crossover.
13:    Quantum mutation.
14: **end while**

The initial population, $Q(t)$ is generated with P_{SIZE} number of quantum chromosomes, i.e., $Q(t) = \{q_1^t, q_2^t, \ldots, q_{P_{SIZE}}^t\}$. AT the beginning (i.e., $t = 0$), all the probability amplitudes are kept same as, $\alpha_{ij}^0 = \beta_{ij}^0 = \frac{1}{\sqrt{2}}$.

5.2   Measurement Operation

In Measurement operation, each quantum individuals are converted to its corresponding binary solutions. After generation of initial population, the individuals are transformed into binary population $P(t) = \{p_1^t, p_2^t, \ldots, p_{P_{SIZE}}^t\}$ by observing each individuals of $Q(t)$, where, $p_i^t = \{x_{i1}^t, x_{i2}^t, \ldots, x_{iM}^t\}$ be a binary chromosome of length M and $x_{ij}^t \in \{0,1\}$. A random number 'r' is generated between (0, 1) and the binary values are obtained by the condition as in Eq. (11). Diversity in the population is ensured since same result can not be achieved by the two consecutive measurement.

$$x_{ij}^t = \begin{cases} 1, & \text{if } r \leq |\alpha_{ij}^t|^2 \\ 0, & \text{otherwise.} \end{cases} \quad (11)$$

5.3   Derivation of Fitness Function

In order to evaluate the chromosomes, the fitness function is derived based on the following given objectives:

Objective 1: f_1 = Minimization of potential position to place CHs.   (12)

Objective 2: f_2 = Coverage of all the sensor nodes by nearset CHs.   (13)

Objective 3: f_3 = Connectivity amongst the CHs along with BS.   (14)

The first objective ensures use of minimum number of CHs. Our second objective implies the coverage of all the deployed sensor nodes by at least one placed CH. the third objective states that connectivity between the deployed CHs along with BS must be maintained such that data can be forwarded to the BS. In order to construct the fitness function, we use weight sum approach (WSA) [21]. To solve the multi-objective optimization problem WSA is found to be so effective. In WSA each objective is multiplied with weight value w_i and added with each other to form a single objective. Finally our fitness value is calculated as follows:

$$Fiteness = w_1 \times (1.0 - f_1) + w_2 \times f_2 + w_3 \times f_3$$
$$= \left\{ w_1 \times (1.0 - \frac{P}{M}) + w_2 \times \frac{1}{N} \sum_{i=1}^{N} COV_{cost}(s_i) \right.$$
$$\left. + w_3 \times \frac{1}{P} \sum_{i=1}^{P} COM_{cost}(c_i) \right\} \tag{15}$$

where, $w_1 + w_2 + w_3 = 1$ and $0 \leq w_i \leq 1$, $\forall i, 1 \leq i \leq 3$. $COV_{cost}(s_i)$ denotes the coverage cost of s_i. It can be calculated as follow.

$$COV_{cost}(s_i) = \begin{cases} +1, & \text{if } |COV(s_i)| \geq 1 \\ -1, & \text{otherwise.} \end{cases} \tag{16}$$

$COM_{cost}(c_i)$ denotes the connectivity cost of c_i. It can be calculated as.

$$COM_{cost}(c_i) = \begin{cases} +1, & \text{if } |COM(c_i)| \geq 1 \\ -1, & \text{otherwise.} \end{cases} \tag{17}$$

Our objective is to maximize the *Fitness* value, i.e.,

$$\text{Objective : Maximize } Fitness \tag{18}$$

5.4 Quantum Parent Selection

In order to select the best parent solutions, selection process is employed similar to that of conventional GA. As in GA, several selection methods like roulette-wheel, tournament, etc. can be applied.

5.5 Quantum Crossover and Mutation

After the selection of parents from initial population, crossover is applied on them to generate a new quantum offspring. There are several types of crossover operations, like single-point, arithmetic, uniform, etc., where parents can exchange their information beyond one or more points. The single-point quantum crossover is shown in Fig. 1.

The quantum crossover operation is followed by the quantum mutation, where randomly chosen qubit value gets flip to produced better quantum offspring. This is same as in GA. Bit-flip quantum mutation is shown in Fig. 2.

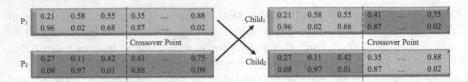

Fig. 1. One point quantum crossover.

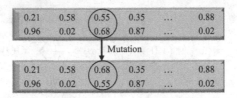

Fig. 2. Quantum mutation.

5.6 Interference

Interference is one of the vital operation to modify the probability amplitudes of individuals. Here, Q-gates are applied to the quantum individuals so that best solution can be achieved. Q-gates can also be designed in accordance with the problem. Depending on the fitness value of the chromosomes, the Q-gate either increase or decrease the amplitude of the qubit of the chromosomes. Among the many Q-gates, rotation gate is widely used. Here, we have also employed the rotation gate as given in Eq. (19).

$$R_{ij}^t(\phi) = \begin{bmatrix} cos(\phi_{ij}^t) & -sin(\phi_{ij}^t) \\ sin(\phi_{ij}^t) & cos(\phi_{ij}^t) \end{bmatrix} \tag{19}$$

Here, i^{th} qubit is diverted towards '0' or '1' depending on its objective sign by the rotation angle represented by the variable ϕ_{ij}^t. The updated qubit is obtained by applying the following formula:

$$(\alpha_{ij}^{t+1}, \beta_{ij}^{t+1}) = R_{ij}^t(\phi). (\alpha_{ij}^t, \beta_{ij}^t) \tag{20}$$

5.7 Evaluation and Replacement

In the evaluation phase, the newly generated offspring from individual parents are evaluated using the fitness function. The evaluation phase is followed by the replacement phase. Like the classical GA, if the generated offspring solutions are better than the parent solutions, then parents are replaced by the offspring; otherwise offspring are discarded.

6 Simulation Results

MATLAB R2012b and C programming language have been used for simulating the proposed QIGA. We performed the simulation in 2-D square fields of two

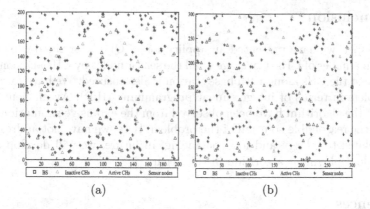

Fig. 3. Initial deployment of 200 sensor nodes with 100 potential positions, (a) first scenario with 64 number of placed relay nodes and (b) second scenario with 68 number of placed relay nodes.

scenarios of 200×200 and $300 \times 300\,\mathrm{m}^2$ area with base station at $(200, 100)$ and $(300, 150)$ respectively. In both scenarios, 200 sensor nodes are randomly deployed with 100 predefine number of potential positions for the placement of CHs as shown in Fig. 3. The communication range of the sensor nodes (R_{sen}) and CHs (R_{CH}) is taken as 40 m and 50 m respectively. To execute the algorithm, we take the initial population of 50 chromosomes with 3% mutation rate. We applied two point crossover operation. After the formation of cluster, an energy balanced routing algorithm as proposed in [22] is employed for CHs to BS data routing. The proposed QIGA based algorithm placed 64 and 68 number of relay nodes out of 100 potential points respectively. Finally, the connectivity amongst the CHs along with BS are shown in Fig. 4.

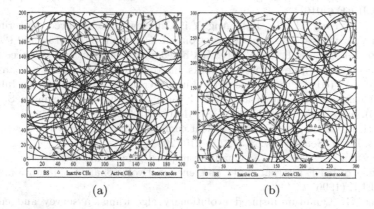

Fig. 4. Connectivity amongst CHs along with BS (a) connectivity amongst 64 CHs and (b) connectivity amongst 68 CHs.

7   Conclusion

In this paper, we have presented an application of QIGA for the deployment of minimum number of CHs. Coverage of all the sensor nodes by CHs and connectivity amongst the CHs along with base station is also ensured. We have formulated the problem in terms of integer linear programming (ILP). An efficient performance of the algorithm have been observed from the extensive simulation. It can find our the reasonable solution of the problem. Here, we have not addressed the issues related to energy and load balancing. In future, we will develop a novel relay node deployment algorithm in this regard.

References

1. Yick, J., Mukherjee, B., Ghosal, D.: Wireless sensor network survey. Comput. Netw. **52**(12), 2292–2330 (2008)
2. Kuila, P., Jana, P.K.: Heap and parameter-based load balanced clustering algorithms for wireless sensor networks. Int. J. Commun. Netw. Distrib. Syst. **14**(4), 413–432 (2015)
3. Kuila, P., Jana, P.K.: Evolutionary computing approaches for clustering and routing in wireless sensor networks. In: Handbook of Research on Natural Computing for Optimization Problems, pp. 246–266. IGI Global (2016)
4. Gupta, S.K., Kuila, P., Jana, P.K.: E3BFT: energy efficient and energy balanced fault tolerance clustering in wireless sensor networks. In: 2014 International Conference on Contemporary Computing and Informatics (IC3I), pp. 714–719. IEEE (2014)
5. Bari, A., Jaekel, A., Bandyopadhyay, S.: Clustering strategies for improving the lifetime of two-tiered sensor networks. Comput. Commun. **31**(14), 3451–3459 (2008)
6. Gupta, S.K., Kuila, P., Jana, P.K.: Energy efficient multipath routing for wireless sensor networks: a genetic algorithm approach. In: 2016 International Conference on Advances in Computing, Communications and Informatics (ICACCI), pp. 1735–1740. IEEE (2016)
7. Low, C.P., Fang, C., Ng, J.M., Ang, Y.H.: Efficient load-balanced clustering algorithms for wireless sensor networks. Comput. Commun. **31**(4), 750–759 (2008)
8. Gupta, S.K., Kuila, P., Jana, P.K.: GA based energy efficient and balanced routing in k-connected wireless sensor networks. In: Mandal, J., Satapathy, S., Sanyal, M., Bhateja, V. (eds.) Proceedings of the First International Conference on Intelligent Computing and Communication. AISC, vol. 458, pp. 679–686. Springer, Singapore (2016). https://doi.org/10.1007/978-981-10-2035-3_68
9. Cardei, I., Cardei, M.: Energy-efficient connected-coverage in wireless sensor networks. Int. J. Sens. Netw. **3**(3), 201–210 (2008)
10. Narayanan, A., Moore, M.: Quantum-inspired genetic algorithms. In: 1996 Proceedings of IEEE International Conference on Evolutionary Computation, pp. 61–66. IEEE (1996)
11. Zhang, G.: Quantum-inspired evolutionary algorithms: a survey and empirical study. J. Heuristics **17**(3), 303–351 (2011)
12. Rathee, M., Kumar, S.: Quantum inspired genetic algorithm for multi-hop energy balanced unequal clustering in wireless sensor networks. In: 2016 Ninth International Conference on Contemporary Computing (IC3), pp. 1–6. IEEE (2016)

13. Tsai, C.-W., Kang, C.-T., Hu, K.-C., Chiang, M.-C.: A quantum-inspired evolutionary clustering algorithm for the lifetime problem of wireless sensor network. Int. J. Internet Technol. Secur. Trans. **6**(4), 259–290 (2016)
14. Mirhosseini, M., Barani, F., Nezamabadi-pour, H.: QQIGSA: a quadrivalent quantum-inspired GSA and its application in optimal adaptive design of wireless sensor networks. J. Netw. Comput. Appl. **78**, 231–241 (2017)
15. Kuila, P., Jana, P.K.: Particle swarm optimization approach: energy efficient clustering and routing algorithms for wireless sensor networks. Eng. Appl. Artif. Intell. **33**, 127–140 (2014)
16. Jia, J., Chen, J., Chang, G., Tan, Z.: Energy efficient coverage control in wireless sensor networks based on multi-objective genetic algorithm. Comput. Math. Appl. **57**(11), 1756–1766 (2009)
17. Zhang, H., Hou, J.C.: Maintaining sensing coverage and connectivity in large sensor networks. Ad Hoc Sens. Wirel. Netw. **1**(1–2), 89–124 (2005)
18. Bari, A., Jaekel, A., Jiang, J., Yufei, X.: Design of fault tolerant wireless sensor networks satisfying survivability and lifetime requirements. Comput. Commun. **35**(3), 320–333 (2012)
19. Gupta, S.K., Kuila, P., Jana, P.K.: Genetic algorithm for k-connected relay node placement in wireless sensor networks. In: Satapathy, S.C., Raju, K.S., Mandal, J.K., Bhateja, V. (eds.) Proceedings of the Second International Conference on Computer and Communication Technologies. AISC, vol. 379, pp. 721–729. Springer, New Delhi (2016). https://doi.org/10.1007/978-81-322-2517-1_69
20. Gupta, S.K., Kuila, P., Jana, P.K.: Genetic algorithm approach for k-coverage and m-connected node placement in target based wireless sensor networks. Comput. Electr. Eng. **56**, 544–556 (2016)
21. Konak, A., Coit, D.W., Smith, A.E.: Multi-objective optimization using genetic algorithms: a tutorial. Reliab. Eng. Syst. Saf. **91**(9), 992–1007 (2006)
22. Singh, D., Kuila, P., Jana, P.K.: A distributed energy efficient and energy balanced routing algorithm for wireless sensor networks. In: 3rd International Conference on Advances in Computing, Communications and Informatics (ICACCI-2014), pp. 1657–1663. IEEE (2014)

Chemical Reaction Optimization to Solve Reconfiguration Problem Along with Capacitor of Radial Distribution System

Sneha Sultana[1($\boxtimes$)], Shivam Singh[1], Ravi Kant Ranjan[1],
Shubham Kumar Sharma[1], and Provas Kumar Roy[2]

[1] Dr. B. C. Roy Engineering College, Durgapur, Durgapur, India
sneha.sultana@gmail.com, shivamsinghme9@gmail.com,
ravikantranjan054@gmail.com,
shubhamthakurgrd@gmail.com
[2] Kalyani Government Engineering College, Kalyani, India
roy_provas@yahoo.com

Abstract. This paper presents, an efficient optimization technique, namely chemical reaction optimization (CRO) algorithm is developed for power loss minimization in radial distribution system by optimal reconfiguration of the network. To check the feasibility and effectiveness the proposed methodology is successfully implemented on two test systems like 33-bus and 69-bus radial distribution systems. Moreover the numerical results are compared with other population based optimization technique like krill herd (KH) algorithm, oppositional krill herd (OKH) algorithm, fuzzy approach show that CRO could find better quality solutions. Finally, convergence graph is given to identify the robustness of above mentioned systems.

Keywords: Radial distribution system · Capacitors · Power loss reduction · Chemical reaction optimization (CRO)

1 Introduction

Effective power distribution is very important subject of interest for not only the electrical engineers but also for researchers and pioneers of science and technology. An important factor for effective power distribution is the minimization of losses in distribution system. Generally speaking in a distribution system there are losses in the conductors, transformers, feeders etc.

The subject of interest in this paper is the minimization of losses in a radial distribution network [1]. The losses witnessed in the above mention network are classified into technical losses and non-technical losses. The above losses in radial distribution network affect the effective power distribution, and to minimize the losses in distribution network capacitor installation method is most widely used. The distribution network where one source feeds the whole network through radial tie-lines and distribution lines is defined as the radial distribution system. A radial network is the simplest of all distribution networks and most widely used one. In a distribution

© Springer Nature Singapore Pte Ltd. 2019
J. K. Mandal et al. (Eds.): CICBA 2018, CCIS 1030, pp. 392–409, 2019.
https://doi.org/10.1007/978-981-13-8578-0_31

network generally reactive power compensation [2] becomes a matter of interest for any electrical engineer. The compensation lagging reactive power losses can be done though placing the capacitors in parallel to the feeders. The capacitors provide leading power factor thus, compensating power loss due to lagging power factor but, it is very important to find out the optimum capacitor value and suitable position to install a capacitor in a distribution network to minimize the losses. The optimal location of the capacitor in the distribution network is important for power flow control, improvement of system's stability and power factor, good voltage profile maintain and loss minimization [3]. In the method of capacitor installation the selection of optimal position is important and then the optimal capacitor size simultaneously to avoid over compensation. One more technique which is frequently used with optimal capacitor allocation is reconfiguration of distribution network. The network reconfiguration technique is a method which helps to mitigate power losses from distribution system. The radial distribution system has sectionalizing switches and tie switches, in reconfiguration the sectionalizing switches and the tie switches positions can be altered by opening and closing them. In normal operating condition the opening and closing of switches can lead to loss minimization, also for further loss minimization optimal capacitor installation can be employed together in the distribution network. Ahmed et al. [4] proposed load flow analysis based method for calculation of reactive and active power losses. It involve the approach of the optimal capacitor placing in a radial distribution system which determines the optimal location and size capacitor with an objective of power loss reduction and maintain input voltage profile.

However, the conventional methods are not suitable for non-linear and non-differentiable problem. Since, capacitor placement in distribution system is a discrete non-linear optimization problem, the classical methods mentioned above are failed to obtain optimum solutions. It is therefore essential to develop new, robust and reliable algorithms, which are capable of handling discrete nonlinear optimization problem.

Recently, many population based optimization have been developed and successfully implemented to solve optimal DG placement problem. Hsiao et al. presented [5] a combination of fuzzy genetic algorithm (GA) method to resolve capacitor allocation problem. Torres et al. used a GA [6] based on edge window decoding technique to optimize power distribution system reconfiguration. Nara et al. represented the GA [7] to solve the RDS problem with minimal losses. Franco et al. used a mixed integer linear programming (MILP) [8] model for reconfiguration of radial distribution system (RDS) considering distributed generation. Gonzoler et al. presented a heuristic algorithm [9] to solve the problem at modern unit distribution system. Singh et al. presented a heuristic method [10] for reconfiguration that performs a sequential switch opening based branch power flow. Arun et al. obtained fuzzy based reconfiguration algorithm [11] for output voltage stability enhancement. Tzong-su et al. developed an ant colony search algorithm [12] to solve for optimal network reconfiguration problem for power loss reduction. Abdelaziz et al. proposed [13] an artificial intelligence tech Particle Swarm optimization technique PSO. Cebrian et al. presented [14] an evolutionary algorithm (EA) to tackle the problem of reconfiguration of radial distribution system.

There is a disadvantage of population based algorithms that they yield extremely large number of unfeasible non radial solutions appearing at each generation will lead to long computation time. So more better algorithm are developed which are based on the artificial intelligence techniques and have much better rate of convergence than any other proposed method so far. The developments in those algorithms are still going on.

In this paper an attempt has been made to derive an effective reconfiguration technique for minimizing the power losses in radial distribution system. A novel optimization technique namely chemical reaction optimization (CRO) algorithm is presented in this paper to obtain the optimal stability of the system.

The proposed algorithm CRO [15, 16] was inspired from the kinetics of chemical reaction. In a chemical reaction the atom or molecules undergo through a chemical process. In any chemical reaction phenomenon the reactants changes to products by creation and obliteration of chemical bonds. Before changing they form a chain of middle species. These small changes are called elementary steps. This means that chemical reactions tend to release energy and this product has less energy as compared to reactants. In terms of stability lesser the energy the system has more stable is the system. Hence the products are always more stable. There is not much difference between the chemical reaction and optimization algorithm. Both aim to have a global minimum, one in energy and another in convergence. With this discovery a new optimization algorithm is used to search the optimal capacitor position and optimal reconfiguration for the minimal power losses. The rest of the paper is as follows. Problem formulation is given in Sect. 2. The key points of the proposed CRO technique are described in Sect. 3. In Sect. 4, the proposed technique tested on reconfiguration problem along with capacitor allocation in radial distribution system is illustrated. Two cases based on medium and large scale power systems are studied and the simulation results are illustrated in Sect. 5. Finally conclusion is drawn in the last section.

2 Problem Formulation

2.1 Objective Function

From the literature [17] it is experimented that sometimes unbalanced deeply loaded conditions involve heavily power losses in a radial distribution system.

The real power loss may be mathematically expressed as follows:

$$P_{RLoss} = \sum_{x=1}^{N} \sum_{y=1}^{N} \frac{R_{x,y}}{V_x V_y} \cos(\delta_x - \delta_y)(P_x P_y + Q_x Q_y) + \frac{R_{x,y}}{V_x V_y} \sin(\delta_x - \delta_y)(Q_x P_y - P_x Q_y)$$

(1)

Here, P_{RLoss} is the real power loss; $R_{x,y}$ resistance of the distribution line connected between busses x^{th} and y^{th}; N is the number of buses in the distribution network; P_x, Q_x are net active and reactive power at the xth bus; P_y, Q_y are net active and reactive power at the yth bus; δ_x, δ_y are phase angle of voltage at x^{th} and y^{th} bus.

2.2   Load Modeling

Here, take account of four types of loads. The expression of active and reactive power loads are specified as:

$$PL(N) = PL_0(N)\left(c_1 + c_2|V(N)| + c_3|V(N)|^2\right) \tag{2}$$

$$QL(N) = QL_0(N)\left(d_1 + d_2|V(N)| + d_3|V(N)|^2\right) \tag{3}$$

Here, (c_1, d_1), (c_2, d_2) and (c_3, d_3) are the arrangements of constant power, constant current and constant impedance loads respectively. Now, the condition for constant power load $c_1 = d_1 = 1$ and $c_2 = d_2 = c_3 = d_3 = 0$; condition for constant current load $c_2 = d_2 = 1$ and $c_1 = d_1 = c_3 = d_3 = 0$; condition for constant impedance load $c_3 = d_3 = 1$ and $c_1 = d_1 = c_2 = d_2 = 0$; condition for composite type load $c_1 = d_1 = 0.4$, $c_2 = d_2 = 0.3$ and $c_3 = d_3 = 0.3$, respectively.

2.3   Constraints

2.3.1   Voltage Limits

Studies reveal that most of the voltage fluctuation and outages in the system are attributed from the distribution system. Though, this can be achieved by proper designing of the distribution network. So, the voltage must be kept within the standard limits of each bus.

$$v_x^{min} < v_x < v_x^{max} \tag{4}$$

2.3.2   Real Power Limit

The real power limit of the different busses must lie within their upper and lower limits. It may mathematically be expressed as:

$$P_x^{min} \leq P_x \leq P_x^{max} \tag{5}$$

2.3.3   Reactive Power Limit

The mathematical expression of reactive power limit is shown below:

$$Q_x^{min} \leq Q_x \leq Q_x^{max} \tag{6}$$

3   Chemical Reaction Optimization (CRO)

The framework of the CRO algorithm [15] can be described as below. It is a population based algorithm and the participating species are molecules. Few characteristics of the molecules are molecular structure, Current kinetic energy, current potential energy and other attributes. The other attributes can vary from problem to problem according to implementation. Users can add or remove any of these properties according to design of the objective function.

The CRO involves some elementary reactions:

3.1 On-Wall Ineffective Collisions

An on-wall-ineffective collision occur when one molecule strikes the wall of any container. The collision can be Elastic or in-elastic. This reaction is not vigorous enough so as to completely change the orientation of the molecule. Only a small change in the molecular orientation (θ) takes place. The molecule tries to transfer from (θ) to (θ^*) in the neighbourhood of (θ) i.e. (θ^*) belongs to (θ) in neighbourhood of (θ). Mathematically it is given as $\theta^* = N(\theta)$, where N is the neighbourhood of θ. The kinetic energy of the molecules before the collision is KE_θ, since after the collision some of the energy are extracted from the molecules. Hence, the new kinetic energy can be derived as

$$KE_{\theta^*} = (PE_\theta - PE_{\theta^*} + KE_\theta)\alpha \qquad (7)$$

Where α belongs to kinetic energy loss rate.

3.2 Decomposition

It is more vigorous than the on-wall effective collision. In decomposition one molecule breaks into one or more different molecules. The orientation of the original molecule say (θ) then after decomposition the orientation of the molecule becomes θ_1^* and θ_2^*. The decomposition reaction possesses much more energy differences from the original molecule. This shows the situation when the exploration moves from the local region θ and decides to explore other region corresponding to (θ_1^*) and (θ_2^*).

3.3 Intermolecular Ineffective Collision

Intermolecular ineffective collision takes place when two molecules beat with each other and then separate. The number of molecules remains unaffected even after the collisions. The flexibility of the algorithm increases with the increase in the number of molecule because the exploration rate for the optimum results will increase. Let us assume that θ_1 and θ_2 are the molecules undergoing ineffective collision. Let the new molecules be (θ_1^*) and (θ_2^*) which are formed in their own neighbourhoods separately i.e. $\theta_1^* = N(\theta_1)$ and $\theta_2^* = N(\theta_2)$, where N is the neighbourhood of θ_1 and θ_2.

3.4 Synthesis

Synthesis refers to a reaction in which two molecules say θ_1 and θ_2 collide and forms a new molecule, this means that the search regions in the neighbourhood of the θ_1 and θ_2 are over and exploration is done in the region of the newly formed territory of the molecule.

4   Algorithm of CRO for Reconfiguration Problem Along with Capacitor

The following steps must be taken to apply the CRO:

Step 1: The preliminary structure of each molecule should be randomly selected while satisfying different inequality constraints of the control variables. In the proposed area, capacitor size and locations are considered as the control variables.

Step 2: Is there any voltage difference across the tie switches and it maximum, go to next step. Otherwise discard that tie switch.

Step 3: Load flow problem have to run to find power loss. Here, a direct load flow algorithm based on the BIBC (Bus-Injection to Branch-Current) matrix and the BCBV (Branch-Current to Bus-Voltage) matrix [18] is used for different test systems.

Step 4: Require to measure the potential energy (fitness value).

Step 5: Update size of capacitor and position using different steps of proposed algorithm like on wall ineffective collision, decomposition, inter-molecular ineffective collision and synthesis process.

5   Test Systems and Results

To make sure the effectiveness of the proposed CRO technique, it is verified in the course of two examples. In this paper standard 33-bus and 69-bus radial distribution systems used to solve reconfiguration with capacitor placement and the aim is to determine the optimal location and size of capacitor in order to minimize active power loss. The verification of the projected CRO can be carried out using two test systems one using a 33-bus system and second using a large 69-bus system. The proposed method is executed in MATLAB software on a personal computer having i3 processor, 2.5 GHz, 4 GB RAM. The proposed CRO algorithm is run for 50 population and 100 iterations for each case.

5.1   Test Case 1 (33-Bus Radial Distribution Systems)

Initially, proposed method is applied on a small 33-bus radial distribution network. This system consists of consisting of 37 branches shown in Fig. 1. For 33-bus distribution system, five tie-switches are used. The full system data are taken from [19] and also illustrated in Appendix A1 and A2 with rated voltage of 12.66 kV. Figures 2, 3 and 4 represent the reconfiguration diagram for three different load cases like constant power type, constant current type and constant impedance type obtained by CRO technique.

Table 1. Outcome of 33-bus system with and without reconfiguration for constant power type load with load multiplying factor of 1.0

	Excluding capacitor placement	Including capacitor placement		
Algorithms used for optimization ⟶		CRO	OKH [2]	KH [2]
Without reconfiguration				
Real power loss (KW)	210.998	153.70	153.80	154.57
Optimal capacitor position	NA	30	30	30
Optimal size of capacitor	NA	997.76	997.15	958.92
Opening branch	NA	NA	NA	NA
Closing branch	NA	NA	NA	NA
With reconfiguration				
Real power loss (KW)		113.17	114.23	115.62
Optimal capacitor position		27	27	27
Optimal size of capacitor		999.23	997.14	856.56
Opening branch		7–8	7–8	7–8
		9–10	9–10	9–10
		14–15	14–15	14–15
		32–33	32–33	32–33
Closing branch		21–8	21–8	21–8
		9–15	9–15	9–15
		22–12	22–12	22–12
		18–33	18–33	18–33

A comparison among CRO, OKH [2] and KH [2] algorithm is made to illustrate the usefulness of CRO for different type of load like constant power, constant current and constant impedance. After load flow, a real power loss without the placement of capacitor at rated load is 210.998 kW. Table 1 pointed out the power losses in a constant power type load along with comparison between OKH [2] and KH [2] algorithm. From Table 1 It is pointed out that after reconfiguration including capacitor placement power loss becomes 113.17 kW by CRO technique which is less compared

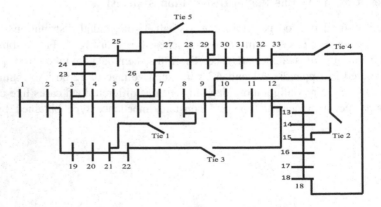

Fig. 1. Sample 33-bus radial distribution system with five tie switches

to OKH [2] and KH [2]. The convergence graph for constant power load type using proposed CRO is shown in Fig. 9.

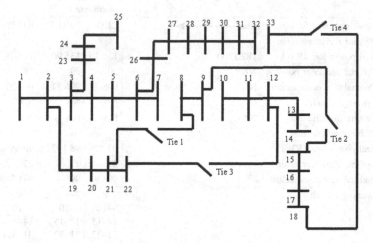

Fig. 2. Reconfiguration figure of constant power load for 33-bus system

Further for different type of load in 33-bus system, CRO yields better result than OKH [2] and KH [2] algorithms which can be demonstrated in Tables 2 and 3. It may be concluded that reconfiguration along with capacitor placement yielded better results.

The performance parameters in a 33-bus system for a constant current load are given in Table 2. When the load flow is allowed then the active power without capacitor placement is 182.176 KW and it is observed that power loss reduced substantially to 97.176 when reconfiguration with capacitor placement is employed. A comparison has also been drawn between different optimization algorithms.

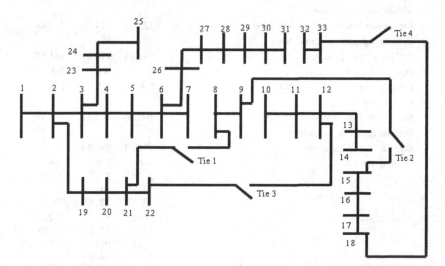

Fig. 3. Reconfiguration figure of constant current load for 33-bus system

Table 2. Outcome of 33-bus system with and without reconfiguration for constant current type load with load multiplying factor of 1.0

	Excluding capacitor placement	Including capacitor placement		
Algorithms used for optimization ⟶		CRO	OKH [2]	KH [2]
Without reconfiguration				
Real power loss (KW)	182.1760	138.43	138.90	144.48
Optimal capacitor position	NA	30	29	28
Optimal size of capacitor	NA	908.47	996.27	902.27
Opening branch	NA	NA	NA	NA
Closing branch	NA	NA	NA	NA
With reconfiguration				
Real power loss (KW)		97.176	98.192	98.6698
Optimal capacitor position		27	27	27
Optimal size of capacitor		998.98	993.49	891.393
Opening branch		7–8	7–8	7–8
		9–10	9–10	9–10
		14–15	14–15	14–15
		31–32	31–32	31–32v
Closing branch		21–8	21–8	21–8
		9–15	9–15	9–15
		22–12	22–12	22–12
		18–33	18–33	18–33

Table 3. Outcome of 33-bus system with and without reconfiguration for constant impedance type load with load multiplying factor of 1.0

	Excluding capacitor placement	Including capacitor placement		
Algorithms used for optimization ⟶		CRO	OKH [2]	KH [2]
Without reconfiguration				
Real power loss (KW)	182.1760	123.78	124.00	127.44
Optimal capacitor position	NA	30	30	31
Optimal size of capacitor	NA	998.64	979.24	881.53
Opening branch	NA	NA	NA	NA
Closing branch	NA	NA	NA	NA
With reconfiguration				
Real power loss (KW)		107.264	107.313	116.793
Optimal capacitor position		6	6	6
Optimal size of capacitor		996.24	982.86	412.30
Opening branch		5–6	5–6	5–6
		9–10	9–10	9–10
		14–15	14–15	14–15
		32–33	32–33	32–33
Closing branch		8–21	8–21	8–21
		12–22	12–22	12–22
		9–15	9–15	9–15
		18–33	18–33	18–33

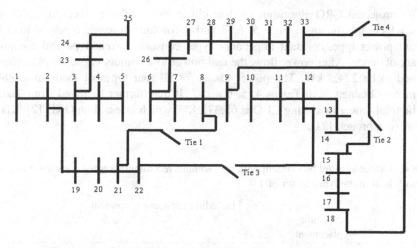

Fig. 4. Reconfiguration figure of constant impedance load for 33-bus system

5.2 Performance Parameters in a 69 Bus System

The validation of proposed algorithm is tested for large scale distribution network; it is implemented on 69-bus test system. It contains 69-buses and 73 branches (including tie branches). The figure of 69-bus system is represented in Fig. 5. The full system data for this system are given in [20] with rated voltage of 12.66 kV.

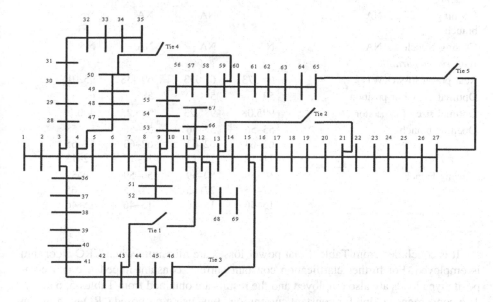

Fig. 5. Sample 69-bus radial distribution system with five tie switches

The projected CRO algorithm used to obtain three different reconfiguration diagrams which are shown in Figs. 5, 6, 7 and 8 for four different types of load like constant power type, constant impedance type, constant current type and composite type are obtained. After power flow, the real power loss without capacitor placement is obtained to be 224.2 kW. The power losses for all four types of loads in a 69-bus system are obtained from Tables 4, 5, 6 and 7. It may further be noted from Table 4 that the total power loss using CRO is 65.373 KW which is less than OKH [2], KH [2] and fuzzy approach [21].

Table 4. Outcome of 69-bus system with and without reconfiguration for constant power type load with load multiplying factor of 1.0

	Excluding capacitor placement	Including capacitor placement			
Algorithms used for optimization		CRO	OKH [2]	KH [2]	Fuzzy approach [21]
Without reconfiguration					
Real power loss (KW)	224.20	156.413	157.457	160.395	186.6
Optimal capacitor position	NA	61	62	62	61
Optimal size of capacitor	NA	996.87	974.10	880.04	400
Opening branch	NA	NA	NA	NA	NA
Closing branch	NA	NA	NA	NA	NA
With reconfiguration					
Real power loss (KW)		65.373	67.653	69.438	95.10
Optimal capacitor position		59	59	58	61
Optimal size of capacitor		995.08	985.23	985.23	400
Opening branch		55–56 62–63 11–12	55–56 62–63 11–12	55–56 62–63 11–12	57–58 64–65 12–13
Closing branch		50–59 27–65 15–46	50–59 27–65 15–46	50–59 27–65 15–46	50–59 27–65 15–46

It is concluded from Table 4 that power losses are minimum when CRO algorithm is employed. For further clarification constant current, constant impedance and composite type loads are also employed and the results are obtained from Tables 5, 6 and 7. The convergence graph for constant current load type using proposed CRO is shown in Fig. 10.

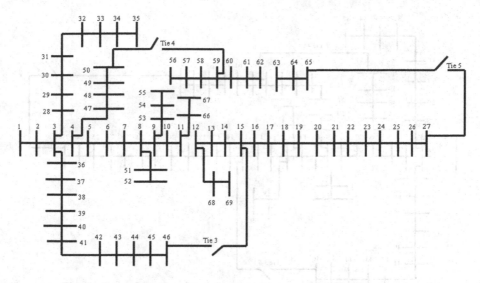

Fig. 6. Reconfiguration figure for constant power load for 69-bus system

Table 5. Outcome of 69-bus system with and without reconfiguration for constant current type load with load multiplying factor of 1.0

	Excluding capacitor placement	Including capacitor placement			
Algorithms used for optimization		CRO	OKH [2]	KH [2]	Fuzzy approach [21]
Without reconfiguration					
Real power loss (KW)	191.0	136.0628	137.487	139.547	161.40
Optimal capacitor position	NA	61	61	61	61
Optimal size of capacitor	NA	997.443	999.49	910.49	400
Opening branch	NA	NA	NA	NA	NA
Closing branch	NA	NA	NA	NA	NA
With reconfiguration					
Real power loss (KW)		59.085	61.441	63.325	95.10
Optimal capacitor position		59	59	58	61
Optimal size of capacitor		986.56	941.17	857.69	400
Opening branch		13–14 54–55 61–62	13–14 54–55 61–62	13–14 54–55 61–62	56–57 64–65 12–13
Closing branch		50–59 27–65 15–46	50–59 27–65 15–46	50–59 27–65 15–46	50–59 27–65 15–46

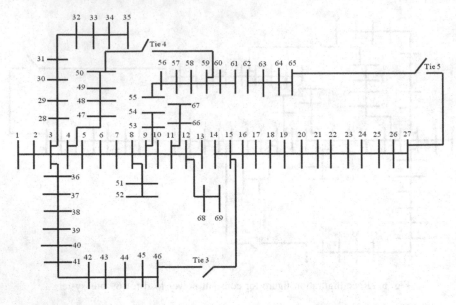

Fig. 7. Reconfiguration figure of constant current and composite type load for 69-system

Table 6. Outcome of 69-bus system with and without reconfiguration for constant impedance type load with load multiplying factor of 1.0

	Excluding capacitor placement	Including capacitor placement			
Algorithms used for optimization		CRO	OKH [2]	KH [2]	Fuzzy approach [21]
Without reconfiguration					
Real power loss (KW)	166.80	121.464	123.047	124.619	142.50
Optimal capacitor position	NA	61	61	61	61
Optimal size of capacitor	NA	997.95	995.88	910.29	400
Opening branch	NA	NA	NA	NA	NA
Closing branch	NA	NA	NA	NA	NA
With reconfiguration					
Real power loss (KW)		32.002	34.755	34.815	79.90
Optimal capacitor position		20	20	26	61
Optimal size of capacitor		655.741	644.44	534.40	400
Opening branch		10–11 57–58 60–61	10–11 57–58 60–61	10–11 57–58 60–61	57–58 64–65 12–13
Closing branch		50–59 27–65 15–46	50–59 27–65 15–46	50–59 27–65 15–46	50–59 27–65 15–46

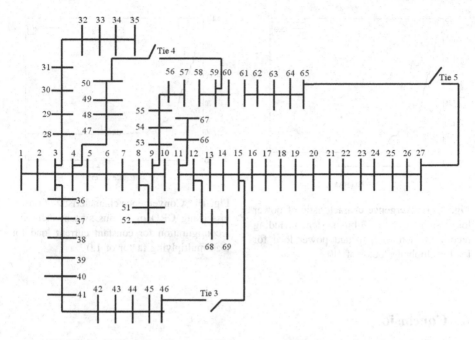

Fig. 8. Reconfiguration figure of 69 bus system with constant impedance load

Table 7. Outcome of 69-bus system with and without reconfiguration for composite type load with load multiplying factor of 1.0

	Excluding capacitor placement	Including capacitor placement			
Algorithms used for optimization		CRO	OKH [2]	KH [2]	Fuzzy approach [21]
Without reconfiguration					
Real power loss (KW)	194.6	139.762	139.883	141.247	164.1
Optimal capacitor position	NA	61	61	63	61
Optimal size of capacitor	NA	987.50	981.98	957.38	400
Opening branch	NA	NA	NA	NA	NA
Closing branch	NA	NA	NA	NA	NA
With reconfiguration					
Real power loss (KW)		59.400	61.397	66.818	87.7
Optimal capacitor position		59	59	57	61
Optimal size of capacitor		992.69	996.56	912.56	400
Opening branch		13–14 54–55 61–62	13–14 54–55 61–62	13–14 54–55 61–62	55–56 64–65 12–13
Closing branch		50–59 27–65 15–46	50–59 27–65 15–46	50–59 27–65 15–46	50–59 27–65 15–46

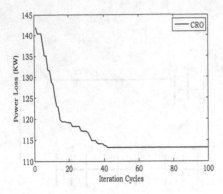

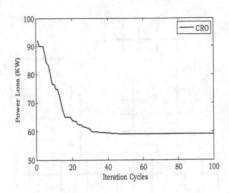

Fig. 9. Convergence characteristic of power loss using CRO of 33-bus system including reconfiguration for constant power load for load multiplying factor of 1.0

Fig. 10. Convergence characteristic of power loss using CRO of 69-bus system including reconfiguration for constant current load for load multiplying factor of 1.0

6 Conclusion

This article contains, a new approach namely chemical reaction optimization (CRO) to solve reconfiguration problem along with capacitor allocation in a radial distribution network. This method is tested on 33-bus and 69-bus radial distribution systems. In order to show the supremacy of the CRO algorithm over other algorithms like KH, OKH and fuzzy logic a comparative study is carried out. The reconfiguration and optimization is carried out in four different loads constant power load, constant current load and constant impedance and composite type load. The study suggests that the efficiency and effectiveness of the proposed method is better than the other population based optimization techniques.

Appendix

Table A1. Line data of 33-bus system

Branch no	Sending end	Receiving end	R (ohms)	X (ohms)	Branch no	Sending end	Receiving end	R (ohms)	X (ohms)
1	1	2	0.0922	0.0477	20	20	21	0.4095	0.4784
2	2	3	0.4930	0.2511	21	21	22	0.7089	0.9373
3	3	4	0.3660	0.1864	22	3	23	0.4152	0.3083
4	4	5	0.3811	0.1941	23	23	24	0.8980	0.7091
5	5	6	0.8190	0.7070	24	24	25	0.8960	0.7011
6	6	7	0.1872	0.6188	25	6	26	0.2030	0.1034

(continued)

Table A1. (*continued*)

Branch no	Sending end	Receiving end	R (ohms)	X (ohms)	Branch no	Sending end	Receiving end	R (ohms)	X (ohms)
7	7	8	1.7114	1.2351	26	26	27	0.2842	0.1447
8	8	9	1.0300	0.7400	27	27	28	1.0590	0.9337
9	9	10	1.0400	0.7400	28	28	29	0.8042	0.7006
10	10	11	0.1966	0.0650	29	29	30	0.5075	0.2585
11	11	12	0.3744	0.1238	30	30	31	0.9744	0.9630
12	12	13	1.4680	1.1550	31	31	32	0.3105	0.3619
13	13	14	0.5416	0.7129	32	32	33	0.3410	0.5302
14	14	15	0.5910	0.5260	33*	21	8	0.0000	2.0000
15	15	16	0.7463	0.5450	34*	9	15	0.0000	2.0000
16	16	17	1.2890	1.7210	35*	12	22	0.0000	2.0000
17	17	18	0.7320	0.5740	36*	18	33	0.0000	0.5000
18	18	19	0.1640	0.1565	37*	25	29	0.0000	0.5000
19	19	20	1.5042	1.3554					

*Tie lines

Table A2. Load data of 33-bus system

Branch no	Sending end	Receiving end	PL (KW)	QL (KVar)	Branch no	Sending end	Receiving end	PL (KW)	QL (KVar)
1	1	2	100.0	60.0	17	17	18	90.0	40.0
2	2	3	90.0	40.0	18	2	19	90.0	40.0
3	3	4	120.0	80.0	19	19	20	90.0	40.0
4	4	5	60.0	30.0	20	20	21	90.0	40.0
5	5	6	60.0	20.0	21	21	22	90.0	40.0
6	6	7	200.0	100.0	22	3	23	90.0	50.0
7	7	8	200.0	100.0	23	23	24	420.0	200.0
8	8	9	60.0	20.0	24	24	25	420.0	200.0
9	9	10	60.0	20.0	25	6	26	60.0	25.0
10	10	11	45.0	30.0	26	26	27	60.0	25.0
11	11	12	60.0	35.0	27	27	28	60.0	20.0
12	12	13	60.0	35.0	28	28	29	120.0	70.0
13	13	14	120.0	80.0	29	29	30	200.0	600.0
14	14	15	60.0	10.0	30	30	31	150.0	70.0
15	15	16	60.0	20.0	31	31	32	210.0	100.0
16	16	17	60.0	20.0	32	32	33	60.0	40.0

References

1. Rezaei, P., Vakilian, M.: Distribution system efficiency improvement by reconfiguration and capacitor placement using a modified particle swarm optimization algorithm. In: Electric Power and Energy Conference. IEEE (2010)
2. Sultana, S., Roy, P.K.: Oppositional krill herd algorithm for optimal location of with reconfiguration in radial distribution system. Int. J. Electr. Power Energy Syst. **74**, 78–90 (2016)
3. Leonardo, W.D.O., Sandoval, C.J., Edimar, J.D.O., Pereira, J.L.R., Ivo, C.S.J., Jeferson, S.C.: Optimal reconfiguration and capacitor allocation in radial distribution systems for energy losses minimization. Int. J. Electr. Power Energy Syst. **32**(8), 840–848 (2010)
4. Ahmed, R., Abul, W.: Optimal capacitor allocation in radial distribution systems for loss reduction: a two stage method. Electr. Power Syst. Res. **95**, 168–174 (2013)
5. Hsiao, Y.T., Chen, C.H., Chien, C.C.: Optimal capacitor placement in distribution systems using a combination fuzzy-GA method. Int. J. Electr. Power Energy Syst. **26**(7), 501–508 (2004)
6. Torres, J., Guardado, J.L., Rivas, F.D., Maximov, S., Melgoza, E.: A genetic algorithm based on the edge window decoder technique to optimize power distribution systems reconfiguration. Int. J. Electr. Power Energy Syst. **45**(1), 28–34 (2013)
7. Nara, K., Shiose, A., Kitagawa, M., Ishibara, T.: Implementation of genetic algorithm for distribution systems loss minimum re-configuration. IEEE Trans. Power Syst. **7**(3), 1044–1051 (1992)
8. John, F.F., Marcos, J.R., Marina, L., Rubén, R.: A mixed-integer LP model for the reconfiguration of radial electric distribution systems considering distributed generation. Electr. Power Syst. Res. **97**, 51–60 (2013)
9. González, A., Echavarren, F.M., Rouco, L., Gómez, T., Cabetas, J.: Reconfiguration of large-scale distribution networks for planning studies. Int. J. Electr. Power Energy Syst. **37**(1), 86–94 (2012)
10. Singh, D., Rakesh, K.M.: Load type impact on distribution system reconfiguration. Int. J. Elect Power Energy Syst. **42**(1), 583–592 (2012)
11. Arun, M., Aravindhababu, P.: Fuzzy based reconfiguration algorithm for voltage stability enhancement of distribution systems. Exp. Syst. Appl. **37**(10), 6974–6978 (2010)
12. Su, C.T., Chang, C.F., Chious, J.P.: Distribution network reconfiguration for loss reduction by ant colony search algorithm. Electr. Power Syst. Res. **75**(2–3), 190–199 (2005)
13. Abdelaziz, A.Y., Mohammed, F.M., Mekhamer, S.F., Badr, M.A.L.: Distribution systems reconfiguration using a modified particle swarm optimization algorithm. Electr. Power Syst. Res. **79**(11), 1521–1530 (2009)
14. Cebrian, J.C., Kagan, N.: Reconfiguration of distribution networks to minimize loss and disruption costs using genetic algorithms. Electr. Power Syst. Res. **80**(1), 53–62 (2010)
15. Lam, Y.S.A., Li, V.O.K.: Chemical-reaction-inspired metaheuristic for optimization. IEEE Trans. Evol. Comput. **14**(3), 381–399 (2010)
16. Bhattacharjee, K., Bhattacharya, A., Haldar, S.: Chemical reaction optimisation for different economic dispatch problems. IET Gener. Transm. Distrib. IET **8**(3), 530–541 (2014)
17. Acharya, N., Mahat, P., Mithulananthan, N.: An analytical approach for DG allocation in primary distribution network. Int. J. Electr. Power Energy Syst. **28**(10), 669–678 (2006)
18. Teng, J.H.: A direct approach for distribution system load flow solutions. IEEE Trans. Power Deliver. **18**(3), 882–887 (2003)

19. Kashem, M.A., Ganapathy, V., Jasmon, G.B., Buhari, M.I.: A novel method for loss minimization in distribution networks. In: International Conference on Electric Utility Deregulation and Restructuring and Power Technologies 2000, City University, London, 4–7 April, pp. 251–256 (2000)
20. Das, D.: Optimal placement of capacitors in radial distribution system using Fuzzy-GA method. Int. J. Electr. Power Energy Syst. **30**(6–7), 361–397 (2008)
21. Banerjee, S., Chanda, C.K., Das, D.: Reconfiguration of distribution networks based on fuzzy multiobjective approach by considering loads of different types. J. Inst. Eng. India Ser. B **94**(1), 29–42 (2013)

QoS-Aware Task Offloading Using Self-organized Distributed Cloudlet for Mobile Cloud Computing

Deepsubhra Guha Roy[(⊠)], Ahona Ghosh, Bipasha Mahato,
and Debashis De

Centre of Mobile Cloud Computing, Department of Computer Science
and Engineering, Maulana Abul Kalam Azad University of Technology,
WB B.F.-142, Sector-I, Salt Lake City, Kolkata 700064, West Bengal, India
roysubhraguha@gmail.com, ahonaghosh95@gmail.com,
mahatobipasha.91@gmail.com, dr.debashis.de@gmail.com

Abstract. Edge-cloud has drawn a significant attention of the IT industries, cloud operators as well as the network service providers and mobile users. To meet the user requirements the service providers have been able to provide various types of services related to the network by applying virtual network functions and deployed cloudlet in Metropolitan Area Network. Our goal is to maximize the number of admitted requests via load balancing by reducing the integrated cost of admissions within a time spare. A problem function is designed to offload set of the tasks in a metropolitan area network, where a particular network related function with a maximum bearable delay is requested by each offloaded task through different network services according to different offloading requests. An algorithm is designed to make a reduced bipartite graph with maximum matching and minimum weight. To save cost we develop an effective prediction algorithm where instances of network functions get created and/or released in different cloudlets considering that the offloading request patterns dynamically changes. Later we have also analyzed that the possible outcome of the proposed algorithm is efficient while distributing the load among the cloudlets into the edge-cloud.

Keywords: Cloudlets · Task offloading ·
Wireless metropolitan area networks · Network function virtualization (NFV) ·
Offloading algorithm

1 Introduction

Mobile devices are becoming an essential part of people's daily lives as they are able provide communication anytime and anywhere. Mobile services are also being developed and user requirements are getting high. But due to the limited processing and storage ability of the devices, the tasks can be transferred to external platform called cloudlet via Wi-Fi or Bluetooth for processing. Recently in 2017, CEO of Facebook Mark Zuckerberg gave a future idea where he stated that in public spaces artists would be able to display virtual network [14] and friends would be able to share study

© Springer Nature Singapore Pte Ltd. 2019
J. K. Mandal et al. (Eds.): CICBA 2018, CCIS 1030, pp. 410–424, 2019.
https://doi.org/10.1007/978-981-13-8578-0_32

materials with each other by mobile smart devices very soon, F8 Developers conference. Quality of service requirements and Network related tasks differ with various offloading tasks. So we can group the jobs together according to their requirement of similar network related tasks and perform the operations in VMs. Challenges of instantiating instance of network function services include

- How many instances will be kept by which cloudlet so that the cost and delay will be minimized?
- How we can minimize the request admission cost by utilizing the instances which already exist?
- How we can predict the amount of required instances?

Here, we deal with the above mentioned challenges in a mobile cloud by studying the task offloading problem. To respond to the dynamic request pattern changes, we form a process which will predict the requirements of upcoming instances by removal or creation of each network function instance in every cloudlet. The paper contributes in the following fields: A WMAN consist of a number of cloudlet servers and access points (APs), we generate a task offloading problem which is aware of QoS and in which each task requires a particular network related function and VNFs vary according to different offloading tasks.

2 Related Works

In the recent past years cloudlet task offloading has been studied widely. Usually the offloading systems model [2, 3] consists of a mobile smart device's client component and a cloudlet server which executes offloading tasks without any physical connection. As the number of user applications is too large for servers to store in the cloudlet, most of the previous works [2, 4, 7] used virtual machines as the offloading platform. Cloudlets execute VM tasks after receiving a mobile device's virtual machine image. Most of the studies considered that a specific VM is connected with every user in the cloudlet but did not take into account the case that multiple users can be served by one VM. However due to the specific position of some applications, assuming multiple users in an area requests same service from cloudlet will be more realistic. In [8] the architecture of task offloading for mobile enlarged reality in museum background has been introduced.

In last few years, a lot of problems on network planning have been done by deploying cloudlets [1, 5, 6]. For example, after developing a heuristic, Jia et al. [9, 10] considered a WMAN assigning user request to different cloudlets. In his algorithm minimization of maximum delay of offloaded tasks which resides in a scattered network of cloudlet was also discussed. Xia et al. [13] worked with task offloading which is opportunity based under energy and bandwidth of mobile smart device [8, 11].

3   Preliminaries

3.1   Methodology

In our proposed model, three layers are there. (i) User layer (ii) Network layer
(iii) Application layer. The user layer gives input to the system. The application layer
checks the user requirements. And the network layer checks the availability of network.
In the other part of the model traffic monitoring, network availability monitoring and
network monitoring functions are there (Fig. 1).

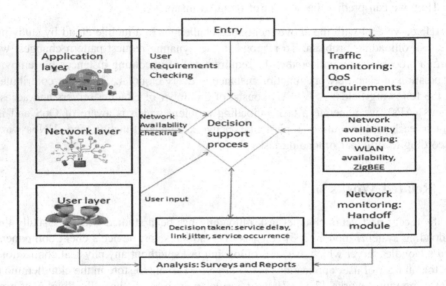

Fig. 1. Three layer decision making system flow diagram

Traffic monitoring takes care of the QoS requirements. Network availability
monitoring is the checking of availability of WLAN or Wi-Fi or ZigBee. And network
monitoring contains the handoff module. All these modules are connected to a decision
support process which is concerned about service delay, link jitter and service occurrence. After the decision making, the analysis is made using surveys and reports.

3.2   System Model

Cloudlet's computing resources instantiate VNFs for implementing offloading requests
of mobile users. So there is a set of virtualized network functions $v_b \in V$ where
$1 \leq b \leq M$ and $M = |V|$ applied in Virtual Machines of cloudlets. If the total time is
distributed to some periods, the accessible resource amount at the starting of the slots
varies. Hence in time instance t, computing capacity of cloudlet c_a is $capacity_a(t)$ where
$1 \leq a \leq n$ and $n = |C|$. Then A WMAN $W = (A \cup C, L)$ where

A = set of AP nodes
L = links between AP nodes
C = set of cloudlet nodes placed with Access Point nodes

We say that an instance of v_b has been implemented when the offloading request implementation with a network related activity $v_b \in V$ requests basic resource of v_b, otherwise if the request implementation requires the v_b resource y times then we say it takes y number of instances of v_b for every $v_b \in V$. The total instances of v_b in c_a at time t is denoted by $m_{ba}(t)$.

A tuple $(id_d, loc_d, VNF_d, \beta_d, f_d)$ represents every user request $r_d \in R(t)$ where id_d = request identity, loc_d = location of the user, VNF_d = Computing service that r_d requests and β_d = packet rate and f_d = requirement of delay by r_d.

3.3 Requirements of End to End Delay of Offloading Requirements

Delay between two ends of a request r_d which has been admitted includes the delay in queuing, processing delay, delay to instantiate and network latency.

3.3.1 Queuing and Processing Delay

Before processing in VM, each offloaded packet having packet rate β_a will have to wait, which leads to both queuing and processing delays. The requests to each cloudlet c_k are divided into N number of groups according to the request service. Here we assume at each cloudlet M/M/n queue for each service $v_b \in V$. The average of queuing delay is:

$$\varepsilon_{da}(\beta) = \frac{1}{m_{ba}(t)\lambda b - \beta'} \tag{1}$$

Where β is the total rate of all packets, λ_b is the rate of data processing and $1/\lambda_b$ is the processing delay.

3.3.2 Instantiation Delay

Without losing generality it is assumed that the delay to instantiate a VNF instance is denoted by a constant e_b^{ins}.

3.3.3 Network Latency

Within the network G, data traffic is assumed to get transferred through the shortest path from the source to destination $(q_{loc(d)}, c_a)$ where loc(d) is the source and c_a is the destination cloudlet. Therefore, the network suffering from an accumulative delay for a request say r_d is considered as network latency and denoted by Eq. 2.

$$l_d^{net} = \sum_{u \in q_{loc(d),ca}} s(u) \tag{2}$$

where delay of link u = s(u).

3.4 Admission Cost

Without violating the delay constraint, a particular network function v_b offloaded a set of request S_{ba} into cloudlet c_a. To measure the operational cost there have to consider two other costs say the transmission cost of data packet and the processing cost $x(VNF_d^b)$ of those data at c_a. If there are enough resources to allocate in cloudlet c_a then the required resources are consumed by r_d through increasing the functional instances for virtual network VNF_d^b in cloudlet c_a. So the total cost of transmitting packet called the admission cost $p(r_k)$, is measured by adding the processing cost with the transmission cost for a new instances to execute r_d in c_a.

3.5   Problem Definition

In a WMAN W (A ∪ C, L) it is assumed that there are some instances for every network related function fi ∈ F are already installed in cloudlet C. The operational cost minimization problem in this situation within the network W is finding a plan of request assignments where the no. of assigned requests is maximized during a particular time instance T.

4   Proposed Offloading Handling Algorithm

Here we firstly consider that, at the starting of each of the time period t, the request admission in R(t) have been performed. After that, dynamic request admissions has been taken into account and an online algorithm has been proposed to minimize operational cost of the problem in W(A ∪ C, L).

4.1   Algorithm to Handle the Offloading Requests at Each Time Instance

At starting of each time slot t, suppose a bunch of requests R(t) is arriving. Offloading request assignment is represented by each matched edge where execution requirement delay, between two ends is described following:

For each cloudlet c_a a bipartite graph $X_a(t) = (Y_a \cup \{y_0, a\}, Z_a, Q_a; w)$ is considered where

Y_a is the VNF instances at c_a
$y_{0,a}$ is the available resources to create new instances
Z_a is the request set $r_d \in R(t)$

Q_a is the set of edges between nodes $y_{ba} \in Y_a$ and $r_d \in Z_a$ if the resource and delay requirements are not violated by resource sharing. We draw an edge between r_d and the instance of v_b in cloudlet c_a when

(i)   The Virtual Network Function of r_d is v_b.
(ii)   The required instance of v_b by r_d is not more than the total no. of instances m_{ba}
(iii)   Other resource delay constraints are not violated by the request admission of r_d
(iv)   The delay caused for assigning r_k is not more than l_d.

The cost to implement request r_k in cloudlet c_f is represented by the weight of the edges. So the edge weights are the total cost of routing, processing and creating instance. If the no. of cloudlets residing in W is n, then the auxiliary graph

$$X(t) = \bigcup_{a=1}^{n} X_a T = (Y(t), Z(t), Q(t); w) \tag{3}$$

is derived from W when

$$Y(t) = \bigcup_{a=1}^{n} \left(Y_j \bigcup \{y_0, a\} \right)$$

$$Z(t) = \sum_{a=1}^{n} Z_j = \{r_1, r_2, \ldots r_n\} \text{ and}$$

$$Q(t) = \bigcup_{a=1}^{n} Q_a$$

For each request entry S(t) at the starting of every time instance t, in the assignment algorithm, $X_1(t) = X(t)$ has granted. In i number of iterations, a maximum matching minimum weight N_i in $G_i(t)$ is seen. Then the requested resources are allocated for the requests in N_i, requests who are matched already, are deleted from Ni and loaded to S(t), the remaining instances and resources of each cloudlet are updated. The graph $G_{i+1}(t)$ is constructed for the next iteration and the process gets terminated when no more matching is found in $G_{i+1}(t)$.

Algorithm 1: Request_Assignment_Algorithm(X(t),R(t))
Input: n cloudlets having resource capacity capacity$_j$(t) where the no. of instances of each $V_f \in F$ and request set R(t) in a piece time instance t
Output: Admitted request maximization (hence R'(t)$\subseteq$ R(t)) in every time instance t minimization of cost. After admission, the request r_d will go to which cloudlet and which instance it will join/create is determined finally.
1. **Start**
/*Admit requests of R(t)*/
2. $N_t \leftarrow \emptyset$ /*Request assignment in R(t)*/
3.   cost$_t \leftarrow 0$ /*Minimization of the cost*/
4.   Generate a weighted bipartite graph X(t)
5. $X_1(t) \leftarrow X(t)$
6. $i \leftarrow 1$
7.   cost$_t \leftarrow 0$
8.   Having a maximum matching there exist a min. weight called N_o in $X_1(t)$ **do**
9.   By calling an algorithm of weighted maximum matching, find the maximum matching minimum weight N_1 in $X_1(T)$
10.   if $N_i \neq 0$,
11. $N_t \leftarrow N_t \cup N_t$
12. $c(N_i) \leftarrow \sum e \epsilon N_i \, w(q)$
13.   cost$_t \leftarrow$ cost$_t$ + c (N_i)
14.   Assign resources to the N_i requests
15.   Update the resource availability and offloading function instance
/* Requests to load into N_o from R (t),when r(N_o) is the requests set in N_o */
16.   R (t) $\leftarrow$ R (t) \ r (N_i)
17. $i \leftarrow i + 1$
18.   Generate $X_i(t)$ taking the modified amount of resource and VNF instances and the set of request R(t)
19.   End if
20. **Return** N_t corresponding to the request admissions in R(t), where cost$_t$ is the cost of implementing resource
21. **End**

4.2   Proposed Algorithm to Minimize the Operational Cost

Previous algorithm has observed to admit offloading requests in a single time period. But in real time scenario, requests come to and go from the system dynamically. Here the present admissions of request will consider their impact on the admission of the future requests.

Some of the VNF instances related with different network functions are generated to admit recently appeared requests. And parallel unoccupied VNF instances moved to the system as they have no chance to be used in the near future. The resources which are released can be handled by us in two ways as follows:

(i)   The VNF instances which can be used in future should not be released
(ii) Immediately release VNF which becomes idle

The first solution indicates that a number of VNF instances will be distributed with some next queued requests. So the VM will keep the resources occupied by them instead of releasing them which will be the reason behind the idleness of more instances. This will result to some unnecessary operational costs and will not allow new requests to be admitted for absence of sufficient VNF instances. However if a request requires a VNF instance just after its release, the delay requirement can be violated as a new instance creation will result to a delay. For avoiding such scenario we make a prediction about VNF creation to guess and releases the idle VNF instance as well as to replace old VNF instance and/or add new VNF construction to minimize the operational cost and it also help to reduce response delay requirements.

Here we demonstrate a technique which will be able to guess the idle instance to be allocated and new instance creations as per requirement of VNF to cope up with the request changing patterns over time. So the system is able to collect resource which were previously allocated but in present staying in idle situation, by releasing those. Then the system cost overhead is maintained those idle VNFs if those are beyond a given threshold. Particularly, if $m_{ba}(t)$ stands for the no. of VNF instances which are to be added (f_i) into the cloudlet c_a at time instant t, then the actual number of instance is $m'_{ba}(t)$ ($\leq m_{ba}(t)$).

Then VNF instances of f_i which are still idle in the cloudlet c_j at time instance t is

$$\Delta_{ba}(t) = m_{ba}(t) - m'_{ba}(t) \tag{4}$$

In cloudlet c_a, let every idle instance v_f causes cost α_{ba} at each time instance, and a cost threshold α ($\geq n_0 \max_{vf \in v} \{c(v_f)\}$) exists there. If cost of some instance is more than the threshold, then the system will release the resource occupied by that instance. At least $m'_{ba}(t)$ instances should be reserved to satisfy the delay requirement of the requests running in $R_{ij}(t)$. But the most undesired situation arises when a VNF instance of f_i has just released to the system, and it has to create that previous instance repeatedly to accept a new request, even in the next time slot. To avoid this scenario, we propose a previous record study or prediction mechanism which is able to determine the expected instances quantity to be kept in each network of the whole system. To predict whether a instance will be removed or replaced or added, we apply a trace (patterns) follow algorithm of offloading request for each cloudlet. The auto-regression technique has used to presumption the number of instances $\tilde{N}_{ba}(t)$ requirement in the next time slot.

$$\tilde{N}_{ba}(t) = \gamma_1 m_{ba}(t-1) + \gamma_2 m_{ba}(t-2) + \ldots + \gamma_k m_{ba}(t-k) \tag{5}$$

Here $\gamma_k =$ constant, $\gamma_k > 0$ and $0 \leq \gamma_{k'} \leq 1$.

If in a network function f_i the number of instances is increased in every time instance, when we add some extra computing resources, some instances of VNF will get added, which will result to some extra cost for creation of each instance. Instead if we want to produce the expected no. of VNF instances at a time to satisfy its upcoming requirement, it can find out while pertain an auto regression technique. Let $z_{ba}(t)$ is new instances number of v_f added at any time slot t into cloudlet c_a. Suppose at time instant t_0 the no. of added instances are started to go beyond the threshold θ, i.e. $\sum_{i=t_0}^{t} b_{ij}$ (1) $\geq \theta$ then the predicted new instances will be

$$b'_{ba}(t) = \beta_1 b_{ba}(t-1) + \beta_2 b_{ba}(t-2) + \ldots + \beta_k b_{ba}(t-k) \tag{6}$$

where $\theta =$ given threshold.

$\beta_k =$ constant where $\beta_k > 0$ and $0 \leq \beta_{k'} \leq 1$.

So after a time slot t the no. of VNF instances to execute through f_i is $b'_{ba}(t) + m'_{ba}(t)$.

Till now we calculate the parameters value when there are enough VNF instance into the cloudlet. But now we will go through that entropy situation when there has no sufficient cloud instance resources to execute the functions into the cloudlet. We have started to reduce fair numbers of instance to create instance shortage from each cloudlet. Let D_{ij} denotes the total no. of required resources and RC_a is the residual resource available into the cloudlet assembly. If there is enough instance is in idle phase $(DI_a > RC_a)$, then required instances will be allocated to execute the task or needed VNF instances have to be created, in other case if $q_a = \frac{RC_a}{DI_a}$ is the residual instance ratio then it will virtually allocated among the cloudlets of the assembly.

$$a'_{ba}(t) = \left\lfloor \frac{a_{ba(t)} C(v_f) q_a}{C(v_f)} \right\rfloor \text{ instances for } v_f \text{ at } c_a. \tag{7}$$

5 Performance Evaluation

5.1 Experimental Settings

A network topology [9] is followed by the WMAN W(A,L) which is made by 100 Access Points, and the network is created by Barabasi-Albert model [12]. Randomly deployed 20 cloudlets are there in G. Each cloudlet is having computing capacity capacity$_j$ between 2000 to 4000 MHz [15]. 20 available network functions are allowed in the cloudlet where each instance requires between 40 to 400 MHz. The time to reach packet from one AP to the destination AP is 2 ms to 5 ms [13]. To execute the proposed scenario a machine has used having a 16 GiB RAM and 3.4 GHz Intel i7-4770 CPU.

The Parameters of Network Are
Here we send 1000 requests per time slot where packet rate of each request is between 10 to 80 packets per second similar to and a delay d_k between 0.2 and 1.2 s. From 20 different network functions we randomly selected the network related function requested by every request. As reference we use the Amazon EC2 instance, assuming the operational cost in every time instance, as 0.25/MHz, where the cost to instantiate a new instance is from 20 to 50. Here it has been assumed that transfer cost of a packet from an AP to another AP grows same with the latency and that is why the cost of transferring packet varies from 0.002 to 0.005.

We assess the performance of our proposed algorithm by comparing it with an algorithm which admits every request r_d having the highest rank where available service and the inverse of cost of implementation are multiplied to calculate the rank. We refer this greedy algorithm by ALGO2 [12] and our proposed algorithm by ALGO1 here.

Algorithm 2: Prediction_of_instance_for_Cloudlet Functions (G(t),R(t))

Input: n cloudlets with available resource capacity$_a$(t), the instance amount of every $v_b \in$ V, and requests in R(t) in every time instance t for t ≤ T ,every idle VNF instance v_b having cost α_{ba} and threshold of cost$_t$.

Output: maximize admission requests (R'(t) ⊆R (t)) $\forall$ t during a limited time horizon hence T with condition 1 ≤ t ≤ T to minimize the sum of all costs.

If above condition is applied to all request r_d for functional execution into the cloudlet, then to predict it will be sent to which cloudlet and further in which instance.

More instances will be added or removed or replaced it is also decided.

Initialization:

Initial predicted Cost ← Null;

Z ← Ø; /* the total admission cost to offload task in the system in a time instance T and admission of request Z */

Start

$\forall$ t in 1 ≤ t ≤ T do

1: Decision is taken if need to release any previously occupied functional resources which is pre ently in idle state.

3. l_{ij} ← t_0 /* The release of resource was done at time instance t_0 with t_0 < t */;

4. for each cloudlet cj do

5. | for all function fi ∈ F do

6. | | if $\sum_{l=t-l_{ba}}^{t} \Delta_{ba}$(l) γ_{ba} ≥ θ then

7. | | Guess m'_{ba} (t): the number of instances of v_f to be kept in c_a

8. | | Keep max{m'_{ba}(t), m_{ba}(t) } instances of v_f in cloudlet c_a

9. | | Release the occupied resources by the rest n_{ij}(t)−max{n'_{ba} (t),n_{ba}(t)} instances of v_f in cloudlet ca

10. | | Update the amounts of available resources at cloudlet c_j

11. | | l_{ba} ← t /* reset the start time of the next instances of fi release in cj */

12. | End if

/* STEP 2: increase the network function instances*/

13. I_{ba} ← t_0 /* the increased v_f instance in the latest time instance t_0 where t_0 < t */

14. for each cloudlet c_a do

15. for each v_f ∈ V do

16. | if $\sum_{l=t-T_{ba}}^{t} a_{ba}(l)\alpha_{ba}$ ≥ θ then

17. | Guess the number of instances $â_{ij}$ of fi which should be increased

18. | | if RC_a is the remaining computing resource of cloudlet c_a and DI_a is the required resource to create new instances

19. | | | if RC_a < DI_a then

20. | | | There will be ⌊RC_a/DI_a · (n_{ba}(t) + $â_{ba}$ (t)) ⌋ instances of v_f in cloudlet c_a In time t

21. | | | else

22. | | | n_{ba} (t) + $â_{ba}$ (t) instances of v_f will remain in cloudlet c_a at time slot t

23. | | | End if

24. | | Modify the existing resources into cloudlet c_a

25. | | I_{ba} ← t /* reset the starting time of the next Increasing VNF instance v_f of cloudlet c_a */

26. | End if

27. End if

/* STAGE two: Admit requests of R(t)*/

28. Zt and cost$_t$ are calculated using Algorithm 1 to X(t)
29. $Z \leftarrow Z \cup Z_t$
30. cost $\leftarrow$ cost + cost$_t$
31. **Return** Z which denotes request assignment, where cost is the admission
    Cost to the system in time T
32. **End**

5.2 Performance of the Algorithm Within One Time Slot

We have analyzed the outcomes of ALGO1 and ALGO2 [12] in a single time instance
is compared with the changes of the request numbers from 575 to 2800 and created
some instances in each cloud randomly of each NFV.

In the Fig. 2, it is observed that ALGO1 accepts more requests than ALGO2 [12]
and incurs less operation cost as seen in Fig. 3. In Fig. 4 we can see that the running
time in case of both the algorithms increases dramatically with the no. of requests.

Number of Requests	ALGO1(Proposed)	ALGO2
575	412	425
800	700	750
1200	712	895
1600	725	957
2000	727	1007
2400	727	1110
2800	728	1230

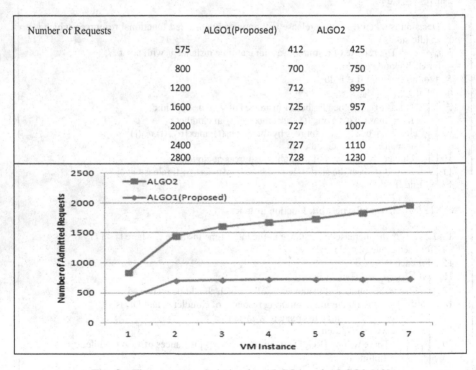

Fig. 2. The requests admission by ALGO1 and ALGO2 [12]

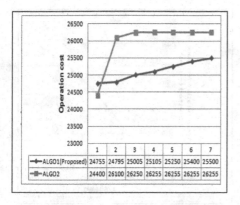

Fig. 3. Operation cost incurred by ALGO1 and ALGO2 [12]

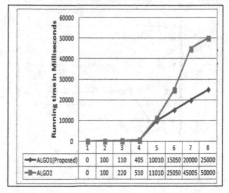

Fig. 4. Running times of ALGO1 and ALGO2 [12] in Milliseconds

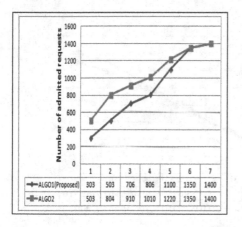

Fig. 5. Request admission by ALGO1 and ALGO2 [12]

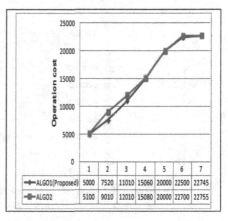

Fig. 6. Operation cost delivered by ALGO1 and ALGO2 [12]

In Fig. 5, it is shown that ALGO1 allows more request admission than ALGO2 [12]. As requests with low cost get assigned first, the rest of the requests are expensive.

Figure 6 shows the operation cost when the number of requests is 1500 and no. of cloudlet is between 4 and 24. Figure 7 shows that running time increases linearly when number of cloudlets increases. Due to the increase in number of cloudlet, the capacity increases, so per round of matching more requests are assigned. Figures 8 and 9 show that as both the algorithms aim for the requests which have the minimum resource requirements, more requests of low cost are admitted. ALGO2 [12] is 31% better than ALGO1 in increasing the resource allocation. Figures 10 and 11 illustrate the effect of

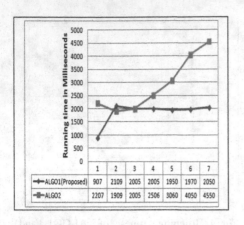

Fig. 7. Running time of ALGO1 and ALGO2 [12] in Milliseconds

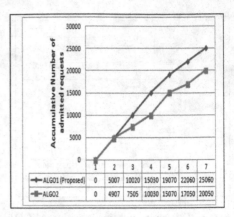

Fig. 8. Admission of request in ALGO1 and ALGO2 [12]

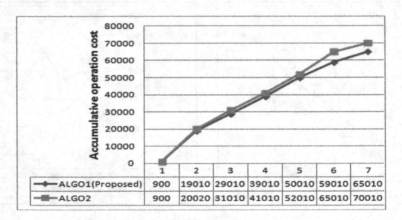

Fig. 9. The total operational cost by ALGO1 and ALGO2 [12]

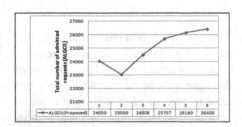

Fig. 10. Request admission by ALGO1

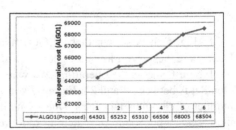

Fig. 11. The cost of operations derived from ALGO2 [12]

cost threshold on total number of request admission and the total cost of operation with 100 time slots. Both ALGO1 and ALGO2 [12] show that request admission operation cost have increased. As amount of resources is limited, the number of request assignment is restricted.

6 Conclusion

A task offloading problem within WMAN for each task of maximized tolerable delay through different services from the cloudlets are required by different requests. We have tried to maximize the number of admitted request to offload the tasks while minimizing the admission cost. We design an algorithm for the problem where a maximum matching minimum weight bipartite graph was generated and helps to create an instance with predicted optimized cost. At last, we evaluate the algorithm performance by experimental simulation which proves that the algorithm proposed by us is of worthwhile and promising.

Acknowledgement. Department of Science and Technology (DST) for sanctioning a research Project entitled "Dynamic Optimization of Green Mobile Networks: Algorithm, Architecture and Applications" under Fast Track Young Scientist scheme reference no.: SERB/F/5044/2012-2013, DST FISTSR/FST/ETI-296/ and TEQIP-III.

References

1. Roy, D.G., De, D., Alam, M.M., Chattopadhyay, S.: Multi-cloud scenario based QoS enhancing virtual resource brokering. In: 2016 3rd International Conference on Recent Advances in Information Technology (RAIT), pp. 576–581. IEEE, March 2016
2. Chun, B.-G., Ihm, S., Maniatis, P., Naik, M., Patti, A.: CloneCloud: elastic execution between mobile device and cloud. In: Proceedings of the Sixth Conference on Computer Systems. ACM (2011)
3. Cuervo, E., et al.: MAUI: making smartphones last longer with code offload. In: Proceedings of the 8th International Conference on Mobile Systems, Applications, and Services. ACM (2010)
4. Kosta, S., Aucinas, A., Hui, P., Mortier, R., Zhang, X.: ThinkAir: dynamic resource allocation and parallel execution in the cloud for mobile code offloading. In: Proceedings of IEEE INFOCOM. IEEE (2012)
5. De, D., et al.: Architecture of green sensor mobile cloud computing. IET Wirel. Sens. Syst. **6** (4), 109–120 (2016)
6. Roy, D.G., De, D., Mukherjee, A., Buyya, R.: Application-aware cloudlet selection for computation offloading in multi-cloudlet environment. J. Supercomputing **73**(4), 1672–1690 (2017)
7. Chen, E.Y., Itoh, M.: Virtual smartphone over IP. In: Proceedings of World of Wireless Mobile and Multimedia Networks (WoWMoM). IEEE (2010)
8. Rodrıguez-Santana, B.G., Viveros, A.M., Carvajal-Gámez, B.E., Trejo-Osorio, D.C.: Mobile computation offloading architecture for mobile augmented reality, case study: visualization of cetacean skeleton. Int. J. Adv. Comput. Sci. Appl. **1**(7), 665–671 (2016)

9. Jia, M., Cao, J., Liang, W.: Optimal cloudlet placement and user to cloudlet allocation in wireless metropolitan area networks. IEEE Trans. Cloud Comput. **5**, 725–737 (2015)

10. Jia, M., Liang, W., Xu, Z., Huang, M.: Cloudlet load balancing in wireless metropolitan area networks. In: Proceedings of INFOCOM. IEEE (2016)

11. Mukherjee, A., De, D., Roy, D.G.: A power and latency aware cloudlet selection strategy for multi-cloudlet environment. IEEE Trans. Cloud Comput. **7**(1), 141–154 (2016)

12. Xia, Q., Liang, W., Xu, W.: Throughput maximization for online request admissions in mobile cloudlets. In: Proceedings of 2013 IEEE 38th Conference on Local Computer Networks (LCN). IEEE (2013)

13. Albert, R., Jeong, H., Barabási, A.-L.: Internet: diameter of the world-wide web. Nature **401**(6749), 130–131 (1999)

14. Knight, S., Nguyen, H.X., Falkner, N., Bowden, R., Roughan, M.: The internet topology zoo. IEEE J. Sel. Areas Commun. **29**(9), 1765–1775 (2011)

15. Facebook f8 developers conference (2017). https://www.fbf8.com/. Accessed 25 Apr 2017

WPD and RBFNN Based Fault Location Estimation on TCSC Based Series Compensated Transmission Line

Kamrul Hasan Mallick[✉], Bikas Patel, and Parthasarathi Bera

Department of Electrical Engineering, Kalyani Government Engineering College,
Kalyani 741235, India
khmallick27@gmail.com, biks.ee@gmail.com,
parthabera1977@gmail.com

Abstract. This paper presents a technique for estimation of fault location on the thyristor control series capacitor (TCSC) compensated transmission line for different types of faults. This technique is developed using wavelet packet decomposition (WPD) and radial basis function neural network (RBFNN) for fast and accurate estimation of fault location. The faulty current signal of 10 ms (half cycle) duration after fault inception is recorded. The fault signals recorded with 40 kHz sampling frequency are decomposed by WPD up to 3rd level with mother wavelet db6 to compute wavelet packet energy (WPE). The features of current signals are extracted by WPD to train the RBFNN for different fault locations. Training and Testing are done by varying fault resistance and position of TCSC. It is found that the combination of RBFNN and WPD coefficient's energy of fault signals can locate the fault with high accuracy.

Keywords: Wavelet packet decomposition (WPD) ·
Thyristor control series capacitor (TCSC) ·
Radial basis function neural network (RBFNN) · Power system fault ·
Feature extraction

1 Introduction

Accurate fault location estimation of long transmission line especially in the hilly area provides a reduction of repair cost, immediate restoration of power supply and improvement of reliability. Failure of fault location estimation leads to prolonged line outage and severe economic losses. Different methods have been found in literature for fault localization on the transmission line. In [1–3], methods for fault analysis on the transmission line have been proposed using wavelet packet transform and artificial intelligence. The article [4] presents the fault detection and location based on travelling waves by Fast Discrete S-transform (FDST) for TCSC compensated lines. Article [5] has shown a hybrid methodology for fault location estimation by the artificial neural network (ANN) and wavelet transform. Different techniques such as combination of wavelet packet decomposition and support vector machine [6], mathematical model for transmission line in the absence of line parameters [7], non-contact lightning current monitoring system [8], Wavelet entropy [9] and wavelet energy [10] have been

© Springer Nature Singapore Pte Ltd. 2019
J. K. Mandal et al. (Eds.): CICBA 2018, CCIS 1030, pp. 425–433, 2019.
https://doi.org/10.1007/978-981-13-8578-0_33

successfully applied in transmission line fault analysis. In [11], back propagation neural network (BPNN) and DWT have been analyzed. Fault detection algorithm for a transmission line with thyristor controlled series compensation is defined in [12]. WPD based traveling wave technique has been elaborated in [8]. For fault location of long transmission lines compensated by series facts devices have been shown in [13, 14]. Radial basis function neural network (RBFNN) has been used for fault diagnosis in controllable series compensated transmission line in [15]. The entropy principle and WPD are discussed in [16–20] as feature extraction tool for fault classification and localization.

This paper presents a fault localization method for a thyristor control series capacitor (TCSC) compensated transmission line using the combination of WPD and RBFNN. The faults at different conditions have been simulated using MATLAB and WPD coefficient's energies of fault current signals are fed to RBFNN for the training and testing.

2 Wavelet Packet Decomposition

Wavelet packet decomposition (WPD) gives better time-frequency resolution than wavelet packet transform (WPT) for non-stationary signal analysis. The transient high-frequency signals are decomposed by WPD to extract important information. The signals are passed through high pass (HP) and low pass (LP) filters to generate approximation and detail coefficients which are denoted by A and D. The signal frequency is decomposed into 2^L frequency bands, where L is the level of decomposition as shown in Fig. 1. Two sequence functions are shown as

$$S_{2n}(t) = \sqrt{2} \sum_{k=0}^{2N-1} h(k)S_n(2t-k) \tag{1}$$

$$S_{2n+1}(t) = \sqrt{2} \sum_{k=0}^{2N-1} g(k)S_n(2t-k) \tag{2}$$

Where $S_0 = \varphi(t)$ and $S_1 = \phi(t)$ are scaling function and wavelet function. Here n is an integer (n = 0, 1, 2.....) which satisfies the above wavelet function and scaling function. So wavelet packet function can be written as

$$W_{j,n,k}(t) = 2^{\frac{-j}{2}}S_n(2^{-j}t-k) \tag{3}$$

The parameters n, k, and j are defined as modulation parameter, time localization parameter, scale parameter respectively. The wavelet packet coefficients are extracted from the decomposition of a signal f(t) by taking the inner product of the signal and the particular wavelet packet function [6] as

$$C_{j,n,k} = \langle f(t), W_{j,n,k(t)} \rangle = \int f(t)W_{j,n,k}(t)dt \tag{4}$$

The WPD coefficient measures the frequency content in the faulty signal and each wavelet packet node represents a specific frequency bands. Features of a signal are combined into an effective manner in which all information of signals remain intact. In this paper, wavelet packet energy is used as fault features and its value for (j, n) node can be calculated as

$$E_{j,n} = \sum_{k=1}^{L} C_{j,n,k}^2 \qquad (5)$$

Where, L is the decomposition level.

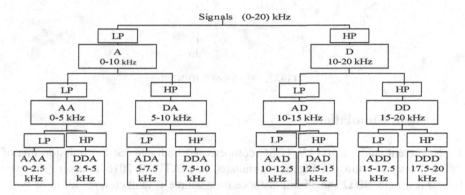

Fig. 1. Decomposition of current signal in WPT

3   Radial Basis Function Neural Network

RBF neural network has been modeled by MATLAB. In present work, RBFNN consists of 24 inputs (8 WPE for each phase current) and one output for fault location estimation. Radial basis function neural network uses radial basis functions as activation functions. For an input vector x and for the jth hidden neuron, the activation function is given by

$$\phi(x, c_j, \delta) = \exp(-\frac{\|x - c_j\|^2}{2\delta^2}) \qquad (6)$$

Where x, c_i, and are input vector centre, activation function and spread factor. In the present work, RBFNN comprises of three inputs and one output layer for estimation of location. The value of spread factor 2 is considered for the location of faults for both ends fed TCSC compensated power transmission networks. The WPD based features extracted from three phase current signals are used to train RBFNN which is shown in Fig. 2.

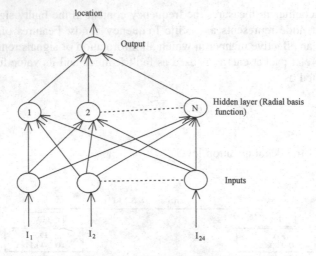

Fig. 2. Model of RBFNN

4 System Simulation

In the present study, a 500 kV TCSC compensated both end fed transmission line of 160 km long as shown in Fig. 3 is simulated in MATLAB 2016 software. For particular resistance 10 Ω and 35 km distance from source 1, fault currents for three types of faults like line to ground (LG) fault, line to line to ground (LLG) fault and three phase (LLLG) fault have been depicted in Figs. 4, 5 and 6 respectively.

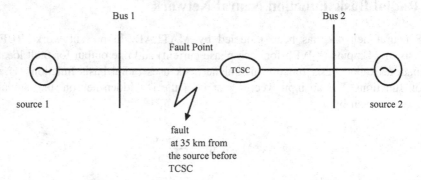

Fig. 3. Single line diagram of a test system

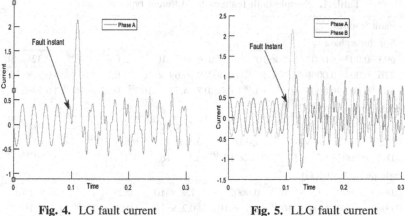

Fig. 4. LG fault current   **Fig. 5.** LLG fault current

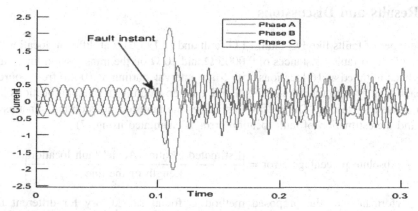

Fig. 6. LLLG fault current (fault occurs at from 35 km from source 1)

5 Feature Extraction Using Wavelet Packet Decomposition

In this paper, wavelet packet energies (WPE) of three phase current signals of half cycle duration after fault are calculated with 3rd level decomposition and mother wavelet db6. These wavelet packet energies are used as fault features to train RBF neural network. Few sample of features for different types of faults at a distance 35 km from source 1 are shown in Table 1.

Table 1. Sample fault features for different types of faults.

Phase current	Fault features							
	For three phase fault (LLLG)							
I_a	693	0.003	0.0007	0.2×10	0.00016	3×10^{-07}	0.6×10^{-08}	0.32×10^{-8}
I_b	276	0.003	0.0008	4.4×10^{-06}	0.00019	0.09×10^{-06}	0.1×10^{-07}	0.2×10^{-07}
I_c	561	0.002	0.0007	0.9×10^{-06}	0.00017	4.76×10^{-07}	0.35×10^{-07}	8.7438
	For double phase fault(LLG)							
I_a	805	0.004	0.0011	1.4×10^{-05}	0.0003	3.5×10^{-06}	8.4×10^{-07}	2.7×10^{-07}
I_b	284	0.005	0.0012	1.4×10^{-05}	0.0002	3.5×10^{-06}	0.6×10^{-07}	2.4×10^{-07}
I_c	36	0.001	0.0002	1.2×10^{-06}	3.4×10^{-05}	3.1×10^{-07}	7.4×10^{-08}	3.4×10^{-08}
	For single phase fault (LG)							
I_a	791	0.0013	0.0007	7.8×10^{-07}	0.0002	1.9×10^{-07}	0.25×10^{-08}	1.6×10^{-08}
I_b	38	0.0005	0.0001	4.9×10^{-07}	0.8×10^{-05}	0.2×10^{-07}	0.08×10^{-08}	1.3×10^{-08}
I_c	35	0.0004	0.0001	0.9×10^{-07}	0.7×10^{-05}	0.2×10^{-07}	0.1×10^{-08}	1.2×10^{-08}

6 Results and Discussions

Three types of faults like LG fault, LLG fault and LLLG fault at different locations are created for two fault resistances of 0.0005 Ω and 10 Ω on the transmission line. Faults have been initiated at 16 locations with 5 km interval starting at 10 km from source 1 for each fault type to train the RBFNN and another 15 uniform random locations have been created for testing. The RBFNN estimates the fault locations on the transmission line and the estimation of fault location error is calculated using (7)

$$\text{Absolute percentage error} = \left| \frac{\text{Estimated location-Actual fault location}}{\text{Length of the line}} \right| \quad (7)$$

The performance of the proposed method is found satisfactory for different fault conditions as shown in Tables 2 and 3.

Table 2. Absolute percentage error (%) with fault resistance 10 Ω

Fault location (km)	Absolute percentage error (%)		
	LLLG fault	LG fault	LLG
15	0.04	0.08	0.02
25	0.01	0.05	0.08
35	0.04	0.11	0.07
45	0.05	0.11	0.02
55	0.05	0.94	0.12
65	0.03	0.05	0.27

(continued)

Table 2. (*continued*)

Fault location (km)	Absolute percentage error (%)		
	LLLG fault	LG fault	LLG
75	0.01	0.06	0.02
85	0.02	0.06	0.15
95	0.04	0.11	0.56
105	0.03	0.12	0.58
115	0.04	0.10	0.52
125	0.02	0.05	0.40
135	0.03	0.02	0.25
145	0.09	0.17	0.06
155	0.07	0.14	0.16

Table 3. Absolute percentage error (%) with fault resistance 0.0005 Ω

Fault location (km)	Absolute percentage error (%)		
	LLLG fault	LLG fault	LG fault
15	0.03	0.17	0.01
25	0.01	0.11	0.07
35	0.03	0.25	0.06
45	0.06	0.27	0.01
55	0.06	0.21	0.06
65	0.061	0.10	0.14
75	0.04	0.15	0.45
85	0.021	0.03	0.17
95	0.06	0.28	0.12
105	0.03	0.26	0.06
115	0.031	0.24	0.13
125	0.032	0.17	0.41
135	0.12	0.02	0.74
145	0.15	0.32	1.23
155	0.13	0.14	0.14

7 Conclusion

In the present article, the features of three phase fault current signals are extracted using wavelet packet decomposition (WPD) and are used to train RBFNN for localization of fault on a TCSC compensated transmission network. The proposed method requires only one end half cycle post-fault current signals which reduce the memory burden. From the result, it is found that combination of WPD and RBFNN can locate the fault with satisfactory accuracy for different types of faults and fault resistances.

References

1. Sedighi, A.R., Haghifam, M.R., Malik, O.P., Ghassemian, M.H.: High impedance fault detection based on wavelet transform and statistical pattern recognition. IEEE Trans. Power Deliv. **20**(4), 2414–2421 (2005)
2. Baqui, I., Zamora, I., Mazón, J., Buigues, G.: High impedance fault detection methodology using wavelet transform and artificial neural networks. Electric Power Syst. Res. **81**, 1325–1333 (2011)
3. Ibrahim, D.K., Tag Eldin, E.S., Aboul-Zahab, E.M., Saleh, S.M.: Real-time evaluation of DWT-based high impedance fault detection in EHV transmission. Electric Power Syst. Res. **80**, 907–914 (2010)
4. Sahoo, B., Subhransu Ranjan, S.: An enhanced fault detection and location and estimation of compensated line connecting wind farm. Electric Power Energy Syst. **96**, 432–441 (2018). https://doi.org/10.1016/j.ijepes.2017.10.022
5. Ray, P., Panigrahi, B.K., Senroy, N.: Hybrid methodology for fault distance estimation in series compensated transmission line. IET Gener. Trans. Distrib. **7**, 431–439 (2013)
6. Yusuff, A.A., Fei, C., Jimoh, A.A., Munda, J.L.: Fault location in a series compensated transmission line based on wavelet packet decomposition and support vector regression. Electric Power Syst. Res. **81**, 1258–1265 (2011)
7. Xiu, W., Liao, Y.: Accurate transmission line fault location considering shunt capacitances without utilizing line parameters. Electric Power Compon. Syst. **39**(16), 1783–1794 (2011)
8. Yao, C., et al.: A novel method to locate a fault of transmission lines by shielding failure. IEEE Trans. Dielectr. Electr. Insul. **21**(4), 1573–1583 (2014). https://doi.org/10.1109/TDEI. 2014.004321
9. Safty, S.E., El-Zonkoly, A.: Applying wavelet entropy principle in fault classification. Electr. Power Energy Syst. **31**, 604–607 (2009)
10. Costa, F.B.: Fault-induced transient detection based on real time analysis of the wavelet coefficient energy. IEEE Trans. Power Deliv. **29**(1), 140–153 (2014)
11. Ngaopitakkul, A., Bunjongjit, S.: An application of a discrete wavelet transform and a back-propagation neural network algorithm for fault diagnosis on single-circuit transmission line. Int. J. Syst. Sci. **44**(9), 1745–1761 (2013). https://doi.org/10.1080/00207721.2012.670290
12. Nale, R., Biswal, M.: Fault detection algorithm for transmission line with Thyristor controlled series compensation (2017). https://doi.org/10.1109/ICCICCT.2016.7987993
13. Ahsaee, M.G., Sadeh, J.: A novel fault-location algorithm for long transmission lines compensated by series FACTS devices. IEEE Trans. Power Deliv. **26**(4) (2011). https://doi. org/10.1109/TPWRD.2011.2166410
14. El-Zonkoly, A.M., Desouki, H.: Wavelet entropy based algorithm for fault detection and classification in FACTS compensated transmission line. Energy Power Eng. **3**, 34–42 (2011). https://doi.org/10.4236/epe.2011.31006
15. Song, Y.H., Jolins, A.T., Xuan, Q.Y.: Radial basis function neural networks for fault diagnosis in controllable series compensated transmission lines (2002). https://doi.org/10. 1109/MELCON.1996.551222
16. Liu, Z., Han, Z., Zhang, Y., Zhang, Q.: Multiwavelet packet entropy and its application in transmission line fault recognition and classification. IEEE Trans. Neural Net. Learn. Syst. **25**(11), 2043–2052 (2014). https://doi.org/10.1109/TNNLS.2014.2303086
17. Ekici, S., Yildirim, S., Poyraz, M.: Energy and entropy-based feature extraction for locating fault on transmission lines by using neural network and wavelet packet decomposition. Expert Syst. Appl. **34**(4), 2937–2944 (2008). https://doi.org/10.1016/j.eswa.2007.05.011

18. Vyas, B., Maheshwari, R.P., Das, B.: Investigation for improved artificial intelligence techniques for thyristor-controlled series compensated transmission line fault classification with discrete wavelet packet entropy measures. Electr. Power Compon. Syst. 42(6), 544–566 (2014). https://doi.org/10.1080/15325008.2014.880961
19. Dasgupta, A., Nath, S., Das, A.: Transmission line fault classification and location using wavelet entropy and neural network. Electric Power Compon. Syst. 40(15), 1676–1689 (2012). https://doi.org/10.1080/15325008.2012.716495
20. Patel, B., Bera, P., Saha, B.: Wavelet packet entropy and RBFNN based fault detection, classification and localization on HVAC transmission line. Electric Power Compon. Syst. https://doi.org/10.1080/15325008.2018.1431817

Implementation of Universal Modulator Using CORDIC Architecture in FPGA

Debarshi Datta[1]([✉]), Partha Mitra[1], and Himadri Sekhar Dutta[2]

[1] Department of Electronics and Communication Engineering,
Brainware Group of Institutions, Kolkata, India
debarshidatta7@gmail.com, pmitra123@gmail.com
[2] Department of Electronics and Communication Engineering,
Kalyani Government Engineering College, Nadia, India
himadri.dutta@gmail.com

Abstract. Implementation of universal modulator in Field Programmable Gate Array (FPGA) is very much useful in many real-time applications for its high throughput, low-cost and short time to market. This paper presents pipeline based CORDIC (COordinate Rotation Digital Computer) algorithm is used in universal modulator such as Amplitude Modulator (AM), Frequency Modulator, Phase Modulator (PM). The CORDIC algorithm basically converts the coordinates from polar mode to rectangular mode. In the absence of multiplier and accumulator in CORDIC architecture, the digital realization system using CORDIC architecture can be efficiently optimized at hardware level. It only requires addition, subtraction, bit shifting, and lookup table and hence the system has become energy efficient and also provides accurate result. The design has been coded in Hardware Description Language (HDL) and synthesized by using Xilinx ISE Design Suite 14.7 with Virtex-6 target device. The implementation result shows that proposed system has less slice-delay product compare to previous architecture.

Keywords: ASIC · AM · FM · CORDIC · FPGA · Universal modulator · HDL

1 Introduction

The modern communication systems consist of fully programmable digital transmitter and receiver with portable antenna. The transmitter modulates the amplitude, frequency or phase according the message signal. CORDIC [1] is a versatile algorithm widely used in digital signal processing applications, communication systems and many more. This algorithm also offers a simple mechanism for computing the magnitude and phase-angle of an input vector; they are highly demand for complex multiplications and estimation of various functions. CORDIC works on the basis of iterative rotation of a two dimensional vector using only add and shift operations. The CORDIC algorithm is used in rotation mode for calculation of sinusoidal angle. In literature, a lot of research work has been published about FPGA-based CORDIC modulators in last few decades. In [2], the authors proposed CORDIC modulator is implemented in FPGA while

© Springer Nature Singapore Pte Ltd. 2019
J. K. Mandal et al. (Eds.): CICBA 2018, CCIS 1030, pp. 434–441, 2019.
https://doi.org/10.1007/978-981-13-8578-0_34

require small memory space. It also provides more quantization accuracy with limitation of word length. Hence, it is useful to generation of low frequency sinusoidal waveform. In [3], a pipelined CORDIC architecture using 2 stages of multiplexer is being proposed for efficient realization of universal modulator such as ASK, FSK, PSK and QPSK modulation system. In paper [4], the authors described implementation of CORDIC based direct digital synthesizer which can applicable in communication system. A novel methodology of CORDIC architecture has been discussed in paper [5]. The complexity of the proposed architecture can be improved upto 25%. An area efficient mux based CORDIC architecture has been implemented in FPGA [6].

The objective of this paper implementation universal modulator using CORDIC algorithm on FPGA [7]. Nowadays, FPGA technology has undergone remarkable advances in higher density, outstanding performance, and low power consumption comparable with Application Specific Integrated Circuit (ASIC). The FPGA also offers design flexibility with optimal device utilization which is often not the case with Digital Signal Processor (DSP) chips. When a design demands the use of a DSP, or time-to-market is critical, or design adaptability is crucial, then the FPGA may offer an enhanced resolution. Hence, FPGA has become the best choice for the design of signal processing system due to its greater flexibility, parallel processing ability and higher bandwidth.

A hardware efficient universal digital modulator is required to generate the modulated signal. The main aim of pipeline CORDIC architecture used in universal modulator is to provide sine and cosine of angle with an improved speed. The proposed modulator is designed and validated in FPGA device. This paper is organized in following sections: The basic theory of CORDIC is explained in Sect. 2. Section 3 designs with universal CORDIC modulator. In Sect. 4, issues related to hardware implementation of CORDIC based universal modulator and results of real time testing are described. At the end, Sect. 5 concludes the paper. In [8] the authors proposed two area-efficient CORDIC algorithms implemented on Xilinx Spartan XC2S200E device. They achieved less slice-delay product.

2 CORDIC Algorithm

This algorithm was specially developed for real time digital computers where the majority of the computation involves trigonometric related function. This CORDIC algorithm is generally implemented on a 2D plane using iterative operation. This algorithm represents a vector 'V' on X-Y plane to solve a function in circular, linear or hyperbolic coordinate system.

The algorithm describes general rotation transform are given below

$$X' = X \cos (\Phi) - Y \sin (\Phi) \tag{1}$$

$$Y' = Y \cos (\Phi) + X \sin (\Phi) \tag{2}$$

Where (X, Y) and (X', Y') are the initial and final value of the coordinates of the vector, respectively and Φ is used in fixed iteration angle.

Rearrange the above two equations can be written as:

$$X' = \cos(\Phi)[X - Y * \tan(\Phi)] \tag{3}$$

$$Y' = \cos(\Phi)[Y + X * \tan(\Phi)] \tag{4}$$

Replace $\tan(\Phi)$ by $2^{(-i)}$, where i is the iteration count. The value of $\tan(\Phi)$ is given in Table 1.

Table 1. Pre-computed $\tan(\Phi)$

Sl no. i =	$\tan(\Phi)$	Φ in deg.
0	1	45
1	0.5	26.6
2	0.25	14.0
3	0.125	7.1
4	0.0626	3.6
5	0.03125	1.8
6	0.015625	0.9
7	0.0078125	0.4
8	0.00390625	0.2
9	0.001953125	0.1
–	—	—

In each iteration i, the new vectors the (3), (4) equations can be modified as

$$X_{i+1} = K_i\left[X_i - Yi * D_i * 2^{(-i)}\right] \tag{5}$$

$$Y_{i+1} = K_i\left[Y_i + X_i * D_i * 2^{(-i)}\right] \tag{6}$$

Where

$$K_i = \cos\left(\arctan 2^{(-i)}\right) = 1/\sqrt{\left(1 + 2^{(-2i)}\right)} \tag{7}$$

$$D_i = \pm1 \tag{8}$$

On each iteration, Di is either 1 or −1, to make a difference between the desired angle and current angle. At the end of rotations, the vector length will be 1, so that vector components will contain cosine and sine values of desired angle as shown in Fig. 1. Hence a new variable known as accumulator is defined as

$$Z_{i+1} = Z_i - Di \arctan 2^{(-i)}$$ (9)

The angle between sine and cosine are calculated in the form of Z_i. Di value should be positive or negative in the following method

$$Di = -1 \sin Z_i < 0$$
$$+1 \sin Z_i \geq 0$$ (10)

The sum of the rotating angles result desired angle

$$\Phi = \Sigma Di \arctan 2^{(-i)}$$ (11)

Due to first tangent value is $2^0 = 1$, the angle can be rotated in any the range $[-\pi/2, \pi/2]$, which is in converge region.

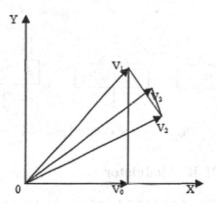

Fig. 1. CORDIC algorithm rotation process

The pipeline CORDIC architecture is shown in Fig. 2 [9]. The sign of Z shows the direction of iteration for every stage as defined by CORDIC equations. The pipeline architecture inputs are taken as angle or phase and produce both sine and cosine for the given input in predetermined number of rotation [10]. In pipeline architecture requires less clock cycles to complete a function. For N stage pipelined, first output obtained after N clock cycles. Each pipeline stage takes exactly one clock period to complete the operation.

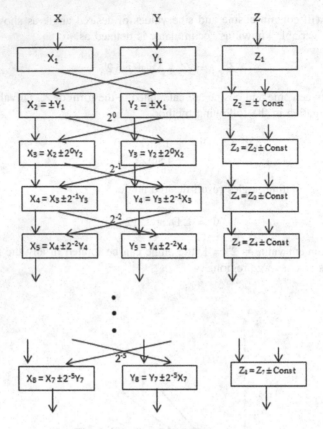

Fig. 2. Pipeline CORDIC processor

3 Universal CORDIC Modulator

There are different types of CORDIC based universal modulators available which having some trade-off between memories and operating speed [11, 12]. Figure 3 shows universal modulator used for AM, FM and PM generation. This modulator consists of

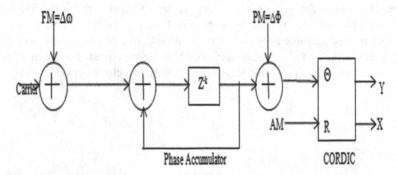

Fig. 3. Proposed Universal CORDIC modulator

adder which provides phase control and phase accumulator which is used to control the frequency component.

For amplitude modulation, the amplitude of the signal is connected to radius R input of the CORDIC processor. CORDIC algorithm is used to convert coordinate from (R, Θ) to (X, Y). The CORDIC algorithm generally increases the radius in rotation mode. As a consequence, the gain of amplifier is changed and does not require consideration for the AM system. The phase of the transmitted signal $\Theta = 2\Pi f_0 t + \Delta\Phi(t)$ can be calculated, where f_0 carrier frequency and $\Delta\Phi(t)$ frequency or phase modulated component. A linear increase phase signal according $2\Pi f_0 t$ is to generate constant carrier frequency and this can be done in accumulator. For FM generation the carrier frequency f_0 is modified by Δf or use of second accumulator compute $2\Pi f_0 t$ and then add two accumulators product to deliver the desire result. In PM generation an offset value is added to the phase of the signal. These phase signals are added and applied to angle $(Z$ or $\Theta)$ input of the CORDIC processor. Initially at beginning of the iterations the register Y is set to zero.

4 Hardware Implementation

This paper has been demonstrated for universal modulator using pipeline base CORDIC algorithm. The universal modulator is realized for AM, FM and PM. Use of pipeline architecture, the design is to calculate continuous input with a small latency. The advantages of this system have high throughput and area efficient computations of sine and cosine functions without using ROM LUTs. An 8 stages pipelined are required to implement the CORDIC architecture design. The coefficient of this proposed modulator is considered 16-bit width. The design has been simulated using Xilinx 14.7 ISE Design Suite and then synthesized the bit streams download into Virtex-6 FPGA board.

The Table 2 represents synthesis report like slices, LUT, IOB and also delay analysis for AM. The operating speed of the proposed modulator in FPGA is of 307.408 MHz for Speed Grade -3. The power consumption report from XPower analysis for the proposed design is of 1.293 W.

Table 2. Device utilization summary of universal modulator for AM implementation

Synthesis parameter	Used	Available	Utilization
Number slice registers	221	54,576	1%
Number of slice LUT	256	27,288	1%
Number of used as logic	237	27,288	1%
Number of IOBs	46	316	14%

A comparison report of AM modulator and FM modulator in terms of slice-delay product are shown in Tables 3 and 4 respectively.

Table 3. Comparison of AM implementation

Architecture	Number of slices	LUT	Slice-delay product
[5]	896	476	88704
[7]	963	502	99189
Proposed architecture	222	250	666

Table 4. Comparison of FM implementation

Architecture	Number of slices	Max. frequency in MHz	Slice-delay product
[5]	915	482	90585
[7]	975	511	100425
Proposed architecture	248	264	744

The result analysis indicate that the proposed pipeline based CORDIC architecture for realization of universal modulator require less slice-delay product in compare with other similar types architectures and also improve its operating speed.

5 Conclusions

Realization of CORDIC based universal modulator is widely applicable in communication system for its versatility and flexibility. Implementation of CORDIC algorithm for all applications as it provides advantage in terms of accuracy and speed of operation. The main use of this CORDIC algorithm is to make high correctness with optimum hardware. This paper presents implementation of pipeline CORDIC architecture used in universal modulator, yield modulated waveform such as AM, FM and PM. The proposed design coded in VHDL and physically tested on Virtex-6 FPGA development board. The design has been compared its performance to other existing design. FPGA Implementation of the proposed design have lower slice-delay product with better of the operating speed.

Acknowledgment. The authors would like to thank the Department of Electronics and Communication, Brainware Group of Institutions for providing the ISE design suite 14.7 and Virtex-6 FPGA board.

References

1. Volder, J.E.: The CORDIC trigonometric computing technique. IRE Trans. Electron. Comput. **EC-8**, 330–334 (1959)
2. Vaishnavi, S., Titiksha, B., Vinay, R. Manikandan, J.: Design and evaluation of universal modulators. In: India Conference (INDICON), pp. 1–5. IEEE Xplore, New Delhi (2015). https://doi.org/10.1109/INDICON.2015.7443273

3. Nandu, K.H., Santosh, S., Praveen, J.: Design and implementation of universal modulator using two-level pipelined CORDIC architecture. Int. J. Innov. Res. Electr. Electron. Instrum. Control Eng. **3**, 123–126 (2015). https://doi.org/10.17148/IJIREEICE

4. Patil, N., Patil, J.H.: FPGA implementation of direct digital frequency synthesizer with CORDIC algorithm. Glob. J. Res. Anal. (GJRA) **4** (2015) https://doi.org/10.15373/22778160

5. Nilson, P.: Complexity reduction in unrolled CORDIC architectures. Electron. Circ. Syst. (ICECS), 868–871 (2009), https://doi.org/10.17148/IJIREEICE.2015.3307

6. Naresh, V., Venkataramani, B., Raja, R.: An area efficient multiplexer based CORDIC. In: International Conference on Computer, Communication and Informatics (ICCCI), pp. 1–5 (2013)

7. Wolf, W.: FPGA-Based System Design. Prentice- Hall, Englewood Cliffs (2004)

8. Vachhani, L., Sridharan, K., Meher, P.: Efficient CORDIC algorithms and architectures for low area and high throughput implementation. IEEE Trans. Circ. Syst. II **56**(1), 61–65 (2009). https://doi.org/10.1109/TCSII.2008.2010169

9. Meyer-Baese, U.: Digital Signal Processing with Field Programmable Gate Arrays, 3rd edn. Springer, Heidelberg (2007). https://doi.org/10.1007/978-3-540-72613-5

10. Garcia, O.E., Cumplido, R., Arias, M.: Pipelined CORDIC design on FPGA for a digital sine and cosine waves generator. In: 3rd International Conference on Electrical and Electronics Engineering, Mexico (2006)

11. Angarita, F., Perez-Pascual, A., Sansaloni, T., Valls, J.: Efficient FPGA implementation of CORDIC algorithm for circular and linear coordinates. In: Proceedings of IEEE International Conference on Field Programmable Logic and Applications, pp. 535–538 (2005)

12. Arvind, S., Brahmaiah, V., Teja, L.: Universal modulator using CORDIC algorithm for communication application. IJAET **6**, 2480–2488 (2014)

Parametric Uncertainty Modeling
and Estimation for Electrical Actuators

Amiya Kumar Roy[✉] and Kaushik Das Sharma[✉]

Department of Applied Physics, University of Calcutta, 92, APC Road,
Kolkata 700009, India
amiyakumarroy1024@gmail.com, kdsaphy@caluniv.ac.in

Abstract. This paper deals with uncertainty modeling and parameter estimation of an electrical actuator popularly utilized in control system design in various applications. The actuator itself is a system which has certain parameters. The parameters need to be estimated properly with their uncertainties. In this present work, a comparative study on the modeling of the actuator employing Monte Carlo method, hidden Markov model and particle swarm optimization are presented. The three modeling approaches are separately used to match the actual motor output and its model output with estimated parameters. The uncertainty range for each parameter is evaluated for entire observation and the real life experimentation successfully demonstrates the usefulness of the proposed study.

Keywords: DC motor · Hidden Markov Model · Monte Carlo method ·
Parameter estimation · Particle swarm optimization · Uncertainty modeling

1 Introduction

Electrical actuators are mostly used to control a system. But the actuator itself is a system which gives response when an input is applied. It has one or more parameters which are essential to compute the output. The actuator may or may not have its parameter datasheet. Also there is deterioration in performance of the actuators due to aging effect. Some time it is not possible to directly measure and make correction in those parameters. We can measure the response and analyze it to study the behavior of the system parameters. Our objective thus is to design a model which will estimate the current parametric values along with the uncertainty range. We can use the new value as the datasheet of the actuator. A DC motor is taken as a representative actuator in this work. There are many techniques available for system modeling. Monte Carlo method, hidden Markov model (HMM) and particle swarm optimization (PSO) are the three approaches utilized in this work to model the system and estimate the parameters.

The work of Refsgaard et al. pictures an idea about system modeling in uncertain condition in ecological model [1]. Various methods for modeling under uncertainty can be used [2–5]. Modeling is needed as a part of managing uncertainty within a system with precision. We have to model parametric uncertainty for DC motor. For understanding the dc motor behavior we go through paper of W. Wu. The small perturbation in torque of the machine is analyzed using the basic transient response equation. An approach to deal the uncertainty and estimation of DC motor parameters are proposed.

© Springer Nature Singapore Pte Ltd. 2019
J. K. Mandal et al. (Eds.): CICBA 2018, CCIS 1030, pp. 442–457, 2019.
https://doi.org/10.1007/978-981-13-8578-0_35

It requires a position sensor and a voltage supply only. The estimated parameters can be used to verify the motor performance [6, 7].

Three methods are used here. Monte Carlo method requires first to define a distribution of the input parameters. Then the randomly a sample is chosen from the distribution. That sample goes through the system and results an output [8, 9]. The HMM is a doubly stochastic process where one process is hidden and exhibit Markov chain. In Markov chain the states transits from one to another with time with certain probabilities. The model has three parameters namely initial state distribution, transition probabilities and emission probabilities. To model HMM structure learning method is used such as Baum-Welch algorithm [10, 11]. Particle swarm optimization is an optimizing search method inspired from the social behavior of herds, schools, flocks and human. These social animals communicate with each other to fulfill an objective. They use their personal behavior and also group behavior to update their movement [12].

The rest of the paper is organized as: Sect. 2 describes the mathematical modeling of the actuator and real life data collection procedure. Section 3 details the main results emphasizing on the Monte Carlo method, HMM and PSO based parameter estimation approaches. Section 4 elaborates the experimental results and Sect. 5 concludes the paper.

2   Actuator Modeling

2.1   DC Motor Model

The circuit diagram and motor parameters are shown in Fig. 1.

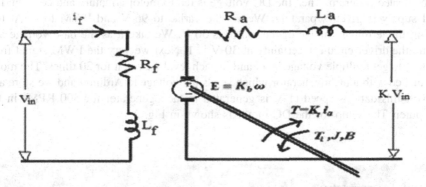

Fig. 1. Circuit diagram of separately excited DC motor. R_a = armature resistance, L_a = armature inductance, B = damping coefficient, J = polar moment of inertia, K_b = emf constant, K_t = torque constant, [Here $K_b = K_t$]

From the transient equation of a DC motor of constant field supply ($K_b = K\Phi$) we can write [13]

$$V_{in} = R_a i_a + L_a \frac{di_a}{dt} + K_b \omega \tag{1}$$

$$T_L + J\frac{d\omega}{dt} + B\omega = K_t i_a \tag{2}$$

Taking Load torque $T_L = 0$, and solving for ω we get

$$\frac{d^2\omega}{dt^2} = -\left(\frac{BR_a}{JL_a} + \frac{K_b K_t}{JL_a}\right)\omega - \left(\frac{R_a}{L_a} + \frac{B}{J}\right)\frac{d\omega}{dt} + \frac{K_t K}{JL_a}V_{in} \tag{3}$$

So we get the motor equation for speed calculation. Here K = driver circuit uncertainty and is unit less. Now in terms of control system a second order differential system can be represented in state space model then the equation becomes

$$\dot{X}_2 = -\left(\frac{BR_a}{JL_a} + \frac{K_b K_t}{JL_a}\right)X_1 - \left(\frac{R_a}{L_a} + \frac{B}{J}\right)X_2 + \frac{K_t K}{JL_a}u(t) \tag{4}$$

$$\text{And } Y = C.X_1 = \frac{60}{2*\Pi}X_1 = \frac{60}{2*\Pi}\omega \text{ (in RPM)} \tag{5}$$

A second order differential equation can be solved by R-K 4th order method [14].

2.2 Training Data Collection and Parameter Estimation

Here an AC variac is sending the power which is further rectified into DC and controlled by an Arduino circuit via sending pulse width modulation (PWM) signal by a sophisticated program. Then the DC voltage is fed to motor armature and constant DC field supply is given separately. We set the variac to 96 V and PWM to 1. At this setting the terminal voltage of the motor is 30 V. We take it as the base voltage and define the driver circuit uncertainty at 30 V is 1. Next we vary the PWM signal from 0.5 to 1 to get multiple voltage level and in each level we run it for 20 times. The motor is attached with a tachogenerator which sends the voltage to Arduino and we store and convert this data as speed (1 V is generated in tachogenerator for 500 RPM) in the computer. The setup for the DC motor is shown in Fig. 2.

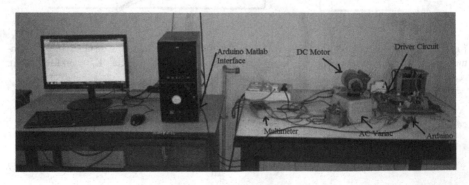

Fig. 2. Experimental setup

After recording the data from the motor we have run different methods to model the motor and our objective is to minimize the error or match the model output with the recorded motor output. The error is represented by IAE (Integral Absolute Error) and is given by

$$IAE = \sum_{t=0}^{T} \text{absolute error between motor recorded output and model output} * (\Delta t) \quad (6)$$

Δt is the step size or time between two successive output

Now in the three modeling methods we will vary the parameters and check for the optimum IAE. More low the IAE is, more is the modeled system tending towards actual system. When the IAE is below desirable limit we can estimate parameters. Now due to uncertainty the parameters will not be at a fixed value. Uncertainty can be included by normal distribution of $\pm3\sigma$ from the mean of parameters which gives 99.7% probability for the estimated parameters to fall within the range.

3 Main Results

3.1 Monte Carlo Method Based Uncertainty Modeling

It is a method based on statistical inferences. For stochastic system conventional approach fails and Monte Carlo method can give us results as it includes probabilistic variation of input and system parameters. In this method we draw samples from a population and the samples exhibits the same property as the population.

The method consist of 4 steps shown in the Fig. 3.

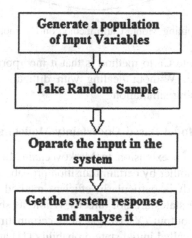

Fig. 3. Monte Carlo method

Here we have six parameters in the DC motor model. We assume the parameters are in Gaussian distribution. So we create a population of each parameter with 3%

standard deviation. Now for six voltage levels (15–30 V) the system model takes samples from the population from the six parameters and process it to get the system response. The model output is then compared with the recorded motor output data and IAE is calculated. The process is shown in Fig. 4. In this method the sampling and testing is done 100 times for a single output data matching and the parameters for which we get minimum IAE is the estimated parameters for a recorded data. Checking for all the recorded data (N number) we get N parameter set. We further calculate mean and range of each individual parameters.

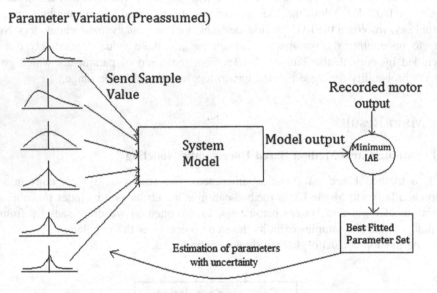

Fig. 4. Appling Monte Carlo method on DC motor model

The advantage of Monte Carlo method is that it incorporates a basic probabilistic approach into the system. Without dealing with difficult calculation we can find probability of an event using simulation.

3.2 Hidden Markov Model Based Uncertainty Modeling

Hidden Markov model is an extension to Markov chain. In Markov chain a system transit from one state to another by certain transition probability (A). The states are the output in Markov chain. It is particularly efficient method for dynamic system. In hidden Markov model the states are not directly visible as shown in Fig. 5.

We observe only the output (Y) we get after certain time interval. The starting probability of the states is called initial state probability (Π) and the probability to emit an output from a state is known as emission probability (B). The interconnection of the states can be shown as state transition graph.

The HMM have three basic problem evaluation, decoding and learning. In parameter estimation first we have to describe the system as a structure of interconnected state. But we don't know the structure parameters (A, B, Π). Taking output from the system we can

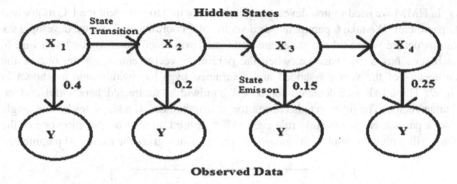

Fig. 5. Hidden Markov model

tune the HMM parameters. After learning, the structure can be used to estimate parameter for any recorded output [15–17]. In simulation the HMM parameters can be found by recording the initial state, transitions and emission by the states which gives minimum IAE for each of the recorded output. We call it best fitted transitions (BFT). Taking the concept from Baum-Welch algorithm and modifying it for simulation we can write

$$\text{Initial state probability } \left(\widehat{\Pi_i} \right) = \frac{\text{Total number of starting from } x_i \text{ state for all BFT}}{\text{Total Number of BFT}}$$

(7)

$$\text{Transition probability } \left(\widehat{A_{i,j}} \right) = \frac{\text{Total number of transition from state } x_i \text{ to state } x_j \text{ for all BFT}}{\text{Total number of transition from state } x_i \text{ for all BFT}}$$

(8)

$$\text{Emission probability } \left(\widehat{B_i} \right) = \frac{\text{Total number of emission from } x_i \text{ state for all BFT}}{\text{Total Number of BFT}}$$

(9)

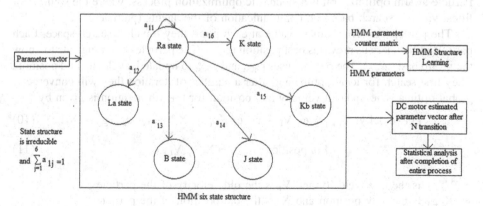

HMM six state structure

Fig. 6. HMM six state structure

In HMM we need to first develop a suitable structure to represent the DC motor and its parameter. We take 6 parameters as a vector of 6 coordinates. Now we develop a six state structure where all the states are connected with each other as shown in Fig. 6. Each state has a rule base i.e. when the parameter vector enters a state, one of the parameters of the vector is added and subtracted by a bandwidth*rand as shown in Fig. 7. Then IAE is calculated for added bandwidth, subtracted bandwidth and no change vector. The fittest one is chosen for next transition. The six states have a single unique parameter modification rule each. After desired number of transition one of the states will emit the output as the parameter vector which gives the estimated parameters.

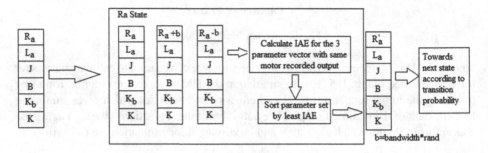

Fig. 7. State rule base

At first HMM parameters are unknown. So we initially assume HMM parameters to have equal probabilities. Next train the HMM parameters with recorded data of 6 voltage level (15–30 V). After learning the modified HMM parameters are used to estimate DC motor parameters and model uncertainty.

The advantage of HMM is that it decompose the system into structures which are time variant. So each individual state can be tuned which increase flexibility for estimation. Tuning the HMM structure is problematic and require more computational time.

3.3 Particle Swarm Optimization Based Uncertainty Modeling

Particle swarm optimization is a stochastic optimization process, where the solution or fittest value is search based on communication of the agents (particles).

The particles evaluate fitness value at each point they travel in search space. Each particle remembers its previous best position (p_{best}). The particles communicate to know the group best (g_{best}). The particle uses p_{best} and g_{best} to update its velocity and position. They first search for local optima and after a number of iteration they will converge to global optima. The updated velocity and position for t + 1th iteration is given by

$$\text{For velocity: } V_{t+1} = \omega . V_t + r_1 . c_1 . (p_t - X_t) + r_2 . c_2 . (g_t - X_t) \tag{10}$$

$$\text{For position: } X_{t+1} = X_t + V_{t+1} \tag{11}$$

- V_{t+1} is the new velocity and V_t is the old velocity of the particle
- X_{t+1} is the new position and X_t is the old position of the particle
- p_t is the personal best position and g_t is the global best position
- ω is the inertia weight
- r_1 and r_2 are random number between 0 and 1

- c_1 and c_2 are the importance of personal best value and group best value
- Number of particle is usually between 10 to 50
- $c_1 + c_2 = 4$ which is empirically chosen, generally $c_1 = c_2 = 2$ [18–20]

In PSO we take a solution 6 parameters set (vector) as a particle. It has a 6 dimensional search space with boundary for each parameter. The particle in each point gives a parameter set and according to it we can calculate model output and compare it with observed output to get IAE. The particles search for the global optima by considering personal best position and group best position. We bound the maximum and minimum velocity of the particle. After several iterations we will find the minimum IAE and corresponding parameter set. By computing the parameters corresponding to least IAE of all observed output we can do statistical analysis. The process is shown in Fig. 8. The advantage of this scheme is it consumes less time for computation and gives high accuracy results.

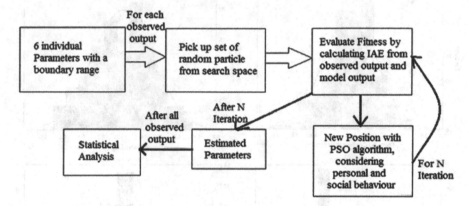

Fig. 8. Block diagram of PSO based approach on DC motor model

4   Experimental Results and Discussion

We take 20 set of output for each voltage level from the DC motor to computer via Arduino for each voltage level and record those data. We use Monte Carlo method, HMM and PSO to estimate the parameters which have minimum error (IAE) for the 30 s run. For the entire 120 set of observations we get 120 set of parameters. Now we do statistical analysis and find the histogram with normal density curve fitting for each parameter. Further we note the mean and range of the parameters and express it in the table form.

We found that the parameter K is voltage dependent. So we calculate K for different voltage level. Verification is done with the average observed output for each voltage level and model output using overall mean parameters and mean parameter of K for each voltage level.

4.1   Parameter Estimation Using Monte Carlo Method

Monte Carlo method is tested first. After running 120 samples we plot the histogram as shown in Fig. 9. And the parameters are shown in Table 1. And Table 2 represents the variation of K due to voltage change. We plot the model output speed all mean parameter and with K depending upon different voltage level as shown in Fig. 10.

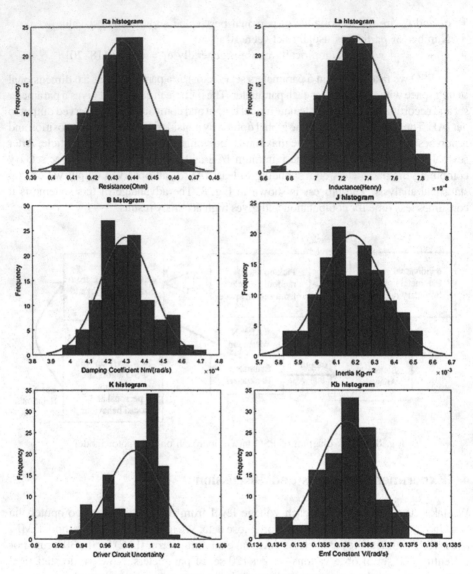

Fig. 9. Histogram of the parameters for Monte Carlo method

Table 1. Estimated parameters using Monte Carlo method

Parameter	Mean and Range	Unit
R_a	0.43442 ± 0.04089	Ohm
L_a	0.00073007 ± 0.00006786	Henry
B	0.00042993 ± 0.00004253	Nm/(rad/s)
J	0.0061844 ± 0.0004811	Kg-m^2
K	0.98529 ± 0.06587	-
K_b	0.13611 ± 0.00197	V/(rad/s)

Table 2. Different values of K for 15–30 V level

Voltage level	Mean and Range of K	IAE for 30 s
15 V	0.94868 ± 0.02960	175.76
18 V	0.96673 ± 0.02018	112.79
21 V	0.99266 ± 0.01837	174.08
24 V	0.99808 ± 0.02506	188.98
27 V	1.00210 ± 0.02513	228.37
30 V	1.00352 ± 0.02115	226.78

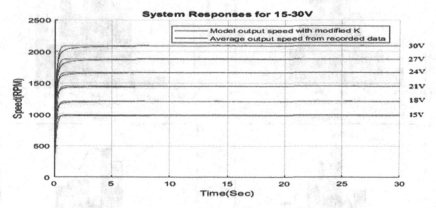

Fig. 10. Speed of motor for different level of voltage

4.2 Parameter Estimation Using Hidden Markov Model

We took the bandwidth as 1%. Transition per observation is taken as 20. We check among 200 runs to get the best fittest transition for one recorded observation. In HMM the parameters of the six state structure is learned and shown

$$\begin{array}{cccccc} R & L & B & J & K & K_b \end{array}$$

Initial State Matrix = $[0.1750 \quad 0.1583 \quad 0.2083 \quad 0.1333 \quad 0.1583 \quad 0.1667]$

Emission Matrix = $[0.1950 \quad 0.1583 \quad 0.1833 \quad 0.1333 \quad 0.1583 \quad 0.1750]$

Transition Matrix =

States	R	L	B	J	K	K_b
R	0.1994	0.1790	0.1942	0.1478	0.1390	0.1405
L	0.2347	0.1683	0.1721	0.1067	0.1665	0.1518
B	0.2318	0.1579	0.1864	0.1565	0.1253	0.1421
J	0.2262	0.1665	0.1867	0.1556	0.1301	0.1348
K	0.2447	0.1483	0.2201	0.1379	0.1038	0.1453
K_b	0.2310	0.1389	0.2139	0.1319	0.1315	0.1528

Next the learned structure is used to determine the DC motor parameter. Here response matching per observation is checked from 50 runs. Results are shown in Fig. 11, Table 3, Table 4 and Fig. 12.

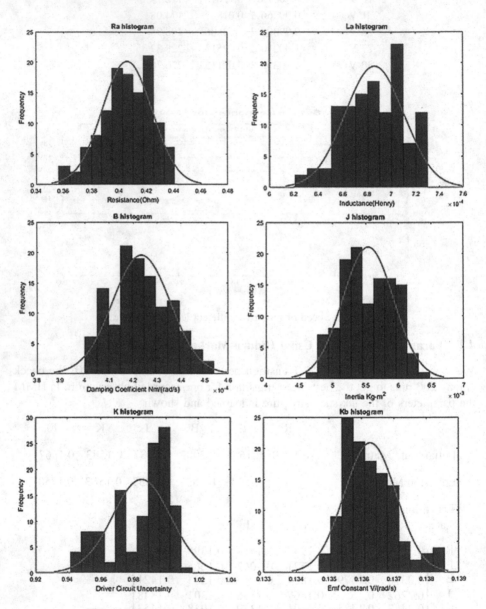

Fig. 11. Histogram of the parameters for hidden Markov model

Table 3. Estimated parameters using hidden Markov model

Parameter	Mean and Range	Unit
R_a	0.40594 ± 0.05429	Ohm
L_a	0.00068608 ± 0.00007299	Henry
B	0.00042343 ± 0.00003602	Nm/(rad/s)
J	0.0055378 ± 0.0011578	Kg-m^2
K	0.98482 ± 0.05327	-
K_b	0.13627 ± 0.00240	V/(rad/s)

Table 4. Different values of K for 15–30 V level

Voltage level	Mean and Range of K	IAE for 30 s
15 V	0.95303 ± 0.01374	278.88
18 V	0.97202 ± 0.00975	259.94
21 V	0.98932 ± 0.01175	202.96
24 V	1.00074 ± 0.01494	143.79
27 V	0.99480 ± 0.02041	479.65
30 V	0.99890 ± 0.01205	381.83

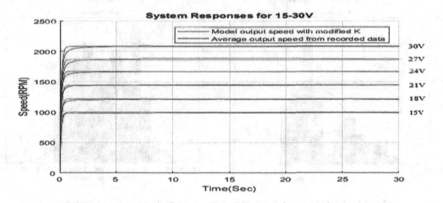

Fig. 12. Speed of motor for different level of voltage

4.3 Parameter Estimation Using Particle Swarm Optimization

For PSO we limit the velocity by,

$$V_{max} = \text{Max parameter position}/1000 \text{ and } V_{min} = -V_{max} \tag{12}$$

The search space is first initialized and random particle position is chosen. They interact with each other and find the optimum position. Based on entire observation we plot the histogram in Fig. 13 and estimate parameter as shown in Table 5. Different values of K are shown in Table 6. Further we plot the speed characteristic in Fig. 14.

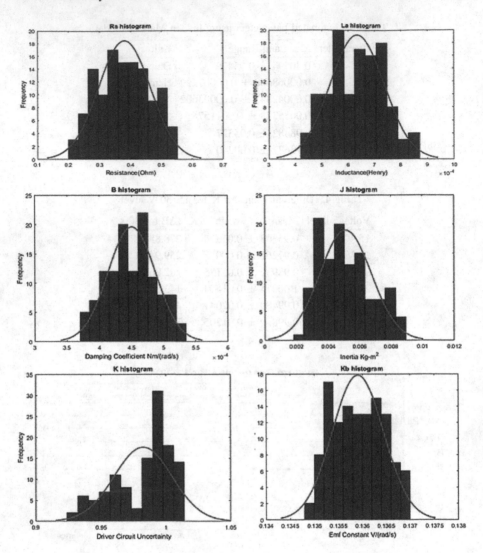

Fig. 13. Histogram of the parameters for particle swarm optimization

Table 5. Estimated parameters using particle swarm optimization

Parameter	Mean and Range	Unit
R_a	0.38036 ± 0.24925	Ohm
L_a	0.00063443 ± 0.00030611	Henry
B	0.00045029 ± 0.00010996	Nm/(rad/s)
J	0.0051238 ± 0.0049236	Kg-m^2
K	0.98233 ± 0.06693	-
K_b	0.13591 ± 0.00161	V/(rad/s)

Table 6. Different values of K for 15–30 V level

Voltage level	Mean and Range of K	IAE for 30 s
15 V	0.94358 ± 0.02649	87.98
18 V	0.96455 ± 0.01525	92.86
21 V	0.98884 ± 0.01394	150.49
24 V	0.99634 ± 0.02282	154.94
27 V	1.00099 ± 0.02457	239.61
30 V	0.99968 ± 0.01322	270.04

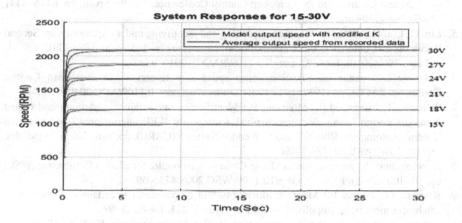

Fig. 14. Speed of motor for different level of voltage

5 Conclusion

Monte Carlo method, hidden Markov model and particle swarm optimization are successfully employed to model the uncertainty present in a real life actuator, namely DC motor. The range of uncertainty has been critically estimated based on the small changes in applied voltage. The uncertainty range is varying with the approach of modeling and PSO based approach outperforms the other two approaches discussed in this paper in terms of accuracy of modeling as well as in terms of computation time for modeling.

We can include various constraints like temperature, humidity and aging effect into our model. We can use Monte Carlo method, HMM, PSO in other electrical actuators to model their performance. We are taking one kind of HMM structure where it is irreducible (every state is connected with all the other states). Other kind of structure can also be tested. Other than PSO we can use genetic algorithm, harmony search algorithm for stochastic optimization.

References

1. Refsgaard, J.C., Sluijs, J.P., Højberg, A.L., Vanrolleghem, P.A.: Uncertainty in the environmental modelling process, a framework and guidance. Environ. Model. Softw. **22**, 1543–1556 (2007)
2. Omlin, M., Reichert, P.: A comparison of techniques for the estimation of model prediction uncertainty. Ecol. Model. **115**, 45–59 (1999)
3. Lambrechts, P., Terlouw, J., Bennani, S., Steinbuch, M.: Parametric uncertainty modelling using LFTs. In: American Control Conference, pp. 267–272 (1993)
4. Marcos, A., Bates, D., Postlethwaite, I.: Control oriented uncertainty modelling using μ sensitivities and skewed μ analysis tools. In: Proceedings of the 44th IEEE Conference on Decision and Control, and the European Control Conference, Seville, Spain, pp. 6436–6441 (2005). https://doi.org/10.1109/CDC.2005.1583194
5. Liu, C., Liu, D., Wang, S.: Situation modelling and identifying under uncertainty. In: Second Pacific-Asia Conference on Circuits, Communications and System (PACCS), vol. 1, pp. 296–299 (2010). https://doi.org/10.1109/PACCS.2010.5626909
6. Wu, W.: DC motor identification using speed step responses. In: American Control Conference (ACC), pp. 1937–1941 (2010). https://doi.org/10.1109/ACC.2010.5531349
7. Salloum, R., Arvan, M.R., Moaveni, B.: Identification, uncertainty modelling, and robust controller design for an electromechanical actuator. In: IEEE International Conference on Control, Automation, Robotics and Embedded Systems (CARE), pp. 1–6 (2013). https://doi.org/10.1109/CARE.2013.6733690
8. Raychaudhuri, S.: Introduction to Monte Carlo simulation. In: Simulation Conference, WSC, pp. 91–100 (2008). https://doi.org/10.1109/WSC.2008.4736059
9. Kuczera, G., Parent, E.: Monte Carlo assessment of parameter uncertainty in conceptual catchment models: metropolis algorithm. J. Hydrol. **211**, 69–85 (1998)
10. Rabiner, L., Juang, B.: An introduction to Hidden Markov models. IEEE ASSP Mag. **3**, 4–16 (1986). https://doi.org/10.1109/MASSP.1986.1165342
11. Zaidi, S.S.H., Aviyente, S., Salman, M., Shin, K.K., Strangas, E.G.: Prognosis of gear failures in DC starter motors using Hidden Markov Model. IEEE Trans. Ind. Electron. **58**, 1695–1706 (2011). https://doi.org/10.1109/TIE.2010.2052540
12. Kennedy, J., Eberhart, R.: Particle swarm optimization. In: Proceedings of the IEEE International Conference on Neural Networks, pp. 1942–1948 (1995). https://doi.org/10.1109/ICNN.1995.488968
13. Dubey, G.K.: Fundamentals of Electrical Drives. Narosa Publishing House, New Delhi (1994)
14. Grewal, B.S.: Higher Engineering Mathematics. Khanna Publishers, New Delhi (1965)
15. Gomes, S.R., et al.: A comparative approach to email classification using Native Bayes classifier and Hidden Markov Model. In: IEEE 4th International Conference on Advances in Electrical Engineering (ICAEE), pp. 482–487 (2017). https://doi.org/10.1109/ICAEE.2017.8255404
16. Poritz, A.B.: Hidden Markov models: a guided tour. In: ICASSP 1988 International Conference on Acoustics, Speech and Signal Processing (1988). https://doi.org/10.1109/ICASSP.1988.196495
17. Zucchini, W., MacDonald, I.L., Langrock, V.: Hidden Markov Models for Time Series, An Introduction Using R. Chapman & Hall, CRC Press, Boca Raton (2016)
18. Zhang, X., Song, K., Li, C., Yang, L.: Parameter estimation for multi-scale multi-lag underwater acoustic channels based on modified particle swarm optimization algorithm. IEEE Access **5**, 4808–4820 (2017). https://doi.org/10.1109/ACCESS.2017.2681101

19. Guo, J., Wang, B.: Particle swarm optimization with Gaussian disturbance. In: IEEE International Conference on Industrial Informatics – Computing Technology, Intelligent Technology, Industrial Information Integration (ICIICII), pp. 266–269 (2017). https://doi.org/10.1109/ICIICII.2017.81
20. Jalal, L., Popescu, V., Murroni, M.: Quality-of-Experience parameter estimation for multisensorial media using particle swarm optimization. In: IEEE International Conference on Optimization of Electrical and Electronic Equipment (OPTIM) & International Aegean Conference on Electrical Machines and Power Electronics (ACEMP), pp. 965–970 (2017). https://doi.org/10.1109/OPTIM.2017.7975095

A Multipath Load Balancing Routing Protocol in Mobile Ad Hoc Network Using Recurrent Neural Network

Arindrajit Pal[1(✉)], Paramartha Dutta[2], Amlan Chakrabarti[1],
and Jyoti Prakash Singh[3]

[1] A.K.Choudhury School of IT, University of Calcutta, Kolkata, West Bengal, India
arindrajit@gmail.com, acakcs@caluniv.ac.in
[2] Visva-Bharati University, Santiniketan, West Bengal, India
paramartha.dutta@gmail.com
[3] National Institute of Technology Patna, Patna, India
jps@nitp.ac.in

Abstract. The route congestion and propagation delay is one of the major issue of the mobile ad hoc network (MANET) which can be overcome by the multi-path communication. But communication through multi-path routing may create a bottle neck problem in the destination node. To select the optimal number of paths between a set of paths can be generated by different parameters. We consider those paths which take minimum time to deliver a data packet from source to destination. Now to distribute the data packets which are generated by source node through these paths in such a way that no path is being overloaded. In this paper, we apply the recurrent neural network based ERNN (Elman recurrent neural network) approach to predict the future load of different paths in the network. This is a time series prediction model using recurrent neural network for evaluating the values in the future time frame. Our experiment shows that this technique can perform very good result in comparison with other state of the art multi-path routing techniques.

Keywords: MANET · Multi-path routing · Neural network ·
Elman recurrent neural network · Time series · RNN

1 Introduction

The artificial neural network (ANN) can be used as a forecasting tool for long period of time. It is a self organizing and a nonlinear learning tool which can predict the output data from the input data patterns. The multilayer perceptron (MLP), backpropagation neural networks, radial basis function are very common neural network training functions which are used for time series forecasting prediction. Other than these forward networks, recurrent neural network (RNN) is considered as the feedback network which can be modeled as the temporal dependencies between the input and output data. The RNN-based prediction

© Springer Nature Singapore Pte Ltd. 2019
J. K. Mandal et al. (Eds.): CICBA 2018, CCIS 1030, pp. 458–464, 2019.
https://doi.org/10.1007/978-981-13-8578-0_36

model ERNN (Elman recurrent neural network) can be used for measuring the time varying predictive control system that can manage the memory of recent facts to forecast the future output. In MANET (mobile ad hoc network), a set of mobile nodes can move within the network area and can communicate with each other without any fixed infrastructure. So, routing between the source and destination mobile nodes is a very challenging part of MANET. To establish a path, initially source node is flooding route request control packets to the network. Receiving these control packets, the destination node replies back these packets to the source node. Most of the time, some intermediate nodes are present as a part of the route for forwarding the packets to the destination. But these unstable moving nodes may move out of their transmission range and create a link failure condition. So, the prediction of stable neighbors of each node can build a steady network. Using these set of stable nodes, many paths can be created between the source and destination nodes. To find a optimal path between the source and destination nodes, there are many algorithms are already developed for this purpose. The common routing algorithms like DSDV [7], DSR [3], LAR [4] and AODV [6] are considered for single path routing technique. But the congestion and the delay for delivering the data packets cannot be overcome with a single optimal path routing. So, from the last decades some multi-path routing algorithms such as LCMR [1], FMLB [5] and MAODV [2] are developed though it is a challenging area in MANET. To determine the time to traverse a packet from source to destination and return back, we can select the optimal set of routes for delivering the packets. The rest of this paper is organized as follows. Our proposed model is presented in Sect. 2. Section 3 contains the simulation settings. The results and discussions are presented in Sect. 4. In Sect. 5 we conclude the article.

2   Proposed Model of Routing

This proposed method first finds the multiple paths from source to destination by using the packet forwarding technique. At the time of searching the routes, it also calculate the traverse time of the packets in different routes. Based on these routing times, our algorithm selects few of the routes among all the routes for communication. After initialization of the routes, say at time t0, the source node transfers the data packets by different routes. The number of packets in each route are inversely proportional to the routing time. This method dynamically changes the packet density of different routes by using the time series prediction based on the ERNN (Elman recurrent neural network) technology.

3   Simulation Model

We used *Network simulator 2* (NS2) for simulation of the proposed network. We have considered the *Random-way Point* (RWP) and *Manhattan Grid* (MHG) mobility models for distribution and movement patterns of the mobile nodes. The mobile nodes are uniformly distributed within an area of $(100 \times 100)\,\mathrm{m}^2$.

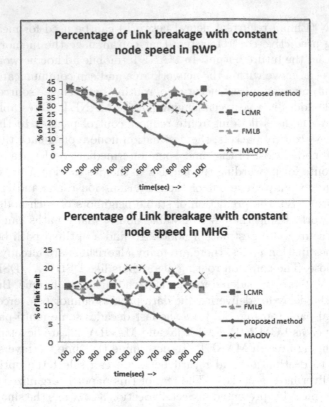

Fig. 1. Percentage of link breakage due to the link failure

The nodes are allowed to move within the network in various direction and in different speed. The speed of the mobile nodes may vary between $V_{min} = 0\,\text{m/s}$ to $V_{max} = 30\,\text{m/s}$. In this experiment, the fixed node speed indicates that the node speed in different time lags may vary but in the same time lag, it is not changed. The communication range of each node is 20 m and it is fixed for entire simulation time. There are 30 mobile nodes are allowed for this network. The source and destination nodes are choose randomly in between 1 to 30. The data packets sends by sender node is about 1000 to 3000 within a specific intervals. The channel bandwidth is 2 MBps. We assume that all the nodes are connected within the simulation area but they may change their neighbors. We can compute the forwarding time of the packets by the source node and the arrival time of the packets in the destination node. If the packets maintain different paths then their intermediate nodes are different and according to this phenomena we can compute the time require to delivery a packet in different routes. Here we also consider the queuing delay and the link delay of all the intermediate nodes due to packet forwarding. In this paper we compare our proposed recurrent neural network based model with three existing multi path routing protocols like *LCMR*, *FMLBRT* and *FLMBHC*. We have also shown that our proposed

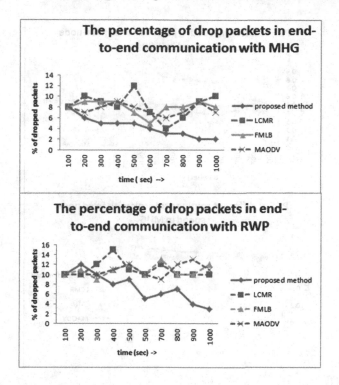

Fig. 2. Percentage of drop packets due to the link failure

model is better than all of them. We consider two mobility models like *RWP* and *MHG* which are two well known and standard mobility models.

4 Results

In this section, we are comparing our proposed model with three other models *LCMR*, *FMLB* and *MAODV*. Our *ERNN* based proposed model selects the low congestion shortest routes which increases the data flow of the multi-path mobile network by considering the two important parameters like speed and position of the mobile nodes in different time frames. This technique has a great impact for multi-path routing. Our first experiment is to calculate the percentage of link breakage with constant node speed for different routing protocols. In Fig. 1, we have studied this experiment with two different mobility models like RWP and MHG. Our RNN based prediction model perform the better result than others. Our model depends on the previous data sets of different time lags. Based on this, it can predict the stable paths between source and destination in future time frame. So, the graph shows that the prediction based model performed well with the increase in time, i.e. the previous data sets help the recursive model for good prediction. Figure 2 shows the effect of *RNN*-based prediction model which performed better than other routing models for counting of dropped

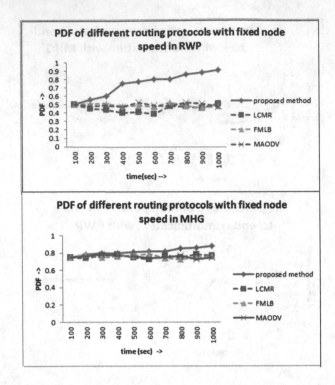

Fig. 3. Packet delivery fraction of different routing protocols

packets within a certain simulation time. The proposed model forwarded the data packets through the stable path and minimized the packet drop at the time of transmission. In the end-to-end communication, several intermediate nodes forwarded the data packets towards the destination node. Our proposed model can select those paths through which the packet lose is minimum. *Packet Delivery Fraction* (PDF) is an important measurement to calculate the efficiency of the network model. It is the ratio between the number of received packet by a node and the number of send packets by that node. High *PDF* value indicates the stability of the network. In Fig. 3 we have calculated the *PDF* of different routing protocols with fixed node speed. It shows that our proposed model performs better results due to the prediction model. Now, we observed the scenario for different node speed with our proposed model and other routing models in Fig. 4. It shows that our model perform better than other routing model and it maintain the percentage of *PDF* almost constant through the simulation time. This happens due to the link stability of our model. It keeps our network stable and maintain the packet flow almost uniform.

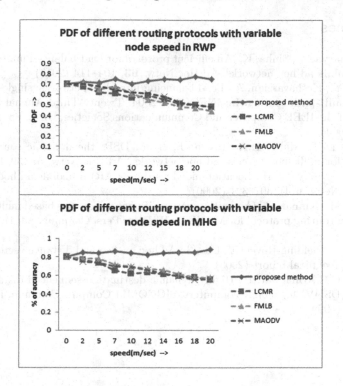

Fig. 4. Packet delivery fraction of different routing protocols in variable node speed

5   Conclusion

We proposed a new recurrent neural network (RNN) based routing model for multi-path communication in MANET. This model selects the paths between the source and destination nodes based on the time series prediction model with the measuring of the previous data values. Our model increases the stability of the network by measuring the congestion and node position of the mobiles nodes. This prediction model actually find out the suitable links between the nodes and calculate the weight or stability factors of those nodes. Based on the weight factors, this model can change the paths to flow the packets from source to destination and the load of those paths dynamically. The other multi-path routing models distribute the data packets by some pre-define measurement techniques which sometimes may not give the highest throughput. But our proposed method always increases the stability and throughput of the network.

References

1. Bhattacharya, A., Sinha, K.: An efficient protocol for load-balanced multipath routing in mobile ad hoc networks. Ad Hoc Netw. **63**, 104–114 (2017)
2. Ganjali, Y., Keshavarzian, A.: Load balancing in ad hoc networks: single-path routing vs. multi-path routing. In: INFOCOM 2004. Twenty-Third Annual Joint Conference of the IEEE Computer and Communications Societies, vol. 2, pp. 1120–1125. IEEE (2004)
3. Johnson, D.B., Maltz, D.A., Broch, J., et al.: DSR: the dynamic source routing protocol for multi-hop wireless ad hoc networks. Ad Hoc Netw. **5**, 139–172 (2001)
4. Ko, Y.-B., Vaidya, N.H.: Location-aided routing (LAR) in mobile ad hoc networks. Wireless Netw. **6**(4), 307–321 (2000)
5. Naseem, M., Kumar, C.: Congestion-aware Fibonacci sequence based multipath load balancing routing protocol for MANETs. Wireless Pers. Commun. **84**(4), 2955–2974 (2015)
6. Perkins, C., Belding-Royer, E., Das, S.: Ad hoc on-demand distance vector (AODV) routing. Technical report (2003)
7. Perkins, C.E., Bhagwat, P.: Highly dynamic destination-sequenced distance-vector routing (DSDV) for mobile computers. SIGCOMM Comput. Commun. Rev. **24**(4), 234–244 (1994)

Performance Analysis of DYMO, ZRP and AODV Routing Protocols in a Multi Hop Grid Based Underwater Wireless Sensor Network

Kamalika Bhattacharjya[✉], Sahabul Alam, and Debashis De

Department of Computer Science and Engineering,
Maulana Abul Kalam Azad University of Technology, West Bengal,
BF-142, Sector- I, Kolkata 700064, West Bengal, India
b.kamalika01@gmail.com, sahabul2009@gmail.com,
dr.debashis.de@gmail.com

Abstract. Underwater Wireless Sensor Network (UWSN), attractive research zone due to suspicious nature of ocean. A numeral sensor nodes and vehicles that collaborate UWSN to gather information and perform cooperative tasks. An efficient network for UWSN is crucial due to sensor nodes and restricted battery power. Exchange or refresh of sensor nodes is difficult by reason of high propagation delay, network dynamics and error probability influence underwater communication. This paper proposed a Multihop Grid based Underwater Wireless Sensor Network (MG-UWSN) and performed analysis on the basis of energy consumption, throughput, average jitter and average delay through the use of QualNet 7.1 simulator. The outcome of the simulation in MG-UWSN depicts that the AODV routing protocol is 2% and 4% higher energy efficient compared to the DYMO routing protocol and ZRP routing protocol.

Keywords: Underwater Wireless Sensor Network · Energy consumption · AODV · DYMO · ZRP

1 Introduction

The water is covered third of the fourth part of the earth's surface therefore life of human exaggerated by the ocean [1]. The sea touches the environment condition, but small section is probed due to the rough nature of the underwater [2–4]. Recently, underwater natural resource, revelation of chemical toxin, oil overflow monitoring has been necessary [5]. Underwater sensor nodes accumulate data, applying point-to-point communication or remote telemetry and construct a small-scale underwater acoustic network (UAN) [6, 7]. Sensor nodes are commonly fixed to buoys or GPS systems or stationary on sea surface in UANs. Low price, minor restricted function and smoothly deployed underwater networks known as underwater wireless sensor network (UWSN) is developed [8]. Wireless sensor network (WSN) performs a significant job to investigate the mystery of underwater environs. Underwater sensor nodes (SNs) perform sensing and monitoring information in UWSNs in an energy efficient manner [9, 10]. Interest on

© Springer Nature Singapore Pte Ltd. 2019
J. K. Mandal et al. (Eds.): CICBA 2018, CCIS 1030, pp. 465–476, 2019.
https://doi.org/10.1007/978-981-13-8578-0_37

internet of underwater things (IoUT) arises to study undiscovered ocean [11] to contribute resolution for military, scientific, security, industrial etc. areas. Energy consumption and link quality to forward data are two primary factors in UWSN [12]. The task of SN becomes difficult and expensive due to water motion [13, 14]. Hop to hop communication is more energy efficient than end to end communication because of rapid change in network topology [15]. A famous reactive routing protocol, Ad-hoc On Demand Distance Vector (AODV) [16, 17] establishes a path between nodes when any node wants to send data to another node in the network. A route table is maintained from source to destination. AODV performs as follows: (i) Route Request Message (RREQ): Message is broadcast to find routes. (ii) Route Reply Message (RREP): Message after route setup (iii) Route Error Message (RERR): Finds data packets forwarding are successful or not. Dynamic MANET On-demand routing protocol (DYMO) [18], reactive routing protocol. Working function of DYMO is very alike to the AODV routing protocol. It takes merely the most basic route discovery and maintenance procedures only. Zone Routing Protocol (ZRP), combines the nature of both reactive and proactive routing protocols i.e. hybrid routing protocol. If source and destination are situated in same zone use already stored routing table by proactive protocol to deliver data otherwise reactive protocol use their functionalities to deliver data. This property reduces overhead of the network. The MG-UWSN is proposed by selecting the coordinator node and cluster head.

Motivation and Contribution

The UWSN is energy restricted. Prolong the underwater network lifetime is the primary challenge of UWSN. There are abundant researches going on the underwater sensor network to increase life span.

The main contributions of this paper are:

- A Multi-hop Grid based Underwater Wireless Sensor Network (MG-UWSN) is proposed.
- The performance parameters like receive energy consumption, idle energy consumption, transmit energy consumption; total energy consumption and average jitter are analyzed.

Related works are provided in Sect. 2. Sections 3 and 4 provide proposed work and simulation environment respectively. The simulation results of multi-hop grid based underwater wireless sensor network are discussed in Sect. 5. Section 6 presents the concluding observations.

2 Related Works

A chain based and energy efficient routing protocol for UWSN is studied in [1] and analyzed the effect of the data packet size and number of data on energy consumption. An energy efficient MAC protocol for UWSN is studied in [19] and perform analysis of transmit energy with respect to the number of nodes, duty cycle and presence of a collision. Analysis of energy in UWSN is performed in [20] and study energy consumption corresponding to distance between nodes in various types of water. Evolution of grid based routing protocol under various mobility models for UWSN is discussed in [21] and analyzed the issues of network density on energy consumption, PDR, end to end delay. Energy consumption in UWSN minimized by improvement of mobicast routing protocol is discussed in [22]. Localization free interference and energy holes minimization routing protocol for UWSNs is discussed in [23] and analyzed total number of dead nodes, packet received at sink, total energy consumption and packet drop.

3 Proposed Work

In this section, Multi-hop Grid based Underwater Wireless Sensor Network is proposed. Location independent relay nodes (RNs) are elected by hop count and RNs conveys the information from normal nodes (NNs) to cluster heads (CHs). SNs present in UWSN sensed data from the deployed areas and transmit data to the Sink node. Data can transmit directly to the base station (BS) via single hop or multi-hop. Data transmission from Sensor nodes (SNs) to sink node through multi-hop is more energy efficient than direct data transmission from SNs to sink node. Here SNs are sonobuoys that means these are enable to track geographical location. Horizontal and vertical direction movements of SNs due to dynamics are 20 km/h [24]. Escalation network lifetime is crucial requirement in UWSN. The reduction of energy consumption increases the network lifetime.

3.1 Network Scenario

In the proposed work, the base station is situated near the border of the surface of an ocean and SNs are deployed in the ocean. Data sensed by SNs are forwarded to BS via radio links. Territories of the sea are divided into sub territories and each sub territories have CH that accumulate data of that territory from SNs. CHs can communicate with the other territories of CHs via Cluster coordinator (CCO) node. CCO aggregates data from other sub territorial CHs and send the information to upper region of CCO. This encourages load balancing on CHs and CCOs. For individual sub territories a chiefly CCO node present that conveys the data of lower sub territories. Conventional localization principle is not befitting for UWSN [25–27]. In case of large area, the region is divided into sub-regions and considers same deployment policy for each sub region. The architecture of MG-UWSN is shown in Fig. 1. In the proposed work, sensor nodes are deployed in a grid manner. Sensor node which has minimum distance from other nodes present in grid selected as CH. All SNs present in grid send data to CH, CH sends data to BS through CCO node.

Algorithm 1: Construct MG-UWSN

Begin
  Step 1. Sensor Nodes (SNs) are deployed in a grid manner.
  Step 2. Deploy coordinator node (CCO).
  Step 3. Deploy sink node or Base Station (BS).
  Step 4. Select cluster head (CH).
  Step 5. CH send data to CCO.
  Step 6. CCO sends data to BS.
End

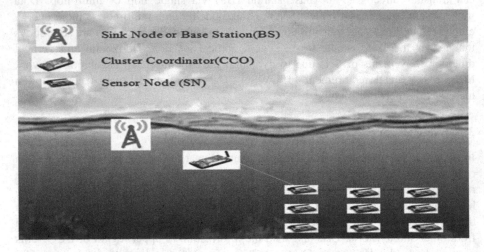

Fig. 1. Architecture of Multi hop Grid based Underwater Wireless Sensor Network

3.2 Network Set up Phase

In network setup phase, every SN has a unique id. In the proposed network scenario, we assume that all SNs are static and SNs are consist of NNs, RNs, CHs and CCOs. Data transfer from source node $SN_s \in UN$ to neighbor node $SN_n \in UN$, where UN is a set of all the underwater sensor nodes. Distance between SN_s and SN_n are equal. Control packet (CP), broadcast information of node with the configuration shown in Eq. (1).

$$CP = <id_s, HC(id_s), DP_{id}>$$

(1)

Where, id_s-identifier of CP, and DP_{id} is defined in Eq. (2).

$$DP_{id} = <id_{sc}, id_{pac}> \qquad (2)$$

Where id_{sc}- source identifier, id_{pac}- data packet identifier.

SN_n ignores the data packet when $HC(SN_n) - HC(SN_s) > 1$, it delimitate that SN_n is situated in farthest distance. The path in water media of the proposed work is SNs transmit data to CH, CHs transmit data to CCO. Finally CCO sends data to the BS.

4 Simulation Environments

The simulation environment is discussed in this section. Proposed MG-UWSN is simulated using QualNet 7.1 software. Some hardware needed besides software to perform simulation. The hardware is processor of 64 bits; 5 GB disk space; CPU of 64 bits; 4 GB free memory; operating system of Windows, Linux etc. Table 1 presents simulation parameter values for simulation of DYMO, ZRP and AODV routing protocols in proposed MG-UWSN.

Table 1. Simulation parameters of MG-UWSN

Parameter	Values
Number of nodes	39
Simulation tool	QualNet 7.1
Area of node deployment (m^2)	1500 × 1500
Routing protocols	AODV, DYMO, ZRP
Mode of node replacement	GRID
Traffic source	CBR
Simulation time (Seconds)	300 s
Energy model	Generic
Radio type	802.11b
Supply voltage (volt)	6.5
Network layer protocol	IPv4
Packet size (bytes)	512, 1024, 2048, 4096
Communication link	Wireless
Battery capacity (mAh)	1200
Battery model	Linear

In MG-UWSN model, the SNs are deployed in grid manner across the area 1500 m × 1500 m for sensing data. This network based on IEEE 802.11b physical and MAC layer specification and uses 39 nodes. In the proposed work, packet size is called item size. Figure 2 represents the snapshot and Fig. 3 represents running view of Multi hop Grid based Underwater Wireless Sensor Network.

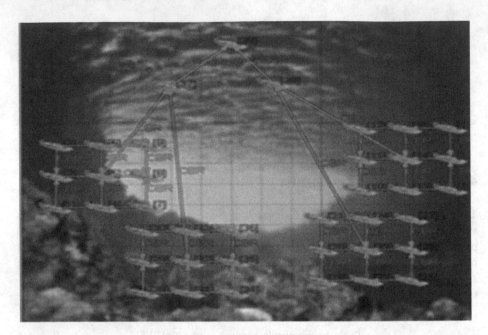

Fig. 2. Snapshot view of proposed Multi hop Grid based Underwater Wireless Sensor Network

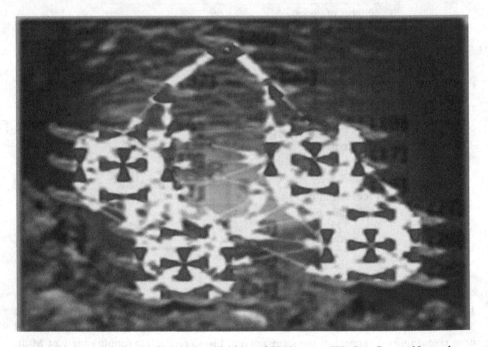

Fig. 3. Running views of Multi hop Grid based Underwater Wireless Sensor Network

5 Simulation Results

This section analyzed the performance of MG-UWSN using three routing protocols DYMO, ZRP and AODV.

5.1 Transmit Energy Consumption in MG-UWSN Using DYMO, ZRP and AODV Routing Protocols

Energy consumed by the nodes for passing data from source to destination. The minimum energy consumed by the AODV routing protocol in the transmit mode than DYMO and ZRP routing protocol is displayed in Fig. 4. As illustrated in Table 2, the AODV routing protocol consumed 26% less energy and 42% less energy than DYMO and ZRP routing protocol respectively.

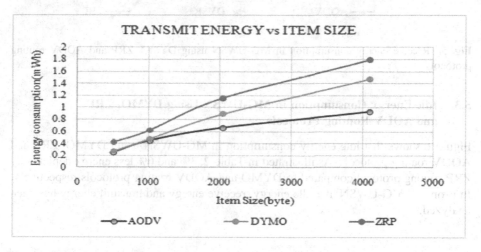

Fig. 4. Transmit energy consumption in MG-UWSN using DYMO, ZRP and AODV routing protocols

5.2 Receive Energy Consumption in MG-UWSN Using DYMO, ZRP and AODV Routing Protocols

Energy consumed for receiving data from source to destination by nodes. Figure 5 shows the receive mode energy consumption using DYMO, ZRP and AODV protocols. In receive mode, the AODV routing protocol received 28% and 44% less energy when compared to DYMO and ZRP routing protocols is shown in Table 2.

472   K. Bhattacharjya et al.

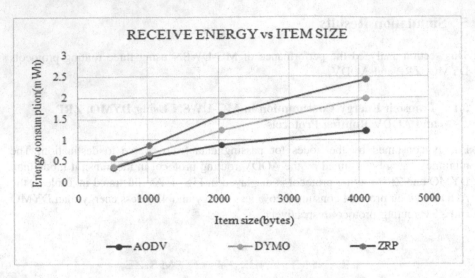

Fig. 5. Receive energy consumption in MG-UWSN using DYMO, ZRP and AODV routing protocols

5.3 Idle Energy Consumption in MG-UWSN Using DYMO, ZRP and AODV Routing Protocols

Figure 6 shows that idle energy consumption in MG-UWSN using DYMO, ZRP and AODV routing protocols. As illustrated in Table 2, 3% and 6% less energy depleted by ZRP routing protocol compared to DYMO and AODV routing protocols respectively. In proposed MG-UWSN, the idle energy, receive energy and transmit energy has been analyzed.

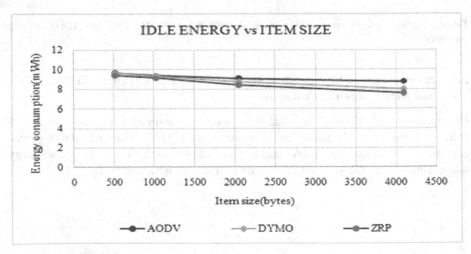

Fig. 6. Idle energy consumption in MG-UWSN using DYMO, ZRP and AODV routing protocols

5.4 Throughput in MG-UWSN Using DYMO, ZRP and AODV Routing Protocols

Information transmitted in network over a certain time termed as throughput. Throughput is defined by Eq. (3). Figure 7 shows throughput of MG-UWSN. It has been observed from Table 2 that the DYMO achieved 26% and 1% higher throughput than AODV and ZRP routing protocol consequences.

$$\Im = \sum_{d=1}^{N}(TP_d)/T \tag{3}$$

Where $\Im$- throughput, TP_d- packet transmitted by dth node, T- total time.

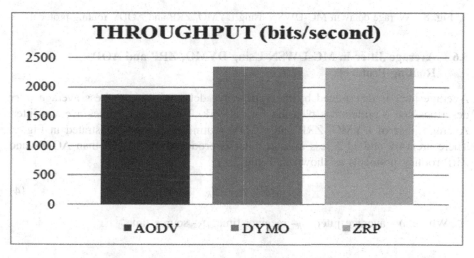

Fig. 7. Throughput in MG-UWSN using DYMO, ZRP and AODV routing protocols

5.5 Average Delay in MG-UWSN Using DYMO, ZRP and AODV Routing Protocols

Average delay of the is defined as the mean number of signals successfully transmit a packet on the network successfully. Comparison of AODV, DYMO and ZRP based on average delay is shown Fig. 8. DYMO routing protocol produces 51% and 45% less average delay than AODV and ZRP routing protocol as shown in Table 2.

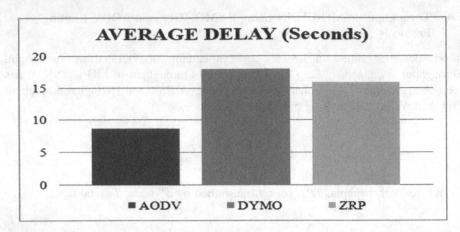

Fig. 8. Average delay in MG-UWSN using DYMO, ZRP and AODV routing protocols

5.6   Average Jitter in MG-UWSN Using DYMO, ZRP and AODV Routing Protocols

Average jitter is determined by the appearance delay of packets. Less average jitter describes that a protocol is pleasing for network. The Eq. (4) defines average jitter. Average jitter of DYMO, ZRP and AODV routing protocol is illustrated in Fig. 9. There are 14% and 11% less average jitter is produced by DYMO than AODV and ZRP routing protocols as shown in Table 2.

$$\delta = d_S - d_R \tag{4}$$

Where, δ - average jitter, d_R- receiver time, d_S- source time.

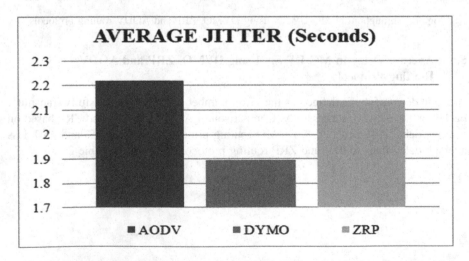

Fig. 9. Average jitter in MG-UWSN using DYMO, ZRP and AODV routing protocols

Table 2. Performance analysis of MG-UWSN using DYMO, ZRP and AODV routing protocols

Parameter	Protocol		
	AODV	DYMO	ZRP
Transmit energy consumption	0.57594	0.782003	0.99691
Receive energy consumption	0.765193	1.064483	1.371905
Idle energy consumption	9.245541	8.952054	8.650753
Throughput	1862.97	2338.37	2320.03
Average delay	8.7344	17.9546	15.851
Average jitter	2.21726	1.89671	2.13705

6 Conclusion

In MG-UWSN, grid based multi-hop data transmission has been used in underwater scenario to reduce energy consumption by transmitting data from the underwater environment to the sink node. The simulation results prove that the AODV routing protocol generates minimum energy than DYMO and ZRP routing protocols. Moreover, the DYMO routing protocol achieves 20% higher throughput and 17% less average jitter compared to AODV routing protocol. The AODV routing protocol achieves better performance than DYMO and ZRP routing protocols in case of average delay. In MG-UWSN, it has been concluded that the AODV routing protocol is energy efficient.

References

1. Rani, S., Ahmed, S.H., Malhotra, J., Talwar, R.: Energy efficient chain based routing protocol for underwater wireless sensor networks. J. Netw. Comput. Appl. **92**, 42–50 (2017)
2. Ayaz, M., Baig, I., Abdullah, A., Faye, I.: A survey on routing techniques in underwater wireless sensor networks. J. Netw. Comput. Appl. **34**(6), 1908–1927 (2011)
3. Meratnia, N., et al.: CLAM—collaborative embedded networks for submarine surveillance: an overview. In: OCEANS, 2011 IEEE-Spain, pp. 1–4. IEEE, June 2011
4. Fang, S., et al.: An integrated system for regional environmental monitoring and management based on internet of things. IEEE Trans. Industr. Inf. **10**(2), 1596–1605 (2014)
5. Proakis, J.G., Sozer, E.M., Rice, J.A., Stojanovic, M.: Shallow water acoustic networks. IEEE Commun. Mag. **39**(11), 114–119 (2001)
6. Heidemann, J., Ye, W., Wills, J., Syed, A., Li, Y.: Research challenges and applications for underwater sensor networking. In: Wireless Communications and Networking Conference (WCNC 2006), vol. 1, pp. 228–235. IEEE (2006)
7. Sozer, E.M., Stojanovic, M., Proakis, J.G.: Underwater acoustic networks. IEEE J. Oceanic Eng. **25**(1), 72–83 (2000)
8. Cui, J.H., Kong, J., Gerla, M., Zhou, S.: The challenges of building mobile underwater wireless networks for aquatic applications. IEEE Network **20**(3), 12–18 (2006)
9. Wang, K., Gao, H., Xu, X., Jiang, J., Yue, D.: An energy-efficient reliable data transmission scheme for complex environmental monitoring in underwater acoustic sensor networks. IEEE Sens. J. **16**(11), 4051–4062 (2016)

10. Han, G., Jiang, J., Shu, L., Guizani, M.: An attack-resistant trust model based on multidimensional trust metrics in underwater acoustic sensor network. IEEE Trans. Mob. Comput. **14**(12), 2447–2459 (2015)

11. Yuan, F., Zhan, Y., Wang, Y.: Data density correlation degree clustering method for data aggregation in WSN. IEEE Sens. J. **14**(4), 1089–1098 (2014)

12. Agarwal, R., Kumar, S., Hegde, R.M.: Algorithms for crowd surveillance using passive acoustic sensors over a multimodal sensor network. IEEE Sens. J. **15**(3), 1920–1930 (2015)

13. Han, G., Jiang, J., Shu, L., Xu, Y., Wang, F.: Localization algorithms of underwater wireless sensor networks: a survey. Sensors **12**(2), 2026–2061 (2012)

14. Lee, S., Kim, D.: Underwater hybrid routing protocol for UWSNs. In: Fifth International Conference on Ubiquitous and Future Networks (ICUFN), pp. 472–475. IEEE (2013)

15. Rani, S., Talwar, R., Malhotra, J., Ahmed, S.H., Sarkar, M., Song, H.: A novel scheme for an energy efficient Internet of Things based on wireless sensor networks. Sensors **15**(11), 28603–28626 (2015)

16. Perkins, C., Belding-Royer, E., Das, S.: Ad hoc on-demand distance vector (AODV) routing. No. RFC 3561 (2003)

17. Manjula, S.H., Abhilash, C.N., Shaila, K., Venugopal, K.R., Patnaik, L.M.: Performance of AODV routing protocol using group and entity mobility models in wireless sensor networks. In: International MultiConference of Engineers and Computer Scientist, vol. 2, pp. 1212–1217 (2008)

18. Teja, G.S., Samundiswary, P.: Performance analysis of DYMO protocol for IEEE 802.15. 4 based WSNs with mobile nodes. In: Computer Communication and Informatics (ICCCI), pp. 1–5. IEEE (2014)

19. Park, M.K., Rodoplu, V.: UWAN-MAC: an energy-efficient MAC protocol for underwater acoustic wireless sensor networks. IEEE J. Oceanic Eng. **32**(3), 710–720 (2007)

20. Domingo, M.C., Prior, R.: Energy analysis of routing protocols for underwater wireless sensor networks. Comput. Commun. **31**(6), 1227–1238 (2008)

21. Alkindi, Z., Alzeidi, N., Touzene, B.A.A.: Performance evolution of grid based routing protocol for underwater wireless sensor networks under different mobile models. Int. J. Wirel. Mob. Netw. (IJWMN) **10**(1), 13–25 (2018)

22. Patil, M.S.A., Mishra, M.P.: Improved mobicast routing protocol to minimize energy consumption for underwater wireless sensor networks. Int. J. Res. Sci. Eng. **3**(2), 197–204 (2017)

23. Khan, A., et al.: A localization-free interference and energy holes minimization routing for underwater wireless sensor networks. Sensors **18**(1), 165 (2018)

24. Emokpae, L.E., DiBenedetto, S., Potteiger, B., Younis, M.: UREAL: underwater reflection-enabled acoustic-based localization. IEEE Sens. J. **14**(11), 3915–3925 (2014)

25. Liang, Q., Zhang, B., Zhao, C., Pi, Y.: TDoA for passive localization: underwater versus terrestrial environment. IEEE Trans. Parallel Distrib. Syst. **24**(10), 2100–2108 (2013)

26. Yu, Z., Xiao, C., Zhou, G.: Multi-objectivization-based localization of underwater sensors using magnetometers. IEEE Sens. J. **14**(4), 1099–1106 (2014)

27. Diamant, R., Lampe, L.: Underwater localization with time-synchronization and propagation speed uncertainties. IEEE Trans. Mob. Comput. **12**(7), 1257–1269 (2013)

Energy Efficient Designing Approach of Flip-Flops Using 2-Dot 1-Electron QCA

Mili Ghosh[1]([✉]), Debarka Mukhopadhyay[2], and Paramartha Dutta[1]

[1] Department of Computer and System Sciences, Visva Bharati University,
Santiniketan 731235, India
ghosh.mili90@gmail.com, paramartha.dutta@gmail.com
[2] Department of Computer Science, Amity School of Engineering and Technology,
Amity University, Kolkata 700156, India
debarka.mukhopadhyay@gmail.com

Abstract. The most concerned phenomena in present era of digital industry is the dimensional crunch of devices in nanoscale. Quantum-dot Cellular Automata (QCA) is an well known alternative technology to transcend the limitations of CMOS technology. One of the newest structural variant of QCA i.e. 2-dot 1-electron QCA grabbing the attention of the research community due to its energy efficiency. In this present article a design methodology of basic flip-flop circuits such as SR flip-flop, JK flip-flop, D flip-flop and T flip-flop. A detailed energy analysis of the proposed circuits have been carried out to check the energy efficiency and robustness of the proposed circuits. The stability of the proposed circuits have also been analyzed for better assessment of the acceptability of the proposed circuits.

Keywords: 2-dot 1-electron QCA · Flip-flops · Energy dissipation · Stability · Energy efficiency

1 Introduction

According to recent studies [1], CMOS technology will achieve its scaling limit shortly such as dimensional restriction. Other shortcomings of CMOS technology are high lithography cost, off state leakage current, decreasing switching performance etc. While nanoscale designs come into play, CMOS technology faces serious challenges. In view of this situation, there is a need of cost effective, efficient technology to overcome the shortcomings of CMOS technology. QCA is an emerging technology capable of offering ultra speed computation along with highly dense structures. The most recent form of QCA is 2-dot 1-electron 1 Electron QCA. The 2-dot 1-electron QCA cell can represent the two binary states by two alternate positions of a single electron. The 2-dot 1-electron QCA can transmit data through inter-cellular interaction. This article proposes some energy efficient design mechanism of flip flops using 2-dot 1-electron QCA. Previous reportings on energy and power analysis of QCA are available in [17] and [2].

© Springer Nature Singapore Pte Ltd. 2019
J. K. Mandal et al. (Eds.): CICBA 2018, CCIS 1030, pp. 477–490, 2019.
https://doi.org/10.1007/978-981-13-8578-0_38

Structurally the article comprises the following: Sect. 2 gives a brief idea about prelude of 2-dot 1-electron QCA. Section 3 suggests the architectures of different flip flops and the output states of proposed flip flop designs are determined in Subsect. 3.1. Relevant analysis is available in Sect. 4. In Sect. 5 the conclusion is drawn.

2   Prelude Discussion

The domain of 4-dot 2-electron counterpart of quantum cellular automata is vastly expired. The binary states are depicted by the electron positions along the diagonals of a planar square cell [14,15]. The most general convention about the cell polarities is shown in Fig. 1. In 4-dot 2-electron QCA architectures, Majority voter (MV) gate with inverter serves as a universal gate. This enables to convert any logic design to convert in its QCA counterpart as done in [3,9,12,16,18].

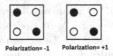

Polarization= -1   Polarization= +1

Fig. 1. Information encoding with 4-dot 2-electron QCA cells

Another form of QCA cell is 2-dot 1-electron QCA cell [7]. As the nomenclature suggests, each cell consists of two semiconductor holes with single electron. The electron is free to move between the holes. The intercell interaction is done by the Coulomb effect between electrons of the neighboring cells. The binary states thus can be encoded by electron's position within a cell, which can have vertical or horizontal alignment as shown in Figs. 2a and b. The elementary architectural blocks are wire to transmit information, majority voter gate (MV gate) to design different logic gates, inverter gate, planar wire crossing which are shown in Figs. 3a, 4, 5, 4c respectively.

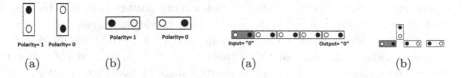

Polarity= 1   Polarity= 0   Polarity= 1   Polarity= 0   Input= "0"   Output= "0"

(a)   (b)   (a)   (b)

Fig. 2. Data encoding with 2-dot 1-electron QCA cell (a) vertically aligned and (b) horizontally aligned

Fig. 3. (a) Wire and (b) Inversion by switching alignment of cell

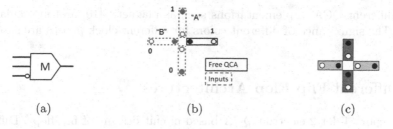

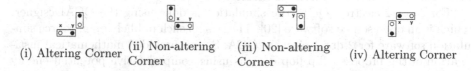

(a)   (b)   (c)

Fig. 4. MV gate (a) Schematic representation and (b) QCA implementation and (c) Planar crossing of wires

(i) Altering Corner   (ii) Non-altering Corner   (iii) Non-altering Corner   (iv) Altering Corner

Fig. 5. Inversion by corner cell placement

2.1 Basics of Clocking

The clocking mechanism is similar for almost every structural variant of QCA. The four phases of the QCA clocking are: **switch, hold, release** and **relax**. Switch phase as the name suggests switches a cell from polarized state to unpolarized state. When this phase is over maximum energy is assumed by an electron and hence the cells become unpolarized. In hold phase, the said unpolarized state is maintained. During release phase, electrons starts to loose its energy and by the end of this phase obtains a definite quantum-dot position. By the end of the release phase electrons get latched and latched cells can act as input cell to its neighboring cells. In course of the relax phase the latched state of the cell is maintained. The four phases of clocking are present in each clocking zone and two consecutive clock zones maintain $\frac{\pi}{2}$ phase difference as shown in Fig. 6b. Some different kind of clocking mechanisms have been reported previously for

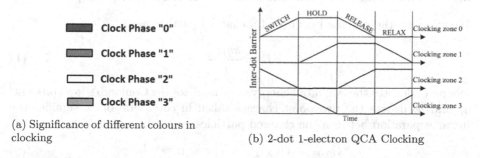

(a) Significance of different colours in clocking

(b) 2-dot 1-electron QCA Clocking

Fig. 6. (a) Significance of different colours in clocking and (b) 2-dot 1-electron QCA clocking

some different QCA implementations such as magnetic [10] and molecular [13] QCA. The significance of different colors for different clock phases are shown in Fig. 6a.

3   Different Flip Flop Architectures

[4,19] report 4-dot 2-electron QCA based circuit designs of flip flops. Different flip flops are constructed with minimum number of 2-dot 1-electron QCA cells ensuring the stability. The stability in any 2-dot 1-electron QCA architecture are assured by some conditions as mentioned in [6].

For 4-dot 2-electron QCA, the simulation is done using the QCADesigner, which is an open source software [20]. There is no such publicly open source simulation software for 2-dot 1-electron QCA. So, we provided mathematical justification of the proposed flip flop designs using comprehensive potential energy calculation. Electron latches at the hole which attains minimum energy. For each of the flipflops, we prove only one state and the other states can be proved accordingly. In the following section, we shall discuss architectures of different flip flops. For simulating circuits developed in the 4-dot 2-electron counterpart of QCA, QCADesigner [20] is widely used.

But no such kind of simulation tool is available for 2-dot 1-electron QCA counterpart. Coulomb's principle is used to justify proposed circuit characteristics. Electron tries to latch at a quantum hole at which it attains the minimum energy. In the proposed circuits, for any input combination potential energy due to influence of neighboring cells is computed for each possible position of electron. In case of 2-dot 1-electron QCA, electron has two possible dot positions in each cell. So, the total potential energy of electron at both the dot positions is computed and the values are compared. Electron will latch at the dot for which the potential energy value minimum. Thus a comparative study has been made to evaluate the most stable electron position by analyzing the potential energy values at each possible quantum hole. We have taken, each 2-dot 1-electron QCA cell length $= 13\,\text{nm}$ and inter cell space $= 5\,\text{nm}$ [11].

3.1   Determination of Output States of Different Flip Flops

We compute the potential energy of a charged particle as:

$$U = \frac{kq_1q_2}{r} \tag{1}$$

where, U denotes the evaluated energy, k symbolizes the Coulomb's law constant, q_1 and q_2 denote the two point charges taken in consideration, r signifies the linear separation between the charged particles.

$$kq_1q_2 = \pm 9 \times 10^9 \times (1.6 \times 10^{-19})^2 \tag{2}$$

The term kq_1q_2 will be evaluated as positive when both the particles are positively charged or both the particles are negatively charged. Within a QCA cell, electron has negative polarity whereas the hole has induced positive charge.

$$U_{Total} = \sum_{t=1}^{n} U_t \tag{3}$$

where, U_{Total} symbolizes the summed up energy value for a specific hole inside a 2-dot 1-electron QCA cell. During potential energy evaluation, the electron and quantum dot within a 2-dot 1-electron QCA cell is named as $e_{cellnumber}$ and $h_{cellnumber}$ respectively. U_{e_ix} is the potential energy between the electron of i_{th} neighbour cell and the electron at x position of the output cell and U_{h_ix} is the potential energy between the quantum dot of i_{th} neighbour cell and the electron at x position of the output cell. The x and y positions corresponding to horizontal and vertical alignments are as per Figs. 7, 8, 9, 10.

SR Flip Flop. The SR flip flop shown in Fig. 7 comprises of one majority voter gate, fan-outs and wires. A majority voter gate has three inputs and eight input states. Here, we will check the correctness for only one input state. The rest others can be proved accordingly. The potential energy evaluations are done according to the calculations shown in Sect. 3.1 as done in [15] and the outcome is reflected in Table 1.

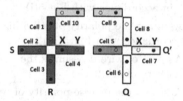

Fig. 7. Design of SR flip flop with cell position

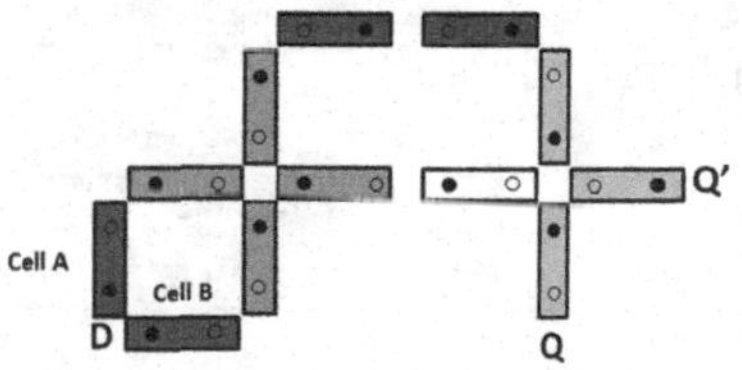

Fig. 8. Design of D flip flop

D Flip Flop. The D flip flop, in Fig. 8 is almost similar to the SR flip flop in Fig. 7 except the S and R inputs in D flip flop are complement of each other. We have shown the potential energy calculations of SR flip flop in Table 1. Similarly, the calculations can be done for D flip flop. For the two extra cells i.e. cell A and cell B in Fig. 8 attain potential energies according to the corner cell placements shown in Fig. 5.

JK Flip Flop. The JK flip flop shown in Fig. 9 comprises of three majority voter gates, fan-outs and wires. Here we will check the correctness for only one input state. The rests can be proved accordingly. The cell numbers are shown in Fig. 9. The potential energy evaluations are done according to the calculations in [15] and are shown in Table 2.

T Flip Flop. The implementation of T flip-flop as reflected in Fig. 10 is almost similar to the JK flip flop shown in Fig. 9 except the J and K inputs in T flip flop are complement of each other. We have shown the potential energy calculations of JK flip flop in Table 2. Similarly, the calculations can be done for T flip flop. The two extra cells i.e. cell A and cell B in Fig. 10 attain potential energies according to the corner cell placements shown in Fig. 5.

Table 1. Output state of SR flip flop determination using potential energy calculation

Cell	Position of electron	Evaluated energy	Remarks
4	x	-13.41×10^{-20} J	Position x will be more stable due to lesser energy
4	y	-1.38×10^{-20} J	
5	-	-	As part of wire it assumes the polarity of cell 4
6	-	-	Assumes the polarity of cell 5 in accordance with Fig. 5(iii)
7	x	6.75×10^{-20} J	Position y will be more stable due to lesser energy
7	y	0.3×10^{-20} J	
8	-	-	Assumes the inverse polarity of cell 5 in accordance with Fig. 5(i)
9	-	-	Assumes the polarity of cell 8 in accordance with Fig. 5(iii)
10	-	-	As part of wire it assumes the polarity of cell 9
1	-	-	Assumes the inverse polarity of cell 10 in accordance with Fig. 5(iv) in next clock phase

4   Energy Analysis

4.1   SR Flip Flop

The SR flip flop is constructed using 2-dot 1-electron cells as shown in the Fig. 7. Here, the SR flip flop is constructed using ten, 2-dot 1-electron QCA cells. The basic components of this design are Majority Voter gate, fan-out and binary wire. In this design, only one Majority Voter gate is used. Each and every cell of the concerned MV gate are in the same zone of clock and the concerned outcome is taken off in the succeeding clock. Thus, stability is ensured in the proposed SR flip flop design using 2-dot 1-electron QCA. In this QCA based SR flip flop design, no race condition exists. When $S = 1$ and $R = 1$, the previous output state is retained. As shown in Fig. 7, the SR flip flop design contains a loop back

Table 2. Output state of JK flip flop determination using potential energy calculation

Cell	Position of electron	Evaluated energy	Remarks
3	x	6.75×10^{-20} J	Position Y is more stable due to lesser energy
3	y	0.3×10^{-20} J	
11	-	-	As part of wire it assumes the polarity of cell 3
13	x	3.33×10^{-20} J	Position Y is more stable due to lesser energy
13	y	0.54×10^{-20} J	
12	-	-	As part of wire it assumes the polarity of cell 13
20	x	13.41×10^{-20} J	Position Y is more stable due to lesser energy
20	y	1.38×10^{-20} J	
18	-	-	Assumes the inverse polarity of cell 20 in accordance with Fig. 5(i)
19	-	-	Assumes the inverse polarity of cell 18 in accordance with Fig. 5(iv)
17	-	-	Assumes the polarity of cell 19 in accordance with Fig. 5(iii)
16	-	-	Achieves the polarity of cell 17 in accordance with Fig. 5(ii)
21	-	-	Assumes the polarity of cell 20 in accordance with Fig. 5(ii)
22	-	-	As part of wire it assumes the polarity of cell 21
23	-	-	Assumes the inverse polarity of cell 22 in accordance with Fig. 5(i)
9	-	-	Assumes the polarity of cell 23 in accordance with Fig. 5(iii)
10	-	-	As part of wire it assumes the polarity of cell 9
8	-	-	Assumes the inverse polarity of cell 9 in accordance with Fig. 5(i)
7	-	-	Assumes the inverse polarity of cell 8 in accordance with Fig. 5(iv)
6	-	-	Assumes the polarity of cell 7 in accordance with Fig. 5(ii)
5	-	-	Assumes the polarity of cell 6 in accordance with Fig. 5(iii)
4	-	-	As part of wire it assumes the polarity of cell 5

input to the Majority Voter gate. This implies that the previous output must be processed with the current inputs. Thus, it is to be ensured that the previous output is available in the next clock for being processed with the current input. We have done a comparative study on the 4-dot 2-electron QCA SR flip flop design with 76 cells in [19] and the proposed 2-dot 1-electron QCA SR flip flop design. The different energy parameters regarding SR flip flop evaluated using the well established energy related formalisms presented in [5,8] are shown in Table 3 and the respective graphs are indicated in Fig. 11. As can be seen in the graphs, electron quantum number plays a significant role in case of energy of any QCA circuit. Through the graphs shown in Fig. 11, a comparison has been made between the flip-flop designs.

4.2   D Flip Flop

The 2-dot 1-electron QCA design of D flip flop is provided in Fig. 8. The number of cells used here is twelve. The D flip flop is constructed by giving complement of S input to R input of the SR flip flop. This design preserved the constraints of stability. In article [11], a D flip flop design has been proposed using 2-dot

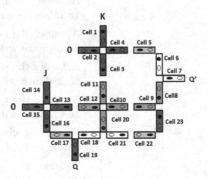

Fig. 9. Design of JK flip flop with cell position

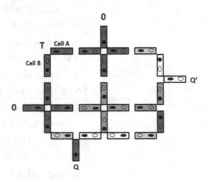

Fig. 10. 2-dot 1-electron QCA design of T flip flop

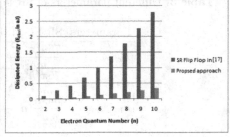

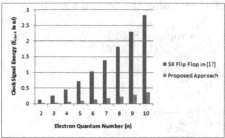

(a) Clock Signal Energy along vertical axis Vs Electron Quantum Number

(b) Dissipation Energy along vertical axis Vs Electron Quantum Number

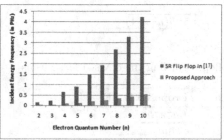

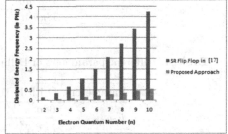

(c) Incident Energy Frequency along vertical axis Vs Electron Quantum Number

(d) Dissipation Energy Frequency along vertical axis Vs Electron Quantum Number

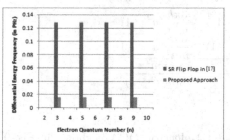

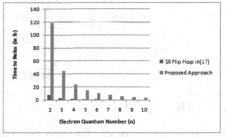

(e) Differential Energy Frequency along vertical axis Vs Electron Quantum Number

(f) Relaxation Time of Electrons along vertical axis Vs Electron Quantum Number

Fig. 11. All the above figures depict different parameters with respect to the electron quantum number for SR flip flop

1-electron QCA. Different parameters regarding the energy flow in the D flip flop architecture is evaluated and tabulated in Table 4 using the proposed formalisms. The comparison in Table 4 is done between the proposed 2-dot 1-electron QCA design of D flip flop and 4-dot 2-electron QCA design of D flip flop with 68 cells in [19]. The respective graphs can be drawn in a similar manner as SR flip flop.

Table 3. Different parameters of SR flipflop regarding the devised formalisms

Parameters	SR FF in [19]	Proposed SR FF
E_{clock}	$\dfrac{76n^2\pi^2\hbar^2}{ma^2}$	$\dfrac{5n^2\pi^2\hbar^2}{ma^2}$
E_{diss}	$\dfrac{76\pi^2\hbar^2}{ma^2}(n^2-1)$	$\dfrac{5\pi^2\hbar^2}{ma^2}(n^2-1)$
v_1	$\dfrac{38\pi\hbar}{ma^2}(n^2-n_1{}^2)$	$\dfrac{5\pi\hbar}{2ma^2}(n^2-n_1{}^2)$
v_2	$\dfrac{38\pi\hbar}{ma^2}(n^2-1)$	$\dfrac{5\pi\hbar}{2ma^2}(n^2-1)$
v_2-v_1	$\dfrac{38\pi\hbar}{ma^2}(n_1{}^2-1)$	$\dfrac{5\pi\hbar}{2ma^2}(n_1{}^2-1)$
τ_2	$\dfrac{ma^2}{38\pi\hbar(n^2-1)}$	$\dfrac{2ma^2}{5\pi\hbar(n^2-1)}$

Table 4. Different parameters of D flipflop regarding the devised formalisms

Parameters	D FF in [19]	Proposed D FF
E_{clock}	$\dfrac{68n^2\pi^2\hbar^2}{ma^2}$	$\dfrac{6n^2\pi^2\hbar^2}{ma^2}$
E_{diss}	$\dfrac{68\pi^2\hbar^2}{ma^2}(n^2-1)$	$\dfrac{6\pi^2\hbar^2}{ma^2}(n^2-1)$
v_1	$\dfrac{34\pi\hbar}{ma^2}(n^2-n_1{}^2)$	$\dfrac{3\pi\hbar}{ma^2}(n^2-n_1{}^2)$
v_2	$\dfrac{34\pi\hbar}{ma^2}(n^2-1)$	$\dfrac{3\pi\hbar}{ma^2}(n^2-1)$
v_2-v_1	$\dfrac{34\pi\hbar}{ma^2}(n_1{}^2-1)$	$\dfrac{3\pi\hbar}{ma^2}(n_1{}^2-1)$
τ_2	$\dfrac{ma^2}{34\pi\hbar(n^2-1)}$	$\dfrac{ma^2}{3\pi\hbar(n^2-1)}$

4.3 JK Flip Flop

The architecture of JK flip flop using 2-dot 1-electron QCA is shown in Fig. 9. The proposed JK flip flop design requires 23 cells. This design includes 3 Majority Voter gates as well as 3 loop back inputs. One of the Majority Voter gate is for J AND Q', another Majority Voter for K AND Q whereas the third one takes as input the outputs from the first two Majority Voter gates and Q. Stability is ensured here. Different parameters regarding the energy flow in the JK flip flop architecture is evaluated and tabulated in Table 5 using the proposed formalisms. For JK flip flop the comparisons are done between the 4-dot 2-electron QCA JK flip flop design with 90 cells in [19] and the proposed 2-dot 1-electron QCA JK flip flop design. The corresponding graphs can be found in Fig. 12.

4.4 T Flip Flop

T flip flop is constructed from the JK flip flop by connecting complement of one input to the other. The implementation of T flip flop is reflected in Fig. 10 which includes 25 cells. As this design satisfies each of the three constraints of

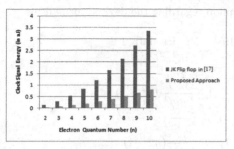

(a) Clock Signal Energy along vertical axis Vs Electron Quantum Number

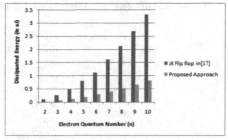

(b) Dissipation Energy along vertical axis Vs Electron Quantum Number

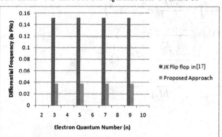

(c) Incident Energy Frequency along vertical axis Vs Electron Quantum Number

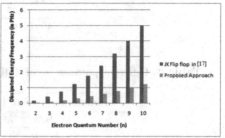

(d) Dissipation Energy Frequency along vertical axis Vs Electron Quantum Number

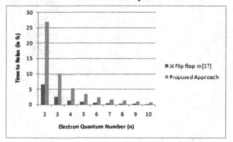

(e) Differential Energy Frequency along vertical axis Vs Electron Quantum Number

(f) Relaxation Time of Electrons along vertical axis Vs Electron Quantum Number

Fig. 12. All the above figures depict different parameters with respect to the electron quantum number for JK flip flop

stability, this design is considered as a stable one. In [11], a design of T flip flop was reported which was based on the XOR gate architecture. The different parameters of T flip flop evaluated using the well established energy related formalisms presented in [5,8] are evident in Table 6. The comparison in Table 6 is done between the proposed 2-dot 1-electron QCA design of T flip flop and 4-dot 2-electron QCA design of T flip flop with 92 cells in [19]. The respective graphs for different flip flops can be drawn similarly as JK flip flop.

Table 5. Different parameters of JK flipflop regarding the devised formalisms

Parameters	JK FF in [19]	Proposed JK FF
E_{clock}	$\dfrac{90n^2\pi^2\hbar^2}{ma^2}$	$\dfrac{23n^2\pi^2\hbar^2}{2ma^2}$
E_{diss}	$\dfrac{90\pi^2\hbar^2}{ma^2}(n^2-1)$	$\dfrac{23\pi^2\hbar^2}{2ma^2}(n^2-1)$
υ_1	$\dfrac{45\pi\hbar}{ma^2}(n^2-n_1{}^2)$	$\dfrac{23\pi\hbar}{4ma^2}(n^2-n_1{}^2)$
υ_2	$\dfrac{45\pi\hbar}{ma^2}(n^2-1)$	$\dfrac{23\pi\hbar}{4ma^2}(n^2-1)$
$\upsilon_2-\upsilon_1$	$\dfrac{45\pi\hbar}{ma^2}(n_1{}^2-1)$	$\dfrac{23\pi\hbar}{4ma^2}(n_1{}^2-1)$
τ_2	$\dfrac{ma^2}{45\pi\hbar(n^2-1)}$	$\dfrac{4ma^2}{23\pi\hbar(n^2-1)}$

Table 6. Different parameters of T flipflop regarding the devised formalisms

Parameters	T FF in [19]	Proposed T FF
E_{clock}	$\dfrac{92n^2\pi^2\hbar^2}{ma^2}$	$\dfrac{25n^2\pi^2\hbar^2}{2ma^2}$
E_{diss}	$\dfrac{92\pi^2\hbar^2}{ma^2}(n^2-1)$	$\dfrac{25\pi^2\hbar^2}{2ma^2}(n^2-1)$
υ_1	$\dfrac{46\pi\hbar}{ma^2}(n^2-n_1{}^2)$	$\dfrac{25\pi\hbar}{4ma^2}(n^2-n_1{}^2)$
υ_2	$\dfrac{46\pi\hbar}{ma^2}(n^2-1)$	$\dfrac{25\pi\hbar}{4ma^2}(n^2-1)$
$\upsilon_2-\upsilon_1$	$\dfrac{46\pi\hbar}{ma^2}(n_1{}^2-1)$	$\dfrac{25\pi\hbar}{4ma^2}(n_1{}^2-1)$
τ_2	$\dfrac{ma^2}{46\pi\hbar(n^2-1)}$	$\dfrac{4ma^2}{25\pi\hbar(n^2-1)}$

5   Conclusion

The present article proposed different flip flop designs using 2-dot 1-electron QCA cells. Further the energy related issues of the proposed circuits are analyzed using some well established formalisms in this regard. The outcomes are extensively indicated by the graphs in Figs. 11 and 12. This analysis helped to understand the energy required to run such an architecture and the energy efficiency of the presented circuits.

Acknowledgment. The authors convey their sincere gratitude towards financial support of the DST INSPIRE Fellowship with serial no. 1513-2012 and INSPIRE reg. no. IF131027 which is given by DST, Ministry of Science and Technology, Government of India to pursue doctoral research.

References

1. International Technology Roadmap for Semiconductor (ITRS) (2004). http://www.itrs.net
2. Blair, E.P., Liu, M., Lent, C.S.: Signal energy in quantum dot cellular automata bit packets. J. Comput. Theor. Nanosci. **8**, 972–982 (2011)
3. Cho, H., Swartzlander, E.E.: Adder designs and analyses for quantum-dot cellular automata. IEEE Trans. Nanotechnol. **6**, 374–383 (2007)
4. Dutta, P., Mukhopadhyay, D.: New architecture for flip flops using quantum-dot cellular automata. In: Satapathy, S., Avadhani, P., Udgata, S., Lakshminarayana, S. (eds.) ICT and Critical Infrastructure: Proceedings of the 48th Annual Convention of Computer Society of India- Vol II. AISC, vol. 249, pp. 707–714. Springer, Cham (2014). https://doi.org/10.1007/978-3-319-03095-1_77
5. Dutta, P., Mukhopadhyay, D.: A study on energy optimized 4 dot 2 electron two dimensional quantum dot cellular automata logical reversible flip-flops. Microelectron. J. **46**, 519–530 (2015)
6. Ghosh, M., Mukhopadhyay, D., Dutta, P.: A 2 dot 1 electron quantum cellular automata based parallel memory. In: Mandal, J.K., Satapathy, S.C., Sanyal, M.K., Sarkar, P.P., Mukhopadhyay, A. (eds.) Information Systems Design and Intelligent Applications. AISC, vol. 339, pp. 627–636. Springer, New Delhi (2015). https://doi.org/10.1007/978-81-322-2250-7_63
7. Ghosh, M., Mukhopadhyay, D., Dutta, P.: A novel parallel memory design using 2 dot 1 electron QCA. In: 2015 IEEE 2nd International Conference on Recent Trends in Information Systems (ReTIS), pp. 485–490, July 2015
8. Ghosh, M., Mukhopadhyay, D., Dutta, P.: A study on 2 dimensional 2 dot 1 electron quantum dot cellular automata based reversible 2: 1 MUX design: an energy analytical approach. Int. J. Comput. Appl. **38**(2–3), 82–95 (2016)
9. Graunke, C.R., Wheeler, D.I., Tougaw, D., Will, J.D.: Implementation of a crossbar network using quantum-dot cellular automata. IEEE Trans. Nanotechnol. **4**, 435–440 (2005)
10. Imre, A., Csaba, G., Ji, L., Orlov, A., Bernstein, G.H., Porod, W.: Majority logic gate for magnetic quantum-dot cellular automata. Science **311**, 205–208 (2006)
11. Iv, L.R.H., Lee, S.C.: Design and simulation of 2-d 2-dot quantum-dot cellular automata logic. IEEE Trans. Nanotechnol. **10**(5), 996–1003 (2011)
12. Kong, K., Shang, Y., Lu, R.: An optimized majority logic synthesis methodology for quantum-dot cellular automata. IEEE Trans. Nanotechnol. **9**, 170–183 (2010)
13. Lent, C.S., Isaksen, B.: Clocked molecular quantum-dot cellular automata. IEEE Trans. Electron Devices **50**, 1890–1896 (2003)
14. Mukhopadhyay, D., Dinda, S., Dutta, P.: Designing and implementation of quantum cellular automata 2:1 multiplexer circuit. Int. J. Comput. Appl. Technol. **25**(1), 21–24 (2011)
15. Mukhopadhyay, D., Dutta, P.: QCA based novel unit reversible multiplexer. Adv. Sci. Lett. **16**(1), 163–168 (2012)
16. Thapliyal, H., Ranganathan, N.: Reversible logic-based concurrently testable latches for molecular QCA. IEEE Trans. Nanotechnol. **9**, 62–69 (2010)
17. Timler, J., Lenta, C.S.: Power gain and dissipation in quantum-dot cellular automata. J. Appl. Phys. **91**, 823–831 (2002)
18. Vankamamidi, V., Ottavi, M., Lombardi, F.: A serial memory by Quantum-dot Cellular Automata (QCA). IEEE Trans. Comput. **57**, 606–618 (2008)

19. Vetteth, A., Walus, K., Dimitrov, V.S., Jullien, G.A.: Quantum-dot cellular automata of flip flop. ATIPS Laboratory, 2500 University Drive, N.W., Calgory, Alberta, Canada T2N 1N4
20. Walus, K., Dysart, T., Jullien, G.A., Budiman, R.A.: QCA designer: a rapid design and simulation tool for quantum-dot cellular automata. IEEE Trans. Nanotechnol. **3**(1), 26–31 (2004)

Author Index

Printed in the United States
By Bookmasters